Contents

Preface

The successful cloning of the sheep Dolly in Roslin, Scotland in 1996 epitomized the impressive achievements of science at the dawn of the new century. The wide gap between the world's scientific achievements and its enormous human problems indicates the extent to which scientific developments have outpaced our ability to solve intractable human problems. When Dolly was born, the world's human problems were salient, including racial, ethnic, cultural, and national conflicts, gender inequality, and the widening gap between the rich and the poor. In the decade between 1980 and 1990, the gap between the rich and the poor widened in the United States.

Scientific achievements such as animal cloning and genetic engineering have not only outpaced social engineering, but have created new human dilemmas, conflicts, and value problems as we illustrate in Chapter 1 with the problem faced by the couple: "Should we join Citizens Against Animal Cloning (CAAC)?" We use this family's decision-problem to describe why citizens in highly technological and scientific democratic societies must take action to preserve democracy and to maintain human dignity as a paramount value. Throughout the world, democracies are fragile and are works-in-progress. They are seriously imperiled in many nation-states.

Global and national events that have occurred in the years between the publication of this fifth edition and the previous edition of this book have reinforced our belief that the main goal of the social studies should be to help students develop the ability to make reflective decisions and to participate in citizen action that will improve the human condition. To become thoughtful decision-makers and citizen actors, students need to master social science knowledge, to clarify their moral commitments, to identify alternative courses of action, and to act in ways consistent with democratic values. Students also need to understand how knowledge is constructed, the purposes it serves, and how it reflects the values and goals of the people who formulate knowledge canons. Understanding how knowledge is constructed will help students to become reflective citizens actors.

Our beliefs about the proper goal for the social studies is based on the assumption that humans will always face personal and social problems, and that all citizens should participate in the making of civic and public policy. The theory of social studies education presented in this book is grounded in democratic beliefs. One of its basic assumptions is that citizenship participation in the making of public policy is essential for the creation and perpetuation of a free, humane, and civic community. This theory also assumes that individuals are not born with the ability to make reflective decisions, but that decision-making consists of a set of interrelated skills that can be identified and systematically taught. It also assumes that people can identify and clarify their values, and that they can be taught to reflect on problems before taking actions to solve them. The main components of decision-making are scientific knowledge, value analysis and clarification, and the synthesis of knowledge and values. Reflective citizens act on many of their decisions.

The organization of this text reflects the basic components of the decision-making and citizen action theory presented within it. Part I describes the rationale for a social studies curriculum that focuses on decision-making and citizen action, and the knowledge and social science inquiry components of such a curriculum. Social studies skills, issues, and materials are described in Part II. Part III describes the social science disciplines and activities and strategies that can be used to teach important social science concepts and generalizations. Each of the social science disciplines provides students with a unique way to view human behavior, one that is essential for reflective decision-making. Exemplary strategies for teaching the key ideas of the disciplines and for helping students to view public issues from an interdisciplinary perspective constitute a major section of Part III. The final section of the book, Part IV, focuses on value inquiry, decision-making, citizen action, and assessment.

This fifth edition has been revised throughout to reflect current developments, research, and issues in social studies education. *Internet Links,* the World Wide Web sites, and the *Feature* sections in Part III are new to this edition. *Internet Links* will enable you and your students to keep abreast of new developments in the social sciences and in social studies education. Each of the *Feature* sections, which opens each chapter in Part III, illustrates an important problem or issue within one of the social science disciplines using a news magazine format and style. We have updated information and references throughout the text.

I wish to thank several colleagues for their contributions to this fifth edition. I am pleased that Cherry A. McGee Banks, who teaches at the University of Washington, Bothell, has joined the authorship team of this book. She enriched this edition and has contributed chapters and indexes to previous editions. Ambrose A. Clegg, Jr. has decided to reduce his contributions to this and future editions. I would like to thank him for revising Chapter 4 for this edition. Christine C. Schaefer contributed and revised Chapter 6 on teaching reading in the social studies.

I wish to thank the following individuals for preparing reviews of the manuscript that enabled us to strengthen it: Janet Elaine Alleman, Michigan State University; Gloria T. Alter, Northern Illinois University; Kenneth Cushner, Kent State University; John C. George, Hood College; Gretchen Kranz Irvine, Augsburg College; Robert L. Leight, Lehigh University; Ann Lockledge, University of North Carolina, Wilmington; Kathleen M. Long, Linfield College; Carole H. Murphy, University of Missouri, St. Louis; Lynn R. Nelson, University of Maine; Pennie Olson, National-Louis University; E. Wayne Ross, State University of New York, Binghamton; and Karen K. Tuttle, Eastern Michigan University.

James A. Banks

The Goals of the Social Studies

Source: Library of Congress, Washington, D.C.

Part I describes the goals of social studies education in a post-industrial world society and sets forth the essential components of an effective social studies curriculum. Chapter 1 describes some of the characteristics of the post-industrial world and the kind of social studies curriculum needed to help students acquire the knowledge, skills, and attitudes needed to become effective citizen actors in our nation and world. It presents a rationale for a social studies curriculum focused on decision-making and reflective citizen action. The essential components of decision-making are discussed and illustrated. They include scientific, interdisciplinary, and higher-level knowledge, value analysis and clarification, and the synthesis of knowledge and values.

Sound decisions must be derived from scientific and interdisciplinary knowledge. Knowledge from any one discipline is too limited to enable the citizen actor to fully understand the complexity of human behavior and to make reflective decisions on personal and public issues. Because each of the social science disciplines provides us with a unique lens with which to view the human drama, the reflective citizen actor must be able to see human behavior from diverse disciplinary perspectives. Chapter 2 illustrates ways in which teachers can conceptualize, plan, and teach interdisciplinary social studies units that are based on higher-level concepts and generalizations and that focus on important topics and social issues.

Reflective citizen actors must not only be able to use interdisciplinary knowledge derived from several disciplines, but they must also understand the nature of social inquiry, be aware of its assumptions, and be able to use the method themselves when it is necessary and appropriate. The first part of Chapter 3 describes the nature of social inquiry and illustrates ways in which teachers can help students to develop social science inquiry skills. The second part of the chapter discusses the nature of social knowledge—facts, concepts, generalizations, and theories—and ways to help students derive this knowledge. Chapter 4 focuses on questioning strategies, which are an integral and important part of social science inquiry and the decision-making process.

CHAPTER 1

The Social Studies: Nature and Goals

THE SOCIAL STUDIES IN A POST-INDUSTRIAL WORLD SOCIETY

The social studies is that part of the elementary and high school curriculum which has the primary responsibility for helping students to develop the knowledge, skills, attitudes, and values needed to participate in the civic life of their local communities, the nation, and the world. While the other curriculum areas also help students to attain some skills needed to participate in a democratic society, the social studies is the only area that has the development of civic competencies and skills as its primary goal. Citizenship is the key goal of the social studies.

Helping students become effective citizens in today's world is a tremendous challenge because of the enormous changes in our global society. Futurists agree that we are living in a world society characterized by rapid and tumultuous changes. The unprecedented changes sweeping our world society are neither temporary nor fleeting, but are signs that we are entering a new society and age in which many of our traditional values, assumptions, and behaviors are being challenged. New value problems and issues are arising, as problems related to such developments as the eroding of the ozone layer of the atmosphere, genetic engineering, human cloning, and the aging of the population in Western societies become increasingly important.

The increasing ethnic, cultural, and racial diversity in nations throughout the world, and the increasing legitimization of this diversity, also pose new problems to societies and nation-states throughout the world.

Futurists use different words to describe the emerging world society. Alvin Toffler (1980) calls it the "Third Wave" society. John Naisbitt (1982) refers to it as the "information society." Daniel Bell (1976) prefers the term "post-industrial society." These writers agree that the emerging world society will differ markedly from the industrial age that dominated Western democratic societies during the 19th and the first half of the 20th centuries. While the industrial age was characterized by the production of goods, the post-industrial society will be increasingly characterized by services and the production of knowledge. Bell believes that a knowledge or information class will emerge.

The post-industrial society will also be characterized by global rather than national economies, international problems that will require global rather than national solutions, and diversity in life styles, values, beliefs, cultures, and political sentiments. Toffler (1982) writes, "we begin to glimpse a new kind of social order—no longer a mass society, but a high-change, high-diversity, de-massified civilization" (p. 35). Toffler believes that almost everyone will be a member of some kind of minority group in the post-industrial society, whether cultural, social, religious, or political.

The futurists also point out that participatory democracy will increasingly characterize post-industrial societies. More people will want to participate in the decisions affecting their lives, not only in politics, but on their jobs (Kanter, 1977; Naisbitt, 1982). Much political activity will occur at the local and regional rather than at the national level. Decentralization, or the dispersal of power and decision-making, will be one of the characteristics of post-industrial society.

A social studies curriculum designed to help students develop the knowledge, skills, and values needed to effectively participate in a post-industrial world society must have characteristics different from traditional social studies curricula. Traditional social studies curricula emphasize the mastery of low-level facts, such as the names of rivers, capital cities, and important dates. Traditional social studies is also characterized by a focus on the Western world, the development of a tenacious and non-reflective nationalism, textbook-centered teaching, and scant attention to citizen action.

A social studies curriculum consistent with the changing world society in which we live must focus on higher levels of knowledge rather than on facts, teach about nations in Asia, Africa, and the Middle East as well as about Westernized nations, use a variety of teaching materials, and help students to develop clarified, reflective, and positive identifications with their local cultures, nation-state, and the world (Banks, 1997).

Helping students to develop a reflective identification with their nation-state is necessary but not sufficient in today's world society. Solutions to many of the most pressing world problems require cooperation by citizens in many different parts of the world. Citizens who have a clarified and reflective identification with the world community are needed to help solve the most pressing problems that face humankind. A modernized social studies curriculum should also help students to develop the knowledge, skills, and commitment needed to participate in action to shape public policy in their communities, nation, and the world.

Teachers can collaborate with their colleagues to learn more about how students can engage in social action to shape public policy in their communities, nation, and world. The teachers in this photograph are attending a conference on prejudice reduction.
Source: Southern Poverty Law Center, Montgomery, Alabama.

THE GOALS OF THE SOCIAL STUDIES

The major goal of the social studies is to prepare citizens who can make reflective decisions and participate successfully in the civic life of their communities, nation, and the world. Goals in four categories contribute to this major goal: (1) knowledge, (2) skills, (3) attitudes and values, and (4) citizen action.

Knowledge

Students must master knowledge in order to make reflective decisions and to participate effectively in their civic communities. Knowledge in the social studies curriculum is usually drawn from the social science disciplines and from history. However, it may also be drawn from the humanities, as well as from other sources if it is needed by the citizen actor to make decisions and to take actions. Philosophy is frequently drawn on in the social studies to help students identify and clarify their values. To make reflective decisions, citizen actors must use higher levels of knowledge, such as concepts, generalizations, and theories. The social science disciplines are discussed in Part III.

Skills

Skill goals are very important in the social studies. They can be categorized as follows:

Thinking Skills: These skills include the ability to conceptualize, to interpret, to analyze, to generalize, to apply knowledge, and to evaluate knowledge (Byer, 1988, 1991).

Social Science Inquiry Skills: These skills include the ability to formulate scientific questions and hypotheses, to collect pertinent data, and to use the data to test hypotheses and to derive generalizations. Social science inquiry skills are discussed in Chapter 3.

Academic or Study Skills: These skills include the ability to locate, organize, and acquire information through reading, to acquire information through listening and observing, to communicate orally and in writing, to interpret pictures, charts, graphs, and tables, to construct timelines, to take notes, to make charts, and to read and interpret maps (Taba et al., 1971).

Group Skills: These skills include the ability to perform effectively both as a leader and as a follower in solving group problems, to participate in group research projects, to help set group goals, to use power effectively and fairly in group situations, to make useful contributions to group projects, to communicate effectively in a group, and to help resolve controversy in groups (Johnson & Johnson, 1991). Skills are discussed in Chapters 3, 4, 5, and 6.

Attitudes and Value Goals

Citizens must develop a commitment to democratic and humane values, such as human dignity and equality, in order to make reflective decisions and to take action consistent with the idealized values of the nation-state. However, it is inconsistent to try to develop commitments to democratic values by using indoctrination approaches. Modern social studies curricula try to help students develop a commitment to democratic values by teaching them a process for identifying the sources of their values, analyzing and clarifying their values, and justifying their values. The social studies should also help students to state the possible consequences of their value choices. A value inquiry model is presented and discussed in Chapter 15.

Citizen Action Goals

The social studies curriculum should provide opportunities for students to participate in projects and activities that will develop a greater sense of political efficacy and teach skills useful in influencing social and civic institutions. The National Council for the Social Studies (1994) emphasizes the importance of citizen action in the social studies. It states, "Social studies is the integrated study of the social sciences and humanities to promote civic competence....The primary purpose of social studies is to help young people develop the ability to make informed and reasoned decisions for the public good as citizens of a culturally diverse, democratic society in an interdependent world" (p. 3).

The social studies curriculum should help students develop the commitment and skills needed to close the gap between the democratic ideals symbolized in our flag and pledge of allegiance and social realities.
Source: Northshore Public Schools, Seattle, Washington.

The primary goal of citizen action projects undertaken in the social studies should be to provide experiences whereby students can attain a sense of personal, social, and civic efficacy, and not simply serve the community. However, the most effective projects contribute to each of these goals. Citizen action is discussed in detail in Chapter 15.

CHARACTERISTICS OF A MODERN SOCIAL STUDIES CURRICULUM

We stated that a modern social studies curriculum helps students develop the ability to make reflective decisions and to successfully participate in the civic life of their communities. We have also noted that it helps students develop mastery in four goal areas: (1) knowledge, (2) skills, (3) attitudes and values, and (4) citizen action. The effective social studies curriculum also has other characteristics.

It helps students develop the knowledge, attitudes, values, and skills needed to deal reflectively with the major social issues and problems in our nation and world. The rights of students with disabilities, the problems of women, ethnic and racial problems, human rights, and the problems of senior citizens are some of the salient and enduring unresolved social issues that continue to evoke controversy within the United States and in other nations. Global and international topics, issues, and problems should also be an important part of the social studies in all grades.

A major goal of the social studies should be to help develop citizens who have the commitment and the skills needed to help close the gap between the democratic ideals of our nation and societal realities. Throughout U.S. history, the rights of various groups have continued to expand. However, there is still a wide gap between our democratic ideals and societal realities. The social studies curriculum should provide a forum in which students can openly examine the conditions of various groups in society, analyze and clarify their values related to these groups and issues, decide on courses of action, and take citizen action when it is appropriate and feasible. Chapter 7 is devoted to teaching social issues.

A modern social studies curriculum is also characterized by units that are organized around topics, key concepts, problems, or issues. Units may or may not be developed cooperatively by the teacher and the students. However, they do provide for both group and individual projects and activities and consequently allow students to play an important role in determining the direction of their own learning. A unit may be organized around a topic such as "Canada: Our Neighbor to the North," around a concept such as culture, or around a decision-problem or issue such as "What Actions Should We Take Regarding World Hunger and Poverty?"

SCOPE AND SEQUENCE IN THE SOCIAL STUDIES CURRICULUM

The social studies curriculum varies within different states, counties, and school districts. However, some characteristics are rather consistent throughout the United States. In the earliest grades the social studies curriculum is usually characterized by units and learning experiences focusing on the most familiar institutions and social systems, such as the home, the family, the school, the neighborhood, and the community. State history is usually studied in the fourth grade. United States history is usually studied in three grades: fifth, eighth, and eleventh.

Within these broad topic categories, a wide variety of approaches are used to teach the social studies in U.S. schools. At the high school level, many schools offer a variety of elective courses, such as sociology, psychology, and problems of democracy. Primary grade teachers use many different approaches to teach about the school, the family, and the community.

Teachers can implement many of the characteristics of a modern social studies curriculum within the traditional scope and sequence pattern that dominates U.S. schools. Primary grade teachers can teach about the family and the community by requiring students to memorize isolated facts. Too often this is done. However, topics such as the family and the community can also be taught by using key concepts from the social science disciplines to organize lessons and units, and to teach students how to conceptualize, to generalize, and to analyze their values. Chapter 2 illustrates how a unit on the family can be organized around key social science concepts. A unit on "Women in American History Textbooks" in Chapter 3 illustrates how topics in U.S. history can be taught while teaching students social science inquiry skills. Throughout this book, we suggest ways in which teachers can teach higher-level concepts and skills, value analysis, decision-making, and citizen action within the context of the dominant social studies curriculum pattern in U.S. schools.

THE EXPANDING COMMUNITIES OF HUMANS

The *scope* (what is taught and in what depth) and *sequence* (when it is taught) pattern that dominates the social studies curriculum in the United States was heavily influenced by Paul R. Hanna (1963). Hanna believed students should study smaller communities first and then increasingly larger ones. Hanna called this sequence the "Expanding Communities of Men." This pattern had dominated the social studies curriculum for many years when Hanna (1963) restated it in an important article. Hanna emphasized that students should study the various human communities in the sequence described below. He noted that the specific grade placement of each of these communities was less important than the sequence suggested.

The child's family community
The child's school
The child's neighborhood
The child's local communities: city, county, metropolis, country
The child's state community
The child's region-of-states community
The U.S. national community
U.S. and Inter-American community
U.S. and Atlantic community
U.S. and Pacific community
U.S. and world community

For a variety of reasons, Hanna's expanding communities of humans concept has been severely criticized by some social studies educators. They question the assumption that students should study only those communities in which they function most intimately and argue that television often brings distant communities within reach of today's youth. They also argue that the expanding communities concept often leads to an overemphasis on the Western world and to the neglect of non-Western nations, women's history and culture, and the experiences of ethnic groups of color in the United States. However, despite strong criticisms, the expanding communities of humans pattern is the most common social studies scope and sequence plan in the United States. However, counties, states, and school districts often implement the plan in diverse and creative ways. The California State Board of Education (California Department of Education, 1997) departed from it significantly in the framework it adopted in 1987 and updated in 1997 (see Table 1.2 on p. 14).

When Superka, Hawke, and Morrissett (1980) studied social studies topics in the United States, they found that the following topics were the most frequently taught at the grade levels indicated. Notice how similar this sequence is to Hanna's expanding communities of humans framework.

Grade	Topic
Kindergarten	Self, school, community, home
1	Families
2	Neighborhoods
3	Communities
4	State history, geographic regions
5	United States history
6	World cultures, Western hemisphere
7	World geography or history
8	American history
9	Civics or world cultures
10	World history
11	American history
12	American government

Table 1.1 contains a list of social studies topics and units that are usually studied in the elementary and junior high school grades. What is taught in each grade varies widely according to school district. However, Table 1.1 describes what might be a typical sequence of topics and units for each grade level.

THE SEARCH FOR SCOPE AND SEQUENCE

Although there is dissatisfaction with the "Expanding Communities" scope and sequence plan among social studies educators, it remains the dominant plan used in the nation's schools in part because social studies educators cannot reach consensus regarding a scope and sequence plan that should replace it. The National Council for the Social Studies has taken the leadership in trying to develop a scope and sequence plan that can be endorsed by the profession. However, its efforts have not been successful. In 1982, it appointed a Task Force on Scope and Sequence to develop a plan for consideration by the profession. The NCSS Task Force did not endorse a particular scope and sequence plan, but it did develop an illustrative scope and sequence plan (National Council for the Social Studies Task Force on Scope and Sequence, 1984). This plan has had little influence on the scope and sequence plans that are used in most school districts.

A HISTORY-BASED SOCIAL STUDIES CURRICULUM

In 1987 the California State Board of Education (California State Department of Education, 1997) adopted a social studies curriculum framework that differs in several significant ways from the expanding communities of humans framework described earlier in this chapter. It is centered in the chronological study of history, emphasizes history as a story or narrative, incorporates the study of literature to deepen historical understanding, and introduces a new curricular approach for grades kindergarten through three (see Table 1.2). Biographies, myths, fairy tales, and historical tales are used extensively in these grades to evoke interest in history

TABLE 1.1. *Examples of Topics and Units for Grades Kindergarten Through Eight*

Kindergarten

Social studies units in kindergarten usually help students to develop a better understanding of themselves and other people. The school, the home, and holidays and celebrations are typical topics.

How are we alike and different?
Rules at home and at school
Holidays and celebrations
Our wants and needs

First Grade

Units in the first grade often deal with relationships in the home and school. A range of social science concepts can be used in the first grade to help students gain new perspectives on family and school life.

What is a family?
Different kinds of families
How we help our families
How families change
How schools and families are alike and different
What people do in schools
Conflict and cooperation at home and at school

Second Grade

Units in the second grade often focus on the neighborhood, people in groups, and groups and neighborhoods in other communities and nations.

What is a group?
Groups we belong to
What is a neighborhood?
Why do groups change?
Why do neighborhoods change?
Cooperation and conflict in groups and neighborhoods
How groups and neighborhoods help us satisfy our needs and wants
A neighborhood in Kyōta (Japan)
A neighborhood in Nairobi (Kenya)

Third Grade

Units in the third grade often focus on local communities, the city, and communities and cities in other nations.

What is a city?
What is a community?
How people meet their needs in communities
How people meet their needs in cities
A comparison of three cities: Washington, D.C., Tokyo, and Rome
How cities are governed
The economic life of cities

TABLE 1.1. *(continued)*

Fourth Grade

Common topics in the fourth grade are the state, the world as the home of humans, and regions of the United States and the world.

The first peoples of our state
The government and economy of our state
The history of our state
Regions of South America
Regions of the United States
The peoples and cultures of Africa

Fifth Grade

The geography, history, and culture of the United States are the most common fifth-grade topics. The early periods of United States history are usually emphasized. The rest of North America and nations in South America are also sometimes studied.

The First Americans
European explorations in America
The growth of the European colonies in America
The quest for independence
The birth of a new nation
The peoples and cultures of the United States
Women in United States history
The cultures and peoples of Latin America
Canada: Our northern neighbor

Sixth Grade

Units in the sixth grade often focus on the geography of the earth and the peoples who live in various parts of the world.

The geographic and cultural regions of the world
The peoples and cultures of Africa
The peoples and cultures of Australia
The peoples and cultures of Asia
The peoples and cultures of Eastern Europe
The peoples and cultures of Western Europe
The peoples and cultures of the Middle East

Seventh Grade

In the seventh grade, students frequently continue the study of world cultures and regions begun in the sixth grade.

Greek and Roman civilizations
The spread of Islam
Medieval days and ways in Europe
The development of nations
Science, reason, and the Enlightenment
Civilizations in Africa, Asia, and the Middle East
Conflict and challenge in the Middle East

TABLE 1.1. *(continued)*

Eighth Grade

The history and development of the United States is studied in the fifth, eighth, and eleventh grades. The intent in the eighth grade is to give students a more in-depth understanding of the nature of United States history and culture than was gained in the fifth grade.

The cultures of North America before the coming of the Europeans
Europeans and the Americans: The meeting of two Old World cultures
Columbus and the Taino Indians
The European colonies in America
The American Revolution
A new nation
The interactions of diverse cultures in the western part of the United States
The westward movement
Ethnic groups in United States history
Women who left their marks on history
Enslaved Africans in the United States and their Communities
A divided nation
The long, sad war
The United States as a world power

and to enhance historical understanding. The California framework emphasizes studying selected historical events in depth rather than covering many events superficially, incorporates a multicultural perspective, and requires the study of world history in three different grades: six, seven, and ten. The California framework also provides for students to participate in school and community service programs and activities. The California framework is unique because the study of U.S. history and geography is limited to the 20th century in the eleventh grade. The California scope and sequence plan has influenced those in several other states.

THE SEARCH FOR STANDARDS IN THE SOCIAL STUDIES

In 1991 President Bush launched America 2000, a long-range plan designed to greatly improve the schools so that students in the United States could compete successfully with students throughout the world. Goal 3 states, "American students will leave grades four, eight, and twelve having demonstrated competency in challenging subject matter including English, mathematics, science, history, and geography; and every school in America will ensure that all students learn to use their minds well, so they may be prepared for responsible citizenship, further learning, and productive employment in our modern economy" (U.S. Department of Education, 1990, pp. 5–6).

The America 2000 project, as well as other social, economic, and political developments, stimulated the leaders of the nation's professional subject-matter

TABLE 1.2. *The History–Social Science Framework for California Public Schools*

Kindergarten	Learning and Working Now and Long Ago
Grade 1	A Child's Place in Time and Space
Grade 2	People Who Make a Difference
Grade 3	Continuity and Change
Grade 4	California: A Changing State
Grade 5	United States History and Geography: Making a New Nation
Grade 6	World History and Geography: Ancient Civilizations
Grade 7	World History and Geography: Medieval and Early Modern Times
Grade 8	United States History and Geography: Growth and Conflict
Grade 9	Elective Courses in History–Social Science
Grade 10	World History and Geography: The Modern World
Grade 11	United States History and Geography: Continuity and Change in the 20th Century
Grade 12	Principles of American Democracy (One Semester) and Economics (One Semester)

Source: Reprinted with permission from *History–Social Science Framework for California Public Schools Kindergarten Through Grade Twelve* (Sacramento: California State Department of Education, 1988), p. 29.

organizations to develop standards for the schools. During the 1990s standards were developed by national organizations and associations for a number of school subjects, including mathematics, science, and arts education.

Standards were also developed by the National Council for the Social Studies (1994). However, because of the fragmented nature of the social studies, standards were also developed for several of the academic disciplines that make up the social studies, including history (National Center for History in the Schools, 1996), economics (National Council on Economics Education, 1997), geography (Geography Education Standards Project, 1994), and civics (Center for Civic Education, 1994).

The National Council for the Social Studies identifies ten themes (key concepts) in its standards and describes examples of how these key concepts can be taught in the early grades, the middle grades, and at the high school level. The ten themes or key concepts that are identified in the NCSS standards are summarized in Table 1.3.

In 1994 the National Center for History in the Schools (1994a,b,c) at the University of California, Los Angeles, published the first edition of the national standards for United States and world history. This is an example from *History for Grades K–4* (National Center for History in the Schools, 1994a):

Standard 1

Students should understand: *Family life now and in the recent past; family life in various places long ago.*

Students should be able to: Demonstrate understanding of family life now and in the past by:

Investigating a family history for at least two generations, identifying various members and their connections in order to construct a time line (p. 32).

TABLE 1.3. *The Ten Themes from the National Council for the Social Studies Standards*

1. **Culture.** The study of culture prepares students to answer questions such as: What are the common characteristics of different cultures? How does the culture change to accommodate different ideas and beliefs?

2. **Time, Continuity, and Change.** Human beings seek to understand their historical roots and to locate themselves in time.

3. **People, Places, and Environments.** The study of people, places, and human-environment interactions assists students as they create their spatial views and geographic perspectives of the world beyond their personal locations.

4. **Individual Development and Identity.** Personal identity is shaped by one's culture, by groups, and by institutional influences.

5. **Individuals, Groups, and Institutions.** Institutions such as schools, churches, families, government agencies, and the courts play an integral role in people's lives.

6. **Power, Authority, and Governance.** Understanding the historical development of structures of power, authority, and governance and their evolving functions in contemporary U.S. society and other parts of the world is essential for developing civic competence.

7. **Production, Distribution, and Consumption.** Because people have wants that often exceed the resources available to them, a variety of ways have evolved to answer such questions as: What is to be produced? How is production to be organized? How are goods and services to be distributed?

8. **Science, Technology, and Society.** Modern life as we know it would be impossible without technology and the science that supports it. This theme draws upon the natural and physical sciences, social sciences, and the humanities, and appears in a variety of social studies courses, including history, geography, economics, civics, and government.

9. **Global Connections.** The realities of global interdependence require understanding the increasingly important and diverse global connections among world societies and the frequent tension between national interests and global priorities.

10. **Civic Ideals and Practices.** An understanding of civic ideals and practices of citizenship is critical to full participation in society and is a central purpose of the social studies.

Source: Adapted with permission from National Council for the Social Studies, *Expectations of Excellence: Curriculum Standards for Social Studies* (Washington, D.C.: Author, 1994), x–xii.

In the first edition of the standards, each standard was followed by examples of student achievement. The examples in the standards evoked a storm of controversy and attacks by conservative educational and government leaders. On October 20, 1994, Lynne Cheney, former chair of the National Endowment for the Humanities, attacked the standards on the editorial page of the *Wall Street Journal* (Nash, Crabtree, & Dunn, 1997). Cheney, like other conservative critics who later spoke out, argued that the standards slighted the founding fathers and other national heroes and emphasized women's history and the history of people of color.

The attacks on the standards focused on the examples used to illustrate the standards rather than on the standards themselves. The attack on the standards culminated when the United States Congress voted overwhelmingly (99 to 1) to reject the standards. The conservative critics successfully mobilized the support of many influential Americans, including Senator Slade Gordon (state of Washington), and Rush Limbaugh, the popular radio and television personality. The defeat of the history standards in the U.S. Senate was an important and disturbing chapter in the construction and making of knowledge. In 1996 an edition of the history standards was published without the teaching examples (National Center for History in the Schools, 1996).

THE CHALLENGES TO THE SOCIAL SCIENCE DISCIPLINES: IMPLICATIONS FOR SOCIAL STUDIES TEACHING

Within the last two decades, the social science disciplines, like the humanities disciplines, have undergone tremendous changes because of the challenges they have experienced from both within and without. Social studies educators should be aware of and sensitive to these changes within the academic disciplines when they design and teach social studies in the schools. The changes within the academic disciplines have important implications for the ways in which the social studies curriculum is conceptualized, planned, and taught. Many of the findings of the social science disciplines about women and people of color, as well as some of the major assumptions about research that are established within the social science disciplines, have been seriously challenged by postmodern scholars, scholars of color, and feminist scholars within the last two decades (Banks, 1996; Rosenau, 1992). The ferment, challenges, and new paradigms that are developing in the social science disciplines should be reflected in the ways in which social studies is taught in the schools. There is a wide gap between the significant changes that are taking place within the social science disciplines and in the ways in which the social studies is taught in the schools. This gap should be closed.

It is important to realize that groups on the margins of society have been questioning the findings, assumptions, interpretations, and uses of mainstream social science since these disciplines were established. These challenges were often heard only within communities of color because the mainstream scholarly and popular communities rarely listened to the voices of groups on the margins of society (Banks, 1997).

Voices on the margins of a society are often able to provide a perspective that enriches and deepens mainstream intellectual and popular thought and discourse. These perspectives are often the most visionary ones within a society and become legitimized over time, often by being appropriated by mainstream society. We call this kind of knowledge *transformative academic knowledge* (Banks, 1996). Brewer (1993) describes how Black feminist scholars have brought new concepts and paradigms into the social science disciplines, such as the "articulation of multiple oppressions," or the ways in which race, class, and gender interact to oppress African American women (p. 13).

Transformative Academic Knowledge

We call the explanations that challenge mainstream academic knowledge, and that expand the historical and literary canon, *transformative academic knowledge* (Banks, 1996) [See Table 1.4]. Transformative academic knowledge challenges some of the key assumptions that mainstream scholars make about the nature of knowledge. Transformative knowledge and mainstream academic knowledge are based on different assumptions about the nature of knowledge, about the influence of human interests and values on knowledge construction, and about the purposes of knowledge.

An important tenet of mainstream academic knowledge is that it is neutral, objective, and uninfluenced by human interests and values. Transformative academic knowledge reflects postmodern assumptions about the nature and goals of knowledge (Rosenau, 1992). *Transformative academic scholars assume that knowledge is not neutral but is influenced by human interests; that all knowledge reflects the power and social relationships within society, and that an important purpose of knowledge construction is to help people improve society* (Code, 1991; Collins, 1991; Harding, 1991). A major aim of transformative knowledge is to understand society so that it may be changed and improved. The primary aim of mainstream academic knowledge is to build theory and explanations.

Concepts such as *feminist standpoint theory* and *positionality* are used by feminist scholars to describe ways that the social, political, and economic situations in which knowers are embedded influence how and what they know. Like the African American scholars who preceded them, feminist scholars recognize that knowledge often labeled objective, neutral, and universal is hegemonic and reinforces dominant social, cultural, and economic arrangements within society. The challenges to the social sciences by feminist scholars and scholars of color reveal how knowledge that is considered objective often contributes to the oppression and voicelessness of marginalized groups.

An influential example of knowledge that was considered objective by many people yet contributed to the marginalization of low-income people and people of color was *The Bell Curve: Intelligence and Class Structure in American Life,* written by Herrnstein and Murray (1994). This book legitimized and perpetuated negative conceptions about the intellectual ability of low-income people and African Americans. The feminist and ethnic projects describe the politicized nature of knowledge (Collins, 1990). Harding (1991) states that every account by humans is "fully political."

DECISION-MAKING: THE HEART OF THE SOCIAL STUDIES

The new paradigms that have been constructed by scholars of color and feminist scholars provide an excellent framework for examining social issues and decision-making in the social studies. Decision-making, like the transformative scholarship constructed by many scholars of color and feminist scholars, is concerned with both knowledge and values and with the ways in which they can be synthesized to guide reflective and humane action.

TABLE 1.4. *Types of Knowledge*

Knowledge Type	Definition	Examples
Personal/Cultural	The concepts, explanations, and interpretations that students derive from personal experiences in their homes, families, and community cultures.	Understandings by many African Americans and Hispanic students that highly individualistic behavior will be negatively sanctioned by many adults and peers in their cultural communities.
Popular	The facts, concepts, explanations, and interpretations that are institutionalized within the mass media and other institutions that are part of the popular culture.	Movies such as *Birth of a Nation, How the West Was Won,* and *Dances With Wolves.*
Mainstream Academic	The concepts, paradigms, theories, and explanations that constitute traditional Western-centric knowledge in history and the behavioral and social sciences.	Ulrich B. Phillips, *American Negro Slavery;* Frederick Jackson Turner's Frontier theory; Arthur R. Jensen's theory about Black and White intelligence.
Transformative Academic	The facts, concepts, paradigms, themes, and explanations that challenge mainstream academic knowledge and expand and substantially revise established canons, paradigms, theories, explanations, and research methods. When transformative academic paradigms replace mainstream ones, a scientific revolution has occurred. What is more normal is that transformative academic paradigms coexist with established ones.	George Washington Williams, *History of the Negro Race in America;* W.E.B. DuBois, *Black Reconstruction;* Carter G. Woodson, *The Mis-Education of the Negro;* Gerda Lerner, *The Majority Finds Its Past;* Rodolfo Acuña, *Occupied America: A History of Chicanos;* Herbert Gutman, *The Black Family in Slavery and Freedom 1750–1925.*
School	The facts, concepts, generalizations, and interpretations that are presented in textbooks, teacher's guides, other media forms, and lectures by teachers.	Lewis Paul Todd and Merle Curti, *Rise of the American Nation;* Richard C. Brown, Wilhelmena S. Robinson, & John Cunningham, *Let Freedom Ring: A United States History.*

profile

RONALD TAKAKI

A Transformative Scholar Who Is Providing a Different Mirror on U.S. History

Ronald Takaki is one of the foremost nationally recognized historians in the United States. The grandson of Japanese immigrant plantation laborers, he holds a Ph.D. in American history from the University of California, Berkeley, where he has been a professor of ethnic studies for more than two decades. His books include *Iron Cages: Race and Culture in 19th Century America, Strangers From a Different Shore: A History of Asian Americans,* and *A Different Mirror: A History of Multicultural America. A Different Mirror* provides a revisionist interpretation of U.S. history. *Publisher's Weekly* describes it as a "brilliant revisionist history of America that is likely to become a classic in multicultural studies." In *A Different Mirror* Takaki writes, "America does not belong to one race or one group, the people in this study remind us, and Americans have been constantly redefining their national identity from the moment of first contact on the Virginia shore. By sharing their stories, they invite us to see ourselves in a different mirror" (p. 17).

Takaki is a transformative scholar who is helping to rewrite American history by incorporating the perspectives of groups of color into the story of how the United States developed. He points out, for example, that just as Ellis Island was an important entry point for European

Americans, Angel Island in the San Francisco Bay was an important entry point for Chinese immigrants to the United States.

References

Takaki, R. (1989). *Strangers from a different shore: A history of Asian Americans.* Boston: Little Brown.

Takaki, R. (1993). *A different mirror: A history of multicultural America.* Boston: Little Brown.

In an important and influential article, Shirley Engle (1960) stated that decision-making should be a major goal of social studies instruction. Later, Engle and Ochoa (1988) developed a curriculum framework for a decision-making–focused social studies curriculum.

We also believe that the social studies should help students attain the skills needed to recognize and solve human problems, analyze and clarify values, and make sound, reflective decisions that will contribute to the perpetuation and improvement of their communities, nation, and world. Our perception of the proper goal for the social studies resulted largely from a realization that citizens—students, homemakers, factory workers, businesspersons, labor leaders, politicians, welfare recipients, and all others—must each day make personal and public decisions that will affect their lives and their community, nation, and world. These are the kinds of nagging decision-problems with which citizens must often deal:

Should I take the job at Tony's or at Bell's?
Should we buy a house, a condominium, or continue to rent?
Should we stop fertilizing our lawn so that more fertilizer will be available for crops?
Would Taylor be a better member of Congress than Kitano?
Should I vote for or against the school bond issue?
Should I become active in Citizens Against Animal Cloning (CAAC)?

Individuals are not born with the capacity to make reflective decisions. Decision-making is a skill that must be developed and practiced. When individuals develop the ability to make reflective decisions, they can act intelligently. *We believe that the most important goal of the social studies should be to develop reflective citizen actors.* We are using citizen to mean a member of a democratic state or nation. Citizen actor refers to an individual who makes a deliberate effort to influence his or her political environment, including its laws, public policies, values, and the distribution of wealth. The activities in which he or she participates are citizen action. Citizen action may, of course, be effective or ineffective.

We are assuming that decision-making skills can be developed, that humans can be trained to reflect before acting on problems, and that individuals can learn to act on their freely made decisions. We cannot expect individuals to act on decisions they have been forced to make. In the decision-making model introduced later in this chapter, the individual must be able to choose freely from many alternative courses of action, consistent with human dignity, before we can characterize his or her behavior as decision-making. This model is discussed in detail in Chapter 15.

Essential Components of the Decision-Making Process

KNOWLEDGE

Reflective decisions cannot be made in a vacuum. Social science knowledge is one necessary component for sound decision-making. If two people (a couple) try to decide whether to join and become active in Citizens Against Animal Cloning (CAAC), they can make a better decision if they know the scientific facts about animal cloning, the extent to which the technology for cloning animals has been developed, and both its possible beneficial and negative effects. By studying historical and political information on animal cloning, the couple would be able to make some informed predictions about the possible consequences of further research and development in animal cloning. They could consequently make a more reflective decision about whether to join and become active in Citizens Against Animal Cloning.

"I knew we shouldn't have had him cloned. All he does is play with himself."

Source: William Haefeli © 1998 from The Cartoon Bank, all rights reserved.

METHODS AND WAYS OF ATTAINING KNOWLEDGE

Knowledge is needed to make reflective decisions. There are many ways of knowing or attaining knowledge. Kerlinger (1984) has summarized four methods of knowing described by Charles Peirce, a philosopher. When people use the *method of tenacity,* they hold firmly to what they know to be true—it is true because they hold firmly to it and have always believed it. Individuals seek out established belief when they use the method of authority. When individuals argue that they know something to be true because it is "agreeable to reason" and self-evident they are using the *a priori method.* Peirce (quoted in Kerlinger, 1984) argues that we need a method to attain knowledge "by which our beliefs may be determined by nothing human....The method must be such that the ultimate conclusion of every man shall be the same. Such is the method of science" (p. 6).

A further discussion of the hypothetical couple mentioned above will clarify the four methods of knowing. When trying to decide whether they should join Citizens Against Animal Cloning, the couple may derive knowledge related to their decision-problem by the *method of tenacity.* The couple may conclude that further developments in human cloning will result in a world in which genetic engineering will be used by powerful groups to eliminate other human groups. The couple reaches this conclusion because they have always believed that human groups are ethnocentric and will use power to defeat or eliminate other human groups.

The couple may have no firm beliefs about animal cloning and little information. They may seek out an authority to get information. The couple may hear a biology professor talk about animal cloning on a television talk show. The professor, who is a strong advocate of animal cloning, argues that it will prove highly beneficial to humans because in time scientists will be able to clone important body organs, such as hearts and lungs, and therefore will be able to save many lives. The professor does not discuss any of the possible ethical, social, or political problems that might occur as a result of the cloning of human organs or of cloning humans.

The couple may use still a different method for obtaining knowledge about animal cloning. They may, without seeking an authority, or sources of information about animal cloning, discuss it and conclude that it is self-evident that animal cloning is required to provide needed scientific development and innovations.

Limitations of Ways of Knowing

It is not difficult to state the limitations of the ways of knowing just discussed and illustrated. Some of the methods have more serious limitations than others. The method of tenacity is not an effective way of gaining knowledge because humans are capable of believing and holding firmly to almost anything imaginable. A brief study of history and anthropology will reveal that humans, throughout history, have held beliefs that they later considered outdated and bizarre. Beliefs in ancestor gods, shamans, witch doctors, and water witching indicate the tremendous range of human beliefs that have existed in many times and places. People's capacity to create beliefs today is as great as in any previous time in history. Some people refuse to live on the thirteenth floor of an apartment building. Others carry charms, such as a rabbit's foot, for good luck. Humankind's ability to create and imagine is one of the most important characteristics that distinguish humans from other primates.

"I can't do this particular book report—I haven't rented the movie yet!"
Source: Joe E. Buresch. Used with permission.

The method of authority is perhaps the most valuable of the three methods discussed above. We could not live organized and productive lives without relying a great deal on authorities because we live in a highly specialized world. When a doctor prescribes medicine, we assume that it will help heal our illness. We depend on authority when we plan trips using a road map, look up words in a dictionary, have our income tax completed by an expert, or act on the advice of a counselor.

While authorities are necessary in our highly specialized world society, a reliance on authority is unwise under certain conditions and in some situations. A biology professor may state publicly that animal cloning is needed to advance science without considering some of the serious ethical issues involved. Individuals are often perceived as authorities although they lack specific training in a given area, or they may be assumed to have conclusive information about problems although the knowledge in the field is scant and sparse. Citizens tend to put too much faith in and to expect too much from "experts."

As Kerlinger (1984) points out, the *a priori* method of knowing is very limited in deriving knowledge, because what is self-evident to one person may not be self-evident to another. People can hold opposite beliefs about the same things. Each will argue that his or her knowledge is self-evident. One person may argue that it is self-evident that animal cloning is essential for the advancement of science. Another may argue just as strongly that it is obvious that animal cloning will result in serious scientific, human, ethnical, and political problems.

The Scientific Method: A Way of Attaining Knowledge

The limitations of the *tenacity, authority,* and *a priori* methods suggest that we need a more reliable way of attaining valid knowledge. We should not be bound either by traditional belief systems or the opinions of authorities. A person should be able to repeat the procedures of the method and derive similar conclusions. Different people who use the method should derive similar conclusions, although these conclusions will be influenced by the researcher's positionality and cultural experiences.

The method should be public rather than private. It should be as independent as possible of the values and biases of the individual using the method. The method that comes closest to meeting these requirements is the scientific method. This is the method used by social scientists to derive knowledge: facts, concepts, generalizations, and theories. We will refer to this method as *social science inquiry* or *social inquiry.* The steps in social science inquiry are discussed in detail in Chapter 3.

If our hypothetical couple (trying to decide whether or not to join Citizens Against Animal Cloning) were to use the scientific method to gain the knowledge needed to make a reflective decision, they would do several specific things. First, they would state clear and researchable questions related to the decision-problem, such as:

What is the status of animal cloning?
What are its possible benefits to science?
What can it contribute to the improvement of human life?
What scientific, ethical, political, and social problems will it cause?

After stating the major questions related to their decision-problem, the couple would then try to define the major concepts in their questions, such as animal cloning, scientific benefits, and ethical problems.

Our hypothetical couple would then state some of their own hunches about animal cloning and its consequences. They would gather data to answer questions and to test hypotheses from a wide variety of sources, including books, magazines, and primary documents. The couple would then evaluate, compare, and analyze the data they had gathered. Even though the couple would use the knowledge in making their decision, they would realize that the knowledge is tentative and must be constantly compared with new findings and discoveries.

Our preference for the scientific method is by now clear. While it is not a perfect method, we believe that it is the most effective and efficient means of obtaining knowledge. Peirce overstates the value of the scientific method when he suggests that "our beliefs are determined by nothing human. . . ." As we will point out in our discussion of values, the scientific method is based on human values and assumptions, and it is limited by the cultural experiences and positionality of the researcher. The scientific method is also based on a set of assumptions, as Bernice Goldmark (1968) has insightfully pointed out. She writes:

The scientific method is based on the assumption that truth is neither absolute nor unchanging. Rather, truth is a judgment that, by the agreement of an informed community, produces desirable results....

It is on this assumption that we argue that all judgments should be held as hypotheses to be tested, evaluated, and reconstructed....(p. 215)

The scientific method also assumes that people can obtain consensus regarding generalizations and statements by using a method that is public, systematic, and repeatable. Persons who accept this method and reject the others value public over private and idiosyncratic knowledge. The *a priori* method, unlike the scientific method, is a private or "internal" method of knowing. An individual using this method derives conclusions on the basis of what is self-evident to him or her. What's self-evident to one person may not be self-evident to another. The scientific method attempts to derive knowledge that can be independently obtained by persons using the method at different times and places. *However, personal values and assumptions do affect the products of this method.* The problems we select and the questions we formulate are determined by our values, purposes, and social environment. These factors influence the outcome of scientific inquiry. However, these factors are less important in social science inquiry than they are in other methods of attaining knowledge.

As we indicated above, knowledge is one essential component of the decision-making process. We prefer the scientific method for attaining knowledge because it is systematic, self-correcting, open-ended, and public. Knowledge used to make reflective decisions must be derived using scientific inquiry. Decisions made on the basis of knowledge derived by intuition or tradition will not satisfy our reflective criteria. Before students can make reflective decisions, they must learn to use methods of social science inquiry to derive knowledge in the form of facts, concepts, generalizations, and theories. *They must also understand how the knowledge they construct is mediated and limited by their values, cultural experiences, and positionality.*

Reflective citizen actors need not independently derive every bit of knowledge they use in making decisions and solving problems. This would be impractical. Not much human progress would be made; few reflective decisions would be possible. However, citizen actors cannot intelligently apply or judge knowledge unless they are aware of the processes used to derive it and are able to use the methods of social scientists to derive knowledge when it is necessary and appropriate (for example, when authorities conflict). In a democratic nation, the scientific method should not be the exclusive property of a scientific elite. It should be shared by all members of the society who make decisions that affect the governing of the community, nation, and world.

INQUIRY AND DECISION-MAKING

Social knowledge, derived by a scientific process, is only one of the essential components of the decision-making process. Before we discuss other elements of the process, it is appropriate (1) to indicate how social science inquiry differs from decision-making and (2) to point out why social science inquiry is necessary but not sufficient for making reflective decisions. In this discussion we will also suggest how the ends of social science inquiry and decision-making differ.

The basic aim of mainstream social science inquiry is to derive knowledge in the form of facts, concepts, generalizations, and theories. The goal is to accumulate as much knowledge as possible. While the social scientist is primarily interested in producing knowledge, the decision-maker or citizen actor is mainly interested in how the knowledge derived by the social scientist can be used to help him or her solve problems and make decisions. The citizen actor, like the transformative scholar, is interested in constructing knowledge that can be used to guide action and to help solve human problems.

Social science inquiry produces knowledge; in decision-making, knowledge is selected, synthesized, and applied. However, as we have previously stated, the reflective consumer of knowledge must be familiar with the methods used by the professional social scientist to derive knowledge and must be able to use the method.

Knowledge in social science inquiry tends to be specialized, although the social science disciplines are becoming increasingly interdisciplinary. Each group of social scientists studies only those aspects of reality they believe are the appropriate concerns of their disciplines. They may ignore many important social problems and issues or study them from a limited perspective. Social scientists fragment reality in order to study it from unique perspectives. Reflective decision-makers and citizen actors must use the knowledge from all the various social science disciplines to solve personal and public problems. In decision-making we select, synthesize, and apply knowledge from diverse sources. No one discipline can adequately help citizen actors to make decisions about the complex problems that confront humankind.

Knowledge alone is insufficient for reflective decision-making. Reflective citizen actors must learn how to synthesize the information they obtain from many sources and apply it to complex social problems. Figure 1.1 and Tables 1.5 and 1.6 indicate how a citizen actor may attempt to decide what actions he or she should take regarding global hunger and poverty. Figure 1.1 illustrates how various social scientists may view the problem. Note how each of the social scientists views the problem from a limited perspective, while the citizen actor attempts to synthesize knowledge from various disciplines and sources (including his or her own inquiries) and use it in making a decision that can guide his or her action regarding the problem of global hunger and poverty. Table 1.5 shows how the decision-maker tries to clarify his or her conflicting values about global hunger and poverty. We have yet to discuss the value dimension, which is an important component of the decision-making process. Table 1.6 illustrates how the citizen actor determines a course of action.

Figure 1.2 illustrates how a reflective citizen actor and a social scientist might show concern about poverty in a hypothetical community. Note that their purposes—and therefore the main problems they formulate—are essentially different. The social scientist is interested primarily in building theory. As Redfield (1947) points out, the social scientist's "main objective is accurate description. Social scientists are scientific in that they are concerned with…what is, not what ought to be" (pp. 1–2). However, citizen actors are interested in both what is and what ought to be.

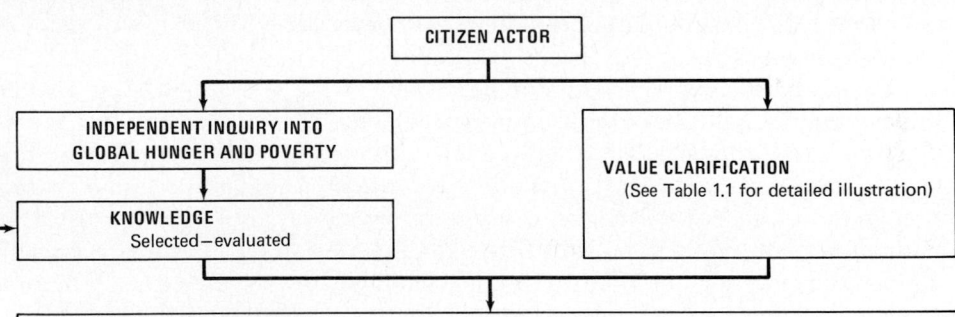

HISTORIAN
Analyzes events that culminated in global hunger and poverty; illuminates similarities between hunger and poverty today and in previous historical periods.

ECONOMIST
Studies the economic factors that contributed to the development of global hunger and poverty. Suggests that the standards of living in the world's affluent nations will have to be reduced if the problems of global hunger and poverty are to be solved.

POLITICAL SCIENTIST
Studies the political consequences of a world community that is made up of *"have"* and *"have not"* nations. Suggests that power struggles and war might result if the world's scarce resources are not more equally distributed among the rich and poor nations.

SOCIOLOGIST
Analyzes the effects of hunger and poverty on the norms, values and socialization practices among the victims of hunger and poverty. Suggests that severe hunger and poverty has a cogent impact on socialization practices.

PSYCHOLOGIST
Analyzes the nature and extent of aggression and frustration that develop among people who are victims of severe hunger and poverty.

ANTHROPOLOGIST
Studies how the responses to severe poverty and hunger are alike and different in various cultures. Concludes that responses to hunger and poverty are influenced by both cultural and biological factors.

GEOGRAPHER
Studies how hunger and poverty influence people's perceptions of their physical environment and their interactions with it.

CITIZEN ACTOR

INDEPENDENT INQUIRY INTO GLOBAL HUNGER AND POVERTY

VALUE CLARIFICATION
(See Table 1.1 for detailed illustration)

KNOWLEDGE
Selected—evaluated

REFLECTIVE DECISION-MAKING
Involves using knowledge acquired to identify alternative courses of action and to predict their possible consequences. An attempt is made by the citizen actor to choose a course of action that is most consistent with his or her values. (See Table 1.2 for a detailed illustration of this process.)

REFLECTIVE CITIZEN ACTION
Acting in a way to promote or realize the ends valued.

Reflective citizen actors synthesize and apply knowledge from many disciplines to help them make decisions about the action they will take regarding global hunger and poverty. They may also apply knowledge that they have derived from their own inquiries. The synthesis of *knowledge* (in the form of facts, concepts, generalizations, and theories) and *values* results in a *decision* which involves selecting a course of action from many possible alternatives, including inactio

Figure 1.1
Citizen actor's decision-problem: What actions should I take regarding global hunger and poverty?

TABLE 1.5. *Value Clarification (Poverty and Hunger)*

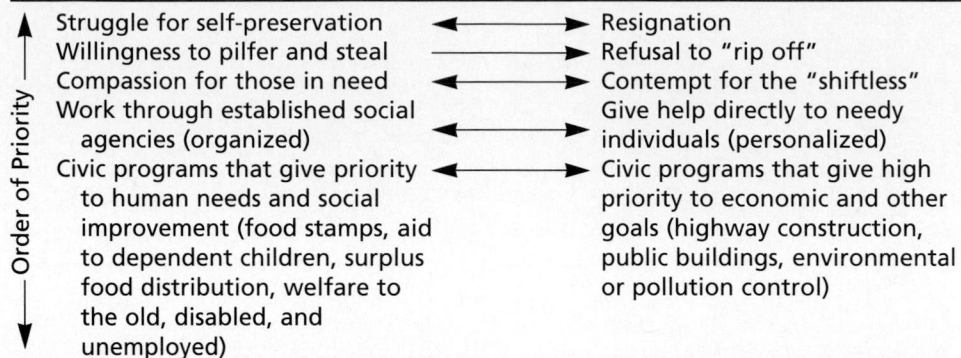

Order of Priority	
Struggle for self-preservation ←——→	Resignation
Willingness to pilfer and steal ——→	Refusal to "rip off"
Compassion for those in need ←——→	Contempt for the "shiftless"
Work through established social agencies (organized) ←——→	Give help directly to needy individuals (personalized)
Civic programs that give priority to human needs and social improvement (food stamps, aid to dependent children, surplus food distribution, welfare to the old, disabled, and unemployed) ←——→	Civic programs that give high priority to economic and other goals (highway construction, public buildings, environmental or pollution control)

In this example, values are conceptualized as existing on a continuum. An individual's value preferences may vary in intensity periodically, but are generally committed toward one end of a continuum. To act intelligently, the individual must arrange his or her values into a hierarchy of preference. The level of commitment to a particular value will greatly determine its place in the hierarchy. In Chapter 15 we present a model for teaching value inquiry. The basic steps of this model are outlined in Figure 1.3.

THE VALUE COMPONENT OF DECISION-MAKING

After they have derived higher-level knowledge from their own and others' inquiries, reflective citizen actors must try to relate the facts, concepts, generalizations, and theories to their own values before deciding to act. What people do with their knowledge depends largely on the values they hold in regard to the decision-problem components.

Thus value inquiry is a very important part of the decision-making process. Value inquiry should help decision-makers identify the sources of their values, determine how they conflict, identify value alternatives, and choose freely from them. *However, students should be required to justify their moral choices within the context of societal values such as human dignity, justice, and equality* (Oliver & Shaver, 1966). If students are not required to justify their moral choices in terms of higher societal values, value teaching will run the risk of becoming relativistic and ethically neutral.

Students must be given the opportunity to freely make value choices. However, individual choice must be defended and made within a framework of societal values (Oliver & Shaver, 1966). The student should be encouraged to predict and to consider the possible consequences of alternative values, and be helped to clarify conflicting and confused values. Not only are conflicting values widespread in the larger society, but individuals have many divergent beliefs, attitudes, and values. Many individuals who are active in religions that preach brotherhood are intolerant of other cultural and religious groups.

Before individuals can make sound decisions and act reflectively, they must be helped to clarify their conflicting and confused values. *We believe that value inquiry and clarification is one of the most important phases of the decision-making process.* Value issues are perhaps the most baffling problems that face both individuals and society. While we probably have the sophistication and means to solve many of our

TABLE 1.6. *The Decision-Making Process (Global Hunger and Poverty)*

A. If I donate money to a world relief organization,

THEN I . . .
1. will be helping an organization that is already set up to help solve the problem of global hunger and poverty.
2. may help save a starving child's life.
3. will feel I am doing something to help eliminate world hunger and poverty.

BUT I . . .
4. will make only a small effort in behalf of my concern.
5. will have to do without some goods I wanted to buy with the money.
6. may be doing little to help starving people because some relief organizations use most of the money they collect to pay overhead costs.

B. If I give up eating meat,

THEN I . . .
1. will be making a strong statement about my concern for global hunger and poverty.
2. will be increasing the amount of meat available on the world's market.
3. will be disassociating myself from "overconsuming" Americans.
4. will be able to eat more cheaply.

BUT I . . .
5. will be doing nothing to assure that the meat that I do not eat will get to the world's starving people.
6. will have to give up a group of foods that I enjoy eating very much.
7. will have to find other foods to substitute for meat.
8. will experience difficulties when I am eating out or eating with others.

C. If I form an organization to help solve the problem of global hunger and poverty,

THEN I . . .
1. will be organizing my efforts in a concerted public way.
2. may involve a substantial number of people who feel much as I do.
3. may be able to get food to many starving children and adults.

BUT I . . .
4. will have to make a heavy investment of time and energy in the organization.
5. may find it difficult to interest enough people to work for and contribute to the organization.
6. may be criticized by existing relief organizations for "duplicating efforts."
7. may not succeed in raising needed funds.

D. If I run for election to a local political office,

THEN I . . .
1. may be able to help reduce hunger and poverty within my own community.
2. could express my views publicly at city council meetings to be reported in the media.
3. could influence or advocate the effective distribution of more food to the poor through changes in local and national laws.
4. could see that such laws were enforced if my views were sustained *and the laws were enacted.*

BUT I . . .
5. may not succeed in getting elected to the city council.
6. might find myself a lone voice without support on the city council.
7. could lose my political effectiveness if I could not engage in tradeoffs on other issues.
8. may risk compromising my views or watering them down to achieve any action related to poverty.

TABLE 1.6. *(continued)*

E. If I choose to do nothing (inaction), *THEN I . . .*	*BUT I . . .*
1. do not really have a strong concern about global hunger and poverty.	4. will not be justified in criticizing others for their inaction on problems related to global hunger and poverty.
2. may not have the courage of my own conviction.	5. will have to live with the fact that thousands of people are starving to death each year while I am living in relative affluence.
3. will not risk taking actions that may not succeed.	

pressing human problems, we have neither clarified our value positions on them nor developed a commitment to solve them.

Let us return to the couple that was trying to decide whether they should join Citizens Against Animal Cloning. We will illustrate how values played an important role in their final decision. The couple gathered data about many different aspects of animal cloning. They read books, magazine articles, and listened to authorities who had conflicting opinions about animal cloning. The couple concluded that both those authorities who argue for the need to continue animal cloning and those who warn about its dangers and problems make compelling points. They believe that the information is far too complex and contradictory to accurately predict the long-term effects of animal cloning. The couple greatly values human dignity, and they decide to base their decision primarily on their value commitments. The couple decides that human dignity is more important to them than scientific advancement. They believe that animal cloning seriously threatens human dignity. They will join and become active in Citizens Against Animal Cloning.

The couple's attitudes and values, more than the knowledge they acquired, determined their decision and consequent action. However, knowledge enabled them to clarify their values and to know what values they considered most important. While knowledge is necessary for sound decision-making, it is not sufficient. The attitudes, beliefs, and values of citizen actors are often the most important determinants of their behavior.

DECISION-MAKING AND THE SOCIAL STUDIES CURRICULUM

The main goal of the social studies should be to help students develop the ability to make reflective decisions and to take successful action to solve personal and public problems. Knowledge, derived by an inquiry process, and values, analyzed and clarified by value inquiry, are essential components of the decision-making process. The relationship between these components is illustrated in Figure 1.3. Decision-makers must select, synthesize, and apply knowledge from various social science disciplines and clarify their values before they can act reflectively on the vexing problems in our global society.

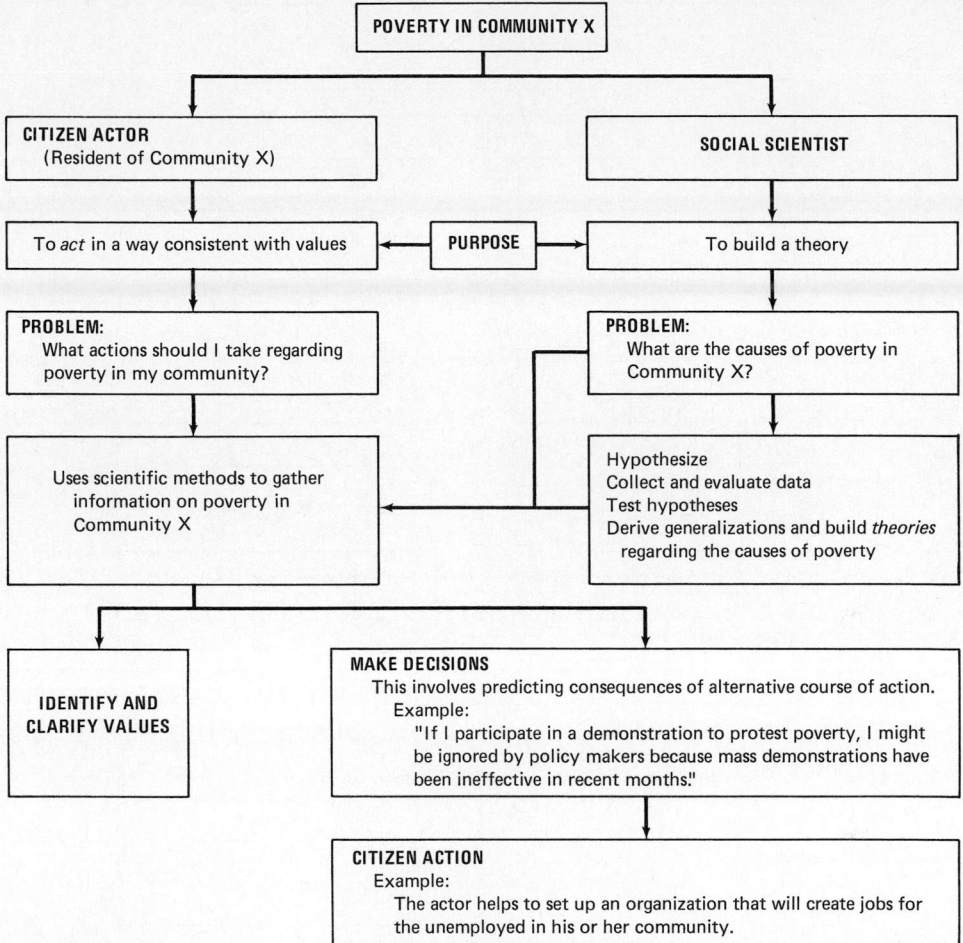

Figure 1.2
How a reflective citizen actor and a social scientist might approach the problem of poverty in community X.

The social studies curriculum should help students gain proficiency in inquiry, valuing, and decision-making skills. Inquiry, valuing, and decision-making each consist of a cluster of interrelated skills, as will become evident in later chapters. Each cluster of skills contains highly interrelated elements. We separate them in this text to facilitate discussion and to emphasize the need for systematic instruction in each. Lessons should also be planned to give the student practice in relating each set of skills to the others, because the ultimate goal of social studies education is to help students make sound decisions and act reflectively.

Historical content illustrating great decisions that people in the past had to make can be used to teach students decision-making skills. In the *Inquiry Strategy* for this chapter, students are asked to decide what decision Thomas Jefferson should make regarding the Louisiana Territory. This case can be used when the class is

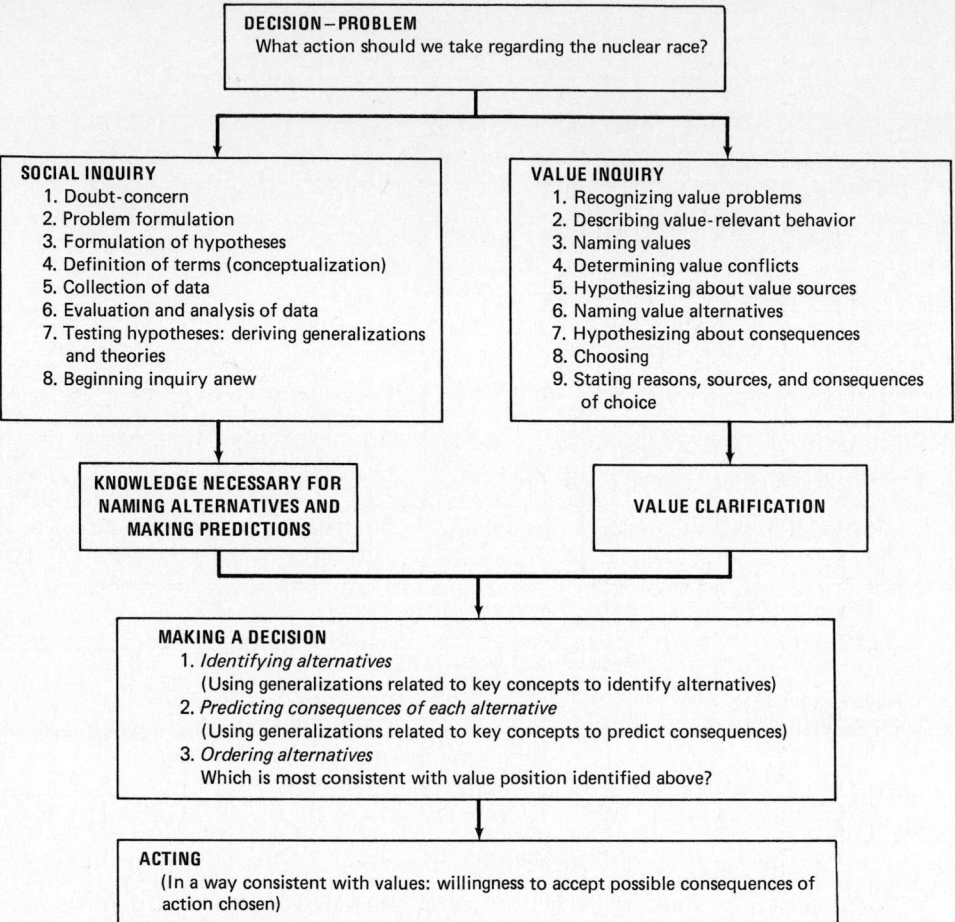

DECISION — PROBLEM
What action should we take regarding the nuclear race?

SOCIAL INQUIRY
1. Doubt-concern
2. Problem formulation
3. Formulation of hypotheses
4. Definition of terms (conceptualization)
5. Collection of data
6. Evaluation and analysis of data
7. Testing hypotheses: deriving generalizations and theories
8. Beginning inquiry anew

VALUE INQUIRY
1. Recognizing value problems
2. Describing value-relevant behavior
3. Naming values
4. Determining value conflicts
5. Hypothesizing about value sources
6. Naming value alternatives
7. Hypothesizing about consequences
8. Choosing
9. Stating reasons, sources, and consequences of choice

KNOWLEDGE NECESSARY FOR NAMING ALTERNATIVES AND MAKING PREDICTIONS

VALUE CLARIFICATION

MAKING A DECISION
1. *Identifying alternatives*
   (Using generalizations related to key concepts to identify alternatives)
2. *Predicting consequences of each alternative*
   (Using generalizations related to key concepts to predict consequences)
3. *Ordering alternatives*
   Which is most consistent with value position identified above?

ACTING
(In a way consistent with values: willingness to accept possible consequences of action chosen)

Figure 1.3
The decision-making process.

studying the period after the War for Independence. Similar strategies are found throughout this book.

Decision-making skills can be taught within the context of the dominant curricular framework found in most school districts and discussed earlier. Table 1.7 shows examples of decision-problems that students can study at the various grade levels. These problems can be studied as part of regular topical social studies units or can be unit topics themselves. The specific ways in which decision-problems can be taught within the context of existing curricula will become clearer as you progress through this book.

TABLE 1.7. *Examples of Decision-Problem Units*

Kindergarten and First Grade: The Home, School, and Community

What should we do as a family to make our community safe?

What should we do as a class and a school to better solve conflicts and problems that occur on the playground and during recess?

What actions should we take in school to help poor families in our community?

Second and Third Grades: Neighborhoods and Communities

What should we do to help reduce pollution in our community?

What should we do to help improve safety in our neighborhood?

What should we do to get to know better the many different kinds of peoples and cultures in our community?

What should we do to get more people in our community to vote for the school levy?

Fourth Grade: State History

What should we do to get the state legislature to provide more money for the schools?

What action should we take regarding the nuclear waste sites in our state?

What action should we take regarding the controversy over Indian fishing rights in our state?

What action should we take to help solve the problems caused by the fact that we do not have a state income tax?

Fifth Grade: United States History

What action should we take regarding poverty in our community and nation?

What action should we take to help women attain more opportunities in our communities and nation?

Because we cannot vote, what actions should we take regarding the current presidential election?

Sixth and Seventh Grades: World Cultures, Geography, and World History

What action should we take regarding the Israeli-Arab dispute in the Middle East?

What action should we take regarding the world's refugee problem?

What action should we take regarding world hunger and poverty?

Eighth Grade: United States History

What action should we take regarding the high rate of unemployment in our nation?

What action should we take regarding discrimination against different groups in our nation?

inquiry strategy

WHAT SHALL THOMAS JEFFERSON DECIDE?

When the class is studying the period after the War for Independence in U.S. history, ask them to read the following case study. Then divide the class into three groups about the same size. One group will develop arguments and evidence to support the purchase of the Louisiana Territory; another group will develop arguments and evidence that Jefferson had insufficient evidence on which to make a defensible decision. The third group will develop arguments and evidence against the purchase of the Louisiana Territory.

THE DILEMMA

Should President Jefferson buy the Louisiana Territory? He has no legal authority to do so. Moreover, such a step might bring on a war with Spain. But not to buy Louisiana might mean losing the chance to add vast new territories to the new nation.

In 1801 Thomas Jefferson came into office as president of the United States. On July 4, 1803, President Jefferson received a letter from Paris. For long, anxious months he had been waiting for this message. But now, before opening it, he hesitated. Was it good news or bad? Had he got what he so badly wanted for the nation? Or was this letter a refusal that would create problems threatening the future of the United States?

The letter was from Robert Livingston, American minister to France. Jefferson had sent him there to make a treaty with Napoleon, the French ruler.

Jefferson opened the letter. As he started reading, he caught a sharp breath of surprise. He continued reading, with growing astonishment and delight. But as he finished the message, his first relief gave way to dismaying second thoughts.

This letter was not the answer he had expected. It went far beyond his greatest hopes. But if he let stand the arrangement that Livingston had made, the consequences might be alarming. Sadly he wondered—if he let this treaty stand, would he ever again know peace of mind?

By Livingston's treaty, Jefferson had bought what would be half a nation. He had bought more land than any human being, before or since, had ever bought. He had bought one million square miles of North America. That had not been Jefferson's intention. He had asked Livingston to try to buy the port of New Orleans from Napoleon. Instead, as Jefferson's agent, Livingston had bought the entire French territory of Louisiana.

But I have no right to buy Louisiana, Jefferson realized. Even though he was president, under the Constitution of the United States he had no authority to buy foreign territory.

His political enemies would pounce on this action. They would accuse him of being a man who violated his most sacred principles. They would charge that

Story written by George Shaftel. Reprinted with permission of the author.

Thomas Jefferson, who insisted so firmly that the Constitution must be upheld with extreme care to obey all its clauses exactly as they were written, now had shamelessly violated it!

Jefferson had maintained that the rights of the states must never be lessened by a strong central government. Now he had plotted to reduce the states' authority and to enormously strengthen the federal power.

Jefferson, who had preached stern economy with treasury funds, now was pouring out many millions of dollars to buy—what? A million square miles of harsh, barren land. That was not the worst, however.

In buying Louisiana, it might be that the United States had bought an enormous amount of trouble. With gloomy foreboding, Jefferson realized that perhaps he had started a quarrel with Spain that would lead to war. Moreover, it was likely that this purchase would arouse political problems that would cause strife and disunity in the nation for generations to come.

Sadly Jefferson tried to reassure himself. He was buying territory from France only to make sure that the growth and prosperity of the United States would be helped, not hindered.

Had he made a ghastly mistake?

There still was time. He could still cancel the purchase.

But should he?

What do you think Jefferson should do? Why?

FOLLOW-UP ACTIVITY

Create a scenario in which Jefferson is meeting with his cabinet to consider the treaty. Have different students role-play the parts of the Secretaries of State, Treasury, and War. What advice might each give Jefferson? What values might each hold? Jefferson was a strong advocate of Republican party principles, yet if he accepted the treaty and all its implications, he would certainly be acting like his despised opponents, the Federalists. How might Jefferson justify his seemingly conflicting value positions? What risks and consequences are involved? The president and the secretaries engage in a lively debate. At the end, Jefferson announces his decision and defends his position.

SUMMARY

We described some of the salient characteristics of a post-industrial society and the kind of social studies curriculum needed to help students become effective citizens in a rapidly changing world. The major goal of the social studies should be to help students attain the knowledge, skills, attitudes, and values needed to become reflective decision-makers and citizen actors. The social studies program should have goals in four major categories: (1) knowledge, (2) skills, (3) attitudes and values, and (4) citizen action. A modern social studies program should also help students deal reflectively with the major social issues and problems that face their communities, nation, and world. Teachers who wish to implement innovations in the social studies must do so within the context of the expanding communities of humans scheme which predominates in most U.S. schools. We have described ways in which this can be done. More examples are given in later chapters.

Developing decision-making skills should be a major goal of the social studies. One of the essential components of decision-making is knowledge. Reflective decisions can be made only when knowledge is scientific, higher-level, interdisciplinary, and reflects the perspectives, points of view, and experiences of diverse groups within society. Reflective decision-makers must not only be able to use and to recognize scientific knowledge, but to derive it themselves when necessary and appropriate. The knowledge on which reflective decisions are based must also be powerful and widely applicable so that it will enable the decision-maker to make the most accurate predictions possible. Higher-level concepts and their related generalizations are necessary for making accurate predictions. Thus the decision-maker must be able to derive these forms of knowledge. Knowledge that serves as a foundation for reflective decisions must also be interdisciplinary. Knowledge from any one discipline is insufficient to help us make reflective decisions on complex social issues such as animal cloning, poverty, and gender inequality.

While scientific, higher-level interdisciplinary knowledge is necessary for sound decision-making, it is not sufficient. Reflective decision-makers must also be able to identify and clarify their values, justify their value choices within the context of societal values (such as human dignity), and relate the concepts and generalizations they formulate to their values. The synthesis of knowledge and values constitutes the process of decision-making. During this process, citizen actors use social science concepts, generalizations, and theories to identify alternative courses of action and to predict their possible consequences. They order their values into a hierarchy and choose a course of action most consistent with their value position and with human dignity. Finally, they take action based on their decisions to resolve personal problems or to influence public policy.

REFLECTION AND ACTION ACTIVITIES

1. Examine several books by futurist authors such as Daniel Bell's *The Coming of Post-Industrial Society,* Alvin Toffler's *The Third Wave,* and John Naisbitt's *Megatrends.* Also look for more recent books that deal with the future. What are the implications of these books for planning the social studies curriculum?
2. Examine several school districts' curriculum guides in the Curriculum Materials Center in your university library or in local school districts. How are the scope and sequence plans in these guides similar to and different from the expanding communities of humans plan described in this chapter? How can a teacher implement a curriculum that focuses on decision-making and citizen action within the context of the expanding communities of humans scope and sequence idea? Develop a sample lesson for a designated grade to indicate how this can be done.
3. What difficulties might teachers encounter when trying to structure a social studies unit or lesson around social issues? What steps might they take to minimize such difficulties?
4. Identify a personal or social problem on which you are required to make a decision, such as "Should I prepare for a career rather than or in addition to teaching?" or "What actions should I take regarding racial and ethnic discrimination in my community?" If you do not currently face such a problem, select one on which you might be required to make a decision.

    a. Make a list of the knowledge you would need (or the questions you would have to ask) to make a decision.

    b. What values do you hold strongly regarding this problem? Try to list them in a hierarchy of preference. (See Table 1.5.)

    c. What are some decisions you might have to make? What consequences might they have? Write down your thoughts in the style of Table 1.6.

5. Recall your own experiences in social studies classes from kindergarten through high school. What were your classes like? What kinds of things did your best social studies teachers do? What activity in social studies do you remember as the one from which you learned the most (or was the most fun or the most exciting)? Compare your experiences with the goals, curriculum, and types of learning activities advocated in this chapter. Are there discrepancies between what you have experienced and what the authors recommend as sound theory and practice? If so, how do you explain these differences?

6. Assume that during a primary-grade valuing lesson you are reading an open-ended story in which two small boys who desperately need some money find a wallet containing ten dollars in cash. At this point the story ends. If, after you ask the students what they would do in a similar situation, a student says he would keep the money and destroy the wallet, what would be your response? What should be your role as a teacher in value education? Why? Do you believe there are certain values teachers have a responsibility to inculcate in students? If so, what are these values? Make a list of such values and compare it with those of other members of your class.

7. Arrange to visit a school where you can observe a social studies lesson being taught. By careful observation, try to identify the key ideas and other major objectives that the teacher is trying to teach. After the lesson, talk with the teacher to determine whether your ideas are consistent with his or hers.

8. Demonstrate your understanding of the following key concepts presented in this chapter by writing or stating brief definitions of them.

    a. citizen

    b. citizen actor

    c. citizen action

    d. decision-making

    e. knowledge

    f. interdisciplinary knowledge

    g. higher-level knowledge

    h. the method of tenacity

    i. the *a priori* method

    j. the method of authority

    k. social science inquiry or inductive method

    l. structure

    m. value inquiry

REFERENCES

Banks, J. A. (1996). The canon debate, knowledge construction, and multicultural education. In J. A. Banks (Ed.), *Multicultural education, transformative knoweldge, and action* (pp. 3–29). New York: Teachers College Press.

Banks, J. A. (1997). *Educating citizens in a multicultural society.* New York: Teachers College Press.

Bell, D. (1976). *The coming of post-industrial society.* New York: Basic Books.

Brewer, R. M. (1993). Theorizing race, class and gender: The new scholarship of Black feminist intellectuals and Black women's labor. In S. M. James & A. P. A. Busia (Eds.), *Theorizing black feminisms: The visionary pragmatism of black women* (pp.13–30). New York: Routledge.

Byer, B. K. (1988). *Developing a thinking skills program.* Boston: Allyn and Bacon.

Byer, B. K. (1991). *Teaching thinking skills: A handbook for elementary school teachers.* Boston: Allyn and Bacon.

California Department of Education, (1997). *History–social science framework for California Public Schools, kindergarten through grade twelve* (1997 updated ed.). Sacramento: California State Department of Education.

Center for Civic Education (1994). *National standards for civics and government.* Calabasas, CA: Author.

Code, L. (1991). *What can she know? Feminist theory and the construction of knowledge.* Ithaca: Cornell University Press.

Collins, P. H. (1990). *Black feminist thought: Knowledge, consciousness, and the politics of empowerment.* New York: Routledge.

Engle, S. H. (1960) Decision-making: The heart of social studies instruction. *Social Education,* 24, 301–304, 306ff.

Engle, S. H., & Ochoa, A. S. (1988). *Education for democratic citizenship: Decision making in the social studies.* New York: Teachers College Press.

Geography Education Standards Project (1994). *Geography for life: National geography standards.* Washington, D.C.: Author.

Goldmark, B. (1968). *Social studies: A method of inquiry.* Belmont, CA: Wadsworth.

Hanna, P. R. (1963). Revising the social studies: What is needed? *Social Education,* 27, pp. 190–196.

Harding, S. (1991). *Whose science? Whose knowledge? Thinking from women's lives.* Ithaca: Cornell University Press.

Herrnstein, R. J., & Murray, C. (1994). *The bell curve: Intelligence and class structure in American life.* New York: Free Press.

Johnson, D. W., & Johnson, F. P. (1991). *Joining together: Group theory and group skills* (4th ed.). Englewood Cliffs, NJ: Prentice-Hall.

Kanter, R. M. (1977). *Men and women of the corporation.* New York: Basic Books.

Kerlinger, F. N. (1984). *Foundations of behavioral research,* 3rd ed. New York: Holt, Rinehart and Winston.

Naisbitt, J. (1982). *Megatrends: Ten new directions transforming our lives.* New York: Warner Books.

Nash, G. B., Crabtree, C., & Dunn, R. E. (1997). *History on trial: Culture wars and the teaching of the past.* New York: Knopf.

National Center for History in the Schools (1994a). *National standards for history for grades K–4: Expanding children's world in time and space* (Expanded ed.). Los Angeles: Author.

National Center for History in the Schools (1994b). *National standards for United States history: Exploring the American experience.* Los Angeles: Author.

National Center for History in the Schools (1994c). *National standards for world history: Exploring paths to the present.* Los Angeles: Author.

National Center for History in the Schools (1996). *National standards for history* (Basic ed.). Los Angeles: Author.

National Council for the Social Studies (1994). *Expectations of excellence: Curriculum standards for social studies.* Washington, D.C.: Author.

National Council for the Social Studies Task Force on Scope and Sequence (1984). In search of a scope and sequence for Social Studies. *Social Education,* 48, pp. 249–262.

National Council on Economic Education (1997). *Voluntary national content standards in economics.* New York: Author.

Oliver, D. W., & Shaver, J. P. (1966). *Teaching public issues in the high school.* Boston: Houghton Mifflin.

Redfield, R. (1947). *The social uses of social science, No. 8013.* Columbus, OH: Charles E. Merrill. Reprinted from *University of Colorado Bulletin,* Vol. 47 (May 24, 1947).

Rosenau, P. M. (1992). *Post-modernism and the social sciences: Insights, inroads, and intrusions.* Princeton, NJ: Princeton University Press.

Superka, D. P., Hawke, S., & Morrissett, I. (1980). The current and future status of social studies. *Social Education,* 44, pp. 362–369.

Taba, H., Durkin, M. C., Fraenkel, J. R., & McNaughton, A. H. (1971). *A teacher's handbook to elementary social studies* (2nd ed.). Reading, MA: Addison-Wesley.

Toffler, A. (1980). *The third wave.* New York: William Morrow.

Toffler, A. (1982, Summer). Civil rights in the third wave. *Perspectives: The Civil Rights Quarterly.*

United States Department of Education (1990). *National goals for education.* Washington, D.C.

FOR FURTHER READING

Banks, J. A. (1997). *Teaching strategies for ethnic studies* (6th ed.). Boston: Allyn and Bacon.

Banks, J. A. (1997). *Educating citizens in a multicultural society.* New York: Teachers College Press.

Cornbleth, C., & Waugh, D. (1995). *The great speckled bird: Multicultural politics and education policymaking.* New York: St. Martin's Press.

Cyrus, V. (Ed.). (1997). *Experiencing race, class, and gender in the United States* (2nd ed.). Mountain View, CA: Mayfield.

Hahn, C. L. (1998). *Becoming political: Comparative perspectives on citizenship education.* Albany: State University of New York Press.

Harwit, M. D. (1996). *An exhibit denied: Lobbying the history of Enola Gay.* New York: Springer-Verlag.

Kolata, G. (1998). *Clone: The road to Dolly and the path ahead.* New York: William Morrow.

Linenthal, E. (1997). *History wars: Enola Gay and other battles for the American past.* New York: Henry Holt.

Nash, G. B., Crabtree, C., & Dunn, R. E. (1997). *History on trial: Culture wars and the teaching of the past.* New York: Knopf.

Parker, W. C. (Ed.). (1996). *Educating the democratic mind.* Albany: State University of New York Press.

Silver, L. M. (1997). *Remaking Eden: Cloning and beyond in a brave new world.* New York: Avon.

Takaki, R. (1993). *A different mirror: A history of multicultural America.* Boston: Little Brown.

Takaki, R. (1995). *Hiroshima: Why America dropped the atomic bomb.* Boston: Little Brown.

CHAPTER 2

Unit and Curriculum Planning

THE NEED FOR AN INTERDISCIPLINARY PERSPECTIVE

The main goal of the social studies should be to help students develop the ability to make reflective decisions so that they can solve personal problems and, through citizen action, influence public policy. Sound decisions cannot be made in a vacuum; they must be based on knowledge. Reflective decisions must be based on scientific knowledge.

Reflective decisions must also be based on interdisciplinary knowledge. The reflective decision-maker should be able to view human events from the perspectives of several different disciplines. Knowledge from any one discipline is insufficient for making personal and public decisions and for understanding the complex nature of human behavior. To understand complex problems such as animal cloning, the feminization of poverty, and racial discrimination, the citizen actor not only needs to use economic concepts, but concepts from disciplines such as political science, sociology, and history.

To successfully influence public policy, the citizen actor must select, synthesize, and apply knowledge from the social sciences, as well as from philosophy and the humanities. The social scientist fragments the universe to study it more easily. The social studies help students view human behavior in a broad context. The behavior of the family is neither economic nor anthropological, but it can be profitably viewed through the special lens of each of these disciplines. When planning interdisciplinary units, it is important for you to realize that the social science disciplines are not specific content but have specialized ways to view the same human behavior. Human behavior is not fragmented. Scientists fragment it in order to study it from unique points of view.

The social science disciplines are discussed extensively in Part III. The separation of the discipline chapters in this book is done to emphasize the contributions that each discipline can make to an understanding of complex social issues, and not to suggest that any one discipline in and of itself is sufficient to explain human behavior or to solve human problems.

TEACHING INQUIRY, VALUING, AND DECISION-MAKING SKILLS

Inquiry, valuing, and decision-making each consists of a cluster of highly interrelated skills. Students should have practice in developing each of these sets of skills, as well as practice relating them. You can plan separate units and lessons that teach social science inquiry, valuing, and decision-making skills, or you can build units to teach all three sets of skills. The long-range goal should be to help students become adept in the processes of decision-making and citizen action. Thus, you should plan units and lessons that will give students practice in relating these sets of skills as often as possible. However, for purposes of emphasis, this chapter discusses and illustrates strategies for social science inquiry. Chapter 15 discusses value inquiry and illustrates how these skills can be combined to help students become reflective decision-makers and citizen actors.

THE INTERDISCIPLINARY UNIT

A unit is a series of interrelated activities designed to attain specific changes in student behavior. Most units contain these components:

1. A major topic or problem
2. Objectives
3. Initiation activities
4. Developmental activities
5. Assessment activities
6. Culmination activities

Social science units should ideally be structured around a number of organizing or key concepts, such as those discussed in Part III. In this chapter, we will illustrate how a conceptual unit can be built within the framework of a traditional social studies curriculum. You will most likely teach in a school that has a traditional social studies curriculum. The final part of this chapter discusses building a conceptual curriculum within schools or districts that wish to change their social studies curricula in substantial ways. Table 2.1 shows the parts of a conceptual unit with examples from a unit on the family discussed later in this chapter.

TABLE 2.1. *The Parts of a Conceptual Unit*

1. **Unit Topic**
   The family
2. **Key Concepts** *(only two are shown here)*
   Scarcity, role
3. **Key Generalizations** *(only two are shown here)*
   Every individual and society faces a conflict between unlimited wants and limited resources. This creates the need for decision-making. *(Scarcity)*
   Every member of a society must function in many different roles. *(Role)*
4. **Subideas**
   Mother and Father often want to buy two or more things when they have only enough money for one of them. *(Scarcity)*
   Father does different things when he goes shopping or to work. *(Role)*
5. **Objectives**
   The students will be able to list examples and nonexamples of *scarcity.*
   The students will be able to list the different *roles* in which they function.
6. **Initiation Activities** *(these activities are designed to start the unit in an interesting and exciting way)*
   The students will be asked what a family is and to state their ideas.
   The students will be shown pictures of different types of families and asked to state how they are alike and different.
7. **Developmental Activities** *(these activities are the heart of the unit)*
   The teacher reads *Aunt Flossie's Hats (and Crabcakes Later)* by Elizabeth F. Howard, an interesting story about a middle-class African American family.
8. **Evaluation Activities** *(these activities, which are ongoing throughout the unit, are designed to determine the extent to which the students are mastering the concepts and generalizations being taught)*
   The students are asked to list three examples of scarcity in their family.
   The students are asked to list several roles performed by themselves and by their parent or parents.
9. **Culmination Activities** *(during this phase of the unit, the major ideas that were studied are highlighted, reviewed, and interrelated)*
   Groups of students are asked to write and present skits that show scarcity.
   The students are asked to list as many different kinds of families as they can.
10. **A Resource Bibliography** *(includes sources for both students and the teacher)*

SELECTING AND ORGANIZING KEY CONCEPTS FOR INTERDISCIPLINARY UNITS

How you select the key concepts that will constitute your units will depend to a great extent on the degree of freedom you have. Most school districts have curriculum guides that provide a basic framework for the local social studies program; their main purpose is to ensure that the instructional program is sequential and developmental. Guides are therefore usually intended to function only as guides, not as blueprints that you are expected to follow without modifications. Curriculum guides may also contain suggested teaching strategies and instructional resources, which you may use in a way that will best enhance student growth and achievement. These comments are not intended to suggest that you should ignore the guidelines provided by your school district; rather, you should implement a program, within your district's guidelines, consistent with modern social studies theory and practice. Theory and research suggest that units should be organized around key concepts and generalizations. Such units will enhance students' understanding, retention, and transfer.

The social studies guides of most school districts specify a number of topics that the teachers of each grade are expected to cover. Those topics usually reflect the "expanding communities of humans" or the "expanding environment" approach; in the primary grades, the students study institutions with which they are most familiar and thus can understand most easily (see Figure 2.1). Most often, the home, school, holidays, community helpers, and the local community are studied in the primary grades. In the middle grades the state, exploration, pioneer days, and the histories of the United States and the Western Hemisphere are studied. World—which includes Europe, Africa, and Asia—and U.S. history usually constitute the program for the junior high school grades.

As the students move through the grades, they study behavior and institutions increasingly more remote from their direct experiences. We will not present a critique of the expanding environment approach, but rather emphasize the fact that you can structure a conceptually oriented curriculum within the framework of a traditional social studies program.

This approach was taken in the Taba Social Studies Program. The directors of this project identified eleven key concepts from the various social science disciplines plus a number of related generalizations and used content samples of the traditional program to develop the key ideas identified. The eleven organizing concepts are *causality, conflict, cooperation, cultural change, differences, interdependence, modification, power, societal control, tradition,* and *values* (Taba, Durkin, Fraenkel, & McNaughton, 1971). In the first grade, content samples are selected from the family, a traditional topic for the primary grades. Content samples are selected from the state, another traditional topic, for the fourth-grade program. While the structure of the Taba Social Studies Program is drastically different from traditional social studies programs, the topics are quite traditional. Approaching curriculum reform using this approach will allow you to maintain a degree of stability in the curriculum. You will also be able to use many of your available instructional materials and resources. There is also a legal reason for approaching curriculum reform within a traditional framework. The study of the

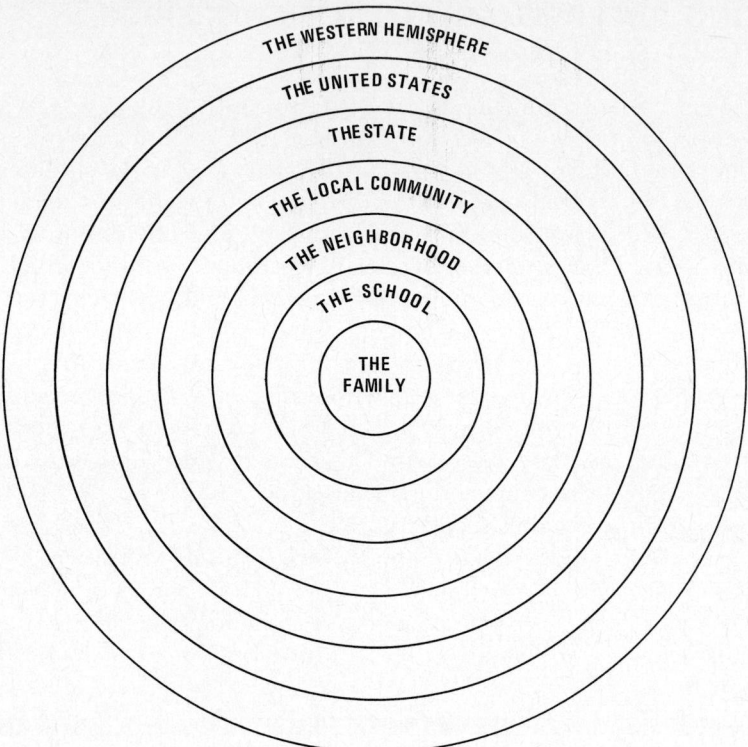

Figure 2.1
The expanding environment approach to curriculum construction. The traditional social studies curriculum is based on the concept of the expanding environment. Students study the human community that is closest to their actual experiences. As they move through the grades, they study increasingly larger communities. Teachers who are required to plan units within this structure can use organizing ideas from the disciplines to help students better understand the communities in which they live.

history of the state and the United States is mandated by most state governments. A final advantage of initiating a new program within a traditional framework is that you will feel more secure and will be more likely to implement it

NEW WINE IN OLD BOTTLES: TEACHING NEW CONCEPTS WITH TRADITIONAL CONTENT

If you have a social studies curriculum guide, you should begin planning your units for the year by carefully studying the topics you are required to teach, such as the home, the school, community helpers, and United States history. You should then study a list of key concepts from the social science disciplines so that you can decide which ones can be most effectively and meaningfully taught with the content you are required to teach. Key concepts from the social sciences are found in Part III. They are listed in Table 2.2.

Teachers must plan jointly to develop a conceptual social studies curriculum that helps students develop an increased understanding of concepts as they progress through the grades.
Source: Southern Poverty Law Center, Montgomery, Alabama.

TABLE 2.2. *Key Social Science Concepts*

History	Sociology	Anthropology
Change	Socialization	Culture
Leadership	Roles	Diffusion
Conflict	Norms and sanctions	Tradition
Cooperation	Values	Acculturation
Nationalism	Social movement	Ethnocentrism
Exploration	Society	Cultural relativism
Historical bias		Rite of passage

Political Science	Economics	Geography
Power	Scarcity	Location
Social control	Production	Spatial interaction
State	Interdependence	Urban spatial patterns
Interest group	Specialization and division	Internal structure of a city
Political socialization	of labor	Cultural diffusion
Political participation	Voluntary exchange	Environmental perception

Criteria for Selection of Concepts

What criteria can you use to select appropriate ideas for development? You should first consider the prior experiences of the students. If they have been introduced to specific concepts in a previous grade, you should further develop and expand these concepts, perhaps introducing new related concepts that will enhance their understanding of their social environment and help them become better decision-makers. You should also select concepts around which a great deal of data and content can be organized. While all key concepts within the social sciences can be used to organize and categorize a great deal of information, some concepts are more powerful than others—that is, they are more encompassing. The concepts selected should have the power to categorize and organize a large number of specific facts and information.

We do not mean to suggest that low-order concepts should never be selected, but the goal should be to select the most powerful ones when all factors are considered. Both *scarcity* and *exchange* are key economic concepts, but scarcity is a much more powerful idea. Taba, Durkin, Fraenkel, and McNaughton (1971) offer the following criteria for selecting organizing or key concepts for a conceptual curriculum:

1. **Validity:** Do they adequately represent ideas of the discipline from which they are drawn?
2. **Significance:** Can they explain important segments of the world today?
3. **Appropriateness:** Are they suited to the needs, interests, and maturational level of the students?
4. **Durability:** Are they of lasting importance?
5. **Balance:** Do they permit development of both scope and depth? (pp. 28–30)

Some consideration should also be given to the content that must be studied when key concepts are selected for study. Some content can be more profitably viewed from certain disciplinary perspectives than from others. For example, it is easier for students to grasp the concept of *culture* when they study U.S. families as well as families in other societies. Students cannot fully appreciate how much we are creatures of our own culture until they have viewed other ways of living and behaving. The concept of *power* can be understood more readily if students study an Indian nation than if they study community helpers, even though certain ideas about the political system can be learned when workers in the community are studied.

You should also select concepts from as many disciplines as is practical and appropriate. In other words, all social studies units should be *interdisciplinary*. The only way to assure that units are interdisciplinary is to select concepts from several disciplines during the initial stages of unit planning. Good judgment and sound selection criteria are important because it will not be possible for you to select concepts from each of the social sciences for every unit. Even though concepts from a particular discipline may not be identified initially, during class discussions you can occasionally help students view the content from other social science perspectives. However, only careful planning will ensure that specific concepts and ideas will be learned by your students.

Identifying Specific Concepts for a Unit

Helping students to view human behavior from the perspectives of the various social sciences will provide them with a sophisticated understanding of their social environment so that they can become reflective decision-makers and citizen actors. They have many daily experiences that can be profitably viewed through the lenses of various disciplines. Without the conceptual tools of the social scientist, students may and often do study topics such as the family, the community, and the school, and memorize a list of disorganized facts that are largely meaningless and quickly forgotten. However, if they learn organizing ideas when they study these topics, they will gain an understanding that can be further developed with new content in later grades. This knowledge will contribute greatly to their understanding of the world in which they live. The following example will illustrate how a first-grade teacher, Mr. Ortiz, who is required to teach "The Family," might select key concepts from the disciplines in order to structure an interdisciplinary unit.

AN INTERDISCIPLINARY UNIT ON THE FAMILY

Mr. Ortiz studies a list of concepts such as those listed in Table 2.2. As he studies the concepts of each discipline, he asks himself this question: "Which concepts from this discipline will best help my students understand the family as a social institution and become better decision-makers and reflective citizen actors?" He first looks over the key concepts of anthropology. Initially, he thinks that culture is a concept with which the students should be familiar, but he decides that they can better understand this concept if they also study families in other cultures. At this time, he does not have the materials necessary to introduce the students to another culture. He therefore decides not to introduce the concept at this time but to introduce culture when the class studies communities later in the year. By that time, his materials on the Hopi Indians will have arrived. He feels that the other anthropological concepts cannot be fruitfully introduced until the students are familiar with the concept of culture, because that is the most important concept in the discipline. Mr. Ortiz is quite familiar with the structure of anthropology and the other disciplines.

Next he studies the key economic concepts in Table 2.2, reviews their meanings, and decides that *scarcity, interdependence, production,* and *voluntary exchange* are not only concepts that the students should know, but are ideas that can be very effectively developed with content samples drawn from the life of a family living in the United States. He believes that he already has selected enough concepts for a unit but remembers that social studies units should be interdisciplinary and not just about economics. He reviews the key concepts in geography and political science. He decides that the only appropriate concept within these two disciplines for his family unit is the political science concept of *social control*. Certainly all students have rules at home that they must obey, and they should gain a better understanding of social control.

In studying the sociological concepts on our list, he immediately sees how closely *role* is related to one of the economic concepts he has selected, *interdependence*. He thus decides to select role. He also selects socialization, norm, and sanction because these concepts are related to the political science concept he chose, *social control*.

If students study laws, they should know how laws relate to norms and sanctions. He is tempted to add other concepts to his list but realizes that it is best for students to gain a working knowledge of a few concepts rather than to learn a large number of them superficially. Let's review the concepts Mr. Ortiz identified and the disciplines from which they were selected:

Discipline	Concepts Selected
Economics	scarcity
	interdependence
	production
	voluntary exchange
Political science	social control
Sociology	socialization
	norm
	sanction
	role

Mr. Ortiz is certain that his unit will be an interdisciplinary one because he has selected key concepts from economics, political science, and sociology, even though he did not select concepts from all the social science disciplines. He believes that it is neither practical nor possible for him to try to teach concepts from all the disciplines in one unit. He will teach other units during the year and at that time will introduce ideas from the other disciplines. He believes that students should be exposed to the ideas and ways of thinking used by all social scientists. As he looks over his list of concepts, he realizes a point that had been made by his professor in social studies methods: Although the social sciences have unique ways of looking at human behavior, the concepts and key ideas they use are far from being mutually exclusive. Political scientists often use key sociological concepts in their research. He notes how the political science concept of social control is related to the sociological concepts of *norms* and *sanctions*. The relationships among the social sciences is far from being a disadvantage to the social studies teacher; rather, it is a great advantage because their interconnections make it easier to plan units that cut across discipline lines.

IDENTIFYING RELATED GENERALIZATIONS

We have explained how Mr. Ortiz, who is required to teach about the family in the first grade, might go about selecting organizing concepts from the disciplines in order to structure an interdisciplinary unit. Once you have identified key concepts for a unit, you must then identify key generalizations. Organizing or key generalizations guide the selection of low-order generalizations or subideas, specific content samples, and teaching strategies. Generalizations that are related to organizing concepts are found in Part III of this book. Like key concepts, key generalizations should be powerful. They should summarize in general terms many facts and a great deal of specific information. They should also be empirical statements that can be scientifically tested. They should not be value or normative judgments.

Some lists of generalizations are value judgments that cannot be scientifically test-ed (see Chapter 3). Mr. Ortiz selects the organizing generalizations shown in Table 2.3 that are related to the key concepts already identified.

Identifying Subideas

After you have identified the organizing generalizations related to the key concepts you wish to develop, you should identify the subideas related to the organizing gen-eralizations. Subideas are low-order statements that relate to the specific content you are required to teach. Examples of subideas that Mr. Ortiz might select for his unit are found in Table 2.3.

TABLE 2.3. *Key Generalizations, Subideas, and Related Concepts*

Generalizations and Subideas	Related Concepts
1. *Generalization:* Every individual and society faces a conflict between unlimited wants and limited resources. This creates the need for decision-making. (Economics) *Subidea:* Mother and father often want to buy two or more things when they have only enough money for one of them.	Scarcity
2. *Generalization:* All members of a society are inter-dependent: individual producers of goods and services exchange with others to get the goods and services they need to satisfy their basic needs. (Economics) *Subidea:* Mother and Father work to make money to buy the goods and services the family wants and needs.	Goods Services Interdependence Production Consumption Voluntary exchange Social control
3. *Generalization:* In every society and institution, regulations and laws emerge to govern the behavior of individuals; individuals usually experience some form of punishment when authorities catch them breaking laws. (Political science) *Subidea:* Father and Mother make rules for children about going to bed, eating, watching television, crossing the street, and playing.	
4. *Generalization:* All human behavior is learned from other human beings through group interaction. (Sociology) *Subidea:* Our parents teach us how to walk and talk.	Socialization Role
5. *Generalization:* Every member of society must function in many different roles. (Sociology) *Subidea:* Father does different things when he goes shopping or to work.	
6. *Generalization:* Norms and sanctions shape the behavior of group members. (Sociology) *Subidea:* We get angry when members of our family do not treat us in expected ways, and we let them know it.	Norms Sanctions

DETERMINING UNIT OBJECTIVES

When you identify the key concepts and generalizations for a social science inquiry unit, most of the objectives of the unit will have been determined, although they have not been articulated. A major objective of a social science inquiry unit is to have the students state or write, in their own words, the organizing generalizations you have identified. The students should also be able to demonstrate an understanding of the key concepts in the unit. When the concepts are named, students can demonstrate their understanding by identifying *examples* and *non-examples* of them. Often you will not choose to teach primary-grade students the labels for concepts used by social scientists, even though you expect them to understand such concepts. In such cases, the objective is for the students to recognize the concept when it is stated in familiar terms. For example, if the concept is *norm,* you might ask the students to list things around the house that "you are expected to do." The students will then be able to respond with examples of the concept.

Another major objective of a social science inquiry unit is for the students to be able to use the method of social science inquiry to derive generalizations. Social science consists of knowledge (concepts and generalizations) as well as a method of inquiry. Because social knowledge is tentative and subject to constant revision, it is extremely important for students to be able to use the method of the social scientist to derive knowledge. While students need knowledge on social issues, knowing the method by which scientific knowledge is derived is more important. Thus, throughout the unit, you should emphasize the process of knowing. (The method of science is discussed in considerable detail in Chapter 3.) Basically, it involves (a) formulation of the problem, (b) formulation of hypotheses, (c) conceptualization, (d) collection of data, (e) assessment and analysis of data, (f) derivation of generalizations, and (g) inquiry into the methods used to solve the problem. You will not be able to provide practice for the students in each of these skills during each unit. However, the goal should be to help them attain maximum proficiency in each skill. These steps in the process and the practice of them should be kept constantly in mind when units and teaching strategies are planned. You might plan specific strategies to develop some of these skills during each unit. For example, during the family unit, you might want to stress how we formulate hypotheses and test them.

The major goals of social science inquiry units that we have identified can be summarized as follows: (1) The students will be able to state or write, in their own words, the organizing generalizations of the unit; (2) they will be able to identify examples and non-examples of the key concepts of the unit; and (3) they will be able to use the process of social inquiry to solve a scientific problem. These objectives are stated in very general terms. However, depending on their purposes, you can state them as specifically as necessary. For example, in his statement of objectives for our sample family unit, Mr. Ortiz might want to write out each of the generalizations the students will be expected to state in their own words, and to list the concepts that they will be expected to understand. Also, the inquiry skills can be stated much more specifically. For example, regarding the skill of hypothesizing, you might state, "When given a problem and sources of data, the student will be able to state a testable hypothesis." This kind of specific statement could be made for each skill that the inquiry process comprises.

Organizing the Unit

When the organizing concepts and generalizations have been identified and the subideas stated, you can organize the unit in a logical and meaningful fashion. In looking over the concepts Mr. Ortiz identified in our example, we note that he identified the following concepts in the order indicated:

1. Scarcity
2. Interdependence, production, voluntary exchange
3. Social control
4. Socialization
5. Role
6. Norms, sanctions

Mr. Ortiz believes that his unit will be more effective if he teaches first some of the concepts that he identified later, and then teaches those he selected earlier. For example, the students can better understand the concept of scarcity if they are acquainted with the idea of role. He decides that role is a basic concept that should be introduced before any of the other ideas. Because people learn their roles through a process of socialization, he decides to teach socialization next. Then norms and sanctions will be taught; they shape a person's behavior during social-ization. Social control is also a part of the socialization process. The concept of interdependence will help students see the relationships among different roles. Scarcity is chosen as the last main concept to develop because Mr. Ortiz thinks that it can be more easily grasped once the other concepts are understood. The prior experiences of the students and the relationships between the key concepts should be the main determiners of the organization of the conceptual-inquiry unit.

Formulating and Outlining Activities: The Developmental Phase of the Unit

The activities and teaching strategies are the heart of any unit. If the organizing con-cepts and generalizations have been carefully selected and stated, they should serve as an effective guide to the formulation of appropriate teaching strategies and learn-ing activities. *The activities and strategies should relate directly to the central ideas of the unit.* No activity should be included within a unit unless you clearly see how it contributes to the development of the ideas and skills you have identified. The subideas related to the key concepts and generalizations are stated primarily to ensure that activities are related to the key ideas and to guide in their formulation. Traditional units often contain a long list of activities and teaching strategies whose relationship to the cen-tral ideas of the unit is not clear. This practice can best be avoided by writing the key concepts and generalizations to be developed on one side of a sheet of paper and the activities or teaching strategies on the other side, as illustrated in Table 2.4. The statement of the activities or teaching strategies can be as general or specific as nec-essary. In our example, we have stated the activities in fairly general terms, largely to conserve space. The major strategies and activities used to develop the key ideas of a unit are referred to as the developmental phase of the unit.

TABLE 2.4. *Concepts, Generalizations, and Activities*

Concepts and Generalizations	Activities
Socialization All human behavior is learned from other human beings through group interaction.	1. Viewing pictures of parents showing children how to do such things as tie their shoes, swim, ski, and eat properly. 2. Naming specific things our parents taught us. 3. Naming the different kinds of clothes we wear to school, to worship, and to play, and who taught us to dress in these ways. 4. Discussing how we treat other people and who taught us how to treat them. 5. Summarizing and generalizing about the things that we learn from other members of our family.
Norms, sanctions Norms and sanctions shape the behavior of group members.	1. Listing ways in which we are expected to speak to our parents. 2. Listing ways in which we are expected to treat our parents and grandparents. 3. Discussing other things members of the family expect us to do. 4. Listing the kinds of things our parents do to us when we do things that they do not expect us to do. 5. Listing the kinds of things members of our families do and say when we do the things they expect us to do. 6. Discussing why members of our family treat us differently when we do things that are expected and things that are not expected. 7. Listing the kinds of things we expect members of our family to do, and what we do and say when they fail to do them. 8. Summarizing and generalizing about family norms and sanctions.

Initiating the Unit

You should plan beginning activities that will stimulate student interest and curiosity. An exciting beginning is one of the best assurances of a successful and meaningful unit. If students are bored at the beginning of a unit, you must seriously doubt whether it will have the intended outcome. The introductory phase of a unit deserves careful thought and planning. To stimulate student interest and questioning, you can arrange materials related to the unit topic around the room. These materials might include captivating pictures, interesting books, and objects the students can handle. You can also read to the students an intriguing story related to the unit topic and encourage them to ask questions about it. A record can be kept of these questions.

To start the unit in our example, you might read a book about family life, such as *Aunt Flossie's Hats (and Crabcakes Later)* by Elizabeth Fitzgerald Howard (1995), which is an interesting story about a middle-class African American family; or *How My Family Lives in America* by Susan Kuklin (1992), which describes life in three families who have recently immigrated to the United States from Africa, Puerto Rico, and Taiwan. A recording or videotape can also introduce units effectively. A unit can also be introduced with a role-playing situation or a dramatic incident. Creative teachers think of many different ways to capture student interest and stimulate curiosity during this important unit phase.

Assessment Activities

You should plan assessment activities that can be implemented throughout the unit. Assessment should be an ongoing and not an end-of-unit activity. It is usually appropriate, however, to plan general kinds of assessment activities for the end of the unit. Because effective assessment is an ongoing process, you might find it helpful to indicate (perhaps with asterisks) which activities within the developmental phase of the unit are intended for assessment purposes. Too often, assessment is considered only as a paper-and-pencil test. Although a test is a legitimate assessment exercise, to think of assessment as merely a written test is much too narrow. Assessment should be thought of in broad terms, and the objectives of the unit should be kept clearly in mind when assessment activities are planned. Checklists, rating scales, role-playing situations, portfolios, and group discussions can all be used as effective assessment exercises (Airasian, 1996). Students may be presented with a problem such as "What kinds of things do we learn from our parents?" and asked to act out the correct answer in a role-playing situation.

When inquiry skills are assessed, it will often be necessary to give students new data to determine whether they are able to state hypotheses, evaluate data, and test generalizations. To test students' ability to identify roles and to form generalizations about them, Mr. Ortiz may read a story about family life among the Hopi Indians and ask the students to describe the roles of the different family members and to state a generalization about these roles. A similar exercise could assess the students' understanding of socialization. If they understand this concept, they will be able to state ways in which the behavior of Hopi children is shaped by the norms and sanctions within their families.

Culminating Activities

You should plan activities that will summarize the various parts of the unit. During this phase of the unit, the major ideas studied are highlighted, reviewed, and interrelated. Culmination activities may consist of reviewing data retrieval charts made during the unit (see Table 4.2), giving oral reports, conducting discussions, participating in role-playing situations, or presenting short skits that highlight the key ideas studied. In the past, culminating activities often consisted of highly rehearsed pageants that were attended by parents and other members of the school community. However, while sharing may be desirable under certain circumstances, the emphasis of culminating activities should be on summarizing the major ideas learned and not on entertaining parents or other students. During the culminating activities, you may also gain helpful ideas about concepts to teach in future units. You may realize that certain concepts and key ideas need further study and clarification. Thus, culminating and assessment activities are not by any means mutually exclusive. The various parts of a unit are discussed separately for purpose of emphasis. In reality, the parts often blend together.

Resource Bibliography

During the early stages of planning, you should start compiling lists of resources you will need to develop the key concepts and ideas of the unit. Some teachers have found it advantageous to collect source material even before actual plans are made. They keep folders in which they place all pictures, clippings, and other materials that relate to specific topics. This greatly facilitates the planning and initiation of a unit. When planning a bibliography, you should consider more than written, factual material. Literature, art, and music are rich sources that can and should be used to help students grasp key ideas in the social sciences. The resources should also include the videotapes, photographs, and computer courseware you plan to use.

All resources should be gathered or requested well in advance. Anyone who has taught can tell a disappointing story about how a lesson was ruined because the book or videotape that was needed at a particular moment was not available. Often these incidents result from poor teacher planning. A videotape may have been ordered too late or the specific location of a book was not rechecked. It is often helpful to have a written list of resources for both the students and you. You will often find it necessary to study a number of books on a topic before you can teach it successfully. Some teachers have found it helpful to duplicate the list of resources available to the students so that they may locate extra copies of resource materials when they want to study the subject in greater detail than is done in class.

The Daily Lesson Plan

Once your unit is constructed, you have clearly in mind the major components of your social studies lessons for several weeks. However, the components of each day's lesson should be planned to assure effective instruction and meaningful learning experiences. The lesson plan should relate directly to the major unit plan. The main components of the daily lesson plan are described in Table 2.5. Like the unit, the daily lesson plan can be as general or as specific as is necessary. In general, the inexperienced teacher will find it advantageous to make more detailed lesson plans than the veteran teacher. The concepts, generalizations, and objectives of the daily lesson plan should be taken from those listed for the major unit plan. As a general rule, you should try to develop no more than one concept and generalization during a daily lesson. Some lessons may only develop concepts; others can be planned to help students develop general statements about concepts. Table 2.5 illustrates how you may develop the concept of role and a related generalization in a daily lesson.

DEVELOPING A SPIRAL CONCEPTUAL CURRICULUM

In the first part of this chapter we discussed how a teacher in a school district with a traditional social studies curriculum can build conceptual units within such a framework. We will now consider a different problem. Some schools and districts are so dissatisfied with the existing social studies curriculum that they wish to develop a

TABLE 2.5. *Example of a Daily Lesson Plan*

1. **Key Concept**
   Role
2. **Organizing Generalization**
   We function in many different roles.
   Subideas:
   a. Family members function in different roles at home.
   b. Family members function in many different roles away from home.
3. **Objective**
   The students will be able to state, in their own words, the organizing generalization above.
4. **Developmental Activities**
   a. Listing things parents do at home.
   b. Listing things parents do away from home.
   c. Listing things children do at home and away from home.
   d. Discussing how roles may conflict.
   e. Viewing pictures of parents functioning in many different roles.
   f. Viewing pictures of children functioning in many different roles.
5. **Summary and Evaluation Activities**
   a. Summarizing and generalizing about how we function in many different roles.
   b. Viewing pictures of a Hopi Indian family and naming the roles of family members.
   c. Contrasting Hopi family roles with those in Anglo American families.
6. **Materials and Resources**
   a. Students' experiences.
   b. Pictures of parents and children engaged in many different activities.
   c. Pictures of a Hopi Indian family engaged in a variety of activities.

totally new one. A curriculum committee made up of teachers in these districts may be asked to develop a new social studies curriculum. You may be on such a committee sometime in the future in your district.

The first step in developing a spiral conceptual curriculum is to identify a list of key concepts the students will study throughout the elementary and junior high school grades, beginning in kindergarten. These concepts will be developed sequentially and in greater depth in each higher grade (see Figure 2.2). The concepts selected should be powerful ones that can encompass many topics and a great deal of information. In the model curriculum discussed below, five key concepts from different social science disciplines are identified: *socialization, scarcity, cultural differences, power,* and *physical environment.* When the committee is selecting key concepts for the curriculum, it should make sure that concepts are selected from a range of disciplines so that the curriculum will be interdisciplinary. When the key concepts are identified, an organizing or key generalization is then selected for each key concept. Related subideas are then selected for each of the key generalizations.

When these parts of the conceptual curriculum have been identified, the committee has the option of specifying content samples to be used to develop the key concepts and generalizations or of concluding its work when a curriculum framework is developed. In most school districts, however, specific content samples for developing the key concepts and generalizations are identified for each grade level.

Figure 2.2
The spiral development of concepts within our model social studies curriculum. The curriculum is organized around five key concepts from the various social science disciplines. Two of the concepts (*socialization* and *cultural differences*) are studied in kindergarten. Three (*socialization, cultural differences,* and *power*) are studied at Level 1. All five of the concepts are studied in Levels 2 through 8. The concepts are developed at an increasing degree of complexity at each successive level.

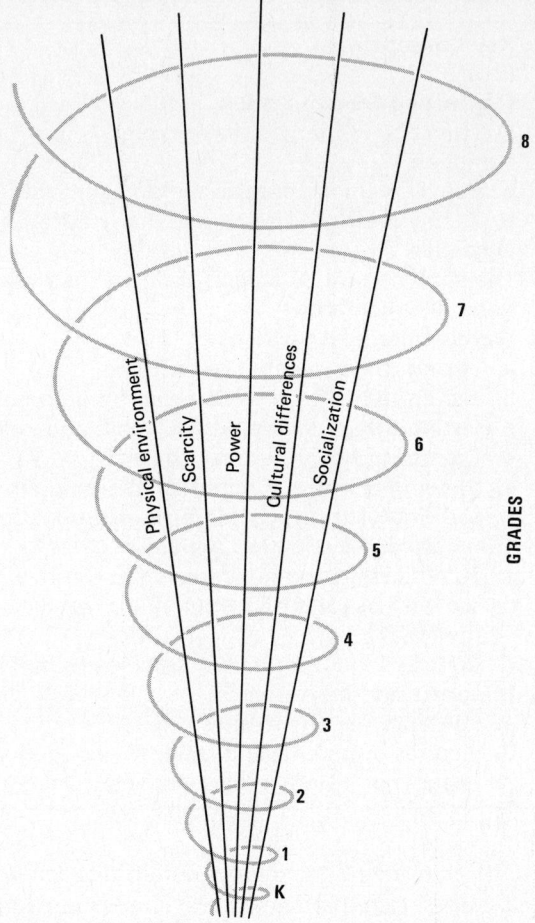

In our model curriculum, specific content for each grade level is not identified (see Table 2.6). However, a major concept, called a focused concept, is identified for each grade level. Several key related questions are also identified for each grade level (see Table 2.7). The focused concepts, such as *human institutions* and *human communities*, are studied from the perspectives of the key concepts and generalizations identified for the total curriculum.

At Levels 2 through 6, each of the focused concepts is studied from the various perspectives of five organizing concepts and related generalizations. At Level 1, only three of the organizing concepts and related generalizations are used to study the focused concept. Only two of the organizing concepts and related generalizations are used to study the focused concept at Level K. Table 2.6 summarizes the conceptual framework for our sample curriculum. The focused grade-level concepts and the key questions are shown in Table 2.7. Our model curriculum is interdisciplinary in two ways. The focused concepts, which are chosen from different disciplines, are viewed from the perspective of concepts from various disciplines. The interrelationship of the focused concepts is illustrated in Figure 2.3.

TABLE 2.6. *A Model Conceptual Curriculum*

Level	Conceptual Focus in Levels	Socialization	Scarcity	Cultural Differences	Power	Physical Environment
		An individual's behavior is influenced by the social system in which he or she participates.	Individuals and groups face a conflict between unlimited wants and limited resources.	Cultural differences influence the behavior of individuals and groups.	Rules and laws govern the behavior of people in a social system.	The physical environment influences the behavior of people in a social system.
Level 6	Social problems and social movements	Individuals join movements to resolve social problems.	Scarce goods and resources cause problems within societies.	Cultural and ethnic differences cause problems in a social system.	Power struggles exist between nations and societies, thus causing international political problems.	Human utilization of natural resources creates social problems.
Level 5	Human cultures	An individual's culture strongly influences his or her behavior and values.	Cultures satisfy their needs for goods and services in many different ways.	Conflict usually results when people from different cultures and subcultures interact.	Laws and rules govern behavior in all cultures.	The physical environment influences how a culture develops.
Level 4	Human societies	Individuals within a society share behavioral characteristics.	Scarcity is a problem in all human societies.	The existence of subcultures within a society increases social conflict.	Political systems emerge in all human societies.	The physical environment influences the nature of a social system.

TABLE 2.6. *(continued)*

Level 3	Human communities	An individual's behavior is influenced by the community in which he or she is socialized.	Members of a community depend on each other to satisfy their needs for goods and services.	Cultural and ethnic minorities within a community usually function in more than one cultural environment.	Individuals frequently form groups to influence political policy.	Different human groups use the same physical environment differently.
Level 2	Human institutions	Institutions help people to meet their needs.	Economic institutions help people to exchange goods and services.	Institutions exist in all cultures.	Political institutions help societies to maintain stability.	The physical environment influences the structure of institutions.
Level 1	Human groups	An individual's behavior is influenced by the groups to which he or she belongs.		Cultures influence the nature of human groups.	Groups are governed by rules and sanctions.	
Level K	Identity	An individual's identity is highly influenced by the people in his or her social environment. An individual's identity strongly influences his or her behavior.		An individual's culture and ethnic group influence his or her identity.		

TABLE 2.7. *Focused Concepts for the Levels and Related Questions*

Level	Focused Concept Level and Related Key Quesions
Level K	*Identity*
	Who am I?
	How did I become the person I am?
	How does my view of myself affect me?
	How do other people become who they are?
	What will I be like in the future?
	What can I do to feel better about who I am? (Decision-making)
Level 1	*Human groups*
	How do people function in groups?*
	How do groups affect people?
	What human needs do groups satisfy?
	What problems do groups experience?
	What problems are groups likely to experience in the future?
	How do, and might, people try to solve them? (Decision-making)
Level 2	*Human institutions*
	How do people function in institutions?*
	How do institutions affect people?
	What human needs do institutions satisfy?
	What problems do institutions experience?
	What problems are institutions likely to experience in the future?
	How do, and might, people try to solve them? (Decision-making)
Level 3	*Human communities*
	How do people function in communities?*
	How do communities affect people?
	What human needs do communities satisfy?
	What problems do communities experience?
	What problems are communities likely to experience in the future?
	How do, and might, people try to solve them? (Decision-making)
Level 4	*Human societies*
	How do people function in societies?*
	How do societies affect people?
	What human needs do societies satisfy?
	What problems do societies experience?
	What problems are societies likely to experience in the future?
	How do, and might, people try to solve them? (Decision-making)
Level 5	*Human cultures*
	How do cultures influence people's behavior?*
	What human needs do cultures satisfy?
	What problems do cultures experience?
	What problems are cultures likely to experience in the future?
	How do, and might, people try to solve them? (Decision-making)
Level 6	*Social problems and social movements*
	What persistent social problems have people experienced throughout history?*
	How have people tried to solve these problems?
	How do social problems affect people?
	How can we solve our social problems today? (Decision-making)
	What major social problems might people face in the future?
	How might these problems be solved?

*These questions will focus on people in both the *past* and the *present*. Thus history will be an integral part of the program. Future studies will also be an integral part of the program because of the parallel questions dealing with the future.

The Valuing and Decision-Making Component of the Curriculum

We stated earlier that knowledge is one of the important components of the decision-making process. This chapter focuses on the knowledge component of decision-making. Students need to master facts, concepts, and generalizations in order to make reflective decisions and to take thoughtful citizen action. Values are another important component of decision-making. The Inquiry Strategy on page 61 is an example of a valuing strategy Mr. Ortiz can use in the unit on the family described earlier in this chapter. Each social studies unit should contain valuing and decision-making exercises.

Values and value inquiry are discussed in Chapter 15. When a curriculum committee designs a conceptual curriculum, it should indicate the kinds of value problems and issues that can be discussed. These problems and issues should be related to the content samples and concepts being studied. The curriculum committee should also indicate what possible decision-problems can be studied when the concepts and content are studied. The valuing and decision-problems identified by the committee should be enduring and persistent problems that it will take many generations of citizens to solve. Problems such as the feminization of poverty, international conflict, and discrimination against various racial and ethnic groups are enduring problems that warrant inclusion in the curriculum.

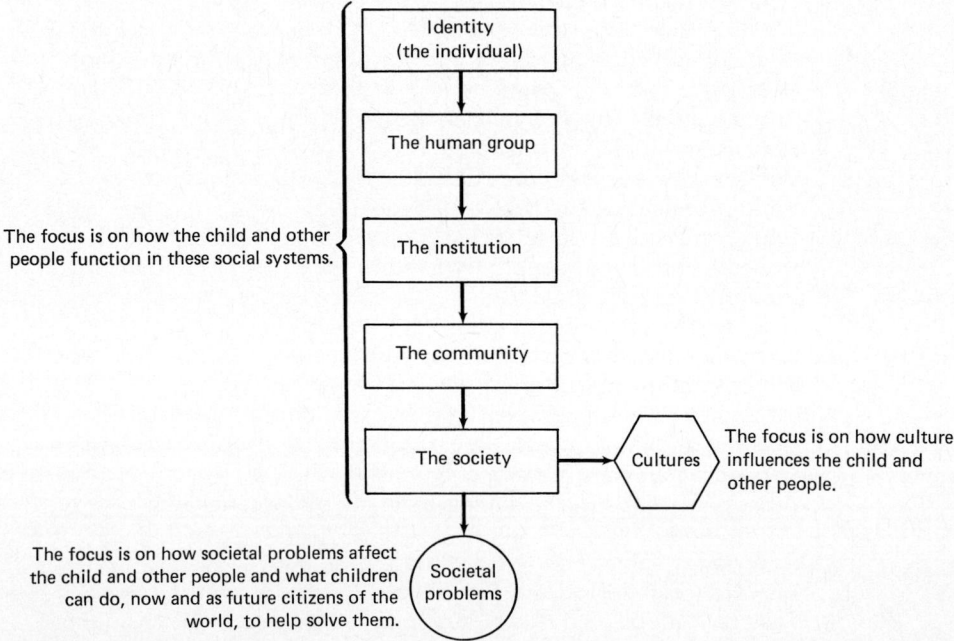

Figure 2.3
The interrelationship of the focused concepts.

inquiry strategy

WHAT SHOULD THE CANGEMI FAMILY DO?

Mr. and Mrs. Cangemi live in Detroit, a very big city in Michigan. They have four children, Kate (14), Bob (12), Randy (9), and Kristin (2). Mr. Cangemi has a good job working in a large factory helping to make new cars. Mrs. Cangemi is a teacher in the high school in their town. Kate, Bob, and Randy help their parents with many of the chores around the house and especially with Kristin, the baby. During the daytime, Kristin goes to a nursery school when Mr. and Mrs. Cangemi are at work. Usually Mrs. Cangemi picks Kristin up at the nursery about 5 P.M. after school.

One day the Cangemis got a telephone call. Mr. Cangemi's mother, who lived far away in Phoenix, Arizona, was 75 years old and had fallen and broken her hip. She lived alone and there was no one to help her. She could not walk or take care of herself, go to the store, or do any of the usual things she did for herself. The doctor said she would need someone to take care of her for six months or more until she fully recovered and could walk again.

The children and parents were very concerned. "What will happen to Grandma? What should we do to help her?" That night at dinner, the whole family, including little Kristin, sat around the table and talked about what they could do about this sudden turn of events in their family. They knew that Grandma liked her home in Phoenix, where it was warm and sunny almost every day. She did not like to come back to Detroit to visit her family because it was often very cold and snowy in the winter, and in the summer it got much too hot. Besides, none of her friends lived there anymore. What should the Cangemi family do?

QUESTIONS

1. Can you retell this story in your own words?
2. What do you think the Cangemi family should do? Can you explain why?
3. Do they have any choices about what they could do? What would be the best choice? The poorest choice? Could you explain why?
4. What choice would Grandma like best? Like least? Why?
5. Is there anything Grandma's friends or neighbors in Phoenix could do to help out? Should they be the ones to help, or should her family in Detroit provide all the help?

The value issues and conflicts in this case study include:

1. Providing care for aging parents who no longer live close by.
2. Readjustment of family life if either parent goes to Phoenix for any longer than a few days.
3. Unplanned financial strain—both parents are already working.
4. The loss of independence for Grandma, leading to loneliness, anxiety, frustration, and helplessness (common among the elderly).
5. Bringing Grandma home to Detroit may be the only option to ensure needed care, but (given her attitudes) it may be very disruptive to the existing family life.

The Skills Component of the Curriculum

Knowledge is the product of social inquiry. Clarified and democratic values are the product of value inquiry. While it is very important for students to master facts, concepts, and generalizations and to develop democratic values, it is just as important, if not more important, for them to gain proficiency in the processes involved in gathering and evaluating knowledge and in deriving democratic values. An important goal of the social studies curriculum should be to help students develop proficiency in social science inquiry and value inquiry skills. A skill is an intellectual or physical process that can be improved through practice.

A social studies curriculum committee should identify the skills that should be introduced and extended in each grade when it formulates a conceptual curriculum. It should identify social science inquiry, value inquiry, decision-making, and citizen-action skills. A model of social inquiry is illustrated in Figure 1.3 and discussed in detail in Chapter 3. Value inquiry, decision-making, and citizen-action skills are discussed in Chapter 15. Chapter 5 discusses a range of skills, including communication skills, map-reading skills, time-space skills, and group participation skills.

The skills discussed in Chapter 5 are subskills of social science inquiry, value inquiry, decision-making, and citizen-action skills. An example will make this point clear. The fifth step of the model of social inquiry presented in Chapter 3 is "Data Collection." The students need a range of other skills in order to "collect data," including skills in locating books, using reference books, reading maps and globes, observing, and note-taking. While we will defer a detailed discussion of the subskills that constitute social science inquiry, value inquiry, decision-making, and citizen action to other chapters, below are examples of the kinds of subskills that students need to carry out these processes:

Social Science Inquiry Skills
 Reading
 Speaking
 Listening
 Concept formation
 Observation
 Gathering and organizing information
 Interpreting maps and globes
 Time-space orientation
 Interpreting graphs and charts
 Summarizing and generalizing

Value Inquiry Skills
 Observing
 Analyzing points of view
 Distinguishing facts from opinions
 Detecting biases
 Critical reading
 Justifying and defending a position

Decision-Making Skills
Identifying generalizations
Evaluating the accuracy of generalizations
Identifying alternative courses of action
Using generalizations to predict alternative courses of action
Relating values to specific courses of action
Defending a particular course of action

Citizen-Action Skills
Working with others in groups
Oral and written communication
Persuasion, compromise, and bargaining
Forming coalitions with other individuals and groups
Communicating a social concern to a large public

SUMMARY

This chapter highlights a basic point underlying the theory of social studies education in this book: students must become reflective decision-makers and citizen actors in order to solve personal problems and influence public policy. Decisions must be based on knowledge; reflective decisions must be based on scientific knowledge. The scientific knowledge the citizen actor uses to make reflective decisions must reflect the perspectives of a number of disciplines; social problems are too complex for a single discipline to provide enough knowledge to help us solve them.

This chapter illustrates how the teacher can build units that teach students to view topics and social problems from an interdisciplinary perspective. Methods for building conceptual units within school districts that have traditional social studies curriculum frameworks were discussed. Ways to structure a conceptual curriculum within districts that are substantially revising their curricula were also discussed and illustrated. The need to include valuing and decision-making skills as components in a curriculum plan was highlighted. The next chapter discusses social science inquiry and its products: facts, concepts, generalizations, and theories.

REFLECTION AND ACTION ACTIVITIES

1. Why is it necessary for students to view social problems from the perspectives of several disciplines in order to make sound decisions?
2. Select a current social problem and develop a teaching plan that will help students to view the problem from the perspectives of history, sociology, anthropology, geography, political science, economics, and psychology. From each of these disciplines, list at least one key concept and related generalization that can help students to better understand the social problem.
3. Structure an interdisciplinary unit on a topic traditionally studied in the elementary and junior high school grades—such as the family, the school, the neighborhood, or the community—including the following components: (1) unit topic, (2) key concepts and generalizations from at least four different social science disciplines, (3) subideas that are related to each of the key generalizations and to the specific institution selected for

study, (4) objectives stated in behavioral terms, (5) initiation activities, (6) developmental activities, (7) assessment activities, (8) culminating activities, and (9) a list of resources for both the students and you.

4. Work with a group of students to structure an outline of a K–8 interdisciplinary social studies curriculum for a hypothetical school district. The outline should indicate the key concepts and generalizations that will be developed, recommended content samples for developing the key ideas, and a list of the units for each grade or level. The rationale and criteria the group will use to identify the key concepts, generalizations, and content samples should also be stated.

5. Examine a school district social studies guide in the curriculum library of your college. Evaluate the guide using the following criteria questions: (1) Does the guide include key concepts and generalizations from all the social science disciplines? (2) Are the concepts and generalizations accurate? (3) Are the key ideas within the curriculum developed with appropriate content samples? (4) Are the key ideas within the curriculum developed at an increasing degree of complexity in successive grades? (5) Are the objectives related to the key ideas stated? (6) Are the objectives stated in behavioral terms? (7) Are the units within the curriculum divided in a way that will facilitate the learning of the key ideas stated? (8) Will the activities develop the major ideas stated in the curriculum? (9) Are sound assessment strategies a part of the curriculum? (10) Does the curriculum contain a sufficient number of resources for both the teacher and the pupils?

6. Demonstrate your understanding of the following concepts and terms by writing or stating brief definitions for each of them. Also tell why each is important:

a. interdisciplinary curriculum
b. unit
c. initiation activities
d. developmental activities
e. assessment activities
f. culminating activities
g. interdisciplinary curriculum skills
h. conceptual curriculum
i. spiral curriculum
j. key or organizing concept
k. key or organizing generalization
l. scope and sequence chart
m. interdisciplinary perspective
n. skills

REFERENCES

Airasian, P. W. (1996). *Assessment in the classroom.* New York: McGraw-Hill.

Howard, E. F. (1995). *Aunt Flossie's hats (and crabcakes later).* New York: Clarion Books.

Kuklin, S. (1992). *How my family lives in America.* New York: Bradbury Press.

Taba, H., Durkin, M. C., Fraenkel, J. R., & McNaughton, A. H. (1971). *Teachers' handbook for elementary social studies* (2nd ed.). Reading, MA: Addison-Wesley.

FOR FURTHER READING

Hunkins, F. P. (1995). *Teaching thinking through effective questioning* (2nd ed.). Norwood, MA: Christoper-Gordon.

Muse, D. (Ed.). (1997). *The New Press guide to multicultural resources for young readers.* New York: New Press.

Parker, W. C. (1991). *Renewing the social studies curriculum.* Arlington, VA: Association for Supervision and Curriculum Development.

Joyce, B., & Weil, M. (1996). *Models of teaching* (5th ed.). Boston: Allyn and Bacon.

CHAPTER 3

Teaching Social Science Inquiry and Its Products: Facts, Concepts, Generalizations, and Theories

THE METHOD OF SOCIAL SCIENCE INQUIRY

The Nature, Goals, and Assumptions of Social Inquiry

To make reflective decisions, students need to master facts, concepts, and generalizations. However, because knowledge changes and often becomes obsolete, they also need to master the skills needed to produce knowledge. Teachers should emphasize the process used to attain knowledge more than the knowledge itself. The process for attaining knowledge can always be used by students to attain the facts, concepts, and generalizations needed to make reflective decisions and to act to influence public policy. We call the process used to attain facts, concepts, generalizations, and theories *social science inquiry* or the *scientific method*.

A major goal of social science inquiry is to build theories and explanations. However, social scientists must formulate facts, concepts, and generalizations in order to build theories. Most social scientists believe that they can best help society by building theories. Theories can be used to understand, explain, predict, and control behavior. Social scientists do not consider theories absolute. The scientific method allows them to constantly expand, change, and reconstruct theories.

Social science inquiry is based on a number of assumptions about the natural world and about human beings. We discussed them briefly in Chapter 1. It is important for teachers and students to know these assumptions so that they are keenly aware of both the strengths and limitations of science. Science assumes that human behavior, like that of all other beings, has causes that can be determined by systematic study. This assumption rejects the notion that human behavior is determined by magical or supernatural forces. Science also assumes that there is enough order, permanence, and uniformity in nature to permit study and generalizations. If things in our environment changed drastically from day to day, we would be unable to make any generalizations about the world and about human behavior. Science also makes these assumptions (Lastrucci, 1963):

> All objective phenomena are eventually knowable....
>
> Nothing is self-evident; truth must be demonstrated objectively....
>
> Truth is relative (to the existing state of knowledge); absolute or final truth may never be achieved....
>
> All perceptions are achieved through the senses; all knowledge is derived from sensory impressions....
>
> Humans can trust their perceptions, memory, and reasoning as reliable agencies for acquiring facts....(pp. 42–46)

In addition to having a number of basic assumptions, the scientific method also has a number of requirements that the scientist must fulfill. Berelson and Steiner (1964) have summarized the basic requirements of science:

> The procedures are public.
> The definitions are precise.
> The data collecting is objective.
> The findings must be able to be reproduced.
> The approach is systematic and cumulative.
> The purposes are explanation, understanding, and prediction.

INQUIRY IN THE SOCIAL SCIENCE DISCIPLINES

Sociologists, anthropologists, economists, and political scientists use similar but not necessarily identical methods to test and to derive knowledge. However, the kinds of questions studied by different social scientists and their respective key concepts, generalizations, and theories distinguish them more than their methodologies. *Participant observation, interviews, sample surveys,* and the *case study* are methods used to collect data in several disciplines. The sociologist's concern for *socialization* and the political scientist's interest in *power* distinguish these two disciplines more than their methodologies. Also, social scientists in one discipline often use the concepts, generalizations, and theories from other disciplines. Thus, the social science disciplines are themselves *interdisciplinary* (Munch & Smelser, 1992; Rosenau, 1992).

Although the methods used by social scientists in the various disciplines have many common characteristics, some of the disciplines use special methods of data

You can use photographs like this one, which shows Mary McLeod Bethune with her students, to help students formulate questions about education in the United States at the turn of the century. Dr. Bethune founded the Daytona Educational and Industrial School for Negro Girls in 1904 in Daytona, Florida.
Source: Library of Congress, Washington, D.C.

collection or use certain research strategies more often than others. The social psychologist uses laboratory experiments perhaps more often than any other social scientist. The sample survey is used frequently in sociology and political science but less often in anthropology. Participant observation and field work are the primary research methods used by anthropologists. Although each group of social scientists sometimes uses unique research methods, an attempt is made below to present a basic model of social science inquiry that is shared by all social scientists. This model is presented in Figure 3.1. It is one that students should use, often in a modified fashion, when they try to answer the questions asked at the beginning of social studies lessons and units.

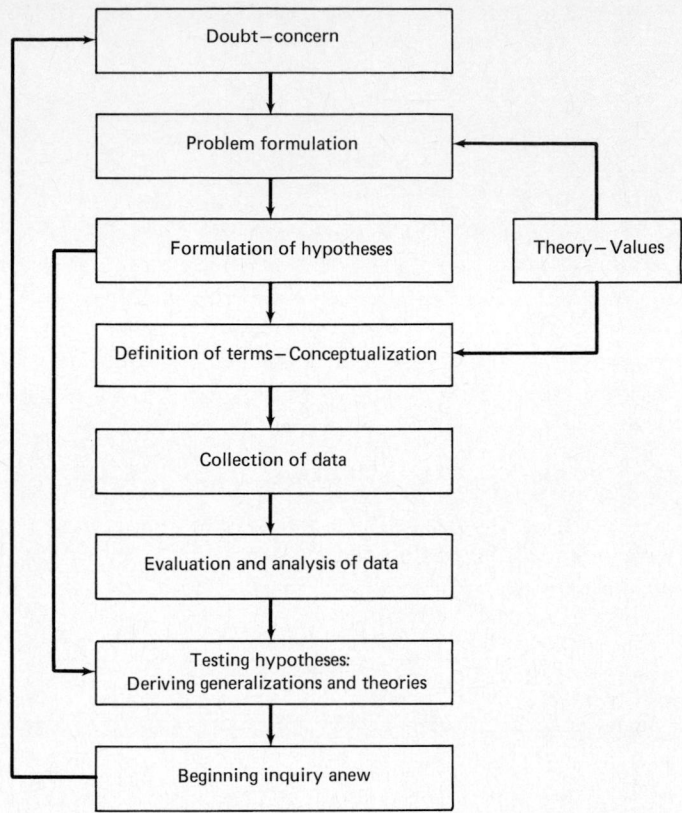

Figure 3.1
A model of social inquiry. Note that in the inquiry model, doubt and concern cause the inquirer to formulate a problem. The problem that he or she formulates does not emanate from a vacuum but is shaped by his or her theoretical and value orientation. Like the social scientist, the elementary school child will need to draw on *knowledge* to be able to ask intelligent and fruitful questions. In social science inquiry, *theory* is the main source of fruitful questions. Although these are the basic steps of social inquiry, they do not necessarily occur in the order illustrated above. This figure indicates that generalizations in social science are continually tested and are never regarded as absolute. Thus, social inquiry is cyclic rather than linear and fixed.

A MODEL OF SOCIAL INQUIRY

Problem Formulation

Before scientists can begin research on any problem or issue, they must clearly state the questions to be answered. Scientists must also have an interest in answering the questions. Scientific questions must be *complete, precise,* and *testable*. *"What were the children's attitudes?"* does not satisfy our criteria because we do not know which children or what kinds of attitudes to study. "What were the attitudes of colonial American children toward school?" meets our criteria of a scientific question because it is complete, precise, and testable.

Some complete and precise questions are not testable because they are not scientific. *"Should I join Citizens Against Animal Cloning?"* is not a scientific question and therefore cannot be answered with social inquiry methods. This is a decision-problem question, and the answer must reflect a synthesis of knowledge and personal values. Scientific inquiry can help us to make decisions and attain goals we value. Value inquiry can contribute to value clarification. However, social science inquiry cannot determine our values. Social science inquiry can help us answer this question: *"How might the cloning of human organs or humans influence the ways in which human life is valued within our society?"* However, regardless of the answers that social science inquiry might provide to this question, different individuals, because of their values, will decide differently about whether they will join Citizens Against Animal Cloning.

Helping students to identify and formulate precise, explicit, and testable questions is one of the most challenging tasks you will face in the inquiry-oriented classroom. The ability to ask good questions is a developmental skill that should be systematically taught beginning in kindergarten. Questioning strategies are discussed in detail in Chapter 4. The inquiries that students make can be no better than the questions they pose.

Example   A junior high school teacher begins a unit with a content analysis of several U.S. history textbooks. The teacher divides the class into several small groups and asks each group to read quickly through one chapter or unit in one of their history textbooks. Each group is asked to list "all the people who are mentioned by name" in their book. Following the completion of the task by the small groups, the teacher makes a list on a projection that contains all the people mentioned by name in the history textbooks. After listing these names, the teacher asks the students to describe different ways of grouping the persons listed (e.g., by occupation, by historical period). One possible grouping will be by gender of the persons listed. After listing all the people mentioned by name and by gender, the students will observe that the list of men is much longer than the list of women.

The teacher asks the class:

Why do you think more men are included in our history textbooks than women?

What kinds of things do people do who are "remembered" in history? What makes a person historically important?

Can you think of any historically important women who might have been included but were not?

Who do you think writes most of the history books we use in school, men or women?

The teacher introduces a new concept:

Written history is what is recorded and passed down about the past. It is not necessarily what actually happened. The teacher further explains the concept of written history.

The teacher asks the students to state questions stimulated by the lesson. The students state these questions, and the teacher writes them on the board:

How are textbooks written?

Who determines what gets included in a textbook?

Who chooses textbook authors?

How do historians determine which women to include in textbooks?

Why are more men than women included in our history books?

Why is written history not always the same as what actually happened in the past?

The teacher tells the students that all of their questions are excellent. He tells them that while they will find some answers to each of these questions during this unit, the main question that they will study is: *Why are more men than women included in our history textbooks?*

Formulation of Hypotheses

After scientists have stated precise and researchable questions, they then make tentative statements to guide their inquiries. We do not actually test questions, but statements related to them. The tentative statements that scientists use to guide inquiries are called *hypotheses. Hypotheses are informed guesses that scientists make when answering their questions.* They are very important in social research. They help to guide and focus it.

Hypotheses must have certain characteristics. They must be related to the questions formulated and be testable. The most effective hypotheses are based on prior knowledge and existing theories. Good hypotheses are not formulated in a vacuum. They are intelligent and not ignorant guesses. If a class were trying to formulate hypotheses about the possible effects of the cloning of human organs and of humans on the ways in which we value human life, the students would state much more informed and useful hypotheses if they had some knowledge about animal cloning (Kolata, 1998). The teacher must provide students with background information before they can formulate useful and intelligent hypotheses. Often a story, a videotape, or a short reading at the beginning of a unit can give the students the information needed to formulate useful hypotheses. A primary resource can also be used to help students to develop and state hypotheses, as is done in the Inquiry Strategy on page 71.

Example   The junior high school teacher continues the unit on women in U.S. history textbooks by setting the stage for the development of hypotheses. First, he shows the students some pictures of men and women in various roles during the colonial and Revolutionary periods of U.S. history.

He also reads selections from several books about women's roles in the development of the United States. The teacher then solicits hypotheses from the students. He says:

"We found that there were 14 times as many men mentioned in our history books as there were women mentioned. Why do you think this is the case? Think of as many different possible ideas as you can and be prepared to support your reasons."

inquiry strategy

DEVELOPING HYPOTHESES USING A PRIMARY RESOURCE

Sojourner Truth, a former slave, became active in both the antislavery and the women's rights movements. Ask the students to read this excerpt from a speech she gave at the Ohio Women's Rights Convention in 1851. Then ask them to state some hypotheses about what rights women had and did not have in 1851. Ask them to do research on the life and times of Sojourner Truth to test their hypotheses. They should note how the rights of African American women and White women were alike and different.

That man over there says that women need to be helped into carriages, and lifted over ditches, and to have the best place everywhere. Nobody ever helps me into carriages, or over mud-puddles, or gives me any best place! And ain't I a woman? Look at me! Look at my arm! I have ploughed, and planted, and gathered into barns, and no man could head [do better than] me! And ain't I a woman? I could work as much and eat as much as a man—when I could get it—and bear the lash as well! And ain't I a woman? I have borne five children, and seen them most all sold off to slavery, and when I cried out with my mother's grief, none but Jesus heard me! And ain't I a woman?

Then they talk about this thing in the head; what's this they call it? That's it, honey [intellect]. What's that got to do with woman's rights?...If my cup won't hold but a pint and yours holds a quart, wouldn't you be mean not to let me have my little half measure full?...

If the first woman God ever made was strong enough to turn the world upside down all alone, these women together ought to be able to turn it back, and get it right side up again! And now they are asking to do it, the men better let them.

Obliged to you for hearing on me; and now old Sojourner Truth ain't got nothing more to say.

Adapted from *Narrative of Sojourner Truth, a Northern Slave* (New York: 1853).

The students state hypotheses and the teacher writes them on the board:

1. Only a few women did anything important back then. If a woman had done something important, she would be in the book the same as a man.
2. Women were busy at home and with children and so they couldn't be explorers and pioneers and politicians. What women did was important, but they didn't do the kinds of things that get written in history books.
3. Men have always written the history books, and they chose to write about what men do. There were just as many important women explorers, pioneers, inventors, and politicians. They were left out of the books on purpose by the men historians.

The students copy the hypotheses the class has formulated, the main question the class will study during the unit, and the other questions the class asked during the problem formulation stage.

Definition of Terms: Conceptualization

At some stage early in the inquiry process, students must try to explicitly define their major terms and concepts. Defining terms so that they have research implications is a major problem for social scientists. There is little consensus about the meaning of many important concepts and terms in social science. *Culture, social class, acculturation,* and *racism* are important social science concepts that are defined differently by various social scientists.

Sometime early in the social studies unit, the teacher and the students must try to operationally define the major concepts that will be studied in the unit. Although we are listing *definition of terms* as a specific step in the inquiry process, in reality it, like the other steps of our inquiry model, may occur at different times during the unit. Each step, while often occurring in the order identified in Figure 3.1, may occur at different times and more than once during the inquiry process. The steps of the inquiry process are not linear, as Figure 3.1 suggests, but complex and multidimensional. In our unit on women in U.S. history textbooks, for example, the teacher felt that the concept *written history* was so important to the unit that he defined it during the problem formulation stage rather than waiting until the other major concepts had been defined. There may be disagreement among social scientists about concepts used in social studies units, but the teacher and the students need to reach agreement about how the concepts will be defined for the purpose of their inquiry.

Example   The teacher asks the students questions about the terms and concepts they will be dealing with so that some agreement on definitions can be reached. The class agrees on the following definitions of the key concepts:

Past events are actual events that occurred only once, never to occur again.
Historical statements (or "facts") are the statements that historians write about past events. They are quite different from the actual event. An infinite number of facts can be stated about any past event.

Historians are people who study the past and write historical statements.

To be *biased* is usually to tell only part of what happened or to tell something only from the point of view of one particular group, race, sex, or nation. Historians may be biased in their choice of subjects to write about, selection of resource materials, organization and presentation of historical statements, and interpretation of material (Appleby, Hunt, & Jacob, 1994).

Historically important people are those who have made significant personal contributions to the course of human events, whether or not they are generally included in history textbooks.

Collection of Data

Questions are answered and hypotheses are tested by the data and information the inquirer gathers. Social scientists use many methods to collect data, to test hypotheses, and to derive generalizations and theories. The *experiment,* the *sample survey,* and the *case study* are three major methods used by social scientists. The *historical study* and *content analysis,* as well as other techniques, are also used by social scientists to gather data. The experiment is a laboratory situation structured by an investigator to determine how concepts (or variables) are related. To determine how one concept influences another, the researcher attempts to control all concepts in an experimental situation.

Using an experiment with students in elementary and junior high school poses many problems: moral and ethical concerns about voluntary participation, concerns about the immaturity of young children, and protecting them from undue invasions of personal privacy. However, role-playing and simulation activities can be effectively used to help students discover how certain situations and concepts affect human behavior. One creative teacher used role-playing to help her students discover how discrimination affects its victims. This simulation is dramatized in the educational film *"Eye of the Storm"* (Peters, 1987). During one class period, the teacher discriminated against students with brown eyes; in another, those with blue eyes. Simulation games such as *Sunshine, Star Power,* and *Bafa Bafa* can also be used to teach students how different situations influence human behavior.

The *sample survey* is widely used in social science to gather data. A sample survey consists of a sample and a survey. A *sample* is a part of a population, usually randomly selected. A *survey* measures some characteristic of a population, such as its attitudes toward African Americans or Jewish Americans.

The sample survey is much easier to use with students than the experiment. Students can develop instruments to sample opinions and attitudes among their own classmates, other students in the school, faculty, and adults in the community. Every community faces an unlimited number of important questions. Students can learn the techniques for conducting sample surveys stratified on the basis of age, section of town, occupation, ethnic origin, and other variables.

Students can learn to sample community attitudes on a proposed highway relocation, a new bond issue, or candidates in an election. They can gather important demographic data by sample surveys concerning occupations, types of homes, businesses, religious preferences, traffic counts on major arterials, air pollution, and the use of public parks, libraries, and museums.

Scientists use the *case study* method when they study the characteristics of one element in a population in depth. Sociologists have used this method widely to analyze the characteristics of cities, political and social institutions, and individuals and groups with special characteristics. Sara Lawrence Lightfoot's (1994) portrait of the lives of six middle-class African Americans, Mitchell Duneier's (1992) study of a group of working-class men, and John Langston Gwaltney's (1980) study of the lives of 41 ordinary African Americans are powerful and influential examples of case studies conducted within the last two decades.

Sociologists often study juvenile delinquents, criminals, mental patients, and other persons with special problems. The case study method is more valuable for deriving fruitful hypotheses than for testing them. This method is limited because the findings derived from it cannot usually be generalized with a high degree of confidence to other individuals and institutions.

A number of possibilities exist for students to engage in the participant-observer type of case study. Students can work for a time in the school cafeteria, the stockroom, the library, or the principal's office to observe work functions and social interactions. They might also serve as street-crossing guards or members of a student council. In the larger sphere, it is not at all unrealistic to think of older students participating in the work of various municipal groups such as the fire or police departments, courts, or social agencies. These activities do suggest, however, that students must plan to spend larger parts of the day outside the school itself, actively engaged in social science inquiry in the real community, and less time studying the artificial world of the textbook.

Example   During the unit on women in U.S. history textbooks, the teacher asked:

> Where can we find some information about our problem of why there are relatively few women mentioned in our history textbooks?

The students responded:

> We could invite a historian from the university to come and tell us how historians get their information to write history books.
>
> We could look for diaries or journals written a long time ago that tell what the lives of women and children were like.
>
> We could go to the school and public libraries and look for biographies of famous American women.
>
> We could check the media center for videotapes or pictures of famous women.
>
> Some of us could watch the same TV program or movie and each write down our own historical statements. Then we could read our statements to the class and see how each person was biased and recorded the event differently.

The teacher replied:

> These are all very good suggestions, and you will no doubt think of even more as you begin to work. Remember that we have three hypotheses we want to test:
>
> > 1. Only a few women are mentioned in our history textbooks because only a few women did anything important.

2. Women did historically important things, but they were not the kinds of things that are generally recorded in history textbooks.
3. There were just as many women who did important things such as invent or explore, but the men historians don't write about them because they are biased in favor of other men and their activities.

How can we divide the work to be done and share the information once we have gathered it?

After much class discussion, the students decided to divide into three committees to gather and present information to the class. Two weeks later each committee made a presentation.

The committee on hypothesis 1 made a large bulletin board that included pictures and capsule biographies of a large number of historically important women who had been "forgotten" in their history books.

The committee on hypothesis 2 divided into subcommittees and prepared written reports and simulated TV shows to dramatize the roles of women and children during each of the main periods of U.S. history (e.g., colonial, Revolutionary, pioneer, WWII). The students decided to emphasize the contributions of women to the development of the new nation in all possible areas of human endeavor, including the arts, sciences, and other frequently neglected areas of history.

The committee on hypothesis 3 searched (in vain) for women explorers in the 15th through 17th centuries, for as many women as men who held important positions in the Revolutionary government, for as many female as male inventors, and for as many female as male military leaders. After some period of indecision and discussion, the committee decided to focus on why many history books concentrated on political, economic, and diplomatic history and not on social history and why women had, in fact, when compared with men, done little in these areas. One subcommittee decided to present a report to the class on the current status of women in the United States and how women's roles are in the process of rapid change (Sicherman & Green, 1980). This group presented reports on contemporary women in politics, economics, and the military, as well as women (and men) in the arts and sciences.

Evaluation and Analysis of Data

Social science inquirers must try to determine the credibility and meaning of their data. The tools they use to gather information have a significant effect on the information's meaning and use. If researchers use instruments that have been tested and validated by other scientists, they can usually put more faith in their data than researchers who construct their own instruments and assume, without adequate evidence, that they actually measure the concepts being studied.

When inquirers are evaluating information, they must carefully examine its source and the methods used to gather it, and try to identify its shortcomings and limitations. Researchers may encounter documents, artifacts, artworks, and other types of evidence whose origin and nature are unknown. They must try to formulate fruitful hypotheses about their origin, relate them to known data, and determine whether they are important for the testing of their hypotheses. Much information that researchers will encounter will be useless for their purposes. The questions and hypotheses that researchers formulate help greatly in identifying pertinent and significant information.

Historical documents may pose special problems for inquirers. Students may not only be required to determine their source and nature, but also whether the authors' statements are accurate or untrue. Letters, reports, and other documents must be rigorously examined by the careful inquirer.

Example   In the unit on women in U.S. history textbooks, the students tried to determine the validity and reliability of their information. Following the presentation of each committee report and the class discussion that followed, the students asked such questions as:

Did the committee consult several sources?

Were authorities consulted, and if so, what were their qualifications?

Did the committee members distinguish between sources that based their arguments on opinion as opposed to facts?

Did the committee try to present findings that supported the hypothesis as well as findings that did not support the hypothesis?

Did the committee often use emotionally charged words? If so, why?

Testing Hypotheses: Deriving Generalizations and Theories

Social scientists begin the research cycle with questions, which are usually related to an existing theory or some other body of knowledge. However, questions per se cannot be directly tested. Hypotheses related to the questions are formulated. When the data are gathered and analyzed, researchers try to determine whether their hypotheses can be verified with the information that has been gathered.

If hypotheses are verified during the process of inquiry, they become generalizations. We can consequently think of *generalizations* as *verified or tested hypotheses.* As different scientists develop generalizations related to the same major concepts, theories are developed and verified. *A scientific theory consists of a system of interrelated high-level generalizations (laws or principles) that have been tested and found to be valid.*

Example   Throughout the inquiry on women in U.S. history textbooks, the students looked at their hypotheses and tried to see how they compared with the information they were gathering. They concluded that the questions raised at the beginning of the unit were complex; there were no simple answers. They rejected hypothesis 1 because it was not supported by their research findings. They found partial support for hypotheses 2 and 3 but thought neither was entirely true. Also, neither was sufficient to answer the major question raised in their unit. The students formulated these generalizations:

In the past, most historians have been men because women were primarily occupied in the home with child rearing and because women received less opportunity for formal education.

The writing of some male historians has reflected their personal biases, the times in which they lived and wrote, and the lack of availability of information written by or about women.

In the past not as many women as men were active in political, diplomatic, and economic affairs because such public activities were not considered proper vocations for women.

Women's roles in the United States are changing rapidly because women now have smaller families, longer life spans, and higher levels of education. Technological developments and the increasing expansion of human rights in the United States are also changing the roles of women.

Beginning Inquiry Anew

When researchers find data to support their hypotheses and theories, they still must continue research to further test them (see Figure 3.1). Although theories can be supported with new data and information, they can never be conclusively established. *Scientific knowledge is neither absolute nor unchanging. It must be viewed as tentative and must continually be tested, evaluated, and reconstructed.* Social inquiry is cyclic rather than linear and fixed. Social knowledge may change when new data are discovered, when new assumptions and ways of viewing behavior emerge, when new ideologies within a society arise, or when a scientific revolution occurs. Kuhn (1970) states that a scientific revolution occurs when a paradigm (or theoretical system) replaces another in a discipline. When behavioral psychology emerged in 1913, it did not replace Freudian or gestalt psychology. However, it seriously challenged these theories and had a revolutionary impact on modern psychology.

Students should learn that generalizations formulated during a unit should be regarded as tentative and not as absolute. They should be encouraged to continue challenging their findings and assumptions, and to continue examining the questions studied during the unit. When they encounter new information about a topic studied in class, they should be encouraged to bring it to class to share and to display on a bulletin board. This bulletin board might be called "New Findings and Insights." It could be used to post new findings related to topics the class has studied in science and the language arts as well as the social studies.

Example   After the students formulated their generalizations during the unit on women in U.S. history textbooks, the teacher asked them:

1. Can we be certain that our generalizations are accurate?
2. What other sources can we use that may give us new information related to our generalizations?
3. Can social scientists ever be certain that their generalizations are completely accurate? Why or why not?
4. Sometimes social scientists change generalizations that they have already published. What kinds of developments do you think cause them to do this?

The teacher gives an optional assignment:

> During the rest of the school year, I would like you to share any news items, magazine articles, or other resources that report new information related to this unit with the class. We will discuss these items briefly near the end of our social studies period and post them on the bulletin board. You can earn five extra points for every news item you bring that meets our criteria.

When giving the assignment, the teacher shared with the class an item he clipped from his newspaper over the weekend that met the criteria he had stated. It read in part:

Western Women: Some U.S. History Books Need Revision

> Whenever scholars gather in the future to ponder the history of the American West, they will have to reckon with the deliberations of an unusual gathering of modern-day women in Sun Valley a few weeks ago.
> . . . Citing recent research, much of it based on diaries and interviews with people who had known women pioneers, conference delegates painted a picture of frontier life either ignored or distorted in earlier accounts.
> The "real" story of Western women of those days was often one of unremitting home-building and homemaking toil mixed with political activism on such issues as suffrage and mining-town labor contracts. Other women went cowboying or homesteading by themselves.
> . . . Sooner or later, a lot of history books will have to be rewritten. (*Seattle Times*, August 28, 1983, p. 18)

THE PRODUCTS OF SOCIAL INQUIRY: FACTS, CONCEPTS, GENERALIZATIONS, AND THEORIES

The method used by the social scientist to derive knowledge was discussed in the first part of this chapter. The importance of the inquiry process is emphasized throughout this book. The results or products of inquiry are also important because facts, concepts, generalizations, and theories help individuals to understand human relationships and to make sound personal and public decisions. Even though the products of social inquiry are subject to constant reconstruction or revision (and thus process is important), citizens must at any given time use the most helpful facts, concepts, generalizations, and theories they can find. This part of Chapter 3 focuses on the nature of knowledge and suggests teaching strategies to help elementary and junior high school students learn facts, concepts, and generalizations.

Facts

Factual knowledge consists of specific data about events, objects, people, or other things that can be or have been verified by the senses. Facts are the particular instancs of events or things that in turn become the raw data or the observations of the social scientist. Facts are usually stated in the form of simple, positive statements.

Albany is the capital of New York State.
There are 1,000 meters in a kilometer.
The earth revolves around the sun.

Factual data are often presented in the form of tables and charts, and in almanacs, gazetteers, or similar reference books. These include quantities of diverse data: populations of cities, tide tables, the number of votes cast in recent presidential elections in various states, counties, cities, and so forth. It should be made clear, however, that facts are the actual data themselves. When readers inspect the data and begin to discover trends, or to compare population data for 1980 and 1990, they are then beginning to interpret the data and to make inferences about the facts. This is a higher-order intellectual skill, part of the process of generalizing that will be discussed later.

Some statements that appear to be factual assertions are colored by perceptual biases or value judgments that may not be entirely obvious to the reader. Let us take the statement *Sir Francis Drake was an English hero*. Most students studying early colonial history would probably be willing to accept that as a verifiable fact because it is repeated so often in their texts. There are also many popular pictures of Drake being knighted by Queen Elizabeth I for his exploits. But what about those exploits? Surely from a Spanish point of view the statement might have been written *Sir Francis Drake was an English pirate*. The gold he brought home to his Queen was taken (stolen?) from captured Spanish treasure ships returning from Mexico.

In short, one queen's hero was another king's pirate. Similar statements could be made about such relative words as *poverty* and *wealth*, or perhaps *starvation* and *adequate diet*.

The Fact/Concept Debate

Considerable debate took place during the last two decades about the extent to which facts should be emphasized, as opposed to concepts and higher-level understandings. Educational critics often claimed that teaching students more facts will increase their academic achievement (Hirsch, 1996).

The way to improve the academic achievement of our nation's citizens and their knowledge about U.S. society is clearly more complicated than teaching them more facts. *We can best improve the historical and cultural literacy of students by teaching them powerful concepts and generalizations of the social sciences, but making sure that these key ideas of the disciplines are buttressed by sufficient factual knowledge.* When teaching about the *acculturation* that has taken place in the United States, for example, teachers should make sure that students can list specific ways in which African American music influenced and became a part of the U.S. mainstream culture, as well as specific ways in which African Americans have assimilated aspects of the mainstream culture. Many of the values that African Americans have about family life and work were taken from the U.S. mainstream culture (Jenkins, 1995).

Concept Learning

A concept is an abstract word or phrase that is useful for classifying or categorizing a group of things, ideas, or events. To illustrate this definition, examine the following list of words:

boy   cat   dog   man   rat

What single word or short phrase can you think of that appropriately names or labels the group? At first glance you might be inclined to say *animal* because all the words describe a kind of animal. If you have recently studied biology, you might add carnivore, mammal, or vertebrate because these are also common characteristics of the group. You might be tempted to include domestic, though that word would not really apply to rat unless we were referring to white rats that might be kept as pets. Teachers who have taught in the primary grades, where reading skills are emphasized, are quick to use such labels as: three-letter words, middle-vowel words, or consonant-vowel-consonant (CVC) pattern. You would undoubtedly discover many other possibilities. The point is that each of these words is a possible label or name for the group because it categorizes each item in the class according to some special characteristic that all share. Words that label or name a group of common objects are called *concepts*.

Several important features of concepts should be noted. For example, among the possible concept terms suggested above, animal and three-letter words are more inclusive than some of the others. Indeed, it might be possible to subordinate some of the terms into a hierarchy such as the following:

I. Animal
   A. Vertebrate
     1. Mammal
       a. Carnivore

In some cases, the concept term applies only partly or in a qualified way to all members of the group, such as the term domestic in the example above. The concept term is also abstract. It is not specific or concrete because it refers to an entire class or group of objects.

Learning to use concepts is a vital part of our thinking processes. They enable us to sort out the great variety of objects, events, ideas, and stimuli with which we come into contact each day. Thus, they help reduce the complexity of the environment by separating the great amount of data to be processed by the brain to more manageable portions. Reflecting this, our English language is filled with many abstract words often expressing very complex ideas. The social studies curriculum provides a number of examples of concepts:

family	government	cooperation	power
community	republic	cultural change	interdependence
society	federal system	conflict	tradition
nation	democracy	law	social control

In addition, concepts have varying degrees of abstractness and can be thought of as existing on a continuum. For example:

Concrete   *Abstract*
family ⟵⟶ nation
fight ⟵⟶ revolution
local ordinance ⟵⟶ international law
village ⟵⟶ megalopolis

One type of abstract concept that requires special attention is the *relational concept. Relational concepts* define a particular association between attributes or distinguishing characteristics. Concepts involving distance and time are perhaps the most common relational ones in social studies: year, century, mile, light-year, outer space, latitude, longitude, great circle route. Other relational concepts are much more abstract: uncle, great-grandfather, mother-in-law, foster parent, compatriot. It is particularly difficult for young children to understand concepts like these because they have not had sufficient experience with the basic facts themselves, or with abstracting the common attributes to establish the particular relation or association involved. For example, it takes considerable practice with a calendar for a six- or seven-year-old child to count up 30 days, learn that that period is called a month, and then recognize that there are approximately four weeks in a month. Most adults are satisfied to think of a century as a "very long time" or have only a foggy notion of the concepts great-uncle and grandniece.

INTERDISCIPLINARY CONCEPTS

Having a knowledge of the basic concepts from the various social science disciplines allows one to consider a problem that spans several disciplines or is interdisciplinary in its scope. Broad ranging topics such as the city, international peace, and poverty can be considered from a variety of perspectives, each avoiding the parochialness of a single point of view. An example of a set of high-order, interdisciplinary concepts used in a social studies curriculum is found in Table 2.6 (pp. 57–58).

HOW CONCEPTS ARE LEARNED

Concept formation is a complex intellectual task. According to the classical approach, it consists of the ability to sort out a group of observations on the basis of one or more common characteristics, to abstract and generalize these discriminating features, and to apply a word or phrase to the observation that appropriately names or labels it on the basis of its discriminating characteristics. In short, *conceptualization is the process of categorizing, classifying, and naming a group of objects.*

Children begin to form concepts very early in life. This becomes evident as soon as they can identify correctly a variety of common objects such as chair, light, table, or dog. By the time most children begin the primary grades, they already have a speaking vocabulary that includes many concept terms. These include concepts for most of the objects in their environment, such as the persons in their immediate family, the things in their homes, and the foods, clothes, and utensils they use each day. Furthermore, television has brought children into frequent contact with many things quite distant from their own environment. They may know more about these than about things that are more immediate and close to them. Children have probably developed a number of relational concepts such as inside, outside, from, to, up, and down, but often have confused and incomplete ideas about the meaning of other important relational concepts such as smaller than, less than, larger, more than, the next one, the one before, double, like, unlike, and the number names for quantities. Nor do children understand just how their close family relatives such as grandparents, uncles, or aunts are related to their own parents and themselves.

Nature of the Learning Experience   As indicated above, many concepts are learned informally before children enter school. Experiences and the many events and things in their environment provide direct and immediate learning situations. The objects encountered are concrete and specific, often with vivid sensory stimuli. Learning in the school classroom, however, tends to be proximate rather than direct, and more symbolic and abstract than concrete. Because the school setting is more formal and structured, you must provide many opportunities for students to gain experience with the events represented by the concept. Young children in the primary grades (to follow Piaget's developmental stages) need frequent experience with concrete realities that can be seen, heard, or manipulated. Older students in the middle and upper grades also need experience with the events or things involved, but the materials may be more abstract or symbolic. For example, primary grade students might use pictures, drawings, or dolls to develop simple aspects of the concept family, whereas students in the fifth or sixth grade might use a diagram with a variety of symbols to chart the familial ties in an extended family. The older students would spend considerably less time on this topic because the more basic elements of the concept family will have already been developed.

Examples and Non-examples of Concepts   Research indicates that concepts are learned most effectively when a number of positive examples of the concept are presented (Yoho, 1986). Students are able to discern the relevant characteristics and to make appropriate discriminations when the examples of a city, such as Boston, Paris, or Tokyo, are not confused with a special case such as Vatican City.

Negative examples illustrate characteristics that are opposite from those positively associated with the discriminating features. For example, liberty may be illustrated by the excesses of license; the need for laws and regulations by the possibility of anarchy; honesty and integrity by the evidence of wrongdoing and corruption. Although it is true that some learning does occur with negative examples, learners are forced to spend an inordinate amount of time inefficiently searching for the appropriate clues leading them to the discriminating characteristic. In addition, they must try to remember all the characteristics that do not apply, which usually far exceed those that are included in the concept. Yet, ironically, most classroom discussions that we have observed on the concepts of liberty, law, or integrity have dealt almost entirely with negative examples. This is not to say that exceptions should not be discussed, only that they should not be introduced until the positive aspects of the concept have been carefully developed so that students can easily make the correct discriminations.

Complexity of Examples   Because the social studies curriculum contains so many complex concepts, it is important that we consider three aspects related to complexity: focusing on the essential characteristics, choosing between realistic versus simulated experiences, and progressing from simple to complex concepts.

Suppose, for example, a class is studying the concept *assembly-line production*. If we were to start by taking the class to a factory without any prior class development of the concept, the students would be overwhelmed by the complexity of factors. Which are the *essential characteristics:* the large stores of materials, the protective clothing worn by the workers, or perhaps the great amount of machinery present? Obviously, the teacher would have had to introduce the idea of a moving table on which the product was placed, and as the table was moved rapidly through various parts of the factory, different groups of workers added something or made some change in the product until it reached its finished form. This could be demonstrated with a videotape, a projected computer presentation, or a set of animated transparencies, each illustrating several different examples (auto production, a meat-packing plant) and non-examples (a jeweler repairing a watch, a shoemaker resoling a pair of shoes).

Once the students have understood the essential characteristics, a field trip to see an assembly line in actual operation would be more profitable. Students could then attend to the essential characteristics and not be diverted by the fascinating but irrelevant cues.

Using the same example, let us examine the problem of choosing between *realistic versus simulated experience* when a concept is being presented for the first time. Abundant research evidence from the areas of industrial and military training has indicated that simplified line drawings, models, animated films, or simulated mock-ups are usually far more effective in teaching a concept than direct observation or involvement. These devices eliminate most of the irrelevant cues and emphasize strongly, often by vivid colors, the essential characteristics. As we indicated above, the field trip to the factory to see an assembly line is a complex learning activity. Undoubtedly, students will see many new and exciting things for the first time, many having little or nothing to do with the concept *assembly line*. As Travers (1964) has pointed out, humans have a limited capacity to handle the onrush of new information, and the brain tends to eliminate those stimuli which it cannot sort out and relate to other existing impressions and ideas. It is very likely that some students will miss entirely the concept *assembly line*, and little will have been gained from the field trip. Thus, a teacher must weigh carefully the value of heightened motivation and interest that will result from a field trip, versus the value of simplicity and accuracy that is to be gained from the use of a simulated experience when a concept is first introduced.

VERBALIZING A CONCEPT

One of the factors related to concept attainment is the ability of the student to verbalize the concept. Verbalizing is distinguishing orally or in writing the discriminating characteristics and giving the concept an appropriate name. Such a skill is important in social studies if students are to use concepts freely and readily in sorting out large amounts of data and if they are to have a repertoire of powerful analytical terms for making comparisons and contrasts in the process of developing generalizations from several samples of data.

Many students at first have some kind of intuitive grasp of the concept and are able to recognize those items that belong to a group and those that do not. They find it difficult, however, to state the basis for their discrimination and can often give no reason for why an item belongs in a particular group other than "Well, because it just does." In short, they may be able to identify (and possibly use) a concept, but not be able to define it adequately in words.

This problem is due not only to the lack of adequate abstract terms in the young child's vocabulary, but also to the fact that the process of conceptualizing involves three separate tasks: *observing, classifying,* and *defining,* all of which involve separate response modes. Studies have demonstrated that the quality of concept definition improves when students are given even limited amounts of practice in making definitions at the same time that they make the discriminations, even when they are not told how good the definition is (Taba, 1966). Teaching strategies should ensure, then, that students are given adequate practice in naming or defining a concept, at the same time that they identify the discriminating features used in classifying the items in the group. Teachers should recognize, too, that students will grope for adequate words to express the concept and will often use awkward phrases because they have not learned the precise abstract word.

One class of third-grade youngsters studying manufacturing agreed on the phrase "things that you make all in a line" as their name for the concept *assembly line.* It was not until a day or two later, when the teacher was certain that most of the students had attained the concept, that she suggested they substitute the more technical phrase *assembly line.* For students with low verbal fluency or poor language development, it is doubly important that the teacher concentrate on the skill of defining as well as the skill of discriminating.

A strategy for teaching concepts based on curriculum and psychological principles is presented in Table 3.1. It consists principally of having the teacher ask a series of questions designed to elicit from the students the essential task of *listing, grouping,* and *labeling.*

ISSUES IN CONCEPT LEARNING

Studies in concept learning have raised a number of issues that challenge the "classical" approach described above (Stanley & Mathews, 1985). These studies present models of the structure of concepts and a theory on the process of how concepts are learned. They also suggest that you as a teacher must be more keenly aware of the cultural context that different groups of students bring with them as they learn to interpret and establish meanings for complex social science concepts.

TABLE 3.1. *Developing Concepts: Listing, Grouping, Labeling, and Defining a Concept*

This task requires students to group a number of items on some kind of basis. The teaching strategy consists of asking students the following questions, usually in this order.

Teacher Asks	Student	Teacher Follow-Through
What do you see (notice, find) here?	Gives items.	Makes sure items are accessible to each student. Lists the items on chalkboard, transparency, individual list, pictures, or item card.
Do any of these items seem to belong together?	Finds some similarity as a basis.	Communicates grouping. For example, underlines in colored chalk, marks with symbols or arranges pictures or cards.
Why would you group them together?*	Identifies and verbalizes the common characteristics of items in a group.	Seeks clarification of responses when necessary.
What would you call these groups you have formed?	Verbalizes a label (perhaps more than one word) that appropriately encompasses all items.	Records.
Could some of these belong in more than one group?	States different relationships.	Records.
Can we put these same items in different groups?†	States additional different relationships.	Communicates grouping.
Can you explain (define) the name or label of this group?	States a definition.	Records the definition.

*Sometimes you ask the same child "why" when he or she offers the grouping, and other times you may wish to get many groups before considering "why" things are grouped together.

†Although this step is important because it encourages flexibility, it will not be appropriate on all occasions.

Source: The Taba Social Studies Curriculum (Menlo Park, Calif.: Addison-Wesley, 1970), vol. 6, p. xxii. Reprinted with permission.

The Structure of Concepts

The classical model of a concept assumes that all the essential characteristics or attributes must always be present. While this may be satisfactory for relatively simple conjunctive concepts (where the elements are additive), it presents serious learning problems for complex, abstract concepts that are often disjunctive in form (that is, some of the elements may or may not be present).

To meet these difficulties, two alternative models have been proposed: the *exemplar model* and the *social context model.* Proponents of the exemplar model have suggested that concepts be identified on the basis of attributes that are most typically present, rather than insisting that all attributes must always be present—somewhat like Wittgenstein's "family resemblance" notion (Rosch & Mervis, 1978; Wittgenstein, 1958). In this model you would present to students a number of best examples (most typical) of the concept with little or no attention to poor examples (least typical). In a study by Yoho (1986), this method of presenting only the best examples proved to be the most effective strategy when compared to three other strategies of concept learning. Thus, many complex concepts in social studies such as *ethnicity, social class, alienation, justice,* or *poverty* might well be taught using this best example (most typical) model.

The *social context model* suggests that the brain forms a unitary representation of a concept, a non-analytic, perhaps intuitive learning, that merges specific instances of a concept within a context of actions, expectations and relationships to other concepts (Nelson, 1974). Consider the concept of a birthday party. For many young children this is an eagerly awaited day, an enjoyable time with family and friends, games, ice cream and cake, gifts, and a vague awareness that they have grown another year older. In this model, while the party itself may be the essential attribute, it is the context of the special day, the expectation of how people, actions, and events are likely to interact, and the relationship of this day to the larger concepts of age or maturity that give meaning to the concept of birthday party. Similarly, the concept of basketball game or playoff tournament has a much larger social context than ball or players, which make up only a part of the concept. Thus, you may find this model much more useful for teaching some complex concepts in social studies such as civil rights demonstration, lobbying, the presidential primary system, or terrorism.

Schemata and the Process of Learning Concepts

Drawing on research in cognition, linguistics, and artificial intelligence, psychologists have proposed the theory that the mind makes use of underlying schemata or frameworks as it organizes and processes information (Millwar, 1980). According to the *schemata theory,* the mind tends to build frameworks which contain slots or place holders into which we put new data or experiences. They are dynamic structures constantly undergoing change. The mind integrates new information by establishing relationships between the new data and what is already known and stored in the long-term memory of the brain. Schemata are the building blocks of cognition or thinking processes (Rumelhart, 1980).

Schemata, or frameworks, are developed out of the cultural background of the student, and prior experiences provide the context for interpreting or deriving meaning from written text or social situations. Thus, students who understand how a neighborhood convenience store functions would have appropriate schemata for understanding the concept of supermarket or department store, but they may have no schemata for understanding the concept of bargaining at a bazaar in Nairobi (Kenya) or bidding at an art auction.

Similes and metaphors seem to enhance the process of relating new information to previously learned data. You might begin a discussion about the concept of election by saying, "Winning a presidential primary election is like winning a state championship in a basketball tournament." The schemata theory has been derived from research studies in sociolinguistics and has had a major influence on the teaching of reading in schools (Anderson & Pearson, 1985; Calfee & Drum, 1986). Scholars cite similar trends beginning to emerge in teaching social studies and urge further investigation into ways that teachers can add new and often conflicting information about culturally different people and societies into students' existing schemata (Armento, 1986; Stanley & Mathews, 1985).

Generalizations

Generalizations are statements of the relationship of two or more concepts. These statements may range from very simple to very complex. Sometimes they are referred to as principles or laws. The following statements are generalizations.

> As people interact with their physical and social environment, both they and the environment are changed.
>
> All persons and groups of persons depend on the other persons and groups for satisfaction of needs.
>
> Conflicts and inequities often result from assigning value to particular categories of differences, such as white skin or high intelligence.
>
> Cultural change is accelerated by such factors as increased knowledge, mobility, and communication, operating both within and between cultures.

Generalizations such as those above provide us with a useful means of expressing the relationship between accumulated facts and information in a highly organized and systematic way. They eliminate the need for us to go back to original statements again and again. In a sense, generalizations become a kind of shorthand for the knowledge that we accumulate during our life experience. They are also useful as a means of helping us explore new situations.

Traditionally, schools have passed on these accumulated generalizations in an expository manner. Teachers have lectured or talked about them. The authors of textbooks have incorporated them as statements of truth. In most cases, they have been presented as statements to be learned and accepted with little or no discussion about their derivation or validity. Typically, generalizations have been used in a deductive manner; that is, students have accepted the truth of the statements and then sought examples that illustrate them in particular detail or in local application.

We believe that students in elementary and junior high schools should have the maximum opportunities to derive generalizations for themselves. While there certainly is a place for deductive learning, it is our position that this mode of learning has occupied far too large a part of students' learning experiences. In contrast, students have had little opportunity to learn the skills and processes involved in deriving generalizations for themselves.

ANATOMY OF GENERALIZATIONS

A generalization expresses a relationship between two or more concepts. For example, let us take two very simple concepts: rain and temperature. What can we say about their relationship? We might be able to make a very simple statement such as "When it is cold, rain changes to snow." While most young children will already have had enough experience in their lifetimes to validate this statement, a more complex generalization might make a statement about the relationship of rainfall and temperature and their effect on vegetation. In such cases, it may be possible to generalize that the combination of warm weather, large amounts of rainfall, and fertile soil produces great amounts of vegetation.

Relationships between two or more concepts are often expressed by verb phrases such as grows larger, declines, is influenced by, is associated with, causes changes in, or varies with. Earlier we spoke of generalizations as "verified hypotheses." It is a good test of a generalization, therefore, to try to recast the statement into the "if...then" form. Not only does this force the relationship into clearer perspective, but it also requires that the concepts be stated in sequence so that their logical cause and effect or other association is plainly evident. Thus, the two examples given above could be rewritten as:

> If it is cold, then the rain will change to snow.
>
> If there is a combination of warm weather, large amounts of rainfall, and fertile soil, then large amounts of vegetation will be produced.

We propose this basic guideline: If a generalization cannot be recast into an "if...then" form, then it is probably only a statement that summarizes factual knowledge.

Some generalizations, of course, are very limited in scope. The data they are derived from may be limited to the experience of a single individual or may refer to a single town or region in the United States. For example, we may have "the growth of the lumber industry in the Pacific Northwest depends in large measure on the annual rainfall." This statement is obviously limited because of the restrictions on the data from which the relationships were derived. The source of evidence is the annual rainfall and the economic growth of the lumber industry in the Northwest. A very different series of generalizations might be developed if we were to analyze the amount of rainfall in Thailand and its effects on the rice crop. These two examples require widely contrasting sources of data. If we extend this by adding the sample data on rainfall and production of rice in Louisiana, and another sample that provides data on the amount of rainfall and the yield of wheat in Russia, we may begin to get some broad inferences from a series of widely divergent samples about the influence of rainfall and temperature on vegetation.

Other generalizations, however, have universal application throughout people's cultural experience. Empirical data from all times and all cultures can be used to support the relationship stated between the concepts. For example:

> In every society rules emerge to govern the affairs of people.
>
> Culture tends to standardize human behavior and to stabilize societies by developing many interrelated and elaborate institutions.

HIGH-ORDER AND LOW-ORDER GENERALIZATIONS

As you can see from the discussion above, generalizations can be classified on the basis of the range of their applications. Some are universal in their scope; others are very limited in their applications. For convenience we have called these *high-order, intermediate-level,* and *low-order generalizations.* In the following paragraphs we have sketched out a progression of generalizations from high to low. As the arrow indicates, these can be read in any direction, from high to low (deductive), or from low to high (inductive).

High-Order Generalizations

These generalizations have universal application. They apply to all people at all times. Generalizations of the highest order are often called laws or principles.

Example: *Interaction between a people and their environment influences the way in which they meet their needs.*

Intermediate-Level Generalizations

These generalizations apply to particular regions of the world, cultures, or historical eras.

Example: *Americans who moved westward from the Eastern Seaboard during the eighteenth and nineteenth centuries modified their life styles to meet the demands of frontier living.*

Low-Order Generalizations

These generalizations are based on data from only two or three small samples, such as a group of cities in a particular region.

Example: *An abundance of moisture together with a long, warm growing season provide good conditions for growing grapes in the San Francisco Bay area and along the southern shore of Lake Erie.*

Summarizing Statements   In contrast to the various levels of generalizations outlined above, summarizing statements tend to sum up a series of facts or observations derived from a single sample, such as manufacturing in Boston, temperature variations in a single town, or even as broad a topic as the American Revolution. No matter how much data may be accumulated on any of these topics, this kind of activity still remains a *summarizing* and not a generalizing statement if the data are drawn from a single sample.

You should not regard long factual summaries as generalizations. *It is not until comparisons and contrast are made with two or more samples and relationships established between important concepts (or variables) that one can be said to be engaged in the process of generalizing.* In one study, this method was found superior to two other methods of teaching economic concepts to fifth-grade students (Betres, Zajani, & Gumieniak, 1984). Table 3.2 illustrates a strategy for teaching students to generalize.

GENERALIZATIONS IN CURRICULUM DESIGN

In planning a unit of study, a teacher usually starts by specifying the end product of the students' learning. This serves as the target or focus for all other planning. Stated in behavioral terms, for example, the learning outcome might be:

> Having completed a unit of study on world cultures, students will write statements that approximate the generalization: *Cultures vary from society to society. Any given culture changes in the course of time. Some behaviors and institutions within a culture are universal while others vary widely, even during the same period.*

TABLE 3.2. *Inferring and Generalizing*

This cognitive task requires the students to interpret, infer, and generalize about data. The teaching strategy consists of asking the students the following questions, usually in this order:

Teacher Asks	Student	Teacher Follow-Through
What did you notice? See? Find? What differences did you notice (with reference to a particular question)?	Gives items.	Makes sure items are accessible—for example, chalkboard, transparency, individual list, pictures, or item card. Choose the items to pursue.
Why do you think this happened? Or, how do you account for these differences?	Gives explanation that may be based on factual information and/or inferences.	Accepts explanation. Seeks clarification if necessary.
What does this tell you about . . . ?	Gives generalization.	Encourages variety of generalizations and seeks clarification when necessary.

This pattern of inviting reasons to account for observed phenomena and generalizing beyond the data is repeated and expanded to include more and more aspects of the data and to reach more abstract generalizations.

Source: Hilda Taba, Mary C. Durkin, Jack R. Fraenkel, and Anthony H. McNaughton, *A Teacher's Handbook to Elementary Social Studies: An Inductive Approach* (Reading, Mass.: Addison-Wesley, 1971), p. 75.

Using this as the final goal toward which all activities should point, the teacher can then begin to plan in reverse the content, materials, and learning experiences that would be appropriate to help the student ultimately arrive at this generalization. Figure 3.2 shows a schematic outline of the process. It should be emphasized again that this diagram represents the teacher's planning activity, which is to a large measure a deductive process. The students' learning activities, however, start from the bottom of the diagram and proceed inductively toward the high-level generalization.

Each of the chapters on the disciplines (Chapters 9 through 14) provides examples of concepts and generalizations from the various social sciences. Sample generalizations from these chapters are presented in Table 3.3. Chapter 2 describes interdisciplinary approaches and illustrates how generalizations from the various social science disciplines can be used to study topics and problems.

You should realize, however, that lists of generalizations are in themselves only lists. When provided in state or local curriculum guides, they are intended to serve as guides. In most cases, it remains for you to work out the practical problem of relating concepts and generalizations to appropriate content, instructional materials, and teaching strategies geared to your students.

Theories: Nature and Examples

Theory is the highest form of knowledge and is a main goal of science. Theories help us to explain and to predict human behavior. Although total agreement on the definition of the term does not exist, most social scientists would agree that a *scientific theory consists of a set of testable interrelated "lawlike" statements or high-level generalizations.* The high-level generalizations that make up a scientific theory must:

1. show the relationship between clearly defined variables or concepts.
2. constitute a deductive system and be logically consistent (unknown principles must be derivable from known ones).
3. be a source of testable hypotheses.

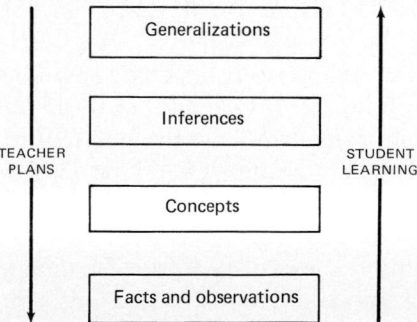

Figure 3.2
Relationship of generalizations, concepts, and facts.

TABLE 3.3. *Key Social Science Generalizations*

Discipline	Generalizations
History	Wherever human beings have lived, conflicts between individuals, groups, and nations have arisen.
	A historian's view of the past is influenced by the availability of evidence, his or her personal biases and purposes for writing, and the society and times in which he or she lives and writes.
Sociology	All characteristically human behavior is learned from other human beings through group interaction.
	The group exerts social control over its individual members through the use of sanctions.
Anthropology	Cultures use a diversity of means to attain similar ends and to satisfy common human needs.
	Cultural exchange takes place when groups with diverse cultures come into prolonged contact. Cultural change may disrupt a society.
Geography	The physical environment influences how a culture develops and how it solves the problems of survival.
	An individual's perception of his or her physical environment is influenced by his or her culture and experiences within that environment.
Political science	In every society and institution, regulations and laws emerge to govern the behavior of individuals and groups.
	Rules and laws reflect the basic values within a society or institution.
Economics	Every individual and society faces a conflict between unlimited wants and limited resources.
	All members of society are interdependent. Individual producers of goods and services exchange with others to get the goods and services they need to satisfy their basic wants.

Unlike physical scientists, social scientists have developed relatively few theories consistent with the definition above. Partly, this is because the social sciences are much newer fields than the physical sciences. Also, data on human behavior are much more difficult to collect and verify than data about our physical environment. However, social scientists have been successful in formulating a number of partial theories. The theories illustrated below are partial because they attempt to explain and predict only limited aspects of human behavior. They try to explain why suicide rates vary among different groups. Grand or inclusive theories try to explain, with a few statements or generalizations, all group behavior or a total class of things. Darwin's theory of evolution, Newton's corpuscular theory of light, and Einstein's theory of relativity are examples of grand theories in the biological and physical sciences. Social scientists have not been able to develop grand or all-encompassing theories universally accepted by the scientific community. However, the Freudian and Marxist theories are grand in scope and attempt to explain most human behavior in a few principles.

EXAMPLES OF THEORIES

Durkheim's Theory of Suicide   One of the first empirical social science theories, Durkheim's theory explains the low suicide rate in Spain (Homans, 1964). Durkheim's system satisfies all the characteristics of a theory described above.

1. In any social grouping, the suicide rate varies directly with the degree of individualism.
2. The degree of individualism varies with the incidence of Protestantism.
3. Therefore, the suicide rate varies with the incidence of Protestantism.
4. The incidence of Protestantism in Spain is low.
5. Therefore, the suicide rate in Spain is low.

Merton's Theory of Suicide   Merton has formulated and tested a theory to explain the lower incidence of suicide among Catholics than among Protestants (Reported in Inkeles, 1965):

1. Social cohesion provides psychic support to group members subjected to acute stresses and anxieties.
2. Suicide rates are functions of unrelieved anxieties and stresses to which persons are subjected.
3. Catholic (and specified additional groups) have greater social cohesion than Protestants.
4. Therefore, lower suicide rates should be anticipated among Catholics than among Protestants.

THEORIES IN THE SOCIAL STUDIES CURRICULUM

Social studies educators have done relatively little work related to the teaching of theories to students. A few writers have suggested that curriculum builders should identify those social science theories that will best help students to make decisions and teach the concepts and generalizations that are part of theories. There are many partial theories in the social sciences that you can use in teaching. These include such theories as Rogers's theory of personality and behavior, Schlesinger's theory of political ambition, and Lenski's theory of social stratification. Arthur M. Schlesinger Jr.'s (1986) interesting theory about cycles in U.S. history—the 30-year alternation of liberal and conservative forces—can provide students in the middle and upper grades with a unique lens through which to view history and contemporary events.

A theory approach to curriculum construction is a promising one. However, we have no models or examples of social studies curricula structured around theories. More work related to the teaching of theory must be done before specific curriculum recommendations can be made. Nonetheless, during a study of some concepts (such as suicide, prejudice, political alienation, and social stratification), especially in the middle and upper grades, you might draw on theories such as those presented above to guide your selection of generalizations to teach and to help your students to better understand and predict behavior (Lemert, 1993). Like all forms of knowledge, social theory has limitations. It is tentative and does not always specify conditions or exceptions. Despite these limitations, theory is the most powerful form of knowledge

TABLE 3.4. *The Relationship of the Categories of Knowledge*

This figure illustrates the relationship between *facts, concepts, generalizations,* and *theories.* Note that each category of knowledge is dependent for its development on the element below it.
Theory: Durkheim's theory of suicide.
Generalization: In any social grouping, the suicide rate varies directly with the degree of individualism.
Concepts: Suicide rate; Individualism.
Fact: Only 7.6 persons per 100,000 committed suicide in Spain in 1965, compared to 16.3 per 100,000 in the United States.*

*Based on data reported in the *Statistical Abstract of the United States* (Washington, D.C.: U.S. Government Printing Office, 1969), p. 81.

that has yet been devised. Table 3.4 illustrates the relationship between the various categories of knowledge discussed in this chapter.

SUMMARY

The main goal of the social studies should be to help students develop the ability to make reflective decisions. They can then influence public policy by participating in effective citizen action. Knowledge is one essential component of the decision-making process. The first part of this chapter discusses the goal and nature of social science inquiry and describes a model students can use to test hypotheses and to derive knowledge. Students must be given systematic practice in each of the skills that constitute this model in order to become adept decision-makers. This chapter also highlights the assumptions, limitations, and basic requirements of science. *Scientific knowledge is neither absolute nor unchanging. It should be regarded as tentative and must be continually tested, evaluated, and reconstructed.*

The second part of this chapter describes the nature of social knowledge. Emphasis in elementary and junior high school social studies should be on the *process* of social science inquiry and not on its *products.* However, the products of inquiry—*facts, concepts, generalizations,* and *theories*—are essential for structuring experiences whereby students can learn inquiry modes, and thus help to solve important personal and public problems. Without higher-level predictive knowledge, or the products of inquiry, the decision-maker is not competent to act. The reflective citizen actor must make use of the best available knowledge.

Factual knowledge consists of specific data about events, objects, people, or other things that can be verified by the senses. Concepts are abstract words useful for classifying groups of facts, events, or ideas on the basis of common characteristics. Generalizations are statements showing a relationship between two or more concepts. A scientific theory is a set of interrelated high-level generalizations capable of explaining and predicting behavior. Partly because of the emerging status of theory in the social sciences, the teaching of social science theory in the schools has not been systematically developed by social studies educators.

REFLECTION AND ACTION ACTIVITIES

1. What are the essential factors that distinguish one social science discipline from another? Give examples to support your answer. What implications does your answer have for planning social studies experiences for elementary and junior high school students?

2. What are the assumptions of science? Why is social science unable to answer many of the questions in which people are most vitally interested? List several questions that social science cannot answer. List several questions that social science cannot answer, but whose resolutions can be aided by the wise use of the scientific method.

3. The model of social science inquiry presented in this chapter consists of a series of skills. Plan lessons designed to help students gain proficiency in:
   a. formulating problems
   b. hypothesizing
   c. conceptualizing
   d. collecting data
   e. evaluating and analyzing data
   f. deriving generalizations.

4. Explain and give examples of how a teacher may help students to implement each of the following types of studies:
   a. the experiment   b. the sample survey   c. the case study
   What difficulties might a teacher encounter in trying to help students implement each type of study? How might these difficulties be overcome?

5. Make a list of 10 facts that can be or have been verified about some important recent event or problem (e.g., the presidential election campaign, consumer protection programs, a racial conflict, a prolonged strike, or a campus controversy). Are any of these "facts" distorted by biased or prejudiced perceptions of the data?

6. Using the list of 10 facts pertinent to any one of the events or problems suggested in Question 5, categorize them into groups and label them with an appropriate concept word or phrase. Can some of the items be interchanged between groups? Does this affect the concept term applied to the groups?

7. The terms *concept* and *generalization* are often confused and substituted for each other. How would you distinguish one from the other?

8. Using some of the concepts you formulated in Question 6, write four generalizations that might be developed from them (assuming the data are available to support them). Test each generalization by recasting it into the conditional "if...then" form to check for the logical relationship among concepts. (The purpose of this exercise is to develop practice in formulating the statement of a generalization, not necessarily in finding the data to verify it.)

9. Think back over the social science courses you have had. With what major theories from one or more of the disciplines are you familiar? To what extent do they meet the criteria for theory identified in this chapter? If students were familiar with this theory, how might it contribute to their understanding of concepts and generalizations? How might it contribute to more effective decision-making?

10. Demonstrate your understanding of the following key concepts by writing or stating brief definitions for each:
    a. social science inquiry (process)
    b. knowledge (product)
    c. hypothesis
    d. conceptualization
    e. experiment
    f. sample survey
    g. participant observation
    h. the requirements of science
    i. the assumptions of science
    j. fact
    k. concept
    l. generalization
    m. theory
    n. hierarchical order of concepts
    o. abstract conceptualizations
    p. concrete concept

q. relational concept
r. interdisciplinary concepts
s. positive examples of concepts
t. negative examples of concepts

u. generalizations
v. high-order/low-order generalizations
w. summarizing statements

REFERENCES

Anderson, R. C., & Pearson, P. D. (1985). A schema theoretic view of basic processes in reading comprehension. In P. D. Pearson, R. Barr, M. Kamil, & P. Mosenthel (Eds.), *Handbook of reading research* (pp. 255–291). White Plains, NY: Longman.

Appleby, J., Hunt, L., & Jacob, M. (1994). *Tell the truth about history.* New York: Norton.

Armento, B. V. (1986). Research on teaching social studies. In M. C. Wittrock (Ed.), *Handbook of research on teaching* (3rd ed.) (pp. 946–947). New York: Macmillan.

Berelson, B., & Steiner, G. A. (1964). *Human behavior: An inventory of scientific findings.* New York: Harcourt Brace.

Betres, J., Zajani, M., & Gumieniak, P. (1984). Cognitive style, teacher methods and concept attainment in social studies. *Theory and Research in Social Education,* 12, 1–18.

Calfee, R. & Drum, P. (1986). Research on teaching reading. In M. C. Wittrock (Ed.), *Handbook of research on teaching* (3rd ed.) (pp. 804–849). New York: Macmillan.

Duneier, M. (1992). *Slim's table: Race, respectability, and masculinity.* Chicago: University of Chicago Press.

Gwaltney, J. L. (1980). *Drylongso: A self-portrait of Black American.* New York: Random House.

Hirsch, E. D., Jr. (1996). *The schools we need and why we don't have them.* New York: Doubleday.

Homans, G. C. (1964). Contemporary theory in sociology. In Robert E. L. Faris (Ed.), *Handbook of modern sociology* (pp. 951–977). Chicago: Rand McNally.

Inkeles, A. (1965). *What is sociology? An introduction to the discipline and profession.* Englewood Cliffs, NJ: Prentice-Hall.

Jenkins, A. H. (1995). *Psychology and African Americans* (2nd ed.). Boston: Allyn and Bacon.

Kolata, G. (1998). *Clone: The road to Dolly and the path ahead.* New York: William Morrow.

Kuhn, T. S. (1970). *The structure of scientific revolutions* (2nd ed.). Chicago: University of Chicago Press.

Lastrucci, C. L. (1963) *The scientific approach: Basic principles of the scientific method.* Cambridge, MA: Schenkman.

Lemert, C. (Ed.). (1993). *Social theory: The multicultural & classic readings.* Boulder, CO: Westview Press.

Lightfoot, S. L. (1994). *I've known rivers: Lives of loss and liberation.* Reading, MA: Addison-Wesley.

Millwar, R. B. (1980). Models of concept formation. In R. E. Snow, P. Federico, & W. E. Montague (Eds.), *Aptitude, learning and instruction,* (vol. 2, pp. 245–275). Hillsdale, NJ: Erlbaum.

Munch, R. & Smelser, N. J. (Eds.). (1992). *Theory of culture.* Berkeley: University of California Press.

Nelson, K. (1974). Cognitive development and the acquisition of concepts. *Psychological Review,* 81, 267–285.

Peters, W. (1987). *A class divided: Then and now* (Expanded edition). New Haven, CT: Yale University Press.

Rosenau, P. M. (1992). *Post-modernism and the social sciences: Insights, inroads, and intrusions.* Princeton, NJ: Princeton University Press.

Rosch, E. H., & Mervis, C. B. (Eds.) (1978). *Cognition and categorization.* Hillsdale, NJ: Erlbaum.

Rumelhart, D. E. (1980). Schemata: The building blocks of cognition. In R. J. Spiro, B. C. Bruce, & W. F. Brewer (Eds.), *Theoretical issues in reading comprehension* (pp. 33–58). Hillsdale, NJ: Erlbaum.

Schlesinger, A. M., Jr. (1986). *The cycles of American history.* Boston: Houghton Mifflin.

Seattle Times, August 28, 1983, p. A18.

Sicherman, B., & Green, C. H. (Eds.). (1980). *Notable American women: The modern period.* Cambridge, MA: Harvard University Press.

Stanley, W. B., & Mathews, R. C. (1985). Recent research on concept learning: Implications for social education. *Theory and research in social education,* 12, 57–74.

Taba, H. (1966). *Teaching strategies and cognitive functioning in elementary school children.* Cooperative Research Bureau Project #2404. U.S. Office of Health, Education, and Welfare, San Francisco State College.

Travers, R. M. W. (1964). Transmission of information to human receivers. *Educational Psychologist,* 2, 1–5.

Wittgenstein, L. (1958). *Philosophical investigations* (2nd ed.). New York: Macmillan.

Yoho, R. F. (1986). Effectiveness of four concept teaching strategies on social concept acquisition and retention. *Theory and Research in Social Education,* 14, 211–223.

FOR FURTHER READING

Ashby, R., et al. (1997). How children explain the "why" of history: The Chata Research Project on Teaching History. *Social Education,* 61 (1), 17–21.

Crisman, F., & Mackey, J. (1990). A comparison of oral and written techniques of concept instruction. *Theory and Research in Social Education,* 18(2), 139–155.

Levstik, L. S., & Barton, K. C. (1996). "They still use some of their past": Historical salience in elementary children's chronological thinking. *Journal of Curriculum Studies,* 28(5), 531–536.

McKinney, C. W. (1985). A comparison of the effects of a definition, examples, and non-examples on student acquisition of the concept of "transfer propaganda." *Social Education,* 49(1), 68–70.

McKinney, C. W., et al. (1987). Effects of a best example and critical attributes on prototype formation in the acquisition of a concept. *Theory and Research in Social Education,* 15(3), 189–201.

VanSickle, R. L., & Hoge, J. D. (1991). Higher cognitive thinking skills in social studies: Concepts and critiques. *Theory and Research in Social Education,* 19(2), 152–172.

Wade, R. (1994). Conceptual change in elementary social studies: A case study of fourth graders' understanding of human rights. *Theory and Research in Social Education,* 22(1), 74–95.

CHAPTER 4

Teaching Higher-Level Thinking with Questions

Making critical decisions about important social issues and problems requires people to use higher-level thinking processes, such as conceptualizing factual data, hypothesizing about possible solutions, and generalizing to larger settings. As a teacher you can help students learn these thought processes by skillfully asking appropriate questions that lead them from simple to complex thinking tasks. Research conducted during the past 20 years has amply demonstrated that student learning improves when teachers use appropriate questioning practices, particularly those that involve higher-order thinking processes (Wilen, 1987; Wilen & Clegg, 1986).

This chapter will examine classroom questions, both oral and written, from a number of considerations: (1) the purpose and function of questions, (2) their use as elements in the teaching strategies related to social inquiry, valuing, and decision-making, (3) various ways of classifying classroom questions, and (4) several simple instruments for observing and analyzing the levels of questioning and for providing feedback to you as the teacher about your own questioning performance.

THE PURPOSE AND FUNCTION OF CLASSROOM QUESTIONS

Although questions may be used to serve a number of purposes, their most frequent use has been as a means of testing students' knowledge, often at the end of a chapter in a book or a unit. The rapid, oral questioning by the teacher has traditionally served as a useful means of review or summary for a lesson, or as a preliminary introduction to new material. To a lesser extent the same function is served by short written tests, or end-of-chapter questions in a textbook. In contrast, the much broader, open-ended questions such as "How do you suppose the Native Americans got to America in the first place?" serve as motivating devices to arouse curiosity and to focus students' thoughts in a particular direction at the start of a lesson or a larger unit of study. Other types of questions focus on both the learning process and the content being studied. The italicized words are a clue to the student about the learning process involved. For example:

> What can you *infer* from this data?
> What *comparisons* or *contrasts* can you make about the economic aspects of 19th-century life in a New England town from their tax records and household inventories?
> What can you *generalize* about the economic life of that period?
> Are those generalizations still *valid* today?
> Can you *predict* (or *hypothesize*) what changes might occur in the economic aspects of New England towns (or cities) in the next three decades?
> How could you *validate* this prediction (or hypothesis)?

Although such questions represent an ideal frequently discussed and encouraged in professional journals and methods textbooks, what actually occurs in the classroom seems to fall far short of these goals. A number of researchers have pointed out that although teachers' objectives are often stated or intended to be at high intellectual levels, the types of questions teachers ask, whether in oral discussion or as written test items, most often require only the recall of a previously learned answer (Gall & Rhody, 1987). Your questions should require more than appropriate content responses. They should also require students to use various learning processes such as forming concepts, proposing hypotheses, and developing generalizations. Especially important is the challenge from students and teachers alike:

> How do you know?
> Where are the data to support that conclusion?
> Why do you feel that way?
> What criteria did you use to judge that solution to be good (or bad)?

In the following pages we will describe how questions such as these can be built directly into the model of social inquiry discussed in Chapter 3.

Students can use texts as a resource to collect and evaluate information.
Source: Library of Congress, Washington, D.C.

A STRATEGY OF QUESTIONING FOR SOCIAL INQUIRY

The model of social inquiry shown in Figure 3.1 (p. 68) is composed of a series of elements: (1) expressing doubt or concern, (2) formulating a problem and recognizing the theoretical position or the values implicit in it, (3) formulating working hypotheses, (4) defining or clarifying the key terms in the hypotheses, (5) collecting data, (6) analyzing and evaluating the data, and (7) testing the hypotheses and deriving generalizations.

Expressing Doubt

To begin a unit of study that involves social inquiry leading to some form of decision-making, first plan for a situation that introduces some form of incongruity, contradiction, or dissatisfaction so that the students will perceive a problem and see some need to solve it. Although the problems will vary with the age of the students and their previous experiences, the essential task remains the same: to arouse the students' curiosity and to motivate them to inquire.

Starting with a Value Question

One approach is to begin with a value question and then shift to a scientific question. A value question is one that asks about a strongly held belief or challenges a deeply held commitment. Because the value question tends to include a strong element of controversy and emotional tone, it quickly arouses interest and motivation. Several examples follow which show how this shift can be made.

PROBLEM 1: PLAYGROUND RULES

Value Questions   After a fight on the playground over the use of the basketball court, you might ask the class: "Do you really think the rules are unfair in this school? Do some students seem to get special favors?"

After some minutes of open discussion, during which students would express their opinions and perhaps vent some pent-up anger or frustration, you might attempt to shift the focus by asking scientific questions related to the problem.

Scientific Questions   Unlike a value question, a scientific question asks for facts or evidence based on observable data. What are the rules regarding the use of the basketball courts? How is time scheduled? Is there a plan for rotating the courts to prevent one group of students from using it all the time? What provision is there for settling disagreements once they arise?

Although the questions posed above deal with a current problem, the same technique can be used to arouse interest in studying problems that have their roots in the past.

PROBLEM 2: CONSTRUCTING A NEW FREEWAY

Value Questions   Should we construct a six-lane freeway through the heart of the central residential district? This will displace 900 or more families. Can they find other places to live that they can afford?

Following some discussion by the class, it might help to shift the focus of the discussion to scientific questions.

Scientific Questions   How many lanes will be needed on the new freeway to handle the expected volume of traffic to and from the city? By 2010? By 2020?

What will be the impact on the community of efforts to link up a major east-west interstate highway with the principal north-south one? How many homes or businesses will have to be relocated? Will the highway effectively cut one part of the community off from another? Are new shopping centers or playground areas being planned? Are homes currently available for those people whose homes will be demolished?

PROBLEM 3: GROUPS OF COLOR IN THE SUBURBS

Value Question   Should African Americans move into White suburbs?

Scientific Questions   How does the presence of ethnic groups of color in a previously all-White community affect the availability of jobs, the quality of education in the schools, etc.? What types of discrimination do Latinos face in predominantly White communities?

PROBLEM 4: DROPPING THE ATOMIC BOMB

Value Question   Should the United States have dropped the atomic bombs on Hiroshima and Nagasaki in 1945 and caused the loss of thousands of lives and the complete destruction of the two cities?

Students who are sensitive to the implications of mass destruction of humanity will have many opinions, views, and feelings on this important topic. To prevent the class discussion from becoming a mere exchange of opinions, the teacher must shift the focus by asking scientific questions related to the strategic decision made by President Truman and his advisors.

Scientific Questions   What were the strategic considerations involved in the decision? What responses had Japan made to the various peace overtures previously made? How did President Roosevelt's "unconditional surrender" doctrine affect the strategic thinking of World War II?

Many of the typical social studies topics can be approached in the same way: topics such as voting rights, "taxation without representation," the westward movement, and the Civil War. The point is that value questions tend to arouse student interest and motivation and, wherever possible, you should capitalize on them to begin a problem of social inquiry. In Chapter 15, we discuss other strategies for teaching value-laden issues.

Starting With a Scientific Question

Not all problems lend themselves easily to starting with a value question. You should vary your procedures so that a class will not become bored by the same approach to every problem. You can skillfully pose what Festinger (1957) has called "cognitive dissonance" by introducing a "discrepant event" as an intellectual teaser to arouse curiosity and motivation. Some examples that might be used are:

1. How can the Eskimos live in the extremes of the Arctic climate when people who have recently moved north from temperate zones have great difficulty adjusting to the new climate?
2. Why does the city of Seattle have so little snow when other cities at the same latitude or even lower, such as Minneapolis, Chicago, Cleveland, Rochester, and Boston, all have so much more?
3. Why can a nation with such a high standard of living as the United States have more than 30 million people living in poverty? (According to the Census Bureau, about 267 million people lived in the United States in 1997.)

These examples illustrate ways of using questions to arouse motivation and interest in a problem. Either of the two approaches shown above may be used. Starting with the value question first has the advantage of introducing a strong emotional element that helps to elicit student interest. You must then take steps to shift the focus of the discussion so that it will center on the scientific questions. If a value question is inappropriate as a starter or the topic does not lend itself, then a scientific question framed in such a way as to create "cognitive dissonance" by posing a discrepant event may be used to arouse interest and motivation.

Finally, we repeat a cautionary note raised in Chapters 1 and 3. While we reassert strongly that values are an essential consideration in social science inquiry and decision-making, we note that some value issues are heavily laden with emotional overtones such as abortion, capital punishment, artificially prolonging the life of the dying, and sexual abuse. Thus, you must judge the merit of the value questions by such criteria as the age and maturity of the students, their ability to understand the issue, and its relevance to the school curriculum. This is not to suggest that difficult or controversial value questions should be avoided, or that unsolved problems of the future should not be raised, but only that you should choose them with care, thoughtfulness, and appropriateness to the curriculum. Teachers should avoid questions that have only shock effect for young students or that invade personal privacy.

Problem Formulation

The next stage of the inquiry process is to take the aroused interest and begin to identify the components of a problem. The problem must be one that is researchable, for which there is some possible answer, about which some hypotheses or test questions can be formulated, data collected, and generalizations drawn.

1. Is smoking marijuana harmful? How is it different from drinking beer or liquor? What are the consequences of using drugs on our personal health? Does smoking marijuana lead to using more powerful drugs such as heroin or cocaine?
2. The American shipbuilding industry has been declining steadily since the 1920s. What has the government done to protect its maritime interests and to prevent almost all its import-export trade from being carried in "foreign flag" vessels?
3. What was our town like in the "olden days"? How did it get that way? How did it change as different groups of people came to live in it?
4. How have democratic societies in the past maintained a balance between the need to achieve a consensus on certain common values and the right of people to dissent?

In the framework described in Chapter 3, these problems are identified as scientific questions. Working hypotheses can be formulated for each, concepts clarified, data gathered and analyzed, and generalizations derived. Each can be verified by repeated inquiries. Each makes use of data from one or more of the social sciences.

Another approach to formulating an inquiry problem is to pose the same questions as value questions, rather than scientific ones. Value questions emphasize the "should" or "ought" of a possible course of action and often imply that some course of action is valued or prized over some other. Here are the same four questions rewritten as value questions:

1. Should we legalize the use of marijuana as we did with liquor?
2. Should the government continue to support the shipping industry but not the trucking industry?
3. Should our town pass a zoning ordinance to prevent the building of a new low-income housing project?
4. The early Puritans banished Roger Williams into the wilderness of Rhode Island for his "obnoxious heresies." Should we take similar action against some of the very outspoken critics of today?

CONTROVERSIAL ISSUES

Questions such as those listed above readily engage student interest and enthusiasm in the topic. At the same time, however, they are also controversial and come quickly to the heart of conflicting values in the community. Although few school officials would deny their rightful place in the school curriculum, they are often relegated to the corner as sensitive topics requiring "special attention." As a result, they are seldom asked in any serious way. Too often, little scientific inquiry has preceded them and no reliable data have been gathered. The teacher is often left with the bland assertion that "people are entitled to their own opinions." True, perhaps. But we strongly take issue with the corollary assertion that "one opinion is as good as another." An unsubstantiated or uncritical judgment is certainly not as good as one that has been carefully made by analyzing relevant data, weighing the alternative options or courses of action, and selecting the choice consistent with one's value system. To help you avoid this uncritical approach, we will deal with strategies for exploring value questions in Chapter 15. For our purpose here, let us simply say that the value question can be used to formulate a worthwhile problem for investigation.

THEORIES AND VALUES

One further issue should be raised: that of formulating a problem within the context of a particular theory or value structure. If the problem were geographic, that is, concerning the development of a city at a particular place, you might help students phrase questions in terms of the city's central location and spatial distance from other cities: "How far is this city from other settlement areas? Is it centrally located and conveniently accessible from all points?" Such questions borrow from the theories of urban geography that attempt to explain the location of cities in terms of space, distance, and function.

In quite the same way, one's value position can also shape the formulation of a problem. The question can be worded so that a normative word or phrase spells out the framework of the question and the dimensions of the problem. Note how the italicized word gives a particular thrust or direction to the following questions:

> What is the most *efficient* route for the construction of this new interstate highway?
> How can school desegregation be accomplished within the concept of the *neighborhood school* pattern?
> What role did English *pirates* such as Sir Francis Drake play in the decline of Spain as a world power?

Note that in the first example given above, efficiency, rather than aesthetic quality or relocation of people, dictates the solution of the highway route. In the second example, desegregation must be accomplished in such a way as to preserve the traditional values of the local school, implying not only the limited use of transportation, but also the retention of residential patterns and local control of school policies. Finally, the word pirates assumes that the English were villainous for having seized the Spanish treasure at sea but makes no similar implication about the Spanish Conquistadors, who plundered the Incas and the Aztecs to obtain the gold in the first place. From another point of view, the title "Sir," designating knighthood, suggests the way in which England's Queen Elizabeth I chose to view the same exploits as heroic deeds furthering England's national interests.

DEVELOPING THE HYPOTHESES

Each of the problems illustrated above is still insufficiently focused to be well researched or to guide the inquirer's research. Before a question can be fruitfully researched, it must be clearly defined, and related hypotheses must be formulated. In Chapter 3, we discussed the key functions of hypotheses and ways of distinguishing them from other kinds of statements. Here we shall introduce several formats for stating hypotheses.

The simplest way of forming a hypothesis is to make a simple statement that tells or predicts the expected relationship between concepts. For example, a class that is studying industrialization might hypothesize: "The development of new technology results in the growth of new industries and increased productivity." A primary class that is studying local communities might hypothesize: "The larger a community is, the more services it provides for its residents." To be sure, statements such as these look much like generalizations, yet it should be made clear that they are merely statements for which we must now gather evidence that supports or refutes the statement. For complex problems, a class might develop several hypotheses, each one related to the problem.

Another way of stating the hypothesis is to use an "if...then" format. This makes unmistakably clear the conditional and tentative nature of the statement. The examples cited above might be rephrased to read: "*If* there is a new development in technology, *then* there will be a growth in the number of new industries and in the amount of productivity." The second hypothesis might be phrased: "*If* the number of people in a community increases, *then* the community will provide more services for the people." The chief value of the "if...then" format is that it requires the student to set the concepts in their correct relationship and makes much more readily apparent any fallacies in the logic of the hypothesis. In addition, the conditional format of the "if" statement allows the students to give fuller reign to their hunches and best guesses. It allows them to send up trial balloons, whereas the statement format tends to suggest a more polished and finished result.

Perhaps a word should be added about the problem of the logic of the conditional "if...then" hypothesis. The teacher must be alert to the problems faced by students when language becomes confusing. If a statement is worded negatively, or double negatives are used when a positive assertion is intended, students will be confused. As a simple rule, it is perhaps best to state the conditional hypotheses in a positive form and avoid the use of negatives wherever possible. If opposite or inverse relationships exist, positively phrased relational concepts should be introduced. Using the example of the community study again, the alternate hypotheses might be: "If the population of a community *declines,* then the community can provide *fewer* services to the residents." This is a much simpler form to deal with than a negatively phrased hypothesis such as: "If the population does not increase, then the community will not expand the services it provides." Not only might the logic be fallacious, but the evidence might not support it either, for many other possibilities may exist under which a community might increase or decrease the services it offers.

Logical fallacies are another problem. For most students, the rules of formal logic are much too abstract and complex to tackle in a straightforward way. These might be better left to upper-grade classes in the junior or senior high schools. Young students, however, can learn to deal with the problem of the sufficiency of evidence and whether the conclusion is warranted from the data presented. Operating in a simple, inductive framework, you can help students question the size of the sample, whether it is representative, and the extent to which the evidence presented validly represents the conditions and the conclusions stated in the hypothesis. Students in grades 4–6 will need considerable practice in learning to weigh and evaluate data in this way.

One further problem to be mentioned in connection with hypothesis formation is the definition of terms. Some words—such as culture, standard of living, productivity, and the like—must be carefully defined so that data can be found about the hypothesis. When complex or abstract concepts are used, it is important to clarify and sharpen the hypotheses by carefully defining terms. This will help to guide and direct the collection of data so that valid conclusions can be drawn.

Collection of Data

Central to the task of social inquiry is the collection of data that bear on the problem. As we indicated above, the carefully formulated hypothesis sets the stage to guide and direct the collection of the data. It sweeps away the irrelevant and focuses sharply on the specific questions at issue. If students have defined the terms in their hypothesis carefully, they can then begin searching for appropriate data. It is important, however, that you see that sources for data are available for the questions that students are most apt to ask, for nothing is more frustrating to students than to have developed fine hypotheses and then have no resources for gathering pertinent data.

Many methods for gathering data are available to the social studies teacher. In Chapter 3, we discussed how the experiment, the case study, and the sample survey can be used in the social studies. Basically, each of these methods asks: Who? What? When? Where? and How?

> What tools did the Iroquois Indians have before they came into contact with the White settlers? Afterward? Where and how were they used? What evidence is available? Is the evidence direct or must we make inferences from other data?
>
> What beliefs did the Iroquois hold about their origin? Life in an afterworld? Or the forces of nature such as the sun, wind, rains, etc.? What evidence do we have? Or must we infer it from some secondary source?

Similar questions can be raised about the problem of technology and industrialization, as well as about the size of the community and the number of services it offers.

As we gather these data, it becomes important to ask questions about the source of and evidence for the data. Is the source primary or secondary? Do we have direct evidence or is it based only on inference? If the class is interviewing a parent or town official, is the interviewee reporting his or her own observations or direct knowledge, or is it perhaps only hearsay (passing along what someone else has said)?

Despite the use of a single textbook in many classrooms, the teacher still has many other options. Publishers have produced supplementary materials or kits that contain original documentary source materials (some in edited form), maps, charts, statistical data, transparencies, videotapes, audiotape cassettes, and computer-based interactive programs that store pictures, data, and sound on CD-ROM disks combined with audiotapes. Software has been developed for classroom microcomputers that will provide large arrays of data for simulating decision-making on such topics as westward expansion, national elections, and agricultural and economic development in developing nations. Moreover, much of this data has been programmed so students can predict and plot out on a graph the trend of the data over time, or the effect if certain variables are altered. Thus microcomputers now make it possible for students to ask "What would happen if …?" and obtain valid data to evaluate a proposed course of action. These newer resource materials are discussed more fully in Chapter 8.

Collecting and Recording the Data

One of the problems associated with data gathering in any investigation is the problem of collecting and recording it in some simple and convenient form. A simple device developed by Hilda Taba and her associates is the data retrieval chart (DRC). This is no more than a chart that allows students to log in the data they have found in answer to a series of questions related to the basic concepts involved in the hypothesis. While Taba envisioned drawing the DRC on the class bulletin board, students can now use a computer spreadsheet to achieve the same results.

The chief value of the data retrieval chart is that it can easily be expanded to include more than one data sample; it allows students to ask the same questions across two or more samples. Thus comparisons and contrasts can be easily made. A data retrieval chart related to the Iroquois Indians is shown in Table 4.1. Each of the questions is related to one of the concepts, and the chart forms an easy method of collecting and recording a relatively large amount of data in an abbreviated form. The exact questions to be asked can be agreed on in a class discussion, and the potential is present for adding additional questions or more concepts as the research progresses. A key point to stress here is the open-endedness of this approach. Students are limited only by the kinds of questions they ask and the data sources available to them.

Deriving Generalizations

A strategy for formulating generalizations was outlined in Chapter 3. In this chapter, we call attention to the types of questions asked and their sequence in relation to the hypotheses that have been formulated and the data that have been gathered. Let us use the problem, "How did the colonists in North America influence the cultures of the Iroquois Indians?" When the data retrieval chart (Table 4.1) is filled in, it is then possible to ask a series of questions about the data that helps to establish relationships, explanations, inferences, and meaning.

> *Discrimination of Data:* What do you notice about the data on the Iroquois's use of tools during these two time periods? About their beliefs and religious practices?
> *Comparison and Contrast:* What similarities do you see? What differences?
> *Relationships:* What things seem to be connected to one another?
> *Explanation:* How do you account for this? What may have caused these events?
> *Inference:* What do these data mean? Suggest? Or infer?
> *Generalization:* What can you conclude from all this? What can you say that is generally true, based on these two data samples?

It is important to stress here that the series of questions listed above is designed to result in the formation of inferences and generalizations, which by their very nature tend to be more abstract than any of the single instances of data, or any summation of them. We stress this because the past practices of teaching have been so heavily loaded in favor of the collection and memorization of vast collections of isolated data. Little or no effort has been made to establish relationships in any meaningful way. What counted most was that the facts were true and verifiable; they could be pointed to with certainty and without equivocation.

In contrast, the process of developing inferences and generalizations takes considerable time and requires much give and take among students and between students and you, the teacher. The students must conceptualize the relationship among data, develop explanations, and seek inferences beyond the literal meaning of the data. Thus, the strategy has much flexibility and a high degree of

TABLE 4.1. *Data Retrieval Chart: Iroquois Indians*

Analytical Concepts and Related Questions	Before Contact with Colonists	After Contact with Colonists
Tools What kind of tools did the Iroquois use: For hunting? For food? For farming? Other uses? What were they made of? Where did they get the material? How plentiful?		
Beliefs What did the Iroquois believe about: Origin of their tribes? Life after death? The forces of nature? Did they have a folklore or mythology? Taboos?		
Religious Practices How did they express their beliefs? Dances, ceremonies? Did they perform special ceremonies in honor of the gods? Was there a special person in charge of ceremonies? Were there special rites at birth, death, marriage, adolescence? Did they wear charms, amulets, or dress that had special meaning?		

open-endedness, provided you are willing to accept student ideas and help the student expand on them.

For the generalization to have a higher level of meaning, data from similar samples of cultural contact must be gathered from other groups and times. Table 4.2 shows how a data retrieval chart might look when additional samples of data are used to study one's own local community and its past.

TABLE 4.2. *Data Retrieval Chart: The Changing Nature of Our Town*

Analytical Concepts	During Indian Days	Period of Early Settlers 1660–1740	Our Town a Century Ago	Our Town Today
Geographical Site Boundaries? Physical features? Climate? Natural resources? How used?				
Technological Development What tools used? New machines invented? Other discoveries?				
Utilization of Place and Space Location of homes? Farms? Businesses? Mills? Factories? Percent of town for each?				
Population Distribution Indians? Farmers? Merchants? Mill hands? Ethnic groups? Religious groups? Density? Rate of growth?				
Connecting Links Main roads? Where to where? New routes? Old or abandoned routes?				

HIGHER LEVELS OF QUESTIONING

In the preceding section we discussed a strategy of questioning based on a model of social inquiry. In this section, we shall describe another strategy of questioning, based on a somewhat different model of thinking processes: Bloom's *Taxonomy of Educational Objectives: Handbook I—Cognitive Domain* (1956).

Bloom and his associates originally developed the taxonomy as a tool for classifying educational objectives. They identified six levels of instructional goals. The first deals with the recall of specified knowledge; the remaining five deal with various cognitive or intellectual skills: comprehension, application, analysis, synthesis, and evaluation. A chart showing the operational definitions of each of these categories is presented in Table 4.3. Let us see how the operational definitions of each category of the Bloom taxonomy can be used to describe different levels of questioning.

Knowledge Questions

A knowledge-level question requires the student to recall specific facts, names, places, trends, previously learned concepts, or generalizations. The key factor is that the student is expected to recall from memory some previously learned knowledge.

CLASSROOM SITUATIONS

Knowledge questions are most often used when students have read material in a text or reference book, watched a film or videotape, or completed a unit of study. The question refers specifically to what has been studied previously. The expected or correct answer is usually a verbatim repetition from the text, a class discussion, or some similar source. Given such settings, typical knowledge-level questions include:

1. List the major cities in the northeast region of the country.
2. Give some of the main reasons for the growth of manufacturing.
3. What were Jefferson's views on liberty?
4. Identify the main causes of the Civil War.

KEY WORDS

A number of key words can be identified in your questions. These give students clues to the cognitive level expected in the reply. There is reason to believe that the use of this kind of "grammar of the interrogative" can be very fruitful in helping students learn to use higher-level cognitive processes.

Some examples of key words usually indicating a knowledge-level question are:

define	identify	name	show	tell
describe	list	recall	state	write

Comprehension Questions

A comprehension-level question requires the student to understand the meaning of an oral or written communication and to make some use of it. Three important subcategories are included within the large category of comprehension: *translation, interpretation,* and *extrapolation.*

In a *translation* question, students are expected to express an idea in similar or equivalent terms. They are not expected to explain or reason with the idea, but only to restate it in a way that approximates its literal meaning. "Tell in your own words…" is one of the simplest forms of a translation question.

TABLE 4.3. *The Taxonomy of Educational Objectives—Cognitive Domain: A Hierarchical Classification of Intellectual Abilities and Skills*

Knowledge (memory)	Comprehension	Application	Analysis	Synthesis	Evaluation:
Ability to recall, to bring to mind the appropriate material, which may include: terminology classification trends criteria methodology generali- zations structure	Ability to know what is being communicated and to be able to make some use of the materials or ideas contained in it. Such behavior involves: *translation* into other forms; *interpretation,* a reordering of ideas and under- standing of their interrelationships; extrapolation, the making of estimates or predictions based on understand- ing, tendencies, trends, or condi- tions described in the communi- cation. **Requires:** Knowledge	Ability to use ideas, principles, and generali- zations in new situations. Involves being able to remember and bring to bear on given new material the appropriate generalizations and principles. **Requires:** Knowledge and comprehension	Ability to identify the component parts of an idea and to establish the logical relationships of the parts to the whole. The activity involved must emphasize the use of induc- tive or deductive reasoning proc- esses in some form. **Requires:** Knowledge, comprehension, and application	Ability to draw on elements from many sources and put these together into a structure or unified organi- zation or whole not clearly there before. **Requires:** Knowledge, comprehension, application, and analysis	Ability to make judgment about the value, for some purpose, of ideas or pro- cedures, solu- tions, methods, materials. Uses criteria (determined by student or given to her or him) for appraising the extent to which particulars are accurate, effective, eco- nomical, or satisfying. **Requires:** Knowledge, comprehension, application, analysis, and synthesis

Source: Adapted from Benjamin S. Bloom, ed., *Taxonomy of Educational Objectives: Handbook I—The Cognitive Domain* (New York: McKay, 1956). Reprinted with the publisher's permission.

Interpretation requires the ability to derive meaning from a passage by relating things to one another, by reordering events, by putting data into some arrangement or sequence, by establishing relationships by comparing or contrasting, or by separating essentials from nonessentials.

Extrapolation requires a student to predict or estimate an event from a known pattern or trend. This frequently includes the ability to project trends on the basis of statistical data or occasionally to interpolate when data are missing. The key factor is the ability to make appropriate inferences as to the probable trend or continued direction of the event, or pattern of ideas that can still be regarded as legitimate extensions of the original data.

CLASSROOM SITUATIONS

From the explanation given above, one can readily see that comprehensive questions have the potential for being a vital part of many classroom activities. The data retrieval charts introduced earlier in this chapter (Tables 4.1 and 4.2) offer many possibilities for teaching students to compare and contrast data, to establish relationships between items, to seek explanations, to state implications, and to make inferences. In the primary grades, students might simply point to different items in a picture and orally explain the relationships involved. In a much more sophisticated way, students in an upper grade might use a graph to predict the probable trend of population increase or decline in large urban centers. In contrast to the knowledge-level questions which involve the recall from memory of a previously learned response, all these activities are new experiences for the student. Thus a comprehension-level test question must use materials or situations different from those used previously in class study. To repeat the same question without change reduces it to the knowledge-recall level. Given such conditions, typical comprehension-level questions might include:

1. Explain how "division of labor" takes place in a factory.
2. Contrast the systems of education found in the United States, France, and Japan. What aspects do they have in common?
3. Explain in your own words the statement attributed to Clemenceau: "Wars are too important to be left to the generals."
4. Given census data for 1970, 1980, 1990, and 2000 for the 10 largest cities in the United States, what trend do you see emerging? What would you predict the population of these cities to be in 2010? 2020?

KEY WORDS

Some key words that usually indicate a comprehension-level question are:

compare	estimate	illustrate	relate
conclude	explain	infer	reorder
contrast	extend	interpolate	rephrase
demonstrate	extrapolate	interpret	tell in your own words
differentiate	predict	give an example of	
distinguish	hypothesize	rearrange	

Application Questions

In an application question, students are required to demonstrate that they can make use of some previously learned relationship or idea. An application question differs from comprehension-level questions in that the student is not told specifically how to apply a particular idea but must be able to select the appropriate idea, concept, or principle and apply it correctly to the given situation. In short, application requires students to transfer their learning to a new situation with little or no direction.

CLASSROOM SITUATIONS

Application questions most often require students to solve a problem, to construct something such as a model farm or town, to put a skill into practice, or to take some appropriate form of action within the social context of the real world outside the classroom. Primary grade students who have studied transportation routes and the exchange of goods and services might apply these concepts and related generalizations by constructing a model town and playacting with toy trains or trucks. Older students can apply ideas and concepts by role-playing a session of the United Nations or a state legislature as it attempts to decide some important issue. Simulation games, such as *Democracy* or *Napoli*, although designed with a set of quite specific rules, require students to apply the principles of the political process to a fast-moving and exciting game that comes very close to approximating real-life situations.

Finally, the social studies classroom meets the real world when students actually apply what they are learning by engaging in social action situations. This may take the form of participation in a student council (provided it has a truly meaningful role in a school and is not simple window dressing), writing letters to the editor, collecting signatures on a petition for some local issue, or ringing doorbells in support of a political candidate. Given such settings, typical application questions might include:

1. Using the sand table, develop a plan for and build a model layout of a medieval manor or estate.
2. Prepare a menu for a modern Thanksgiving dinner by locating material on the Pilgrims' first Thanksgiving using the Internet and various reference materials in the school library.
3. Write a play (or role-play a scene) that illustrates the controversy about whether or not the United States should have joined the League of Nations after World War I.
4. Develop a plan for calling the community's attention to the seriousness of homelessness in the community. Gather the necessary data and be prepared to present it at a public hearing on the topic. (Assume that the class has recently completed a study of poverty and homelessness.)

KEY WORDS

Some key words that usually indicate an application-level question are:

apply	demonstrate	build
develop	construct	solve

Analysis Questions

The analysis-level question requires a student to break down an idea into its component parts and distinguish these parts with a conscious knowledge of their relationship to one another. This involves three different abilities.

First, the student must be able to distinguish assumptions from conclusions, to determine whether a conclusion is warranted from the evidence presented, or to detect the presence of an unstated but implied assumption that may invalidate the initial premises. Second, the student must be able to recognize the relationship of part to whole, to recognize which facts are essential to support the main thesis, or to distinguish relevant from irrelevant data. Third, the student must be able to recognize the form or organizational structure of a statement or set of ideas and to relate this to the overall intent or meaning. Thus, a student can recognize various parts, such as the major theme and local variations in a political candidate's speech, the techniques of persuasion in advertising or propaganda, or the viewpoint or bias of a writer in a historical account.

The difference between interpretation and analysis questions depends on the extent to which the student is aware of and makes use of the formal processes of reasoning. At the interpretation level, a student may make inferences and generalizations, or formulate hypotheses, without reference to the formal processes involved. For the same processes to be at the analysis level, the student must be consciously aware of these intellectual processes and the organizational structure of the material being studied.

CLASSROOM SITUATIONS

The strategies of teaching for social inquiry, valuing, and decision-making discussed in this book offer many possibilities for analytical thinking. It should be noted, however, that thinking at the analysis level involves a considerable degree of abstract reasoning. The processes identified above dealing with the logical quality of thought, and the form of expression they take, are rather high level and complex. All too often students simply have no experience with this type of thinking process. It is important that students have sufficient practice and experience with thinking at the analysis level. The inductive strategies described on the preceding pages for making inferences and generalizations should provide the kind of experience necessary to help develop abstract thinking.

Given sufficient experience with this mode of thinking, then, it is possible for students to distinguish a fact from an opinion, a hypothesis from a generalization, or to determine whether the evidence gathered is sufficient to warrant the conclusion that is drawn. Upper grade students can learn to detect unstated assumptions in arguments, or identify elements of form and style in primary source materials that indicate personal points of view, biases, or prejudices, as distinguished from objective evidence. They can also learn to identify specific techniques of persuasion borrowed from mass media advertising, now being used frequently in political campaigns. Commonly available material, such as bumper stickers, lapel buttons, billboards, newspaper ads, and TV spot commercials for political candidates all can be used to illustrate such techniques as the half-truth, the catchy slogan, the appeal to selected values, stacking the deck in favor of one side, the sound byte, the deliberate distortion, and the big lie. For students to be able to recognize the intentional use of these techniques when they come upon them in campaign literature or in public statements gives evidence of analytical thinking. Given such settings, typical questions at the analysis level might be:

1. Analyze the following slogans. What techniques of persuasion are used in them?

> Keep your local police force independent.
> The United States: Love it or leave it.
> Every American has the right to own a gun.
> Buy American.
> English only.
> No Nukes.

2. Having studied the problem of cultural change following contact between the Iroquois Indians and the White settlers, a class might formulate the generalization: "A technologically less advanced society will quickly adopt aspects of the technology and belief systems of a more technologically advanced society when such societies come into extended contact." You might challenge this generalization by asking: "What data support the notion that the change will occur quickly? Or that the belief system will necessarily change because the technology is adopted? Isn't there an assumption that all technologically less advanced societies will react this way? Are the data from one case study sufficient to warrant this broad generalization?"

3. Analyze the views of White slaveholders as described by Frederick Douglass, an ex-slave, in his autobiography, *Narrative of the Life and Times of Frederick Douglass,* and by former slaves in Botkin's *Lay My Burden Down: A Folk History of Slavery.* Make a similar analysis of the accounts written by historians such as Ulrich B. Phillips, John Hope Franklin, Kenneth P. Stampp, and Eugene D. Genovese. What evidence is there in the choice of words, style, or form to indicate the writers' viewpoints about the White slaveholder?

KEY WORDS

Some key words that usually indicate analysis-level questions are:

analyze	compare	discriminate
categorize	contrast	distinguish
classify	detect	recognize

Note that while some of these key words are the same as those used for comprehension-level questions, at the analysis level they must focus on the logical relationship of the parts of a passage such as the assumptions, bias, use of propaganda techniques, or organizational structure (e.g., introduction, statement of a problem, evidence, recommendations, and conclusions).

Synthesis Questions

In a synthesis question, students are expected to be able to respond by combining or integrating a number of facts into some arrangement that is new for them. This often takes the form of a plan, a proposal, or some product such as a story, a report, a play, or even a mural on the classroom wall. Synthesis differs from application in that the form of the final product is not specified, nor are the ways in which the elements may be combined. It is this feature that makes the synthesis a unique and creative activity.

In contrast to the types of questions discussed above, where each implies a particular form of thinking process, the synthesis question usually gives no cues to the student and is intended to be broad and open-ended. It does not imply any right answer, but instead assumes a variety of possible solutions, any or all of which could be acceptable. In short, it seeks divergent, rather than convergent, thinking.

CLASSROOM SITUATIONS

There are many possibilities for using creative synthesis questions in the social studies class. In the elementary school, the many reasons for early exploration can be synthesized into a fictional story or a carefully written paragraph. Other common forms of synthesis include writing a short play, a role-playing scenario, preparing a mural, a bulletin board, or a showcase display. Most frequently overlooked, especially in the primary grades, is the short oral statement synthesizing (but not merely restating) a group of explanations for some event into a broader proposition. Here, too, is the chance for students to speculate freely and imaginatively on possible courses of events or actions, using factual data, interpretations, or new relationships to support their conjectures. "What would happen if...?" "What are the possible courses of action...?"

Given the settings described above, typical synthesis questions might include:

1. Write a report that describes some solutions that might be proposed for the problems of air pollution in Los Angeles?
2. Create a play of a Los Angeles City Council meeting in which your committee proposes solutions for air pollution and they are debated by council members and the mayor. Make a videotape of your play to review and study later.
3. Create a role-playing scenario about the solutions that might have been open to President Truman immediately prior to the beginning of the Korean War.
4. Present a committee report on the many different ways prisoners in jails can engage in rehabilitation programs? Debate the report with members of your city or county council.
5. Create a mural on a class bulletin board that creatively depicts the Whites moving westward toward California and Oregon in the 1840s. Include the early expedition of Lewis and Clark. Show some of the hazards and difficulties they encountered. Describe orally to the class each of the elements in the mural.

KEY WORDS

Some key words that usually indicate a synthesis-level question are:

| create | formulate a solution | propose a plan |
| develop | make up | put together |

Evaluation Questions

The evaluation question asks the student to make a judgment about the worth, merit, or value of something. Is it good or bad, beautiful or ugly, trivial or worth-while? Students must appraise, assess, or criticize some idea, statement, or plan on the basis of specific standards or criteria that they have developed or that may be provided by the teacher. Thus, students must indicate the criteria on which they have made their judgment and supply appropriate data to justify their positions. In short, the evaluation level requires much more than an unsubstantiated opinion based purely on personal whim or opinion.

CLASSROOM SITUATION

There are many situations in which a student can make an evaluative judgment, especially in the decision-making mode of inquiry discussed in Chapter 1. If several alternatives are given, a student must select one, using some appropriate criteria. Under these conditions, the evaluation level is heavily cognitive, even though a judgment about worth or value is being made.

Typical evaluation questions might be:

1. Evaluate the three plans that are now before the City Council that deal with homelessness. Which do you consider to be the best plan? Explain why? What criteria did you use to arrive at your judgment?
2. Evaluate (judge the merit of) the plan you chose in No. 1 in terms of cost, practicality and community acceptance.
3. You have read several books about cowboys and pioneers of the Old West. Which book would you judge to be the best book. Consider such factors as characters, plot, action, suspense, excitement, and adventure.
4. There is constant bickering among classmates about who can use what part of the playground for what games and when. With help from the teacher, three groups of students work on different plans to try to solve the problem. The class holds a meeting to present and discuss the plans and then will vote for the best plan. Ask each student to evaluate (judge) the three plans. Which do you consider the best plan based on (a) fairness to all, (b) sharing balls and equipment, and (c) rotating between using the soccer field, the swings, and the seesaws?

It is important to note that the student must make an *informed judgment* on the worth, merit, goodness, or evil of something, based on a set of criteria and supporting data. Helping the students learn to identify appropriate criteria is just as important as making the value judgment. The evaluation must be supported by data. It is important to recognize, however, that different students can arrive at different evaluations depending on the criteria established and the data presented to them. Thus, students are not necessarily right or wrong in the evaluation they make. Rather, it is the appropriateness of the criteria and how well they have supported the judgment with data or a rationale.

KEY WORDS

Key words that would indicate an evaluation-level question are:

choose	evaluate	select
decide	judge	which do you consider?

"Think of the variety of questions they're asking for on that test! Are we human computers?"
Source: Joe E. Buresch. Used with permission.

Creative and Divergent Questions

Finally, we wish to stress the importance of creative and divergent thinking in social studies and the need to ask questions that stimulate these intellectual processes. Creative thinking involves the formation of new ideas, novel or unconventional approaches to old problems, or some different arrangement of existing parts or ideas in order to create something entirely new. It is the opposite of rote memory, copying, imitating, or making minor variations in a familiar pattern. Closely related is the term "divergent thinking," which refers to open-ended, unconventional or nontraditional thinking. It is in sharp contrast to convergent thinking, which emphasizes the single, limited, or traditionally approved "right answer." We do not underestimate the importance of accuracy in basic factual knowledge, or the knowledge of established traditions; nevertheless, problem-solving and decision-making in the 21st century will surely require new insights, unique approaches, and radical departures from many of our customary or traditional ways of thinking.

There is a thin line between the creative and imaginative response and fantasy. Indeed, the fantasy or science fiction written by Jules Verne in the 1890s about travel to the moon and other planets has become the scientific reality of our day. Thus, a teacher should not label a student's novel or unusual solution to a problem as "silly" or "impossible," but should rather encourage the student to explain the chain of reasoning or new insights that led to the solution. Schools should do everything possible to encourage the creative abilities in students. You should also be slow to criticize or dismiss highly unusual ideas, nonconformist approaches, or challenges to conventional mores or wisdom.

It is a sad commentary on the history of science that the insights and theories of some of our most brilliant scientists—Galileo, Newton, Darwin, Freud, and Einstein—were for many years rejected and dismissed by teachers, scientists, and intellectuals as impossible or bizarre. Yet, ultimately, each revolutionized our thinking and changed the course of developments in their fields.

For these reasons we encourage you to ask and prod students with questions such as these:

1. How many different ways could that be done?
2. What new approaches could you suggest to remedy the weakness of this plan?
3. Could we rearrange the parts of this mural on exploration and discovery to create a new effect?
4. Are there some approaches that have not been tried yet? What would it take to make them feasible or workable?

SUMMARY

Two questioning strategies were presented in this chapter. The first was based on the model of social inquiry developed in Chapter 3. It suggested a variety of questions that could be used for each step of the inquiry model. The other strategy was based on the six levels of cognitive processes identified in Bloom's *Taxonomy*. We discussed the cognitive activity required at each level and identified a series of key words that could be used to form questions at each cognitive level. Lastly, we discussed the importance of creative and divergent questions in helping students to develop new, unique, or unconventional approaches to problem-solving and decision-making.

REFLECTION AND ACTION ACTIVITIES

1. Students in the primary grades often study some aspect of their local community. Write some questions that might be used to express doubt or concern to begin the process of social inquiry. Write a value question first followed by several scientific questions.
2. Take several conventional topics such as the westward movement, the American Revolution, the writing of the U.S. Constitution, or the Age of Exploration and prepare an opening value question for each. Then show how the discussion could be shifted by asking appropriate scientific questions.
3. A social inquiry problem can often be begun by introducing a "discrepant event" as an intellectual teaser to arouse curiosity and motivation. Select three such situations and write questions involving a discrepant event that could be used to start an inquiry study.
4. Using the questions you prepared in Questions 1 through 3, write suitable hypotheses for each that could be used in a social inquiry study. Write each first in the statement form, and then in the "if...then" format.
5. The use of the conditional "if...then" form for stating hypotheses has been described in this chapter. What are some of the advantages and limitations of this approach?
6. Using any of the hypotheses you wrote for Question 4, prepare a data retrieval chart for gathering appropriate information. Be sure you identify the major concepts from the hypothesis and list a number of related questions that will help guide the search for data under each concept. Identify two or more possible samples (time periods, cultures, nations, etc.) that would provide good sources for making comparisons with the data found (see Tables 4.1 and 4.2).
7. Classroom questions can be written at a variety of cognitive levels. Take any one of the areas you identified above for social science inquiry. Write a question at the knowledge level of Bloom's *Taxonomy*. Then expand the same topic into six questions, one at each of the levels of the taxonomy.
8. Select a social science inquiry problem different from the one used in Question 7. Write several creative or divergent questions.
9. Define and illustrate each of the following terms:
   a. value questions
   b. scientific questions
   c. cognitive dissonance
   d. "if...then" proposition
   e. data retrieval chart
   f. taxonomy
   g. cognitive domain
   h. the six categories of the Bloom Taxonomy (knowledge, comprehension, application, analysis, synthesis, evaluation)
   i. convergent questions
   j. divergent questions
   k. creative questions

REFERENCES

Bloom, B. S. (Ed.). (1956). *Taxonomy of educational objectives: Handbook I—Cognitive domain.* New York: McKay.

Festinger, L. (1957). *A theory of cognitive dissonance.* Stanford: Stanford University Press.

Gall, M. D., & Rhody, T. (1987). Review of research on questioning techniques. In W. W. Wilen (Ed.), *Questions, questioning techniques, and effective teaching.* Washington, D.C.: National Education Association.

Wilen, W. W. (Ed.). (1987). *Questions, questioning techniques, and effective teaching.* Washington, D.C.: National Education Association.

Wilen, W. W., & Clegg, A. A., Jr. (1986). Effective questions and questioning: A review of research. *Theory and Research in Social Education, 15*(2), 153–161.

FOR FURTHER READING

Beyer, B. K. (1991). *Teaching thinking skills: A handbook for elementary school teachers.* Boston: Allyn and Bacon.

Beyer, B. K. (1991). *Teaching thinking skills: A handbook for secondary school teachers.* Boston: Allyn and Bacon.

Hunkins, F. P. (1995). *Teaching thinking through effective questioning* (2nd ed.). Norwood, MA: Christopher-Gordon.

Skills, Issues, and Materials

• PART II •

Part II focuses on several important components of a sound social studies curriculum: skills, social issues, and materials. While reflective citizen actors must master facts, concepts, and generalizations, it is also essential that they gain proficiency in the processes involved in gathering, evaluating, and processing knowledge. Reflective citizen actors need thinking skills, social science inquiry skills, academic or study skills, and the skills needed to function effectively in group discussion and research. Chapter 5 discusses these important skills. Most of the materials used to gain proficiency in social studies skills are reading materials.

Chapter 6 describes ways that social studies teachers can help students to improve their reading skills.

Reflective citizen actors frequently use their knowledge and skills to help them make decisions on important social issues. Some of the important social issues within our nation and world are described in Chapter 7. Activities that can be used to help students gain information about these issues are also described. Social issues are society's unresolved problems. These problems deeply concern large numbers of citizens, and citizens strongly disagree about their causes and solutions. Citizens also have deep value commitments to social issues. Social issues can be used effectively to help students develop decision-making and citizen action skills.

To gain the knowledge needed to participate successfully in a democratic society, citizen actors need to use a wide variety of resources. Information from any one source will not enable citizens to acquire the range of views and perspectives needed to make reflective decisions and to take successful citizen action. Chapter 8 discusses a range of resources that you can use to help students formulate concepts and generalizations, clarify their values, make decisions, and participate in reflective citizen action.

CHAPTER 5

Teaching Social Studies Skills

The social studies curriculum is designed to help students attain the knowledge, attitudes, and skills needed to participate effectively in a democratic society. Chapter 3 describes the knowledge components of the social studies curriculum, which include higher-level concepts and generalizations needed by citizens to make reflective decisions. Skills are an important component of the social studies and are discussed in several chapters in this book. Social science inquiry skills are discussed in Chapter 3; value inquiry and decision-making skills in Chapter 15. This chapter discusses skills that should be an important part of a decision-making-focused social studies curriculum: thinking skills, map and globe skills, time and chronology skills, group skills, and writing skills.

TEACHING THINKING SKILLS

Helping students develop and increase their proficiency in thinking skills should be an important goal of the social studies. While this is an accepted goal of social studies education, it is difficult to find a clear definition and a specification of thinking skills in the educational literature. Beyer (1987), who has done extensive work on teaching thinking skills, defines thinking as a search for meaning and as a "mental process by which individuals make sense out of experience" (p. 16). He identifies two major components, or operations, of thinking: cognitive and metacognitive. Individuals engage in the cognitive operation when they generate or attempt to find meaning. Metacognition involves thinking about thinking. The major cognitive operations in thinking identified by Beyer are shown in Table 5.1.

Thinking consists of a number of processes, including describing, inferring, analyzing, conceptualizing, generalizing, applying, and making decisions. We will discuss how you can help students develop and increase their competence in each of these skills.

TABLE 5.1. *Major Cognitive Operations*

I. Thinking Strategies

Problem-Solving	**Decision-Making**	**Conceptualizing**
1. Recognize a problem	1. Define the goal	1. Identify examples
2. Represent the problem	2. Identify alternatives	2. Identify common attributes
3. Devise/choose solution plan	3. Analyze alternatives	3. Classify attributes
4. Execute the plan	4. Rank alternatives	4. Interrelate categories of attributes
5. Evaluate the solution	5. Judge highest-ranked alternatives	5. Identify additional examples/nonexamples
	6. Choose "best" alternatives	6. Modify concept attributes/structure

II. Critical Thinking Skills

1. Distinguishing between verifiable facts and value claims
2. Distinguishing relevant from irrelevant information, claims, or reasons
3. Determining the factual accuracy of a statement
4. Determining the credibility of a source
5. Identifying ambiguous claims or arguments
6. Identifying unstated assumptions
7. Detecting bias
8. Identifying logical fallacies
9. Recognizing logical inconsistencies in a line of reasoning
10. Determining the strength of an argument or claim

III. Micro-Thinking Skills

1. Recall	*Reasoning*
2. Translation	inductive
3. Interpretation	deductive
4. Extrapolation	analogical
5. Application	
6. Analysis (compare, contrast, classify, seriate, etc.)	
7. Synthesis	
8. Evaluation	

Source: Reprinted with permission from Barry K. Beyer, *Practical Strategies for the Teaching of Thinking* (Boston: Allyn & Bacon, 1987), p. 27.

Describing

Students must learn to make careful observations in order to write accurate descriptions. Students cannot make sound inferences or formulate concepts and generalizations unless they are able to carefully observe and to accurately describe their observations. To help students develop and enhance their observation and describing skills, you must give them ample opportunities to observe and describe behavior in a variety of situations. Role-playing episodes, photographs, videotapes, sound recordings, and World Wide Web sites can be used to enhance students' observational skills. Here are some activities that can be used to teach students to make careful observations and accurate descriptions:

> One group of students in the class role-plays the open-ended story "Tell-Tale" by George Shaftel (Shaftel & Shaftel, 1982). After the role-play, the students make a list of the major actions that occurred in the story.
>
> A group of students makes observations in the cafeteria for a one-week period to determine the most popular foods.
>
> A group of students conducts a small study to determine whether men or women buy more groceries at a particular store on a Saturday morning between 9:00 A.M. and 12:00 noon.

Language should not be a barrier to teaching higher-level thinking skills. This teacher is helping students make accurate descriptions.
Source: Library of Congress, Washington, D.C.

The students watch television commercials for a one-week period to determine how women are depicted.

The students view Medieval, Renaissance, and French impressionist paintings and describe the characteristics of the paintings of each period.

Making Inferences

When social scientists observe and describe, they try to tell exactly what happened without making guesses about what the observed behavior means. When they interpret and develop hypotheses about what their observations mean, social scientists are making inferences. Social scientists make inferences in order to try to understand and explain behavior. Students should be given practice in both making *observations* and *making inferences* about what they observe. However, they should be keenly aware of the differences between observation and inference and know when they are practicing each skill.

After students have made observations and descriptions while participating in the kinds of activities described above, they can then make inferences about the behavior they observed. If they find during the observation of food preferences in the cafeteria that hot dogs are more popular than beef stew, they can make some inferences about why this is the case. However, the students should realize that, while many of their inferences may be correct, the inferences are actually *hypotheses* which must be tested before they can be accepted as valid knowledge. While students may assume that hot dogs are preferred to beef stew because hot dogs taste better than beef stew, their inference will become less certain if they do a survey and find that the most important factor that influences choice of a dish at lunchtime is the dish chosen by close friends.

Analyzing Information

The ability to make careful observations and to formulate inferences will help students analyze information. When students analyze information, they identify its parts and establish a logical relationship of the parts to each other and to the whole. You can use reading, visual, and audiovisual materials to help students increase their skills in analyzing information. The following questions and activities can help students to develop and increase their ability to analyze materials:

This list contains both facts and inferences about animal cloning. Which are facts and which are inferences?

In this selection on the removal of the Cherokee from their Georgia homeland to Oklahoma in 1838–1839, the author makes a number of conclusions and generalizations. Do the facts he presents support his conclusions and generalizations? Explain.

What are the major points made in this passage? What other points are made? How are the major points and subpoints related?

Which of the following statements best describes the videotape on the feminist movement we viewed?

Conceptualizing

The ability to conceptualize is important because concepts are needed to formulate important generalizations and principles. Hilda Taba (1971) and her colleagues developed some useful strategies for helping students attain and develop concepts. Some of these strategies are discussed in Chapter 3.

In the Taba strategy for *developing a concept,* begin by having the students generate a list of items by asking them a question and writing their responses on the board or on an overhead projector. After the class has studied a unit on urbanization, you can ask a question such as "Why do families move from the city to the suburbs?" Each of the reasons the students state is listed on the board or projector. When the students have listed as many reasons as they can, ask them to group the items in as many different ways as they can. Each student can be asked to form a group. Tell the students that the items can be grouped in many different ways and that items placed in one group by one student can also be placed in another group by a different student. They should be encouraged to group items in many different ways.

Once the students have grouped the items, ask them to name or label the groups. They will find that labeling a group is the most difficult part of the process of conceptualizing, which in this strategy consists of *listing, grouping,* and *labeling.* When the students have made a list of items, grouped them, and labeled the groups, they can be asked to think of ways the groups may be changed and extended to include other items on the list. They should also be encouraged to think of other ways the items on the list may be grouped.

Another Taba strategy is called *attaining a concept.* This is a deductive strategy in which you first introduce the concept label, such as *rite of passage,* then ask students to repeat the label, and finally present them with an example of the concept, such as a description of a puberty ceremony in a preliterate culture. You can then present the students with other examples. You might have them read a description of a traditional Jewish wedding, view a videotape on a birth ceremony in a preliterate society, and read a description of a funeral in an American novel. You can then offer students non-examples of the concept and ask them to define the concept. You can determine the students' level of mastery by asking them to identify examples from a list of examples and non-examples. (See Table 5.2.)

Generalizing

When students form generalizations, they formulate statements which show how concepts are related. It is therefore important for students to be able to develop and to attain concepts before they are asked to formulate generalizations. It is also important for students to be able to make accurate descriptions, to infer, to analyze data, to differentiate, and to compare and contrast before they can formulate generalizations. The ability to formulate accurate and valid generalizations is one of the most important and sophisticated skills in the social studies.

To formulate valid higher-order generalizations, students must study several different content samples, determine how the data from different cultures and societies are alike and different, and formulate valid statements for the different sets of

TABLE 5.2. *The Taba Strategy for Attaining Concepts*

Teacher	Student	Teacher Follow-Through
1. Say this word after me . . .	Repeats word.	Makes sure the word is pronounced correctly.
2. This is an . . .	Looks at object, listens to description given,	Checks for any who may not be able to see or hear.
3. This is also an . . .	or reads statements which are illustrative examples of the concept.	
4. This is *not* an . . .	Looks at new object, or listens to new description, or reads statements which are not samples of the concept (but which may be similar, in similar form, etc.)	Checks again.
5. Show me an . . . or Tell me what you think an . . .is or Which of these describes an . . . or Is this an . . .	Points to object. Defines the concept. Selects from one or more descriptions.	Shows additional objects or gives fresh descriptions to test. Has students write down their definitions.
6. Asks: How then would you define an . . .	Gives summary generalization (definition) of concept.	Checks for accuracy.

Source: Hilda Taba, Mary C. Durkin, Jack R. Fraenkel, and Anthony H. McNaughton, *A Teacher's Handbook to Elementary Social Studies* (Reading, Mass.: Addison-Wesley, 1971), p. 71.

data. If students are studying the political system in three different nations—the United States, the United Kingdom, and Russia—the class can be divided into three research groups. Each group could study the political system of each nation in depth. When the students come together as a whole class to share and to pool their information, they can enter their data on a data retrieval chart such as the one in Table 5.3. Data retrieval charts can help students to formulate generalizations because they enable them to clearly see relationships. After studying the three political systems, the students may develop generalizations such as these:

TABLE 5.3. *The Political System in Three Nations*

	The United States	The United Kingdom	Russia
What major individuals make binding political decisions?			
What major groups or bodies make binding political decisions?			
How are these individuals and groups chosen?			
In what ways can individual citizens participate in the political system?			
What is the level of citizen participation in the political process?			
To what extent can political views be freely expressed?			
What are the major political parties?			
To what extent are the rights of minority political parties protected?			

In each of the three nations, some individuals and groups are authorized to make decisions that all citizens must obey.

The ways in which the three nations determine which groups will make binding political decisions differ.

Decision-Making and Citizen Action

Decision-making problems and situations give students opportunities to apply the concepts and generalizations they formulate. Using concepts and generalizations to identify alternative courses of action and to predict their possible consequences is an important part of the decision-making process. When students study a social issue—such as racial discrimination—and try to determine what course of action they should take regarding it, generalizations help to identify alternative courses of action as well as to predict possible consequences. Courses of action that a class may identify when studying this issue include (1) taking no action, (2) joining and supporting a local or national civil rights organization, (3) writing letters to members of Congress, and (4) initiating a project to reduce racial discrimination in their school.

Generalizations about racial and ethnic discrimination will enable the students to predict that alternative 1 will most likely result in the continuation of racial discrimination in society. Generalizations about influencing public policy will enable the students to predict that if they choose alternative 2, they might have some influence on reducing racial discrimination because they will have more influence joining and working with a national group than working alone as a small class. They are also more likely to develop a sense of personal and political efficacy if they choose alternative 2 rather than alternative 1. They will also realize that they took some action to help reduce racial discrimination, even though their chances of having a large influence on a national scope is minimal. They may conclude that alternative 2 is more consistent with their values than alternative 1.

Generalizations about ways to influence national policy will enable the students to predict that writing letters to senators and congressional representatives is one of the least effective ways to affect public policy. Letters have little influence on legislators unless they are received in massive numbers. What the students will most likely conclude, after considering these and other alternatives, is that as a class they can have little influence reducing racial discrimination in the nation. However, they can take some small actions, such as joining a national civil rights organization or working to reduce racial discrimination in their school (alternative 4). Thus, reflective courses of action for them are joining and contributing to a national or local civil rights organization, and working to reduce racial discrimination in their own school.

Some students in the class, however, may choose to take no action. They have read the same information in the class as the other students but have decided that they do not wish to take action, either because they do not have a personal commitment to take such action or think that the action will not be effective. In a decision-making unit or lesson, students must be able to freely choose alternatives consistent with their values within a democratic classroom atmosphere. They should, however, be encouraged to examine and to reflect on their values and to consider value alternatives and different ways to interpret data.

Students need to think about issues in social studies classes. Thinking does not occur in a vacuum. Thinking is also more fruitful if the issue is important to students. Important social issues, to which students have strong attachments and commitments, should be used frequently in social studies classes to give students opportunities to practice and reinforce their thinking skills. Thinking serves its most important purpose when it enables students to make better decisions and to take action that helps solve problems and improve the human condition.

TEACHING MAP AND GLOBE SKILLS

Social studies teachers should help students develop space and time concepts. Social studies content often deals with people, problems, and issues that are distant in both time and space. When students study medieval Europe, you should help them understand how very long ago that period was in Western history and how far removed Europe is from their homes and communities. Timelines and work with dates can help students to better understand time concepts. Map and globe concepts and skills can increase understanding of spatial relationships.

Introducing Maps

A map is a drawing of a part or all of the earth's surface. You can introduce the concept of a map to young children by working with them to make a map of their classroom. When preparing the map of their classroom, you should make sure that the students understand that when a map is made, the view is looking down from above. You can reinforce the concept of a map by asking the students to draw a map of one

"I love our hideaway. I only wish we could find it."
Source: Joseph Farris. Used with permission.

of the rooms in their homes, which they can share and discuss in class. The students can also build maps with blocks and mold them in clay.

You can prepare the class for doing a map of a section of their neighborhood by taking them on a walking tour of the section and asking them to observe and note various buildings and landmarks. If possible, you should take the students to a tall building from which they can observe the section of the neighborhood they will be showing on their map. This will help them to see the neighborhood from a map-like perspective.

To keep the map simple, only several important buildings can be included on the map, as illustrated in Figure 5.1. This map can be used to introduce the students to several important concepts related to maps, including *legend* (or key) and *grid*. You can work with the class to make a new copy of the map, using symbols rather than written descriptions to show the locations of the school, the church, the hospital, the drugstore, the barber shop, and the department store. The class might decide that it will use the symbols shown in Figure 5.2 to represent the buildings.

Teachers whose students are in the middle and upper grades can draw vertical and horizontal lines on the map to make a grid system. Numerals and letters can be used to label the grids. The students can be taught to use the grid system by locating buildings such as the school, the church, the hospital, and the department store on the map.

Introducing the Globe

Students should be introduced to the globe in the primary grades. It is important for students to be introduced to a globe early because maps greatly distort the land and water forms on the earth and their relationships. Students who memorize the relationship of the continents shown on a Mercator projection have a very distorted concept of the size of Greenland and the relative distance of Asia from North America. Students must also be introduced to the globe in order to understand the cardinal directions.

You can introduce the globe to students by showing them an illustration of the nine planets that revolve around the sun and explaining that the earth is one of these nine planets. You can explain that the globe is a small model of the earth.

THE CARDINAL DIRECTIONS

When the globe is introduced, you can introduce some of its important features and help students to learn the cardinal, or most important, directions. You should point out the imaginary line around the center of the globe called the *equator*. The North and South Poles should also be introduced. You can then tell the students that north is toward the direction of the North Pole and that south is toward the direction of the South Pole. The students should also learn that when they face north, their back is toward the south, their left hand is toward the west, and their right hand is toward the east. Asking the students to observe the direction in which the sun rises and sets will help them to better understand the cardinal directions. The sun rises in the east and sets in the west. The students can also observe the sun on a sunny day to help them locate the cardinal directions. Shadows point toward the north at noon because the sun is south.

137

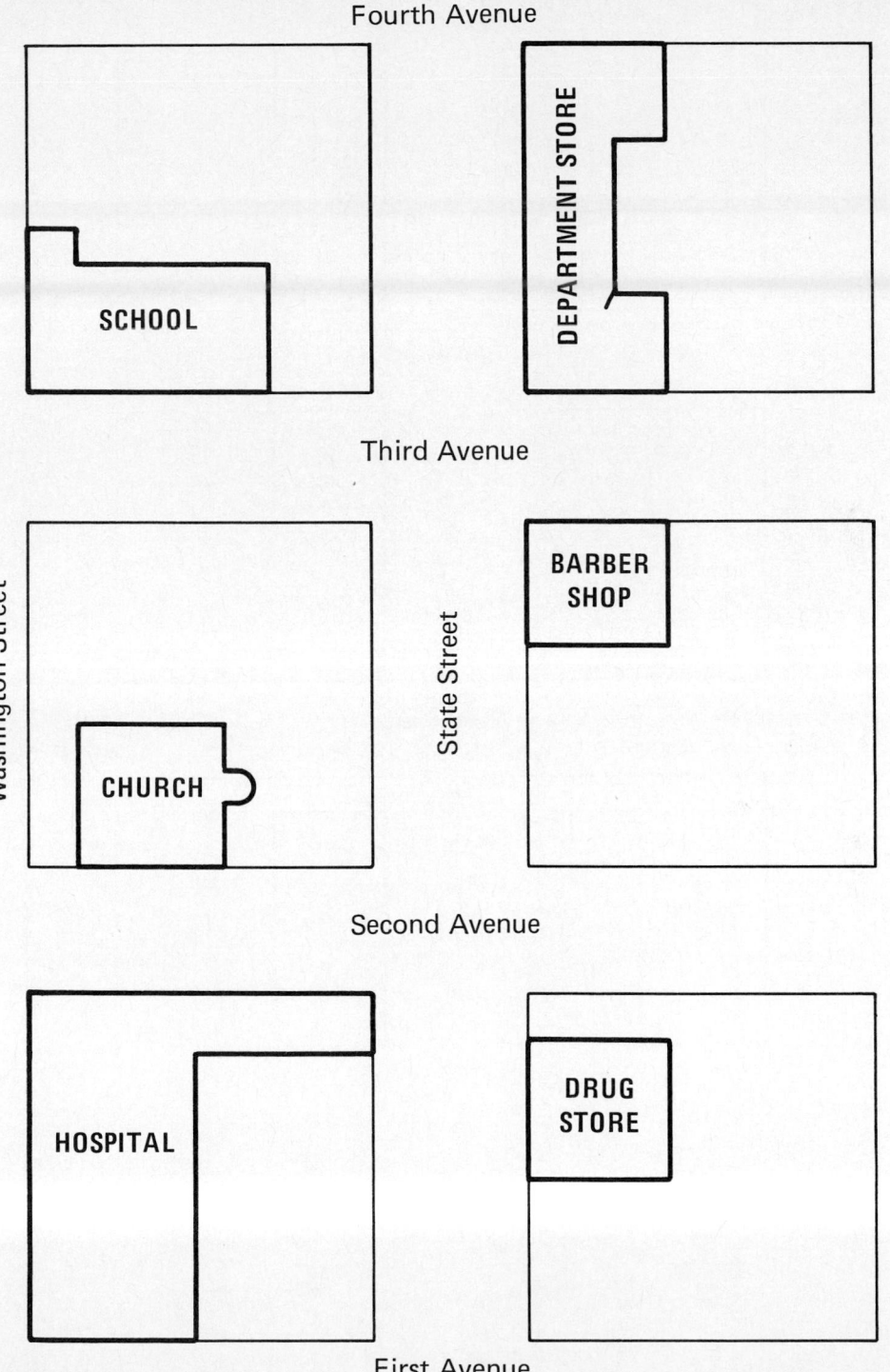

Figure 5.1
A neighborhood map.

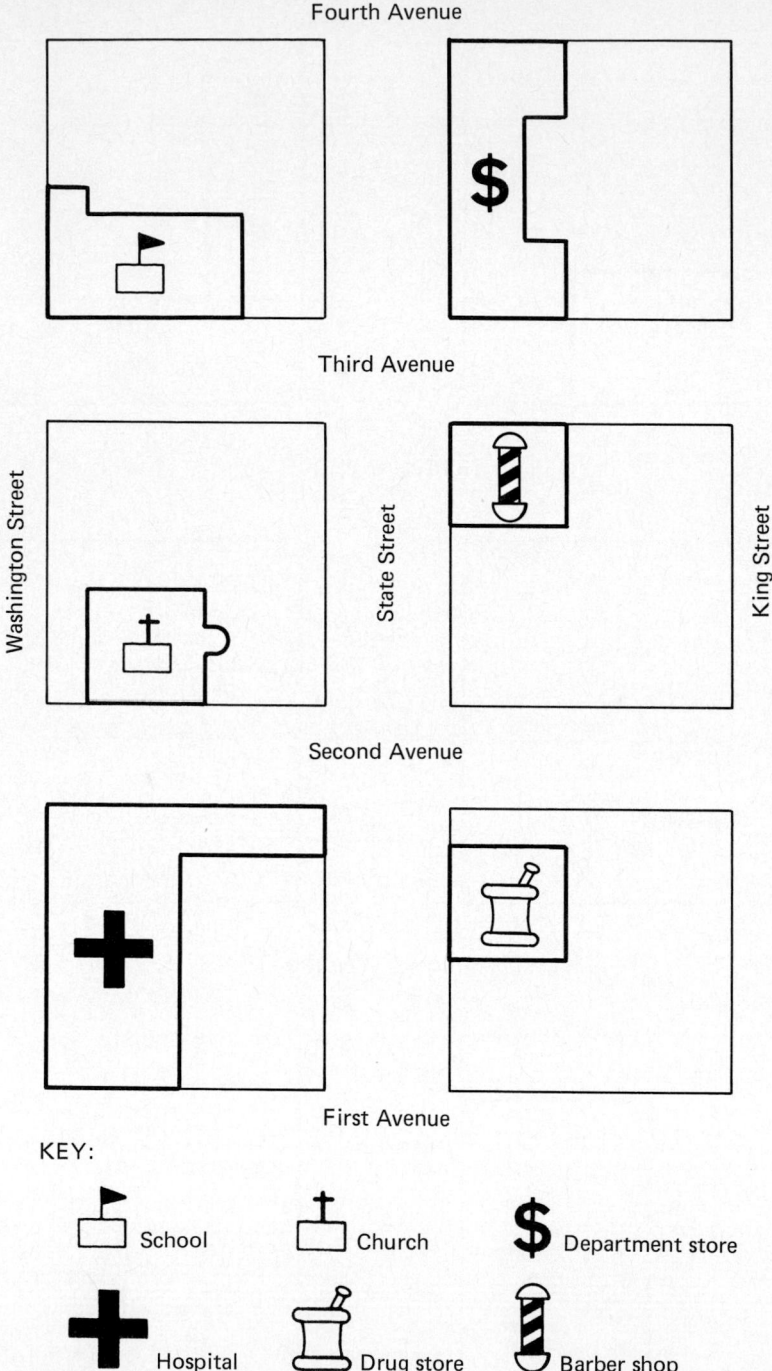

Figure 5.2
A neighborhood map with a pictorial legend.

Students often learn the misconception that north is up and south is down on a map because this is the case on most of the maps they see. Unfortunately, some teachers also reinforce this misconception. This common misconception should not be taught or reinforced for several reasons. Up is away from the center of the earth and down is toward the center of the earth. Where north appears on a map depends on the kind of map projection being viewed. On a map projection showing only the Northern Hemisphere (see Figure 5.3), for example, north and south are seen from a perspective that belies the notion that north is at the top of the map.

HEMISPHERES AND PROJECTIONS

The students should be helped to see how the earth as a sphere can be conceptualized as consisting of two hemispheres. A hemisphere is half of a sphere. The *equator,* the imaginary line equidistant from the North and South Poles, divides the earth into the Northern and Southern Hemispheres. The earth can also be conceptualized as

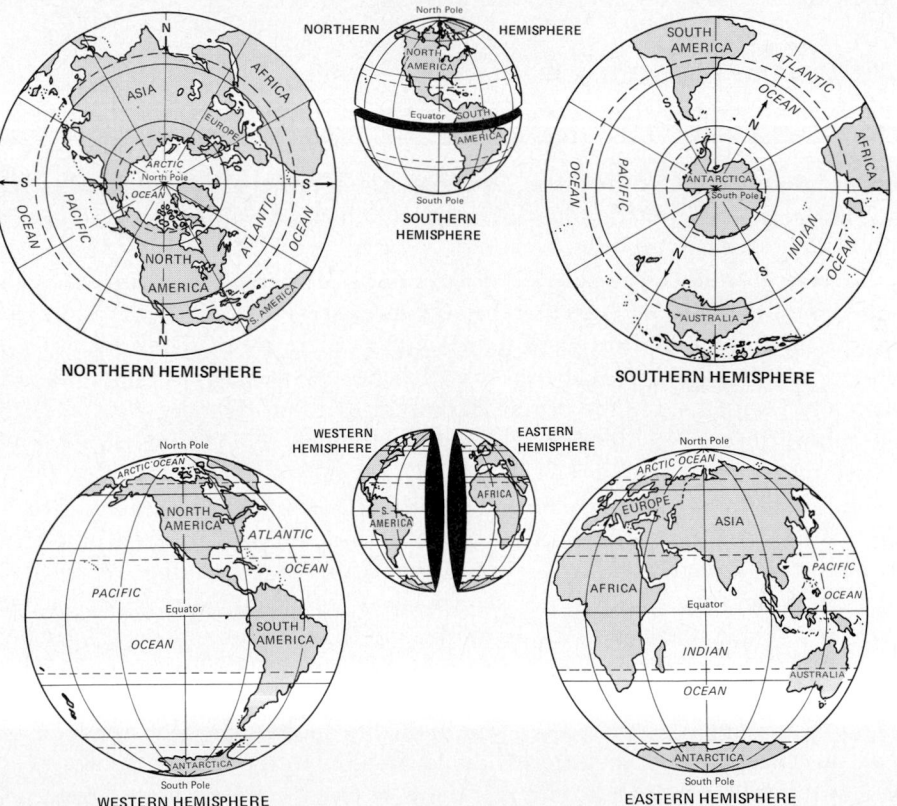

Figure 5.3
The hemispheres.
Source: Reprinted from Herbert J. Gross, compiler, *Follett Student Atlas,* Chicago: Follett Publishing, 1983, p. 9.

Eastern and Western Hemispheres when it is divided into two equal parts along an imaginary line that runs north and south. The Northern, Southern, Eastern and Western Hemispheres are illustrated in Figure 5.3.

After the students have been introduced to the concept of hemispheres, they can then be introduced to various kinds of projections of the earth's surface. It is not possible to show a sphere like the earth on a flat surface like a map without distortions. However, maps were created and are frequently used because they are much more convenient to carry than a globe, enable us to view the whole earth at once, and can show much more detail than globes. Mapmakers have created more than 200 kinds of projections, which are ways to draw a flat map of the earth's surface.

The purpose of a map largely determines the kind of projection a mapmaker uses. All flat maps distort the earth's surface. However, some types of projections are more accurate than others. Figure 5.4 illustrates three common types of projections: the *Mercator,* the *Mollweide,* and the *Broken* projection. These projections can be used to help students discover the different ways in which maps depict and distort the land and water forms of the earth. They can notice, for example, the extent to which Greenland is oversized on the Mercator map and the accuracy of the size, but distortion in shape, of the land forms on the Mollweide projection.

LATITUDE AND LONGITUDE

A knowledge of the parallels of latitude and the meridians of longitude will deepen students' understanding of the globe and help them use these concepts to locate land and water forms on the globe. Students should understand that parallels of latitude and meridians of longitude are imaginary lines drawn on maps and globes to help locate places on the earth.

You can introduce the parallels of latitude by locating the equator on a globe and explaining to the students that the equator is at 0 degrees latitude and that the latitudes north of it are north and those south of it are south. The lines north and south of the equator are numbered from 1 degree to 90 degrees of latitude at the North and South Poles. One degree of latitude is about 69 miles. Parallels of latitude run in an east-west direction and are used to pinpoint locations north or south of the equator.

Meridians of longitude are imaginary lines that run in a north-south direction. They are used to pinpoint locations in an east-west direction. Meridians of longitude are measured by degrees in an east or west direction from the Prime Meridian. The Prime Meridian runs through the original site of the Royal Observatory located in Greenwich, England, which is a suburb of London. The east and west meridians of longitude run from 0 degrees at the Prime Meridian to 180 degrees where they meet at the International Date Line. The days change at the International Date Line. It is Sunday east of the line and Monday west of the line at the same time. Students learn about the importance of the International Date Line in the Inquiry Strategy. Figure 5.5 shows parallels of latitude and meridians of longitude on a globe. You can ask students to use parallels and meridians to locate land and water forms on the earth. However, map and globe skills practice should take place within the context of ongoing social studies units and lessons as often as possible. They should not be isolated exercises that relate to little else in the social studies curriculum.

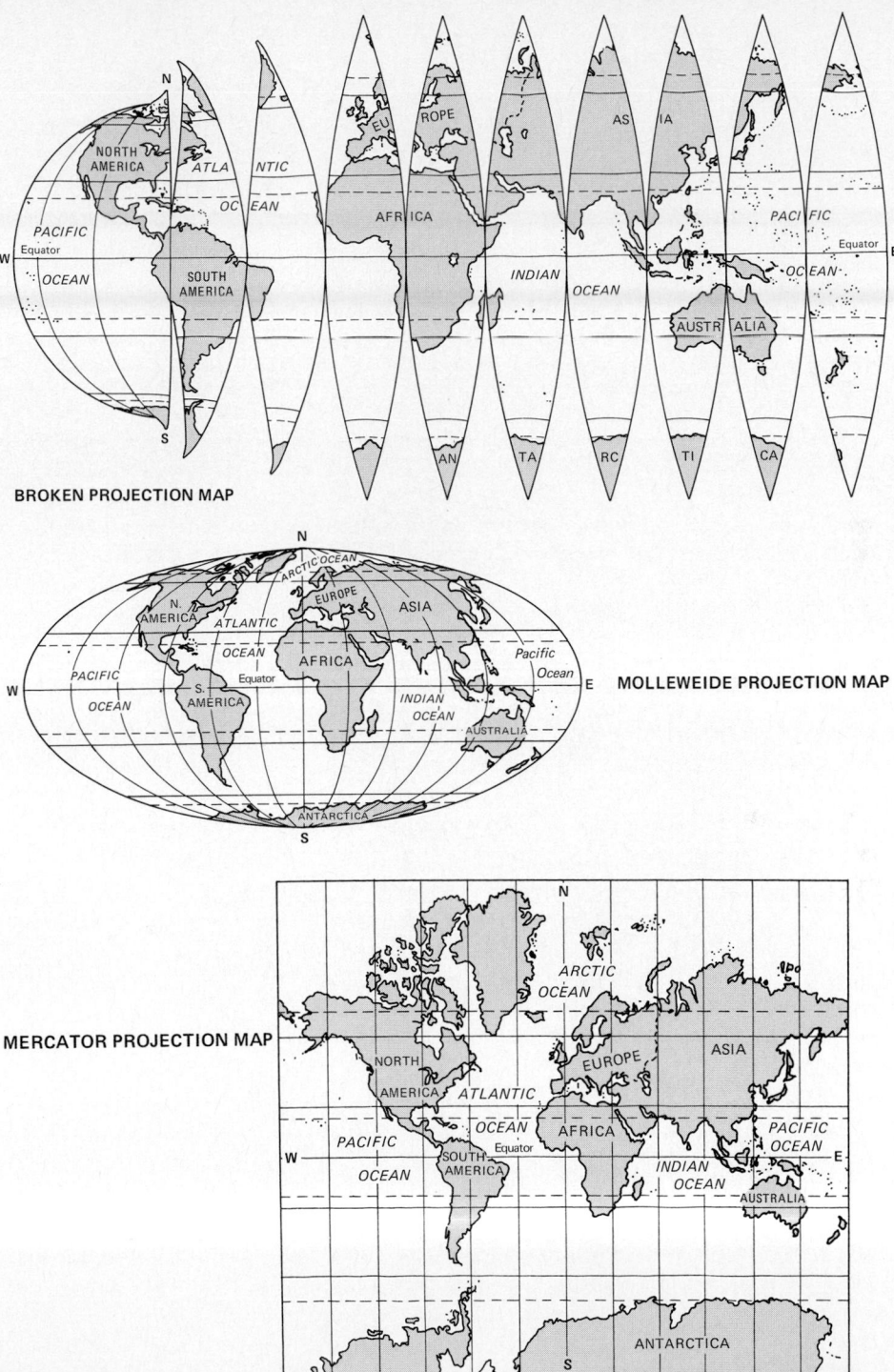

BROKEN PROJECTION MAP

MOLLEWEIDE PROJECTION MAP

MERCATOR PROJECTION MAP

Figure 5.4
Map projections.
Source: Reprinted from Herbert J. Gross, compiler, *Follett Student Atlas*, Chicago: Follett Publishing, 1983, p. 8.

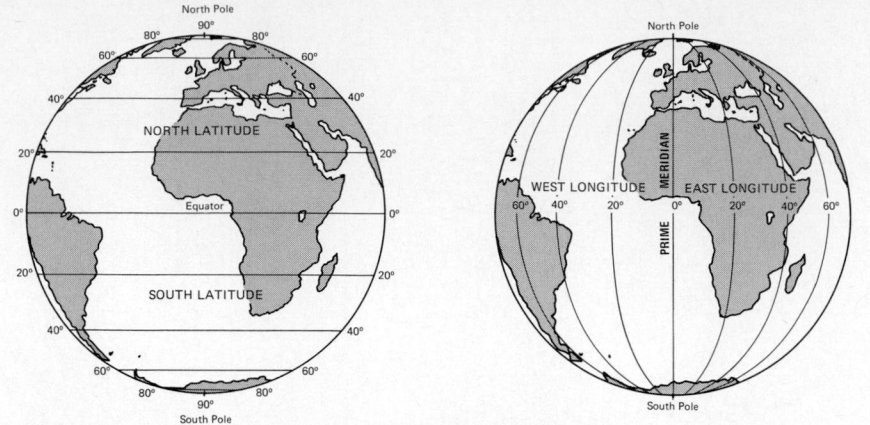

The parallels on globes or maps show the degrees of latitude north or south of the equator. The equator is 0°, the poles are 90°.

The meridians show the degrees of longitude east and west of the Prime Meridian. Both east and west longitude run from 0° to 180°, where they meet.

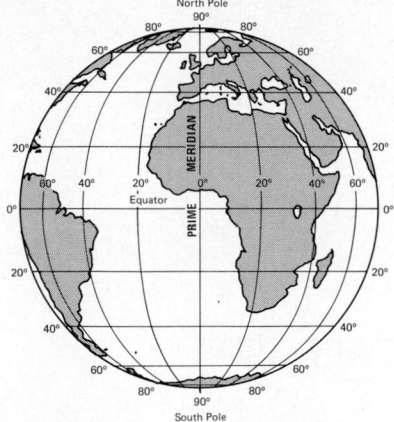

On a globe, notice that 180° east or west longitude is on the opposite side of the world from the Prime Meridian. This is where the International Date Line is located. Here the days change. When it is Sunday east of the line, it is Monday west of the line.

Figure 5.5
Parallels of latitude and meridians of longitude.

Source: Reprinted from Herbert J. Gross, compiler, *Follett Student Atlas,* Chicago: Follett Publishing, 1983, p. 10.

inquiry strategy

AN IMAGINARY WINTER HOLIDAY TRIP TO ANOTHER LAND

This activity is designed to teach the students about time zones and the International Date Line, how the seasons differ above and below the equator, foreign currency, and how the celebration of Christmas or Chanukah is influenced by the type of climate and cultural setting.

1. The students will break up into groups and plan a winter holiday vacation to another land. Students in North America or Europe should plan a trip to Sydney, Australia. Students in Australia or New Zealand should plan a trip to New York City, in the United States. Teachers in other parts of the world should adapt this lesson accordingly. We describe the trip as if it were being planned in North America or Europe.

2. One group of students should plan the trip itinerary. Working with a travel agent, they should obtain information about flights to Sydney, the time and day they would leave their city, and the time and day they would arrive in Sydney. They should choose the most convenient flight from their home city to Sydney. Given this information, they should determine how many hours the flight takes and why the day changes when they fly from their city in North America to Sydney.

3. A second group should obtain information about vacationing in Australia from the library, from travel agents, and by writing to the Australian Consulate-General (1 Bush Street, San Francisco, CA 94104-4413).

4. A third group should determine the rate of exchange between Australian and U.S. dollars and find out the cost of hotels and other goods and services in Sydney. This group will also tell the students how and where they can convert U.S. dollars to Australian dollars and what the current exchange rate is. They can find the current exchange rates in the daily financial sections of the *Wall Street Journal* and the *New York Times*. You can create more interest in this activity by exchanging several U.S. dollars for Australian currency at a local commercial bank and showing it to the class. (Make the request in advance, because some commercial banks require several days to acquire foreign currency.) Students are quite interested in currency of other nations.

5. A fourth group should complete a report on how Christmas or Chanukah is celebrated in Sydney, as well as how these celebrations in Sydney differ from those in their home city in North America. They can read various sources, in addition to interviewing people who have lived in Australia or who have traveled there at Christmastime. They will discover, for example, that the celebration of Christmas in Sydney is influenced by the fact that it takes place in the summer (as compared to the winter in New York City) and that Christmas in the United States tends to be celebrated much longer and with many more commercial aspects than Christmas in many other parts of the world.

6. Each of the groups will share its report when the class takes an imaginary trip to Sydney during the Christmas or Chanukah season.

READING AND INTERPRETING MAPS AND GLOBES

Middle- and upper-grade students can be introduced to more complicated maps and globes and taught more complex map and globe concepts. They can be taught the concept of *scale* and can make a correctly scaled map of a small area. Locations on maps and globes must be drawn on a scale that is many times smaller than the actual area of the earth shown. The makers of maps indicate the extent to which the water and land forms on a map have been reduced in the map's key or legend. The scale is often made in a statement such as "one inch equals 1,000 miles," or expressed as a ratio: 1:1,000. The scale may also be shown with a line divided into segments showing how many miles each segment of the line represents. When introducing the concept of scale, you should point out to the students that every place on the map has been reduced to the scale stated in the map's legend. If the students decide to develop a map to scale of a small area, such as a room or the school grounds, they will be required to use precise measurements and quantification techniques. Making a map to scale of a small area is a fruitful activity that students can undertake as a mathematics–social studies project.

Students in the middle and upper grades should be introduced to the various kinds of special-purpose maps and to the way in which color is used to delineate political boundaries, distinguish bodies of land from bodies of water, and to show various levels of elevation. Maps that show political boundaries between cities, states, and nations are frequently used in the social studies. Other special-purpose maps, showing climate, population, and the distribution of resources and occupations, are also used in social studies lessons and units. Combination maps, showing political boundaries, vegetation, and national boundaries, can be used successfully with upper-grade students but are often not appropriate for students in the primary and intermediate grades. Road, city, and state maps can frequently be used to help students better understand the location of places within their communities.

INTRODUCING LAND AND WATER FORMS

When they study the globe, students in the middle and upper grades should learn to identify the major land and water forms that make up the earth. They should also learn how to locate some of the major nations they will be studying. While studying the globe, the students will quickly discover that most of the earth's surface is made up of water rather than land. There is over two times more water than land on the earth's surface.

You should ask the students to locate the continents on the globe (the major land forms): Asia, Africa, North America, South America, Antarctica, Europe, and Australia. The students can explore a number of interesting questions when studying the continents, such as:

In which continents do most of the world's population live?
In which continents are the world's most technologically developed nations located?
In which continents do we find the poorest nations of the world? Why?

After students have located the major continents, they can identify the major water forms, the oceans. The major ones are the Pacific, the Atlantic, the Indian, and the Arctic. When studying about the oceans, students can investigate their importance in the history of the development of Western nations and their economic and political importance in today's world.

TEACHING TIME AND CHRONOLOGY

Social studies materials often contain references to time. Many of these refer to definite time concepts, such as month and year; others refer to indefinite time concepts, such as a long time ago, a generation, a period, or an era. Time concepts are relational concepts. Relational concepts define a particular association between attributes or distinguishing characteristics. Relational concepts are difficult for young children to understand. They have not had sufficient experience with the basic facts, or with abstracting the common attributes, to establish the particular relation or association involved. For example, it takes considerable practice with a calendar for a six- or seven-year-old child to count up 30 days, learn that that period is called a month, and then recognize that there are approximately four weeks in a month.

The development of a mature sense of time and chronology is a slow, complex, sequential, and cumulative task (Geography Education Standards Project, 1994). Consequently, it is not realistic for elementary and junior high school teachers to expect their students to completely master time and chronology concepts. Your goal should be much more modest: to help students increase their ability to understand and interpret time concepts and to understand how past and present events are interrelated.

The teaching of time concepts should be done primarily within the context of social studies content and units. If time concepts are taught in isolation, they will be less meaningful to students and will not help them to understand how past, present, and future historical and social events are interrelated.

You should identify the major time concepts and historical periods in the content and materials you plan to teach during the year. Once these concepts and periods are identified, you can formulate activities and teaching strategies that will help students master them within the context of particular units. You can best help students to master time and chronology concepts by personalizing them and making them as concrete as possible. Definite time concepts that you will want your students to develop include second, minute, hour, day, week, month, year, decade, and century. Indefinite time concepts—such as long ago, a short time, and an era—are more difficult for students to understand than definite time concepts. You will also need to help students understand concepts such as B.C. and A.D. when they are studying the early development of societies and nations. You can use activities such as the following to help students increase their skill in using time concepts:

1. To teach the idea that time is relative, ask the students to be silent for five minutes and then to clock five minutes when they are playing one of their favorite games.

2. Ask the students to make a family tree. Have them write birthdates for their parents and grandparents and relate those dates to famous historical events.

3. The students can make a personal time line, including such events as their birthdates, when they started school, when they moved into their new home, and when their parents were born.

4. The students can bring and share photographs of themselves at various points in their lives.

5. The students can keep a multiple time line for the school year on which they pictorially note events that were happening at the same time in the various locations and cultures studied.

6. The students can construct a time line of the history of their school. They can also include other important historical events on the timeline.

DEVELOPING GROUP SKILLS

The Nature and Importance of Groups

Human beings are socialized within groups and learn their basic values, beliefs, and behaviors from other individuals within group situations. People become human by interacting with other human beings in groups. Thus groups are important for the survival of humankind as well as for teaching people how to become human. A mere collection of individuals does not constitute a group. Rather, a group is a collection of individuals sharing certain purposes, goals, a sense of identity, and a relatively long-term relationship (Levine & Moreland, 1998). Johnson and Johnson (1991) write, "Groups are networks of human relationships, and a group is effective only if members are effective in cooperating with each other. Whenever two or more individuals join together to achieve a goal, a group structure develops" (p. 16).

Individuals belong to many different kinds of voluntary and involuntary groups which help them to satisfy a wide range of needs. Babies and young children depend on the family for survival. Religious groups help individuals to satisfy their spiritual needs and to answer complex questions about life, death, and morality. Other groups help individuals to satisfy their need to belong, for companionship, and for status. Groups are especially important in a highly modernized society characterized by widespread alienation and an erosion of traditional community beliefs, norms, and moral authority.

Many traditional groups and group attachments have fallen victim to modernization and urbanization. As a result, many individuals in modernized Western societies have experienced an acute sense of alienation and often search to satisfy group needs in unorthodox and socially unacceptable ways. Cults and other nontraditional groups and organizations to some extent reflect the search by individuals in modernized societies for important group attachments and affiliations. Humans have a need for both individuality and group membership.

The Need to Develop Group Skills

Individuals need to develop competency in group skills because of the importance of the group in a democratic society. Individuals who have highly developed thinking skills and are very knowledgeable are not likely to become effective citizens if they cannot function competently in groups. They must know how to exert influence within a group. Effective citizens in a democratic society must be able to exert influence in public affairs by convincing groups of the importance of the goals to which they are committed and to mobilize group support for their goals. Individuals also need proficient group and human relations skills in order to perform successfully on their jobs. Most people who have problems on their jobs have the technical skills to perform successfully but lack essential human relations skills.

Students should be helped to gain increased proficiency in group skills in each of the subject areas in elementary and junior high school. However, the social studies has a special responsibility to help students develop proficiency in group skills. One of the major goals of the social studies is to help students become effective citizens in a democratic society. Effective group skills are essential for this role.

The Nature of Group Skills

You must be aware of the nature of group skills in order to help students increase their proficiency. Students must have opportunities to practice group skills in order to become more competent in group situations. Just as students must practice baseball to increase their ability to play, they must have repeated opportunities to function in group situations to become more skilled group participants. However, for students to increase their group skills, certain conditions must exist in the practice situation. Some of these conditions are discussed and illustrated below.

The task given to the group of students must be within their ability range. Students must experience success in group situations to increase their proficiency in group skills. If a group of students is given a task beyond their skill level, they will be frustrated and the group situation is likely to contribute little to their skill development. As a matter of fact, when a group of students is given a task beyond their skill level, they are likely to develop negative attitudes toward group work and to view it as a waste of their time.

You should carefully tune group task assignments to the skill level of the students within the group. If a group of students who are poor readers are given a group assignment to prepare a report that requires extensive reading, the group experience will be frustrating and unrewarding. However, if they are given a group task that requires them to make a construction, a map, or to present a role-play of an incident from a story the class has read, they will be more likely to have a successful experience and to further develop their group skills.

Group tasks should be motivational and meaningful to each group participant. Each member of the group must feel that he or she can both contribute something to and gain something from it. Unless students feel that they both contribute to and gain something from a group experience, they will view the experience negatively. If the group task is such that some of the students feel that they can accomplish it more successfully working alone than working in a group, the group experience is likely to be viewed negatively. Consequently, when group assignments are made, you should make sure that they can be done better by a group than by individual students working alone. You should provide opportunities for students to complete tasks and assignments both individually and in group situations. Some tasks are completed more successfully by individuals; others are completed more successfully by groups. A book report and reports on the lives of individuals are usually best done by one student; a dramatization, a construction, and a research report on an entire nation can usually best be done by students working in groups.

The task and goals for the group should be clearly understood both by the leader and by all group members. When you give group assignments, make sure that students clearly understand the task. When group tasks are given to students who have had little experience in group situations, you will need to monitor the group as it works to make sure that it is carrying out the assigned task. When you begin group work in class, it is a good idea to start with one group, gradually creating more groups as the year progresses. As more students gain proficiency in group skills, you can eventually have all the students working on group projects at the same time.

Both participation and leadership should be distributed among all group members. All students have a need to participate and to make meaningful contributions, but they also need to exercise some leadership functions. Both teachers and chairs of committees and study groups should be sensitive to this principle of group life. If care is not exercised with a group, one or two individuals are likely to dominate the group and do most of the work. While most groups in social studies classes need a chair, the chair should be sensitive to individuals' needs to exercise leadership. Many opportunities arise for individuals other than the chair to exercise leadership functions. The chair can help by asking different individuals within the group to assume responsibilities for various tasks. As the teacher, you can make sure that all individuals within a group have the opportunity both to participate and to exercise leadership by carefully monitoring the groups as they work and encouraging reluctant students to participate and contribute. Ask those who like to dominate to share the participatory and leadership functions with others in the group.

Groups function best when power and influence are distributed equally, based on expertise, ability, and access to information rather than on authority (Johnson & Johnson, 1991). If this principle is applied, each member of the group will have an opportunity to exercise influence and power sometime during the life of the group.

Every group will experience problems when disagreements and conflicts arise and minority opinions are expressed. In an effective group, conflicts among members with different views and opinions are encouraged and dealt with openly in a negotiated way (Johnson & Johnson, 1991). You will need to help students develop conflict-resolution skills to learn how to resolve conflicts within groups successfully.

Table 5.4 summarizes some of the important characteristics of effective and ineffective groups. You should keep these characteristics in mind when you plan group experiences.

The Improvement of Group Skills

Students need to develop a range of group skills to become effective citizens in a democratic society. They need to learn how to become successful leaders, effective followers, and how to make productive contributions to groups. The ability to be a good listener, to express a strong opinion as well as to compromise, and to identify with others in situations different from one's own are also important group skills. Effective group members are able to see things from a different frame of reference and to empathize with others in diverse situations. Effective group members are also able to communicate successfully and to negotiate and compromise. They have a strong sense of identity with group goals and respect the rights and opinions of other group members.

TABLE 5.4. *Comparison Between Effective and Ineffective Groups*

Effective Groups	Ineffective Groups
Goals are clarified and changed to give the best possible match between individual goals and the group's goals; goals are cooperatively structured.	Members accept imposed goals; goals are competitively structured.
Communication is two-way and the open and accurate expression of both ideas and feelings is emphasized.	Communication is one-way and only ideas are expressed; feelings are suppressed or ignored.
Participation and leadership are distributed among all group members; goal accomplishment, interval maintenance, and developmental change are underscored.	Leadership is delegated and based upon authority; membership participation is unequal with high-authority members dominating; only goal accomplishment is emphasized.
Ability and information determine influence and power; contracts are built to make sure the individual goals and needs are fulfilled; power is equalized and shared.	Position determines influence and power; power is concentrated in the authority positions; obedience to authority is the rule.
Decision-making procedures are matched with the situation; different methods are used at different times; consensus is sought for important decisions; involvement and group discussions are encouraged.	Decisions are always made by the highest authority with little group discussion; members' involvement is minimal.
Controversy and conflict are seen as positive keys to members' involvement, the quality and originality of decisions, and the continuance of the group in good working condition.	Controversy and conflict are ignored, denied, avoided, or suppressed.
Interpersonal group and intergroup behavior are stressed; cohesion is advanced through high levels of inclusion, affection, acceptance, support, and trust. Individuality is endorsed.	The functions performed by members are emphasized; cohesion is ignored and members are controlled by force. Rigid conformity is promoted.
Problem-solving adequacy is high.	Problem-solving adequacy is low.
Members evaluate the effectiveness of the group and decide how to improve its functioning; goal accomplishing, internal maintenance, and development are all considered important.	The highest authority evaluates the group's effectiveness and decides how goal accomplishment may be improved; internal maintenance and development are ignored as much as possible; stability is affirmed.
Interpersonal effectiveness, self-actualization, and innovation are encouraged.	"Organizational persons" who desire order, stability, and structure are encouraged.

Source: David W. Johnson and Frank P. Johnson, *Joining Together: Group Theory and Group Skills*, 4th ed. (Englewood Cliffs, N.J.: Prentice-Hall, 1991), p. 20. Reprinted with permission of the publisher.

Students will differ greatly in the level of their group skills. Individual students will be strong in some group skills and weak in others. Some students will be highly capable of taking leadership functions within the group but will lack the ability to be good followers and participants when they are not functioning in leadership roles. Other students will be good followers but will lack the ability to function adequately in leadership roles. Students need to develop the skills to be good followers as well as good leaders. One of the teacher's major responsibilities is to carefully observe students in group situations and to give them feedback about their skill development. Feedback is essential to help students improve their group skills. You can use a checklist similar to the one in Table 5.5 to observe and record student behavior in group situations.

TABLE 5.5. *Group Observation Checklist*

Name of Student: Group Situation Observed:	Grade: Date:		
	Rarely	**Sometimes**	**Always**
1. Carefully listens to others.			
2. Contributes useful ideas to the group.			
3. Functions well as a group leader.			
4. Takes every opportunity to lead.			
5. Functions well as a follower.			
6. Helps the group stick to the task.			
7. Has a strong interest in the group.			
8. Shows interest in opinions different from his or her own.			
9. Demonstrates his or her ability to compromise and to help resolve conflict.			
10. Is able to express his or her opinions clearly.			
11. Is able to exercise influence within the group.			
OTHER COMMENTS:			

Group Activities and Projects

Students must have practice in group situations to improve their group skills. You should begin to give students experience in group situations in the primary grades. Groups in the primary grades should be kept small and their tasks should be simple. Two students might be given group assignments, such as erasing the board for a day, watering the plants, or making a house with blocks.

In the middle and upper grades, groups can be assigned more academically oriented tasks. During a unit on Latin America, sixth-grade students might be divided into research groups to study the four nations covered in the unit: Colombia, Brazil, Argentina, and Chile. This kind of assignment can be made only after the students have developed sufficient research and group skills. When establishing research groups to study a topic, you should make sure that the scope of the group task is clear and limited. In our example, the class could develop an outline that would be used by each study group. The outline might include the following as major topics: the political system, education, industry, agriculture, and religion.

A range of instructional goals can be achieved in group situations in the middle and upper grades. Writing a script based on a story the class has read, producing and presenting the story in a school assembly, making charts and graphs, collecting pictures and artifacts, making videotapes, interviewing, and various kinds of reports and discussions are tasks that can be successfully achieved in groups.

Reports and discussions are frequently used in social studies classes. You can help students increase their skills in discussion groups. You can help students formulate guidelines for participating in discussions, provide students feedback on their own behavior in discussion groups, and give them opportunities to observe other students in discussion groups.

TEACHING WRITING SKILLS IN THE SOCIAL STUDIES

The rich content in the social studies provides many opportunities for you to extend and enrich students' speaking, listening, and writing skills. While the major goal of the social studies should be to help students to develop the knowledge and skills needed to become competent citizens, the reinforcement of literacy skills is an important component of the social studies curriculum. Effective citizens must be able to write, speak, and listen competently. Competence in these skills will also enable students to better attain goals more germane to the social studies.

Writing as a Form of Thinking

When teaching and extending writing skills in the social studies, you should realize and help students to understand that writing is primarily a form of thinking. Clear and effective writing results when the writer has carefully thought about the subject or topic, clearly organized his or her ideas, and formulated them in lucid English. Thus the first and most important step in effective writing is to determine the purpose of the composition, its intended audience, and the form and content that will best enhance the purpose. Purpose and audience should be the main determiners of the nature and structure of the writing project. A successful persuasive essay on the societal consequences of animal cloning will differ significantly from an essay designed mainly to inform the reader about animal cloning. Both essays might be factually accurate. However, the writer who wants to persuade and convince will select a different set of facts than the writer who merely wants to inform. The tone of the essays is likely to be different. The persuasive writer will, for example, use more emotion-evoking adjectives than the writer who wants to inform.

Summary Writing

You should provide practice in writing for different purposes during social studies lessons and units. In the primary grades, students can be given ample practice in summary writing. The major purpose of summaries is to accurately summarize the works of other authors in the students' own words. Summary writing can be taught successfully to primary grade students, to students who have had little previous writing experience, and to students who have poor writing skills. Summary writing does not require students to formulate new ideas but merely to express the ideas of other writers in their own words. However, students must have a sufficient level of understanding of a written work to summarize it successfully.

When teaching summary writing in the primary grades, you can ask the students to summarize topics, paragraphs, or excerpts that they have read, viewed, or listened to during social studies lessons. You can list the students' summary statements on the board or overhead projector in simple but clear and complete sentences. During a unit on the community, you can ask students to state three major points made about communities in a textbook selection or a videotape. When you write these statements on the board, make sure they are accurate summaries of the text or videotape. They should also be in complete sentences (not sentence fragments) and grammatically correct.

After the students have had ample practice in dictating summaries of materials as a class, you can ask them to work in small groups and then individually to prepare summaries (in lists). Eventually, they should be required to formulate their lists of sentences into paragraphs and to complete their writing assignments independently. When teaching students to formulate their lists of sentences into paragraphs, you should introduce or review the concept of a paragraph and the topic sentence. The topic sentence states the main idea of the paragraph as briefly as possible. In the middle and upper grades, you can require students to prepare summaries of materials in short compositions that consist of a number of interrelated paragraphs.

Synthesis Writing

In the middle and upper grades, students can be introduced to synthesis writing. In this form of writing, students are required to research a topic, such as "Women in the West," and to synthesize the ideas from at least two different authors. Synthesis writing requires higher-level thinking skills than summary writing. The writer is required to summarize the ideas of two or more writers and to integrate them into a single composition. Outlining skills will help students to successfully synthesize and interrelate ideas, interpretations, and facts from two or more authors on a single topic.

When students do research and read to prepare a composition on "Women in the West," they should jot down main ideas and subideas related to major topics and subtopics in outline form. Main topics for the outline might include:

I. Work
II. Recreation
III. Health
IV. Raising children
V. Religion

Often a writer will need to do exploratory reading before knowing what the appropriate main topics and subtopics should be for a particular composition.

When teaching composition and outlining skills, you should not convey the idea that research and writing is a rigid process, such as first developing a detailed outline, reading, and then writing. In reality, these processes might go on at the same time. Writers often do exploratory reading on a topic, develop a skeleton outline, begin a rough draft of the composition, and outline the composition in more detail mentally as they write without developing a highly detailed outline like those often found in English composition textbooks. The microcomputer, with word processing software, has greatly influenced the writing process for many writers. Because editing and changes are very easy to make when writing on a word processor, writers tend to be more tentative in their planning of compositions, more exploratory, and more prone to make significant changes during the writing process.

When you first assign synthesis compositions, an example of the assignment should be done with the class as a whole. The scope of the assignment should be limited and explicit. A first synthesis writing assignment might be to ask the students to use two references (an encyclopedia and a trade book) to describe the Jamestown settlement in 1607.

When students prepare synthesis writing assignments, they should be taught how to summarize the authors' ideas in their own words, to interrelate the ideas of several authors, to identify a direct quotation, and to cite references in a simple way. Students should learn as early as possible that an author's words belong to him or her just as other kinds of property, and that an author's works should always be respected and credited.

Analytical and Critical Writing

In both summary and synthesis writing, the writer is concerned primarily with accurately summarizing the ideas of other authors. Students in social studies classes also need to develop and refine higher-level thinking and writing skills, such as thinking about and extending ideas they read, hear, or view, critically analyzing them, determining perspectives and points of view, evaluating the validity of arguments, and distinguishing facts from opinions. Students practice these skills when they do analytical and critical writing.

You can provide practice in analytical and critical writing by asking students to write responses to newspaper editorials, to analyze the treatment of women in television commercials, and to compare the treatment of the Civil War in two different textbooks. To successfully write analytical and critical compositions, students will need many in-class opportunities to identify the biases, points of view, and frames of reference of different authors. One effective way to help students develop skills in analytical and critical writing is to work with them as a class in identifying and naming the perspectives and points of view of writers and contrasting them with their own views and the views of other writers.

EXERCISES FOR TEACHING ANALYTICAL AND CRITICAL WRITING SKILLS

1. Read the account of the American Revolution in our textbook. List the major assumptions the author makes about (1) the British and (2) the American colonists.
2. Read this editorial (provided by the teacher) on the new immigrants that have come to the United States since 1970. Write one or two paragraphs that present another point of view.
3. In a short essay, compare and contrast the ideas of Booker T. Washington and W.E.B. DuBois about the education of African Americans in the 19th century.
4. Read several accounts of animal cloning and its possible effects on society. Summarize the major assumptions and points of view of each author in a brief composition. In the last part of the composition, state your own views about animal cloning.
5. Read one of the books on this list (provided by the teacher) and write a critical review of it in 500 words. Do not summarize the book. Assume that the reader is familiar with its contents. Use all of your 500 words to critically discuss the book.
6. After viewing the videotape *Wings of Change, Part 1: A Matter of Promise,* write a short paragraph which describes the ways in which Native Americans and their struggles are depicted. Describe another way these events may have been viewed.

Creative Writing

Content in the social studies can serve as an excellent springboard for creative writing. In creative writing in the social studies, the student is asked to assume various roles and positions in different historical periods and to write diaries, speeches, letters, editorials, and other compositions from particular points of view and perspectives.

To write successful creative essays in the social studies, the student must have in-depth knowledge of the historical period, the culture, the people, and the particular role of the person he or she assumes. Creative writing assignments provide an excellent opportunity for students to synthesize and apply the knowledge gained in social studies lessons and units. During the culminating phase of a unit on medieval life, the students can be asked to write a composition on "My Life as a Knight." While the specific events in the essay will be fictitious, the composition should accurately reflect the culture and times of the medieval period. The students can also be asked to assume roles from the past and to complete writing assignments such as those listed below.

CREATIVE WRITING ASSIGNMENTS IN THE SOCIAL STUDIES

1. You are Harry S. Truman in 1945. Write a speech explaining why you decided to authorize the dropping of the atomic bomb on Japan at Hiroshima (August 6) and Nagasaki (August 9).
2. You are a mother and an enslaved African American living in South Carolina in 1850. Two of your three children have just been sold to the owner of another plantation in another state. They will be taken from you and sent to the new owner in a few days. Write an entry in your diary about this event and describe your feelings.
3. You are a newspaper writer living in San Francisco in 1942. You work for William Randolph Hearst. Japanese Americans are being sent to internment camps. Write an editorial about the internment for your newspaper.
4. The year is 1885. You are an immigrant from Italy who has settled in New York City. You have found a job in a factory. Write a letter home to Italy telling about your new country, your job, problems, hopes, and dreams.

Making Writing Assignments in the Social Studies

Students in the middle and upper grades are frequently asked to write book reports, short research papers, biographies of important people, and answers to examination questions in social studies classes. When making these kinds of assignments, you should make sure that they require students to use higher-level thinking skills. As often as possible, these assignments should require students to do analytical, critical, and creative writing. Writing assignments in the middle and upper grades that only require students to summarize or to regurgitate information they have read, heard, or viewed are rarely justified. However, some assignments may justifiably require students to accurately summarize information and then to interpret, evaluate, and analyze it. Book report assignments may require students to briefly summarize a book and then to spend most of the report evaluating and analyzing it. We cannot overemphasize the importance of teaching students the difference between *summary* and *analysis;* this difference frequently eludes college students when they prepare book reports and research papers.

You should carefully review writing assignments to make sure that they require students to use higher-level thinking skills (see Figure 5.6). Social studies seat work assignments and essay examinations frequently require students to regurgitate information they have memorized. Frequent use of higher-level questions, discussed and illustrated in Chapter 4, will enable you to make sure that social studies writing assignments are meaningful, challenging, and rewarding for your students.

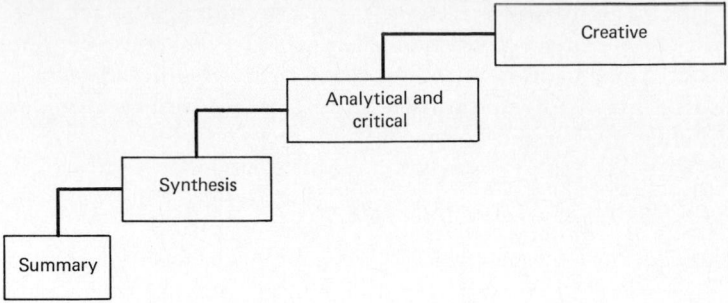

Figure 5.6
A typology of writing skills in the social studies. Writing in the social studies should reinforce skills that students learn in the language arts and help them develop increasingly higher-level thinking and writing skills using social studies content.

SUMMARY

The social studies curriculum is designed to help students develop the knowledge, attitudes, and skills needed to become successful participants in a democratic society. This chapter discusses skills that should constitute an important component of a decision-making-focused social studies curriculum: thinking skills, map and globe skills, time and chronology skills, group skills, and writing skills. To help students develop proficiency in these skills, you need to give them sufficient practice and feedback and teach skills within the context of ongoing social studies units and lessons.

REFLECTION AND ACTION ACTIVITIES

1. Plan a series of activities to provide students with practice in (1) describing, (2) making inferences, and (3) analyzing information. If you are teaching or student teaching, try these activities with a class or group of students to evaluate their effectiveness.
2. Develop several lesson plans using the Taba strategies described in this chapter to teach students to conceptualize and to generalize. If possible, try these strategies with a group of students.
3. Develop a lesson plan for introducing globes and maps to students in the primary and intermediate grades.
4. What problems might you experience in teaching the cardinal directions to students? How might these problems best be overcome?
5. Develop a plan for teaching students the concept of map projections.
6. How can young children best be taught time and chronology concepts?
7. What are some of the major principles of group participation discussed in this chapter?
8. Develop activities for involving students at the following grade levels in group projects: primary grades, intermediate grades, and upper grades.
9. Develop a creative writing social studies assignment for students in the intermediate grades.

10. Demonstrate your understanding of the following concepts and terms by writing or stating brief definitions for each of them. Also tell why each is important:

   a. describing
   b. inferring
   c. analyzing
   d. map
   e. projections
   f. globe
   g. parallels of latitude

   h. meridians of longitude
   i. group skills
   j. summary writing
   k. synthesis writing
   l. analytical and critical writing
   m. creative writing

REFERENCES

Beyer, B. K. (1987). *Practical strategies for the teaching of thinking.* Boston: Allyn and Bacon.

Geography Education Standards Project (1994). *Geography for life: National geography standards.* Washington, D.C.: Author.

Johnson, D. W., & Johnson, F. P. (1991). *Joining together: Group theory and group* skills (4th ed.). Englewood Cliffs, NJ: Prentice-Hall.

Levine, J. M., & Moreland, R. L. (1998). Small Groups. In D. T. Gilbert, S. T. Fiske, & G. Lindzey (Eds.), *The handbook of social sociology* (4th ed., Vol. 2, pp. 415–469). Boston: McGraw-Hill.

Shaftel, F. R., & Shaftel, G. (1982). *Role playing in the curriculum* (2nd ed.). Englewood Cliffs, NJ: Prentice-Hall.

Taba, H., et al. (1971). *A teacher's handbook to elementary social studies.* Reading, MA: Addison-Wesley.

FOR FURTHER READING

Beyer, B. K. (1988). *Developing a thinking skills program.* Boston: Allyn and Bacon.

Cohen, E. (1994). *Designing groupwork: Strategies for the heterogeneous classroom* (2nd ed.). New York: Teachers College Press.

Cohen, E. G., & Lotan, R. A. (Eds.). (1997). *Working for equity in heterogeneous classrooms: Sociological theory in practice.* New York: Teachers College Press.

Johnson, D. W., & Johnson, R. T. (1991). *Learning together and alone: Cooperative, competitive, and individualistic learning* (3rd ed.). Englewood Cliffs, NJ: Prentice-Hall.

Lederman, L. C. (1995). *Asking questions and listening.* Dubuque, IA: Kendall/Hunt.

Stahl, R. (1994) (Ed.). *Cooperative learning in social studies: A Handbook for teachers.* Menlo Park, CA: Addison-Wesley.

CHAPTER 6

Teaching Reading in the Social Studies

The reading load in social studies classes can be immense and difficult, with textbooks, trade books, and primary source material available for student use. Therefore, helping students become better readers of these materials is an important responsibility for the social studies teacher that requires careful planning. Social studies materials contain difficult, often new and unfamiliar concepts, which make them hard to understand and remember. Furthermore, the expository nature of most of these materials compounds the difficulties. These structures are more complex and less commonly encountered in earlier grades than the more familiar narrative structures of stories. This chapter is designed to help you become more aware of the reading process, the problems students encounter when they read social studies materials, and techniques you can use to help students become more successful readers of the materials in your classes. An integrated approach to improving reading is stressed, one that combines teaching of social studies content with a concern for the techniques necessary for reading social studies materials successfully. Such an approach is supported by research, but it requires positive teacher attitudes for success (Berryhill, 1984).

This chapter is contributed by Christine Caverhill Schaefer, Ph.D., Seattle Urban Center, Western Washington University.

Teachers must support students' efforts to read materials within their subject areas. It is not reasonable to expect language arts teachers, whose focus is more often on narrative text forms, to teach students how to read material in other classes. Teachers in each subject area must assume some responsibility for teaching students how to learn from the texts important in that subject from the perspective of the subject-area specialist.

KNOWING WHEN WE KNOW

An important part of any learning activity is developing an awareness of how and when learning is taking place and the learner's role in making it happen. Students must get into the habit of evaluating how much they know about a subject and how

"We don't want any of your money. We just want an audience to listen to Jason reading from his own works."
Source: Joseph Farris. Used with permission.

much they learn when they read. They should learn to ask themselves such goal-setting questions as the following:

> What is my purpose for reading this text?
> What will I do with the information?
> How should I read to fulfill my purpose?

They should also ask themselves such questions as these to evaluate their learning:

> Do I understand what I've just read?
> Does it make sense?
> How is it related to what I knew before I read?
> Does all the information go together?

They should learn to ask themselves questions in an attempt to fix any lack of comprehension that might be discerned during the process:

> What can I do to understand this better?
> Shall I read it again?
> Shall I read it differently?
> Shall I ask someone else?

This self-analysis is called *metacognition,* or metacognitive awareness. Metacognition has been described as "knowing about knowing" and "knowing how to know" (Brown, 1978). Metacognition is an awareness of what must be done in order to learn, an awareness that allows readers to determine if and when they have understood. Paired with conscious, manipulative reading strategies to increase understanding, it develops flexible readers who can alter their activities to match their purposes for reading, to allow or compensate for their own backgrounds and preparation for the task, and to recognize text characteristics that will help or interfere with successfully fulfilling the learning task.

Research has shown that the ability to control comprehension strategies is in general a developmental process, that is, as children get older, this ability increases. This is also affected, however, by the explicitness of the text, how the material is presented, and how familiar the reader is with the topic (Pearson, Roehler, Dole, & Duffy, 1992). In one study, fifth-graders who were above-average readers adjusted how much time they spent on reading tasks, increasing the time when the tasks became more difficult. The below-average readers, however, failed to make this adjustment. In fact, they spent less time as the tasks became harder (Guthrie, 1982). This indicates that either the poorer readers did not know when they did not understand, or that they recognized when the tasks became more difficult and gave up.

Poor readers do not see themselves as being in control of what they do when they read (DiVesta, Hayward, & Orlando, 1979; Dole, Brown, & Trathen, 1996). They do not understand that they must rely on their own prior knowledge and background information to comprehend as well as on the textual material. They tend to see reading as decoding only—figuring out the words—rather than as

Students can use the four steps for monitoring comprehension to develop their megacognitive awareness. In this photograph, a teacher is helping a student review his notes from a reading selection.
Source: Northshore School District, Seattle.

understanding the ideas in the text (Gambrell & Heathington, 1981), and they are poor at monitoring comprehension (Baker & Brown, 1984; Brown, Armbruster, & Baker, 1986; Wagoner, 1983.)

However, you can help teach your students to develop metacognitive awareness. In several studies (Andre & Anderson, 1979; Baker, 1979; Mangano, Palmer, & Goetz, 1982; Dole, Brown, & Trathen, 1996), younger and less able readers began to learn through training what proficient readers already seem to know:

Part of being a good student is learning to be aware of one's own mind and the degree of one's own understanding.…[T]he problem is not to get students to ask us what they don't know; the problem is to make them aware of the difference between what they know and what they don't. (Holt, 1964)

Four steps for monitoring comprehension have been identified by Fitzgerald (1983):

1. Students must know when they do and do not know something.
2. Students must know what they know.
3. Students must know what they need to know.
4. Students must know the usefulness of techniques that help them to learn.

Metacognitive awareness requires active participation in self-monitoring and self-evaluation, which are essential for learning. This internal process of quality control must be a reader's constant companion. For students to develop metacognitive awareness, however, teachers must teach and encourage them to monitor their own learning activities. Asking students for reflective information about reading and study strategies they already use is a good way to start the process (Baker & Brown, 1984; Garner, 1992). Garner suggests asking questions such as these:

Are any sentences in a paragraph more important than others?
Are reading to study and reading for fun the same?
What things does a person have to do to become a good reader?
What makes something difficult to read?
How do you answer a question in your textbook if you remember that you read about the topic, but you do not remember the answer?
How can you tell what an author thought was important in a passage?
How do you write a short summary of a long piece of text?
What do you do if you come to an unfamiliar word in something you're reading for homework?
How do you put something "in your own words"? (p. 239)

Many students will find that they cannot answer some of these questions, which will signal where instruction can take place.

The concerns for developing metacognitive awareness in student readers has led to a vast body of literature regarding the effectiveness of using different strategies for reading different kinds of materials for different purposes, and for different backgrounds. Unlike innate skills, which seem to operate automatically, strategies are applied consciously by expert readers, who choose strategies to be consistent with text cues to achieve comprehension (Chambliss, 1995). Strategic readers:

Search for connections between what they know and the new information they encounter in the texts they read.
Monitor the adequacy of their models of text meaning.
Take steps to repair faulty comprehension once they realize they have failed to understand something.

Learn early on to distinguish important from less important ideas in texts they read.

Are adept at synthesizing information within and across texts and reading experiences.

Draw inferences during and after reading to achieve a full, integrated understanding of what they read.

Sometimes consciously, and almost always unconsciously, ask questions of themselves, the authors they encounter, and the texts they read. (Pearson, Roehler, Dole, & Duffy, 1992, pp. 153–154)

Metacognitive awareness is essential for becoming a strategic reader. (A further look at developing reading strategies will be found later in the chapter in the section titled Developing Flexible Reading Strategies.) All of the other topics discussed in this chapter depend on metacognitive awareness, the aspect of learning that gives the learner control over the material and options for learning from it.

CHARACTERISTICS OF SOCIAL STUDIES READING MATERIALS

When young children first learn to read, they read fiction. They learn to develop expectations about the structure of stories, or narratives, and those who have been read to at home have an advantage in developing and internalizing these structures. However, the skills students develop to understand narrative structures for fiction cannot be applied directly to social studies materials for several reasons. First, most social studies materials are nonfiction, and the expository structures of most nonfiction materials differ greatly from those of fiction. Narrative structure is generally linear, with an identifiable beginning, middle, and end, which is meant to be read from beginning to end so readers can see how the plot unfolds and how the characters develop.

Social studies materials, however, are not written as linear narratives. Social studies textbooks, for example, are organized more like a series of embedded outlines. The largest outline is the entire book, and by looking at the table of contents, you can see the major topics, which on a traditional outline would be represented by Roman numerals. Each unit, section, and chapter also resembles a fleshed-out outline, but of smaller proportions. Each smaller piece of the text can be read as a unit on its own, and yet each smaller piece is a part of the next larger one, which is a part of the next larger one, and so on, up to the entire book. Within an individual chapter, each major idea, often represented by a subheading, is explained in detail and then followed by the next major idea and its detail. If students read these materials from beginning to end as they would with a story, the chapter and section headings—the main points in the outline—are generally ignored, the major ideas get lost among the details, and the advantage of the structure is squandered.

The second way textbooks differ from narrative text is in the specialized vocabulary used. These words are the labels for complicated concepts that can be abstract, and therefore more difficult to understand. An example is the abstract term *agricultural assets.* This term could be used to apply to anything from land, to machinery, to chicken feed, to all of these things together. The abstractness of this label makes it difficult to interpret and to understand, more difficult than the label *pigs*, which has a concrete referent, rendering it substantially easier to understand. Without some planning and teaching on your part, your students may have difficulty making the connection between the two terms. Frequently, the abstract concepts will also be new to your students, and large numbers of new, complex concepts increase the difficulty of the materials. You must be concerned about how many new concepts are introduced, how they are explained, and how much prior knowledge the author assumes readers have (Bullock & Hesse, 1981), as well as the levels of abstraction of the concepts.

The third way that social studies textbooks differ from narratives is in the purposes for reading them. Gathering and remembering information, interpreting, and connecting to other information are important, with different outcomes involved—taking tests, writing reports, discussing, and applying the information to new situations. "Reading to learn" replaces "learning to read" as the primary reading activity.

A final way these materials differ from stories is in the authors' purposes for writing the materials. The primary purposes are no longer to entertain, to give practice in the process of learning to read, or to give insights into the human condition through creative narratives, but to give information, to persuade, to compare and contrast, to present problems and their solutions, to present and defend points of view, to give insight into the human condition through real events. Your students need to read critically so that they can learn to recognize an author's purposes for writing, whether the purposes are stated or not.

These various aspects of text change again when students are confronted with primary source material. The organization might then be random or tightly structured but in unfamiliar formats. The language might be archaic as well as abstract, or the terms might have very different meanings from the terms in modern times. Students' purposes change as well when they are interpreting primary sources rather than relying on the credibility of those who have interpreted them for textbooks or for other secondary sources. Finally, the authors' purposes might be very different from those of the authors of textbooks, and students must learn to interpret these also. Few of these materials will be written as narratives in the same sense that stories are written as narratives.

Unfortunately, however, many students read social studies materials as if they were reading fiction, losing opportunities for comprehension. Without help, they do not understand that the differences in the materials themselves and in their reasons for reading them require different reading strategies. Without help, they might not understand the different expectations you have for them as they read the materials; they might not understand different outcomes expected for their having read the material. Sadly, many of our students are ill-prepared for the reading demands of expository text (Garner & Gillingham, 1987), and many subject-area teachers do not help them because they do not consider it part of their job.

STRATEGIES FOR READING TEXTBOOKS

Before you teach your students how to read social studies materials, show them how the information is organized. A great deal of research supports the notion that a reader who understands the structure of text will have a better chance of understanding the text itself (Meyer, Brandt, & Bluth, 1980; Taylor & Beach, 1984; Armbruster, Anderson, & Ostertag, 1987; Zabrucky & Ratner, 1992; Moore, 1995). A reader who understands the structure of the text will attend to the ways in which the author develops ideas and uses the structure metacognitively. At the first level, for example, teach your students to find and use the different parts of textbooks (see Chapter 8). Make it a game by using a scavenger hunt. Ask students to tell you where they can find the meaning of abolition, on which page they can find the date and effects of the Marshall Plan, in which section they can find a map of modern India. Make sure they must use every part of the book to finish the game so that they have some experience with each section and with the kind of information it contains.

Help your students get a preview of what is contained in the materials. Rather than making connections among units of chapters, students often think of their reading assignments as being separate, unconnected collections of facts. Show them how to use a table of contents to discover the material's scope and the connections among the different parts. If they realize how the authors have organized the material, they can understand better how the various sections fit together. Smaller sections of the materials, such as textbook chapters, also have identifiable structures that can help your students read them successfully.

Teach students how to preview the material and encourage them to preview each reading assignment. Let's use a textbook chapter as a convenient example to show how this should be done, because authors and editors include features for the express purpose of helping readers understand the material included in each chapter. Most chapters have an introduction, subheadings, and a summary or conclusion. Teach your students to read these first and in that order. That will give an overview of the most important points in the chapter. If they know what the most important points are, they can spend more time on and attention to these to understand them and to see how they fit together. They should also look at graphical information and read the questions at the end of the chapter. All of these things should help readers understand what the author thinks are the most important aspects of the text. Only after reading this "skeleton" or outline of the chapter should students go back to read for detail.

This simple and quick strategy, called variously previewing, surveying, preceding, or overviewing, may well be the most important reading strategy you can teach your students for reading nonfiction: It will save them time and help them understand material better and review efficiently. When they do not preview reading assignments, they run the risk of getting bogged down in detail because they often cannot tell what is important and what is not, especially if their background for the subject is limited. Getting an overview first is a critical step in their learning to sift out the less important information and to emphasize the most important.

You should also encourage other useful applications for the process of previewing text. Previewing should be done *before* any notes are taken on text and *before* any underlining is done, because the important information must be identified first for these activities to be thoughtful, efficient, and helpful when the notes or underlining are reviewed. Similarly, this technique is a fast way to review material before a test or discussion because it allows students to get another exposure to the main ideas and to recognize quickly which ideas were not remembered or adequately understood. Previewing, then, can help guide the students' attention, help them formulate questions, and show them where more work is necessary. When students are short of time for studying, previewing is a more efficient strategy than merely reading as far as they can in the time they have, because the information they encounter will represent the most important ideas unencumbered by less important details.

Encourage your students to read their social studies textbooks in this way by showing them how much they can learn and remember from previewing. First, teach them the strategy and give them practice using it. Then give them a quiz on that information or an activity that requires they use it. If you reinforce the strategy in these ways after several previewing sessions, you will probably notice that they use the strategy more carefully, first for the purpose of doing well on the quiz or activity, but later for the amount of information they realize they can gain so easily. You can also model how it can streamline note-taking and reviewing. Your students must see how useful it is and how much time it saves before they will use the technique regularly. A teacher's commitment and enthusiasm are important for overcoming old, inappropriate reading habits.

However, many students find the strategy unnatural at first because it requires that they skip text, and they will probably resist it. The students who read very slowly and with little or no comprehension, but are also very diligent, need this strategy the most, perhaps, and they are probably the ones who will resist it the most. They frequently cling to the notion that they will not be able to understand the text unless they read every word in order, a holdover from reading fiction. For these students, you can underline what they should read during the preview and then reinforce how much information they gain from it. This will not be easy for many of your students, but the rewards will be worth your efforts.

PAIRING TEXTBOOKS WITH TRADE BOOKS

Because of the fact and sequence orientation of many social studies textbooks, many students see them as dry collections of unconnected facts, stacked like firewood. Making them see social studies as the history, culture, and concerns of real people like themselves can help them learn to see the importance of these studies. One way of doing this is to use trade books—novels, biographies, autobiographies, in fact, any book that is not a textbook—in conjunction with the textbook. A good historical novel, for example, can often give a better flavor for a period or for an issue and its effects on regular people, enticing a student to want to know even more about it. A biography, an autobiography, or a memoir can help students see in more detail the motivation of important people in our past.

Source: Joseph Farris. Used with permission.

Chosen well and used judiciously, trade books can add an element of interest that a textbook might not be able to provide. Furthermore, trade books can often provide background that will better enable readers to understand the textbooks. Sometimes it is a matter of interest, and sometimes it gives students a more familiar text style—narrative—with which they will have had more experience, which will make the materials easier for them to read.

Trade books can also be used in order to clarify concepts or a consciousness of a period. For example, having students read a book such as *Ragged Dick* (Alger, 1990) can teach them the concept of pulling oneself up by one's bootstraps, a concept that the media and political parties still refer to, especially when welfare and poverty are discussed. This concept has become a part of the American consciousness, and Alger's books illustrate it well.

Using a book such as *Number the Stars* (Lowry, 1989) can show the ethos of the Danish people as they saved virtually overnight nearly the entire Jewish population in Denmark by evacuating them in fishing boats to neutral Sweden. Or use *The Devil's Arithmetic* (Yolen, 1988) to put students inside a German concentration camp. These fictional stories that portray real events vividly show the conflicts and courage of people in those times and can draw the readers into the situations more dramatically than the brief, objective historical accounts that appear in textbooks. Memoirs, such as *Having Our Say* (Delany, Delany, & Hearth, 1993), give personal accounts of individuals living through difficult times and good times in a way that is impossible in textbooks. The textbooks, of course, have to consider space limitations, and so the human emotions are frequently minimized or omitted. In addition, the experiences and contributions of different ethnic and cultural groups in the U.S. are sometimes given little attention in textbooks. Nonfiction trade books such as *Free at Last* (Bullard, 1993), for example, give much more information about the people who were killed during the Civil Rights Movement during the 1960s than most textbooks.

Using a book such as *Maniac Magee* (Spinelli, 1991) can help students understand race relations from different perspectives and in different situations that might help them understand their neighbors and themselves better. Judicious use of television programs, such as offerings from public television stations, Arts & Entertainment, and the History Channel, can also help students view events from different perspectives. In fact, the History Channel has a website through which teachers are encouraged to print educational materials that include vocabulary, discussion questions, and research activities for their programs (http://www. historychannel.com/class). Listings of upcoming programs are given in advance to make it easy to include them in the syllabus.

You can also combine efforts with literature teachers. Find out what books your students are reading in English classes to see whether you can coordinate topics and issues. If, for example, literature classes are reading *The Scarlet Letter* (Hawthorne, 1997), use concepts or period references as points of comparison or contrast with social studies concerns.

THE IMPORTANCE OF BACKGROUND EXPERIENCE

Background experience is necessary for understanding concepts and events. It provides a point of reference and a structure for the world. In order to learn, we must link new information to information we already know (Pearson & Johnson, 1978). Try explaining what quiche is, for example, to someone who has never heard of it or seen it before. You would probably say something like, "It is like a pie, but it's made with cheese rather than fruit or custard." Or try to explain rap music to someone who has not heard it. Comparisons to chants, rhythms, tunes, even jump-rope rhymes, might be used, but these cannot fully describe this unique musical form.

These kinds of explanations, however, are very common. We do the best we can with what we already know in trying to understand new things. We have a natural tendency to compare new ideas and new things to those we already understand because making these connections leads us to an understanding of the new ideas and also helps us communicate these ideas with others. Some psychologists refer to "working memory" as the place where these connections are recognized and made (Royer, 1986). This term indicates that the process of learning through these connections is active and dynamic, a crucial link in the learning chain.

Resnick (1984) arranges background experience into three categories: topic-specific knowledge, general world knowledge, and text-organization knowledge. Good readers use all three of these to comprehend, interpret, and remember information from text. To read effectively, all three are necessary. When we read, we must constantly call on background information in order to interpret the information in the text. Background is so important to understanding that one theorist has gone so far as to call reading "only incidentally visual" (Kolers, 1969), indicating that what the reader brings to the page is more important than the text itself. Not everyone will go that far in recognizing the contributions of the reader to comprehension, but it is clear that both the text and the reader's knowledge are critical for comprehension to occur.

Schema theory is an attempt to show how background information is acquired, stored, retrieved, and altered, and how it helps us use that information to learn new things, to make sense of things already learned, and to make connections among them (Pearson & Spiro, 1980). First, let's see what is meant by *schema*. If you were asked if you were familiar with going to restaurants, you would probably say yes, but you probably would think about the experience in general, not about any particular experience in a restaurant. Your schema for restaurants is a generalized composite of all your experiences with them. From these experiences, you can probably identify the critical aspects that characterize restaurants: a customer, a server, and the exchange of money for food.

Every time you go into a restaurant, you compare the new experience with your schema, although you are probably not aware of this process unless something unexpected happens. Suppose that in your whole life you have gone only to fast food restaurants. Your schema for restaurants would have to include lines for placing your order, low prices, and the ubiquitous hamburger and fries. After this limited background, suppose you go for the first time to an expensive French restaurant. Two things would probably happen: First, you would recognize this as being "like a restaurant" but with high prices, linen tablecloths, candles, and waiters in evening clothes. In other words, you would compare this new experience with your established schema. Second, you might store this information away as a kind of subset, or subschema, for future reference. The more experiences like this new one you encounter, the more useful the subschema would seem, and the more complete your restaurant schema would become. In fact, these experiences might cause you to restructure the schema so that fast food restaurants would be reinterpreted, appearing as only one kind of restaurant in a much more complete and complicated schema that included an extensive array of restaurant types. Suppose for a moment you could actually remember your absolutely first experience in a restaurant. With nothing in your set of experiences to match this experience, you would miss several of the details and you would probably understand only pieces of it.

This same phenomenon happens to students when they read about topics with which they have little or no experience. Even if they have familiarity with the type of text organization and general world knowledge, deficiencies in topic-specific information might lead to their not understanding main ideas, missing details, and attending to superfluous information disproportionately. They will not understand as much as they would if they had a topic schema to which they could compare it.

word is presented in sentences within the chapter. Then ask your students to discuss why those words go together or ask them to analyze the sentences and try to decide what the words mean. Also teach them to be suspicious about word meanings by modeling analysis processes: "The space shuttle has 250,000 tiles on its surface. If they were as heavy as bathroom tiles, wouldn't the shuttle be too heavy to be launched? I'd better not assume they are the same kind of tiles. I'd better look for more information to clarify that point" (Schaefer, 1983).

A fairly common vocabulary activity is to ask students to use the alphabet as the framework for finding words important to a unit. In a brainstorming session in a whole class or in smaller groups, have students find words about the topic for each letter of the alphabet. Post the list so that as the unit progresses, students can add words to the list. Toward the end of the unit, have your students determine which are the most important words, the words they have seen and heard over and over again, and then make them responsible for these words. Students of all ages get involved in this activity with enthusiasm, and with the list posted, you and your students will be encouraged to use the words from the list, further reinforcing the vocabulary.

Two cautions must be considered when teaching vocabulary. First, for direct vocabulary instruction, do not overdo it: Choose only the most important terms from the lesson. If you teach 25 words from each chapter, you will have considerable trouble ever getting as far as assigning the reading. Research has shown that students will remember the words we teach them and the concepts related to them, whether the words are important to the text selection or not (Wixson, 1986). Do not spend time directly teaching vocabulary that is not necessary for the students' understanding of the most important concepts in the text. You can, however, mention a word or two you think they might not know, but don't spend a lot of time on it. Second, do not ask students to copy definitions out a dictionary or glossary. This method is not effective for teaching vocabulary words in social studies classes because copying requires no thought, no comprehension, and little attention. Students rarely reread these definitions, and knowing the definition does not mean they know the word, the concept it represents, or how to use it. Active involvement with the words as they are used in social studies materials will help students understand and remember their specialized meanings. This teaches usage and appropriate contexts for the words rather than static definitions that are without meaning for students.

MATCHING TEXT CHARACTERISTICS AND READING ABILITIES

The Text—Readability

Readability is the level of difficulty of written material, with high readability levels being more difficult than lower ones. Most formulas that measure readability do so by accounting for such things as word difficulty (often measured by word frequency or length), and sentence length. These factors are used because longer words are usually less common and less likely to be part of a student's vocabulary. Longer sentences are assumed to be more difficult, more complex, and therefore harder to read and understand.

Thinking about the difficulty levels of social studies materials is important because they are often hard to read. Difficult concepts with which the students are unfamiliar are common, and the format of materials can also make them more difficult. Furthermore, materials are often used in social studies classes that were not written especially for students, so there is little if any control over their level of difficulty or the modernity of the vocabulary.

Publishers usually apply readability formulas to school texts and report the results in teacher's manuals and promotional material. If you use materials that have not been measured for readability, and you are curious about how it is measured, you can figure a rough estimate very easily yourself. The Fry Readability Formula (Fry, 1977) is among the most commonly used because it is quick and easy. This formula uses the average number of sentences and syllables in randomly selected, 100-word passages. The results are plotted on a graph separated by grade-level scores (see Figure 6.3).

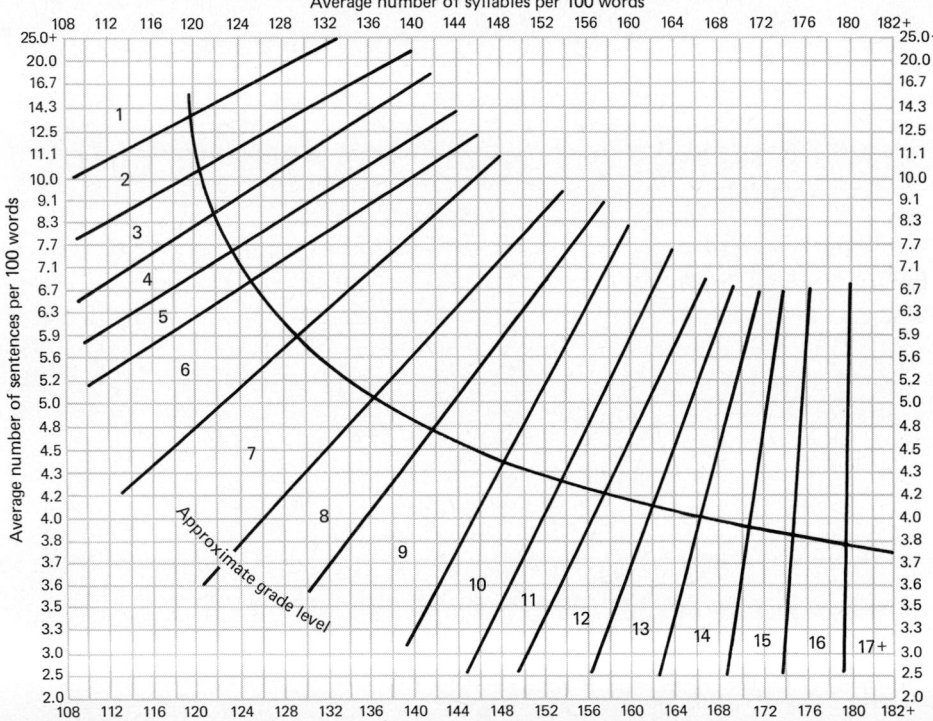

Figure 6.3
Graph for estimating readability—extended. This extended graph does not outmode the earlier (1968) version or render it inoperative or inaccurate. It is an extension.
Source: Edward Fry. Reprinted from *Journal of Reading,* December 1977. Reproduction permitted. No copyright.

Expanded Directions for Working Readability Graph

1. Randomly select three (3) sample passages and count out exactly 100 words each, beginning with the beginning of a sentence. Do count proper nouns, initializations, and numerals.
2. Count the number of sentences in the 100 words, estimating length of the fraction of the last sentence to the nearest one-tenth.
3. Count the total number of syllables in the 100-word passage. If you don't have a hand counter available, an easy way is to simply put a mark above every syllable in each word; then when you get to the end of the passage, count the number of marks and add 100. Small calculators can also be used as counters by pushing numeral 1, then pushing the + sign for each word or syllable when counting.
4. Enter onto the graph with average sentence length and average number of syllables; plot a dot where the two lines intersect. The area where dot is plotted will give you the approximate grade level.
5. If a great deal of variability is found in syllable count or sentence count, putting more samples into the average is desirable.
6. A word is defined as a group of symbols with a space on either side; thus, *Joe*, *IRA*, *1945*, and *&* are each one word.
7. A syllable is defined as a phonetic syllable. Generally, there are as many syllables as vowel sounds. For example, *stopped* is one syllable and *wanted* is two syllables. When counting syllables for numerals and initializations, count one syllable for each symbol. For example, *1945* is four syllables, *IRA* is three syllables, and *&* is one syllable (Fry, 1977).

Alternatively, you can type passages into a word processing program that measures readability by averaging the results of several readability formulas.

Extreme care must be used in interpreting readability formulas, however, because the results of these formulas are neither absolute nor precise, regardless of how precise they appear to be. They give merely a rough description of limited aspects of the text alone, with no consideration for how much the readers know about the topic, with no consideration for text clarity or cohesion, with no consideration for whether it makes any sense. Putting too much faith in the measured readability level is neither warranted nor wise, and their use has led to some rather unreasonable recommendations.

Be suspicious, for example, if you are advised to rewrite materials to lower the readability by substituting simple, common words for difficult ones and breaking long sentences into shorter ones. This advice is impractical and undesirable for several reasons. First, few teachers have enough extra time to rewrite materials. Your time is better spent preparing students to read the materials you already use and finding other suitable materials. Second, simplifying vocabulary may yield short-term results that are actually rather costly. The most difficult words in social studies materials are often technical terms necessary for discussing the topics. If students do not learn the precise words, they will no longer be able to discuss the topics with others who understand them, and they will not be adequately prepared for more advanced classes in which they are expected to know these terms and the concepts they represent. Sacrificing precision for the sake of "easy" readability is an extremely poor choice that can have dire results for your students.

Finally, sentence length is not always a measure of sentence complexity. Shortened, simplified sentences might not be able to support the complex ideas they must communicate. Research suggests that using short sentences to decrease the measured readability can actually make materials harder to understand (Pearson & Johnson, 1978). Complex relationships stated explicitly in longer sentences can become implicit when the sentence is broken into shorter ones, thus putting the burden of inference on readers who may not have enough background to make reasonable or appropriate inferences.

For example, the following sentence contains an explicitly stated cause-and-effect relationship:

I stayed home from school because I was sick.

To decrease the measured readability level of a passage, such a sentence is easily broken into two sentences:

I stayed home from school. I was sick.

To the good reader, both examples are easy to understand, and with supporting context, the meaning would probably be clear. However, the cause-and-effect relationship in the pair of shorter sentences is implicit, placing the demand for inference on the reader. Among the options for combining these sentences are the following:

I stayed home from school after I was sick.
I stayed home from school when I was sick.
I stayed home from school until I was sick.
I stayed home from school unless I was sick.

Adverbs being the most portable words in English, we have these options as well:

After I stayed home from school, I was sick.
When I stayed home from school, I was sick.
Until I stayed home from school, I was sick.
Unless I stayed home from school, I was sick.

Each of the eight variations changes the meaning of the primary ideas in some way because their relationships change. The surrounding context of such sentences would help direct us to combine the thoughts in the most appropriate way. Imagine, however, that you are reading about a topic about which you know very little. In that case, the surrounding context might not give enough information for you to be able to make a reasonable inference. Because making inferences requires a higher level of comprehension than understanding literal statements, the shorter sentences—the ones that readability formulas tell us are the easier ones—can actually be more difficult to understand.

Students face enormous difficulty when they read about social studies concepts and events for which they have little background. Without adequate schemata, students are unlikely to recognize the relationships and to make the necessary inferences required in falsely labeled "readable" texts. Furthermore, a preponderance of short, choppy sentences is esthetically undesirable, and does not give good models of prose structure and rhythm. In addition, important words that signal the author's direction of ideas are also frequently lost when sentences are shortened. Such words and phrases as *because, however, on the other hand,* and *similarly* are not simple space-fillers but contribute to the cohesion and logical organization of text. Loxterman, Beck, and McKeown (1994) rewrote social studies materials in their study, altering measured readability from 5.7 to 9.1. Students found the "more difficult" material easier to understand because the logical connections were added that made the information make sense.

Readability formulas can be useful, however, if you use them wisely and remember what they can and cannot do. They give a rough measure of superficial text difficulty independent of readers and their capabilities and backgrounds. The formulas cannot measure students' backgrounds, experiences, or cultural identification with a topic; they cannot measure the clarity and cohesion of the text; they cannot measure students' interest in or motivation for reading. These factors are critical for determining whether or not a reader can or will understand text. "Nonreaders" can surprise their teachers by fluently reading materials that interest them, while being unable to read school assignments. However, as a rough estimate, readability formulas provide a starting point. An interesting use of a readability formula is to have your students apply it to their own writing passages, most easily accomplished with a word processing program with a readability feature. This can help them become more aware of their own writing patterns and encourage them to avoid short, choppy sentences and to consider the best ways of expressing complicated ideas.

The Text—Beyond Readability

Other factors to consider when determining whether a text will be appropriate for your students are considerateness of text and text structures. For example, a text that is considerate sets up expectations on the part of the reader and also fulfills them. A *first* will always be followed by a *second;* a promise of four reasons will be found easily because the author has used appropriate signal words to let you follow the structure. Terms will be clearly used or defined; ideas that go together will be clearly seen in juxtaposition. Subheadings will give definite clues about what will be covered within the section that follows; foreign words will be clearly translated or defined. Inconsiderate text, on the other hand, does not take into account the probable knowledge base of the intended audience, leaving the readers confused or annoyed. Here is an example of inconsiderate text:

> Sir Walter Raleigh brought over a small company in 1584, and he named the land where they settled *Virginia,* in honor of the Queen, Elizabeth I (Holder, Eckerson, Schubert, & Withers, 1958, p. 5).

The intended eighth-grade audience would be unlikely to know why a place was named Virginia after someone named Elizabeth, which is never made clear in this textbook. Apparently the editors thought a discussion about the Virgin Queen inappropriate for eighth-graders, but the result is text that does not make sense.

Teaching your students to understand and use the structure of expository text is another way to help them understand text better, and text structure is another factor not measured by readability formulas. Generally speaking, expository text is organized in large sections in these basic structures: *description* (also called *enumeration* or *collection*), *sequence, compare and contrast, cause and effect,* and *problem-solution.* For example, a textbook chapter might explore the westward movement as a set of problems and solutions or as a series of cause-and-effect relationships. Within that chapter, other text structures will be used to clarify points, but students need to be aware of the overall structure first in order to follow the information and arguments presented by the author. This can actually be rather difficult, because one chapter might use each of the text structures within the body of the text.

Authors indicate which structures they use by using appropriate signal words, which readers should use to follow the arguments the author has set forth. Typical signal words for these structures follow:

Description: The text describes, defines, or explains.
Signal words: first, second, then, next, finally, furthermore, also, for example, for instance, in fact
Sequence: The text shows events in order of occurrence.
Signal words: now, then, when, before, later, first, second, finally
Comparison and Contrast: The text shows similarities and differences between items.
Signal words (compare): and, also, as well as, similar to, same as, in addition to, both
Signal words (contrast): but, yet, however, on the other hand, on the contrary, although, unless
Cause and Effect: The text shows the results of events, the causation and the result.
Signal words: because, since, thus, therefore, caused, resulted in, if . . . then, consequently, accordingly
Problem-Solution (Result): The text describes how a problem was solved, which sometimes leads to a new problem-solution relationship.
Signal words: because, since, thus, therefore, if . . . then, consequently, according, solved by, resulted in, the problem, the concern, the solution

When students understand these structures, their comprehension of and memory for the material improve. In one study with ninth-grade subjects, students taught to use four of these structures nearly doubled the amount of information they recalled, as compared to their own pretraining scores and over those of a control group (Meyer & Rice, 1984). Those students who were able to recognize and use the structures remembered more information from the passages when tested immediately and one week later, remembering more major and minor details than those students who did not. In general, when the text structure was recognized, the students used this structure as the basis for remembering the information, which served as an important memory hook for the information.

Miller and George (1992), who developed special study guides that emphasized the expository text structures, found similar results with sixth-graders. The subjects who completed these study guides not only improved in reading, but also in writing, because they tended to use the structures when they wrote. These students comprehended the text better and recalled more information than control students, and they were also able to transfer the skill to other, similar material. Armbruster, Anderson, and Ostertag (1987) found a similar result with fifth-grade students. After being trained in using a problem-solution structure, students in the experimental group wrote higher-quality essays that contained a higher proportion of important ideas than the essays written by students in the control group.

However, Garner and Gillingham (1987) found that students have limited awareness of these structures and difficulty putting their knowledge of them to use. This suggests that students receive little instruction and reinforcement in this important aspect of expository text.

Of the five structures discussed here, *comparison and contrast, cause and effect*, and *problem-solution* are the most useful, easier to understand and remember, because of the way the information is linked. Those three structures show more integrated relationships: If you can remember a solution, you perhaps have a better chance of remembering the problem, and vice versa; if you can remember the result of something, you might better recall the cause, and vice versa. We already have seen that comparing and contrasting is a fairly natural activity, which is also supported by research (Richgels, McGee, Lomax, & Sheard, 1987). Students must be taught to recognize the role of signal words in telling them how the author has organized information and presented arguments.

The Students—Reading Levels

Students in every class vary widely in their reading abilities. An individual student will vary in ability to read course materials from class to class as well. To find out how well your students are going to understand the materials in your classes, you can construct some informal silent reading tests, a variation of Informal Reading Inventories (IRIs), for quick, specific information.

To construct an IRI, choose sample passages from your textbook that you consider represent different levels of difficulty. You can judge this by how well students in the past have understood the sections, or you could combine this with using a readability formula. Try to begin with the easiest passage, with each subsequent passage being more difficult, but do not assume that earlier sections of a book are necessarily easier, especially if multiple authors are involved. Follow these guidelines:

1. Choose passages from your materials that are at least 100 words long. These passages must make sense when taken out of the context of the rest of the selection.
2. Write a brief introductory sentence or brief paragraph to give your students some background for the passage.
3. Check their comprehension by asking questions for each passage. You can ask a general question that requests a summary of the main point, or you

can ask several questions that are more specific and at different levels of comprehension. For example:

a. Write one or two literal questions that are answered explicitly in the test passage.
b. Write one or two inferential questions, requiring students to go beyond the literal information given in the passage.
c. Write one question that asks students to go beyond the inferential level to evaluate the accuracy of the passage, to project what might happen next, to determine the author's purpose, or the like.
d. Write one or two vocabulary questions that ask the students to give the meaning of a word as it is used in the passage.

When you administer the IRI, ask your students to read the passages silently in the way they would read a regular assignment. They should know why you are doing this, to help them become better readers of their social studies materials. Either give them a time limit for reading and answering the question on paper or ask them to time their reading only. Comparing their speed with their comprehension is also important to get a better picture of their reading skills.

You might want to give two different kinds of IRIs that examine very different kinds of reading tasks. On some IRIs, let students look back at the text, and on others, have them answer questions from memory. These tasks require different skills—recognition versus memory. If you decide to give an IRI, be clear about what you want to know about your students to help determine what kind of task you give them.

Results from these tasks gives you specific information about how well your students can handle the material. You are better able to determine the severity of the gap between text difficulty and the reading abilities of your students. This information will help you discover how much extra help they will need for reading and understanding their social studies materials. Traditionally, IRI results show three reading levels that describe your students' abilities:

1. If a student answers 90 percent of the questions correctly, that passage represents the level at which he or she can read *independently*.
2. If comprehension is between 70 and 89 percent, that passage represents his or her *instructional* reading level. At this level, the material is appropriate for the student with instruction from the teacher.
3. If comprehension is below 70 percent, that student has reached a level of *frustration*. Students should not be asked to read at this level.

After giving your students some instruction in reading the materials, you might try administering some of these passages again to see if there is improvement for those who had trouble with them.

Less formal procedures for assessing how well your students are handling their reading assignments are, of course, ongoing. Monitoring discussions, asking for summaries, having group presentations of dramatic reenactments, creating tableaux, radio plays, and drawing are ways to determine comprehension of materials. In addition, do not forget to ask students how well they think they understand and why they think so. Journal entries for this purpose can be very revealing.

DEVELOPING FLEXIBLE READING STRATEGIES

Many people believe that good readers are fast readers, but this definition is too narrow. The mark of a good reader is not great speed but flexibility in speed of reading and the application of appropriate strategies. Flexible readers use a variety of speeds and strategies depending on the difficulty and structure of the text, their backgrounds in the subject matter, and the purposes for reading it (Holmes & Singer, 1966). Inflexible readers muddle through everything at the same rate, regardless of what they know or why they are reading. We have already begun the discussion of reading strategies in earlier sections of this chapter: Knowing When We Know, Strategies for Reading Textbooks, and Setting Purposes for Reading.

Strategies are "conscious plans under the control of the reader" that emphasize the "reasoning process readers go through as they comprehend text" and emphasize the "adaptable nature of the comprehension process" (Pearson, Roehler, Dole, & Duffy, 1992, p. 169). A strategic reader is one who participates fully and efficiently in trying to comprehend text, making decisions about the best way to achieve comprehension in a very active way. Helping students become strategic readers of social studies textbooks and other social studies materials is done most efficiently within the social studies classroom (Simonson & Singer, 1992). Making suggestions and helping students see when certain strategies are appropriate should become part of reading assignments.

Good readers know and developing readers need to be reminded, for example, when less information is sufficient for the task at hand, when a preview is all that is required, and when to slow down and read more carefully. *Skimming* and *scanning* are strategies that give students reading flexibility. Teach your students to skim to get an overview—the first few paragraphs, the first sentence of each paragraph, and the last few paragraphs. (They should recognize that skimming is a variation of previewing.) Skimming is very rapid because much of the text is ignored. Its purpose is to gain a general understanding of the main ideas in the material but not to read for details.

Scanning is also rapid reading, but it differs rather importantly from skimming. Your students should scan material when they need to look for specific, precise information, such as a date, a number, or a name. But they should also learn to scan intelligently, by using chapter or section headings to find the most probable location of the information required. They should examine that section, looking only for the kind of information they need. If they are looking for a date, for example, they should pay attention only to numbers. As each one is found, they should examine the text around it to see if it is the right number. If not, the process continues.

Study reading is quite different from skimming and scanning, but it is the logical companion of these fast rates of reading. Once students have received prereading directions, have skimmed or previewed their reading assignment, and determined a purpose, then they must read carefully and much more slowly. This reading requires paying attention to details as they relate them to the overall information, weighing accuracy of information, making connections between new and known information, and making critical judgments. It also involves rereading, taking notes, and checking meanings of words. Study reading also requires that students understand the purpose for reading that particular assignment, what they must do with the information, and if they have understood. In short, they must understand if they have learned and what they have learned.

PLAN is a study-reading strategy that has been used successfully with readers from middle school to college (Caverly, Mandeville, & Nicholson, 1995). It uses four steps: (1) Students first *predict* content and structure of the text using the chapter title and subtitles, highlighted words, and graphics, creating a diagram of the information. (2) Next, they *locate* known and unknown information on the map, so that they are assessing their familiarity with the material before reading. (3) Next, students *add* information to their map as they read the chapter. They can also clarify, extend, or confirm information. (4) In the last step, students *note* and use the new information. Sometimes this might mean reconfiguring the original map into a different format to reflect a different text structure than the one anticipated, or to rearrange main ideas to make them appear more prominent.

Teaching a *thinking-aloud strategy* (Loxterman, Beck, & McKeown, 1994) can promote active participation and thinking while reading. Sixth-grade students taught this strategy outperformed a silent-reading group on tests of recall immediately and one week after reading the material. The effect was especially powerful when used on well-written, coherent texts. *Talk through* strategies (Simpson, 1995) teach students how to rehearse aloud the important concepts of material after reading, using their own words and organization of the material or transforming it in some way, and adding their own examples or applications to it. This helps them monitor their comprehension because without understanding the text, these tasks will not be possible, and the students will recognize their deficiencies.

Making inferences, a cornerstone of comprehension, can be taught to poor readers, traditionally thought of as lacking in this ability. Winne, Graham, and Prock (1993) found that poor readers in third, fourth, and fifth grades improved in making inferences from text when given explicit feedback that included explaining and demonstrating ways to combine text information. When the application of readability formulas to textbook material deletes the information that makes inferences easy, teaching students how to combine ideas for this purpose becomes even more critical.

Reciprocal teaching is a highly successful program, one aspect of which focuses on summarizing information by applying four strategies to text: (1) summarizing the text; (2) asking questions to get at what is important; (3) trying to clarify the most difficult parts; and (4) predicting what will come next (Palincsar & Brown, 1984). As with the thinking-aloud strategy, the effect of these strategies is to encourage the reader's active involvement with text.

Strategy instruction is important for students' academic survival, because they are responsible for reading longer and more demanding assignments as they get older. They must learn to read strategically and flexibly to complete their assignments successfully. To do that, they must learn when particular strategies are appropriate and when careful reading is necessary. You should already be helping them understand *why* they read their assignments. Also help them learn to vary their rate and approach by helping them understand *how* they should read each assignment. All assignments should include suggestions for how the material should be read, determined by the expected outcome (Bullock & Hesse, 1981). After your students become accustomed to the idea of using reading strategies, let them help determine what is appropriate. They should learn to match their purpose for reading with their backgrounds and the appropriate reading strategies so that this process can become an automatic part of reading and studying. All of this instruction should emphasize that reading is an active, thoughtful, and purposeful process.

CRITICAL READING

The ability to read critically is essential for making decisions, for solving problems, and for effective citizen participation. Because critical reading is a higher-level comprehension skill, it requires an understanding of literal information and the ability to make reasonable inferences. Critical readers must be able to make judgments about accuracy, to understand the author's purposes, and to evaluate text. They must also be able to decide if the material they read fulfills their purposes for reading. Becoming a critical reader is difficult because students must learn to trust their own judgments without being swayed by the power of the printed word. To do that, they must realize that politicians, advertisers, and members of special interest groups often use personality and skills of persuasion to sway people to their points of view.

Skills that are commonly taught in reading classes have a direct application for helping students become critical readers of social studies materials. Sequence, for example, is an important concept in social studies materials as well as in reading textbooks. Recognizing the sequence of events that led to the dropping of the atomic bombs on Hiroshima and Nagasaki, or the sequence of events that led to President Richard M. Nixon's resignation from office, helps students understand these events. Linking the decisions in the sequence of events with their consequences also helps students recognize cause-and-effect relationships.

Other skills traditionally found in reading classes—distinguishing between statements of fact and statements of opinion, drawing conclusions, and predicting outcomes—are essential for students to become critical readers. They must learn these skills, however, by examining issues systematically. You can use the inquiry method to provide a framework for your students' reading.

The inquiry method involves gathering, categorizing, and evaluating information. For example, if your students are examining the issues surrounding the nuclear arms race, they must be clear about alternatives, points of view, and potential consequences. Because students must gather facts, they must learn to distinguish facts from opinions, as well as understand how different interpretations of the same set of facts can lead to different conclusions, attitudes, and actions. They must learn to evaluate the source of the information—a news article, an editorial, a promotional piece, a tabloid story. They must learn to consider why the material was written and for whom it was intended—the author's motives or purposes for writing. They must determine who wrote the material and what the author's qualifications are. These are all important aspects of critical reading.

TABLE 6.1. *Summary of Chart on Slavery*

Source	Author's Purpose	Intended Audience	Details	Conclusions
Editorial	Persuade	Contemporary readership (1864)		
News article	Inform-persuade	Contemporary readership (1864)		
Textbook	Inform	Modern (1984)		

You can encourage critical reading in prereading exercises by helping students establish criteria for comparing and evaluating information. You can encourage it in post-reading exercises by asking good questions at several levels of comprehension. Good questioning can lead your students from literal understanding to inference, to evaluation, and to critical analysis. You can also use charts to summarize information so that it can be weighed and evaluated (see Table 6.1). This evaluation leads to drawing conclusions on which decisions for action can be based, and predicting the outcomes of the decisions that are made. When students systematically examine different points of view, they can make decisions and understand the complexities of social issues. They can also learn to understand their own values through this process. Make the issues immediate and help your students feel involved by asking them to take a stand and by helping them realize when they need more information to do so. (See the Inquiry Strategy on page 188.)

Your students must become involved in the issues and understand why they are important. Even more essential, however, is that they understand why their involvement is important. They must learn that they can help shape events when they are informed and prepared to make decisions. To do this, students must recognize the relationship between social studies concepts and the world (Gaskins, 1981). When students learn to evaluate what they read and to make thoughtful decisions, they will have become critical readers, well prepared to accept their responsibilities as citizens of the U.S. and the world.

Teaching Students About Questions

Students are asked myriad questions during the course of a school year, yet some never seem to understand how to go about the task of answering them. Some exciting research has emerged that suggests that students can be taught an effective metacognitive approach to the task of answering questions.

Much has been written about the need for teachers to ask questions at different levels of comprehension (see Chapter 4), as well as creating clusters of questions that represent a line of questioning (Pearson, 1985). A further step has been taken in teaching students what tasks the different kinds of questions represent. Using these question-answer relationships (QARs), the readers who can identify the

inquiry strategy

READING CRITICALLY

DIRECTIONS

Have your students read materials from sweepstakes offers, time-share introductory offers, pyramid schemes, and the like. When they are finished, break them into groups of four or five students to answer the questions that follow. When they have completed the questions, the whole class should come together to discuss their results. (Note: This lesson is designed to accompany the many materials that most people receive in the mail stating that they "may have already won" a sum of money or one of the fabulous prizes in Column A, or that they can make $250,000 merely by selling reports to other people through the mail. Look to your junk mail for ideas.)

THE PROBLEM

Your family has been inundated with get-rich-quick opportunities in the mail and on the telephone. Examine each situation and decide which are responsible enough to warrant participation.

QUESTIONS

1. What language (specific words and phrases) do the materials use to encourage you to participate?
2. How do they make you feel that you are only one step away from being wealthy?
3. What are your chances of winning or earning money from any of these? How can you tell? Find specific words and phrases that are clues.
4. Is it usually possible to get something for nothing? Find examples. How frequently does this happen?
5. What are the consequences of participating in each of the schemes? For example, what will it cost you in time and money, and what are the chances of reward?
6. What will you advise your friends who are tempted to participate in one of the more expensive ventures?

kinds of questions asked have a better chance of actually being able to answer them because they understand where to go to find the information.

In one study students were taught to identify literal, inferential, and beyond-inferential questions (Raphael & Wonnacott, 1985). The researchers used this terminology in teaching the students:

> *Right-there questions* (because readers can find the answers *right there* in the text).
> *Think-and-search questions* (for which readers have to put together information from different places in the text in order to draw an inference).

On-my-own questions (which require students to use background knowledge and the text in order to answer the questions. For example, a question in this category for "Goldilocks and the Three Bears" is "Should Goldilocks have to pay for the property she ruined?"). This type of question requires that students understand the text, but their answers must also be based on outside experiences. (Sometimes this category is subdivided into *Author and me* and *On my own,* which differ in how closely one must rely on the text.)

In the study by Raphael and Wonnacott (1985), above-average, average, and below-average readers were trained by their teachers to identify the kinds of questions being asked before answering them. The above-average readers in the study did not make significant gains as a result of the training (probably because they already possessed the skills). However, the average and below-average readers were greatly helped by this strategy, which gave them more control over the task. In some instances, the poorest readers who received the training did as well as the good readers in the control group, who had not received the strategy training.

This study indicates that a metacognitive approach—What is my task? What do I need to do in order to fulfill it?—is of great value to learners and can be taught effectively to the students who need it most. It reveals to the students who need the help the secrets of how fluent and able readers approach tasks. The encouraging results of this study indicate that teaching students new strategies for monitoring their learning processes will increase their reading skills. We need to emphasize high-level reading tasks among students to prepare them to be responsible and active citizens.

SUMMARY

Concern about reading is certainly not new. In the 18th century, Samuel Johnson stated that "People in general do not willingly read, if they can have anything else to amuse them" (Boswell, 1964). Those students who avoid reading today may do so because they have not learned to actively compare new information with existing schemata, have not learned to monitor and evaluate their own learning processes metacognitively, and have not learned the joy that can come from successful and satisfying reading. The inability to fulfill reading tasks successfully can lead to an unwillingness to try.

Because social studies materials are often difficult to read, helping students develop the skills necessary to understand them must be an important part of social studies instruction. Developing background information, introducing important vocabulary, teaching the structures of the materials, and encouraging flexible reading are all important for helping students read social studies materials more successfully. Students must develop an awareness of their purposes for reading and of any appropriate background information needed to read each assignment successfully. Students must also become critical readers who are able and willing to evaluate what they read so they can make good decisions and assume the rightful role of reflective citizen actors.

 *internet links*

TEACHING READING

The Kids Only Browser (in AOL) has several classroom categories, which include math, science, and social studies.

Yahooligans has a "Homework Answers" section, and has links to Cognito! Student Research (www.cognito.com).

The History Channel (www.historychannel.com/class) offers vocabulary, discussion questions, and research activities to accompany their programming. These education materials can be reviewed and printed.

PBS offers information about the American presidents at www.pbs.org.

Through America Online (AOL), it is possible to select under the Learning and Culture category "History":

Civil War Forum

Congressional Quarterly

History Channel

Holocaust Information

Military History Forum

Revolutionary War Forum

Time Life Photo Perspectives

Castles of Wales

Genealogy Forum

REFLECTION AND ACTION ACTIVITIES

1. For one chapter in a social studies textbook, prepare materials to help students understand the text more easily by building their schemata: for example, structured overviews, guiding questions or directions, videotapes, field trips.
2. Identify the vocabulary words from one textbook chapter that should be taught before your students read the material and decide the best way to present them. Look for items in these categories:
   a. Technical terms
   b. Acronyms and initials
   c. Figurative language
   d. Common words with specialized meanings
3. Prepare a scavenger hunt worksheet that will introduce your students to every part of their textbook.
4. Prepare a lesson plan to show your students how to read social studies materials. It should include previewing, skimming, scanning, and study reading. It should also call attention to the structures of the material.

5. Do each of the following:
   a. Prepare a lesson plan that compares an editorial, a news story, and a political cartoon on the same topic. How do they differ in language, point of view, vocabulary, purpose?
   b. Prepare a lesson plan using these materials to help your students understand the concepts.
   c. Explain why critical reading is important. What can happen to students if they do not become critical readers?
6. Do each of the following:
   a. Evaluate your text for text structures. Choose one chapter and decide what the overall structure is intended to be.
   b. Find examples of other text structures used to explain information in the same chapter. What signal words are used to show the direction of the author's ideas?
   c. Evaluate the same chapter for logical connections, clear writing, and considerateness.
7. Prepare a set of three Informal Reading Inventory (IRI) passages and questions. Choose passages that differ in difficulty.
8. Demonstrate your understanding of the following terms by writing or stating brief definitions for each of them. Also tell why each is significant.

   a. schema theory
   b. text structures
   c. metacognition
   d. critical reading
   e. question-answer relationships (QARs)
   f. purpose for reading
   g. guiding questions
   h. previewing
   i. flexible reading

REFERENCES

Alger, H. (1990). *Ragged Dick*. New York: NAL/Dutton. (Originally published in 1867.)

Anderson, R. C., & Freebody, F. (1981). Vocabulary knowledge. In J. T. Guthrie (Ed.), *Comprehension and teaching: Research reviews* (pp. 77–117). Newark, DE: International Reading Association.

Andre, M. E., & Anderson, T. H. (1979). The development and evaluation of a self-questioning study technique. *Reading Research Quarterly, 14,* 605–623.

Armbruster, B. B., Anderson, T. H., & Ostertag, J. (1987). Does text structure/summarization instruction facilitate learning from expository text? *Reading Research Quarterly, 22,* 331–346.

Baker, L. (1979). *Comprehension monitoring: Identifying and coping with text conclusions.* Technical Report No. 145. Urbana IL: University of Illinois, Center for the Study of Reading.

Baker, L., & Brown, A. L. (1984). Metacognitive skills and reading. In P. D. Pearson (Ed.), *Handbook of reading research* (pp. 353–394). White Plains, NY: Longman.

Banks, J. A., with Sebesta, S. L. (1982). *We Americans: Our history and people, Vol. 2.* Boston: Allyn and Bacon.

Berryhill, P. (1984). Reading in the content area of social studies. In M. Dupuis (Ed.), *Reading in the content areas: Research for teachers* (pp. 66–81). Newark, DE: International Reading Association.

Blanton, W. E., Wood, K. D., & Moorman, G. B. (1990). The role of purpose in reading instruction. *The Reading Teacher, 43*, 486–493.

Boswell, J. (1964). *Life of Samuel Johnson.* New York: McGraw-Hill. (Originally published 1791.)

Bransford, J. D., & Johnson, R. (1972). Conceptual prerequisites for understanding: Some investigations of comprehension and recall. *Journal of Verbal Learning and Verbal Behavior, 11*, 717–726.

Brown, A. L. (1978). Knowing when, where and how to remember: A problem of metacognition. In R. Glaser (Ed.), *Advances in instructional psychology* (Vol. 1, pp. 77–165). Hillsdale, NJ: Erlbaum.

Brown, A. L., Armbruster, B. B., & Baker, L. (1986). The role of metacognition in reading and studying. In J. Orasanu (Ed.), *Reading comprehension: From research to practice* (pp. 49–75). Hillsdale, NJ: Erlbaum.

Bullock, T. L., & Hesse, K. D. (1981). *Reading in the social studies classroom.* Washington, DC: National Education Association.

Bullard, S. (1993). *Free at last.* New York: Oxford University Press.

Caverly, D. C., Mandeville, T. F., & Nicholson, S. A. (1995). PLAN: A study-reading strategy for informational text. *Journal of Adolescent and Adult Literacy, 39*, 190–199.

Chambliss, M. J. (1995). Text cues and strategies successful readers use to construct the gist of lengthy written arguments. *Reading Research Quarterly, 30*, 778–807.

Delany, S., & Delany, A. E., with Hearth, A. H. (1993). *Having our say: The Delany sisters' first 100 years.* New York: Kodansha International.

DiVesta, F. J., Hayward, K. G., & Orlando, V. P. (1979). Developmental trends in monitoring text for comprehension. *Child Development, 50*, 97–195.

Dole, J. A., Brown, K. J., & Trathen, W. (1996). The effects of strategy instruction on the comprehension performance of at-risk students. *Reading Research Quarterly, 31*, 62–88.

Fitzgerald, J. (1983). Helping readers gain self-control over reading comprehension. *The Reading Teacher, 37*, 249–253.

Fry, E. (1977). Fry's readability graph: Clarifications, validity, and extension to level 17. *Journal of Reading, 21*, 242–252.

Gambrell, L. B., & Heathington, B. S. (1981). Adult disabled readers' metacognitive awareness about reading tasks and strategies. *Journal of Reading Behavior, 13*, 215–222.

Garner, R. (1992). Metacognition and self-monitoring strategies. In S. J. Samuels & A. E. Farstrup (Eds.), *What research has to say about reading instruction* (pp. 236–252). Newark, DE: International Reading Association.

Garner, R., & Gillingham, M. G. (1987). Students' knowledge of text structure. *Journal of Reading Behavior, 19*, 247–259.

Gaskins, I. W. (1981). Reading for learning: Going beyond basals in the elementary grades. *The Reading Teacher, 35*, 323–328.

Gould, S. J. (1989). *Wonderful life: The Burgess Shale and the nature of history.* New York: W. W. Norton.

Guthrie, J. T. (1982). Metacognition: Up from flexibility. *The Reading Teacher, 35*, 510–512.

Hawthorne, N. (1997). *The scarlet letter.* Austin, TX: Holt, Rinehart & Winston, Inc. (Originally published in 1850.)

The History Channel in the Classroom. http://www.historychannel.com/class.

Holder, G., Eckerson, O., Schubert, E. H., & Withers, R. (1958). *Journeys in American literature.* New York: Globe.

Holmes, J., & Singer, H. (1966). Speed and power of reading in high school. *Cooperative Research Monograph No. 14,* Superintendent of Documents Catalog No. FS 5.230:30016. Washington, DC: U.S. Government Printing Office.

Holt, J. (1964). *How children fail.* New York: Dell.

Kolers, P. A. 1969). Reading is only incidentally visual. *Psycholinguistics and the teaching of reading.* Newark, DE: International Reading Association.

Lowry, L. (1989). *Number the stars.* New York: Houghton Mifflin.

Loxterman, J. A., Beck, I. L., & McKeown, M. G. (1994). The effects of thinking aloud during reading on students' comprehension of more or less coherent text. *Reading Research Quarterly, 29,* 352–367.

Mangano, N. G., Palmer, D., & Goetz, E. T. (1982). Improving reading comprehension through metacognitive training. *Reading Psychology, 3,* 365–374.

Mason, J. E., Knisely, E., & Kendall, J. (1979). Effects of polysemous words on sentence comprehension. *Reading Research Quarterly, 15,* 10–56.

Meyer, B. J. F., Brandt, D. M., & Bluth, G. J. (1980). Use of top-level structure in text: Key for reading comprehension of ninth-grade students. *Reading Research Quarterly, 16,* 72–103.

Meyer, B. J. F., & Rice, G. E. (1984). The structure of text. In P. D. Pearson, R. Barr, M. Kamill, & P. Mosenthal (Eds.), *Handbook of reading research* (Vol. 1, pp. 319–352). New York: Longman.

Miller, K. L., & George, J. E. (1992). Expository passage organizers: Models for reading and writing. *Journal of Reading, 35,* 372–377.

Moore, S. R. (1995). Focus on research: Questions for research into reading-writing relationships and text structure. *Language Arts, 72,* 598–606.

Palincsar, A. S., & Brown, A. L. (1984). Reciprocal teaching of comprehension-fostering and comprehension-monitoring activities. *Cognition and Instruction, 1,* 117–175.

Parker, W. C. (1988). Personal communication.

Pearson, P. D. (1985). Changing the face of reading comprehension instruction. *The Reading Teacher,* 724–738.

Pearson, P. D., & Johnson, D. D. (1978). *Teaching reading comprehension.* New York: Holt, Rinehart and Winston.

Pearson, P. D., & Spiro, R. J. (1980). Toward a theory of reading comprehension instruction. *Topics in Language Disorders, 1,* 71–88.

Pearson, P. D., Roehler, L. R., Dole, J. A., & Duffy, G. G. (1992). Developing expertise in reading comprehension. In S. J. Samuels & A. E. Farstrup (Eds.), *What research has to say about reading instruction* (pp. 145–199). Newark, DE: International Reading Association.

Raphael, T. E., & Wonnacott, C. A. (1985). Heightening fourth-grade students' sensitivity to sources of information for answering comprehension questions. *Reading Research Quarterly, 20*, 282–296.

Resnick, L. B. (1984). Comprehending and learning: Implications for a cognitive theory of instruction. In H. Mandl, N. L. Stein, & T. Trabasso (Eds.), *Learning and comprehension of text* (pp. 431–443). Hillsdale, NH: Erlbaum.

Richgels, D. J., McGee, L. M., Lomax, R. G., & Sheard, C. (1987). Awareness of four text structures: Effects on recall of expository text. *Reading Research Quarterly, 22*, 177–196.

Rickards, J. P. (1976). Processing effects of advance organizers interspersed in text. *Reading Research Quarterly, 11*, 599–622.

Royer, J. M. (1986). Designing instruction to produce understanding: An approach based on cognitive theory. In G. D. Phye & T. Andre (Eds.), *Cognitive classroom learning* (pp. 83–113). New York: Harcourt Brace Jovanovich.

Schaefer, C. C. (1983). *The effects of metacognitive processing on immediate and delayed memory of extended discourse.* Unpublished doctoral dissertation, Seattle: University of Washington.

Simonsen, S., & Singer, H. (1992). Improving reading instruction in the content areas. In S. J. Samuels & A. E. Farstrup (Eds.), *What research has to say about reading instruction* (pp. 200–219). Newark, DE: International Reading Association.

Simpson, M. L. (1995). Talk throughs: A strategy for encouraging active learning across the content areas. *Journal of Reading, 38*, 296–304.

Spinelli, J. (1991). *Maniac McGee.* New York: HarperCollins.

Taylor, B. M., & Beach, R. W. (1984). The effects of text structure on middle-grade students' comprehension and production of expository text. *Reading Research Quarterly, 19*, 134–146.

Wagoner, S. A. (1983). Comprehension monitoring: What it is and what we know about it. *Reading Research Quarterly, 18*, 328–346.

Winne, P. H., Graham, L., & Prock, L. (1993). A model of poor readers' text-based inferencing: Effects of explanatory feedback. *Reading Research Quarterly, 28,* 52–66.

Wixson, K. K. (1986). Vocabulary instruction and children's comprehension of basal stories. *Reading Research Quarterly, 21*, 317–328.

Yolen, J. (1988). *The devil's arithmetic.* New York: Puffin Books.

Zabrucky, K., & Ratner, H. H. (1992). Effects of passage type on comprehension monitoring and recall in good and poor readers. *Journal of Reading Behavior, 24*, 373–391.

FOR FURTHER READING

Cioffi, G. (1992). Perspective and experience: Developing critical reading abilities. *Journal of Reading, 36*, 48–52.

Cooter, R. B., Jr., & Chilcoate, G. W. (1990). Content-focused melodrama: Dramatic renderings of historical text. *Journal of Reading, 34*, 274–277.

Edwards, P. R. (1992). Using dialectical journals to teach thinking skills. *Journal of Reading, 35*, 312–316

Gillespie, C. (1990). Questions about student-generated questions. *Journal of Reading, 34,* 250–257.

Grant, R. (1993). Strategic training for using text headings to improve students' processing of content. *Journal of Reading, 36,* 482–488.

Ryder, R. J. (1991). The directed questioning activity for subject matter text. *Journal of Reading, 34,* 606–612.

To-Dutka, J. (1991). Developing self-monitored comprehension strategies through argument structure analysis. *Journal of Reading, 35,* 200–205.

CHAPTER 7

Teaching Social Issues and Human Rights

SOCIAL ISSUES AND CITIZEN ACTION

Social issues are society's unresolved problems that deeply concern many citizens. Citizens usually have strong value commitments related to these problems and frequently disagree about both their causes and ways to solve them. Social issues can be adequately understood only when studied from an interdisciplinary perspective. Scientific data are necessary but not sufficient for resolving social issues. Social issues have value dimensions and are deeply rooted in emotional attachments. They provide an excellent means for teaching decision-making skills and for providing opportunities for citizen action.

Social issues can be one of the most interesting and important components of the social studies curriculum. They add vitality to the curriculum and help make it significant to both students and teachers. The study of social issues gives students an opportunity to get a better understanding of the dynamic and changing nature of our society, their responsibilities as citizens in a democracy, and the importance of concepts such as equality and human dignity in maintaining a democracy.

Even though social issues are an important and necessary component of the social studies curriculum, there is evidence that many schools are bypassing their responsibility to help students learn how to examine them. Teachers are reluctant to teach social issues for many reasons. These include fear of pressure groups, lack of knowledge about how to teach social issues, and a desire to keep society's serious problems hidden from students.

Highly organized pressure groups are active in some communities. Such groups often try to keep topics they consider inappropriate out of the classroom. Fear of controversy, however, should not prevent teachers from helping students deal reflectively with social issues. You should review your school district's policy on teaching about controversy before teaching social issues. If a school district does not have a policy on teaching controversial issues, you should inform the parents and the principal about the issues you plan to teach well in advance. This is not intended to suggest that teachers should acquiesce. However, if parents and administrators are fully informed in advance, any resulting criticism can be properly channeled toward a full and free discussion of the right to raise such issues in the classroom, rather than centered on the personality of a particular teacher. Review the procedures listed in table 7.1 and decide how you would handle complaints.

Some teachers are reluctant to teach social issues because they feel uneasy when teaching about controversy. Their uncertainty, to some extent, reflects the value conflicts in our society. Some educators advocate indoctrination while others advocate the uncritical transmission of our cultural heritage as the best way to develop loyal and intelligent citizens. Though widely used, both of these approaches are inappropriate.

When studying social issues, students should be encouraged to examine original sources and to reach their own conclusions. Indoctrinating teachers lack a deep faith in democracy, for individuals who strongly endorse democratic ideals believe that democracy will sustain the most intense scrutiny. If students arrive at their own

TABLE 7.1. *Procedures for Responding to Complaints*

If a complaint is made, consider using the following procedure:

1. Inform the complainant about her or his rights and the school district's procedure for expressing concerns about curriculum and texts.

    If the district does not have a policy, a review committee should be formed to develop one. The committee, which should represent the school community and include parents, teachers, administrators and students, should:

    - read, view, or listen to contested material
    - check general acceptance of the material by consulting with experts
    - determine the extent to which the material is age appropriate and fits curriculum goals
    - file a written report

2. Ask the complainant to submit a written statement describing her or his concern and identifying her or his desired outcome.

3. Inform the principal or other appropriate administrator about the complaint.

4. Continue teaching about the issue during the review process.

5. The principal or other administrator should inform the complainant of the decision.

---

conclusions, their convictions will be strong and rooted in reason, not merely emotional. Emotion easily gives way to persuasion. Sound, reflective convictions will sustain the most intense challenge.

Some teachers are reluctant to teach social issues because they believe students should be shielded from society's serious problems. Whether in school or out, students eventually learn about the deep value conflicts in U.S. society. They are often star witnesses in the social conflicts of our times. Television programs, the daily newspaper, and lunchroom conversation often reflect current conflicts. Students will, perhaps more in the future than at any time in the past, be required to confront and find ways of dealing with vexing social problems. You should help students to reflectively examine these problems. Unless students are aware of the problems in our society, have accurate information about them, and begin thinking about effective ways to help solve them, they cannot help close the gap between our ideals and actual behavior or become reflective citizen actors.

"I'm going to watch the news. Do you know where my rose-colored glasses are?"
Source: Joseph Farris. Used with permission.

HUMAN RIGHTS: A FRAMEWORK FOR TEACHING SOCIAL ISSUES

Human rights is a unifying theme that connects the social issues discussed in this chapter. Human rights, by definition, is a global issue. Human beings everywhere in the world want to live in dignity. The quest by groups such as women, groups of color, and people with disabilities to secure equality in the United States and other parts of the world are all human rights movements.

Studying about the quest for human rights in the United States as well as throughout the world will help students to understand that the United States is neither the only nation whose documents promise its citizens basic human rights nor the only one with a wide discrepancy between its democratic ideals and its historical and current realities. The Magna Carta (1215), the British Bill of Rights (1689), and the writings of John Locke (1632–1704), the English philosopher renowned for his writings on freedom, are historical precedents to the major documents establishing equality and human rights in the United States in the late 1700s. Viewing the struggle for human rights within a global context enables students to better understand how the U.S. Declaration of Independence (1776), the Constitution (1788), and the Bill of Rights (1791) are related to earlier efforts to establish human rights in the United Kingdom and other Western European nations. Without viewing problems such as racism, sexism, handicappism, and militarism from a global perspective, students, especially those in the early and middle grades, are likely to conclude that these problems are uniquely U.S. ones.

The global approach to the study of the social issues described in this chapter will help students not only to understand that these problems are global in scope, but also to see that they are unlikely to be solved without international cooperation among nations throughout the world. The right to work is an example of such an issue. It is one of the basic human rights stated in the Universal Declaration of Human Rights, adopted by the United Nations General Assembly on December 10, 1948. The right to work, however, does not exist in a vacuum. It intersects with other issues. For example, ethnic problems and tensions are increased in the United States when immigrants from Mexico enter the United States illegally because they are unable to find jobs in their native land. In 1994 anti-immigrant feelings resulted in California residents approving Proposition 187, also known as the Save Our State proposition, which denied schooling and other benefits to children of illegal immigrants. Ultimately, the ban on schooling was declared unconstitutional.

The final topic discussed in this chapter, law-related issues, is a key and integral component of the quest for human rights because most of the documents and legislation establishing and guaranteeing individuals human rights have been created by national governments or by international bodies with the power to make national or international laws. Although national governments usually have the power to enforce the laws they make, bodies that establish international laws, such as the United Nations International Court of Justice, usually have little enforcement power.

U.S. President Jimmy Carter and Egyptian President Anwar Sadat shake hands at the conclusion of discussions initiated by President Carter that led to a formal peace treaty between Egypt and Israel.
Source: Library of Congress, Washington, D.C.

HUMAN RIGHTS IN A GLOBAL WORLD SOCIETY

Human rights are rights that every man, woman, and child have—by birthright—to live a dignified life that is free of poverty, illiteracy, and cultural and political repression (Banks, 1982). Without protection of these basic human rights, people become dehumanized to the extent that they lose opportunities to live dignified lives. One of the most important characteristics that distinguish humans from other beings on earth is their ability to create cultures that regard human life as sacred and that promote human dignity and creativity.

Today our world is one of paradox. While we are experiencing tremendous technological growth, there are ominous threats to human rights and human welfare. Poverty, hunger, limited wars, authoritarian governments, racism, sexism, illiteracy, and international terrorism also present serious threats to human rights. The problems posed by such threats are intractable and overwhelming. Yet, as teachers and human beings, we have an inescapable responsibility to do what we can to help solve them and to improve the human condition.

It is far easier to affirm our commitment to improve human rights in the world than to take actions that will achieve this goal. It is very difficult to enforce international human rights pronouncements and laws. Some very significant documents, such as the Universal Declaration of Human Rights (1948), the Declaration on the

Right to Development (1986), the Declaration on the Protection of All Persons from Enforced Disappearance (1992), and the International Covenant on Civil and Political Rights (1966), are designed to protect human rights throughout the world. Yet how do nations committed to the protection of these rights bring sanctions successfully against nations that violate them? Often, citizens and groups within nations focus on their unique concerns and show little interest in the rights of other citizens within their own or other nations.

A major challenge that we face in international human rights is how to create an international constituency that is not only committed to the protection of human rights throughout the world, but that also can effectively mobilize to bring decisive sanctions against nations that consistently violate those rights. Strong commitments to community and nation-state, along with a tendency to focus on their unique concerns and issues, often prevent citizens and groups from taking actions related to global issues and concerns.

It is essential for a nation's citizens to experience equity and human rights before they can realistically be expected to participate in actions to protect the human rights of other people within or outside their national borders. Citizens who are struggling to survive, who are illiterate, who feel that they have few basic rights, or who are structurally excluded from their own political system are likely to show little interest in the human rights of other groups. Consequently, the most important contribution that teachers can make to promoting international human rights is to help create conditions in social and political institutions that promote equity and human rights and that help students to see how their own human rights are inextricably bound to the human rights of other peoples throughout the world.

Violations of human rights in one nation usually have important consequences in others. When Haitian and Cuban refugees fled from their nations to the United States, they had a significant influence on the Miami area. Ethnic conflict in Miami increased. Immigrants from nations such as China, the Philippines, and Mexico also affect jobs and educational opportunities for the Chinese, Filipinos, and Mexicans already living in the United States. Yet citizens who are preoccupied with protecting and attaining their own basic rights often do not see the interrelationship between their rights and those of other world citizens.

As the difficulties involved in enforcing international human rights make clear, we can protect human rights in the international community only when a critical mass of citizens throughout the world is committed to their protection and when these citizens are able to mobilize for effective social and political action.

To help future citizens develop a commitment to international human rights, we must create situations in their communities, schools, and nations in which they are treated with dignity and equity. You can best contribute to the promotion of international human rights by creating a classroom and school environment that respects the human rights of students. The school, wrote John Dewey (1912), should be a model democracy. Human rights should be promoted, exemplified, and protected in the classroom and school. Within this kind of atmosphere, the teaching of concepts related to international human rights will make sense to students because their experiences will be consistent with what they are being taught. Attempts to teach and promote human rights in an authoritarian atmosphere will be rightfully dismissed by students as empty rhetoric and hypocrisy.

STRATEGIES FOR TEACHING SOCIAL ISSUES AND HUMAN RIGHTS

The social issues component of the social studies—taught within the framework of international human rights—should be consistent with and help to extend the goals of the social studies stated in Chapter 1: to help students develop decision-making skills and the ability to influence public policy by participating in effective citizen action. To make effective decisions related to issues such as sexism, racism, and handicappism, students must master knowledge in the various social science disciplines related to these issues.

When the students have sufficient historical and sociological knowledge about an issue, such as the development and dropping of the atomic bomb on Hiroshima on August 6, 1945, they can then begin to clarify their values regarding the issue, to discuss whether they think President Truman's decision to drop the bomb was justified, and what actions they think we should take regarding the control of nuclear energy and nuclear weapons today. It is important for students to understand the historical context in which a decision was made in order for them to discuss the decision reflectively. When they consider President Truman's decision to authorize dropping the atomic bomb on Hiroshima in 1945, they should know that the United States believed that Germany was developing an atomic bomb, that many American soldiers were being killed daily in Asia, and that Japan's government was controlled by military leaders. They should also be knowledgeable about the catastrophic consequences of dropping the atomic bomb (Takaki, 1995). Knowledge is an important requisite for reflective decision-making and value inquiry.

AN EXPANDING CONCEPT OF HUMAN RIGHTS IN THE SOCIAL STUDIES CURRICULUM

The study of social issues in the social studies should not be isolated but should be a continuing and integral part of daily lessons and units. While you may want to teach one or more units a year that focus on human rights issues, every unit you teach during the year has content that will enable you to deal with issues related to social issues and human rights. Social and human rights issues can be related to the content as well as to the developmental levels of the students. Students in the primary grades are concerned about fairness in their families, in the classroom, and on the playground. You can use incidents that actually happen in the classroom and on the playground, as well as case studies, to enable students in the primary grades to think about and to make decisions related to human rights issues.

The social world of young children, however, is not confined to their own families, schools, and communities. Television, books, and travel enable most primary-grade students to greatly expand their social world. You can use books, videotapes, and photographs about families in other cultures and times (both within and outside the United States) to enable students in the primary grades to learn about human rights issues and problems that children their age experienced in the past or still experience today. You can also use books written about children and families in other nations to acquaint primary-grade students with how human rights issues, as experienced by families in other parts of the world, are alike and different from those in the United States. An excellent source for books about children in the United States and in other lands is *The New Press Guide to Multicultural Resources for Young Readers,* edited by Daphne Muse (1997). The global dimension of human rights and social issues teaching should be an integral component of all lessons and units.

As students progress through the grades, they can deal effectively with increasingly complex content, case studies, and decision-problems related to human rights. Students often study the history of their state in the fourth grade. As they do, students can examine issues and problems related to the status of women, ethnic groups, and people with disabilities. They can determine the laws that exist in their state to protect the rights of these groups, the extent to which they are enforced, and the unresolved human rights issues related to these groups in their state. Native American fishing and treaty rights, as well as affirmative action for women and people of color, are examples of issues that are still controversial and unresolved in many states.

The study of U.S. history in the fifth and eighth grades will give the class an opportunity to examine the development of the major documents (such as the Constitution and the Bill of Rights) that established human rights and equity in the United States, the limited groups to which human rights applied when these documents were first formulated, and the ways in which human rights have been expanded through the centuries to include more groups. For example, it is important to help students understand the meaning of the phrase "All men are created equal." When written in the Declaration of Independence in 1776, this phrase referred to White males with property (Franklin & McNeil, 1995). However, the strength of documents such as the Declaration of Independence and the Constitution is that the ideas within them were able to be interpreted to include more and more groups through the years. The story of the expansion of equality and human rights in the United States, and the active role that groups such as women and people of color played in the expansion, is an important story that students should learn (Banks, 1997a). They should also be helped to understand that full justice in the United States, as well as in other nations, is still an ideal and not a reality. Table 7.2 lists some landmark events in the development of human rights. These events should be incorporated into a study of human rights in the United States and in the world.

Students can add events to this timeline throughout the year as they study various human rights issues. The study of nations in various parts of the world in the upper grades gives students many opportunities to examine human rights issues and problems in a global context. You can focus on the major issues and problems related to human rights and social issues that are still unresolved, such as the conflict between Israelis and Arabs in the Middle East and political repression in various parts of the world. Important violations of human rights in the past, such as slavery in the United States and the Holocaust in Europe during World War II, should also be studied. The important documents developed by the United Nations to protect human rights throughout the world, formulated since World War II, should also be examined, such as the Universal Declaration of Human Rights (1948) and the Declaration of the Rights of the Child (1959). Case studies, such as those in the Inquiry Strategy on pages 205–206, can be used to integrate a study of social issues and human rights into the social studies curriculum.

TABLE 7.2. *Human Rights Timeline*

1215	The Magna Carta
1689	The British Bill of Rights
1690	Publication of *Two Treatises on Civil Government* by John Locke
1776	The Declaration of Independence (United States)
1788	The United States Constitution
1791	The Bill of Rights (amendments to the U.S. Constitution)
1792	Publication of *Vindication of the Rights of Woman* by Mary Wollstonecraft
1848	The Declaration of Women Sentiments (issued at the Seneca Falls Convention)
1851	A resolution supporting female suffrage presented in the House of Lords (Great Britain)
1859	Publication of *On Liberty* by John Stuart Mill
1865	The Thirteenth Amendment to the U.S. Constitution abolishing slavery
1866	Civil Rights Act
1868	The Fourteenth Amendment to U.S. Constitution making Blacks citizens
1869	Formation of the National Women Suffrage Association (led by Susan B. Anthony and Elizabeth Cady Stanton)
1870	The Fifteenth Amendment to the U.S. Constitution giving Blacks voting rights
1893	Granting the right to vote to women in New Zealand
1902	Granting the right to vote to women in Australia
1906	Granting of suffrage to women in Finland
1910	Formation of the National Association for the Advancement of Colored People (NAACP)
1913	Granting of suffrage to women in Norway
1917	Granting the right to vote to women in the Soviet Union
1920	The Nineteenth Amendment to the U.S. Constitution giving women the right to vote
1946	Granting suffrage to women in Mexico
1947	Independence of India from Great Britain
1948	Adoption by the United Nations General Assembly of the Universal Declaration of Human Rights
1954	Segregation in public schools declared unconstitutional by the Supreme Court
1959	Adoption by the United Nations General Assembly of the Declaration of the Rights of the Child
1960	Full independence of Nigeria from Great Britain
1963	The March on Washington (a landmark civil rights demonstration of the 1960s)
1964	Civil Rights Act of 1964 (the most comprehensive to date)
1965	Voting Rights Act
1966	Formation of the National Organization for Women (NOW) (over 400 local chapters by the early 1970s)
1975	Public Law 94–142, expanding educational opportunities for students with disabilities in public schools
1990	The German Democratic Republic (East Germany) and West Germany reunited after 45 years
1994	South Africans of all races can vote in national election (The beginning of majority rule in South Africa)
1994	Israeli and PLO leaders sign accord resolving a number of issues on Palestinian self-rule in the Gaza Strip and Jericho
1996	Treaty banning nuclear arms from the African continent signed by most African nations

inquiry strategy

HUMAN RIGHTS CASE STUDIES

Ask the students to read the following case studies. Then have the students respond to the questions and complete the exercise after the questions.

CASE 1

A group of women factory workers in Birmingham (England) have discovered that their hourly wages are about 30 percent less than those of the men who work in the factory. The women have about the same level of education, work experience, and responsibility as the men.

CASE 2

James and Ethel Brewer lived near Three Mile Island (Pennsylvania) in 1979 when an accident occurred in the nuclear generating plant there. They have two children, ages 6 and 14. James has just been told that he has terminal cancer and that he has less than one year to live. Several medical authorities believe, like the Brewers, that James's cancer is a direct consequence of the large amounts of radioactivity he was exposed to when the nuclear accident occurred at Three Mile Island.

CASE 3

Jenny Willis is the only blind student who attends her small school in an isolated rural community in the deep South. The principal of the school has told Jenny's parents that the district does not have the resources to offer Jenny the special instruction she needs. They have advised the parents to enroll Jenny in the state boarding school for the blind, which is located in the state capital, about 400 miles from Jenny's home. Jenny's parents believe that it is wrong to send her away to a boarding school and that the school has both a moral and legal responsibility to provide Jenny with the special kind of instruction she requires.

CASE 4

African American students attending a predominantly White university have been the victims of several racist incidents within the last several months. A skit was performed by an all-White student group that included a student with a painted black face who played a stereotypic African American character. Anti-Black graffiti has been found on several campus buildings. A conservative campus student newspaper has published several inflammatory articles that most African American students and faculty consider insulting and demeaning.

> **QUESTIONS AND EXERCISES**
> Ask the students:
> 1. In what ways are the case studies alike?
> 2. In what ways are they different?
> 3. What words or labels can we use to describe these case studies as a group? Try to elicit concepts such as discrimination and unfair treatment. Introduce the concept of human rights and explain how each of the cases is an example of how human rights are violated.
> 4. Divide the class into four groups. Give each of the groups one of the cases above. Ask each group to identify the problem the protagonists face in each case and what they should do to try to solve it. Members of each group should try to reach a consensus about what they would do if they were the protagonists. Individual students should be free to make a decision different from that of their group.

SOCIAL ISSUES AND HUMAN RIGHTS

The first two sections of this chapter discuss a rationale for including a study of social issues in the curriculum and illustrate how human rights can be used as an organizing framework and unifying theme for teaching social issues. The sections that follow describe five social issues that should be an integral part of the social studies curriculum:

> Global citizenship awareness
> Gender equity
> Ethnic issues
> Social justice for physically challenged individuals
> Law-related issues

The final section of this chapter discusses law-related education because laws are often used to guarantee the rights of individuals and groups.

Global Citizenship Awareness

We live in an age of global realities, which affect not only our national policies, but also many aspects of our everyday lives. The U.S. economy is one of the many components of American society that reflect global realities. It is influenced by the actions of people living within the U.S. as well as by people in other nations.

The U.S. economy is an example of the interdependent nature of life in the 20th century. When Arab oil-producing nations decided to increase the price of oil in the 1970s, Americans started buying smaller, more fuel-efficient cars. Most of these cars were not manufactured in Detroit but by manufacturers in other nations. Car sales for Detroit automakers decreased in the United States and those for small, foreign-made cars sharply increased.

It is important to note, however, that while the United States was importing large numbers of foreign-made automobiles, American auto makers were exporting American-made cars to other nations. In 1977, Ford Motor Company received 42 percent of its income selling cars to countries outside North America. Exports and foreign investments continue to account for a significant percentage of multinational American corporations' income. In 1996, U.S. companies exported $624.8 billion in merchandise, making the United States the world's leading exporter in merchandise trade (Statistical Abstract of the United States, 1997). That year, General Motors ranked first and Ford Motor Company ranked second on the *Fortune* 100 World's Largest Industrial Corporations (Wright, 1997).

In addition to manufactured goods, agricultural and other products, chemicals, and capital are also being imported to and exported from the United States. In 1981 Americans had just over $109 million invested in assets abroad. In that same year there were nearly $78 million in foreign assets invested in the United States (Statistical Abstract of the United States, 1997). These facts point out the difficulty of isolating one nation's economy, culture, or politics from that of other nations. It is difficult today, and will perhaps be even more difficult in the future, to delineate significant components of our lives that are uniquely American and untouched by the influences of other nations.

Through the years there has been a great deal of cultural exchange both within and outside the borders of the United States. Important components of U.S. culture are shared with people in other nations. U.S. citizens have borrowed food, clothing, music, and languages from other nations. Today it is possible to buy a McDonald's hamburger in downtown Paris or Amsterdam. You can see young people dressed in jeans in the Ginza in Tokyo as well as on Fifth Avenue in New York City. Jazz is popular in both Moscow and New Orleans.

There are many reasons for the rapid cultural exchange among nations. Sophisticated telecommunication systems make it possible for Americans to witness events in distant lands as they are occurring. Some observers have suggested that the daily battles that were shown on the evening news were one of the reasons that anti-Vietnam war sentiment grew in the United States. We are also coming in contact with more people from other nations. Thousands of foreign students enroll in U.S. colleges and universities each year.

Americans continue to have a strong national identity. However, our knowledge of the people and cultures of other lands, our internationally based economy, and our growing awareness of earth as a spaceship with finite supplies is increasing our knowledge of the interrelated nature of the world.

Global studies offers an excellent opportunity for interdisciplinary teaching. It also provides a vehicle for teaching social studies skills, including decision-making, valuing, and the ability to conceptualize and generalize. The world, not a nation-state, becomes the unit of analysis. Instead of learning about the culture, geography, or economy of one nation, students are taught to compare and look for relationships among the cultures, geographies, or economies of several nations. Students learn to view their actions and the actions of their government from both national and international perspectives. Most important, they have an opportunity to view themselves as citizens of the world and to explore the importance and responsibility of that role.

GOALS, CONCEPTS, AND ACTIVITIES FOR TEACHING ABOUT GLOBAL REALITIES

Goal 1

To help students increase their awareness and understanding of the interlocking relationships among all people and nations of the world.

Concept

Interdependence—the interaction among nations in a variety of areas, including finance, trade, communication, and travel that transcend national boundaries.

Activities

1. Take students on an electronic field trip to the United Nations at [http://www.pbs.org/tal/un].
2. Many churches, unions, and community groups such as sororities and fraternities are transnational. Invite a person from one of these groups to talk to your class about why his or her organization is interested in people in other nations.
3. Have your students write to a large bank such as Chase Manhattan to request an annual report. Using the annual report as a resource, ask students to identify all the nations that have borrowed money from the bank.

Goal 2

To help students develop the ability to look at the world and world events as part of an interrelated system, not as separate, isolated nations and events.

Concept

Global perspective—a conception of the world as an integrated whole.

Activities

1. Immigrants from Europe have settled in many nations including Mexico, South Africa, and Australia. Have students compare the influence of European immigration on the native populations of these nations.
2. Have students research Esperanto. Esperanto, which has been in use for more than a hundred years, is a language created to facilitate communication among people from different countries. Then have them debate whether there is a need for an international language. You can find information on Esperanto on the Internet at Esperanto.Net (http://www.esperanto.net).
3. Select a multinational company such as General Motors, Mitsui, Royal Dutch/Shell Group, or Daimler-Benz-Chrysler. Have students put a pin in a world

map where the company has its headquarters. Then have them put different colored pins in the map to represent where the company has plants, where it gets its raw materials, and where its products are sold.

Gender Equity

Using the work of early feminist reformers as their foundation, modern-day feminists began a movement that helped change the way women are viewed in our society. The publication of Betty Friedan's book *The Feminine Mystique* (1963) marked a new beginning for the women's movement. Friedan's position—that women had the potential and the need to work in a wide range of occupations and professions outside the home—was considered radical when the book was published. Many of the people who debated the merits of gender equity in the 1960s knew little of the 19th-century reform movements or of the efforts of women like Sojourner Truth and Susan B. Anthony to secure basic rights for women. Studying about women and gender equity gives students an opportunity to see how past events can affect those in the present and future.

Students need to examine both the past and the present experiences of women to fully understand U.S. society. The culture, status, development, and achievement of women as a group should be explored. Women are not a monolithic group, making their study a complex and often difficult task. There are many different women, and differences in race and social class often result in diverse experiences for women (Andersen & Collins, 1997). A sound curriculum must reflect both similarities and differences. A distinction should also be made between sex and gender. *Sex* refers to the biological characteristics that make an individual male or female. *Gender* describes behaviors that result from social, cultural, and psychological factors associated with masculinity and femininity within a society. Appropriate male and female roles result from the socialization of the individual within the group.

The study of women often has an emotional dimension. In some cases, emotions can make it difficult for students to examine facts related to women's issues. In other cases, you can help students use their emotions to reach an effective understanding of what it means to be a male or a female in our society. In either case, you should realize that emotions are an important factor.

Many of the questions raised by the women's movement are related to sexism. *Sexism* is prejudice and discrimination directed at individuals on the basis of their sex. Sexism in education confronts every classroom teacher, whether it is part of the formal curriculum contained in books and materials or part of the hidden curriculum communicated through behavior and attitudes, and it can have an important effect on students. For example, while the role of women in U.S. society is changing, many questions related to gender equity, such as income, are unresolved. In 1996, 59.3 percent of women were in the labor force. According to the U.S. Bureau of Census, this is up from 37.7 percent in 1960 (Wright, 1997). However, even though the percentage of women working outside the home is increasing, women continue to earn less than men. In 1996 women who worked full-time in year-round executive, administrative, and managerial positions had a median yearly income of only 61 percent of the median income for men in the same occupational group.

The percentage varies and is higher in some fields. However, women received less income than their male counterparts in most major occupation groups reported by the U.S. Census (Wright, 1997).

Language is one way that sexism is reflected in our society. Words and phrases such as *mankind, manpower, chairman,* and *early man* can leave students with the notion that women have not been active participants in the development of civilization. Even when words used to describe men have a female counterpart, the female word may have a very different meaning. A case in point is the word bachelor, whose feminine counterpart is spinster, a word with a very different denotation. Increased teacher awareness can play an important role in helping students understand the importance of language. You can model nonsexist language as well as point out and correct sexist language in textbooks and other materials.

When you review your class lists at the beginning of the school year, you should realize that gender is a possible factor in the academic development of your students. Many girls start out in first grade equal to or ahead of boys in reading, mathematics, and science (Gollnick & Chin, 1997). However, as they progress through school, girls tend to fall behind boys in science and mathematics. You should also realize that the girls in your class with high grade point averages will tend to have lower occupational goals than boys with similar grade point averages. In addition, girls will tend to have less confidence in their potential for academic and occupational success than boys (Gollnick & Chin, 1997). This kind of knowledge can help you to successfully intervene and support your students.

While much of the literature on sexism in education focuses on women, sexism also affects men. The study of women can provide an opportunity to explore how the treatment and condition of women in our society relates to the experiences of men. Boys are much more likely to be identified as having learning or behavioral problems or to be diagnosed as hyperactive than are girls (Gollnick & Chin, 1997). Boys are expected to be strong and not to cry even if they are hurt. After being told, year after year, not to cry and to act like a man, it is not surprising that many young men have trouble communicating their feelings and are unable to show a full range of emotions.

Sex-role stereotyping denies both men and women freedom of choice and can prevent students from developing their full potential. Students need an atmosphere that encourages them, not one that limits their hopes and dreams. Students should be helped to expand their concepts of male and female roles and to understand that gender should not determine what men and women are able to do. Teachers who use books and materials that show both men and women in nontraditional roles will help their students understand that most roles in society can be filled by both women and men (Sadker & Sadker, 1994).

profile

SANDRA HARDING

A Feminist Scholar Who Challenges Mainstream Knowledge

An important assumption within mainstream Western science is that knowledge can be produced that does not reflect the cultures, experiences, and gender of knowledge producers. Transformative scholars, including feminist scholars such as Sandra Harding, have challenged this assumption. They contend that all knowledge reflects the values and cultural experiences of researchers and scientists, and that knowledge is valid and objective to the extent that the values of researchers and social scientists are made explicit. Harding is an influential proponent of "feminist standpoint theory," which tries to "construct knowledge from the perspective of women's lives" (p. vii). Feminist scholars maintain that objectivity is also increased when knowledge incorporates the diverse voices within a society and when the politicized nature of knowledge is acknowledged.

In a series of important and influential books, Harding challenges mainstream academic knowledge, argues that it has marginalized the experiences of women, and describes the need for knowledge that reflects the diverse groups within U.S. society. A more objective and inclusive knowledge, she argues, must incorporate the perspectives, experiences, and epistemologies of women. Her books include *The Science Question in Feminism, The "Racial" Economy of Science: Toward A Democratic Future,* and *Whose Knowledge? Whose Science? Thinking From Women's Lives.* Harding, who was a professor of philosophy for 10 years at the University of Delaware, is now Director of the Center for the Study of Women at the University of California, Los Angeles (UCLA). She is also a professor of education and women's studies and adjunct professor of philosophy.

References

Harding, S. (1991). *Whose knowledge? Whose science? Thinking from women's lives.* Ithaca: Cornell University Press.

Harding, S. (Ed.). (1998). *Is science multicultural?* Bloomington: Indiana University Press.

GOALS, CONCEPTS, AND ACTIVITIES FOR TEACHING ABOUT WOMEN

Goal 1

To increase student awareness and knowledge of women in our society.

Concept

Sexism—prejudiced beliefs and behaviors that are directed against women because of their gender.

Activities
1. Have students examine their textbooks for sex biases.
2. Help your students develop a nonsexist dictionary. Give them a list of sexist words and have them suggest alternatives.
3. Read and discuss the poem "What Are Little Boys Made Of?" Ask your students to rewrite the poem.
4. Ask your students to look at specified television programs for a one-week period to find out how women of color are depicted and in what kinds of roles.
5. Make a list of all the extracurricular activities at your school. Ask your students to find out if both males and females participate in each of the activities and in what proportions. Discuss their findings in class.

Goal 2

To help students examine how sex-role stereotyping influences the behavior of men and women.

Concept

Role—sex-role stereotyping. Sex-role stereotyping involves using traditional definitions of feminine and masculine to limit the behavior of males and females.

Activities
1. To open discussion of sex-role stereotyping, show your students a picture of a woman and a man and ask the students to name some jobs that each of them can do. List the jobs on the board. Then ask your students if the woman can do all the jobs listed for the man and if the man can do all the jobs listed for the woman.
2. Have students examine the roles of women and men at different periods in U.S. history, such as the late 1700s, and compare those to the roles men and women function in today.
3. Ask your students to pretend they are journalists who give advice to readers. Tell them to respond to a man who wants to know if he should become a househusband and stay home with his two preschool children while his wife runs the family business full-time.

Ethnic Issues

In recent years, school districts throughout the nation have attempted to modify their curricula to more accurately reflect the ethnic and cultural diversity within U.S. society (Banks & Banks, 1997). Much of the curriculum reform related to ethnic studies and ethnic heritage programs has taken place in the social studies because the social studies deal with human behavior and the relationships among groups.

To fully understand the cogent role that race and ethnicity play in our society, ethnic studies must be broadly defined to include European American ethnic groups as well as ethnic groups of color. When ethnic studies is broadly defined it provides an opportunity for students to learn about a wide range of ethnic groups. They are able to compare and contrast the experiences of a wide range of ethnic groups and gain valuable insights into U.S. society. Ethnic studies deals with such ethnic groups as Anglo Americans, Italian Americans, and Polish Americans, as well as with ethnic groups of color such as African Americans and Mexican Americans. Conceptualizing ethnic studies and ethnic content broadly enables the curriculum builder to select content about different types of ethnic groups so that students, by comparing and contrasting them, can develop higher-level concepts and generalizations about race and ethnicity within U.S. society.

Ethnic identification and affiliations are important for many groups of Americans, including African Americans, Mexican Americans, Irish Catholics, Jewish Americans, and Greek Americans. It can be a factor in selecting a marriage partner, voting in an election, and joining a social club. Because ethnicity is an important factor in American life, infusing ethnic content into the curriculum provides an excellent opportunity for teachers to examine its assumptions, purposes, and nature. Rather than viewing ethnic studies as an addition to the regular social studies curriculum, it should be viewed as a process of curriculum reform. One of the most promising aspects of ethnic studies is that it can serve as a vehicle for general curriculum reform. As such, it can result in the creation of an innovative curriculum based on new assumptions and new perspectives. Such a curriculum can help students gain novel views of the American experience and a new conception of what it means to be American (Banks, 1997b).

We need to teach U.S. history and culture from diverse ethnic and cultural perspectives rather than primarily or exclusively from the points of view of mainstream American historians and writers. J. A. Banks (1997c) has described four approaches that are used to integrate ethnic and multicultural content into the curriculum: the Contributions Approach, the Additive Approach, the Transformative Approach, and the Decision-Making and Social Action Approach. (See Figure 7.1.)

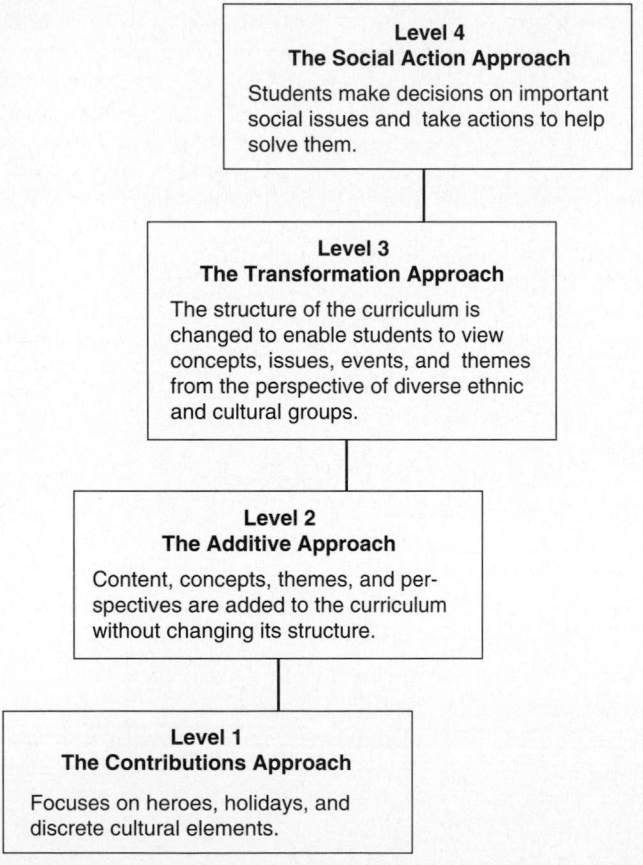

Figure 7.1
Banks levels of integration of ethnic content.

The Contributions Approach, which is the easiest approach for teachers to use to integrate the curriculum with ethnic and multicultural content, is most frequently used by teachers in the primary grades. In this approach, ethnic content is limited primarily to special days, weeks, and months related to ethnic events and celebrations. Cinco de Mayo, Martin Luther King's Birthday, and Black History Week are examples of ethnic days and weeks that are celebrated in the schools. During these celebrations, teachers involve students in lessons, experiences, and pageants related to the ethnic groups being commemorated. While this approach has some advantages, including requiring relatively little time and resources for implementation, it has some important drawbacks. Students do not attain a global view of the role of ethnic and cultural groups in U.S. society. Rather, they see ethnic issues and events primarily as an addition to the curriculum, and consequently as an appendage to the main story of the development of the nation and to the core curriculum. Most importantly, the Contributions Approach can reinforce stereotypes and misconceptions and trivialize ethnic cultures, presenting them as having strange and exotic characteristics. When the focus is on the contributions and unique aspects of ethnic cultures, students are not helped to understand them as complete and dynamic wholes.

Another approach to the integration of ethnic and multicultural content to the curriculum is the Additive Approach. This approach introduces ethnic content, concepts, themes, and perspectives into the curriculum without changing its basic structure, purposes, and characteristics. This approach allows the teacher to incorporate ethnic content into the curriculum without restructuring it, which takes substantial time, effort, training, and rethinking of the curriculum and its purposes, nature, and goals. This approach can be the first phase in a more radical curriculum reform effort designed to restructure the total curriculum and to integrate it with ethnic content, perspectives, and frames of reference. However, it shares several disadvantages with the Contributions Approach. Its most important shortcoming is that it usually results in students viewing ethnic content from the perspectives of mainstream historians, writers, artists, and scientists because it does not involve a restructuring of the curriculum. The events, concepts, issues, and problems selected for study are selected using Mainstream-Centric and Euro-Centric criteria and perspectives. The Additive Approach also fails to help students to view society from diverse cultural and ethnic perspectives and to understand the ways in which the histories and cultures of the nation's diverse ethnic, racial, cultural, and religious groups are inextricably bound.

The Transformative Approach differs fundamentally from the Contributions and Additive Approaches. This approach changes the basic assumptions of the curriculum and enables students to view concepts, issues, themes, and problems from several ethnic perspectives and points of view. The key issue in the Transformative Approach is the infusion of various perspectives, frames of reference, and content from various groups that will extend the students' understanding of the nature, development, and complexity of U.S. society. The emphasis is not on the ways in which various ethnic, racial, and cultural groups have contributed to mainstream U.S. society and culture. The emphasis, rather, is on how the common U.S. culture and society emerged from a complex synthesis and interaction of the diverse cultural elements that originated within the various cultural, racial, ethnic, and religious groups that make up American society.

A historian's experience and culture, including his or her ethnic culture, influence his or her views of the past and present. However, it would be simplistic to argue that there is one mainstream American view of history and contemporary events, or one American Indian view. Wide differences in experiences and perceptions exist both within and across ethnic groups. However, those who have experienced a historical event or a social phenomenon, such as racial bigotry or internment, often view the event differently from those who have watched it from a distance. There is no one mainstream American perspective on the Japanese American internment during World War II, just as there is no one Japanese American view of it. However, accounts written by those who were interned, such as Takashima's (1971) powerful *A Child in Prison Camp,* often provide insights and perspectives that cannot be provided by people who were not interned. Individuals who viewed the internment from the outside can also provide us with unique and important perspectives and points of view. Both perspectives should be studied in a sound social studies curriculum.

The Social Action Approach includes all the elements of the Transformative Approach but adds components that require students to make decisions and to take actions related to the concept, issue, or problem they have studied in the unit. In this approach, students study a social problem such as "What actions should we take to reduce prejudice and discrimination in our school?" They gather pertinent data, analyze their values and beliefs, synthesize their knowledge and values, identify alternative courses of action, and finally decide what, if any, actions they will take to reduce prejudice and discrimination in their school. Major goals of the Social Action Approach are to teach students thinking and decision-making skills, to empower them, and to help them acquire a sense of political efficacy. More information on the approaches to multicultural curriculum reform can be found in Banks (1997c).

GOALS, CONCEPTS, AND ACTIVITIES FOR TEACHING ABOUT ETHNIC GROUPS

Goal 1

To help students become more aware of how different ethnic groups have influenced American culture.

Concept

Acculturation—the exchanging of cultural traits among ethnic groups.

Activities
1. Ask students to name their favorite foods. Then have them research how those foods became a part of the American diet.
2. Have students compare the values that are the basis for the environmental movement with values expressed by American Indians in the 1800s.

3. Many Americans set off fireworks on the Fourth of July. Ask your students to find out how this tradition started and what other cultures use fireworks for celebrations.

Goal 2

To help students gain a new view of who is an American and what it means to be American.

Concept

Ethnocentrism—the belief that your own ethnic group is superior to all others.

Activities

1. Show your students a photograph of a group of people representing a variety of ethnic and racial groups. Then ask them to select the person in the photograph that they feel represents an American. Have them discuss why they made that choice.
2. In 1998 Ron Unz led a statewide campaign in California to greatly restrict bilingual education. Unz's efforts resulted in the passage of the Unz-Tuchman California Ballot Initiative, which limits bilingual instruction to one year. Immediately after its passage, the initiative was challenged in the California courts. Ask your students to use news sources such as *U.S. News,* the *Los Angeles Times, Time* magazine, and *Newsweek* to analyze the bilingual education debate in the popular media. Then ask them to take a position on bilingual education. Discuss how ethnicity often plays a role in how we perceive and respond to issues.

Social Justice for Physically Challenged Individuals

Physically challenged people have been a part of United States society since its beginning. However, because they were isolated and hidden, they were generally unknown to most people in their communities. In the past, people with disabilities were sometimes not even accepted by their own families. Fear, shame, and a lack of understanding caused some families to disown relatives with disabilities.

Until the 19th century, people with disabilities without families to care for them were "farmed out." The government paid people to provide room, board, and care for people with disabilities. The person who put in the lowest bid was often the one who got the contract. Public concern grew as people with disabilities were starved or frozen to death by their caretakers. Reforms resulted and people with disabilities were sent to institutions for care.

In the 1800s most people with disabilities were put into poorhouses in which conditions were generally unsanitary and overcrowded (United States Commission on Civil Rights, 1983). Between 1870 and 1890, state institutions located outside cities were developed to provide more specialized care for people with disabilities. One of their main goals was to protect people with disabilities from society.

By the early 1900s, there was a marked reversal in society's attitude toward people with disabilities. Many people back then believed society needed protection from people with disabilities. Social Darwinism was popular and it was widely believed that most social problems were the result of unfit people having unfit children. People with disabilities were referred to as "mere animals," "subhuman creatures," and "waste products." Today these terms are completely unacceptable. Yet it is this history that both non-physically challenged and physically challenged citizens must examine if they are to know and understand people with disabilities in today's society.

PREJUDICE AND HOW IT AFFECTS PEOPLE WITH DISABILITIES

As a society, we have many reactions to people with disabilities. Sometimes response to people with disabilities is accepting and compassionate. However, unless this attitude is accompanied by respect, it can result in pity and be patronizing. One of the most common reactions is for people who are not physically challenged to see themselves as superior to people who are. Because people with disabilities are often isolated, we do not get many opportunities to learn about their abilities or disabilities. Stereotyping often results. People with Down's syndrome are often believed to be incapable of showing emotions. Many people believe that individuals who do not have use of their arms and legs are not able to live alone (United States Commission on Civil Rights, 1983).

Because people sometimes feel uncomfortable or embarrassed when they interact with individuals with disabilities, they tend to avoid them. Some sales clerks are slow to wait on them. Restaurants will often seat them in places where they are not likely to be seen by other customers. People on the street commonly look away, as if to pretend that they aren't there. Many of the problems experienced by people with disabilities result from prejudice and discrimination. Lessons about people with disabilities can profitably focus on some of the same concepts as lessons about women and ethnic groups (Shaver & Curtis, 1981).

WHO ARE THE PHYSICALLY CHALLENGED?

Public Law 94-142 identifies the physically challenged as individuals who are mentally retarded, hard of hearing, speech-impaired, hearing-impaired, orthopedically impaired, visually disabled, learning disabled, or seriously emotionally disturbed (Shaver & Curtis, 1981). Many people see individuals with disabilities only in terms of their disability. People with disabilities are a diverse group and should be viewed as individuals who share both similarities and differences. They have the same interests and are as diverse as individuals without disabilities. Persons with disabilities, such as Franklin D. Roosevelt and Helen Keller, have made major contributions to society. Consequently, many physically challenged persons prefer that their disabilities be described with adjectives and not with nouns. Thus, the phrase "a person with epilepsy" would be preferred to "an epileptic."

It is difficult to determine the exact number of people with disabilities in the United States. The various agencies that collect data on people with disabilities use different methods. This makes the data difficult to compare. In 1994, 9.9 percent of the U.S. population—about 26 million people—had severe disabilities. The U.S.

Census estimated that from 3.4 to 10.4 percent of adults in the United States from age 21 to 64 had disabilities that limited their ability to work in 1994 (U.S. Census Bureau [http://www.census.gov]). Special education programs are required for 5.1 to 7.4 percent of the resident population of the United States from birth to 21 (Heward & Cavanaugh, 1997). Most have speech impairments or learning or mental disabilities.

Older people have a greater probability of having a disability than younger people. In 1994 the rate of disability for adults between the ages of 55 and 64 was 21.9%. It was 11.5% for people between the ages of 45 and 54, and 6.4% for individuals between 22 and 44 (U.S. Census Bureau [http://www.census.gov]. People with disabilities are less likely to get married and more likely to separate or divorce than people without disabilities.

WHY TEACH ABOUT PEOPLE WITH DISABILITIES?

Teaching about people with disabilities can be an important part of citizenship education. Many of the beliefs and attitudes related to persons with disabilities have tended to deny them the opportunity to participate fully in the political, economic, and social life of our nation. Many of the laws enacted to protect citizens with disabilities from discrimination are often misunderstood and sometimes interpreted as giving them privileges that are not available to other citizens. Studying about citizens with disabilities gives students an opportunity to examine fundamental issues such as equality, responsibility, and rights in a democracy.

GOALS, CONCEPTS, AND ACTIVITIES FOR TEACHING ABOUT PEOPLE WITH DISABILITIES

Goal 1

> To make students aware of policy issues regarding citizens with disabilities and to become better able to discuss and act on that knowledge.

Concept

> Mainstreaming—resulted from the Education for All Handicapped Children Act of 1973, which requires that physically challenged students be placed in the "least restrictive environment." This means that many students with disabilities who, in the past, were educated in classes with other physically challenged students are now required to be integrated into regular classrooms.

Activities
1. Have students write a letter to the school board to find out their school district's policy on mainstreaming.
2. Have students discuss how they would feel and act if they had a severely disabled person in their class. Help your students understand that disabilities are on a continuum. Most people have some type of disability, such as being nearsighted or farsighted.

3. Have your students investigate where and how severely disabled people in your community are educated. Ask them to interview a person who teaches students with severe disabilities. Then have the students discuss whether or not they believe citizens with disabilities are receiving all the educational benefits to which they are entitled.

Goal 2

To provide students with varying perspectives and information on the physically challenged.

Concepts

Disabilities and handicaps—there is some disagreement over the use of these terms. Some writers use disability to refer to a medical condition and handicap to refer to a person's status as a result of the disability. Often a combination of several definitions is used by agencies.

Activities

1. Disabled in Action (DIA) and the American Coalition of Citizens with Disabilities are groups that promote civil rights for people with disabilities. Invite a disability rights activist from such a group to speak to your class.
2. Have students read about the disabled rights movement. Then have them role-play a rally for equal employment opportunity for people with disabilities.
3. Have students evaluate library books on disabilities and on people with disabilities. Ask them to report their findings to the class.

Law-Related Issues

Since the 1960s, educators and legal professionals have developed law-related curricula and materials. In 1963, a group of concerned educators, lawyers, and other legal professionals met in Chicago under the leadership of the Chicago Bar Association. The initial plan for an educational program to promote the study of law in the schools was developed at that meeting. The Law in American Society Foundation was established to conduct teacher-training workshops and to develop curricula. The Foundation's initial work was supported by federal funds. The Foundation's program has grown and expanded since then through the development of a nationwide network of associated projects. It sponsors a number of publications, including a quarterly journal, *Law in American Society: Journal of the National Center for Law-Focused Education*. Significant contributions to the growth and development of law-related education have also been made by organizations such as Law in A Free Society and the Constitutional Rights Foundation.

Law-focused education is designed to help students obtain the knowledge and skills needed to participate more effectively in our legal institutions. A major goal of law-focused education is to help students attain the knowledge, skills, and attitudes needed to obtain their maximum rights within our legal system. Students are also taught about the responsibilities that all citizens must exercise to make our legal system work more effectively and justly.

Major attention is given to local laws, legal institutions, and law enforcement within a sound law-related curriculum. Many of the encounters that people have with the law involve county or city laws and ordinances, and not federal laws. Enforcement of these regulations varies greatly from one locality to another. The norms of the particular agency and the values and beliefs of the individuals who are enforcing or administering the law also vary greatly. When students are knowledgeable about the laws in their communities, they can increase their chances for obtaining their legal rights.

The case study method and inquiry approaches are often used to teach law-focused components of the social studies program in both elementary and secondary schools. When examining case studies, especially controversial ones such as the case involving Christine Craft, students explore both the moral and legal implications of the case. They also examine their own feelings and attitudes toward the issues and people involved. Craft, a former television news anchor, sued her employer for sex discrimination. She won a half-million-dollar verdict in her first trial. However, that verdict was overturned and a new trial was ordered. This case gives students opportunities to enhance their decision-making skills and abilities. The teacher can have students role-play controversial legal cases like the Craft case and designate different students to play the judge, the jury, defense and prosecuting attorneys, and the defendant. If the case has already been decided, the students can discuss why their verdict in the case is similar to or different from the verdict in the actual case.

Law-related education is an important component of a sound social studies curriculum. It gives students an opportunity to explore social issues from a legal perspective. Many social and human rights issues have a legal dimension. Examining the legal aspects of social issues can help students understand and appreciate the complexity as well as the promise of our democratic society. They are able to examine the wide discrepancies that often exist between our legal ideals and realities, and consider what they might be able to do to help close this gap. Law-related education also provides an opportunity to recognize and respect the legal rights and entitlements of diverse groups. Each of the social issues discussed in this chapter has important legal dimensions and has been affected by important legislation, court cases, or treaties.

GOALS, CONCEPTS, AND ACTIVITIES FOR TEACHING ABOUT LAW-RELATED ISSUES

Goal 1

To help students develop an understanding of their constitutional rights and responsibilities and to become familiar with landmark Supreme Court decisions that reflect American values.

Concept

Justice—a cardinal principle of impartial, fair action in the assignment of rewards or punishments.

Activities

1. The historic 1954 Supreme Court decision in *Brown vs. Board of Education of Topeka, Kansas,* legally outlawed *de jure* school desegregation. Linda Brown was prevented from attending her local elementary school in Topeka because she was Black. Her family sued the local school board, and the case went through the Kansas State court system and was eventually appealed to the Supreme Court. The Supreme Court held that school segregation was unconstitutional. Have your students review the *Brown* decision. Then ask them to pretend that they are Linda Brown in 1954 and tell how they feel about:
   a. her local school
   b. her parents' suing the school board
   c. the Black school she is attending
   d. the Supreme Court justices who ruled on her case

   As a final activity, ask your students to write a one-page statement about how the *Brown* decision has changed our society and the problems encountered when school districts have tried to implement it. Discuss with the students why some people feel that school desegregation protects equality for groups of color but denies both groups of color and Whites freedom of choice.

2. Contact your local Bar Association and request a speaker to come to your class and discuss the judicial power of the Supreme Court. Ask the speaker to explain how the Court, during the 1960s, expanded the protection given to people who are accused of committing a crime. Three important cases reflecting this expansion are (1) *Miranda vs. Arizona,* which requires the police to inform arrested persons of their rights, including the right to remain silent; (2) *Gideon vs. Wainwright,* which guarantees defendants subject to jail sentences the right to legal counsel; and (3) *Mapp vs. Ohio,* which provides protection against illegal search and seizure. At the end of this presentation, divide your class into small groups and ask each group to discuss this question: How does our society as a whole and how do you as individuals benefit from laws that protect the rights of people accused of crimes? Ask each group to summarize its discussion for the class.

3. Have your students visit a law library to gather information on the Supreme Court's position on the rights of children. Ask the librarian to explain how to use the library and to help the students locate and make copies of Supreme Court decisions in cases like *Oregon vs. Mitchell.* The Supreme Court upheld the right of 18-year-olds to vote in this case. When the students get back to their classroom, they can make posters highlighting some of the rights they have as children. The posters can be displayed in the classroom or throughout the school.

Goal 2

Help students to understand our society's need for rules and laws, their origin and modification, and the seriousness and potential consequences of their violation.

Concept

Responsibility—being accountable for your actions and obligations.

Activities

1. Ask your students to act out a situation in which they are stranded on an island with no adults. None of the children know where they are. They don't know what, if anything, is being done to rescue them. They only have enough food and water for two days. After the students have acted out this situation, ask them the following questions.
   a. Was it necessary for them to decide on certain rules?
   b. If not, how did they make decisions about things like shelter and food?
   c. What are some of the benefits of having rules?
   d. Should everyone obey rules?
   e. What happens to the group when people do not obey rules?
   f. Ask students to summarize why rules and laws are necessary.

2. When our Constitution was written, women were not given the right to vote. That right was granted to women by the Twenty-first Amendment to the Constitution in 1920. Ask each of your students to pretend that he or she is a famous suffragist, such as one of the Grimke sisters or Elizabeth Cady Stanton. Then ask each student to write a five-minute speech to present to the class telling why women should have the right to vote.

3. Have your students identify several rules or laws, such as the law against shoplifting, that are sometimes violated by young people. Then have them survey all the students at their school to find out how many students are aware of the penalties for breaking those rules or laws. Finally, ask your students to prepare and distribute to all students in the school a flyer listing several rules or laws and explaining the possible consequences for violating them.

SUMMARY

Social issues are society's unresolved problems. These problems are enduring and are not likely to be solved in the foreseeable future. They touch the lives of large numbers of citizens and therefore can add vitality to the curriculum and help make it significant to the lives of teachers and students. The controversial nature of social issues provides excellent opportunities for teaching decision-making and citizen-action skills. Social issues also provide excellent opportunities for students to analyze their values and to develop clarified commitments to important human concerns. Human rights is a unifying theme that connects the social issues discussed in this chapter.

REFLECTION AND ACTION ACTIVITIES

1. Define "social issue." Find three news stories in a local newspaper that deal with social issues. Bring the news stories to class for a discussion of current social issues.
2. Discuss the similarities and differences among the following concepts:
   a. racism
   b. sexism
   c. handicappism
   d. ethnocentrism

3. Write key generalizations that are related to social issues using the following concepts:
   a. role
   b. stereotype
   c. inclusion
   d. interest group
   e. change
   f. freedom

4. List five citizen action strategies that can be effectively used by elementary and middle school students to show their concern about animal cloning.
5. Interview several teachers to find out if they teach about social issues. If they do, find out what issues they teach and the methods used to teach them.
6. Demonstrate your understanding of the following concepts by writing brief definitions for each and telling why each is important.
   a. transformation approach
   b. feminist
   c. physically challenged
   d. human rights
   e. global interdependence
   f. law-focused education
   g. social issue

REFERENCES

Andersen, M. L., & Collins, P. H. (1997). *Race, class, and gender: An anthology* (3rd ed.). Belmont, CA: Wadsworth.

Banks, J. A. (1982). Foreword. In M. S. Branson & J. Torney-Purta (Eds.), *International human rights, society, and the schools.* Bulletin 68 (pp. v–viii). Washington, D.C.: National Council for the Social Studies.

Banks, J. A. (1997a). *Educating citizens for a multicultural society.* New York: Teachers College Press.

Banks, J. A. (1997b). *Teaching strategies for ethnic studies* (6th ed.). Boston: Allyn and Bacon.

Banks, J. A. (1997c). Approaches to multicultural curriculum reform. In J. A. Banks & C. A. M. Banks (Eds). *Multicultural education: Issues and perspectives* (3rd ed., pp. 229–250). Boston: Allyn and Bacon.

Banks, J. A., & Banks, C. A. M. (Eds.). (1997). *Multicultural education: Issues and perspectives* (3rd ed.). Boston: Allyn and Bacon.

Dewey, J. (1912/1966). *Democracy and education.* New York: Free Press.

Franklin, J. H., & McNeil, G. R. (Eds.). (1995). *African Americans and the living Constitution.* Washington, D.C.: Smithsonian Institution Press.

Friedan, B. N. (1963). *The feminine mystique.* New York: Dell.

Gollnick, D. M., & Chin, P. C. (1997). *Multicultural education in a pluralistic society* (5th ed.). St. Louis, MO: Mosby.

Heward, W. L., & Cavanaugh, R. A. (1997). Educational equality for students with disabilities. In J. A. Banks & C. A. M. Banks (Eds.), *Multicultural education: Issues and perspectives* (3rd ed., pp. 301–333). Boston: Allyn and Bacon.

Muse, D. (Ed.). (1997). *The New Press guide to multicultural resources for young readers.* New York: New Press.

Sadker, M., & Sadker, D. (1994). *Failing at fairness: How America's schools cheat girls.* New York: Scribner's.

Shaver, J. P., & Curtis, C. K. (1981). *Handicappism and equal opportunity: Teaching about the disabled in social studies.* Reston, VA: Foundation for Exceptional Children.

Statistical Abstract of the United States 1997 (117th ed.). Washington, D.C.: U.S. Government Printing Office.

Takaki, R. (1995). *Hiroshima: Why America dropped the atomic bomb.* New York: Little Brown.

Takashima, S. (1971). *A child in prison camp.* Montreal, Canada: Tundra Books.

United States Commission on Civil Rights (1983). *Accommodating the spectrum of individual abilities.* Washington, D.C.: U.S. Commission on Civil Rights.

Wright, J. W. (Ed.) (1997). *The New York Times 1998 Almanac.* New York: Penguin.

FOR FURTHER READING

Human Rights

Banks, J. A., & Banks, C. A. M. (Eds.) (1997). *Multicultural education: Issues and perspectives* (3rd ed.). Boston: Allyn and Bacon.

Hasan, A. (1998). *Human rights dilemmas in contemporary times: Issues and answers.* Bethesda, MD: Austin and Winfield.

Horowitz, I. L. (1996). *Taking lives: Genocide and state power* (4th ed.). New Brunswick, NJ: Transaction Press.

Ignatieff, M. (1998). *The warrior's honor: Ethnic war and the modern conscience.* New York: Henry Holt.

Lawson, E. (Ed.). (1996). *Encyclopedia of human rights.* Bristol, PA: Taylor and Francis.

Perry, M. (1998). *The idea of human rights: Four inquiries.* London: Oxford University Press.

Global Realities

Brown, Lester R., et al. (1998). *State of the world 1998: A worldwatch institute report on progress toward a sustainable society.* New York: Norton.

Diaz, M. (1997). *Global education.* New York: Prentice Hall.

Gannon, M. J. (1994). *Understanding global cultures: Metaphorical journeys through countries.* New York: Sage.

Merryfield, M. M., Jarchow, E., & Pickert, S. (1996). *Preparing teachers to teach global perspectives: A handbook for teacher educators.* Thousand Oaks, CA: Corwin.

Gender Issues

Barber, J. D., & Kellerman, B. (Eds.) (1986). *Women leaders in American politics.* Englewood Cliffs, NJ: Prentice-Hall.

Bassnett, S. (1986). *Feminist experiences: The women's movement in four cultures.* Boston: Allen and Unwin.

Klein, S. S. (Ed.). (1992). *Sex equity and sexuality in education.* Albany, NY: State University of New York Press.

Kleinfeld, J. (Ed.). (1992). *Teaching in the North: Gender tales.* University of Alaska, Fairbanks, Center for Cross-Cultural Studies.

Middleton, S. (1993). *Educating feminists: Life histories and pedagogy.* New York: Teachers College Press.

Sadker, M., & Sadker, D. (1995). *Failing at fairness: How America's schools cheat girls.* New York: Simon and Schuster.

Race and Ethnicity

Banks, J. A. (1994). *Multiethnic education: Theory and practice* (3rd ed.). Boston: Allyn and Bacon.

Banks, J. A. (1997). *Teaching strategies for ethnic studies* (6th ed.). Boston: Allyn and Bacon.

Grossman, H. (1995). *Educating Hispanic students: Implications for instruction, classroom management, counseling and assessment* (2nd ed.). Springfield, IL: Charles C. Thomas.

Jones, J. M. (1997). *Prejudice and racism* (2nd ed.). New York: McGraw-Hill.

McInnis, K. M., Petracchi, H. E., & Morgenbesser, M. (1992). *The Hmong in America: Providing ethnic sensitive health, education, and human services.* Dubuque, IA: Kendall/Hunt.

Pang, V. O., & Cheng, L. L. (Eds.). (1998). *Struggling to be heard: The unmet needs of Asian Pacific American Children.* Albany, NY: State University of New York Press.

Physically Challenged Individuals

Downing, J. E. (1996). *Including students with severe and multiple disabilities in typical classrooms: Practical strategies for teachers.* Baltimore, MD: Paul H. Brookes.

Nielsen, L. B. (1996). *The exceptional child in the regular classroom: An educator's guide.* Thousand Oaks, CA: Corwin.

Pijl, S. J., Meijer, C. J., & Hegarty, S. (1996). *Inclusive education: A global agenda.* New York: Routledge.

Rosenberg, M. S., O'Shea, L.J., & O'Shea, D. J. (1997). *Student teacher to master teacher: A guide for preservice and beginning teachers of students with mild to moderate disabilities* (2nd ed.). New York: Prentice Hall.

Westwood, P. S. (1997). *Commonsense methods for children with special needs: Strategies for the regular classroom* (3rd ed.). New York: Routledge.

Law-Related Issues

Hepburn, M. A. (Ed.). (1983). *Democratic education in schools and classrooms.* Bulletin 70. Washington, D.C.: National Council for the Social Studies.

Keller, C. W., & Schillings, D. L. (Eds.) (1987). *Teaching about the constitution.* Bulletin 80. Washington, D.C.: National Council for the Social Studies.

CHAPTER 8

Selecting and Using Instructional Materials and Resources

To solve scientific, valuing, and decision-problems, students must collect, analyze, and evaluate data from a wide variety of resources. Information and data from any one resource are insufficient to help students solve problems and answer the range of questions that will arise in the units, lessons, and problems they study. Information and data from multiple media sources present students with diverse perspectives and points of view and stimulate their different senses. Learning is enhanced when it is reinforced by different communication forms.

Students need to use data from a wide range of communication forms in order to formulate and test concepts and generalizations, analyze and clarify their values and those of others, make reflective decisions, and plan thoughtful citizen action. In this chapter we discuss a variety of data forms that can be used to introduce, extend, and enrich social studies learning. We have classified these materials as (1) reading materials, (2) technology, (3) role-playing, creative dramatics, and simulation, and (4) the community as a learning resource.

SELECTING AND USING APPROPRIATE DATA SOURCES

The textbook is the most frequently used data source in the social studies classroom. It consists primarily of verbal and visual symbols. The textbook is consequently one of the most abstract teaching tools. However, abstract materials are not always more difficult than direct experiences. Some simple explanations in textbooks (visual symbols) are much less difficult than some complex demonstrations or field trips during which students view and participate in situations and events with many complex and distracting clues.

You should determine which data source can be used to teach a concept most efficiently and accurately and which will be the most meaningful to your students. The textbook or other reading sources might best be used to introduce many concepts. Demonstrations, field trips, and dramatized experiences might best be used to extend and reinforce them. Once students have mastered the concept *assembly line* as explained in their textbooks, they might then be able to greatly benefit from a field trip to visit an assembly line at a local automobile factory. Field trips are often poor vehicles for introducing concepts. Students see many distracting and irrelevant clues on a field trip and often find it difficult to focus on the essential attributes of the concepts being studied.

Each of the data sources used in teaching the social studies, such as the textbook, the videotape, and the field trip, has unique characteristics making it effective for some instructional purposes and ineffective for others. The most important criteria for deciding which data source to use for a particular lesson are the lesson's objective and the nature of the learning activity. A textbook account of the South during the 1930s can help students acquire the facts about the discrimination that took place during this period of U.S. history. However, a powerful work of historical fiction, such as *Roll of Thunder, Hear My Cry*, by Mildred Taylor, will enable students to experience the bigotry and heroism of these times when they identify with the heroine, Cassie Logan, and the other African American and White characters who represent the broad spectrum of human characteristics.

Our major point is that no one data source, including the textbook, the field trip, or the dramatized experience, is appropriate for each learning situation and purpose. Each data source has strengths and limitations and is appropriate for specific learning activities, purposes, and goals. No one data source should be regarded as *the* source for the social studies curriculum. Rather, you should use a wide range of data sources to help your students attain instructional goals.

READING MATERIALS

Social Studies Texts

For many teachers in elementary and middle schools, textbooks often serve as the main source of information used in the classroom, a guide for curriculum planning, and a compendium of ideas about teaching activities. This is not only true for the social studies, but for other subject areas as well, such as reading, language arts, mathematics, and science. According to some reports, between 70 to 90 percent of students' instructional time is spent focusing on information contained in textbooks (English, 1980).

Textbooks are criticized for being boring to read, for the way in which they are developed and written (usually by teams of authors and editors), and for being shaped primarily by market rather than educational considerations. Each of these criticisms contains grains of truth as well as exaggerations. The textbook, like any human creation, has both strengths and limitations.

Many of the poor teaching practices associated with textbooks result more from the way they are used rather than from the nature of textbooks themselves. The authors, editors, and publishers of textbooks do not intend them to be the only source of information for a particular subject. However, common statements such as "My social studies book is too big for me to cover in one year" and "I think I will be able to cover my textbook this year" indicate the extent to which many teachers regard the textbook as the curriculum. When teachers equate the textbook with the curriculum, they minimize their ability to make instructional decisions, and the textbook becomes the major if not the only source of information available to students. Textbooks should be viewed as one of many important instructional tools in an effective social studies curriculum.

Most social studies textbooks are well organized, readable, attractively illustrated, and contain important if highly selective information. The social studies as presented in the textbook is the best social studies curriculum that some students ever experience. This may be because the teacher has a scant background in the social sciences, little interest in teaching the social studies, or assigns the social studies a low priority. Often most of the teacher's time in the elementary and middle school grades is spent teaching reading, the language arts, and mathematics. Consequently, little time is spent teaching either science or the social studies. Social studies and science are taught only a few times a week in many elementary schools. When the social studies program is thin and sporadic, the textbook is a blessing because it is the only social studies curriculum that exists.

The best way to have an effective social studies curriculum in a school that devotes most of its time to teaching reading, the language arts, and mathematics is to integrate social studies concepts and content into the reading and language arts curricula. This is best done with interdisciplinary units requiring the use of a wide variety of data sources.

Another advantage of textbooks is that the teacher is usually supplied with useful and carefully developed supplementary materials, such as a teacher's guide or edition which includes answers to questions in the textbook, tests, and teaching activities. Most textbooks also have supplementary materials for the students, such as workbooks, duplicating masters, and other aids. When used wisely and selectively, and adapted for use with their particular units, lessons, and students, these materials can be helpful. However, supplementary materials can be easily abused. This happens when teachers use a teacher's guide without adapting it to their unique situations and classes. Student workbooks are often abused when teachers use them to give students busy work that is not clearly related to instructional goals.

UPDATING TEXTBOOKS

To use a textbook effectively, it must be supplemented, enriched, and updated. It is necessary to supplement and enrich textbooks because of the limited space textbooks can devote to any one topic. It is also better to relate the topics, issues, and concepts taught in the textbook to your own students and the communities and cultures in which they live. The content of textbooks also needs to be extended and enriched because they become quickly outdated. The use of old textbooks is often a serious problem in school districts that face financial problems. During financial hard times, school districts are reluctant to replace old books with new ones because of the high costs involved.

Textbooks often need to be updated when a new president is elected, an international crisis arises, or new problems grip the nation. You should use reliable local, national, and international news sources to keep abreast of current events that should be incorporated into textbook lessons. National newspapers such as the *New York Times* and the *Wall Street Journal,* national news magazines such as *Time* and *Newsweek,* and international news magazines such as the *Economist* and *World Monitor* contain valuable information that can help you keep textbooks current. These resources are not only available in print form but can be accessed through the Internet. Web addresses or URLs (Universal Resource Locators) can be found in Table 8.1. Using resources such as these, you can collect important and timely news items, cartoons, and editorials, group them by categories, and file them for use at appropriate times during lessons or units. Possible categories for grouping news items and stories are:

Crime and Violence
Diversity, Social Justice, and Equity
Environment
Hunger and Poverty in the United States
Local Issues
World Peace and Understanding

In addition to updating the content in social studies textbooks, you need to update pictures, charts, tables, and other visual aids when these materials become dated. You may wish not only to update pictures in the textbook but to present the students with other visuals that show different aspects of a city, nation, or situation. A unit on Nigeria or Colombia may show pictures of rural villages but not of cities. Consequently, the students may acquire visual misconceptions about Nigeria and Colombia, not realizing that there are major cities such as Lagos, Nigeria, and Bogota, Colombia, in developing nations.

One of the best sources of pictures to supplement the social studies textbook is magazines such as *Life* and *National Geographic.* Ethnic magazines such as *Ebony* and *Hispanic* magazine contain pictures of ethnic groups not usually found in large numbers in magazines such as *Life* and *Time,* the news magazine. Parents are a good source of old copies of these magazines because many families periodically discard old magazines. A useful PTA project is to form a clearinghouse to collect discarded magazines from parents that can be used for instructional purposes. You can clip pictures from the magazines discarded by your own family. Pictures can also be downloaded from the Internet. You should keep an ongoing file of pictures and group them by categories such as those listed above. To preserve and display them in an attractive way, pictures should be laminated.

You can use a variety of sources to update statistics, charts, tables, and other information in textbooks. One of the most useful sources for this purpose is the

TABLE 8.1. *Internet Resources for Updating Textbooks*

The Britannica Internet Guide—http://www.ebig.com

Ebony magazine—http://www.ebonymag.com/

The Economist—http://www.economist.com/

The Education Network—http://www.EducationNetwork.com

The History Channel—http://www.historychannel.com/class

Kathy Schrock's Guide for Educators—http://www.capecod.net/schrockguide

National Council for the Social Studies—http://www.ncss.com

National Geographic Society—http://www.nationalgeographic.com/main.html

New York Times—http://www.nytimes.com

Pathfinder Network—http://www.pathfinder.com/welcome/

    CNN

    Fortune

    Life

    Money

    Time

Population Reference Bureau—http://www.prb.org

Smithsonian Institution—http://www.si.edu/newstart.htm

Social Studies School Service—http://SocialStudies.com

U.S. Bureau of the Census—http://www.census.gov

Wall Street Journal: Classroom Edition—http://info.wsj.com/classroom/

---

information and data published by the Bureau of the Census. The Bureau publishes a series of useful and timely publications. One of the most helpful is the *Statistical Abstract of the United States.* Published annually, it contains census data on a wide range of topics, including population, vital statistics, immigration and naturalization, elections, energy, and foreign commerce and aid. The *Bureau of the Census Catalog,* issued periodically, contains a complete list of the Bureau's publications, grouped by topics such as agriculture, business, and foreign trade. Census data can also be accessed from the Internet at [http://www.census.gov].

Almanacs, published annually by a number of commercial publishers, also contain valuable statistical information on a wide range of topics and issues. Most of the yearly almanacs are available in inexpensive paperback editions. The annual almanacs usually go on sale near the end of the year and are still available during the first part of the next year. The annuals that are published by encyclopedias such as *Britannica* and *World Book* also contain articles and statistics which can be used to update social studies textbooks. These are usually received each year by school and public libraries.

The Population Reference Bureau is an excellent source of information and publications that can be used to update your social studies textbook. Its informative periodic publications cover such topics as immigration, minorities throughout the United States and the world, education, health, and demographic information. The Population Reference Bureau also publishes an annual *World Population Data* sheet that contains demographic data and estimates for the countries and regions of the world. Its website address is [http://www.prb.org].

You should be sensitive to the need to update the maps in textbooks. National boundaries change from time to time, especially within the developing areas of the world and in regions, such as the Middle East, where there is ongoing conflict. Many African nations changed their names when they gained independence. During the 1990s several new Eastern European countries were created when communism was overthrown in those nations. However, older maps of Europe do not show the new countries. On those maps, Georgia and Ukraine are part of the Soviet Union or the Union of Soviet Socialist Republics. National boundaries are also changing in Asia. In 1996 Hong Kong reverted to the People's Republic of China. It is important that students learn the new rather than the old names and geographical boundaries of these nations and regions. Current editions of standard atlases, such as those published by Hammond and the National Geographic Society, can be used to update the maps in textbooks.

ENRICHING TEXTBOOKS

While it is necessary to update textbooks with both visual aids and information, you also need to enrich and supplement textbooks with other kinds of resources. Different points of view on issues, concepts, and events, information that relates directly to the community and cultures of your students, and art and literary resources are the kinds of materials that are needed to enrich textbooks. Art and literature, as well as other kinds of data sources, are discussed later in this chapter. We will now discuss a few other ways in which textbook lessons can be extended and enriched.

Primary grade textbooks usually include units on families, the individual, the community, the neighborhood, and the school. During a study of the textbook unit on families, you can ask the students to bring pictures of their families, discuss the kinds of families they have, and make a list of the things their families do for fun or recreation. The students can also make a list of the rules they have at home. When the community is being studied, you can survey the parents of your students to learn about their jobs. The parents' jobs can be discussed. Several of the parents can be invited to class to tell about their jobs. To culminate the unit, a field trip can be taken to places where several of the parents work.

In the fifth grade, textbooks often have units that relate to "Our Country and Other Lands." During a study of these units, the class can undertake a historical study of their community by interviewing citizens who have lived in the community for many years and by visiting community museums, newspaper offices, churches, and cemeteries. You can integrate this experience with the language arts and require the students to write up their community history in narrative form. It can be duplicated and shared with other classes, parents, neighbors, and other members of the community. During their study of other lands, you can survey the parents to find out which nations they have visited. Some of the parents can be invited to give their impressions of the nations they have visited and share their slides, photographs, art, and artifacts.

When using the textbook as a major data source, you should use the experiences and resources of the students, the parents, and the community to enrich and extend textbook lessons. Primary sources found in documentary histories, diaries, conflicting accounts of the same historical events, political cartoons from current newspapers, and dramatic and role-playing techniques can all be used to enrich and extend textbook learning and experiences.

INTRODUCING THE TEXTBOOK TO STUDENTS

You should not hand out the textbook to students during the first few days of the school year until you have developed a plan for introducing it. While introducing the textbook to the students, you should explain that, although the textbook is an important resource, it will be only one of many resources that will be used during the year. Some students might come to your room, because of previous experiences, with the idea that the textbook is the social studies curriculum.

You should introduce the textbook to the students by asking them to note the authors, the title, and the publisher. It is a good idea for the students to learn something about the authors of their textbooks. If biographical sketches of the authors are not included in the book (which is often the case in school textbooks), you might be able to obtain information about the authors of the textbook from biographical sources such as *Who's Who in America* or from one of the regional *Who's Who* books. Information on authors who are university professors can be accessed through the Internet web pages for their universities.

You should explain the parts of the book to the students, including the front matter (title page, table of contents, preface, etc.) and the end matter (the appendixes, glossary, index, and other special features). You should explain the purpose of each of these sections of the book and ask the students to complete a number of activities, such as those below, that will help them to increase their skills in using the textbook:

> How many units are in the book? (Using the table of contents)
> Turn to the first page of the unit on the Civil War. (Using the table of contents)
> Find the first page on which Abraham Lincoln is mentioned. (Using the index)
> Turn to the first page where the Constitution is discussed. (Using the appendix)
> How does the author define Civil War? (Using the glossary)
> Find the maps that show the states which made up the Confederacy. (Using the guide to maps)
> Locate the names of the original 13 colonies. (Using the index to locate charts)

Reference Books

You should introduce reference books to students in the primary grades and help them increase their skills in using reference books in each subsequent grade. One of the first reference books that students should learn to use is the dictionary. Picture dictionaries can be used to introduce primary grade children to the dictionary. These dictionaries define words, such as *river* and *school,* with both words and pictures. Some dictionaries for young children, such as *The Magic World of Words: A*

Very First Dictionary (Macmillan), define each entry simply but show pictures of only some of the concepts. As students progress through the grades, they should be introduced to increasingly comprehensive and complex dictionaries and helped to attain the skills needed to use them.

There are a number of good dictionaries on the market designed for upper elementary and middle school students, including *The Oxford Children's Dictionary* and the *Macmillan Dictionary for Students*. You can help students to acquire skills in using a dictionary by asking them to do activities such as the following:

> Rearrange a group of words into alphabetical order.
> Write sentences illustrating the various ways in which *culture* is defined in the dictionary.
> Tell how the words citizen, citizenry, and citizenship are alike and different.
> Define these words and use them correctly in sentences that are related to the behavior of people: artifact, norm, behavior, values.
> Find the origins of these words: delicatessen, pretzel, tortilla, enchilada, chow mein, smorgasbord.

Students should also be introduced to other reference books, such as encyclopedias and almanacs, in the primary grades. As students progress through the grades, they should be given assignments that will help them increase their skills in using reference books. In the primary grades, you can use reference books such as those in the *Childcraft* series to introduce children to the concept of a reference book. *Childcraft* includes several volumes that treat topics typically studied in elementary social studies, including *Places to Know, How We Get Things, Children Everywhere,* and *Holidays and Customs.* You can introduce young children to these books by reading aloud from them. When the students learn to read, you can make simple assignments requiring them to use these kinds of resources independently or in small groups.

Beginning in the middle and upper grades, social studies teachers frequently give students assignments that require use of the encyclopedia and other reference sources. *Encarta* (Microsoft) and *Britannica* are two encyclopedias that are available on compact disks (CDs). Students are often asked to prepare written or oral reports which require the use of reference books. Not infrequently, teachers will assign a written report when the students do not have the skills to select appropriate readings needed to prepare the report, to locate the needed resources, and to organize and write the report. What often happens in these circumstances is that parents do a lot of work on the reports or the students copy verbatim from encyclopedias and other reference works. In the first instance, the report is a product developed largely by parents. In the latter case, the student report is primarily a random collection of quotations from authorities.

To reduce these problems, you should make sure that the students have the skills needed to complete an oral or written report prior to assigning it. This should be done even if the skills were taught in a previous grade. Students' knowledge and skills often become rusty over the summer months. Students also attain skills at highly varying levels when they are introduced.

One way to make sure that students have the skills to complete oral and written reports is to do such a report with the class prior to making the assignment. During a unit on "Leaders and Leadership," a fourth-grade teacher asked each of the students to prepare a written report on one of the nation's presidents. However, before giving the assignment, the teacher chose one president, George Washington, and worked with the class to prepare a report on Washington. The class first did some general reading on Washington. They then made a list of major topics they wanted to cover in the report, including his childhood, education, and early career. They then made a list of resources they could use to find information about George Washington. Their list included encyclopedias, informational books in the school and public library, and U.S. history textbooks that they could borrow from the fifth grade.

The class gathered these materials and read them together. As they read the sources, they took notes and listed the main ideas from the sources under the major topics they had identified. The class then organized their notes and prepared a final outline. Finally, they wrote, edited, revised, and rewrote their report on Washington until it was polished.

Informational Books

Informational trade books intended for a general audience are another important resource you can use to enrich social studies units and lessons. These books are not intended for use as school textbooks and consequently tend to cover a wide range of topics in considerable depth. Informational trade books for children are usually written by single authors. The authors of these books can usually express points of views and positions more freely than textbook authors.

Each year, hundreds of children's books are published, many of them informational books that can be used to enrich the social studies. *Children's Books in Print*, the *Elementary School Library Collection, Horn Book*, and the *Best in Children's Books* by Zena Sutherland can help you locate appropriate informational books for use in the social studies. Each spring, usually in April, *Social Education*, the official journal of the National Council for the Social Studies, publishes an annotated list of "Notable Children's Trade Books in the Field of Social Studies." This list includes both fiction and informational books that can be particularly useful.

Informational books that can be used to enrich the social studies cover a range of topics, from early colonial days to current social issues and problems. Such books can be used to initiate a unit, to test hypotheses, for dramatic and role-playing incidents, and as references when students prepare written and oral reports. Informational books can usually be found in the school and public libraries. They can also be identified and ordered through the Internet using [http://www.amazon.com]. You will need to help the students acquire the library and computer skills needed to locate informational books.

Using Fiction to Enrich the Social Studies

There is a gold mine of fiction that can be used to enrich the social studies. When used properly, fiction not only makes the social studies more interesting, but it also provides the students with valuable insights into historical periods that cannot be obtained easily from textbooks and informational books. Fiction used in social studies should be carefully selected and effectively used. Fiction not only enriches and adds interest to social studies units; it can help students to answer major unit questions.

Historical fiction, novels, poems, stories, and other literary forms can give students keen insights into the hopes, dreams, aspirations, and behavior of peoples who lived in the past and who live today. Students should be taught the difference between fact and fiction. However, they should also be helped to understand how literature provides unique insights into the behavior and world views of peoples.

When the fifth-grade students at one school studied the ancient Romans, they used a children's version of the *Aeneid* to help answer such questions as "How did the Romans feel toward the pagan gods?" "What were the characteristics of an ideal Roman?" and "What were the favorite legends of the Romans?" Each of these questions was related to the central problem of the unit: "How did the ancient Romans live, think, and feel?" These and other questions were identified in the early part of the unit. The students were encouraged to use a variety of sources to find the answers.

Copies of the *Aeneid* were in the room. The teacher anticipated many of the questions the students raised in the first stage of the unit and realized that the *Aeneid* would provide answers to many of them. After reading the *Aeneid* and factual sources, the students concluded that the Romans held their gods in high esteem, and that an ideal Roman, personified by Aeneas, sacrificed personal wishes for the good of his country. They also knew the legendary history of the founding of Rome.

If fictional writers thoroughly research the period they write about, their words can give the reader keen insights into the past . In the *Devil's Arithmetic* by Jane Yolen, a young girl resents her Jewish heritage until she travels back in time to a small Jewish village in Nazi-occupied Poland. This book will give students an appreciation for the human dimension of World War II.

Fiction can be used to make the social studies more meaningful and interesting to students. However, fictional works used in the social studies should be carefully chosen and used only when they help solve the central problems and questions raised in units and lessons. Their purpose in the unit or lesson should be clear to both students and the teacher. Students should be helped to distinguish fact from fiction. However, they should also be helped to appreciate the social and historical validity of powerful and authentic fiction.

VISUAL, AUDIO, AND AUDIOVISUAL MATERIALS

Visual materials, such as pictures, illustrations, and charts, are often used in the social studies to introduce concepts, reinforce learning, and extend understanding. We have already discussed how pictures can be used to update the content of textbooks. Audio materials such as records, tapes, and radio can also be used to enrich the social studies program. Videos, which combine pictures, sound, and motion, can help students to experience powerful examples of concepts, value dilemmas, and decision-making opportunities.

Audio materials such as tapes can be combined with texts to enrich the social studies program.
Source: Northshore School District, Seattle.

The objectives for a lesson should be the main consideration when deciding which form of material to use and how to use it. When introducing a concept such as culture, photographs or artifacts might be more appropriate than a videotape on the Netsilik Eskimo. Most videotapes have many distracting clues and examples and are better used to reinforce rather than to introduce concepts.

When you use media materials with your classes, you should prepare, present, and follow up. Brown, Lewis, and Harcleroad (1983) have identified five steps you should follow:

1. prepare yourself
2. prepare the environment
3. prepare the class
4. use the item
5. follow up

You should prepare for using an item such as a video by deciding what objectives the item is designed to attain, previewing it, developing questions and activities related to it, and arranging for the delivery of the item. It is important that arrangements for the delivery of the item to your classroom be made well in advance of when you plan to use it. You should also check to make sure that the physical setting is appropriate for the item. You might need to obtain a videocassette recorder (VCR) to show a video in your room.

Prepare the class for the use of the item by giving the students an overview of it and explaining how it relates to the other unit experiences. The students should have a clear idea of what you expect them to understand from a video. Giving the students a list of key questions is one effective way to help them focus while viewing it.

After viewing a videotape or listening to a recording, the class should discuss the major points it presented, relate these points to other learnings in the unit, and evaluate the item. The class may conclude that the videotape or recording was a valuable learning experience or that some other kind of experience might have been more valuable. Another possibility is that the students will conclude that, although the videotape or recording was excellent, they would have gained more from it had it been shown earlier in the unit.

Enriching the Social Studies with Art

The use of art in the social studies can add depth, meaning, and interest to social studies units and lessons. Students in the elementary and middle school grades can be taught the visual literacy skills needed to derive social science concepts from works of art. Works of art such as paintings, drawings, sculpture, basketry, pottery, and architecture can help students to derive and test hypotheses about peoples who lived in the past and who live today.

After studying a unit on the ancient Greeks that includes a study of their architecture and a discussion of Doric, Ionic, and Corinthian orders, fifth-grade students can be helped to formulate the concept of cultural borrowing by looking at a picture of the Roman Pantheon. When they begin their study of the ancient Romans, the students can be asked a question such as "What features of the Roman Pantheon are similar to the Greek Temple of the Olympian Zeus (the Olympium) and other Greek temples we have discussed?" The students will quickly discover that both buildings use Corinthian capitals. Knowing that the Greeks developed the Corinthian order, they will correctly hypothesize that the Romans borrowed it from the Greeks.

The concept of cultural borrowing is paramount in the social sciences. You can use other examples of art to develop and extend it. Roman art is especially conducive to teaching cultural borrowing because it is highly eclectic. The Romans borrowed many art forms from the Egyptians, the Etruscans, and the Greeks. To further extend the concept of cultural borrowing, you can ask the students to name buildings in their community that use Greek and Roman architectural innovations. This may require some field research. Hardly a student will be disappointed, because nearly every community has public buildings that use classical architecture.

When studying medieval times, the students can discuss the symbolic meaning of the pointed arch and other features of medieval cathedrals. After reading several accounts of the Middle Ages and viewing pictures of medieval cathedrals, the students will be able to conclude that medieval people were preoccupied with life after death and that the medieval cathedral was the ultimate expression of this preoccupation. The pointed arch was especially effective in guiding the worshipper's eyes toward heaven. Medieval people were awed by the potent otherworldly impact of the magnificent cathedrals.

When shown a detail from a medieval stained-glass window, such as one from the cathedral in Chartres, students can be asked to tell whether they think the figures look like real individual people or like types and symbols. The students will discover that the medieval artist was not concerned with individuals but with symbols and types. In the artist's preoccupation with the other world, individuals *per se* were not important. Instead, Virtue, Purity, and Evil were personified.

The students can compare medieval with Renaissance paintings. They will discover that the artists of the Renaissance were more interested in this world and in individuals rather than in types and symbols. This is evident by the tendency toward portraiture during this period, by the expensive imported silks, other fabrics, and jewelry in high Renaissance paintings, and by the de-emphasis of strictly religious subjects. In the architecture and sculpture of the period, the students can see a revival of the classical Greek and Roman traditions. Michelangelo's *David* is an excellent example of this trend. Using the Internet, students can visit great museums throughout the world. They can travel to Paris to visit the Louvre Museum at [http://www.paris.org/Musees/Louvre] or to the Smithsonian Institution at [http://www.si.edu] in Washington, D.C.

The art and architecture of today, like that of the Middle Ages and the Renaissance, mirror central concerns. While the cathedral was the ultimate expression of the ideals of medieval Europe, the present-day preoccupation with commerce and industry is reflected in the office buildings that dominate our cities. Louis Sullivan's Guaranty Building (Buffalo), Hood and Howells's Daily News Building (New York), and many other modern office buildings of architectural merit can be viewed. The students can be taken on a field trip to study important modern office buildings in their community and their architects. Several of the architects could be invited to class to share their views of what they were trying to achieve and express in their buildings.

The students can examine works of contemporary American artists and the works of artists in their local communities. Several local artists can be invited to class to share and discuss their works. When the students study contemporary

Western art, they can be helped to discover ways in which the freedom and individualism in contemporary art reflect some of the salient characteristics of modern society.

In a number of important ways, art forms can be used to enrich social studies lessons and units. The use of art to reinforce social studies learning heightens students' interests and historical insights. It also gives them a deeper appreciation for the cultural heritage of humankind.

Records, Radio, and Audiotapes

Sounds from the past and the present can enrich social studies lessons and units. Using recordings and audiotapes is often more convenient than arranging for the showing of a videotape. Record players and tape recorders are easily accessible in most schools. Many elementary and middle school students own their own tape recorders.

A number of commercial records and tapes are available for use in social studies lessons. John F. Kennedy's inspiring inauguration address, Martin Luther King's hopeful "I Have a Dream" speech, and Adlai E. Stevenson's poignant words when he conceded defeat to Eisenhower in November 1952 are examples of excellent commercial recordings. Alex Haley tells the story of the search for his roots on a commercial recording.

You and your students can make recordings. Recordings can be made of important presidential speeches and news conferences to be played and discussed in class. Your students can also make audiotapes for use in their class reports. There are some excellent programs on the radio that can be used to enrich the social studies. In our highly visually oriented age, we tend to forget that the radio is a valuable and effective tool for information as well as entertainment.

Films and Videotapes

Films and videos combine pictures and sound. They are an effective teaching tool. They can also be stopped at any point to answer student questions and to clarify and extend points made in the presentation. Commercial films and videos are available on an infinite variety of topics studied in social studies classes, such as Colonial America, the Civil War, and the post–World War II era.

Many educational films and videos on social studies topics are produced each year. Some films and videos designed for other purposes, such as television documentaries, are also available at public libraries and can be rented or purchased by educational institutions. If used properly, films and videos can add vitality and interest to social studies lessons and units. An excellent source of videotapes and other social studies materials, such as books and simulation games, is Social Studies School Service, located in Culver City, California. They publish an annual catalog. Their website address is [http://SocialStudies.com].

However, films and videos should be carefully chosen, clearly related to the major objectives of the unit, be of a high technical quality, and be appropriate for students. The use of videotapes in schools is often abused. Sometimes they are shown as fillers, to kill time or merely to entertain. At other times videos are shown when their relationship to what's being studied is unclear to the students. Almost nothing is done in these instances to relate the videotape to instructional goals.

The discussion and activities that take place before and after a videotape is shown are in some ways more important than the videotape itself. These activities extend and clarify the understanding presented in the videotape and relate them to the other learnings in the unit. Without pre- and post-discussion and activities, the screening of a videotape might result in little learning.

Video recorders and videotapes can be used creatively in the social studies. Students can use the video recorder to record role-playing incidents and to make class presentations. The portable video recorder can be used to record observations made in the community and on field trips.

Television

Television is a salient part of most students' lives. However, too much television can affect students' academic performance. A study sponsored by the U.S. Department of Education found that students in both 4th and 8th grades who watched 3 or fewer hours of television each day had a higher level of proficiency in U.S. history than those who watched 4 or more hours of television each day. In 12th grade, students who watched 1 hour or less of television each day had higher average history proficiency scores than did those who watched 2 or more hours each day (U.S. Department of Education, 1996). You should help students become more critical viewers of television. You should use television as an instructional medium when it is an effective and feasible alternative.

Television is frequently harshly criticized. Its critics claim that its primary purpose is to sell products rather than to inform and entertain, that the quality of most programs is very low, and that it frequently manipulates viewers. Despite the criticisms, there are some excellent programs, on both public and commercial television, that you can use to extend and enrich social studies learning.

Documentaries, historical fiction, and news programs can all be used to extend and enrich the social studies. Alex Haley's *Roots,* shown on commercial television, combined imagination with facts to present a powerful and entertaining saga about African Americans. *Holocaust* and *The Winds of War* were historical novels serialized on commercial television. *Holocaust* gave keen insights into the experiences of Jews during World War II. *The Winds of War* enabled the audience to share the experiences of one American family during World War II. Excellent documentaries are often shown on public television. *The Civil War,* produced by Ken Burns, was a powerful and informative public television documentary.

Programs such as *Roots, Holocaust,* and *The Civil War* are not aired on commercial television frequently. You should periodically check sources that announce outstanding forthcoming television programs. You need to be aware of the programs in advance in order to give students viewing assignments. Most public television stations provide schedules of their forthcoming programs to subscribers. *Social Education* periodically announces upcoming quality television programs and provides its members with viewing guides that can be used with their students. When television viewing assignments are made, their purpose and relationship to the total social studies curriculum should be clear.

Teaching Visual Literacy Skills

The social studies curriculum, as well as the language arts, should help students develop and increase their visual literacy skills. Whether watching a news presentation or a documentary, students should realize that the director of a film, like the author of a book, has biases and a point of view. Most visual presentations present selected perspectives on events and issues while omitting others. Students should be helped to analyze visual media critically, just as they are taught to analyze and evaluate the printed word.

Several curriculum projects are designed to help students increase their visual literacy and critical viewing skills. Public television station WNET/13 (New York) developed a text that helps students view television more critically (*Critical Television Viewing*, 1980). It states that critical television viewers:

1. Analyze what they see and hear on television.
2. Make informed judgments of what they watch.
3. Express their evaluations in discussion, in writing, or in a choice of reading.
4. Distinguish television fiction from life's reality.
5. Understand television's relationship to the printed word.
6. Make judicious use of their viewing time.

Cortés and Richardson (1983) have developed teaching strategies that help students analyze the media. The strategies are:

1. Determination of perspective
2. Evaluation of the logic of analysis
3. Analysis of the topic being discussed
4. Analysis of supplementary materials
5. Analysis of connections with other phenomena
6. Projecting into the future
7. Analysis of self

In step 5, students discuss the future implications of the presentation. In the final step, they examine their own beliefs, attitudes, and perceptions.

The techniques developed by WNET and Cortés and Richardson can help you devise strategies and questions that will enable students to develop and increase their skills in critically analyzing visual media. When students view a film or television presentation, they should be asked questions to increase their skills in analyzing the director's point of view and the perspectives from which the presentation is made.

The Computer in the Social Studies

The technological landscape in schools has changed dramatically over the last decade. It is common for elementary and middle school students to be computer literate. Students have access to computers in their classrooms and many schools have extensive computer labs. Between 1985 and 1995, the number of computers in U.S. public schools increased from one computer for every 75 students to one for every 11 students (Quality Education Data, 1995). In 1997 and 1998, U.S. schools spent $5.2 billion on technology. With the change in the number of computers per student, there has also been a change in the way computers are used. Computers are moving from the periphery of the classroom where they were primarily used for drill and practice to a more central place in the school curriculum where students are integrating Internet-based resources into their schoolwork.

Early uses of computers consisted of computer-assisted instruction using software stored on floppy disks. Floppy disks have been replaced by hard drives with more storage capability, compact disks (CDs) and videodiscs. The most revolutionary change in the technological landscape, however, is the arrival of the information superhighway, the Internet. The Internet, a worldwide information network, and its hypermedia environment, the World Wide Web (WWW), give students almost instant access to the world's great museums and libraries, opportunities to dialogue with people who live in distant places, and the most up-to-date information on topics of interest. In 1997, 29.2 percent of K–12 public school classrooms had access to the Internet, and 72 percent of schools reported that they had Internet access in some location (Quality Education Data, 1997). More information on the use of technology in schools can be found at the website for Quality Education Data (QED), [http://www.qualityeducationdata.com].

Web browsers, such as *Netscape Navigator* and Microsoft Internet *Explorer,* can be used to explore the Internet by providing access to *Yahoo, Lycos, Alta Vista,* and other search engines. Directions for using each search engine can be found on its homepage. It is also possible to go directly to an information source on the Internet by entering the web address or URL (Universal Resource Locator) into a web browser. URLs are provided throughout this book to help readers locate web pages that can help them access relevant social studies information. It is important to remember that although many websites are relatively stable, some are experimental and are discontinued. Others are discontinued because maintaining a website can be time-consuming and costly. If a website contains information that you plan to use, be sure to download it.

Web pages frequently include electronic communication links such as e-mail, newsgroups, and listservs (see Table 8.2). Electronic communication links such as these are an exciting way to put students in touch with people who are different from them and thus explore different values and the implications of those values. Teachers can set up listservs that provide an opportunity for their students to work collaboratively with students in other regions or countries.

Computer technology is an important resource for the social studies. However, in addition to the opportunities that stem from computer technology, such as easy access to relevant and timely data, challenges also exist. Those challenges include the lack of clear authority, misinformation, and information overload. The dichotomy that is inherent in computer technology can be overwhelming to students who do not have critical thinking skills. Information on the Internet, for example, may be inaccurate, incomplete, or misleading. There are few gatekeepers to evaluate the quality of the information posted there. Students need to learn how to organize, evaluate, and make meaning from the information they identify on the Internet. Students have to determine what is fact and what is opinion. In addition

TABLE 8.2. *Glossary of Computer Terms*

Browsers   Computer applications such as Netscape Navigator and Microsoft's Internet Explorer. Browsers access the World Wide Web by decoding and displaying documents written in HyperText Markup Language (HTML).

CD-ROM   Compact disc (CD) used as a Read-Only-Memory (ROM). Data is stored on CDs in a form that is readable by a laser. This form results in CDs having great capacity to store and access data.

E-mail   Electronic mail consists of messages sent from one individual to another using telecommunications links between computers.

Homepage   The hypertext document you see when you first enter a website.

Internet   The world's largest computer network. The Internet consists of networks that cooperate to form a seamless network for their collective users. It provides file transfer, remote log in, electronic mail, news, and other services.

Listservs   A special form of e-mail in which a person can send a message to everyone who subscribes to the listserv. Subscriptions to listservs are free.

Search Engines   Computerized databases of files. Search engine files can be text, graphic, or audio. Yahoo, Lycos, and Alta Vista are three examples of popular search engines.

URL   The Universal Resource Locator serves as a mailing address that can be entered into a web browser. The URL for the National Council for the Social Studies (NCSS Online) is [http://www.ncss.org].

World Wide Web (WWW)   The World Wide Web is a hypertext-based system for finding and accessing Internet resources.

---

to determining the accuracy of the information, they must judge its worthiness and authenticity as they consider how it relates to other data sources.

Even though computers are increasingly becoming a standard part of the hardware in elementary and middle schools, students will have varying levels of computer literacy and skills. Some students will enter your classroom with rather sophisticated computer literacy and skills, and you will need to have the appropriate computer skills to guide their learning. Other students will have few computer skills. Therefore lessons and activities using the computer will need to be highly individualized.

The teaching of computer literacy and basic computer skills should begin in the primary grades and continue throughout the elementary and middle school grades. Computer awareness lessons should help students understand the nature of computers, how they follow instructions and manipulate information, and how they help us to solve problems. The students should understand the various parts of the microcomputer and the functions of each part, such as the keyboard, the disk drives, and the monitor. The way information is stored on a diskette and how it can be retrieved should also be a part of computer awareness instruction.

A number of computer simulations and decision-making software are available for schools. These programs give students an opportunity to step into social, political, or historical settings, make decisions, and respond to the consequences of those decisions. Students are able to explore situations that would not be available

"We keep Amos around just in case the computer breaks down."
Source: Joseph Farris. Used with permission.

to them in any other way. Popular programs include *The Oregon Trail* and *Fur Trader Choices,* in which students make decisions as they travel west, and *Where in the World Is Carmen Sandiego? Where in the U.S.A. Is Carmen Sandiego?,* and *Where in Europe Is Carmen Sandiego?,* the popular geography simulations in which students use geography clues and reference books to locate Carmen Sandiego. These kinds of programs can be integrated into the curriculum by having students write about their experiences on the Oregon Trail, develop maps of the fur trader's expedition across Canada, or calculate the number of miles traveled by Carmen Sandiego as she moved from one location to another.

Selecting appropriate courseware is a difficult and time-consuming task, and one that is not made easier by the paucity of excellent programs and by the fact that courseware made for one kind of computer will not necessarily run on others. Magazines such as *The Computing Teacher, Personal Software*, and *Softalk* contain software reviews. Before purchasing software, be sure that it is appropriate to the goals and objectives of the social studies program. Make sure that the objectives of the courseware and the objectives of your instructional program are consistent, that the courseware will run on your computer, and that it will interest and motivate your students. Develop criteria that you can use to evaluate social studies software. Several books contain excellent criteria for selecting courseware (Jung, 1994; McConnell, 1997).

The criteria can also serve as a departure point for thinking about assessing student learning. Unfortunately, very little work has been done on how to determine what a student knows and can do as a result of spending time on the Internet, engaging in e-mail conversations, or participating in a listserv. For example, you will need to devise ways to assess the extent to which students compare and contrast information from one website to another and engage in critical thinking when playing simulation games, and the extent to which access to computer technology influenced student learning. You can ask students to respond to the information found at the site by writing papers, role-playing an incident, or debating an issue. You can also ask students to compare and contrast similar and divergent data from multiple sites.

Technology will increasingly become apart of social studies instruction and you will not be able to ignore computer technology. Computers will become more central to the social studies classroom because more and more students will come to school computer literate. Students, parents, and employers will expect schools to develop and refine students' computer skills and knowledge. In addition, information that you need to make your curriculum relevant and timely will be available through the Internet. This is particularly important when funds limit the purchase of new materials and when rapidly changing events quickly make new books outdated. Your challenge is to take advantage of computer technology by using it effectively while simultaneously avoiding its inherent limitations.

ROLE-PLAYING, CREATIVE DRAMATICS, AND SIMULATION

Role-playing, creative dramatics, and simulation are techniques that can be used to bring more reality into the social studies classroom. Each of these techniques allows students to experience the feelings, perspectives, and points of view of other people. These techniques can be set in historical or present times.

Role-playing, creative dramatics, and simulation are similar in many ways. However, each technique is also unique. The Shaftels (1982) describe role-playing as "a group problem-solving method that enables young people to explore human problems in spontaneous enactments followed by guided discussion" (p. 12). In role-playing situations, several people usually face a problem and are required to make a decision. In their role-playing strategies, the Shaftels present students with a problem story and ask them to identify courses of action and their possible consequences. The students are also asked to make a decision by choosing one of the alternatives. In

"You've got to watch what you program with that computer!"
Source: Joseph Farris. Used with permission.

addition to using open-ended stories, the teacher can use problem situations and dramatic episodes to involve students in role-playing. See the Inquiry Strategy on page 249 for an example of a role-play situation that involves making decisions.

In creative dramatics, students work with a teacher or leader to play through a problem in order to discover alternative solutions and examine the results of those solutions. Students are allowed to express their feelings and behavior in creative dramatics. They express the thought and feelings of the playwright in formal drama (Heinig, 1993). Students can often develop dramatic presentations that are based on books they read in the social studies. The class that read the *Aeneid* when they studied ancient Rome wrote and produced a play based on the book.

Most of the simulations appropriate for use in social studies classes are models of social, economic, or political situations. In simulations, the reality represented is reduced in size so that it is manageable (Hostrop, 1990). Only selected aspects of the real situation are included in a simulation. Developers of simulation reduce and simplify reality so students can focus on selected aspects of reality and because of the impossibility of including all of reality in a model or simulation.

There are some excellent commercially available simulations that you can use to extend and reinforce social studies learning. Some creative teachers and their students also develop their own simulations, based on situations, problems, and events they are studying. Simulations can help students to experience realities that other materials cannot. In *Gateway: A Simulation of Immigration Issues in Past and Present America*, students are helped to appreciate the problems of immigrants, learn more about governmental response to immigrants, and examine ethnic pride.

In *Democracy*, students experience the dilemmas faced by members of Congress when they try to make decisions balancing their values with the values and wishes of their constituents. Students experience some of the problems faced by a community hit by a natural disaster in *Disaster*. *Trade Wars: The Game of Gobble Commerce* gives students a realistic view of international commerce. With fluctuating currency, students buy and sell corporations, form trusts and cartels, collect earnings, and pay debts in pounds, pesos, yen, and dollars. In *Rafa Rafa* the participants live with and cope with a different culture. Students select artifacts that will be buried for 30 years in *Time Capsule: An Interaction Unit Preserving a Record of Today's Culture for the Next Generation's Discovery and Analysis*. There is a wide range of commercial simulations for use in the social studies.

When you use role-playing, creative dramatics, and simulations, every effort should be made to select a technique that is appropriate for a particular lesson or unit and that contributes to the attainment of the unit objectives. These techniques are highly motivating, and students usually enjoy them. They are not infrequently used to motivate students when they are not directly related to the unit goals and objectives.

When these techniques are used, a discussion should take place before and after their use. The primary goal of the discussion before the activity is to help the students to see how it relates to the other learning in the unit and to identify its major intended outcomes. The debriefing that follows the use of the technique should summarize and evaluate it.

inquiry strategy

MAKING DECISIONS IN A ROLE-PLAY SITUATION

DIRECTIONS

1. Ask the students to carefully read the open-ended story "What Should Arlean Do?"
2. Then ask them to divide into groups of four. One member of the group should serve as the group leader. The other three members of the group should play the roles of:

   Arlean Evans, the daughter

   Bruce Evans, the father

   Ruth Evans, the mother

3. The group leader should conduct a discussion with the three role-players so that they will have a clear and definite understanding of their roles. They should understand the points below. The group leader should facilitate the role-play and the discussion that follows.
4. The role-players should forget their own values and try to act out the values of the characters in the story as they interpret them from their careful reading of it. The role-players must understand that they are not themselves, but Arlean, Bruce, and Ruth Evans.
5. The primary task in the role-play is to resolve the problem presented in the story.
6. The role-playing should begin where the story ends. In other words, the role-players should assume that they have participated in the events described in the story. Their job in the role-playing situation is to improvise conversation.
7. To end the role-play, the group leader should stop the other members either when a solution has been reached by the role-players, when time is becoming limited, or when the role-playing situation has reached its logical conclusion, even though a solution may not have been attained. The primary function of the role-playing episode is to serve as a springboard for discussion.
8. After the role-playing has ended, each small group should discuss the questions below. The leader of the group should act as a reporter and recorder. She or he should give a brief report of the role-play and the discussion in the group when the large group reassembles.

QUESTIONS FOR DISCUSSION

1. What is the main problem in this case? Discuss the main problem rather than ancillary problems.
2. Was the problem resolved in the role-playing situation? If so, is the solution an effective one? Why or why not? If the problem was not resolved, how would you resolve it? What are the possible consequences of the solution you propose?
3. What should Arlean do? Why?

WHAT SHOULD ARLEAN DO?

Arlean Evans is an attractive, bright, 11th-grade African American girl who goes to school at Maplewood High. Arlean is one of a handful of African Americans who attend this mainly White school, although about 5 percent of the students are Asians, mostly Japanese and Chinese. Maplewood High is the only high school in the affluent community of Maplewood, which is located in the suburban area of a major city. The Evans family, which consists of Arlean, her brother George, and her parents, have lived in Maplewood all of her life. She attended nearly all-White elementary and junior high schools in Maplewood.

Arlean spends most of her time in her home community. Most of the kids she knows and all of her friends are White. She occasionally visits African American families in the city, which are her parents' and not her friends. She knows some of their children, but only casually. Once in a while she attends a predominantly African American church in the central city with her parents. Her world, however, is primarily White and middle-class. Arlean feels good about being Black and wishes she had more African American friends.

Arlean is trying to make one of the most difficult decisions of her life: where to go to college. Her best friend, Peggy, has decided to go to State University. Arlean has been accepted there. However, because of her outstanding SAT scores, she has also been accepted at Hamilton, the nation's oldest and most prestigious university. She will receive some financial aid if she goes to Hamilton. Bruce, Arlean's father, is a medical doctor. Members of his family have attended Frederick Douglass University, a highly regarded, predominantly Black institution, for three generations. He feels strongly that Arlean should go to Frederick Douglass, not only to follow family tradition but, in his words, "to make lifetime friends." He is putting strong pressure on Arlean to go to Frederick Douglass. Because of pressure from her father, Arlean applied to and has been accepted at Frederick Douglass. Ruth, Arlean's mother, is very concerned that if Arlean does not go to Hamilton, she might miss the educational opportunity of her life. Ruth respects Frederick Douglass and Bruce's family tradition but believes that Arlean's academic possibilities at Hamilton are more important. Arlean is genuinely conflicted.

THE COMMUNITY AS A LEARNING RESOURCE

The community is a rich learning resource that you should not overlook. Institutions and agencies such as factories, museums, zoos, aquariums, newspaper publishers, churches, civil rights organizations, and art galleries are some of the rich resources found in most communities. You can make use of these resources either by taking the students to these institutions (field trips) or by inviting speakers from these institutions to come to the classroom and share their experiences and expertise with the students.

When you decide to make use of a community resource, you will need to determine whether it is more appropriate to take the students to the institution, invite a speaker from the institution to the school, or use some other activity, such as a videotape, to achieve your objectives. When making this decision, you should consider whether your objectives warrant the time and energy that a field trip involves. Inviting a speaker to the classroom from the institution might accomplish your instructional objectives just as well or more effectively. The decision to take a field trip should be made only when it is the best or only way to achieve instructional objectives. Successful field trips require a great deal of preparation, organization, and energy.

Whenever you decide to make use of a community resource, a great deal of preparation must be made. A speaker must be chosen with extreme care. Speakers should be able to give the students the information they need, communicate effectively with young students, and be acceptable to the school and local community. When you invite speakers to class, you should carefully communicate what you expect from them. You should also inform the principal so that appropriate courtesies can be extended.

You should allow ample time to plan a field trip because careful and extensive planning is required for successful field trips. Here are some guidelines:

1. Visit the institution and find out exactly what experiences the students will have when they arrive.
2. Carefully prepare the students for the trip. Explain why they are taking the trip, how it relates to the other learnings in the unit, and exactly what they will be expected to learn and remember.
3. Prepare a list of questions for the students to answer while on the field trip. Ask only a few good questions. Otherwise the students will spend more time writing answers to questions than looking and listening.
4. Get the principal's permission to take the field trip.
5. Send permission forms to the parents for their signatures.
6. Arrange transportation. A bus is usually preferable to a carpool. Volunteer drivers must be arranged if a carpool is used.
7. Ask several parents to volunteer to go with the class. Having about one adult for every five students will make your job a lot easier. Carefully inform the volunteers of their roles and responsibilities.
8. Check to see what the legal responsibilities are for you and the school prior to taking a field trip and make sure that the school has the appropriate insurance coverage in case of accidents or other problems.
9. Make sure that the students have lunch and restroom facilities during the field trip.
10. Find out what procedures should be followed in the event of an unexpected illness or emergency.

Before a guest speaker or a field trip, the students should discuss the purpose of the activity, the questions they might ask, and how they might use the information collected. The class might be able to get permission to tape the guest lecture or to tape lectures during the field trip and to take pictures. When the guest lecture or the field trip is over, the students should summarize and evaluate the experience. They should carry out the plans for the use of the information they made earlier. The students should also send a thank-you note to the guest speaker or to the institution they visited.

SUMMARY

Students need a wide range of data sources to answer the questions and to solve the problems they study in social studies units and lessons. It is necessary to use a variety of data sources because different sources present diverse perspectives on events, problems, and situations. When a variety of media is used in the social studies, the teacher is able to select the most appropriate media form to teach different concepts and to attain various instructional objectives. No media form is appropriate for all learning situations and for all instructional goals. Some media forms are appropriate for some instructional purposes and not for others. It is also necessary to use a variety of media forms in the social studies because students differ greatly in their learning styles. Different students learn best when different media forms are used.

In this chapter we have described how a variety of media forms can be used in the social studies, including reading materials, and visual, audio, and audiovisual materials. We have described some possible uses for the computer in social studies classrooms. Role-playing, creative dramatics, and simulation are also forms of data; they help students gain feelings, attitudes, and points of view that are difficult to attain from other materials. The community is a rich learning resource. However, like the other forms of information, the community must be used wisely and only after careful and thoughtful preparation.

REFLECTION AND ACTION ACTIVITIES

1. Locate a social studies textbook designed for the grade you plan to teach. You will be able to find one in the instructional materials center of your college or university. Select a unit in the book such as "Your Community and State." Develop and write a plan that you can use to update and enrich the unit and make it more meaningful to the students in your community.
2. Choose a social studies unit topic that can be taught at a particular grade level or that you can teach in a class you are student teaching or teaching. Develop a picture file for the topic and obtain pictures from newspapers, magazines, and the Internet. Develop activities for using these pictures.
3. Develop an assignment requiring students to use reference books. How is the assignment related to the unit objectives? How will you make sure that the students have the skills to complete the assignment?
4. List the units in a social studies textbook. Locate and prepare annotations of five informational and five fiction books that can be used to enrich the units. How can these books best be used to enrich and extend the information in the textbook?
5. Develop a social studies unit plan. Make sure that you include each of the following types of materials in your unit plan. Describe an activity using each type of material:

   a. informational book
   b. fiction book
   c. pictures
   d. recordings or tapes
   e. art (including architecture)
   f. role-playing, creative dramatics, or simulation
   g. television
   h. microcomputer
   i. videotape
   j. guest speaker or field trip

6. Demonstrate your understanding of the following terms by writing or stating brief definitions for each of them. Also tell why each is important.
   a. textbook
   b. reference book
   c. informational book
   d. fictional book
   e. art forms
   f. audiovisual resources
   g. visual literacy
   h. simulation
   i. role-playing
   j. creative dramatics

REFERENCES

Brown, J. W., Lewis, R. B., & Harcleroad, F. F. (1983). *AV instruction: Technology, media, and methods* (6th ed.). New York: McGraw-Hill.

Cortés, C. E., & Richardson, E. (1983). Why in the world: Using television to develop critical thinking skills. *Phi Delta Kappan, 64,* 715–716.

Critical television viewing: A language skills work-a-text (1980). Teacher's annotated edition. New York: Cambridge.

English, R. (1980). The politics of textbook adoption. *Phi Delta Kappan, 62,* 275–278.

Heinig, R. B. (1993). *Creative drama for the classroom teacher.* Paramus, NJ: Prentice-Hall.

Hostrop, R. W. (1990). *United States history simulations, 1925–1964.* Palm Springs, CA: ETC Publications.

Jung, H. (1994). *Barriers and bridges.* New York: Peter Lang.

McConnell, S. (1997). *Software project survival guide.* Dunmore, PA: Microsoft Press.

Quality Education Data, (1995). *Technology in Public Schools.* Denver: Author.

Quality Education Data, (1997). Educational technology trends (10th ed.). Denver: Author.

Shaftel, F. R., & Shaftel, G. (1982). *Role playing in the curriculum* (2nd ed.). Englewood Cliffs, NJ: Prentice-Hall.

U.S. Department of Education, National Center for Education Statistics, National Assessment of Educational Progress. (1996). *1994 NAEP U.S. history report card.* Washington, D.C.: U.S. Government Printing Office.

FOR FURTHER READING

Ackermann, E. (1997). *Learning to use the world wide web: Academic edition.* Wilsonville, OR: Franklin Beedle.

Braun, J. A., Fernlund, P. F., & White, C. S. (1996). *Teaching social studies with technology.* Wilsonville, OR: Franklin Beedle.

Budin, H., Kendall, D. S., & Lengel, J. (1986). *Using computers in the social studies.* New York: Teachers College Press.

Heinig, R. B. (1981). *Creative drama for the classroom teacher* (2nd ed.). Englewood Cliffs, NJ: Prentice-Hall.

Knapp, L. R. and Glenn, A. D. (1996). *Restructuring schools with technology.* Boston: Allyn and Bacon.

Muir, S. P. (1996). Simulation games for elementary and primary school social studies: An annotated bibliography. *Simulation and Gaming: An International Journal of Theory, Practice, and Research 7,* 41–73.

Muse, D. (Ed.). (1997). *The New Press guide to multicultural resources for young readers.* New York: New Press.

Patton, W. E. (Ed.). (1980). *Improving the use of social studies textbooks.* Washington, DC: National Council for the Social Studies.

Ryder, R. J., & Hughes, T. (1998). *Internet for educators.* Upper Saddle River, NJ: Merrill.

Schug, M. C., & Berry, R. (Eds.). (1984). *Community study: Applications and opportunities.* Washington, DC: National Council for the Social Studies.

Steen, D. A., Roddy, M. R., Sheffield, D., & Stout, M. B. (1995). *Teaching with the internet: Putting teachers before technology.* Bellevue, WA: Resolution Business Press.

The Social Science Disciplines: Structure, Concepts, and Strategies

• PART III •

Source: Library of Congress, Washington, D.C.

While all the social science disciplines study human behavior, each of them views human events and situations from a somewhat unique and different perspective. Each of the social science disciplines also uses research techniques. Each consists of concepts, generalizations, and theories that can make unique and useful contributions to the design and teaching of the social studies in the elementary and middle school grades.

Part III is designed to acquaint readers with the methods of inquiry and the structures of the various social science disciplines. With this basis, they can create learning experiences for students that will enable them to master both the methods and products of social inquiry. Each of the chapters in this part opens with a *Feature,* written in a news magazine format and style, that is designed to pique the interests of students and to enable them to see ways in which the social science disciplines are involved in the complex social and human problems of our times.

Activities and teaching strategies are an important component of this part of the book. Activities for teaching each of the key social science concepts discussed in each of the chapters in this part are described. Strategies for teaching key social science generalizations are also found in the last part of each chapter in this section. This part of the book is designed to help readers become more knowledgeable about the social science disciplines and to learn creative ways to teach key social science concepts and generalizations.

CHAPTER 9

History: Structure, Concepts, and Strategies

*f*EATURE

REWRITING HISTORY: THE WOMEN WHO STARTED THE MONTGOMERY BUS BOYCOTT

An examination of the events that culminated in the Montgomery Bus Boycott that began on December 5, 1955, will give students an opportunity to understand how history is written and rewritten. Popular and widespread views of the Montgomery bus boycott that are often repeated in textbooks are: (1) the arrest of Mrs. Rosa Parks was the cause of the boycott, and (2) Mrs. Parks refused to give up her seat when asked by the bus driver because she was tired from working hard all day.

Two important autobiographies by women who played key roles in the boycott enable historians to rewrite the history of the boycott. One is by Jo Ann Gibson Robinson, who was an English professor at Alabama State College and who served as president of the Women's Political Council (WPC) (Garrow, 1987). The other autobiography is by Rosa Parks (1992).

The WPC was founded in 1946 by professional African American women in Montgomery to provide leadership, support, and improvement in the Black community and to work for voting rights for African Americans. Many of the WPC members were professors at Alabama State College; others were Black public school teachers.

In 1953, African Americans in Montgomery brought more than 30 complaints about abuses they had experienced from bus drivers to the WPC. Robinson and the other WPC members worked with the city leaders to improve the treatment of Black bus riders but to no avail. About 70 percent of the bus riders in Montgomery were African Americans.

African American bus riders continued to experience intimidation and demeaning and hostile encounters with bus drivers, such as being asked to give up their seats to Whites even when seated in the "Negro" section of the bus. They often had to pay their fares in the front of the bus and were forced to exit and reenter through the back door. Sometimes the bus drove off and left them before they could make it to the back entrance. In 1951 an African American man who had been drinking was killed by a police officer after he was involved in an encounter with a bus driver.

As the negative incidents directed against African American bus riders mounted, the WPC concluded that only a boycott against the bus system would end hostile bus incidents toward Blacks and bus segregation. It began to plan for a boycott and to wait for the "right" incident to use to launch it. Writes Robinson:

> The women felt not that their cup of tolerance was overflowing, but that it had overflowed; they simply could not take anymore. They were ready to boycott. On paper, the WPC had already planned for fifty thousand notices calling people to boycott the buses; only

the specifics of time and place had to be added. And, as tempers flared and emotions ran high, the women became active. (Garrow, 1987, p. 39)

On March 2, 1955, Claudette Colvin, a 15-year-old high school student, was arrested when she refused to give up her seat for White riders. She was seated in the "Negro" section of the bus. Robinson observes:

> When she refused, they dragged her, kicking and screaming hysterically, off the bus. Still half-dragging, half-pushing, they forced her into a patrol car which had been summoned, put handcuffs on her wrists so she would do no physical harm to the arresting police, and drove her to jail. There she was charged with misconduct, resisting arrest, and violating the city segregation laws. (Garrow, 1987, p. 38)

Claudette Colvin was later found guilty and released on probation. The African American community was enraged by the verdict. Mary Louise Smith, an 18 year old, was arrested and fined for refusing to give up her seat in October, 1955. Then, on December 1, 1955, Rosa Parks was arrested for refusing to give up her seat for White riders. Parks (1992) writes:

> People always say that I didn't give up my seat because I was tired, but that isn't true. I was not tired physically, or no more tired than I usually was at the end of a working day. I was not old, although some people have an image of me being old then. I was forty-two. No, the only tired I was, was tired of giving in.
>
> The driver of the bus saw me still sitting there, and he asked was I going to stand up. I said, "No." He said, "Well, I'm going to have you arrested." Then I said, "You may do that." These were the only words we said to each other.

As I sat there, I tried not to think about what might happen. I knew that anything was possible. I could be man-handled or beaten. I could be arrested. People have asked me if it occurred to me that I could be the test case the NAACP had been looking for. I did not think about that at all. In fact if I had let myself think too deeply about what might happen to me, I might have gotten off the bus. But I chose to remain. (p. 116)

Fed up with mistreatment, intimidation, and the violence they experienced daily from bus drivers, the African American women of Montgomery, led by the WPC, called for a boycott of the city buses that would take place the day after Rosa Parks was arrested, Friday, December 2, 1953. Robinson describes how she prepared for the boycott.

I sat down and quickly drafted a message and then called a good friend and colleague John Cannon, chairman of the business department of the college, who had access to the college's mimeograph equipment. When I told him that the WPC was staging a boycott and needed to run off the notices, he told me that he too had suffered embarrassment on the city buses. Like myself, he had been hurt and angry. He said that he would happily assist me. Along with two of my most trusted students, we quickly agreed to meet almost immediately, in the middle of the night, at the college's duplicating room. We were able to get three messages to a page, greatly reducing the number of pages that had to be mimeographed in order to produce the tens of thousands of leaflets we knew would be needed. By 4 A.M. on Friday, the sheets had been duplicated, cut in thirds, and bundled. Each leaflet read (in part):

Another Negro woman has been arrested and thrown in jail because she refused to get up out of her seat on the bus for a White person to sit down....This has to be stopped. Negroes have rights, too, for if Negroes did not ride the buses, they could not operate. Three-fourths of the riders are Negroes, yet we are arrested, or have to stand over empty seats. If we do not do something to stop the arrests, they will continue. The next time it may be you, your daughter, or mother. This woman's case will come up on Monday. We are, therefore, asking every Negro to stay off the buses Monday in protest of the arrest and trial. Don't ride the buses to work, to town, to school, or anywhere else on Monday. (Garrow, 1987, p. 45)

WHAT IS HISTORY?

History has at least three separate components. All *past events* can be thought of as history. This part of history is sometimes called history-as-actuality. The *method* used by historians to reconstruct the past is another element of history. The *statements* historians write about past events are also a part of history. Documents, textbooks, and other historical narratives are made up of historical statements.

The feature above, *Rewriting History*, indicates how difficult it is for historians to write accurate and complete accounts of events such as the Montgomery bus boycott. Many historians wrote that Rosa Parks did not give up her seat for a White rider because she was tired, yet Rosa Parks strongly refutes that statement. What becomes clear from a reading of her autobiography is that Rosa Parks came from a family with a strong commitment to civil rights and had worked as the secretary for the local chapter of the National Association for the Advancement of Colored People (NAACP). Her refusal to give up her seat was the culmination of a life's commitment to civil rights and action.

The *Rewriting History* feature also points out that when historians reconstruct or write historical statements about past events, they often leave out important people and events, such as the significant role that Jo Ann Gibson Robinson and the Women's Political Council played in creating, initiating, and sustaining the boycott. Martin Luther King Jr., rather than the women who were highly influential in the boycott, is usually emphasized in textbook accounts of the Montgomery bus boycott.

The views that historians have of the past are influenced by the availability of evidence, their personal biases and purposes for writing, and the society and times in which they live and write. Although history consists largely of accounts of events from particular points of view, it is often taught in school as a body of truth not to be questioned, criticized, or modified. This approach to the teaching of history stems largely from the teacher's confusion about the nature of history and the popular belief that history contributes to the development of patriotism. Much confusion about the nature of history would be eliminated if teachers distinguished *historical statements* (such as accounts of the Montgomery bus boycott in textbooks) from *past events* (such as the actual events that made up the Montgomery bus boycott). The historical statement, often referred to as the historical fact, is quite different from the actual event. The event itself has disappeared, never to occur again. An infinite number of "facts" can be stated about any past event.

When historians in the late 21st century try to reconstruct the Montgomery bus boycott, they will uncover an infinite number of facts, autobiographies, personal accounts, documents, and secondary accounts related to this pivotal event in the civil rights movement. They will find enough facts to fill volumes. However, historians will be neither interested nor able to completely reconstruct the events related to the boycott. Their investigations will be limited by the statements and other evidence recorded by eyewitnesses, newspapers, magazines, radio, television, and other sources. They will not use all of the facts or information they uncover because their purposes, biases, and the times and cultures they live in will determine the statements they will regard as important and valid. White males, African American males, White females, and African American females might write very different accounts of key events in the civil rights movement of the 1950s and 1960s (Hine, 1986).

Historians often encounter conflicting accounts of events when they try to reconstruct the past. On April 9, 1775, shots were fired in Lexington, Massachusetts, and the American Revolution began. Who fired the first shot, the British or the American colonists, is a problem for historians. Accounts of the Lexington incident written by British commanders and the American colonists often conflict (Bennett, 1970). Historians face similar problems when they try to write accurate descriptions of institutions such as slavery. Accounts written or dictated by slave masters and enslaved persons, and by field- and house-enslaved persons, often conflict (Blassingame, 1977). The historian's problems are complicated by the fact that field-enslaved persons on the same plantation often had very different views of slavery.

Because historical sources conflict and historians can never discover all the information about any single event or present all the data they uncover, they must use some criterion for selection. Their criteria are highly personal. Current needs and purposes deeply influence historians' interpretations of the past. Becker (quoted in Snyder, 1958, p. 59), the noted historian, writes: "The past is a kind of screen upon which we project our vision of the future; it is…a moving picture, borrowing much of its form and color from our fears and aspirations." Historical facts are products of the human mind, because the historian must use sources and artifacts to reconstruct past events.

THE HISTORICAL METHOD

Historians write conflicting accounts of the same events (Bennett, 1970). Historical interpretations of events vary greatly in different times and cultures. Historians debate the extent to which history is a science whose major purpose is to develop generalizations and theories. Historians also disagree about the objectivity of methods of data collection in history.

Historians try to use the method of inquiry used by the behavioral scientist, although they admit that this method must be modified in historical research. Most historians are narrative historians. Narrative historians such as Arthur Schlesinger Jr. and Henry Steele Commager believe that the historical method is to some degree scientific but is at the same time highly personal. Narrative history is a combination of science and art (Commager & Muessig, 1980; Schlesinger, 1970). Gottschalk (1963) points out that a clear gap separates past events from written history and that this gap can be filled only by an imaginative process akin to art.

Objective data collection is an ideal and not a reality in each discipline. Historians are keenly aware of the effects of bias on their research. Becker (Snyder, 1958) has referred to the researcher's bias as the "personal equation" and argues that it inevitably affects the scientist's conclusions. Becker points out that there is bias in the choice of subject, bias in the selection of material, bias in its organization and presentation, and bias in its interpretation. He argues that historians are "creatures of their time, their race, their faith, their class, their country—creatures, and even prisoners" (Snyder, 1958, p. 56). Perhaps an overstatement, it does emphasize the strong influence of bias on the writing of history.

Feminist Historians and Historians of Color
Critique Mainstream History

Feminist historians and historians of color have severely criticized mainstream history during the last two decades. They have argued that mainstream history is male dominated, Western-centric, and too focused on military and political events. These historians have also argued that the histories of women, people of color, and workers have been largely ignored. They have not only critiqued traditional history but have written a score of important articles, books, and monographs that describe the histories of women, people of color, and workers.

Important histories that focus on women include *Women, Work and the Family* by Louise A. Tilly and Joan Wallach Scott (1987), *Pioneer Women: Voices from the Kansas Frontier* by Joanna L. Stratton (1981), *Labor of Love, Labor of Sorrow: Black Women, Work and the Family: From Slavery to the Present* by Jacqueline Jones (1985), and *Women and the American Labor Movement,* edited by Philip S. Foner (1982).

Scholars of color have also written rich, informative, and innovative histories of the experiences of people of color within the last two decades. These histories are written from "insider" perspectives and points of views and describe how people of color interpret their own experiences. In the past, most historical and social science accounts were written from "outsider" perspectives and points of view. Important and influential works in this genre include *Puerto Ricans Born in the U.S.A.* by Clara E. Rodriguez (1989), *Strangers from a Different Shore: A History of Asian Americans* by Ronald Takaki (1989), *Asian Americans: An Interpretive History* by Sucheng Chan (1991), *Black Folk Here and There* by St. Clair Drake, 2 volumes (1987, 1990), and *Occupied America: A History of Chicanos,* 3rd ed., by Rodolfo Acuña (1988).

Narrative Histories: The Goal Is Description

Sociologists and psychologists attempt to formulate a body of concepts and generalizations that can be tested and verified by other researchers, and thus contribute to building theories. Narrative historians typically study and describe single past events and approach them in a somewhat personal fashion. Narrative historians describe events rather than attempt to test generalizations and theories. Conflicting findings and interpretations are found more often in narrative history than in the behavioral sciences.

Narrative historians have serious doubts about their ability to formulate scientific generalizations and theories. They regard the reconstruction and description of past events as their primary and proper goal. They also believe that the narratives they write should be interesting and appealing. Some narrative historians believe that history is a branch of literature and that it serves some of the purposes and is governed by some of the principles of literature (Commager & Muessig, 1980). Narrative historians are primarily interested in description rather than the formulation of generalizations and theories that explain behavior. They often study specific and unique events rather than a large class of different events having common characteristics.

SCIENTIFIC AND QUANTITATIVE HISTORIANS

While most historians use narrative to imaginatively reconstruct the past, some historians are interested in using quantitative data to test hypotheses and to derive generalizations. These historians are called scientific or social science historians. Scientific historians often use quantitative data to test hypotheses and to formulate generalizations and theories. Many political and economic historians use quantitative data in their research. Their subfields are known as the "new political history" and the "new economic history."

Scientific historians use quantitative techniques to study such topics as the composition of the British House of Commons, social mobility using census data, public opinion in the past, trade in the Old Northwest, and ethnic groups and voting patterns. The data in Figure 9.1 might be used by scientific historians to formulate hypotheses about Nazism and the population distribution of European Jews during the 1930s and 1940s. Scientific historians such as William O. Adelotte (1970), Lee Benson (1970), Allyn G. Bogue (1970), and Fogel and Engerman (1974) are optimistic about the contributions scientific and quantitative history makes to historical inquiry and knowledge. However, humanist historians such as Commager (1980) and Schlesinger (1970) believe that many of the most important questions in history must be studied using the approaches and techniques of the humanist rather than those of the scientist. The debate between narrative and scientific historians continues as each group enriches the discipline, which has elements of both science and the humanities.

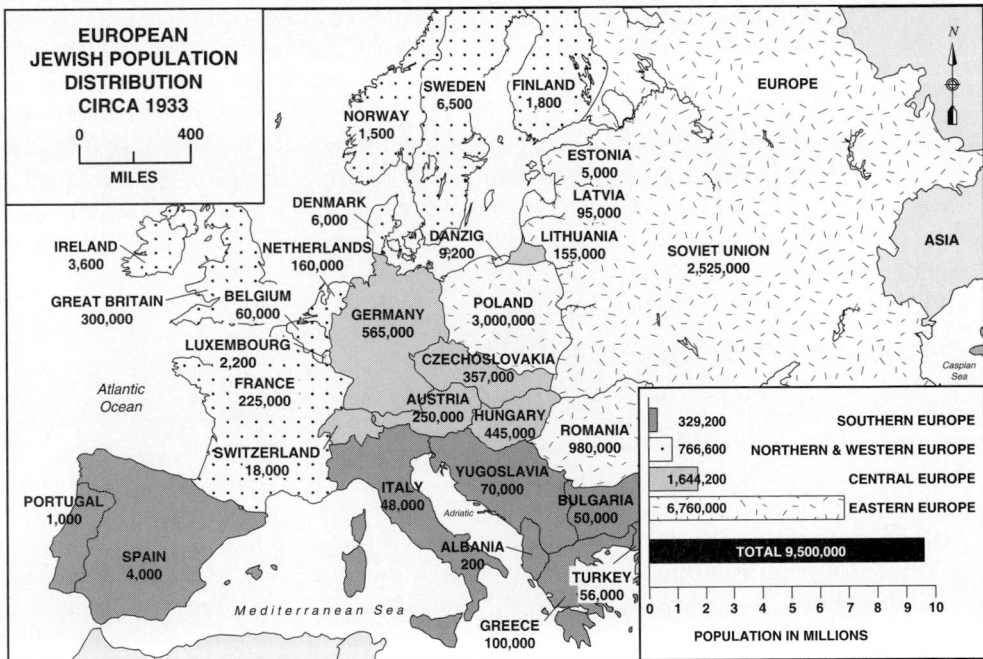

Figure 9.1

European Jewish Population Distribution Circa 1933. During their study of events that culminated in the Holocaust, students can use the information in this map to formulate hypotheses about Nazism and the population distribution of European Jews during the 1930s and 1940s.

Reprinted with permission from United States Holocaust Memorial Museum, *Historical Atlas of the Holocaust,* New York: Simon and Schuster Macmillan, 1996, p. 14.

HISTORY: A MODIFIED SCIENCE

History is scientific because historians try to use the scientific method of inquiry. However, they use it differently from most other researchers. Historical data have large gaps which historians are unable to fill because the events which they study took place in the past and will never occur again. When they study the makeup of Congress or the census in the late 1800s, they often find that the data have large gaps and were frequently compiled and categorized differently in various historical periods. History is also scientific because most historians consciously strive to approach historical problems objectively.

History, however, has a number of nonscientific characteristics. Most narrative historians concentrate on unique problems and events, not on patterns and trends. Most historians do not try to formulate concepts, generalizations, and theories. However, scientific historians try, with difficulty, to formulate concepts, generalizations, and theories. Historians must also act scientifically when they fill in the gaps created by the lack of concrete evidence, try to recreate imaginatively, and write in a literary style.

However, historians who formulate broad statements to describe events and look for evidence to support them are behaving scientifically. Although historians and historian-educators have formulated a number of generalizations that can be used for classroom instruction, scientific historical theories are rare. Brinton's (1962) attempt to identify and verify a system of interrelated generalizations about revolutions is one of the most fruitful efforts by a historian to formulate a scientific theory. Lee Benson (1970), a leading scientific historian, believes that past behavior can be studied scientifically and that powerful concepts and theories can be developed and tested in history. He believes that this will not happen until historians first collect, systematize, and widely disseminate data and master the techniques needed to analyze the data.

DEVELOPMENTS IN HISTORY

A number of important changes took place in historical research during the last three decades. Political history became much less dominant and is no longer the focal point in historical scholarship (Kammen, 1980). Historians are still interested in studying political leaders and developments. However, many historians today are keenly interested in the lives of ordinary citizens and how political, economic, and social developments influence their lives. The study of the activities and outlook of ordinary people is called social history (Stern, 1982). The popularity of social history since the 1980s has resulted in excellent studies of the lives of women, children, enslaved persons, ethnic groups, factory workers, and the family (Foner & Lewis, 1989; Jones, 1985; Takaki, 1993). Social historians study history from the bottom up and describe the total lives of peoples and groups. Their work helps historians to write the total histories of institutions, societies, and nations.

Oral history also became popular during the last three decades. When oral history first emerged, prominent individuals were usually interviewed. However, during the last three decades ordinary men and women were the subject of such popular history books as Race: How Blacks and Whites Think and Feel About the

profile

DARLENE CLARK HINE

Giving Voice to African American Women in History

Darlene Clark Hine, the John A. Hannah Professor of American History at Michigan State University, studied little about African American women while she pursued her B.A. degree at Roosevelt University (Chicago) and her Ph.D. degree in U.S. history at Kent State University, which she received in 1975. Hine's interest in the history of African American women was triggered when Shirley Herd, an elementary school teacher and president of the Indianapolis section of the National Council of Negro Women, asked her in 1980 to write a history of Black women in Indiana. At the time, Hine was an associate professor of history at Purdue University in West Lafayette, Indiana. Hine tried to explain to Herd that she could not write a history of Black women in Indiana because she was not an expert on the history of African American women. Herd persisted and brought a station-wagon load of historical documents on the role of Black women in Indiana to Hine's home. Hine was eventually persuaded by Herd and wrote *When the Truth Is Told: Black Women's Community and Culture in Indiana*, 1875–1950, which was published in 1981.

The publication of *When the Truth Is Told* marked the transformation of Hine's academic research and career. Since 1981 she has written scores of papers, articles, and books on the role of African American women in U.S. history, thus giving them voice and visibility. Today, she is one of the nation's leading authorities on the subject.

Hine worked with Herd and others to establish the Black Women in the Middle West Project, which assembled a permanent archive on the history of Black women in Illinois and Indiana. In 1986 she edited *The State of Afro-American History*. This book resulted from a conference sponsored by the American Historical Association that she coordinated. Hine edited the 16-volume series, *Black Women in United States History: From Colonial Times to the Present*, an important collection of reference works published by the Carlson Publishing Company in Brooklyn, New York.

One of Hine's most significant contributions is the landmark book that she edited, *Black Women in America: An Historical Encyclopedia*, published in 1993. This massive, two-volume work includes over 800 entries that chronicle the history of African American women, organizations, and historical developments from the 17th century to the present. Elsa Barkley Brown of the University of Michigan and Rosalyn Terborg-Penn of Morgan State University, two other African American women historians, served as associate editors of this reference work.

Reference

Darlene Clark Hine, ed., *Black Women in America: An Historical Encyclopedia*, Brooklyn, NY: Carlson Publishing, 1993, pp. xix–xxii.

American Obsession by Studs Terkel (1992) and All God's Dangers: The Life of Nate Shaw by Theodore Rosengarten (1974).

Other important changes have occurred in historical research during the last three decades. A "new" political history and a "new" economic history emerged. In these two subfields particularly, and in history generally, historians tried to become more analytical, quantitative, and scientific. Many historians "tried harder than ever before to theorize and generalize, but also to respect the particularities of place and time—in sum, not to violate the pastness of the past" (Kammen, 1980, p. 30). Historians tried to be both more analytical and more richly descriptive (Kammen, 1980). Historians also tried to use more quantitative methods and computer technology to answer questions and to test hypotheses (Fogel & Engerman, 1974).

Historians became less nationally chauvinistic and more inclined toward national self-criticism in their writings during the last three decades. However, they also became more inclined to inject moral positions into their writings and to view history as a moral science. Wrote Gordon Wright (1976), "Our search for truth ought to be quite consciously suffused by a commitment to some deeply held humane values." Historians have heavily borrowed methods, theories, and concepts from other disciplines in recent years. This has enriched history and resulted in more diversity in the discipline. Some historians have borrowed generously from anthropology. Kammen (1980) writes: "It is now acceptable for [historians] to plot kinship and child-rearing patterns, analyze festivals, and describe idiosyncrasies of village celebrations" (p. 41).

HISTORICAL CONCEPTS

Substantive

The key concepts, generalizations, and theories of a discipline are part of its structure. These knowledge components enable the social scientist to view human behavior from restricted perspectives. Students must study these higher levels of knowledge in order to become adept decision-makers and reflective citizen actors. Thus an important goal of the social studies should be to help students learn the key concepts and generalizations within the disciplines. Students should also learn how these key concepts were constructed, as well as how to construct their own concepts and meanings (Banks, 1993). Constructivist approaches, such as conceptualized by the Russian psychologist Lev Semenovich Vygotsky, should be used to teach students historical concepts and generalizations (Wertsch, 1985).

Conceptual approaches to instruction enable students to view behavior from diverse disciplinary perspectives and to understand higher levels of knowledge. Other elements of structure are the modes of inquiry used by social scientists to solve problems and to derive concepts, generalizations, and theories. Students must use scientific modes of inquiry to derive higher levels of knowledge.

In Chapter 2 we described the advantages of using conceptual approaches to instruction. However, it is difficult to draw concepts from some of the disciplines for instructional purposes, either because the field's leaders have not focused much attention on their special concepts or, more frequently, because social scientists are unable to agree on what the key concepts within their disciplines are.

Identifying key concepts in history to guide instructional planning poses special problems. While the behavioral sciences use specialized conceptual frameworks to view human behavior, *history's uniqueness stems from the fact that it views behavior that has taken place in the past and is interested in the totality of the human experience.* Because it is concerned with the past, it uses a modified mode of scientific inquiry.

Whereas the sociologist and the political scientist are mainly interested in *socialization* and *power* respectively, the historian may be interested in how each of these concepts is exemplified in past human behavior. History, then, is a truly interdisciplinary field because historians, in principle, are interested in all aspects of past human behavior. Thus it is difficult to speak about unique historical concepts. Yet every discipline makes use of the historical perspective and has historical components. When a sociologist studies norms and sanctions in colonial America, and the economist describes how the colonists produced goods and services, they are both studying history.

A quick review of lists of the historical generalizations found in school district and state education departments' curriculum guides will reveal how history uses concepts that originate in other social science disciplines. Note these two examples of historical generalizations prepared by a state department of education (State Superintendent of Public Instruction, n.d.):

1. Communities today differ from communities of earlier times.
2. The rate of cultural change varies from one country to another.

The key concepts within these two statements are *communities* and *cultural change*. Community and cultural change are sociological and anthropological concepts, respectively.

Some sources suggest that *change* is a key historical concept. It is true that we cannot verify statements about change without the use of historical data. However, when we speak of change, we must also use some other concept. Change describes the status of concepts at different points in time. Thus change is a relational concept (see Chapter 3). Although change is a historical concept, we must recognize that we can't study change unless we talk about it in concepts usually associated with other disciplines. For example, we can write generalizations about *cultural change* (anthropology), change in *goods and services* (economics), or change in *regions* (geography). Both historical data and concepts within other disciplines are necessary to state and test generalizations about change.

Whereas the behavioral scientist uses specialized conceptual frameworks to view human behavior, the historian can and sometimes does use concepts from different social science disciplines to study the past. The historical perspective should be concerned with the totality of the human past. Traditionally, however, many historians have studied the past primarily from a political science perspective. As we point out above, however, more historians are now studying the totality of the human past from different disciplinary perspectives. Social historians study ordinary people. Other historians study political events, leaders, economic events, and institutions.

There is a tremendous lag between historical scholarship and school history. School history textbooks still largely reflect political history. A glance at the table of contents of almost any history textbook will reveal the predominance of political concepts—wars, treaties, revolutions, political leaders, and national movements. However, writers of some history textbooks have been influenced by the new developments in historical scholarship. Today's history textbooks include more information about the lives of ordinary people, families, women, ethnic groups, and factory workers. The more innovative history textbooks often include excerpts from the letters and diaries of ordinary men and women (Garcia, 1993).

Methodological

The concepts discussed above are related to the content (product) of history. We have noted the difficulty involved in identifying substantive historical concepts. However, history consists of more than its products or conclusions. History is also a *process*. The mode of inquiry historians use to solve problems and to derive generalizations is also part of the structure of history. While the concepts within history are interdisciplinary, the method used by historians to solve historical problems is unique; historians are the only group of researchers whose research is limited to the reconstruction of past events. Their problem is complicated by the fact that past events have taken place and will never recur. Sociologists can always study a new family situation. Political scientists can observe a future national election.

It is important to teach concepts and generalizations about historical method, as well as concepts related to historical conclusions (products). In the Teaching Strategies section, later in this chapter, we state a generalization related to historical research and describe strategies for teaching it.

The study of historical method (historiography) should constitute a substantial part of the social studies curriculum in the elementary and middle school grades. A study of the historian's method will enable students to gain an appreciation of the difficulties involved in reconstructing the past, strengthen their inquiry skills, and enable them to become more thoughtful consumers of history.

The concepts used by historians are borrowed from the other social sciences. Historians have written very little about the concepts they use and their place in the social studies curriculum. Fenton (1967), the historian-educator, believes that historians are uncomfortable with concepts. He states that the analytical questions that historians ask—rather than key concepts and generalizations—make up the heart of history.

Examples of Concepts

Historians have not written very much about the concepts they use. In a book edited by Edward N. Saveth (1964), a number of historians describe how concepts such as *group structure, mobility, social structure, role, leadership,* and *power* can be studied using historical data. Some of the major social science concepts frequently used by authors of history textbooks are described below. Examples of activities that can be used to teach them are also described. Most of these concepts deal with the products (conclusions) of history; one relates to the historical method. Students can be helped to gain historical insights and understanding by studying these concepts using data about past human behavior.

CHANGE

Things in our social and physical environment are constantly becoming different each day, week, and year. It is very important for students to understand the factors that cause change and be able to adjust to and accept change. Historical data must be used to develop this concept effectively, although it is interdisciplinary. You can use concepts from each social science discipline to help students understand the dynamics of social and cultural change.

Activities
1. Ask students to study their childhood pictures at different ages and to tell how they are alike and different.
2. Ask students to state the differences noted in pictures taken in their community recently and those taken 20 years earlier.
3. Compare the roles of women now and in the late 1800s.
4. Compare the culture of the Iroquois today with their culture in the 1840s.

LEADERSHIP

Leadership is the exercise of influence and authority by an individual or group within a social relationship. The democratic leader respects the right of all group members to participate in decision-making and the setting of group goals (Theodorson & Theodorson, 1969). The authoritarian leader determines the goals and rules for the group and does not allow other group members to help determine group goals. No leader is entirely democratic or authoritarian. Leaders are more or less democratic or authoritarian.

Activities
1. Study national leaders whose birthdays we celebrate, such as George Washington and Martin Luther King Jr.
2. Discuss some of the groups the students belong to, such as Blue Birds and the Boy Scouts. List the characteristics of these groups' leaders. Discuss what makes a person or group a leader.
3. Have each student research one U.S. president and discuss ways in which these presidents were alike and different.
4. Interview community leaders and ask several to talk to the class.
5. Study leaders of social movements such as Susan B. Anthony, Cesar Chavez, and Jane Addams. Discuss the extent to which the movements these leaders led were successful.

CONFLICT

Throughout history, disagreements and hostilities have arisen between individuals, groups, and nations when they had divergent goals or different ideas about how similar goals could best be attained. While conflict, like change, is an interdisciplinary concept, historians spend much of their time documenting conflicts and wars. Most past conflicts have had both positive and negative consequences.

Activities
1. Observe disagreements on the playground and note why they occur.
2. Read selections about the American Revolution, the Civil War, and the civil rights movement of the 1960s. Generalize about what causes conflict, its consequences, and ways to resolve conflict.
3. Read about the cultural conflicts experienced by Polish immigrants when they came to the United States near the turn of the century.
4. Identify the major causes of the conflict in the Middle East and explain how it developed.
5. Study the concept *revolution*. A revolution takes place when an existing government is abruptly overthrown and a different group assumes power. Study the following revolutions and generalize about the causes and sequence of events during a revolution: American (1776), French (1789), Russian (1917), and Algerian (1962).

COOPERATION

Cooperation occurs when individuals or groups work together to achieve the same goals. Students will acquire a skewed view of history if they study about conflict but do not learn about the ways in which individuals and groups have cooperated in the past—and still cooperate today—to solve problems and to bring about social and political change.

"I'd like to have lived during the decline and fall of Rome. Boy! Then they really had some current events!"
Source: Joe E. Buresch. Used with permission.

Activities
1. List ways families work together to get jobs done around the house.
2. List ways people in the school work together to attain goals.
3. List ways various workers and members of the community work together to improve it.
4. Describe ways Native Americans helped the colonists to learn to plant and grow crops in America.
5. Study the history and functions of the United Nations (UN), the North Atlantic Treaty Organization (NATO), and the Organization of American States (OAS) and list ways different nations work together to promote peace and economic development.

EXPLORATION

Historians devote a great deal of attention to men who traveled into lands unknown to them. Exploration is a geographical concept. In extolling the virtues of European explorers, historians have sometime distorted or omitted any discussion of the cultures of the people who inhabited the lands before the coming of the Europeans. When using historical data to teach students about exploration, the teacher should help them to view exploration from both the perspectives of those who were exploring as well as from the perspectives of the peoples who inhabited the native lands.

Activities

1. Ask the students to name men and women today who are going to unknown places or discovering new things. Point out that astronauts, archeologists, and scientists are explorers.
2. Read to the students the part of Columbus's diary that describes how he first landed in the West Indies and met the Taino Indians. Then read them accounts of the Tainos' lives (Rouse, 1992). Ask the students to tell how the Tainos might have reacted to Columbus's description of them.
3. After the students have studied Cortez's exploration of what is now Mexico, ask them to role-play a meeting between Cortez and a group of Aztec Indians.
4. Study the impact of European exploration into Africa during the 15th century.
5. Research the impact of the westward movement in the 19th century on American Indian cultures.

HISTORICAL BIAS

No matter how hard they try, historians are unable to completely reconstruct a past event. Many of the sources and artifacts they uncover contain contradictory and inconsistent information. They must judge the accuracy and authenticity of the data. Their data selection is greatly influenced by their personal biases, the nature of the data, their audience, and the culture and times in which they live. Because of the limitations of the historical method, it is very important for students to learn how history is written so that they will be critical readers of the conclusions in their textbooks and in other sources.

Activities

Activities that can be used to teach this concept are in the Teaching Strategies section of this chapter.

HISTORICAL GENERALIZATIONS

Scientific historians are keenly aware of how difficult it is for historians to agree on facts and interpretations. Nevertheless, they believe that historians can agree enough to formulate generalizations. Haskins (1966) states that historical generalizations can be formed because "historic events follow the same natural laws as the objects of science" (p. 24).

Most narrative historians distrust generalizations. However, a historian cannot describe a single event or institution without making some kind of generalized statements. "The serfs in France were angry" and "The kings of France were arbitrary" are lower-level generalizations about the French Revolution. The second generalization could be written at a higher level if more examples were encompassed within it. It would then read, "The monarchy in 18th-century Europe was arbitrary."

Gottschalk (1963), who edited a book on generalizations in history, concluded that all historians make generalizations. However, often historians make generalizations and are not aware that they are making them. Sometimes historians know they are generalizing, but they try to limit generalizations to the event or period they are studying. Scientific historians deliberately try to form generalizations that can apply to a large range of trends and events. They sometimes make generalizations that have implications for future events. During his study of the British, American, French, and Russian revolutions, Crane Brinton (1962) derived the generalizations listed below. They not only describe past events, but suggest the nature of future revolutions. Brinton, like other scientific historians, would not argue that these conditions will always emerge whenever and wherever a revolution occurs. However, he does suggest that if a revolution occurred in a society similar to those he studied, the conditions described by these statements will very likely emerge.

Generalizations about Revolutions
> In a revolutionary state, vocal critics emerge who create a myth about the coming of a utopian society and decry the evils of the existing regime.
> In revolutionary societies, moderate leaders take over after the old regime is overthrown; the moderates are eventually overruled by extremists.
> When extremists take control of the government during a revolution, a reign of terror ensues.

Teaching Historical Generalizations

Explicit generalizations are as rare in history textbooks as they are in most narrative histories. Despite the limitations of the historical method and the paucity of historical generalizations, you can help students in the elementary and middle school to generalize using historical data. However, historical generalizations must consist of concepts from other disciplines, such as *conflict, exploration*, and *nationalism*. Historical generalizations state how social science concepts were related in the past. Higher-level generalizations are difficult to formulate in history because of the historical method's limitations (Benson, 1972; Delzell, 1977). While students should be taught to derive and test historical generalizations, they should be keenly aware of their limitations. When students derive statements about the French Revolution, they should realize that a revolution occurring in a society significantly different from France in 1789 may be characterized by a different sequence of events.

Because most history textbooks are organized chronologically and give scant attention to generalizations, you will need to identify the historical generalizations you wish your students to learn during the year, and then to select the appropriate materials and teaching strategies. The generalizations chosen for study may be limited by the topics and content you are required to teach in a particular grade. However, U.S., state, and world history is rich with data that can be used to teach a wide range of generalizations.

You can find lists of historical generalizations in a variety of sources, including conceptual frameworks for basal social studies series, methods books, and school district curriculum guides. You should realize that generalizations on lists can vary widely in quality. Some are of a very low order. Many are not empirical statements at all but are value claims. Others lack empirical support and contain dubious concepts.

Even an excellent list of generalizations is only a list and should only be used to plan and guide instruction. Students must derive generalizations for themselves if they are to have any meaning. Memorizing meaningless generalizations is not essentially different from memorizing a list of unrelated facts, a practice most educators now publicly criticize. We should not repeat the same kinds of mistakes when teaching students key concepts and generalizations.

inquiry strategy

THE WORLD AND YOUR FAMILY

This lesson is designed to enable your students to dig into their families' pasts and to determine what was happening in their families when some major U.S. and world events were occurring.

Give the students the following list of key events in world and U.S. history. Ask them to interview family members to find out what important events were happening in their families at these times. They might find out such things as where their ancestors (on the mother's side, father's side, or both) were living when the Women's Rights Convention was held in 1848. One student may discover, for example, that in 1848 her ancestors on her mother's side were living in New York while those on her father's side were in Russia.

Some students will be unable to find out where their families were or what they were doing in some of the years listed. However, almost every student in your class will be able to find out something about his or her family during at least one of those years. Encourage your students to find out such things as where their families were living (such as what city, state, and nation), what kinds of jobs they had, and what kinds of positions they took on such events as the civil rights movement of the 1960s and 1970s and the Vietnam War. Also encourage them to find out whether their families experienced any special situations, problems, or good times during the years listed. They should also try to determine if any members of their families took an active part in any of the events listed, such as the civil rights movement or the Vietnam War.

Allow the students to skip any events for which they cannot find information about what their ancestors or families were doing.

BENCHMARK EVENTS

1848	Women's Rights Convention, Seneca Falls, New York
1917	United States' entry into World War I (The Great War)
1929	The stock market crash, signaling the beginning of the Great Depression
1941	United States' entry into World War II when Japan attacks Pearl Harbor
1954	The *Brown* decision, in which the Supreme Court rules that school segregation is inherently unequal
1955–56	The Montgomery Bus Boycott, which signaled the beginning of the civil rights movement of the 1960s
1963	The March on Washington and Martin Luther King Jr.'s "I Have a Dream" speech
1968	With half a million U.S. combat troops in Vietnam, a controversy rages about whether the U.S. should continue to participate in the war. The war ends in 1975 with a communist victory, when Richard Nixon is president. No war since the U.S. Civil War divided the nation so deeply.
1980	Ronald Reagan is elected president of the United States
1992	Bill Clinton is elected president of the United States

Examples of Historical Generalizations

Because history, in principle, is concerned with the totality of the human past, it is a truly interdisciplinary discipline. It can and sometimes does use concepts from all the social science disciplines to explain the past. We have identified several generalizations below that can be considered historical, and indicated the social science concepts and disciplines to which they are related. This list of historical generalizations can be used to guide the planning of historical studies in the elementary and middle school grades.

Change (History–Sociology)
   Human society is characterized by change.

Conflict (History–Political Science)
   Whenever human beings have lived, conflicts between individuals, groups, and nations have arisen. Although conflicts have some negative effects on society, they are often the impetus for effective change.

Cooperation (History–Sociology)
   Throughout history, individuals and groups with different cultures and experiences have worked together to achieve common goals, especially when they were threatened by outside forces.

Revolution (History–Political Science)

Revolutions tend to occur in societies where organized groups perceive their conditions, which are beginning to improve, as intolerable, public officials as unresponsive to their needs, and legitimate channels for alleviation of grievances as ineffective.

Culture (History–Anthropology)

Wherever humans have lived, they have developed systems of artifacts, beliefs, and behavior patterns that enabled them to satisfy their physical and social needs.

Exploration (History–Geography)

The explorations people made into what were to them strange territories resulted in tremendous cultural exchange as well as conflict between different cultural and ethnic groups. In general, more technologically advanced cultures have assimilated or destroyed cultures that were less technologically developed.

Historical Bias (History)

A historian's view of the past is influenced by the availability of evidence, his or her personal biases and purposes for writing, and the society and times in which he or she lives and writes.

NATIONAL HISTORY STANDARDS

What history to teach and how to teach it became the center of a contentious debate in 1994 with the publication of the National History Standards (NHS). The NHS is a series of guidelines for teaching U.S. and world history that provide a framework for teachers and students to uncover unlearned lessons from the past and to study U.S. history from multiple points of view. The NHS were viewed by conservatives as devoting too much attention to women and people of color and not focusing on what was most worth knowing in history. Protests led by critics of the NHS, many of whom were not historians, resulted in a revision of the standards (Nash, Crabtree, & Dunn, 1997). The revised NHS were released in the spring of 1996 and reduced from three volumes to one. Both versions were directed by Charlotte Crabtree and Gary B. Nash at the National Center for History in the Schools at the University of California, Los Angeles, and funded by the National Endowment for the Humanities and the U.S. Department of Education.

The NHS, which are listed in Table 9.1, focus on historical thinking skills and historical understandings. Historical thinking skills enable students to differentiate past, present, and future time; raise questions; seek and evaluate evidence; compare and analyze historical stories, illustrations, and records from the past; interpret the historical record; and construct historical narratives of their own. Historical understandings define what students should know about the history of families, their communities, states, nation, and world. These understandings are drawn from the

TABLE 9.1. *National Standards for History*

Standard 1. Chronological Thinking
A. Distinguish between past, present, and future time.
B. Identify the temporal structure of a historical narrative or story.
C. Establish temporal order in constructing students' own historical narratives.
D. Measure and calculate calendar time.
E. Interpret data presented in time lines.
F. Create time lines.
G. Explain change and continuity over time.

Standard 2. Historical Comprehension
A. Identify the author or source of the historical document or narrative.
B. Reconstruct the literal meaning of a historical passage.
C. Identify the central question(s) that the historical narrative addresses.
D. Read historical narratives imaginatively.
E. Appreciate historical perspectives.
F. Draw upon data in historical maps.
G. Draw upon visual and mathematical data presented in graphs.
H. Draw upon the visual data presented in photographs, paintings, cartoons, and
    architectural drawings.

Standard 3. Historical Analysis and Interpretation
A. Formulate questions to focus their inquiry or analysis.
B. Compare and contrast differing sets of ideas, values, personalities, behaviors,
    and institutions.
C. Analyze historical fiction.
D. Distinguish between fact and fiction.
E. Compare different stories about a historical figure, era, or event.
F. Analyze illustrations in historical stories
G. Consider multiple perspectives.
H. Explain causes in analyzing historical actions.
I. Challenge arguments of historical inevitability.
J. Hypothesize influences of the past.

Standard 4. Historical Research Capabilities
A. Formulate historical questions.
B. Obtain historical data.
C. Interrogate historical data.
D. Marshal needed knowledge of the time and place, and construct a story,
     explanation, or historical narrative.

Standard 5. Historical Issues Analysis and Decision Making
A. Identify problems and dilemmas in the past.
B. Analyze the interests and values of the various people involved.
C. Identify causes of the problem or dilemma.
D. Propose alternative choices for addressing the problem.
E. Formulate a position or course of action on an issue.
F. Identify the solution chosen.
G. Evaluate the consequences of a decision.

Source: Reprinted from *National Standards for History,* Basic Edition, (1996), Los Angeles. National Center for History
    in the Schools, pp. 15–16.

record of human aspirations, strivings, accomplishments, and failures in at least five spheres of human activity: the social, political, scientific or technological, economic, and cultural (the philosophical, religious, or esthetic), as appropriate for students.

The extent to which the NHS will influence what teachers teach is questionable. The standards require a significant amount of classroom time to teach, as well as a highly skilled and knowledgeable teacher. Perhaps one of the most interesting aspects of the NHS, for social studies teachers, is the political controversy surrounding them. The NHS can be used as a case study of how politics influence school knowledge (Nash, Crabtree, & Dunn, 1997).

Goals for Teaching History

Major public policies in our nation and world are frequently made with little regard for history and often reflect a preoccupation with the present. When a nation pays little attention to its history, it loses much of its capacity to understand its present and to shape its future. Because of the persistent and complex problems that our nation and world face, we need historical insight to help us understand our world. We also need historical insight to shape alternative futures that are rooted in historical realities rather than in myths and illusions. Thus a major goal of history teaching should be to help students develop historical understanding and insight.

Students should not only study the products of history as found in their textbooks and other sources; they should also solve historical problems using the methods of the historian. By using the historical method, students will derive generalizations that help them understand human behavior in the past, present, and future. Historical generalizations will also help students appreciate the pace and extent of change in the modern world.

Helping students to understand and use the methods of the historian should be important objectives of the social studies. We cannot teach what actually happened but must teach historical accounts from various perspectives. By using this approach to history, you will help your students discover that written history is largely made up of accounts of events from particular points of view. *You will also enable them to construct their own interpretations of historical events and situations.* Studying the methods of the historian will also help students realize that there are many ways of looking at identical events and situations. Their own reasoning and critical powers will be used and strengthened. If students are taught to treat history as assured knowledge, they are likely to believe that seeing information in print is sufficient evidence of its credibility.

Learning the method of the historian is also valuable because history is not only an account of the past but a method of inquiry. It develops through a process of asking questions and attempting to find answers. In addition, it involves evaluating the importance and authenticity of artifacts and documents and using them skillfully to understand the past. Just as baseball players cannot become skillful by watching baseball games, students cannot fully understand history by simply reading historical accounts. They must use the historical method. We teach students the historical method so they will learn to appreciate the difficulties involved in reconstructing past events and become more reflective readers of history.

TEACHING STRATEGIES

Generalization

A historian's view of the past is influenced by the availability of evidence, his or her personal biases and purposes for writing, and the society and times in which he or she lives and works.

Primary Grades

1. After a class field trip, ask each of the students to summarize in one or two sentences what happened. Write their responses on the board. Ask them how their responses are alike and different, and why they are different. Help them to discover that their own personal feelings and experiences shaped their perceptions and memory of the field trip.

2. Ask the students to write or state in one sentence what happened during the art period yesterday, or some other day. Have them compare their responses and see how they are alike and different. Ask them why they wrote or gave different versions of what happened.

3. Read the students a story, and ask them to summarize what happened in one or two sentences. Have them compare their responses to see how they are alike and different. Ask them why they are different.

4. If the students are in their second year of school, ask them to describe their previous year in one or two sentences. Have the pupils compare their responses, and ask them why, since they were in the same room, they gave different versions of the year's experience.

5. Show the class a picture or a drawing that shows enslaved African Americans happy and singing. Show them another in which the enslaved persons are bound in chains and looking sad. A third picture might show the enslaved persons being sold on a market. As you show each picture, ask questions such as "What is happening in this picture?" "Do these people look happy or sad?" "Why?" When you have finished, ask: "How are all of these pictures alike?" "How are they different?" "Why do you think they are different?" "How can we tell which artist is telling the truth?" The pupils might be asked to write a caption for each of the pictures.

6. Read several short conflicting versions of the life of a person such as Abraham Lincoln or Crispus Attucks. Ask the class why different versions are written about the same person. Ask them which version they think is most nearly correct and why. Ask them to tell how we can go about finding out which version is probably nearest to the truth.

Intermediate Grades

1. Read a short story of the American Revolution to the students. Emphasize the battle of Lexington. Tell the students about the controversy regarding who fired the first shot. Read them some of the conflicting documents that the British and Americans have written about the event. Ask them whether we can determine what really happened, and why or why not.

2. Stage a role-playing situation for the class (using several members of the class as participants). Ask each student to write what he or she saw happen in the situation. The accounts should be written independently. When the reports have been written, ask the class to compare them to see how they are alike and different. The class should use their accounts to answer these questions:

   a. Can different accounts be written about the same event?
   b. What does the answer to Question 1 tell us about the writing of history?
   c. Are two people who witness an automobile accident likely to give identical reports of it?
   d. Are two historians who read the same documents about a particular historical event likely to write identical accounts of the event? Why or why not?
   e. Are two people who participate in or observe the same historical event likely to write identical accounts of the event? Why or why not?
   f. What are some of the factors that cause historians to write different accounts of the same events?

3. You can help students to better understand bias in history by asking them to compare and contrast accounts of the treatment of events such as the American Revolution, the War of 1812, and World War I in different U.S. textbooks and in British, Canadian, and Australian textbooks. Many publishers have offices in foreign countries. They are willing to help teachers obtain copies of foreign textbooks for classroom use at regular cost plus air postage. Collecting foreign social studies textbooks for use in the social studies is an interesting and informative project.

Upper Grades

1. Plan a historical investigative unit. Assemble about 10 primary documents related to a specific historical event or institution, such as the life of the enslaved African Americans, the life of colonial women, the life of colonial children, or the relationship between the first Jamestown colonists and the American Indians. Identify with the class the major questions that can be answered using these documents, such as "What was life like for the enslaved African Americans?" and "What was the role of women in colonial America?"

   After the students have stated questions and hypotheses related to the problem in the unit, divide the class into four research groups. Assign a leader and a recorder for each group. Give each group a copy of each of the 10 documents. The goal for each group should be to write a brief history, using their primary documents and several library secondary sources. Their brief histories should be in narrative form, should answer the major questions formulated at the beginning of the unit, and should be grouped into subtopics.

   When each group has written its history, the four histories should be shared and compared. The class should then discuss why the histories written by each group were similar and different.

2. Researching and writing a *community history* can help students learn about the difficulties historians have reconstructing the past and how this leads to bias in historical accounts. Divide the class into groups to reconstruct the history of their community. The groups might study these specific topics: the people in the community, the beginnings of the community, the town, business and industry, trade and communication, labor, the professions, education, the arts and crafts, government, and recreation (Lord, 1967). As the students gather data in their various groups, ask them to identify conflicting information they have uncovered, and to think of ways they can solve the problems that conflicting data cause.

When the students pool their data from the various groups, they should identify consistent and conflicting data and ways to resolve the conflicts. They should also identify gaps in their data. They should discuss how both gaps in data and conflicting data cause problems for historians and how historians try to solve them.

When doing their community history, the students should incorporate ideas from social history and oral history. Social history would require them to work with a broad concept of the community, which encompasses the history of women, children, factory workers, and ethnic groups. They can use oral history techniques by interviewing senior citizens and recording them with an audio tape.

SUMMARY

History consists of three components: (1) the past, (2) statements about the past, and (3) a method of inquiry. It is important for you to understand how these aspects of history differ in order to organize effective lessons in historical studies and to help your students view social problems from the historical perspective. Historians are never able to reconstruct past events totally because of the lack of available data. Furthermore, they are not able to use all the data that they locate. To write a meaningful narrative, they must select from the data they uncover what they regard as most valid and reliable. *Their selection of data is influenced by their personal biases, their purposes for writing, and the society and times in which they live and write.* Because history is highly influenced by the personal and cultural experiences and biases of historians, it is extremely important for students to develop skills in historical inquiry so that they will become more reflective readers of history.

History differs from the other social disciplines in several ways. It includes elements of both science and the humanities. The historians' interest in writing exciting narratives and their tendency to describe unique events relate the discipline closely to the humanities. However, history is "scientific" because historians use the scientific method in modified form and value objective description. Objectivity is an ideal within the discipline. Thus, history is considered a modified science in this book.

History is distinguished from the other social sciences not by its special concepts but by its concern for the past and its mode of inquiry. Although the other social sciences are characterized by their tendency to view human behavior from special conceptual frameworks, history, in principle, is concerned with the totality of the human past and thus is in one sense a highly interdisciplinary discipline. While this is the case in principle, in the past historians often used political science concepts. Today's historians, however, are using concepts from the other disciplines more and more frequently to explain the past. This trend will undoubtedly continue as historians become more familiar with concepts in the behavioral sciences. Because historians attempt to reconstruct the past, they experience unique research problems. While all social science disciplines have historical components, history is the only discipline primarily concerned with the past. To help students view problems from the historical perspective, you should teach concepts and generalizations related to the conclusions (products) of history, as well as those that relate to history as a process.

REFLECTION AND ACTION ACTIVITIES

1. Locate several accounts of controversial historical events, such as the American Revolution, slavery and the Civil War, or the War of 1812, that were written in different periods of history, in different states, and in different countries (see Barendsen, et al., 1976; Kellum, 1969; McKitrick, 1963; Phillips, 1918; Robinson, 1969; Thomas, 1965). After the accounts are located and analyzed, answer these questions: (a) How are the accounts alike? (b) How are they different? (c) Why are they different? (d) What generalizations can you make about controversial historical events? (e) What generalizations can you make about the nature and writing of history?
2. Obtain a copy of a fifth-grade United States history textbook in your curriculum library. Study the treatment of the American Revolution in it. How would you use this account to help students learn how history is written?
3. Write three lesson plans to teach the following generalization to students at the *primary, intermediate,* and *upper grade* levels:

   A historian's view of the past is influenced by the availability of evidence, his or her personal biases and purpose for writing, and the society and times in which he or she lives and works.

   What difficulties might you encounter in teaching this generalization at these three levels? How might these difficulties be overcome?
4. Study the treatment of women, African Americans, Mexican Americans, and Native Americans in a sample of U.S. history textbooks written for the elementary and middle school grades. What generalizations can you make about the treatment of these groups in the sample of books that you studied? What implications do your generalizations have for teaching history in the elementary and middle school grades?
5. Carefully study the table of contents of a history textbook and list the major concepts discussed and illustrated in the book. After listing the concepts, classify them according to the discipline to which you feel they belong. For example, *revolution* is usually considered a political science concept, *culture* an anthropological concept, and *scarcity* an economic concept. To which discipline do most of the concepts belong? What implications do the results of your investigation have for the teaching of history in the elementary and middle school grades?

 *internet links*

TEACHING HISTORY

The World Wide Web is an important resource for teaching and learning on the Internet. It provides an extensive source of information for teachers and for classroom use. What follows are several examples of websites that can be used to teach history.

1. *The American West* (http://www.AmericaWest.com). Information on the history of the American West can be accessed from this web page. It also links to the National Archives, where images of western figures and sites can be downloaded, and to home pages for Native American nations, organizations, and institutions.

2. *K–12 History/Social Studies* (http://execpc.com/~dboals.html). This web page was designed to encourage history and social studies teachers to use Internet resources by providing easy access to information on the World Wide Web. Teachers, for example, can download materials catalogs as well as link to the National Council for the Social Studies, the Library of Congress, information on critical thinking, and other resources from this web page.

3. California Social Studies WWW Project (http://www.burbank.k12.caus/~luther) and *The History Guide* (http://www.gate.net/~stevek). These two websites are dedicated to helping students learn U.S. and world history. They contain study guides and information on topics that are typically covered in secondary social studies and history classes.

4. *The History of the World* (http://www.hyperhistory.com/). Teachers and students can access a small sample of the World History Chart, view historical maps, study timelines on the development of major civilizations, and access information on key historical figures from this interactive web page. They can also link to HyperHistory Online where a chart of world history covering 3,000 years of history from David and Solomon to Einstein, Picasso, Roosevelt, and Churchill is being constructed.

5. The History Channel (http://www.historychannel.com). Teachers can use this site to stay up-to-date on topics covered on the history channel and to link to information sources addressed in those topics.

REFERENCES

Acuña, R. (1988). *Occupied America: A history of Chicanos* (3rd ed.). New York: Harper & Row.

Aydelotte, W. O. (1970). Quantification in history. In R. P. Swierenga (Ed.), *Quantification in American history: Theory and research* (pp. 25–35). New York: Atheneum.

Armitage, S., & Jameson, E. (Eds.). (1987). *The women's west.* Norman: University of Oklahoma Press.

Banks, J. A. (1993). The canon debate, knowledge construction, and multicultural education. *Educational Researcher, 22,* (5) 4–14.

Barendsen R. D., et al. (Eds.). (1976). *The American Revolution: Selections from secondary school history books of other nations.* Washington, DC: U.S. Government Printing Office.

Bennett, P. S. (1970). *What happened at Lexington Green? An inquiry into the nature and methods of history.* Menlo Park, CA: Addison-Wesley.

Benson, L. (1970). Quantification, scientific history and scholarly innovation. In R. P. Swierenga (Ed.), *Quantification in American history: Theory and research* (pp. 25–35). New York: Atheneum.

Benson, L. (1972). *Toward the scientific study of history.* Philadelphia: Lippincott.

Blassingame, J. W. (Ed.). (1977). *Slave testimony: Two centuries of letters, speeches, interviews, and autobiographies.* Baton Rouge: Louisiana State University Press.

Bogue, A. G. (1970). United States: The "new" political history. In R. P. Swierenga (Ed.), *Quantification in American history: Theory and research* (pp. 36–52). New York: Atheneum.

Brinton, C. (1962). *The anatomy of revolution.* New York: Vintage.

Chan, S. (1991). *Asian Americans: An interpretive history.* Boston: Twayne.

Commager, H. S., & Muessig, R. H. (1980). *The study and teaching of history.* Columbus, OH: Merrill.

Delzell, C. F. (Ed.). (1977). *The future of history.* Nashville: Vanderbilt University Press.

Drake, St. C. (1987/1990). *Black folks here and there.* 2 vols. Los Angeles: UCLA, Center for Afro-American Studies.

Fenton, E. (1967). A structure of history. In I. Morrisett (Ed.), *Concepts and structure in the new social science curricula* (pp. 52–53). New York: Holt.

Fogel, R. W., & Engerman, S. L. (1974). *Time on the cross: The economics of American Negro slavery.* Boston: Little Brown.

Foner, P. S. (1982). *Women and the American labor movement: From the first trade unions to the present.* New York: Free Press.

Foner, P. S., & Lewis, R. L. (Eds.). (1989). *Black workers: A documentary history from colonial times to the present.* Philadelphia: Temple University Press.

Garcia, J. (1993). The changing image of ethnic groups in textbooks. *Phi Delta Kappan.* 75 (1), 29–35.

Garrow, D. J. (Ed.). (1987). *The Montgomery bus boycott and the women who started it: The memoir of Jo Ann Gibson Robinson.* Knoxville: University of Tennessee Press.

Gottschalk, L. (Ed.). (1963). *Generalizations in the writing of history.* Chicago: University of Chicago Press.

Haskins, R. W. (1966). History. In J. U. Michaelis & A. Montgomery Johnston (Eds.), *The social sciences: Foundations of the social studies* (pp. 25–74). Boston: Allyn and Bacon.

Hine, D. C. (1981). *When the truth is told: Black women's community and culture in Indiana, 1985–1950.* Indianapolis, IN: National Council of Negro Women, Indianapolis Section.

Hine, D. C. (1986). Lifting the veil, shattering the silence: Black women's history in slavery and freedom. In D. C. Hine (Ed.), *The state of Afro-American history: Past, present, and future* (pp. 223–249). Baton Rouge: Louisiana State University Press.

Hine, D. C. (Ed.). (1993). *Black women in America: An historical encyclopedia.* Brooklyn, NY: Carlson.

Hoover, H. T. (1980). Oral history in the United States. In M. Kammen (Ed.), *The past before us: Contemporary historical writing in the United States* (p. 391–407). Ithaca, NY: Cornell University Press.

Jones, J. (1985). *Labor of love, labor of sorrow: Black women, work, and the family from slavery to the present.* New York: Basic Books.

Kammen, M. (1980). The historian's vocation and the state of the discipline in the United States. In M. Kammen (Ed.), *The past before us: Contemporary historical writing in the United States* (pp. 19–46). Ithaca, NY: Cornell University Press.

Kellum, D. F. (1969). *American history through conflicting interpretations.* New York: Teachers College Press.

Lord, C. L. (1967). *Teaching history with community resources.* New York: Teachers College Press.

McKitrick, E. L. (Ed.). (1963). *Slavery defended: The views of the old South.* Englewood Cliffs, NJ: Prentice-Hall.

Nash, G. B., Crabtree, C., & Dunn, R. E. (1997). *History on trial: Culture wars and the teaching of the past.* New York: Knopf.

Parks, R., with Haskins, J. (1992). *Rosa Parks: My Story.* New York: Dial.

Phillips, U. B. (1918). *American Negro slavery.* New York: Appleton.

Robinson, D. W. (Ed.). (1969). *As others see us: International views of American history.* New York: Houghton Mifflin.

Rodriguez, C. E. (1989). *Puerto Ricans born in the U.S.A.* Boston: Unwin Hyman.

Rosengarten, T. (1974). *All God's dangers: The life of Nate Shaw.* New York: Avon.

Rouse, I. (1992). *The Tainos: Rise and decline of the people who greeted Columbus.* New Haven, CT: Yale University Press.

Saveth, E. N. (Ed.). (1964). *American history and the social sciences.* New York: Free Press.

Schlesinger, A., Jr. (1970). The humanist looks at empirical social research. In R. P. Swierenga (Ed.), *Quantification in American history: Theory and research* (pp. 30–35). New York: Atheneum.

Snyder, P. N. (Ed.). (1958). *Detachment and the writing of history: Essays and letters of Carl L. Becker.* Ithaca, NY: Cornell University Press.

State Superintendent of Public Instruction (n.d.). *A conceptual framework for the social studies in Wisconsin schools* (Social Studies Bulletin No. 4, Curriculum Bulletin No. 14. Madison, WI: State Superintendent of Public Instruction.

Stern, P. S. (1982). Social history and the teaching of history. In M. T. Downey (Ed.), *Teaching American history: New directions* (pp. 51–63). Washington, DC: National Council for the Social Studies.

Stratton, J. L. (1981). *Pioneer women: Voices from the Kansas Frontier.* New York: Simon and Schuster.

Takaki, R. (1989). *Strangers from a different shore: A history of Asian Americans.* Boston: Little, Brown.

Takaki, R. (1993). *A different mirror: A history of multicultural America.* New York: Little, Brown.

Terkel, S. (1992). *Race: How Blacks & Whites think & feel about the American obsession.* New York: New Press.

Theodorson, G. A., & Theodorson, S. G. (1969). *A modern dictionary of sociology.* New York: Barnes & Noble.

Thomas, J. L. (Ed.). (1965). *Slavery attacked: The abolitionist crusade.* Englewood Cliffs, NJ: Prentice-Hall.

Tilly, L. A., & Scott, J. W. (1987). *Women, work and the family.* New York: Routledge

Wertsch, J. V. (1985). *Vygotsky and the social formation of mind.* Cambridge: Harvard University Press.

Wright, G. (1976). History as a moral science. *American Historical Review, 81,* 1–11.

FOR FURTHER READING

Appiah, K. A., & Gates, H. L., Jr. (Eds.). (1997). *The dictionary of global culture.* New York: Knopf.

Brophy, J., & VanSledright, B. (1997). *Teaching and learning history in elementary schools.* New York: Teachers College Press.

Downey, M. T. (Ed.). (1985). *History in the schools.* Washington, DC: National Council for the Social Studies.

DuBois, E. C., & Ruiz, V. L. (Eds.). (1990). *Unequal sisters: A multi-cultural reader in U.S. women's history.* New York: Routledge.

Eldridge, L. D. (Ed.). (1997). *Women and freedom in early America.* New York: New York University Press.

Gifford, B. R. (Ed.). (1988). *History in the schools: What shall we teach?* New York: Macmillan.

Grossman, J. R. (1989). *Land of hope: Chicago, Black southerners, and the great migration.* Chicago: University of Chicago Press.

Hampton, H., & Fayer, S. (Eds.). (1990). *Voices of freedom: An oral history of the civil rights movement from the 1950s through the 1980s.* New York: Bantam.

Hine, D. C., & Thompson, K. (1998). *A shining thread of hope.* New York: Broadway Books.

Huang, F. (1997). *Asian and Hispanic immigrant women in the work force.* New York: Garland.

Jones, M. A. (1993). *American immigration* (2nd ed.). Chicago: University of Chicago Press.

Lerner, G. (1997). *Why history matters: Life and thought.* New York: Oxford University Press.

Linenthal, E. T., & Engelhardt, T. (1996). *History wars: The Enola Gay and other battles for the American past.* New York: Metropolitan Books.

Nash, G. B., Crabtree, C., & Dunn, R. E. (1997). *History on trial: Culture wars and the teaching of the past.* New York: Knopf.

Said, E. W. (1993). *Culture and imperialism.* New York: Knopf.

Said, E. W. (1992). *The question of Palestine.* New York: Vintage.

Schlissel, L. (1982). *Women's diaries of the westward journey.* New York: Schocken.

Watkins, W. H. (1993). Black curriculum orientations: A preliminary inquiry. *Harvard Educational Review,* 63 (3), 321–338

Zinn, H. (1995). *A people's history of the United States* (rev. ed.). New York: Harper & Row.

CHAPTER 10

Sociology: Structure, Concepts, and Strategies

*f*EATURE

THE HOUSEWORK GENDER GAP

Who does the housework in the family when a husband and wife both have paid jobs? Over the past three decades, U.S. women have begun to work outside the home in record numbers. Even so, most married women continue to spend far more time than their husbands on the kinds of household tasks that have been traditionally performed by women.

Since time is a precious and finite commodity, the way spouses negotiate personal time use is an important gender issue. How we spend our time outside of working hours can add to stress or improve the quality of life.

When dual-earner married couples were interviewed in the late 1980s in the National Survey of Families and Households, women reported spending (on average) almost 26 hours per week on traditional "female" tasks—preparing meals, washing dishes, cleaning house, washing, ironing, and mending. Men spend about 7 hours on these tasks.

A counter gender gap operates for tasks that have been traditionally performed by men—such as auto repair or household maintenance—but these tasks generally do not involve as much time. Husbands spend about seven hours per week on these tasks, compared with two hours for their wives.

There are also "gender-neutral" tasks—paying bills or running errands—which tend to be divided somewhat more evenly. Wives spend about six hours on the gender-neutral tasks, husbands about four.

Among dual-earner families, women spend on average about twice as much time on housework as their husbands—almost 34 hours per week for women versus 18 hours for men. This is over and above hours spent taking care of children, an area in which fathers are spending more time than in the past, but not as much time as mothers do.

Narrowing the housework gender gap requires that men take on more of the disproportionately time-consuming, traditionally female tasks.

We know from previous research that when wives work longer hours, husbands tend to increase their time spent on housework, including traditional "women's work." But this is not the whole story. Even more important are the work schedules of couples—that is, the extent to which spouses work different hours. In particular, the more off-work hours a man has when his wife is at the workplace, the greater his share of traditionally female tasks. This is especially true for husbands who work evenings, nights, or rotating shifts, and thus are home during daylight hours when their wives are at work.

In general, the more highly educated men do the greatest share of traditionally female housework. However, the relative job status and income of spouses has an effect also. Husbands whose wives have occupations of similar or higher positions than their own, or who earn more than they do, perform a greater share of female housework than other husbands. But this is because the wife spends relatively less time at it, not because the husband does more. Women in this situation may tend to be more willing (and able) to pay for domestic help than other women or to reduce their maintenance standards. The more children at home, the more both spouses increase their hours doing traditionally female housework. But since wives put in more additional hours, the husband's relative share goes down.

And how much influence do gender-role attitudes have on this division of household labor? Little or none, according to this analysis. Neither traditional nor nontraditional ideologies concerning roles for women on the part of either husband or wife predicted how a couple would split their time on traditionally female tasks. Bridging the housework gender gap may depend more on the work schedules of spouses and the couple's socioeconomic achievements, and less on changing ideologies concerning gender roles.

Source: Harriet P. Presser, "The Housework Gender Gap," *Population Today*, Vol. 21, No. 7/8 (July/August, 1993), p. 5. Used with permission of the Population Reference Bureau, Inc.

THE SOCIOLOGICAL PERSPECTIVE

In our chapter Feature, a sociologist, Harriet B. Presser, who teaches at the University of Maryland, describes how gender roles in the home are influenced by the work schedules and socioeconomic status of the family. Sociology is the study of human group life. All sociologists, like Professor Presser, are interested in the interrelationships of human groups such as families, institutions, communities, and societies.

The largest group studied by sociologists is a society, which is a large, permanent, self-sufficient group sharing common values and beliefs. Sociologists try to explain why human activity is characterized by a system of stable social relationships. Sociologists often use the concept *social system,* which exists when two or more people interact, when studying group interactions. Sociologists study the community, institutions such as the family and education, religious and economic institutions, and social movements. Sociologists also study social-category systems such as *gender, age, social class,* and *ethnic groups.* Sociologists are also interested in social problems.

Sociologists make several assumptions about the characteristics of groups and their influence on behavior. They assume that individuals need the group for survival, that their behavior is greatly influenced by group norms and sanctions, and that the group helps individuals acquire the behaviors and characteristics needed to adapt to their cultural and physical environments. Sociologists believe that groups have independent characteristics and identities. Groups are more than an aggregate of individuals. Groups have a continuity that transcends the lives of individuals. Sociologists are also interested in the role of individuals in the group and how individuals influence the group.

Sociologists use unique concepts and theories to guide their research and questions. If two sociologists were trying to determine the causes and effects of divorce in U.S. society, they might start by asking what *roles* each spouse is expected to fulfill in marriage, and what *norms* and *values* are associated with these roles. They would also be interested in sanctions used to assure fulfillment of role expectations, and the conditions under which these sanctions break down. They might also investigate how modernization has influenced traditional roles, norms, values, and sanctions.

The researchers might also try to determine whether the divorce rate varies in different types of *communities* and within different *social classes.* They would probably be interested in how each spouse is socialized for the marriage role, and the effects of divorce on an individual's *status* in society, as well as on *institutions.* The italicized words are concepts sociologists might use to help them determine what to study about divorce and to some extent how to study it.

Each of the social science disciplines has unique concepts, but often uses concepts from other disciplines. The social science disciplines are becoming increasingly *interdisciplinary.* Social scientists are discovering they cannot answer all of their important questions by using concepts only within their own disciplines. Historians sometimes use concepts from sociology. Sociologists use concepts from psychology, political science, and anthropology. *Culture,* an anthropological concept, is frequently used by sociologists. In introductory college sociology textbooks, an entire chapter is often devoted to culture and socialization.

While each of the social science disciplines uses concepts from other disciplines, there are core concepts each discipline often uses that are traditionally associated with it. Thus a psychologist, an anthropologist, and an economist might use different concepts and ask different questions about divorce. A Freudian psychologist might investigate the extent of tension and aggression in marriages ending in divorce. An anthropologist might compare the consequences of divorce in different cultures throughout the world. An economist might investigate how divorce rates affect the money and wealth in a society.

THE NATURE OF SOCIOLOGY

Most sociologists accept scientific objectivity as an ideal but realize the difficulties of attaining complete objectivity when studying human behavior. Sociologists are aware of their bias and try to minimize its effects on their research. Because they are students of socialization, sociologists are keenly aware of how society's values and norms shape an individual's view of social systems and social relationships.

Sociologists believe that, despite the bias that exists in their field, sociology is scientific because its major goal is to build theories that can explain and predict behavior. Sociologists assume, with other behavioral scientists, that human behavior is patterned and systematic and that law-like statements about human behavior can be discovered. Most sociologists, unlike most narrative historians, are not necessarily interested in single cases and events. While a narrative historian might write a biography of a noted leader, a sociologist is interested in studying a number of leaders in order to form and test generalizations and theories about leadership.

The sociologist is primarily interested in studying classes of behaviors and their common characteristics. Sociology is a generalizing discipline. While sociologists sometimes use the case study method to study single cities, individuals, and events, they usually try to derive hypotheses from case studies. These hypotheses can later be tested with a larger population.

SOCIOLOGICAL THEORIES

A scientific theory consists of a system of interrelated high-level generalizations (principles or laws) that constitute a deductive system. The development of theory is the major goal of a science. Social science theories can be used to explain and predict behavior. Grand or large theories are very abstract and inclusive theories that explain most of the facts in a discipline and place most of its general laws and principles into a coherent system. In the older physical sciences, such as physics and chemistry, most of the knowledge in the discipline is explained by a small number of highly interrelated large theories, such as Sir Isaac Newton's gravitation theory and Albert Einstein's theory of relativity.

A number of factors, including the complexity of human behavior and bias in social science research, have prevented sociologists, as well as other behavioral scientists, from developing large empirical theories that are universally accepted in the discipline. Traditionally, theorists and empirical researchers (data gatherers) in sociology have been different people and have not worked closely together. The result was that large "armchair" theories were developed by the theorists but rarely tested in the real world by empiricists. Empiricists, on the other hand, often collected data that did not fit into a theory. This is not as true in sociology today as it has been in the past. Many sociologists today are both theorists and empirical researchers. There are many large theories in sociology. However, many are neither universally accepted in the discipline nor data based. Some of the major large theories in sociology are functionalism, macrofunctionalism, structural functionalism,

profile

WILLIAM JULIUS WILSON

A Sociologist Who Studies Poverty

One of the most serious challenges to educating citizens in U.S. society today is the widening gap between the rich and the poor. In 1990 about one of every five students in the U.S. lived below the official government poverty line. William Julius Wilson, Malcolm Wiener Professor of Social Policy at the Kennedy School of Government at Harvard, is one of the most widely read and important voices speaking and writing on race and poverty. Wilson was named one of "America's 25 Most Influential People" by *Time* magazine. His 1978 book, *The Declining Significance of Race*, triggered a storm of controversy. Wilson's intent in the book was to describe how the African American community was becoming increasingly differentiated by class and the factors that contributed to class stratification other than race. Wilson believes that his book was widely misread and misinterpreted.

Wilson published another important and influential book in 1987, *The Truly Disadvantaged*. He wrote this book to focus attention on low-income residents in the inner-city. Wilson believes that his message about the growing underclass in the inner-city was overshadowed in his previous book by the debate about whether the significance of race in the U.S. was declining. In *The Truly Disadvantaged* Wilson explains why poverty is concentrated in inner-city communities and proposes thoughtful public policies for addressing related problems. Wilson thinks that public policies must "address the broader problems of societal organization, including economic organization" and advance "a social democratic public-policy agenda" that all racial, ethnic, and social-class groups will support (p. viii).

In his most recent book, *When Work Disappears: The World of the New Urban Poor* (1996), Wilson describes the powerful effects of joblessness on inner-city communities. He explains how joblessness erodes the social structure of a community. Wilson argues that "the disappearance of work and the consequences of that disappearance for both social and cultural life are the central problems" in inner-city communities (p. xix). One of the reasons for the widespread joblessness in inner-city communities is that many jobs that were once in these communities have moved to the suburbs.

Reference

Wilson, W. J. (1996). *When work disappears: The world of the new urban poor.* New York: Knopf.

---

social action or Weberianism, conflict and symbolic interactionism, and modern systems (Coser, 1971; Kuhn, 1970; Merton, 1968; Shils, 1980; Warshay, 1975).

Sociologists have been more successful in developing empirical partial or small theories than they have been in developing empirical large ones. Partial theories explain only a part of group behavior, while large theories try to explain all of it. Probably the first empirically tested sociological theory was the theory of suicide developed by Emile Durkheim and presented in his book, *Suicide*, published in 1897. Most sociologists use small or partial theories rather than large ones when they do research. Small theories include role theory, reference group theory, alienation theory, social integration theory, and the theory of cultural and structural assimilation developed by Gordon (1964) and summarized below.

1. With regard to *cultural behavior*, differences of social class are more important than differences in ethnic group.
2. With regard to *social participation* in primary groups and primary relationships, people tend to confine these to their own social class segment within their ethnic group, that is, *ethclass*.
3. With a person of the same social class but of a different ethnic group, one shares behavioral similarities but not a sense of peoplehood.
4. With those of the same ethnic group but of a different social class, one shares a sense of *peoplehood* but not behavioral similarities.

THE FEMINIST CHALLENGE IN SOCIOLOGY

The feminist movement in U.S. society has echoed within sociology during the last 20 years (Bernard, 1987; Giele, 1988). Feminists in sociology have accused the discipline of focusing primarily on issues that relate to men and of viewing women's issues from a male perspective even when they study them. Bernard (1987) cites examples of two leading sociologists during the 1960s—Ruth S. Cavan and Talcott Parsons—who perpetuated sexist ideas in their analyses and conclusions. Cavan, an expert on the family, concluded that many feminists had become bitter while working to attain rights and that these feelings harmed families when they created conflict between men and women. Parsons concluded that the separation of men and women into occupational and domestic roles was functional for society because it reduced competition between men and women.

The research by feminist sociologists has been rich since the 1970s (Tong, 1989; Tuchman, 1992). In a path-breaking article, "Equality Between the Sexes," Alice S. Rossi (1964) set forth new interpretations about gender relationships that challenged existing paradigms and that reflected the standpoint of women. Giele (1988) has summarized some of the major categories of feminist research in sociology:

> *Liberal feminist theory* drew on the Enlightenment ideas of individual rights, justice, and freedom...
> *Traditional Marxist feminist* theory traced oppression of women to relations in production and advocated the abolition of private property as the principal vehicle for the liberation of women...
> *Radical feminist theory* focused on the immutable physical differences between the sexes as the principal source of women's oppression...
> *Socialist feminist theory*...combines the insights of both traditional Marxist and radical theories. (p. 293)

SOCIOLOGICAL CONCEPTS

Sociologists, like other social scientists, try to develop concepts that have precise meanings and are universally accepted in the discipline. Concepts such as *institutions, social structure, community,* and *value* are rarely defined in identical ways. This can cause research problems. Two sociologists who are studying the social structure of middle-class U.S. communities might reach different conclusions if they have different working definitions of social structure.

Although sociological concepts are rarely defined identically by sociologists, there are important similarities in the definitions of key sociological concepts. There is also much consensus within the field about what the major concepts are in sociology. Most sociologists would agree that concepts such as *group, socialization, status, role, institution, society, social stratification, social structure, collective behavior,* and *culture* are among their most important concepts. We will now discuss some of the major sociological concepts and describe ways in which they can be taught in the elementary and middle school grades. The interrelationship of these concepts is illustrated in Figure 10.1.

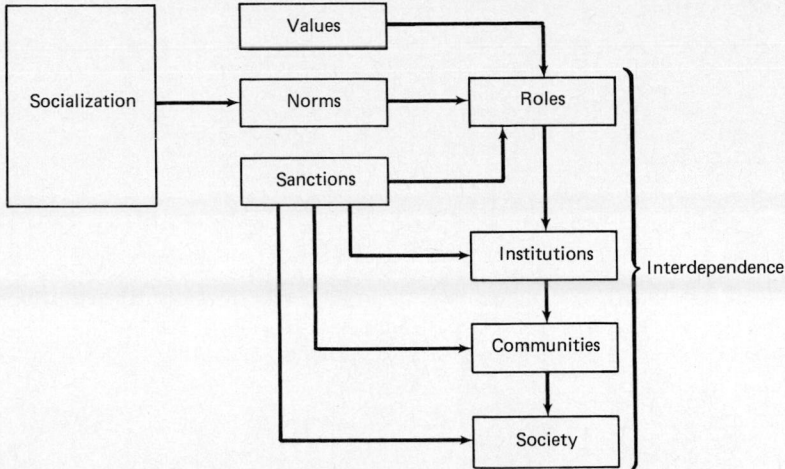

Figure 10.1
Concepts in sociology. This figure illustrates the relationships of some of the key concepts in sociology. Through socialization, individuals acquire the values and norms that shape the roles they must fulfill in human groups. Sanctions are used to ensure fulfillment of role responsibilities; individuals also learn these during socialization. Sets of related roles constitute institutions, such as political, economic, and educational institutions. Institutions exist within communities. Society is the all-encompassing group. All units are guided by norms, values, and sanctions; all are interdependent.

Socialization

Sociologists assume that individuals are not born human but are made human by interacting with and learning from the persons in their social groups. Socialization is the process by which individuals become a part of their social group by learning its culture and their roles. Children attain the attitudes, values, and behaviors needed to survive in their communities from other people in their social group. Some sociologists also use socialization to describe the learning of any new role, such as when a child has to learn to become a member of the Girl Scouts or a new teacher has to learn how to function in her role.

Activities
1. Ask the students to name some things they learned from their mother, father, brother, sister, and teacher, such as how to tie their shoes, clean the house, and read.
2. Ask the students to name things they have learned from the groups to which they belong, such as the Girl Scouts and the Boy Scouts. Ask them to tell how they learned these things.
3. Study about different religions and identify ways they influence their members' behavior.
4. Examine ways boys and girls in different nations and cultures learn to act differently.
5. Read the story *The Country Mouse and the City Mouse* and discuss ways the city mouse taught the country mouse how to survive in the city.

Students become socialized to the school as a social system and learn about norms, roles, and sanctions as they interact with their schoolmates and teachers.
Source: Library of Congress, Washington, D.C.

Roles

Roles are sets of behavior regularly expected of individuals. Each day, almost everyone must function in many different roles. These roles often conflict. Elementary school teachers are expected to teach social studies on school days; yet teachers may have family responsibilities in the evening, such as caring for the lawn, cooking, or entertaining, that prevent them from being properly prepared the next morning. A knowledge of the roles people are expected to fulfill will help students to better understand their own roles and obligations.

Activities
1. Ask the students to list some things they are expected to do at home, at school, at church, synagogue, or temple, and in groups to which they belong. Introduce the concept of *role*. Ask the students to state how their roles sometimes conflict.
2. Ask the students to list some things their parents do at home and away from home.
3. Ask the students to name some of the workers in their community and to list what they are expected to do to help the community. Discuss what happens when these workers do not fulfill their role expectations.
4. Compare the roles of women in the United States in the 19th century with the roles of women today.

Norms and Sanctions

A norm is a standard or code that guides behavior. Norms tell us when our behavior is right or wrong, proper or improper. In our society, people are often expected to dress differently on various occasions and in different social settings. Children are often expected to act and talk in "respectful" ways around adults. Adults are usually expected to act in certain ways around children. Norms vary not only in different times and cultures, but also among different social classes and cultural groups within the same society. Many norms within the United States have changed within the last decade.

Sanctions are rewards and punishments used by groups to ensure that norms are followed and that role expectations are fulfilled. Groups use a variety of pressures and controls to ensure that norms are obeyed. Gossip, embarrassment, and praise are often used as sanctions. Students who get caught cheating on tests are embarrassed when the teacher catches them. Teachers who are popular with parents are usually praised by their principals. We occasionally violate norms, but more often we conform to them because we internalize most of the norms and values of our culture when we are socialized.

Activities

Activities for teaching norms and sanctions are in the Teaching Strategies section in this chapter, beginning on page 304.

Values

Values are aspects of a society or culture to which groups attach a high worth or regard. Individuals acquire the values of their society during the process of socialization. Values are generalized rather than specific and consequently serve as standards for concrete behavior. Human dignity, justice, equality, and freedom of expression are some of the major values expressed in the national documents of the United States, such as the Constitution and the Declaration of Independence. People often agree on general values but disagree about actions that exemplify them. Individuals have different ideas about what constitutes human dignity, equality, and freedom of speech. Values such as freedom of speech and equality often conflict. One individual's freedom of speech might deny equality to another.

Activities

1. Read *The Three Little Pigs* and ask the students to list some things important to each character. Give them at least two examples.
2. Ask the students to make a list of rules they have to follow at home and at school. Ask: Are these rules fair? Why or why not?
3. Discuss the Bill of Rights and list the major values it expresses.
4. Read the following speeches and identify the values each expresses: Lincoln's Gettysburg address, John F. Kennedy's inaugural address, and Martin Luther King's "I Have a Dream" speech.
5. Ask the students to name the three persons they most admire and to name the values that each of these individuals exemplifies.

inquiry strategy

VALUES AND NORMS IN CONFLICT

DIRECTIONS
Read the following story to your class and ask the questions that follow.

ALTERNATIVE
Read the story to the class. Break the class up into four equal groups. Ask each group to decide what Susan should do. After each group has made a decision, the group decisions are shared with the class. The class then discusses the questions that follow the story.

STORY
Susan and Ronald Cortes have been married for nearly 20 years. During most of that time, Susan has strongly supported Ronald and their two children, Kate and Joseph, in whatever they wanted to do. Before their children were born, Susan worked full-time while Ronald completed medical school. She resigned from her middle school teaching job when Kate, their older child, was born. She wanted to spend more time with Kate and to support Ronald in his efforts to establish a successful medical practice. After Joseph entered school, Susan enrolled in graduate school with Ronald's encouragement. She completed her master's degree by going to school part-time. However, she was such an outstanding student that she received a doctoral fellowship to study for her Ph.D. degree. With Ronald's strong encouragement and support, Susan completed her Ph.D. degree in sociology after six years of study. Her professors consider her one of the most promising Ph.D. students ever to finish at State University. State University has one of the top-rated sociology departments in the United States.

After two years of trying to find a job teaching sociology at a local college, the best that Susan has been able to find is a part-time job at the community college teaching two courses a year. There is no possibility for a permanent position at the college. Her professors recommended her for a sociology position at one of the nation's best universities. It is located on the East Coast of the United States, about 3,000 miles from their home on the West Coast. It was tough to get an interview at such a prestigious university. However, Susan was interviewed and has been offered the job.

The Cortes family, which is close-knit, faces a dilemma. Ronald has a well-established medical practice in the city in which they now live. He does not want to start over in a new city. Kate is in her second year of high school and does not want to leave her friends. Joseph is in the sixth grade. While he doesn't want to leave his friends, he is quietly excited about the possibility of living on the East Coast. Susan is strongly committed to her family but wants to pursue her career at a university that will give her opportunities to do research and to realize her promise and talents.

QUESTIONS
1. What is the main problem in the case?
2. What values and norms are in conflict?
3. How does this situation challenge traditional norms and values about the roles of men and women in the family?
4. Which of Susan's values are in conflict?
5. What are the choices available to the Cortes family?
6. What are the possible consequences of each choice?
7. Should Susan take the job on the East Coast? Why or why not?

Social Movement

A social movement takes place when large numbers of people organize and try to promote or resist change in a group or society. Sociologists consider social movements a form of collective rather than group behavior because they do not have the amount and type of interaction and organization that characterize groups. Collective behavior is interrelated but is primarily unstructured. People get together but interact very little (Kitchens & Muessig, 1980; Smelser, 1963). Social movements sometimes give birth to formal organizations. The social movement that arose during the 1800s to improve conditions for U.S. workers resulted in the establishment of labor unions. The feminist and the civil rights movements of the 1960s and 1970s also gave birth to organizations, such as the Southern Christian Leadership Conference (SCLC) and the National Organization for Women (NOW). During their study of both historical and contemporary events and issues, students in the elementary and middle school grades will have many fruitful opportunities to study the influence of social movements on society.

Activities
1. View pictures of people who participated in the civil rights movement of the 1960s and 1970s.
2. Prepare and present a dramatic presentation chronicling the struggles, riots, and mass movements in which workers participated during the 1800s to gain higher wages and better working conditions.
3. Read documents revealing the ways colonists resisted British tax laws during the events leading to the American Revolution.
4. Make a collage showing highlights from the feminist movement of the 1960s and 1970s.

Society (Community, Neighborhood, Institution)

The largest unit sociologists study is society. A society is an independent unit in the sense that it includes all of the social institutions needed to meet human needs. It is not necessarily economically independent but is capable of surviving for a long period of time (Theodorson & Theodorson, 1969). Societies are made up of communities, neighborhoods, and institutions.

A community exists when a group of people frequently interact, live in close geographical proximity, and have a sense of belonging. A sense of a common bond and a shared identity are among the most important characteristics of a community. A community can also exist when a group of people have a shared identity and interests but live in separate geographical areas. The African American, Jewish, and Mormon communities in the United States are examples of this kind of community. Communities are made up of smaller units called neighborhoods, in which people have local ties and face-to-face relationships.

A set of roles organized to attain a specified goal constitutes an institution. Education is an institution organized to help children and adults learn. Educational institutions, such as schools, are made up of roles, each having a definite function and expectation. Roles include those of the superintendent, principal, teachers, and students. Sociologists usually study educational institutions, the family, and religious, economic, and political institutions, as well as others.

Activities
1. Ask the students to state what they think a family is and what needs they think families help individuals satisfy.
2. Ask the students to tell what they consider their neighborhoods. Ask them to tell what needs they are able to satisfy in their neighborhoods.
3. Discuss how neighborhoods and communities are alike and different. Name the communities in the region.
4. List institutions in the community and state their functions and their services. Invite community leaders to speak to the class.
5. Discuss how a society differs from a neighborhood, a community, and an institution. Compare and contrast norms, values, and behaviors in the United States and Japan. Discuss how U.S. society and Japanese society are alike and different.

SOCIOLOGICAL GENERALIZATIONS

The following generalizations (and related concepts) can be used to guide sociological studies in the elementary and middle school grades (Advisory Committee on the Social Studies; 1967; Michaelis & Johnson, 1965). The words and phrases in italic type are concepts. The statements below them are related generalizations. The learning experiences planned for students are far more important than a list of generalizations. Generalizations should be used to guide instruction. They should not constitute it.

Socialization
　　All characteristically human behavior is learned from other human beings through group interaction.

Groups
　　People live in social groups of two or more individuals. (These groups help them satisfy their needs.)

The group exerts social control over individual members through the use of sanctions (rewards and punishments).

The group enforces its norms by the use of sanctions.

Social Organization

All societies develop social institutions that may be defined as complex sets of folkways, mores, and laws integrated around the major functions (or needs) of the society.

Societies develop specific institutions to carry out their basic functions.

Institutions are characterized by division of labor and specialization.

Every society consists of smaller social units such as social classes, racial and ethnic groups, communities, clubs, associations, and neighborhoods. Each of these participates in a different way in the total culture.

Social Change

All societies are in constant change.

No society is completely harmonious: Some form of social disorganization is present in all societies.

Conflict

In all societies conflict develops between persons and groups.

Controlled conflict sometimes leads to social change that facilitates the attainment of desired goals.

Stratification

All members of a society are ranked into levels of prestige and power called social classes.

Human Ecology

People's social relationships and behavior are affected by their spatial distribution in geographic space.

Communication

Communication is basic to culture and group existence. Individuals and groups communicate in many ways other than by language. However, every type of communication involves symbolism of varying meanings.

Interdependence

Individuals, families, neighborhoods, communities, organizations, and other groups help each other meet their basic needs.

Discrimination

Groups are often the victims of discrimination and prejudice because of age, gender, race, religion, or cultural differences.

*f*EATURE

RACE STILL MATTERS IN THE UNITED STATES

On July 20, 1993, the National Association for the Advancement of Colored People (NAACP) office in Tacoma, Washington, was bombed (Wallace, Houston, & Penhale, 1993). The bombing of the Tacoma NAACP office was part of a well-organized and orchestrated national effort by White supremacist groups to target African American and Jewish civil rights organizations, churches, and synagogues. That same summer, the FBI uncovered a plot to bomb the largest African Methodist Episcopal (AME) church in Los Angeles—a church attended by some of the best-known Black entertainers in Hollywood. The plot to bomb an AME church in Los Angeles was part of a plan to start a race war by White supremacists. Synagogues were also the targets of ethnic hate in the early 1990s.

The extreme acts by White supremacist groups like the Skinheads are only the tip of the iceberg of the racial crisis in U.S. society. Throughout the early and middle 1990s African Americans, Asian Americans, and Jews were victims of racial and ethnic hate in their communities and on college campuses. In a posh upper-middle-class suburb of Seattle, Washington, an African American family experienced months of anguish caused by terrorist acts by White teenagers who attended the local high school with their son. Their son's car was bombed in the middle of the night while it was parked in the driveway of their home. He was also the victim of other hostile racial acts perpetrated by some of his White male classmates. The community was mobilized, greatly facilitated by the parents'

going public and appearing on a local television program. Eventually the teenage perpetrators were caught and brought to trial.

As onerous as blatant acts of racial and ethnic hate are, they are only symptomatic of the deep structural and institutionalized racism in the United States that is subtle and covert. It victimizes people of color each day. These acts include housing and job discrimination and well-meaning but hurtful acts and statements. In his *New York Times* best-selling book, *Race Matters* (1993), Cornell West, an African American professor at Harvard University, tells how he waited an hour for a taxi in New York City. Every taxi passed him by without stopping. Finally he walked three long blocks and took a subway. He arrived for his appointment late and out of breath.

In *A Different Mirror: A History of Multicultural America* (1993), Ronald Takaki, a Berkeley professor of Japanese American descent, describes a stinging and hurtful racist question he received from a Norfolk, Virginia, taxi driver:

> "How long have you been in this country?" he asked. "All my life," I replied, wincing. "I was born in the United States." With a strong Southern drawl, he remarked: "I was wondering because your English is excellent." Then, as I had many times before, I explained: "My grandfather came here from Japan in the 1880s. My family has been here, in America, for over a hundred years." He glanced at me in the mirror. Somehow I did not look "American" to him: my eyes and complexion looked foreign. (p. 1)

Near the end of his thoughtful and informative book, *The Color Line: Legacy for the Twenty-First Century* (1993), John Hope Franklin, the eminent American historian, gives sage advice about how to confront and deal with racism in U.S. society:

> Perhaps the very first thing we need to do as a nation and as individual members of society is to confront our past and see it for what it is. It is a past that is filled with some of the ugliest possible examples of racial brutality and degradation in human history. We need to recognize if for what it was and is and not explain it away, excuse it, or justify it. Having done that, we should then make a good-faith effort to turn our history around so that we can see it in front of us, so that we can avoid doing what we have done for so long. (p. 74)

SOCIOLOGICAL STUDIES IN THE ELEMENTARY AND MIDDLE SCHOOL

The social science content in the first four grades is primarily sociological. Usually, in kindergarten and first, second, and third grades, institutions such as the home, school, community, and family are studied. These institutions are often taught with a topical rather than a conceptual approach, as recommended in this book. When social studies units are planned in the elementary grades, the teacher identifies the topics (or lower-level concepts) to be taught, such as "Our Family," and then formulates teaching strategies. Too often, the end result is mastery of unrelated and disorganized facts. These are quickly forgotten.

The family is an institution that can be analyzed and studied from diverse perspectives. Psychologists look at it very differently than do sociologists. More effective units are structured when teachers identify key or organizing concepts and generalizations that they want the students to master before they select content, lower-level concepts, materials, and teaching strategies. This procedure allows teachers to freely select content samples that are meaningful to students, and that are also timely, diverse, and more appropriate for a greater variety of ability levels. If, for example, third-grade students are expected to study norms, you can use a variety of content samples to illustrate how norms are formed and how they shape behavior. Norms in such institutions as the family, school, and community could be examined.

This ideal way to plan instruction often is not practical for many teachers. In designated grades the teacher is frequently required to plan units dealing with specific topics and lower-level concepts, perhaps the home and school in kindergarten, and the family in first grade. If you find yourself in this situation, you should carefully study the required content, and identify key concepts and generalizations that the content can be used to illustrate. Higher-order or organizing concepts, such as norms and values, can be illustrated with a wider variety of content than can lower-level concepts such as *Our Town*, which is referred to above as a topic. (See Chapter 3 for a discussion of concept levels.)

The social studies program should be sequential, but scope and sequence should be based on the development of central, organizing concepts and generalizations rather than on topics or lower-level ideas. A conceptual approach to the study of institutions, such as the family and community, will help militate against the superficial way that they are often presented in the primary grades. When you try to help pupils master the concept *role,* you can use materials on families from many different groups to increase students' understanding. You can use a variety of content samples to help students discover that the roles of the mother in homes with one and with two parents working outside the home might be quite different.

Because any content can be studied from many different perspectives, *you should select organizing concepts from several disciplines when planning social studies units.* However, one discipline may be emphasized more than others in a particular unit. When studying the family, for example, sociological concepts may be stressed, because sociology is the study of human groups (the family is a group). However, economic and political science concepts will also help students to understand important aspects of family life. Chapter 2 discusses effective ways to plan interdisciplinary units. The point emphasized here is that you should have key, organizing concepts and generalizations in mind when you plan and teach units even if you are required to work within the limits of previously identified content. As we noted before, the conceptual approach to social studies instruction greatly facilitates comprehension, transfer, and mastery of content.

Sociology is rich with concepts and generalizations that can be used throughout the social studies program to help students better grasp traditional subjects, understand their social environment, and make decisions on important social issues. A study of institutions, such as the family and school, can help young children understand essential aspects of *socialization,* a key sociological concept. These institutions can also be used to teach such concepts as *values, norms,* and *sanctions,* because roles in all institutions are guided by norms and sanctions. A sound unit on community helpers can help pupils to understand such central sociological concepts as *institution, status,* and *role. Society* can be taught when intermediate- and upper-grade pupils study the United States and various nations of the Eastern and Western hemispheres.

TEACHING STRATEGIES

Generalization

The group enforces its norms by the use of sanctions.

Primary Grades

Read the following situation to the class and ask the questions that follow:

> During recess, the boys in Ms. Jones's class hurried outside to play with the big, red ball that Ms. Jones had just bought for her pupils. Ms. Jones had wanted the boys to play a game with the girls that morning, but the boys, led by Joe, had begged her to let them play with the big, shining ball. When she pulled the ball out of the closet, Joe and Johnny grabbed it. They ran toward the large play area, which was a

distance from where Ms. Jones usually stood to watch the children play. Joe and Johnny threw the ball to each other and to their friends. Carl, who was not too well liked by some of the leaders in the crowd, didn't get a chance to catch the ball very often. When Carl and Joe were struggling for the ball, it rolled out of the playground into the street. It was crushed by a speeding car. Stu ran and told Ms. Jones exactly what had happened.

1. Did Joe and Johnny treat Carl in a way that would have been approved by Ms. Jones? Why or why not?
2. When children are playing, what are some ways that adults expect them to act? (List statements [norms] on the board or overhead projector.)
3. Did Stu act in a way that the other boys would approve? Why or why not?
4. When children are playing, what are some things that they expect each other to do and not to do? (List norms on board or overhead projector.)
5. What are some things that Ms. Jones might do to make Joe and Johnny treat Carl differently? (List sanctions on board.)
6. What might the other boys do to make Joe and Johnny treat Carl differently? (List sanctions on board.)
7. What might the boys do to stop Stu from tattling? (List sanctions on board.)

Intermediate Grades

1. Read the students the story of Joan of Arc. Ask them to state the kinds of behavior and belief she exemplified that those in authority would not tolerate. The concept of mores could be introduced. Mores are protected by very strong sanctions, some as extreme as death. Ask the students whether they can identify some mores we have today.
2. Have the students read novels and accounts of the Salem witch trials in colonial America (e.g., Speare, 1958). Help them to identify why some people were called witches, and why they were persecuted. Ask the class: "What behavior codes (norms) did people called 'witches' violate? What punishments (sanctions) did the group give witches?"
3. During a study of the Middle Ages, read the class selections dealing with the many aspects of chivalry. Help the students identify the kinds of behavior expected of men and women during those times, and the sanctions that were used to enforce them.
4. Have the class read books and selections dealing with life in the United States during the settlement of the West. Ask them such questions as "What did the community probably think of women who went to taverns? Why? Of women who carried guns? Why? What would the people have said about a woman who wanted to run for public office?"

Upper Grades

Read the following case and ask the questions that follow.

Albert Roberts's parents live in a beautiful, large house in one of New York City's most exclusive suburbs. Mr. Roberts, his father, is a very successful lawyer who drives to and from the city every day. Ms. Roberts is a psychologist and a Sunday school teacher. Albert was a straight-"A" student in elementary and high school. He was able to get most of the things he wanted from his parents. When he left home to attend Green University, his parents gave him a new car. When Albert came home for Christmas vacation, his hair was longer than his sister's. He was smoking strange cigarettes that had a peculiar odor. His clothes were dirty and ragged. His parents were very upset when they saw him. They told him that he could not stay at home during the vacation period unless he cleaned up, cut his hair, and stopped smoking the strange cigarettes.

1. What did Albert do that his parents did not think a young man should do? (Solicit norms.)
2. How did they show their disapproval? (Solicit sanctions.)
3. Have you ever done anything of which your parents strongly disapproved?
4. What did they do to show their disapproval?

Ask the students to list:

1. The kinds of behavior they usually expect of:

   a. parents   h. the principal
   b. teachers   i. senior citizens
   c. brothers   j. neighbors
   d. sisters   k. close friends
   e. ministers   l. strangers
   f. store clerks   m. relatives
   g. the letter carrier

2. The kinds of behavior they do not expect of the individuals and groups named above.
3. The kinds of behavior they display to show disapproval of unexpected behavior from the persons and groups named above.
4. The kinds of behavior that the individuals and groups named above expect of them.
5. The kinds of behavior that the persons and groups named above would display to show disapproval of the students' unexpected behavior.

SUMMARY

Sociological concepts and generalizations can help students to make decisions related to social problems and to better understand the groups in which they live. Sociology is primarily concerned with group influences on individual behavior, and the relationships between different groups. Students must understand the structure of human groups and the interrelationships between groups in order to make reflective decisions on social issues. They must also be familiar with the ways their own behavior is shaped by their social groups.

Students can be introduced to sociological concepts and generalizations in the earliest grades; these key ideas can be developed and expanded in later grades. There are many opportunities for the teacher in the primary grades to introduce sociological concepts, because the topics traditionally studied in these grades are primarily sociological. The family, community, school, and neighborhood are usually studied in primary grade social studies. You can help your students understand these institutions by organizing your units around key sociological concepts. When students study an institution such as the family, they can be introduced to such key concepts as *socialization, role, norm, sanction,* and *values.*

The family plays a major role in socializing individuals and in preparing them to satisfy their societal needs. Each individual within a family has roles he or she is expected to fulfill. *Norms* tell people whether they are performing their roles properly, and *sanctions* are used to reward individuals for properly fulfilling their role expectations and to punish them when they fail. Both norms and sanctions reflect the values found in institutions such as the family. Although key concepts such as socialization, role, norm, sanction, and values can be introduced in the primary grades, these ideas can be developed at a more sophisticated level in the higher grades, with different content samples. When students study such topics as large urban centers, our state, United States history, and the Eastern and Western Hemispheres, they can learn key sociological concepts. When they study large urban centers, students can compare or contrast the ways in which socialization in the city family differs from that in the rural or less urbanized areas. The roles, norms, and sanctions present in urban institutions can also be examined. When studying the history of the United States and regions such as the Eastern and Western Hemispheres, students can determine the ways in which roles, norms, and values differ within various periods of U.S. history, and the many ways in which individuals are socialized in different parts of a region.

While certain units during the year might emphasize concepts from various disciplines, every unit should contain sociological concepts because of sociology's focus on group interactions and the ways in which the group influences an individual's behavior. Students must often view human behavior from the perspective of sociology in order to understand the complexity of human relationships.

REFLECTION AND ACTION ACTIVITIES

1. Examine an introductory sociology college textbook and make a list of these knowledge forms discussed in it: (1) key concepts, (2) key generalizations, and (3) key theories. Make a lesson plan for teaching one of the key concepts and several related generalizations to a group of students in one of the following grade levels: (a) primary grades, (b) intermediate grades, or (c) upper grades.
2. Examine several primary units in the curriculum library of your college dealing with such topics as the family, the community, the neighborhood, and the school. What key sociological concepts are stated in these units? Are the concepts accurate? Will the activities contained in the unit develop the concepts supposedly taught? What key sociological concepts could you add to the unit to enable students to gain a better perspective of the ways in which groups influence the behavior of individuals? What teaching strategies would you use to develop the key concepts that you would add to the unit?
3. Structure a unit on the family for the primary grades and plan teaching strategies to teach the concepts socialization, role, norm, sanction, and values. Which of these concepts is easiest for young children to understand? Which is the most difficult for them to understand? What special methods will you use to ensure that the students will gain an understanding of the most difficult concepts?

4. Select a current social problem dealing with an issue such as race relations, gender equity, war, or poverty. Illustrate, with a teaching plan, how students could use sociological concepts to better understand the situation and make decisions regarding the issue. While completing this exercise, review the decision-making model presented in Chapter 1.

 *internet links*

TEACHING SOCIOLOGY

The Internet can add a new and important dimension to teaching sociological concepts. Students can access needed information for sociological research, and teachers can make sociology more meaningful by providing opportunities for students to participate in virtual field trips and engage in critical thinking. What follows are several examples of websites that can be used to teach sociological concepts.

1. Intercultural E-mail Classroom Connection (http://www.stolaf.edu/network/iecc). Teachers who are interested in establishing e-mail pen-pal projects will find this web page helpful. It provides information on cross-cultural e-mail exchanges and includes an electronic mailing list where teachers can post requests for help with specific classroom projects that involve e-mail.

2. 1990 Census (http://www.census.gov). This web page offers speedy access to important social and demographic data. It also features *Map Stats,* a hands-on opportunity for students to use data and geographical information that can provide important information related to sociological concepts. Students can use *Map Stats* to access detailed maps and statistical profiles for states and congressional districts and learn how to process statistical information.

3. National Archives and Records Administration (NARA) (http://www.nara.gov). Teachers will be especially interested in the Digital Classroom, which can be accessed from this web page. The Digital Classroom provides classroom materials, information on teaching with primary sources, sample lessons, and quizzes. It also includes information on workshops and summer institutes for teachers.

4. The National Museum of the American Indian (http://www.si.edu/nmai) and the U.S. Holocaust Museum (http://www.ushmm.org). Students can experience virtual field trips to museums like the National Museum of the American Indian and the U.S. Holocaust Museum through the World Wide Web. Students who access the U.S. Holocaust Museum will be able to view photographs from the museum's archives, visit on-line exhibitions, and read excerpts from the official record of the Nuremberg Trial. The National Museum of the American Indian includes information on educational programs and resources as well as films and videos on Native Americans. This web page also links to the Smithsonian Institution.

REFERENCES

Advisory Committee on the Social Studies (1967). *A guide for concept development in the social studies.* Denver: Colorado Department of Education.

Bernard, J. (1987). Re-viewing the impact of women's studies on sociology. In C. Farnham (Ed.), *The impact of feminist research in the academy* (pp. 193–216). Bloomington: Indiana University Press.

Coser, L. A. (1971). *Masters of sociological thought* (2nd ed.). New York: Harcourt Brace Jovanovich.

Franklin, J. H. (1993). *The color line: Legacy for the twenty-first century.* Columbia: University of Missouri Press.

Giele, J. Z. (1988). Gender and sex roles. In N. J. Smelser (Ed.), *Handbook of sociology* (pp. 291–323). Newbury Park, CA: Sage Publications.

Gordon, M. M. (1964). *Assimilation in American life.* New York: Oxford University Press.

Kitchens, J. A., & Muessig, R. (1980). *The study and teaching of sociology.* Columbus, OH: Merrill.

Kuhn, T. S. (1970). *The structure of scientific revolutions* (2nd ed., enlarged). Chicago: University of Chicago Press.

Merton, R. K. (1968). *Social theory and social structure* (enlarged ed.). New York: Free Press.

Michaelis, J. U., & Johnson, A. M. (1965). *The social sciences: Foundations of the social studies.* Boston: Allyn and Bacon.

Rossi, A. S. (1964). Equality between the sexes: An immodest proposal. In R. J. Lifton (Ed.), *Woman in America* (pp. 98–143) Boston: Beacon Press.

Shils, E. (1980). *The calling of sociology and other essays on the pursuit of learning.* Chicago: University of Chicago Press

Smelser, N. J. (1963). *Theory of collective behavior.* New York: Free Press.

Speare, E. G. (1958). *Witch of blackbird pond.* Boston: Houghton Mifflin.

Takaki, R. (1993). *A different mirror: A history of multicultural America.* New York: Little Brown.

Theodorson, G. A., & Theodorson, A. G. (1969). *A modern dictionary of sociology.* New York: Barnes & Noble.

Tong, R. (1989). *Feminist thought: A comprehensive introduction.* Boulder: Westview Press.

Tuchman, G. (1992). Feminist theory. In E. F. Borgatta & M. L. Borgatta (Eds.), *Encyclopedia of sociology* (pp. 695–704). New York: Macmillan.

Wallace, J. , Houston, E., & Penhale, E. (1993, July 30). Terror campaign revealed. *Seattle Post Intelligencer,* Vol. 130, No. 181, pp. A1, ff. A6.

Warshay, L. H. (1975). *The current state of sociological theory: A critical interpretation.* New York: David McKay.

West, C. (1993). *Race matters.* Boston: Beacon Press.

FOR FURTHER READING

Antler, J. (1997). *The journey home: Jewish women and the American century.* New York: Free Press.

Brooks, R. L. (1990). *Rethinking the American race problem.* Berkeley: University of California Press.

Bryan, G. J., & Soroka, M. P. (1992). *Sociology: Cultural diversity in a changing world.* Boston: Allyn and Bacon.

Edelman, M. W. (1987). *Families in peril: An agenda for social change.* Cambridge: Harvard University Press.

Fine, M. (1997). *Off white: Readings on race, power, and society.* New York: Routledge.

Franklin, J. H. (1993). *The color line: Legacy for the twenty-first century.* Columbia: University of Missouri Press.

Hamburg, D. A. (1992). *Today's children: Creating a future for a generation in crisis.* New York: Random House.

Hill, H., & Jones, J. E., Jr. (Eds.). (1993). *Race in America: The struggle for equality.* Madison: University of Wisconsin Press.

Hochschild, A. R. (1989). *The second shift: Working parents and the revolution at home.* New York: Viking.

Kozol, J. (1988). *Rachel and her children: Homeless families in America.* New York: Fawcett Columbine.

Mindel, C. H., Habenstein, R. W., & Wright, R., Jr. (1988). *Ethnic families in America: Patterns and variations* (3rd ed.). New York: Elsevier.

Rossides, D. W. (1997). *Social stratification: the interplay of class, race, and gender* (2nd ed.). Upper Saddle River, NJ: Prentice-Hall.

Skolnick, A. S., & Skolnick, J. H. (1992). *Family in transition: Rethinking marriage, sexuality, child rearing, and family organization* (7th ed.). New York: Harper Collins.

West, C. (1993). *Race matters.* Boston: Beacon Press.

CHAPTER 11

Anthropology: Structure, Concepts, and Strategies

*f*EATURE

REWRITING ARCHAEOLOGY: CHANGING INTERPRETATIONS OF THE MAYAN CULTURE

The Maya are Indians who are ethnically and linguistically related. They live in an area comprising parts of the Yucatan peninsula and parts of Mexico, Guatemala, and Honduras. Today they number about 6 million (Coe, 1993). Mysteries about the Maya and their sophisticated civilization, which included massive pyramids and complex religious beliefs, practices, and rituals, have baffled the public as well as archaeologists since the mid-19th century. The Mayan civilization experienced a glorious period between A.D. 250 and 900. However, their impressive civilization mysteriously disappeared.

Archaeologists, by using artifacts and the well-developed Mayan hieroglyphics, are trying to reconstruct the sophisticated civilization and daily life of the Maya and to explain why their highly developed civilization vanished. Limited by a small number of Mayan remains and perplexing artifacts, Mayanism—as the field is called—is a fast-changing field in which old paradigms and explanations are being discarded and replaced by new ones. The newer ones, while benefiting from new technology such as radiocarbon procedures for dating artifacts, are characterized by thin evidence, conflicting interpretations, and much archaeological speculation. Some archaeologists estimate that only 1 percent of the original Mayan artifacts are preserved. Much about their history and culture is still unknown.

During the 1950s, Mayanism was dominated by theories developed by two highly respected archaeologists, J. Eric Thompson and Sylvanus Morley. Today, however, their theories have been rejected and replaced. Lemonick (1993) states some of their ideas that have been overturned:

> That the city centers of the Classic Maya were used primarily for ceremonial purposes, not for living; hieroglyphic texts described esoteric calendrical, astronomical, and religious subjects but never recorded anything as mundane

as rulers or historical events; slash-and-burn agriculture was the farming method of choice; and...the Maya lived in blissful coexistence with one another. (p. 47)

Coe (1993) also describes how knowledge about the Maya has changed. He writes:

> The past two decades have seen great advances in our knowledge of Maya civilization in both the Preclassic and Classic epochs, often in ways that earlier generations of scholars would not have approved. For a picture of the Maya that emphasized peaceful theocracies led by priest astronomers, ruling over relatively empty "ceremonial centers," we now have highly warlike city-states led by grim dynasts obsessed with human sacrifice and the ritual letting of their own blood. Although traditional "dirt" archaeology has contributed to our current view of the ancient Maya, the contributions of epigraphy and art history have been, in my opinion, truly revolutionary. (p. 7)

THE ANTHROPOLOGICAL PERSPECTIVE

Anthropology literally means the science (logos) of man (anthropos). Human behavior is studied in all of the social sciences. However, anthropology is concerned with people's behavior and their physical traits. Anthropology's interest in the relationship between culture and human biological traits is unique. Humans' long period of dependence, bipedal locomotion, large brain, and ability to symbolize are among the biological traits that enable them to create and acquire culture.

As this chapter's *Feature* on the changing interpretations of the Mayan culture indicates, knowledge in archaeology and cultural anthropology, like knowledge in all fields, continues to change and to be transformed. The changing nature of knowledge in anthropology is influenced by the discovery of new data and information, by the times in which anthropologists live and work, and by their personal experiences and frames of reference (Marcus & Fischer, 1986).

All of the concepts, generalizations, and theories in anthropology are related to those activities, artifacts, and belief systems that anthropologists call *culture*

(Marcus & Fischer, 1986; Harris, 1993). Although many animals are social and live in groups, people are the only animals that have culture (Munch & Smelser, 1992). The dominant interest in the concept of culture and the "holistic" method of studying it also distinguish anthropology from the other behavioral sciences. Anthropologists use a holistic approach when studying culture; they study all parts of a cultural system. Culture, they assume, is an integrated whole (Stigler, Shweder, & Herdt, 1990). Therefore, cultural traits cannot be understood in isolation from the whole. When anthropologists study a society, they collect data on all its aspects, including history, religion, geography, economy, technology, and language. To derive valid generalizations about a cultural complex, such as marriage, anthropologists believe that they must be familiar with all of society's other institutions.

Ethnography is the unique research method within anthropology that distinguishes it from the other social sciences. Marcus and Fischer (1986) define ethnography as "a research process in which the anthropologist closely observes, records, and engages in the daily life of another culture—an experience labeled as the *fieldwork method*—and then writes accounts of this culture, emphasizing descriptive detail" (p. 18) [emphasis added].

The comparative approach to culture and affinity with history and the humanities are more important to anthropology than to any of the other behavioral sciences. In the past most anthropologists were interested in studying nonliterate rather than modernized societies. They concentrated their work on nonliterate societies because it was easier to study whole cultures in small homogeneous societies than in complex, modern ones. Also, anthropologists wanted to test their generalizations in cultures very different from their own. Isolated, nonliterate societies served as laboratories for most earlier anthropologists (Benedict, 1934; Boas, 1938). The interests of today's anthropologists extend far beyond nonliterate societies. Most modern anthropologists view their discipline as a general biocultural study (Pelto & Muessig, 1980; Stigler, Shweder, & Herdt, 1990). They study nonliterate as well as highly modernized societies and the institutions within them. Themes in Japanese culture, the culture of the U.S. school, and African American culture in the United States are among the kinds of cultures and subcultures that anthropologists study in Westernized societies.

A number of important ethnographies of schools have been conducted within the last three decades. These include John U. Ogbu's (1974) study of education in an urban neighborhood, Susan Philips's (1983) study of communication in classroom and community on the Warm Springs Indian Reservation, and Alan Peshkin's (1991) study of a multiethnic community and its only high school. George Spindler (1982), an educational anthropologist, has edited an important book that includes a number of school ethnographies.

The formulation of the concept of culture and the study of nonliterate societies are two of the most significant contributions that anthropology has made to social science and the modern world (Geertz, 1973, 1983). Many of the traits and characteristics that had been considered "human nature" were reexamined when anthropologists such as Ruth Benedict (1934) and Margaret Mead (1928) found that these traits and characteristics were not always the same in nonliterate and modernized societies. As a result of the work of anthropologists such as Benedict and Mead, social scientists began to understand better the cultural influences on human behavior.

In the 1980s, however, the research assumptions and methods of anthropologists such as Benedict and Mead were seriously questioned by anthropologists who believe their research methods were not sufficiently rigorous. In a controversial and highly publicized book, *Margaret Mead and Samoa: The Making and Unmaking of an Anthropological Myth,* Derek Freeman (1983) refutes the conclusion Mead reached in her book *Coming of Age in Samoa,* published in 1928. In her book, Mead concludes that adolescence is not a universally traumatic period as social scientists claim, because the adolescent period in Samoa is tranquil. Freeman argues that Mead's conclusion is invalid because she went to Samoa to reinforce her environmental biases, was given inaccurate information by her informants (because they gave her the information she wanted rather than facts), and because Mead did not sufficiently understand the language and culture of Samoa. Despite the criticisms that have been made of earlier anthropologists such as Benedict and Mead, their important contributions to the study of culture and to anthropology are widely recognized and appreciated by most social scientists.

Historical approaches and elements are probably more important in anthropology than in any of the other behavioral sciences. Throughout the brief history of the discipline, anthropologists have shown a keen interest in the historical origins of cultural traits, and later a concern for unique and particular cultural elements. One area of anthropology, archaeology or prehistory, is devoted exclusively to reconstructing early human history, such as the Mayan culture in this chapter's *Feature.* Anthropology is also closely akin to the humanities. Books such as Benedict's (1934) *Patterns of Culture,* Mead's (1928) *Coming of Age in Samoa,* and Marvin Harris's (1974) *Cows, Pigs, Wars and Witches: The Riddles of Culture* are interesting, engrossing, and informative.

THE FIELDS OF ANTHROPOLOGY

Because of the broad scope of the discipline, anthropologists usually specialize in one of the subfields of anthropology. Although most of the areas are closely related, some are linked primarily by their common interest in humans. Physical anthropologists, who study the evolution of humans and their relationships with other animals, particularly other primates, are more akin to biologists than to social scientists. However, social and cultural anthropologists depend on physical anthropologists for information regarding the unique biological traits of humans, which are essential for the formation of culture. Weston LaBarre (1954), in *The Human Animal,* argues that biological drives and needs are the basis for many human institutions, such as the family. Physical anthropologists are also interested in the concept of race and have devised various schemes for classifying and identifying races (Montagu, 1997).

Cultural anthropology is often considered the main area of the discipline because it is concerned with the study of whole cultures, including *cultural change, acculturation,* and *diffusion.* An area called social anthropology has also emerged, primarily in England. Social structure rather than culture is the key concept in social anthropology. Its leaders refer to it as "comparative sociology" and contend that social anthropology searches for laws and generalizations while cultural anthropology is concerned primarily with tracing the history of cultural traits (Harris, 1968). They regard cultural anthropology as primarily historical and social anthropology as mainly explanatory.

Other areas of anthropology include ethnography, the accurate description of living cultures, and ethnology, which is mainly concerned with comparing and explaining the similarities and differences in cultural systems. Linguistics is devoted to the description and analysis of languages (Salzmann, 1993). Anthropologists have discovered that the language systems of cultures reveal much about their beliefs, ideology, and behavioral patterns.

Archaeologists, or prehistorians, attempt to reconstruct the history of peoples without a written history by digging up artifacts and other cultural elements. Elementary and middle school students will find the techniques and methods used by the archaeologist interesting as well as revealing. Within the last two decades, archaeologists have used a number of chemical processes both to locate artifacts and to determine their age. When applications of these processes revealed how very old our earth is, the archaeologists made a significant contribution to scientific knowledge.

RESEARCH METHODS IN ANTHROPOLOGY

The two most frequently used methods in anthropology are *participant observation* and *interviewing,* which are used when anthropologists do fieldwork (Pelto & Pelto, 1978). When anthropologists study a culture, they live with the people, learn their language, and take an active part in the daily affairs of the community. They cook with the women, go hunting with the men, participate in the ritual ceremonies, and help with the harvest. They take field notes while actively participating in the culture. Anthropologists face a number of problems when trying to keep their methods of data-collecting objective. Sometimes anthropologists must take notes several hours after they have observed or participated in an event. While other social scientists usually select their subjects for an interview randomly, anthropologists interview persons with whom they can establish rapport, or persons from whom they feel they can get accurate and detailed information. The accounts they receive from different subjects are often conflicting and contradictory. Anthropologists attempt to minimize errors in their data by observing as well as by interviewing, and by making cross-checks with other informants when they detect contradictory information. In the past, anthropologists made little use of the written questionnaire, largely because most of their subjects were not literate.

Data collection in anthropology tends to be more exploratory and personal than in the other behavioral sciences. Some of the difficulties anthropologists face in collecting data are inherent in the discipline itself; others reflect a tradition in anthropology that tends to regard suspiciously data-gathering procedures preventing anthropologists from directly observing the wholeness of cultures.

Anthropologists are concerned about the claim by some social scientists that ethnographic studies are often not objective. Within the last three decades, they have tried to make their research methods more objective and rigorous without "abandoning altogether the informal and personalized methods that have been the hallmark of fieldwork" (Pelto & Muessig, 1980, p. 42). A number of anthropologists have combined such techniques as random sampling, structured interviews, and quantitative methods with traditional ethnographic fieldwork. Anthropologists also use cameras, videotapes, and other research equipment to improve the objectivity of their data-collecting methods.

One development that has helped to foster objectivity in anthropology, as well as to save many hours of fieldwork, is the Human Relations Area Files, which include a large range of data on a variety of topics about cultures throughout the world. By using these files, the anthropologist can randomly select samples from many cultures and test hypotheses dealing with such topics as child-rearing practices, magic and religion, and marriage rites. Some anthropologists, however, think that this procedure is invalid because it does not permit them to study whole cultures.

*f*EATURE

THE HUMAN SIDE OF FIELDWORK

Hortense Powdermaker (1896–1970) was a well-known anthropologist who studied with Bronislaw Malinowski, one of the founders of anthropology, at the London School of Economics. She spent her teaching career at Queens College in New York. Her books include *Hollywood: The Dream Factory* (1950) and *Stranger and Friend: The Way of an Anthropologist* (1966). In the selections below from *Stranger and Friend*, Powdermaker describes the human side of doing fieldwork at Lesu, a small village on the southwest Pacific island of New Ireland. This human side of doing ethnography is rarely found in published ethnographies.

> A day or two later, my anthropologist friends left me to return to their own work. As I waved good-bye, I felt like Robinson Crusoe, but without a man Friday. That evening as I ate my dinner, I felt very low. I took a quinine pill to ward off malaria. Suddenly I saw myself on the edge of the world, and alone. I was scared and close to panic. When I arrived I had thought the place was lovely.

Everything seemed in harmonious accord: the black natives, the vividness of the sea and of the wild flowers, the brightly plumed birds, the tall areca palm and coconut trees, the delicate bamboo, the low thatched-roofed huts, the beauty of the nights with the moon shinning on the palm trees. But now the same scene seemed ominous. I was not scared of the people, but I had a feeling of panic. Why was I here, I asked myself repeatedly. (p. 53)

…While I was immersed in gloom, visitors arrived: Ongus, the *luluai,* who had competently directed the finishing of my home, with his wife Pulong, and their adolescent daughter Batu. With Pulong and Batu I had only previously exchanged greetings. They presented me with a baked taro, and I asked them to sit down. (p. 58)

I was no longer alone. I had friends. I went to bed and fell asleep almost immediately. No more thoughts of madness or leaving entered my mind. Several years later I learned that a definition of panic is a state of unrelatedness. (p. 59)

THEORIES IN ANTHROPOLOGY

In Chapter 3 we defined a *theory* as a set of interrelated statements (propositions) or laws that can be tested. In Chapter 10 we discussed two kinds of theories: *partial* (or small) and *grand* (or large). Partial or small theories explain only a part of behavior. Large or grand theories attempt to explain most of the findings in a discipline. Cultural anthropology is primarily historical and descriptive rather than theoretical. In this respect, anthropology is akin to history. Anthropologists devote most of their time to the description and comparison of cultures rather than to building generalizations and theories. However, anthropologists such as Marvin Harris (1980) and Clifford Geertz (1983) are interested in formulating generalizations and theories about culture. Anthropologists have formulated a number of important generalizations about culture that can be incorporated into the elementary and middle school grades.

Empirical partial theories are as scarce in anthropology as they are in history. However, during its brief history, a number of grand theories, schools of thought, and approaches have been developed in anthropology. These are referred to as theories in the anthropological literature and are summarized in Table 11.1.

THE FEMINIST CRITIQUE OF ANTHROPOLOGY

As in the other social and behavioral sciences, a feminist critique emerged within anthropology during the 1970s (Lamphere, 1987). One of the first feminist publications in anthropology was *Women, Culture and Society,* a book edited by Michelle Rosaldo and Louise Lamphere, published by the Stanford University Press in 1974. In this collection of essays, the authors attempted to define the major issues related to women in anthropological research and concluded that the fact that women bore children led to their subordination in most societies.

Later feminist anthropologists criticized the early feminist conclusions described in *Women, Culture and Society* as well as the major concepts within anthropology. These anthropologists argued that, while men and women have different roles in societies, they are often equally valued and important. The Hopi and Eskimo societies were sometimes used to illustrate the equally valued roles of men and women within different societies (Briggs, 1975; Schlegel, 1977).

Within the last decade, feminist anthropologists have critiqued the methods and major concepts used within anthropology. They have argued that these concepts are male dominated. Feminist anthropologists have critiqued the *man the hunter* conceptualization and have argued that it needs to be supplemented by the *woman the gatherer* hypothesis. In her analysis, Lamphere (1987) concludes that, while feminist scholarship has become a rich subfield within anthropology, this new scholarship has had limited influence on mainstream anthropology. She writes:

> Perhaps the most clear-cut example is that the research and writing on woman the Gatherer has failed to make an impact on textbooks' analyses of human evolution. Textbooks in the late 1960s and early 1970s...discussed human evolution in terms of "man." (p. 25)

TABLE 11.1. *The Development of Anthropological Theories*

Theory	Description	Leaders	Major Contributions to Anthropology
Evolutionism	An evolutionary theory of cultural development. All human cultures had experienced the same developmental stages; each higher phase represented more progress. Preliterature cultures typified the earliest stages of human cultural development. Western European civilization was the highest stage of culture that people had attained. Formulated in the 1800s.	Edward B. Taylor Lewis H. Morgan Sir James Frazer	Formulated the concept of culture. Stimulated research by others.
Historicism	Produced ethnographies indicating that the development of culture traits had not been uniform and unilinear. Within the same culture area could be found traits associated with each of Morgan's developmental levels. Advocated studying the historical origin of each culture trait through extensive fieldwork.	Franz Boas	Started the tradition of empirical fieldwork in anthropology.

ANTHROPOLOGICAL CONCEPTS

As in history and sociology, the concepts in anthropology tend to be broadly defined, and they are used differently by various anthropologists. Anthropological concepts are more standardized than historical concepts but less refined than those in sociology. We find less agreement among anthropologists than among sociologists about what the key concepts in their discipline are and what they mean. However, cultural anthropologists do agree that *culture* is the most important concept in the discipline, although there is considerably less agreement about what culture means. After surveying the literature, Kroeber and Kluckhohn (1963) found 164 different definitions of culture. They defined culture as the "patterns, explicit and implicit, of and for behavior, acquired and transmitted by symbols, constituting

TABLE 11.1. *(Continued)*

Theory	Description	Leaders	Major Contributions to Anthropology
Diffusionism	Cultural traits and elements had been invented in only a few areas of the world and had spread from these areas to all other culture regions.		Emphasized the importance of borrowing in the formation of cultures.
Functionalism	Each element in a culture exists to fulfill the needs of individuals. Every cultural system is an integrated whole, and each culture element fulfills definite functions. All cultures must meet three kinds of needs: primary or biological needs, derived or instrumental needs, and integrative or synthetic needs.	Bronislaw Malinowski A. R. Radcliffe-Brown	Stimulated discussion and debate in anthropology.
Configurationalism	Cultures do not consist of separate elements but are organized wholes. Cultures as wholes can be characterized according to the dominant ideologies, values, and ideas embraced by the individuals.	Ruth Benedict	Introduced the idea that cultures may have themes or patterns.

the distinctive achievement of human groups, including their embodiments in artifacts" (p.357).

Some anthropologists point out that, while the development of well-defined concepts is a goal in the discipline, anthropology lacks standardized concepts because of the newness of the field. Writes Keesing (1958), "No two anthropologists think exactly alike, or use precisely the same operating concepts or symbols. The science is too new, and the struggle to give sharp meanings to what are usually everyday terms still too wide open" (p. 152). Although anthropologists often define the same concepts differently, there is usually some degree of similarity in their meanings. We discuss some of the key concepts in anthropology below and describe activities that can be used to teach them to elementary and middle school students.

profile

SHIRLEY BRICE HEATH

An Anthropologist Who Studies Language, Life, and Work in Communities and Classrooms

Shirley Brice Heath, a professor of English and linguistics at Stanford University, is an anthropologist and former classroom teacher. She studies communities and classrooms. Heath brings to her ethnographies about communities and schools the keen insights of a teacher concerned about improving education. Her best known and most influential book is *Ways With Words: Language, Life, and Work in Communities and Classrooms,* published in 1983. In this book, she describes and interprets her findings related to the use of language in two communities: "Roadville," a White working-class community, and "Trackton," an African American working-class community. Heath describes the significant cultural differences between these two communities, especially in the ways in which they use and learn language. She also describes how differences in language are related to social relationships.

Heath's most recent book, *Identity and Inner-City Youth: Beyond Ethnicity and Gender,* is edited with Milbrey W. McLaughlin and published by Teachers College Press.

Culture

Culture comprises the behavior patterns, belief systems, artifacts, and other human-made components of a society. It includes the foods people eat, the tools they use, their clothing, myths, religion, and language. It consists of those elements humans use to adjust to their physical and social environments. It is their solution to the problem of survival. The unique biological structure of humans and their ability to symbolize make them the only animals able to create and acquire culture.

Because culture is human-made, students will be able to conclude that cultures vary greatly in different parts of the world, in different societies, and among different peoples. Students should be helped to discover that a culture system is an organized whole. Any drastic external or internal changes are likely to disrupt it. Culture is the key concept in cultural anthropology. Because all the other concepts are related to it, culture should be given special attention and focus in anthropological studies in the elementary and middle school.

When teaching the concept of culture, you may find it helpful to introduce three closely related concepts: *culture element* (trait), *culture complex,* and *enculturation.* A culture element is the smallest unit of culture. A tool such as an ax, a custom such as tipping the hat when greeting a person, and a word such as house are all culture traits. A set of functionally interrelated traits is a culture complex. The marriage complex in U.S. society usually consists of a period of courtship, a formal engagement, and an elaborate ceremony. Often culture traits are in the form of complexes when they spread from one culture area to another. Enculturation is the process by which individuals learn to participate in the culture of their society. Sociologists use the term socialization to describe this process.

You can also introduce the concepts *macroculture* and *microculture* when teaching about culture. A macroculture is a large culture. United States culture and Japanese culture are examples. Microcultures are subcultures that are part of a macroculture. Ethnic cultures such as the Italian American, African American, and Japanese American, and religious cultures such as the Muslim and Mormon, are examples of microcultures in the United States.

Activities
1. Show the students symbols such as a flag, a cross, and a stop sign. Ask them to tell what each of these symbols means. Point out that they are all examples of culture because they represent ideas that humans use to communicate.
2. Read the students descriptions of life in different subcultures in the United States, such as in Appalachia, in New York City, and on a farm in Texas. Ask them to identify ways in which life styles in these various places are alike and different.
3. Study the various cultures of Native American groups in the United States and describe ways in which they are alike and different.
4. Compare and contrast the life of children in the United States with the life of children in nations such as the United Kingdom, Nigeria, Japan, and Lebanon.
5. Divide into groups and make lists of what each group thinks makes up U.S. culture. Pool the ideas of each group and make a master list of what the class thinks constitutes U.S. culture.

Language is an important part of culture. In this photograph, the teacher is providing instruction in Spanish.
Source: Library of Congress, Washington, D.C.

inquiry strategy

AN ARCHEOLOGICAL CULTURAL ODYSSEY

DIRECTIONS
Read the following scenario to the students. Then give them the items described in the "artifacts" list that follows the scenario.

SCENARIO
It is 1,000 years from now. You have landed in an unknown land and are conducting an archaeological dig. You know nothing about the people who lived in this land 1,000 years ago except what you can detect from the following items that you find on the dig. This unknown land is the United States.

Your task is to try to describe the culture of the United States in 1999 as revealed in the items listed below. For example, on the front side of the one dollar bill is found a photograph of George Washington. On the back, the seal of the United States appears. It includes an eagle and the words *E Pluribus Unum*. Also on the back of the one dollar bill are the words "In God We Trust." What do these symbols and words, as well as those in the other items in this activity, tell you about the culture of the United States?

Break up into groups of five to complete this activity. Appoint a leader and a recorder for each group. Each group independently will make a list describing what these items reveal about the culture of the United States.

Each person in each group should also draw a circle or a box and make a personal "seal." The seal should contain words or symbols that reveal what is most important to you personally and to your cultural or ethnic group.

When these two steps have been completed, assemble in a large group. Ask the recorder from each small group to share the list it developed and the highlights from the group's discussion about the personal seal.

ARTIFACTS

1. Photograph of a one dollar bill, showing details of both the front and back. (Actual one dollar bills may also be used.)
2. Photograph of a U.S. postage stamp that shows a famous American or a symbol about American society. (Actual postage stamps can also be used.)
3. The following excerpt from the Declaration of Independence (1776):

> We hold these truths to be self-evident, that all men are created equal, that they are endowed by their creator with certain unalienable rights, that among these are life, liberty, and the pursuit of happiness. That, to secure these rights, governments are instituted among men, deriving their just powers from the consent of the governed. That, whenever any form of government becomes destructive of these ends, it is the right of the people to alter or to abolish it, and to institute new government, laying its foundation on such principles, and organizing its powers in such form, as to them shall seem most likely to effect their safety and happiness.

4. The poem, "I, Too, Sing America" by Langston Hughes, in Langston Hughes and Arna Bontemps, eds., *The Poetry of the Negro, 1746–1970* (Garden City, N.Y.: Doubleday, 1970), p. 182.
5. Excerpts from Martin Luther King, Jr., "I Have a Dream," in *The Annals of America*, Volume 18, 1961–1968 (Chicago: Encyclopedia Britannica, Inc., 1968), pp. 156–159.

Diffusion

A culture area is a geographical region that shares a number of culture traits and complexes. Anthropologists have identified the following culture areas for American Native cultures: the Eskimo, the Pacific Northwest coast, the Plains, and the Southwest. The spreading of culture traits from one culture area to another is called *diffusion*. A concept related to diffusion is *invention*, the process of independently developing a new cultural trait or artifact.

Anthropologists have discovered that most of the traits that make up a culture were borrowed, not invented. However, all cultures have made independent inventions. Many of the words, customs, behavior patterns, and artifacts that are very important components of United States culture were invented in other culture areas. Culture traits may spread from one microculture to another within the same macroculture, as well as from one macroculture to another.

Activities
1. Study the origins of words in U.S. English that came from other nations, such as *enchilada, pizza,* and *bon voyage.*
2. Study the invention and spread of architectural forms to various nations, such as the post and lintel construction, the dome, and the Doric, Ionic, and Corinthian orders.
3. Research the evolution, domestication, and uses of the horse and how the horse spread to and was used by various cultures.
4. Research the factors that gave rise to French Impressionism and its influence on art in various Western nations.
5. Ask the students to list the major values stated in the United States Declaration of Independence and the Constitution. Help them to identify the European writers and philosophers that strongly influenced the ideas of the founders of the United States.

Tradition

A social custom, behavior pattern, or belief that has been part of a culture for a long period of time is a tradition. Folkways, mores, and myths are part of the traditions of a society. Traditions in the United States include decorating a tree for the Christmas season, eating turkey on Thanksgiving Day, and wearing a ring to indicate marital status. Traditions help a society to maintain stability and to socialize children. However, as Durkin (1969) points out, "Societies and the groups and individuals within them tend to retain many traditional ways of living and dealing with current problems, whether or not that behavior is appropriate" (p. vi).

Activities
1. Study the origins of holidays such as Christmas, Chanukah, New Year's Day, and St. Valentine's Day.
2. Compare and contrast the ways in which nations such as Colombia, Brazil, Canada, the United Kingdom, and the United States celebrate Christmas.
3. Study U.S. traditions that originated within, and are celebrated primarily by, ethnic groups within the United States, such as Jewish Passover, Yom Kippur, and Kwanzaa.
4. Students can learn how difficult it is to start a new national holiday by studying the history of the development of Labor Day and Martin Luther King's Birthday as national holidays. Ask them to identify the major factors involved when a day is made into a national holiday.
5. Ask the students to make a list of special traditions that exist in their families, such as having a family reunion every five years or going to grandmother's house for Christmas.

Acculturation

The cultural exchange that takes place when two unlike cultures experience extended contact is called *acculturation*. Acculturation often takes place when powerful groups capture or subjugate less powerful ones. Much cultural exchange took place when the American colonists invaded the areas inhabited by the Native Americans. It is extremely important for students to understand that acculturation is a two-way process. While most Americans are aware of how the Native American cultures were affected by Anglo-Saxon culture, our great cultural debt to the Indians is less well-known and less acknowledged (Weatherford, 1992).

Acculturation is a selective process; cultures accept only those elements from a foreign culture that blend with their own cultural elements. When they use traits from another culture, they modify them. Forced cultural change can disrupt a culture because cultures are organized wholes. Many of the forced cultural changes that the Native Americans experienced had a profoundly negative effect on their life styles. If you and your students make extensive use of this concept in the early grades, when they are learning about Native American and Eskimo groups, the study of these peoples will be less superficial and ethnocentric than it currently is in many classrooms.

Activities

1. Study ways in which the Native American cultures changed after the arrival of the English colonists.
2. List the things that the Native Americans taught the early colonists that enabled them to survive the harsh winters in New England.
3. Research ways African American culture has influenced mainstream American culture, especially in music and the arts.
4. Identify the ways foods in the United States have been influenced by other nations.
5. Examine the ways United States culture has influenced other nations.

Ethnocentrism

Every group tends to think its culture is superior to all others. Writes Spain (1975): "Many groups…refer to themselves by using names which translate as 'true humans' or 'people,' while the names for 'others' are the equivalent of such words as 'savage,' 'barbarian,' or other more descriptive indications of their distinctive and inhuman qualities such as 'the-ones-who-walk-on-their-heads' " (p. 5). A knowledge of this concept will help elementary and middle school students to better understand the pervasive ethnocentrism in the United States and the world.

Activities

1. Ask the students to list epithets they have heard used to refer to different cultural, ethnic, religious, and gender groups. Discuss why people use such negative terms to refer to outside groups.
2. Read documents written by various European explorers to the Americas and discuss words they used to describe the Native Americans. Discuss why they used these words.

3. View drawings of Native Americans that were done by Europeans in the 19th century and discuss ways in which they exemplify ethnocentrism.
4. View pictures of Africa in textbooks and other sources and list ways that they show ethnocentrism.
5. Study the role ethnocentrism played in leading Japan and Germany to World War II.

Cultural Relativism

Cultural relativism means we can gain a full understanding of the behavior within a group only if we look at it from the perspective of that group's culture. Many cultural practices, such as water witching, the vision quest among the Plains Indians, and the revival meetings of southern fundamentalist Baptists, often seem strange and perplexing to outsiders unless they view them from the perspectives of the cultures in which they are practiced.

Cultural relativism is often interpreted to be a moral position which indicates that cultures should not be judged with other cultures' criteria. However, as Swartz and Jordan (1976) point out, cultural relativism need not be an ethical concept. They write, "Being able to understand the forces that influence behavior is one thing and evaluating that behavior is quite another. Cultural relativism, seen as an intellectual tool, is very different from cultural relativism as an instrument of moral judgment").

When interpreted as an ethical concept, cultural relativism can be abused. It can be used to justify the destruction and exploitation of human lives. However, students should be aware of this concept because it can help them to see that behavior in other cultures that they may consider bizarre is often quite meaningful and useful to the people who practice it. They should also be aware of the limitations of cultural relativism when used in an ethical context.

Activities
1. Identify current practices and customs in U.S. society, such as beliefs about ghosts, the four-leaf clover, and the rabbit's foot and explain how these customs emerged and why people believe in them.
2. Do a survey to find out how many modern office buildings in your community do not have a 13th floor, and find out why.
3. Read about the customs related to witches in American colonial society and discuss why they ended.
4. Read about customs in traditional Native American and Eskimo cultures that are perplexing to most Americans and explain what they meant to the people who practiced them.
5. Identify some of the customs in several of the major world religions, such as Christianity, Judaism, and Islam, and discuss why these practices are perplexing to outsiders and what they mean to those who practice them.

Rite of Passage

A rite of passage is a ceremony marking an important change in an individual's life. The individual moves from one status to another. Ceremonies related to birth, puberty, marriage, and death are rites of passage. Rites of passage are important to individuals because they clearly mark important changes in their lives and provide them with emotional support.

Activities
1. Make a list of the ways the students celebrate their birthdays.
2. Share pictures of important events in the students' lives, such as birthdays and baptisms.
3. Read about the Jewish *bar mitzvah* and *bas mitzvah* ceremonies and identify their nature and major purposes.
4. Do research to find out ways in which marriage ceremonies are similar and different in various cultures.
5. Do research to find out ways in which death ceremonies are similar and different within various United States subcultures and within different nations.

ANTHROPOLOGICAL GENERALIZATIONS

Most anthropological generalizations are based on cross-cultural samples and deal with the discipline's key concept, *culture*. A number are also interdisciplinary, because anthropologists study many problems of interest to other behavioral scientists. The following generalizations can be used to guide anthropological instruction in the elementary and middle school grades. The generalizations are grouped under major concepts.

Culture
Every society consists of a human-made system of artifacts, beliefs, and behavior patterns, called culture. Culture enables individuals within it to meet their needs according to their physical and social environment.
Because of their unique biological traits, humans are the only animals able to create and acquire culture.
Culture is an integrated whole. Changes in one part are reflected in nearly all other components.
Cultures use a diversity of means to attain similar ends and to satisfy common human needs.

Symbols
Making and using symbols is an essential component of every culture.

Diffusion
Every culture consists of a variety of borrowed cultural elements. However, cultures are selective in the traits they borrow. Societies adapt borrowed cultural elements to their own particular life styles.

Acculturation
Cultural exchange takes place when groups with diverse cultures come into prolonged contact. Cultural change may disrupt a society.

Magic and Religion

In all human societies, magical and religious practices arise to help individuals explain perplexing phenomena in the universe, and to attain a sense of control over their environment.

Rites of Passage

All societies have traditional ceremonies and rituals to signal and mark important status changes in a person's life.

Traditions

All societies have a set of traditions that help to maintain group solidarity and identity.

ANTHROPOLOGY IN THE ELEMENTARY AND MIDDLE SCHOOL

Many units in the primary and middle grades have content dealing with preliterate societies that can be profitably studied from an anthropological perspective. When students are taught about Eskimos, Native Americans, and Africans, the exotic and strange behavior of these peoples are often emphasized. As a result, students often conclude these groups are not very human. They seem very different from the students, and they do many things that seem inhuman or absurd, such as sending the aged into subzero weather to freeze to death or dancing to make it rain. Most young children think that behavior very different from their own is bizarre. Too often social studies units reinforce students' misconceptions about other cultures, rather than help them to understand the meaning of the "puzzling" behavior to the people who practice it.

Social studies units on groups such as Indians, Asians, and Africans often include songs, dances, and materials that reinforce stereotypes of these cultural groups. Units on Indians often present the stereotypic image of Plains Indians. Rarely is the tremendous diversity among Indian tribes accurately described in social studies units for young children. Africa is often presented in the curriculum as a land that consists only of preliterate cultures. The modernized cities in Africa and the tremendous diversity of the peoples and cultures that make up Africa are rarely described in elementary school units. Units on Africans and Native Americans often describe traditional cultures without indicating the tremendous ways in which these cultures have changed as a result of modernization. Units on Native Americans and Africans should be taught from anthropological perspectives and help students understand the tremendous diversity both within and across Native American and African cultures.

Units on Indians and Eskimos, if approached from an anthropological perspective, *can help students to broaden their understanding of what it means to be human, and enable them to better understand their own culture and life styles.* Students should be helped to discover that although people are born with the physical capacity to become human, individuals become human only by learning the culture of their group. Anthropologists call this learning process *enculturation.* Because cultures are human-made, there are many ways of being human. The middle-class Anglo Saxon Protestant life style is one way; the Navajo Indian culture represents another. Studying these important anthropological generalizations helps students to appreciate humankind's great capacity to create a diversity of life styles and to adapt to a variety of environments.

During their study of preliterate cultures, students can learn that although human beings have many of the same basic needs—such as love, protection, and food—different cultures have devised a great variety of means to satisfy them. The rain dances of the Hopi Indians, the Shaman among some African groups, and water witching in the United States all represent attempts by humans to control and manipulate their environment. Once students understand preliterate people's behavior, they will be less likely to consider it exotic and bizarre. With understanding may come tolerance.

While you should help students see and understand differences, you should also make them aware of the many ways in which all human groups are alike. For example, all human societies have families, a system of government, the incest taboo, and divisions between male and female roles. However, these institutions often take diverse forms. Nevertheless, you should not emphasize differences to the neglect of important similarities. Students should know how closely they are related to all human groups—both biologically and culturally. Anthropologists call the many ways in which all human cultures are alike *culture universals.*

Anthropology can also help students better understand their own culture. By studying about other ways of being and living, students will see how bound they are by their own values and prejudices. The fact that most Americans think romantic love is the most important part of marriage indicates how much we are creatures of our culture. Individuals in some cultures would be shocked by the idea that marriage could be based on such flimsy grounds. Kluckhohn (1965) writes, "Studying preliterates enables us to see ourselves better. Ordinarily we are unaware of the special lens through which we look at life....Anthropology holds up a great mirror to man and lets him look at himself in his infinite variety" (p. 19).

You can use a conceptual approach to the study of preliterate societies to militate against perpetuating stereotypes and misconceptions. You can begin by identifying a number of key anthropological concepts that will serve as an organizing framework for your units. Once you have identified a number of organizing concepts such as *culture, tradition, acculturation,* and *diffusion,* you should select several generalizations related to these concepts, such as "Cultures employ a diversity of means to attain similar ends and to satisfy common human needs" and "Culture exchange takes place when groups with diverse cultures come into prolonged contact." After key concepts and generalizations are identified, you can select teaching materials and devise appropriate teaching strategies.

If you select the first generalization named above, you could identify three cultures for content samples, such as the Navajo Indians, the Iroquois Indians, and the Netsilik Eskimos, or you could select one of these groups and use mainstream U.S. culture as a comparison group. Selecting a small number of cultures and covering them in depth is better than selecting a large number of cultures and covering them superficially. Selection of content samples should be based primarily on the materials available, interests of the students, recommendations in the district curriculum guide, teacher competency and interests, and the prior experiences of the students. If the students studied the Navajos in a previous year, it would be better to select the Iroquois for the new unit.

TABLE 11.2. *Data Retrieval Chart: Comparison of Cultures*

Concepts and Related Questions	Navajo	Iroquois	Netsilik Eskimo
Food What foods are eaten? How are they obtained?			
Protection What kinds of shelter exist? How are they made?			
Recreation What do people do for fun?			
Esteem How do people gain recognition?			

When teaching the generalization "Cultures employ a diversity of means to attain similar ends and to satisfy common human needs," you could construct, with the pupils' help, a data retrieval chart similar to the one illustrated in Table 11.2. You could begin by asking the students to name some needs that all human beings have. Their responses may include food, protection from extreme weather, love, esteem, recreation, and a need to explain the origin of the universe and people's place in it. Their responses could be used to structure categories on universal human needs. Once these categories are structured, the class can identify a number of questions related to the categories that can be asked about each of the cultures studied. The names of the cultures should be listed on the chart. The students should participate in a variety of activities—such as reading, role-playing, and viewing videotapes—in order to gain the information needed to complete the chart. Once the chart is complete, the students will be able to derive the generalization stated above.

TEACHING STRATEGIES

Generalization
The making and use of symbols is an essential component of every culture.

Primary Grades

Show the class these symbols. Then ask the questions that follow.

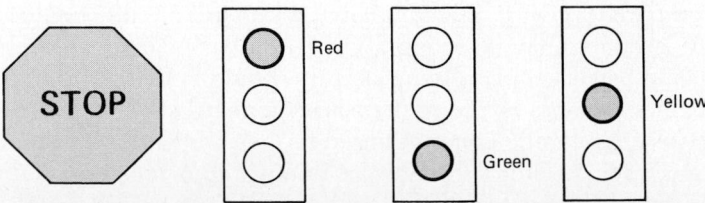

1. Look at these signs. Have you ever seen them before? Where? What does each mean? Can you think of other signs? (Recalling meanings of specific symbols.)
2. Did you always know what the first sign means? How did you find out what it means? (Cultures pass on meanings of symbols.)
3. Do these signs help people? How? (Symbols help people adjust to their environments.)
4. What would happen if we didn't have these signs?

Ask the following questions

1. Did anyone ever tell you that you were a little monkey? Why would anyone call you a little monkey? Would you like to be called by that name? Why or why not? (Example of a symbol.)
2. Draw a line between the animal and the thing it stands for. (Matching symbols with meaning.)

mouse	courageous, brave
lion	quiet, tiny
elephant	clever
fox	good memory

3. Isn't it funny that we think of animals in these ways? Do you think a mouse is really quiet? Think about the other animals and the words we use to describe them. Do these words and animals fit? (Questioning the relationship between the symbol and its meaning.)
4. Did you ever hear a story about a house where "nothing was stirring, not even a mouse"? Why don't we say, "where nothing was stirring, not even a horse"? Which phrase makes the house seem quieter? Why? Does it help to use animal names to tell about things? How? (Examining the use of symbols in descriptions.)

Read the class a story about Indians or Eskimos that tells about totem poles and includes characters that have animal names such as Running Bear or Crazy Horse. Then ask the children to write a story in which they use animal names to describe characteristics of people and things. (Application: Using symbols.)

Ask the following questions

Do you ever pretend to be a driver of a car or a fisherman in a boat? Do you sometimes walk around the house in your mother's or father's shoes? Do you ever pretend to ride horses or drive trucks and trains? Why? (Identifying feelings that are symbolized in action.)

Tell the class

England is a country that is on the other side of the Atlantic Ocean. (Show on a globe.) There, when you are old enough, you get the key. Children are given the key to their house when they are big enough.

Ask the following questions

> Would you like to be big and have a key to your house? Would your parents give a key to a one-year-old child? Why not?

Say

> We would call the key a symbol of being big because you get one only when you are old enough to take good care of a key and will not lose it. You get a key when you are big. (Determining the reason for particular meaning of symbol.)

Ask

> Can you think of other symbols of being big? If we had no symbols of being big, would you ever know if you were grown up? (Remembering, predicting, and hypothesizing result of loss of symbols.)
>
> Ask the children to act out, tell a story about, draw pictures of, or write about someone's acting in a way that shows or symbolizes what he or she would like to be. (Applying knowledge.)

Intermediate Grades

Tell the class

> Every year in Mexico, as in many other countries, there is a retelling of the story of Jesus' birth. In a symbolic journey, a girl and a boy, representing Mary and Joseph, walk each night for nine days. On the last day an innkeeper gives them shelter and Jesus is born.

Ask the following questions

> 1. Is Jesus really born each time the boy and girl walk through the journey in the story? (Recognition of symbolic nature of the action.)
> 2. What do people in other countries do to symbolize the birth of Jesus? (Memory; comparison of similar symbols.)
> 3. Why do you suppose the people have this festival every year? (Determining meaning of symbolic tradition.)
> 4. Have you ever seen a cross? What does a cross mean? Why do some people wear a cross? (Analyzing a concrete symbol.)

Ask the following questions

> 1. In scouting, Boy Scouts, Girl Scouts, and Campfire Girls receive emblems for each skill attained and demonstrated. How is this practice similar to the markings of the Native Americans? How is it different? (Comparing symbol systems.)
> 2. Military organizations also use symbols to designate achievement levels. How are military symbols similar to the ones we have discussed? How are they different? (Comparing symbols.)

Ask the students to complete the following activities

> 1. Select flags from three African nations. Investigate the meanings or symbolism behind each color used and also the meanings of the designs on the

flags. (Identifying symbolic meanings.) Each student will discuss with the class the flags he or she selected, indicating all symbols involved.

2. Discuss things to which you could feel loyal, like your family, friends, class, city, state, religion, and country. What other things could you feel loyal to? What could be symbols of the things you named? (Identifying feelings, creating symbols.)

3. Select something to which you feel you are loyal and create a flag, using symbols to express important aspects of it. (Identifying feelings, creating symbols.)

Tell the class

Before you had money to buy some of the things you wanted, you could collect things and trade them for items that you didn't have.

Ask

What things could you collect when you were smaller? What could you trade them for?

Upper Grades

Read the class the following summary of an Eskimo anthropologist's report of one aspect of American life.

Many peoples in the world pay close attention to time, but none more than Americans. Though it might be denied, time seems sacred in the United States.

This is apparent from the American language. It is generally regarded as sinful to "waste time." One of the greatest American philosophers has said: "Dost thou love life? Then do not squander time, for that is the stuff life is made of."

But to be specific. Nearly all Americans carry idols that represent time. Larger idols that show time are displayed throughout American igloos and in public places.

Even when busy, Americans often gaze at such idols and regulate their lives according to them. They start when they get up in the morning, and they hardly stop until they go to bed. Many students and workers seem more interested in the time idol than they are in their tasks.

If time worship can be considered a religion, Americans may be the most religious people on earth. (*Anthropology in Today's World: Case Studies of Peoples and Cultures*, 1965, p. 7)

Ask these questions

1. What did the Eskimo anthropologist say about Americans and time? (Memory.)

2. Do Americans worship idols of time? Why or why not? (Analyzing symbolism about time.)

3. Do you agree with the Eskimo anthropologist? Why or why not? (Evaluating the interpretation of symbols.)

4. What does this selection tell you about making assumptions about other people? (Evaluating method of interpretation.)

Say to the class

Words are symbols. They stand for ideas and values that people have. Ask your parents and your grandparents what words they used to describe things they liked when they were your age. What words do people your age use for things they like? Are they the same as they were when you were five years younger? Why or why not? Do you think that you will use different symbols or words for things you like when you are five years older? Why or why not? (Changing of symbols through time.)

Find out how people from different countries greet each other. We greet each other with "Hello," "Hi," "How are you?"; in parting we may say "Good-bye," "Peace," or "Take it easy." The Navajo say "Ya ta hey"; it is used to say "Good-bye" or "Peace." The Jewish people may say "Shalom," which means "Peace be with you," or also "Hello" or "Good-bye." The Chinese say "Ni Hâu Ma" for "How are you?"

Ask

How are these symbols alike? Different? What would we do without them? (Comparing symbolic systems.)

Ask the class the following questions

There has been a change through time in the symbols for peace. Native Americans had a few peace symbols. Can you name one? (Pipe and broken arrow.) Can you name three symbols for peace used later in this country? (Dove, eagle with olive branches, and two fingers making a V.) Find out ways in which peace is symbolized in other societies. Create your own symbol of peace. (Identification of meaning, recall of symbols, comparison of symbols with same meaning, and application of knowledge by creating a new symbol.)

SUMMARY

Anthropology is distinguished from the other social sciences because of its focus on culture—the behavior patterns, belief systems, artifacts, and other human-made components of a society. Anthropologists use a *holistic* approach when they study culture; they believe that valid generalizations can be made only when all the elements of a cultural system are studied as an integrated whole. The comparative study of preliterate cultures is also a unique characteristic of anthropology. The main research method used in the discipline is participant observation. Anthropologists live in the cultures they study. Because of the nature of the discipline and its traditions, anthropological research is more exploratory than research in the behavioral sciences like sociology and psychology. Most anthropologists are more interested in describing particular cultures than they are in formulating empirical theories about many different cultures. Anthropological generalizations are often interpretive judgments rather than empirical statements. The participant observation method does not facilitate the making of hard generalizations. Thus anthropology is akin to both the humanities and history. Theory development has been retarded in the discipline because of its research aims and methods and a nonempirical tradition involving the search for single-factor theories to explain the emergence of individual cultures.

Despite the scientific status of anthropology, its focus on culture and its concern for preliterate cultures make it an excellent vehicle for helping students to broaden their conception of what it means to be human and understand how bound they are by their own cultures, prejudices, and biases. In all societies, people tend to think that their way of doing things is the right way or the only way. Such chauvinistic ethnocentrism is especially detrimental in our increasingly small and interdependent world, where peoples of many different cultures, races, and ideologies must learn to live together if the human race is going to survive the challenges of the 21st century. Anthropology can help students to learn that there are other ways of living and being that are just as valid as the ways with which they are familiar. With understanding, tolerance sometimes comes. Anthropology merits a special place in the schools because it gives students a unique lens to view other humans—and themselves.

REFLECTION AND ACTION ACTIVITIES

1. Read one of the classic books in anthropology, such as *Mirror for Man* by Clyde Kluckhohn, *Patterns of Culture* by Ruth Benedict, or *Coming of Age in Samoa* by Margaret Mead, or a more recent book or ethnography, such as *Cows, Pigs, Wars and Witches: The Riddles of Culture* by Marvin Harris, or "Deep Play: Notes on a Balinese Cockfight" by Clifford Geertz in *The Interpretation of Cultures,* and answer the following questions:
   a. What key concepts and generalizations are discussed in the book or ethnography?
   b. What kinds of data are used to support the generalizations made by the author?
   c. What methods of research were used to gather the data discussed by the author?
   d. How does the writing style of the book or ethnography compare with that in studies you have read in other disciplines? (For example, is the book or ethnography more interesting than books that you have read in other subject areas?)
   e. What were the major strengths and limitations of the book or ethnography?
   f. In what ways can the information reported in the book or ethnography help you to plan and organize a unit on culture for students in the elementary and middle school grades?
2. Examine a primary grade social studies unit in your curriculum library dealing with the cultures of preliterate groups, such as some Native American, Eskimo, or African societies. What key concepts and generalizations are developed within the unit? Are the concepts and generalizations accurate? If not, in what ways are they inaccurate? Are the facts used to teach the concepts and generalizations accurate? Are the activities designed to teach the concepts and generalizations effective? What concepts and generalizations would you add or take out of the unit in order to make it more effective? What learning activities would you add or take out of the unit to make it more effective?
3. Select one of the following generalizations and write a series of activities (similar to the ones in this chapter) that can be used to teach it to students in the (1) primary grades (2) middle grades, and (3) upper grades.
   a. The making and use of symbols is an essential component of every culture.
   b. Cultures use a diversity of means to attain similar ends and to satisfy common human needs.
   c. Cultural exchange takes place when groups with diverse cultures come into prolonged contact. Cultural change may disrupt a society.
   d. All societies have traditional ceremonies and rituals to signal and mark important status changes in an individual's life.

4. Examine an introductory college textbook in anthropology and list the key concepts and generalizations within it that could serve as a guide to a social studies curriculum committee.

5. Assume that you are an anthropologist who is studying a primary grade classroom.
   a. State the key concepts you would use to guide your analysis of the culture within the classroom.
   b. List key questions related to the concepts you would raise.
   c. State related hypotheses.
   d. Indicate how you would test your hypotheses.
   e. If possible, carry out the study.

6. Can students in the upper elementary grades implement an anthropological study of their classroom, school, or community? If you think that they can, tell how. If you feel that they cannot, state why.

 *internet links*

TEACHING ANTHROPOLOGY

The Internet is a tremendous resource of information on culture, tradition, symbols, and other key concepts in anthropology. Teachers can use the Internet to increase their knowledge about anthropology as well as to help students develop critical thinking skills. Several examples follow of websites that can be used by teachers and students.

1. Egyptian Educational site (http://pharos.bu.edu/Egypt). This web page is one of the most comprehensive websites available on Egypt. It contains information on a wide variety of topics ranging from demographic information to recipes for Egyptian food. It also links to news groups and current events on Egypt and information on Egyptology.

2. The American Anthropological Association Homepage (http://www.ameranthassn.org/). Teachers who are interested in anthropology will find this web page helpful. It can connect teachers to the publications, conferences, and annual meetings of a professional organization that focuses on anthropology. This web page also links to a wide range of anthropological resources on the internet.

3. Maya Adventure (http://www.sci.mus.mn.us/sln/ma/). This web page provides a basis for teachers to integrate science and social studies. The site, which was developed by the Science Museum of Minnesota, includes images from the museum's anthropological collections and highlights science activities and information related to ancient and modern Maya culture.

4. UC Berkeley Tel Dor Archaeological Expedition (http://www.qal.berkeley.edu/~teldor/). Tel Dor offers a unique opportunity for teachers and students to learn about an archaeological dig that is currently in progress. A team from the University of California, Berkeley, is excavating the temple area and city center in a major Phoenician, Jewish, Persian, Greek, and Roman city on the coast of Israel.

REFERENCES

Anthropology in today's world: Case studies of peoples and cultures (1965). Middletown, CT: American Education Publications Units Book.

Benedict, R. (1934). *Patterns of culture.* Boston: Houghton Mifflin.

Boas, F. (1938). *The mind of primitive man.* New York: Macmillan.

Briggs, J. (1975). Eskimo women: Makers of men. In C. J. Matthiasson, (Ed.), *Many sisters.* New York: Free Press.

Coe, M. D. (1993). *The Maya* (5th ed.). New York: Thames and Hudson, Inc.

Durkin, M. C. (1969). *The Taba social studies curriculum* (Grade 5: United States and Canada). Menlo Park, CA: Addison-Wesley.

Freeman, D. (1983). *Margaret Mead and Samoa: The making and unmaking of an anthropological myth.* Cambridge, MA: Harvard University Press.

Geertz, C. (1973). *The interpretation of cultures.* New York: Basic Books

Geertz, C. (1983). *Local knowledge: Further essays in interpretive anthropology.* New York: Basic Books.

Harris, M. (1968). *The rise of anthropological theory: A history of theories of culture.* New York: Crowell.

Harris, M. (1974). *Cows, pigs, wars and witches: The riddles of culture.* New York: Vintage Books.

Harris, M. (1980). *Cultural materialism: The struggle for a science of culture.* New York: Vintage Books.

Harris, M. (1993). *Culture, people, nature: An introduction to general anthropology* (6th ed.). New York: Harper & Row.

Heath, S. B. (1983). *Ways with words: Language, life, and work in communities and classrooms.* New York: Cambridge University Press.

Heath, S. B., & McLaughlin, M. W. (1993). *Identity and inner-city youth: Beyond ethnicity and gender.* New York: Teachers College Press.

Keesing, F. M. (1958). *Cultural anthropology: The science of custom.* New York: Holt Rinehart and Winston.

Kroeber, A. L., & Kluckhohn, C. (1963). *Culture: A critical review of concepts.* New York: Vintage Books.

Kluckhohn, C. (1965). *Mirror for man.* Greenwich, CT: Fawcett.

LaBarr, W. (1954). *The human animal.* Chicago: University of Chicago Press.

Lamphere, L. (1987). The struggle to reshape our thinking about gender. In C. Farnham (Ed.), *The impact of feminist research in the academy* (pp. 11–33). Bloomington: Indiana University Press.

Lemonick, M. D. (1993, August 9). Secrets of the Maya. *Time*, 142 (6), 44–50.

Marcus, G. E., & Fischer, M. J. (1986). *Anthropology as cultural critique: An experimental moment in the human sciences.* Chicago: University of Chicago Press.

Mead, M. (1928). *Coming of age in Samoa.* New York: Mentor Books.

Montagu, A. (1974). *Man's most dangerous myth: The fallacy of race* (6th ed.). Walnut Creek, CA: AltaMira Press.

Munch, R., & Smelser, N. J. (Eds.). (1992). *Theory of Culture.* Berkeley: University of California Press.

Ogbu, J. U. (1974). *The next generation: An ethnography of education in an urban neighborhood.* New York: Academic Press.

Pelto, P. J., & Muessig, R. H. (1980). *The study and teaching of anthropology.* Columbus, OH: Merrill.

Pelto, P. J., & Pelto, G. H. (1978). *Anthropological research: The structure of inquiry* (2nd ed.). New York: Cambridge University Press.

Peshkin, A. (1991). *The color of strangers, the color of friends: The play of ethnicity in school and community.* Chicago: University of Chicago Press.

Philips, S. U. (1983). *The invisible culture.* New York: Longman.

Powerdermaker, H. (1950). *Hollywood, the dream factory: An anthropologist looks at the movie-makers.* Boston: Little, Brown.

Powerdermaker, H. (1966). *Stranger and friend: The way of an anthropologist.* New York: Norton.

Rosaldo, M., & Lamphere, L. (Eds.). (1974). *Women, culture and society.* Stanford: Stanford University Press.

Salzmann, Z. (1993). *Language, culture and society: An introduction to linguistic anthropology.* Boulder, CO: Westview Press.

Schlegel, A. (1977). *Sexual stratification.* New York: Columbia University Press.

Spain, D. H. (Ed.). (1975). *The human experience: Readings in sociocultural anthropology.* Homewood, IL: Dorsey Press.

Spindler, G. (Ed.). (1982/1988). *Doing the ethnography of schooling.* Project Heights, IL: Waveland Press.

Stigler, J. W., Shweder, R. A., & Herdt, G. (Eds.). (1990). *Cultural psychology: Essays on comparative human development.* New York: Cambridge University Press.

Swartz, M. J., & Jordan, D. K. (1976). *Anthropology: Perspectives on humanity.* New York: John Wiley.

Weatherford, J. (1992). *Native roots: How the Indians enriched America.* New York: Fawcett Columbine.

FOR FURTHER READING

Carrithers, M. (1992). *Why humans have cultures: Explaining anthropology and social diversity.* New York: Oxford University Press.

Coe, M. D. (1993). *The Mayan Code.* New York: Norton.

Coe, M. D. (1994). *From the Olmecs to the Aztecs* (4th ed.). New York: Thames and Hudson.

Diop, C. A. (1991). *Civilization or Barbarism: An authentic anthropology.* Chicago: Lawrence Hill Books.

Fagan, B. M., & Beck, C. (Eds.). (1996). *The Oxford companion to archaeology.* New York: Oxford University Press.

Geertz, C. (1995). *After the fact: Two countries, four decades, one anthropologist.* Cambridge, MA: Harvard University Press.

Harris, M. (1989). *Our kind: The evolution of human life and culture.* New York: Harper & Row.

Jameson, J. H., Jr. (Ed.). (1997). *Presenting archaeology to the public: Digging for truths.* Walnut Creek, CA: AltaMira Press.

Leonardto, M. (Ed.). (1991). *Gender at the crossroads of knowledge: Feminist anthropology in the postmodern era*. Berkeley: University of California Press.

McGrane, B. (1989). *Beyond anthropology: Society and the other*. New York: Columbia University Press.

Mead, M. (1977). *Letters from the field*. New York: Harper & Row.

Moore, H. (1988). *Feminism and anthropology*. Minneapolis: University of Minnesota Press.

Munch, R., & Smelser, N. J. (Eds.) (1992). *Theory of Culture*. Berkeley: University of California Press.

Spindler, G. D., & Spindler, L. (Eds.). (1994). *Pathways to cultural awareness: Cultural therapy with teachers*. Thousand Oaks, CA: Corwin Press.

Wright, R. (Ed.). (1996). *Gender and archaeology*. Philadelphia: University of Pennsylvania Press.

CHAPTER 12

Political Science: Structure, Concepts, and Strategies

*f*EATURE

INFLUENCING PUBLIC POLICY THROUGH SOCIAL ACTION: ELIMINATING CHILD LABOR

In 1995 Craig Kielburger read a newspaper article about Iqubal Masih, a young boy who began working in a carpet mill in Pakistan when he was four years old. Iqubal was sold to the owner of the carpet mill to pay off his parents' debts. Even though bonded labor is illegal in Pakistan, the law is rarely enforced and about 7.5 million Pakistani children are involved in bonded labor. The United Nations estimates that there are 250 million child laborers throughout the world.

Craig and Iqubal were both 12 years old when Craig first learned about the circumstances of Iqubal's life. He was particularly struck by the difference between his comfortable life in Ontario, Canada, and the cruelty Iqubal suffered on a daily basis. Craig began investigating child labor and found that children in a number of countries, including Haiti and Brazil and several Asian countries, worked full-time at jobs such as repairing cars, weaving carpets, and making fireworks and sports equipment. With that information in hand, Craig and his classmates formed, Free the Children, an organization committed to stamping out child labor.

Craig and the other members of Free the Children gathered data and attempted to influence public policy on child labor by interviewing children involved in child labor, testifying before U.S. congressional committees, holding press conferences, and meeting with Canadian Prime Minister Jean Chrétien. In 1996 Craig was presented with the Reebok Human Rights Youth in Action Award for his efforts to end child labor.

As a result of Craig's efforts Iqubal Masih was eventually freed and began to attend school. In December 1994 Iqubal visited Broad Meadows Middle School in Quincy, Mass., and talked to the students about his experiences as a bonded laborer. A few months later Iqubal was murdered. The students at Broad Meadows Middle School were so moved by Iqubal's experiences that they wanted to join the effort to eliminate child labor. With the help of Amnesty International, the students opened a website called "A Bullet Can't Kill a Dream." You can visit their website at http://mirrorimage.com/igubal/index.html or write to the organization at 50 Calvin Road, Quincy, MA 02169. The students also raised $130,000 to build a school in the Punjab region of Pakistan and help 50 families buy back children sold into bondage.

Craig Kielburger's concern about a young Pakistani boy resulted in the development and implementation of a social action project. Craig's social action project demonstrates that young people can influence public policy and can make a difference. When asked to identify the achievement he is most proud of, Craig said, "Young people are starting to realize the power they have to improve in their community, whether they fight child labor, organize a food drive or give clothes and blankets to people on the streets." To learn more about Free the Children, visit their website at [http://freethechildren.org], or you can write to the organization at 16 Thorn Bank, Thornhill, Ontario, Canada, L4J 2A2.

Sources: Free the Children: Young People Fight to Stamp Out Child Labor. *Update on Law-Related Education.* Chicago: American Bar Association Special Committee on Youth Education for Citizenship, Spring 1997, Vol. 21, No. 2, p. A6–A7.

Students Fund a School: A School Is Built in Pakistan. *Update on Law-Related Education.* Chicago: American Bar Association Special Committee on Youth Education for Citizenship, Spring 1997, Vol. 21, No. 2, p. A7.

THE NATURE OF POLITICAL SCIENCE

We described sociology as the study of human groups and anthropology as the study of culture. However, it is difficult to briefly define political science because there are many different types of political scientists. They ask very different kinds of questions, have different research aims, and use many different concepts and approaches.

Political scientists' views of their discipline vary as much as the approaches within it. Some political scientists define the discipline as the study of the legal government of the state. Other political scientists consider this view too narrow. They point out that it does not reflect the study of the many informal groups and processes that are not part of legal government. These include interest groups, lobbying, bargaining, and logrolling. The first view of political science is also problematic because there are many different definitions of state. One author reports that he found 145 such definitions (Easton, 1981).

Some political scientists define the discipline as the study of the struggle of competing groups for power. Like state, power has many different definitions.

Consequently, it does not clearly define the boundaries of political science. Some political scientists cannot accept the power definition because they believe it does not specify unique behavior for them to study. They point out that power exists in all institutions, including a gang, a family, and a church. While the power definition is in one sense too inclusive, it is too restrictive in another. Political behavior is not limited to a struggle for power (Easton, 1981). The power definition of the discipline is not accepted by some political scientists because of these problems. However, it is a very popular definition that is accepted by many political scientists.

David Easton (1981), a leading political scientist, defines political science as the "study of the authoritative allocation of values for a society (p. 117)." He points out that people have competing values, demands, and aspirations that they would like to become part of public policy and enforced in society. The political system is the process by which people decide which demands and goals will become public policy. This system prevents disruptive struggles among competing individuals and groups.

Eaton's definition specifies the boundaries of political science more clearly than do the state and power definitions. Political scientists study all the processes by which the goals and demands of competing groups become public policy when they use Eaton's definitions. They do not study just legal government and formal institutions. If political scientists were trying to determine how the Welfare Reform Bill* was passed in 1996, they would not merely study the formal ways by which the bill became law. They would also study the informal acts that influenced its passage—lobbying, logrolling, filibustering, and speeches by President Clinton, which were designed to influence public opinion. Eaton's definition is more precise than the power definition. It does not suggest that political scientists study all competing goals and values within a society, only those that are enforced by legitimate public authorities. Despite its strengths, some political scientists find Eaton's definition unclear. Others disagree about what it means (Galston, 1993).

We have discussed three definitions of political science: the study of the legal government of the state, the struggle for power, and the authoritative allocation of values for a society. They reflect the diversity of methods and approaches within the discipline. While all the definitions have competed for acceptance within political science, each has been only partially accepted. Each of them has a place within the discipline, but neither reigns supreme.

APPROACHES IN POLITICAL SCIENCE

The Normative Approach

The first political scientists were armchair theorists who were primarily concerned with describing the ideal political system—one that would result in the best possible life for people. These theorists were mainly interested in value questions such as "What should be the proper political system?" rather than scientific questions. They considered themselves philosophers and tried to advise political leaders and

---

*The official name of the Welfare Reform Bill of 1996 is the Personal Responsibility and Work Opportunity Act of 1996.

to influence public policy. Political philosophy (as this approach is sometimes called) is still an important part of modern political science. Political thinkers such as Aristotle, Plato, Locke, and Marx are often studied by political theorists in order to develop ideas about the best type of political system (Galston, 1993).

Normative political theorists are very critical of the more scientific trends in the discipline. They believe that such approaches tend to ignore value questions—the most important questions facing people—and to study trivial, narrow questions whose answers will not contribute to the improvement of human life. Scientific political scientists contend that they do not ignore value questions but study values instead by describing them, just as they do other behavior. They try to avoid advocating values or forms of government best for society.

The Legal-Institutional Approach

The first professors of political science were members of law faculties; thus a strong legal tradition has existed within the discipline since it first emerged. In this approach, an attempt is made to understand a political system primarily by describing and analyzing the laws, codes, constitutions, and other documents that are a part of legal government. The legalist studies the U.S. Constitution to discover the functions of the legislative, executive, and judicial branches of American government.

The institutional approach, closely related to the legal method, focuses on describing the functions of various governmental bodies and officials, such as the roles of judges, jurors, and congresses. The roles of formal institutions are described in great detail. However, little attention is given to the individual voter, the personalities of leaders, or to informal political institutions, such as interest groups and other organized lobbyists.

While many insights can be gained about a political system by studying its legal codes and formal institutions, the information that can be gained from this approach is greatly limited. Laws are interpreted variously by different authorities and in different time periods. The effect on the political system of informal groups and the personalities of political leaders is as great as—if not greater than—the effect of formal codes and institutions. The legal powers of the president were no different in the 1930s than they were in the 1950s, yet Franklin D. Roosevelt exercised much more power than Dwight D. Eisenhower. An approach that largely ignores the role of individuals and personalities in the shaping of public policy—as this approach does—cannot provide keen insights into how a political system actually works.

The legal-institutional approach has traditionally dominated American political science. It has retarded the theoretical development of political science because it focuses on the accurate description of laws and formal institutions rather than on the development of generalizations and theories about political behavior.

Closely related to the legal-institutional approach is the historical tradition. When political science first emerged, it was primarily political history. The historical tradition, with a focus on particulars and unique events, shaped the development of political theory much as it influenced the growth of theory in history and anthropology. Most school and college textbooks are heavily influenced by the legal-institutional approach to the study of political behavior.

profile

JAMES MACGREGOR BURNS

A Political Scientist Who Writes History

James MacGregor Burns integrates his work as a political scientist with the skills of a historian and the perspectives of an active participant in the world of government. His award-winning biographies of Franklin D. Roosevelt and John F. Kennedy and his Pulitzer Prize book *Leadership* are highly regarded for their historical accuracy and their political insight. Burns's contributions to the field of leadership have inspired and influenced the work of scholars and practitioners. Active in civil liberties, civil rights, and labor groups, Burns does not believe scholars should remain ensconced in the ivy-covered halls of academia. He believes there is a place for the scholar in politics and sees no conflict between his work as a professor and his interest in the practical world of government. He served as a delegate to the Democratic National Convention in 1952, 1956, 1960, and 1964, and in 1958 was a candidate for the U.S. House of Representatives for the 1st District in Massachusetts. An important theme that is woven throughout Burns's writing is the need for effective political leadership sustained by centralized and disciplined political parties.

James MacGregor Burns is Woodrow Wilson Professor of Government, Emeritus, Williams College and Senior Scholar, Center for Political Leadership and Participation, University of Maryland at College Park.

The Behavioral Approach

In the years following World War II, a protest movement developed within political science that caused sweeping changes within the field. It started a bitter struggle between the newly trained political scientists and those more traditional (those who endorsed the approaches described above). The protest movement emerged because a significant number of young political scientists, such as Harold Lasswell, David Easton, and Robert A. Dahl, were very dissatisfied with the scientific status of the discipline. They were unhappy about its research goals, methods, and the body of accumulated knowledge.

The new group of political scientists wanted the discipline to become more scientific and less concerned with trying to describe the "best" political system or the "good life." They argued that these goals were not scientific. They wanted political scientists to study less about values, legal documents, and institutions (Straayer & Muessig, 1980). They wanted the discipline to focus on the study of the behavior of people in a political system, to use rigorous research methods, and to make scientific theory development its major goal.

This movement is known as the behavioral approach because its leaders are primarily interested in studying the behavior of political actors, rather than legal codes and institutions. While they are not uninterested in the legal duties of the president and of senators, they are primarily concerned with developing scientific generalizations about their behavior. Behaviorists believe that the main concern of the political scientist should be the activity within and the behavior around the political institution (Isaak, 1988).

Behaviorists can also be distinguished by their research methods and strategies. They often use techniques such as opinion surveys, content analysis, case studies, and experimental studies. Behaviorists also frequently quantify data and use sophisticated statistical techniques. Most of their field research consists of voting studies. Behaviorists also try to unite political scientists more closely to the other behavioral sciences. They use many of the key concepts, theories, and research methods from psychology, sociology, and anthropology. Subfields such as political sociology and political psychology reflect the interdisciplinary nature of behaviorism. The behaviorists have also tried to make political science concepts more precise, measurable, and meaningful.

The behavioral orientation has won a place within the discipline, but it has neither escaped harsh criticism nor displaced the more traditional legal-institutional, historical, and normative approaches. However, behaviorism nearly dominated political science during the 1960s. It also polarized and created more reform and soul-searching within the discipline than any other previous movement. The attacks on it have been severe. Sometimes they are sound, but just as often they are short-sighted and subjective. Behaviorism has its shortcomings, as its leaders are keenly aware. In their zest for information about political actors, behaviorists have not always appreciated the contributions that legal, institutional, and historical approaches can make to the development of political generalizations. The emphasis on the individual political actor has sometimes prevented full consideration of the political group and the political system.

The most serious attack on the behaviorists has come from normative political theorists, who believe that the discipline's primary goal should be to improve human life by searching for the best possible political system and recommending it to policy makers. These theorists accuse the behaviorists of neglecting values, and therefore of avoiding the most important questions that face humankind.

BEHAVIORISM: THE SYSTEMS APPROACH

Some behaviorists have tried to focus their research in the discipline by conceptualizing the political process as an interrelated system. The political system is conceptualized as one of a number of interrelated but somewhat independent social systems that make up society. The orientation of this approach is essentially scientific. It is more inclusive than a behavioral approach that focuses primarily on individual political actors. It not only attempts to develop generalizations about individual political actors but also tries to explain how organized pressure groups influence the making of public policy. Systems theorists focus on developing generalizations about how the competing demands and inputs of political actors become public policy or outputs. David Easton (1985), a leading systems theorist, believes that the major research task of the approach is to "identify the inputs and the forces that shape and change them, to trace the processes through which they are transformed into outputs, to describe the general conditions under which such processes can be maintained, and to establish the relationship between outputs and succeeding inputs of the system" (p. 140). Figure 12.1 illustrates the relationships among the central concepts in Eaton's systems theory.

The Postbehavioral Movement

The tremendous social changes within U.S. society during the 1960s and 1970s deeply affected many political scientists and gave birth to a new movement within the discipline. This movement arose as a reaction against the strong behaviorism that had gripped the discipline by the late 1960s and as a response to the major problems that the nation faced (Saxonhouse, 1993). These included a controversial war in Vietnam that deeply divided the nation, the quest for civil rights by

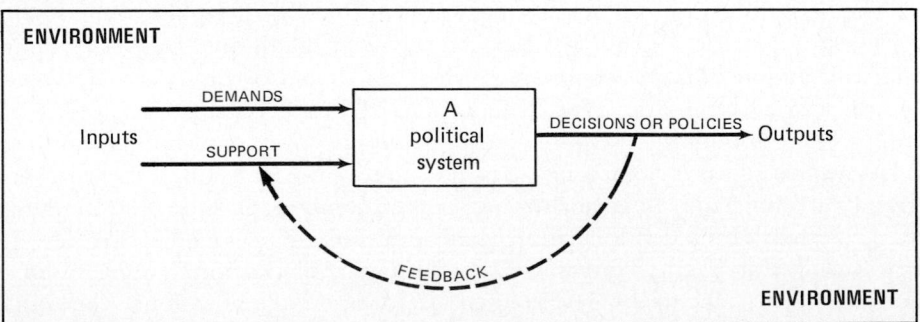

Figure 12.1
Easton's System Theory.
Source: Reprinted from David Easton, "An Approach to the Analysis of Political Systems," *World Politics* 9:3 (April 1957), p. 394. Reprinted by permission of The Johns Hopkins University Press.

groups of color and women, and a new awareness about the wide gap dividing the rich from the poor in the United States.

The postbehaviorists argued that the behaviorists, by devoting almost all of their attention to research methods and theory, were showing no concern for the value conflicts and problems that were threatening the nation. The postbehaviorists believe that social scientists have a moral responsibility to use their knowledge and expertise to help solve human problems. They said that political science had become too removed from human affairs in the 1970s and that political science research was conservative and supported the status quo.

The postbehavioral call for political scientists to become more involved in value issues and in public policy created tremendous debate and conflict within the discipline. The movement had a significant influence on many political scientists. David Easton (1969), one of the leaders of the behaviorist movement, discussed the postbehaviorists in his presidential address to the American Political Science Association in 1969. He urged political scientists to heed the call of the new revolutionaries within the discipline. He agreed that political scientists needed to pay more attention to their value assumptions, to get more involved in the urgent social problems of the day, and to play an important role in the formation and implementation of public policy. At the same time, however, Easton urged political scientists to continue to do research aimed at building theory. He believes that the discipline should both respond to the concerns of the postbehaviorists and continue to pursue its traditional goals. The movement has enriched the diversity of political science. Like the movements before it, it will find a place within political science but will not replace the discipline's other approaches and traditions. Table 12.1 summarizes the major approaches within political science.

THEORY AND RESEARCH IN POLITICAL SCIENCE

The goal of science is the building of theory that can be used to explain, predict, and understand behavior. The building of scientific theory is not the goal in any of the more traditional approaches within political science. The aim of political philosophy is to describe the ideal political system. The legal-institutionalists regard the accurate descriptions of legal codes and formal institutions as their primary goal. The emphasis is on describing unique codes and institutions and not on developing high-level generalizations about them. Many traditional political scientists do not believe that high-level political science generalizations can be developed because of the complexity of human behavior.

Only in the newer approaches to political science—the behavioral and systems orientations—is the expressed goal the building of scientific theory. While the newer approaches have theory-building as their goal, the discipline is largely void of tested theories. However, attempts have been made, and are still being made, to formulate and test partial theories. A major challenge facing the discipline is the clarification of goals, that is, whether political science will become a scientific discipline whose major goal is to build theory, a discipline that will have major policy goals and make prescriptions for society, or whether it will try to accommodate each of these orientations.

TABLE 12.1. *Approaches in Political Science*

Approach	Description	Major Goals
Normative	Focuses on the examination of the ideas of such political theorists as Plato, Locke, and Marx.	To describe the ideal political system and how it can be attained.
Legal–institutional	Focuses on description and analysis of legal documents and the functions of governmental bodies and officials.	To accurately describe legal institutions and the roles within them.
Behavioral	Primarily interested in studying the behavior of political actors.	To develop theories about political behavior that can be used to predict and control behavior.
Systems	Focuses on organized political behavior and its effects on the political system.	To develop generalizations and theories about the competing demands and inputs that are parts of the political process within a political system.
Postbehavioral	Focuses on public policy, issues, and social problems.	To use political science knowledge to help solve social problems and improve the human condition.

POLITICAL SCIENCE CONCEPTS

The concepts within all of the political science approaches tend to be vague rather than precise. Such terms as state and government, which are central to traditional approaches, and such concepts as power, legitimacy, and authority, essential to newer approaches, are often defined differently. However, the behaviorists make concerted efforts to make their concepts precise and to operationalize them for measurement purposes.

Any attempt to identify the key concepts in political science is destined to be futile because of the variety of approaches within the discipline. Each approach, to some extent, uses a unique set of concepts. The concept of natural law is important in political philosophy but foreign to the systems approach.

A selected list of concepts from each of the orientations within political science should be an integral part of the social studies curriculum for the elementary and middle school grades. However, although some concepts from the traditional approaches should be taught (such as constitution), you should select most of the concepts you teach from the more modern approaches for two reasons: (1) These approaches build scientific generalizations about political behavior, and (2) traditional approaches are easily abused by teachers. When teachers use traditional approaches, the emphasis easily shifts to requiring students to memorize the duties and powers of various offices,

"You were extremely funny. It's a pity the butt of your humor was me."
Source: Joseph Farris. Used with permission.

and away from helping them derive generalizations about political behavior. The normative approach permits teachers to moralize, without evidence, about the merits of particular institutions, the values of which are not fully demonstrated. It also places undue emphasis on the views of authorities, whether classic (Plato, Aquinas, Crotius, or Locke) or more contemporary (Lippmann, Lasswell, or Hyneman). We describe some key political science concepts, and activities that can be used to teach them, below.

Power

Power is the ability of one individual or group to influence, change, modify, or in some other way affect the behavior of others. Power may be attained in a variety of ways. An individual or group may have formal authority over others. Political leaders have authority when they are able to make decisions and laws that are legally binding for the individuals within a political system.

They may be elected by the people, appointed by leaders, or take authority by force, as during a coup d'etat or revolution. However, for a political system to function smoothly, it is necessary for authority to be legitimate. A government is regarded as legitimate when the individuals affected by its policy accepts its authority as valid. If an authority is not viewed as legitimate, authorities have to expend a great deal of energy enforcing their decisions.

Activities
1. List examples of the individuals who exercise power in the family. Discuss the source of their authority.
2. Discuss why and how authorities exercise power in the school and why.
3. Ask the students to investigate ways in which the governor and the state legislature try to exercise power over each other.

Social Control

Social control is the regulation of human behavior by outside social forces. It is maintained by laws and rules that emerge within every society and institution. Every institution must have ways to control the behavior of its members in order to attain its goals and to maintain an environment in which individuals and groups can satisfy their wants and needs. The laws that govern behavior within a society are usually found in written documents, such as legal codes and constitutions. Laws reflect the norms and values of a society. Norms that are very important to a society usually become laws, and the violators of these norms are punished by the state.

Activities
1. Ask the students to list some of the rules they have at home and to tell why their families have them. Ask the students to tell what they think of these rules.
2. List the rules at school and discuss whether the school should have them and why or why not.
3. Make a list of county and state laws and discuss why they were made.

State

The concept of state is central to traditional approaches in political science. Political science is often defined by traditionalists as the study of the legal government of the state. Although this concept has been defined in many different ways, it is sometimes defined as the institution that has ultimate responsibility for maintaining social order, usually within a geographically and legally defined territory. Closely related to the concept of state is the concept of government. Government is an agency of the state and is used by it to maintain social control. Deutsch (1980) defines state as "the organized machinery for the making and carrying out of political decisions and for the enforcing of the laws and rules of government."

Activities
1. Introduce the concept of nation and point out that when political scientists use the term state they are usually referring to the nation-state.
2. Discuss the relationships among the federal, state, county, and city governments in the United States.

Representative Ronald V. Dellums represents California's 9th District in the United States House of Representatives. When studying the concept of state, students can learn more about the House of Representatives and take a virtual tour of the Capitol by visiting the website for the House at http://www.house.gov.
Source: Library of Congress, Washington, D.C.

3. List the duties and functions of the executive, legislative, and judicial branches of the United States federal government.

Interest Group

An interest group is a collection of individuals who share common concerns and goals; they organize in order to more effectively attain those goals. Individuals with similar goals join interest groups to influence political bodies because they realize that they are more likely to influence public policy when working in groups than when working alone. Interest groups are sometimes called special interest groups or pressure groups.

Activities
1. Identify a current bill before Congress or the state legislature and role-play a situation in which various interest groups try to persuade the legislative body.
2. Interview a lobbyist who works in the state capitol and represents an interest group, such as the state education association, farmers, or the state medical association.
3. Interview members of the city council or the state legislature about how they are influenced by lobbyists and interest groups when they vote and make decisions.

Political Socialization

The process by which individuals acquire their attitudes, beliefs, and perceptions of the political system is called political socialization. Behavioral political scientists have shown a great deal of interest in this concept. Their research suggests that, of the many institutions affecting the child's attitudes toward the political system, the family is the most important. People are usually members of the same political party as their parents. Research indicates that children's basic political attitudes are formed during their early years, when they are between the ages of 3 and 13.

Activities
1. Sing "America the Beautiful" and "The Star-Spangled Banner" and discuss the attitudes and beliefs these songs help children develop toward the U.S. political system.
2. Recite the Pledge of Allegiance and discuss the ideas it expresses about U.S. democracy. Discuss the extent to which these ideals are realities in the United States.
3. Conduct a survey to find out whether students have political beliefs that are similar to their brothers, sisters, and parents.

Political Participation

Political participation is the "actions of private citizens by which they seek to influence or to support government and politics" (Milbrath & Goel, 1982). Political scientists conceptualize political participation to include not only voting and lobbying, but activities such as campaigning, attending political meetings, and running for office. Political scientists often do research to determine which personal, social, and economic factors are most closely related to political involvement.

Activities
1. Vote on some decisions that need to be made in the classroom and discuss the factors that influenced the way individuals voted.
2. Send a class letter to a member of Congress or to a state legislator, expressing an opinion on an important bill that is up for a vote.
3. Make a class visit to the state legislature or city council to present views on a bill that will soon be up for a vote.

inquiry   strategy

WHO VOTES?

GOAL

The right to vote is only one factor in determining who votes. A range of sociological, psychological, and economic factors influence people's decision to vote or not to vote. The goal of this Inquiry Strategy is to help students better understand the multiple factors that influence who votes.

INTRODUCTION

Explain to students that voting is an important component of the democratic process. Voting is important for its symbolic value and for the ways in which it links citizens to the political process and legitimizes the democratic system.

In the past, a number of barriers prevented many U.S. citizens from voting. These barriers included gender, racial, and economic requirements that limited voting to White men who owned property. Even though those and other restrictions, such as poll taxes and literacy requirements, have been eliminated, many Americans fail to exercise their right to vote.

In 1994, 45 percent of U.S. citizens over the age of 18 voted. This was an off-year election in which candidates were elected to a number of local, state, and national offices including positions on school boards, city councils, state assembles and the U.S. Senate (U.S. Census/Internet). In 1996, a presidential election year, voter turnout rose to 54.2 percent. Almost 46 percent of the individuals who were eligible to vote did not.

LESSON

Ask students to brainstorm reasons that more U.S. citizens do not vote. Write the students' responses on the board or overhead projector. After the students have completed this exercise, tell them that when investigating why people vote, social scientists frequently examine factors such as access to political information, political interest, party identification, and feelings of political efficacy. Those factors frequently relate to age, education, race, and income.

Divide the class into four groups and assign each group one of the following factors: age, education, race, and income. Ask students to investigate voter turnout as it relates to their assigned factor. Students can use data from the U.S. Census reports and the following websites:

Percent Reported Voted and Registered by Race, Hispanic Origin, and Gender from 1964 to 1996 (http://www.census.gov/population/socdemo/voting/history/vot01.txt)

Percent Reported Voted by Age and Gender: November 1964 to 1996 (http://www.census.gov/population/socdemo/voting/history/vot05.txt)

Voting and Registration in the Election of November 1996 (http://www.census.gov/population/socdemo/voting/history/vot23.txt)

Information on voter turnout in 1996 by age, education, race, and income is also summarized in Table 12.2.

Ask each group to assemble its data in charts and tables and simulate a press conference in which each group reports its findings. After the press conference, lead the class in a large group discussion of this question: What factors will result in more people voting?

It will be important for you to help students understand that when political organizations mobilize, even disinterested citizens turn out to vote. Increasing citizen participation in voting to a great extent is related to the skills of political groups rather than the public's concern about an election. The data generated by the students can help them better understand who votes and can serve as a departure point for learning more about the concerns of politically alienated citizens and ways to communicate civic issues to them.

Once students have generated a list of things that could be done by elected officials and others, ask them to identify one thing they could do. This lesson could serve as the basis for a student-generated social action project.

TABLE 12.2. *Voter Turnout in 1996*

The U.S. Census reports the following voter turnout in the 1996 election by gender, age, race, education, and employment status.

Gender
   52.8 percent of men voted
   55.5 percent of women voted
Age
   31.2 percent of 18 to 20 year olds voted
   33.4 percent of 21 to 24 year olds voted
   49.2 percent of 25 to 44 year olds voted
   64.4 percent of 45 to 64 year olds voted
   67.0 percent of people 65 years old and older voted
Race
   50.6 percent or African Americans voted
   26.7 percent of Hispanics voted
   56 percent of Whites voted
Education
   29.9 percent of people who did not attend high school voted
   33.8 percent of people with some high school voted
   49.1 percent of people with a high school diploma voted
   60.5 percent of people with some college including an associate degree voted
   72.6 percent of people with a bachelor's degree or higher voted
Labor Force
   54.3 percent of the people in the labor force voted
   55.2 percent of employed people in the labor force who voted
   37.2 percent of unemployed people in the labor force who voted
   54.1 percent of the people who were not in the labor force voted

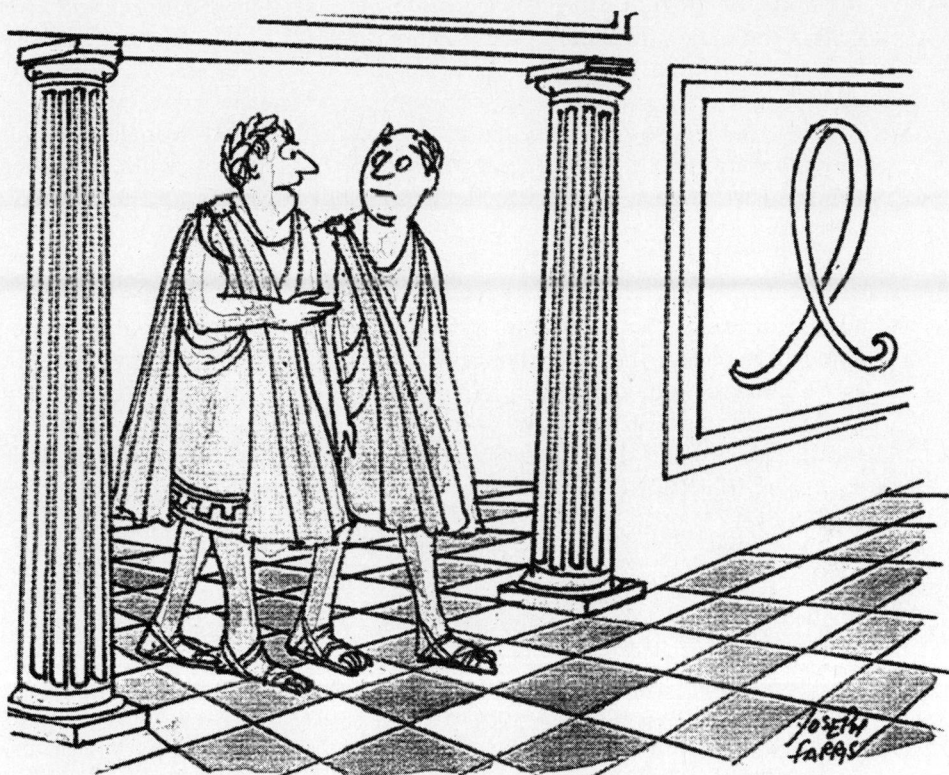

"What Caesar doesn't understand is that all politics is local!"
Source: Joseph Farris. Used with permission.

POLITICAL SCIENCE GENERALIZATIONS

Much of what we have said about political science concepts is also true of political generalizations, because generalizations state relationships between concepts. Generalizations in political science, like those in the other behavioral sciences, vary greatly in the extent to which they can be applied to help us understand behavior. In selecting generalizations to guide political studies in the elementary and middle school grades, you should only select scientific statements. Many lists of political science generalizations in state and school district curriculum guides contain a large number of value statements such as these: "Young people respect and obey parents and teachers"; "Autocracy, or similar centralization of power in one man or body, develops when citizens shirk their responsibilities." Below is a list of political science generalizations that can be taught in the elementary and middle school grades. They are grouped under concepts related to them.

Social Control
 In every society and institution, regulations and laws are formed to govern
  the behavior of individuals; individuals usually experience some form of

punishment when authorities catch them breaking laws. • Rules and laws reflect the basic values of a society or institution.

Government

Within every society, some individual or group is authorized to make binding decisions and to allocate values. • Many different types of political systems are used in various societies to determine public policy and to regulate behavior.

Interest Groups

Organized interest groups attempt to influence the making of public policy when they believe that such policy will affect their goals. • Individuals are more likely to influence public policy when working in groups than when working alone. • Individuals and groups resort to extreme methods to change public policy when they believe that authorities are unresponsive to their needs or that legitimate channels for the alleviation of grievances are ineffective.

Authority

Authorities may be violently replaced if they remain unresponsive to the demands of the citizens in their state. • When authorities feel that the basic ideology and well-being of their political system is threatened, they may take extreme action against individuals and groups, denying them the basic rights guaranteed under the laws of the state. • Authorities tend to resist any change they feel will reduce their power and influence. • Authorities attempt to legitimize their power in order to maintain control (i.e., convince their constituency that they have a right to rule because of divine right, the constitution, etc.) and to ensure a stable political system.

Leadership

Leaders emerge when individuals are able to articulate and personify the wishes and goals of groups; leaders lose their power and influence when groups perceive their goals as different from those of the leaders.

POLITICAL STUDIES IN THE SCHOOLS

Political studies are usually either ignored or treated superficially in the early and middle grades, and taught with the historical and legal-institutional approaches in middle school. Political studies are neglected or poorly taught largely because the goals of political education are unclear, confusing, and conflicting.

The most often stated goal of political studies is to develop patriotic citizens, loyal to the nation and committed to American democracy. However, patriotic citizen is rarely defined clearly. In order to perpetuate its dominant values and system of government, every nation-state must socialize its citizens in such a way that it inculcates its prevailing ideology. Thus, developing loyal and patriotic citizens is a sound goal of political education.

However, political studies are often taught poorly because of the way teachers and textbook authors interpret patriotism. A patriotic citizen is often regarded as one who votes regularly, obeys the laws, respects the flag, and rarely criticizes our political leaders and national policies. Teachers and textbook authors often emphasize the strengths of the United States and the problems of other nations when trying to help students become patriotic citizens with strong national loyalties.

The major goal of political education should be to help students develop a reflective patriotism and become thoughtful citizen actors. Citizens with reflective patriotism are committed to American democratic ideals, are aware of the gap between ideals and realities in our nation, and are committed to taking action to help close the gap. To develop reflective citizens, we must teach students about the ideals of American democracy, the extent to which these ideals have been attained, and the work that must still be done to fully realize them. To attain this goal, the curriculum must teach about the hopes and promises of U.S. democracy, as well as about the problems the nation faces. The quest for civil rights by women and people of color, poverty, and the problems that plague American cities should be an important part of a political education curriculum. A sound political education curriculum should also have an important global dimension. Students should realize that the most complex problems facing humankind today, such as genetic engineering and animal cloning, can only be solved by nations working together.

Political studies in the elementary and middle school should also emphasize political behavior rather than the description of legal documents and institutions. In the legal-institutional approach to civic education, students spend a great deal of time memorizing the legal powers and responsibilities of various political posts and the functions of the different branches of government. The emphasis is on memorizing facts and giving them back to teachers.

A focus on documents and institutions will give students a misconception of the political system. To understand how a bill is actually passed, one cannot merely study the Constitution but must know how competing pressure groups work to influence the making of public policy. Simulation games such as *Democracy* and *Napoli* can help students understand informal political processes, such as bargaining, logrolling, pledging support in return for another's support on other issues, wheeling and dealing, compromising, welching on promises, misleading others, and other political tactics. We must help students learn about the realities of political life, while at the same time helping them develop a commitment to American democratic values and ideals. This is a challenging task because these goals often conflict.

NATIONAL STANDARDS FOR CIVICS AND GOVERNMENT

The National Standards for Civics and Government can help teachers develop learning opportunities that foster the skills and perspectives needed for civic participation. They are designed to encourage educators to consider ways to enhance students' understanding of and commitment to the goals of American constitutional democracy. The standards are not a series of course outlines or lesson plans. They are exit standards that specify what students should know and be able to do in the field of civics and government when they complete the 4th, 8th, and 12th grades. As such, they can enhance political studies in schools by stimulating the development of curricular frameworks, course outlines, and professional development programs.

The development and dissemination of the standards, which were published in 1994, was facilitated by the Center for Civic Education. The standards are divided into five broad areas with specific standards flowing from each of the areas for students at the K–4, 5–8, and 9–12 grade levels. Table 12.2. contains the curricular questions specified in the standards.

TABLE 12.3. *National Content Standards for Civics and Government*

In grades K–4, curricula should be designed to help students answer the following questions:

- What is government and what should it do?
- What are the basic values and principles of American democracy?
- How does the government established by the Constitution embody the purposes, values, and principles of American democracy?
- What is the relationship of the United States to other nations and to world affairs?
- What are the roles of the citizens in American democracy?

In grades 5–8 and 9–12, curricula should be designed to help students answer the following questions:

- What are civic life, politics, and government?
- What are the foundations of the American political system?
- How does the government established by the Constitution embody the purposes, values, and principles of American democracy?
- What is the relationship of the United States to other nations and to world affairs?
- What are the roles of the citizen in American democracy?

Source: Reprinted with permission. *National Standards for Civics and Government.* (1994). Calabasas, California: Center for Civic Education, pp.13–14, 43–44.

TEACHING STRATEGIES

Generalization

Conflict arises within a political system when individuals or groups have competing goals or interpret the meaning of laws differently; rules and laws reflect the basic values of a society or institution.

Primary Grades

Ask the students

"What are some of the rules you have at home for going to bed, for eating, and for playing?"

Responses might include "Be in bed by 8:00, be in bed by 9:00, eat everything on your plate, eat everything you serve yourself, take at least one bite of everything on your plate, play in your own yard, no playing after dinner." List the responses on the board in the categories indicated and any additional ones that student responses suggest.

Ask the following questions
1. Why were there different times listed for going to bed?
2. Why are there rules for eating?
3. Why are there rules for playing?
4. What sentence could we write that would be true of rules in all our families? (Rephrase the question as necessary to solicit the response, "While all families have rules, each family has different ideas about them.")
5. What do these rules tell us about the importance of children to their parents? (Rephrase the question as necessary to solicit the response that reflects the idea that taking good care of children is an important value in our society.)

Ask the students
"What are some rules at school that the principal and teachers think are important, but you feel are unimportant?"

Write the responses on a chart such as the following.

School Rules Not Important to Me   Why

_____   _____

_____   _____

_____   _____

_____   _____

_____   _____

After the responses are recorded, ask the students why they think these rules are unimportant. Write their responses under the "Why" column. A sample response might be "Don't talk in the hall." "Why?" "Because I like to talk to my friend and can never talk to him in class." You might plan and carry out an experiment related to some of the rules the children have identified as unimportant. The following activity, relating to talking in the corridors, could be planned and carried out with another teacher and his or her class.

Have the students from another class walk by your classroom and talk loudly while your students are taking a spelling test. Afterward, ask each of your students to record whether or not the noise made by the other students affected his or her performance on the spelling test. On another day, the classes should switch roles. Have your class make loud noises near the door of the other class while the students in it are taking a test. Put together the observations made by both classes. Discuss the results and how the students feel about the school rule after the experiment.

The following activity will help students discover how conflict may arise when individuals interpret the meanings of rules differently. Ask several students to role-play a classroom situation that has the agreed-on rule that no one should talk during the daily math test. The rule also states the punishment. The test paper of the person who is caught talking is automatically torn up by the teacher. While he is taking his math test one morning, Johnny breaks the lead in his pencil. He quietly asks Sue for an extra pencil. After the test, some members of the class insist that Johnny's test paper be torn up. However, Johnny becomes upset and argues that the rule does not apply to him because he was not talking but was just asking for a pencil that he badly needed to complete his test. After the role-playing situation, ask each member of the class to tell whether he or she thinks Johnny's paper should be torn up. Help the students to derive the generalization that even though we may have laws to govern behavior, conflict often arises when individuals interpret those laws differently. Discuss with the students the idea of freedom of speech as set forth in the First Amendment to the Constitution. Write the phrase "freedom of speech" on the board. Ask the following questions:

1. What is speech?
2. What is freedom? Give some examples. (A possible response might be "Doing anything you want to.")
3. Let's put the ideas of these two words together. What does "freedom of speech" mean? (List responses on the board.)
4. What are some things the idea of freedom of speech does not mean?

An example, such as the following, may be necessary here.

Boys and girls, if you are having trouble answering this question, listen to this story. Jane is in the first grade. She told all the children in her class that Sam always steals things from her desk, that she saw him take a banana from her lunch, that he stole her library book from the coat room, and that he even stole some candy from Mr. Jones's store. Soon the children were saying to Sam, "You are a robber." "I'm not going to play with you." "You can't touch my things, Sam." "You are a thief." Jane's teacher found out that Jane was lying. Is Jane's use of speech an example of what is meant by "freedom of speech"? Why or why not?

Pair the students and give to each pair some pictures torn from magazines. Have them group these pages into examples of "freedom of speech" and "nonfreedom of speech." The discrimination made between pictures representing freedom and nonfreedom of speech will depend on individual interpretations of the pictures. Encourage the students to talk about this as they make their judgments. An example of nonfreedom of speech might show a father scolding his child without giving him a chance to defend himself. An example of freedom of speech might show a politician making a speech in a public forum. The students can cut out the pictures from the pages and glue them onto two labeled charts to develop collages representing the two categories discussed.

Intermediate Grades

Select six students from the class and divide them into two equal groups. Give Card 1 to one group and Card 2 to the other. Direct the students to read the cards and follow the directions written on them.

Card 1

George is accused of stealing a typewriter from the school office and selling it to a pawnshop in order to buy a new football of special design, which his parents told him that he could not have. George is an "A" student and is on the student council. He is also captain of the baseball team and a real leader. Most of the boys and girls in his class respect him highly. George is known to be a friend to everyone and is always helping out the other guy. His parents are well known in the community; his father is a doctor. George says he is not guilty. Prepare a statement to present to the class on why George should or should not be charged with the crime.

Card 2

Joe is accused of stealing a computer from the school office and selling it to a pawnshop in order to buy Christmas presents for his family. Joe is a very poor student who gets mostly D's and sometimes C's. He is often in the principal's office for being late to school, not paying attention in class, and fighting on the playground. He is a sloppy dresser, wears dirty clothes, and doesn't participate in sports. His only friend is Mike, who lives in the same run-down apartment building in a poor neighborhood. Joe's father works in the flour mill. Joe says he is not guilty. Prepare a statement to present to the class on why Joe should or should not be charged with the crime.

Have each group read the case descriptions and present their arguments to the class. Have the class vote on the following:

1. George should be charged with the crime and brought before the appropriate authorities. Yes or No
2. Joe should be charged with the crime and brought before the appropriate authorities. Yes or No

Tape record the session, and save the tape and results of the class vote for the next day's lesson.

Play yesterday's tape, directing students to listen for the facts and assumptions that supported or rejected charging each boy with the crime. These observations should be listed on a chart similar to Table 12.4. Stop the tape after each case presentation to make suggested notations.

Display a chart on which Section 1 of the Fourteenth Amendment to the Constitution of the United States is written, and ask the questions that follow.

Section 1. All persons born or naturalized in the United States, and subject to the jurisdiction thereof, are citizens of the United States and of the State wherein they reside. No State shall make or enforce any law which shall abridge the privileges or immunities of citizens of the United States; nor shall any State deprive any person of life, liberty, or property, without due process of law; nor deny any person within its jurisdiction the equal protection of the laws.

TABLE 12.4. *Supporting and Rejecting Facts*

Supporting Facts	Assumptions Made from Facts
George:	
Joe:	

Rejecting Facts	Assumptions Made from Facts
George:	
Joe:	

1. How do the data collected relate to this Amendment?
2. Did our actions yesterday violate this Amendment? Why or why not?
3. Were the assumptions made justified? Why or why not?
4. Why did yesterday's vote turn out as it did?
5. How does this vote reflect our value systems?

Write the First Amendment to the Constitution of the United States on the board:

> Congress shall make no law respecting an establishment of religion, or prohibiting the free exercise thereof; or abridging the freedom of speech, or of the press; or the right of the people peaceably to assemble, and to petition the Government for a redress of grievances.

Divide your class into research groups of five students each. Direct each group to formulate an interpretation of the meaning of this statement that reflects a unanimous decision of the group. In this interpretative statement they should give examples of what they think citizens can and cannot do without violating this Amendment. After the students have completed this task, ask these questions:

1. What problems occurred in your groups when you were trying to reach a unanimous decision? Why?
2. What was the source of your problems?
3. If no problems occurred, why?

Type the data collected, and reproduce the material so each student can have a copy. Direct students to read all the reports and prepare for a discussion on the similarities and differences in interpretations. During a class discussion, ask the students to explain the differences and similarities in interpretations.

Ask your students to read the newspapers for a week and collect examples of articles that relate to the First Amendment. Have students mount these articles on construction paper and write a one-sentence heading for each article saying "In this article the First Amendment is interpreted to mean that...". Display these articles on a bulletin board. Direct students to read them as they are displayed. After numerous articles are collected, discuss them and ask the students whether they agree or disagree with the various interpretations of the Amendment demonstrated in the articles, and why. Ask: "What in your life experience causes you to make that judgment?"

Upper Grades

Have a group of three students collect and research the current laws in your state concerning drug usage, and duplicate their findings for the entire class. Discuss the laws within the following framework: (1) statement of the laws themselves, (2) legal interpretation of the laws, (3) student interpretations of the laws, (4) society's behavior toward the laws, (5) reasons for society's behavior, (6) resulting conflicts, (7) possible ways to resolve conflicts, (8) values the laws represent, and (9) values that conflict with the laws.

Have students research affirmative action as a method of attaining equal job opportunities. Direct them to find five examples of methods used to implement affirmative action in five different states. Then divide the class into debating teams, one for affirmative action and one against affirmative action. The rules for the debate are: (1) All debating must be done from a legal base, from the laws and governing documents at the national and state levels; (2) the debaters should state the laws and then tell how they either support or outlaw affirmative action; and (3) students should point out when local and national laws conflict.

After the research is carried out, have the groups select formal spokespersons to direct the presentation of the material collected. Audio tape or videotape the presentations if possible. After the debates, discuss the following questions:

1. What were the major differences in interpretations? (List on board).
2. Why did the differences occur? (Rephrase this question as necessary to solicit responses focusing on the conflicting values within our society.)
3. Why does conflict occur in instances such as these?
4. What ways can you suggest to resolve some of these conflicts?

Activity for the next day: Give each of the students a sheet of paper listing the laws and part of the governing documents that the students used to support their ideas. Leave room on these sheets so that during the debate, while they listen to the tape replay, the students can write notes on the various interpretations made of these laws. The tape replay on the following day serves several purposes: (1) It can be replayed to check points, and (2) it allows students to focus on the variety of interpretations of the laws during a session, separate from the debate itself. The emotional reactions generated during the debate should have cooled so that the students can discuss the laws objectively. Discuss the student observations of each law.

1. How do the interpretations relate to the Declaration of Independence and the Constitution? Are they consistent with these documents? Why or why not?
2. How can we explain the differences in interpretations?
3. How can these differences be resolved?

Have students research several current controversial legal cases. Direct students to consider the following points in their research:

1. With what laws have these persons come in conflict? Find the specific laws and their sources.
2. How do these laws relate to the First Amendment of the United States Constitution?
3. What were the circumstances surrounding the conflict in which these people found themselves?

After research has been completed, discuss:

1. What do these cases have in common?
2. How are they different? Chart the responses:

Alike	Different
_____	_____
_____	_____
_____	_____
_____	_____
_____	_____

3. On the basis of your research and the First Amendment, under what conditions is it legal to demonstrate and speak out on controversial subjects?

Have the students vote on the case for which they would most like to role-play a mock trial. Guide the students in determining the roles that should be included in the trial, such as judge, jury, defense attorney, prosecuting attorney, witnesses, and research teams. After each role has been determined, give the students time to research their roles in the trial and prepare for their performance. Then carry out the trial in its entirety.

SUMMARY

Political science is a discipline with many different structures and traditions. It has been defined as the study of the legal government of the state, the struggle of competing groups for power, and the study of the authoritative allocation of values for a society (Easton, 1981). The latter definition is accepted by many political scientists because it defines the boundaries and sets a focus for the discipline.

The earliest political scientists were normative theorists who believed that their main goal should be to describe the ideal state and the means by which it could be attained. The legal-institutional approach, another tradition within the discipline, focuses on describing political laws and institutions. In the period after World War II, a new tradition, known as the behavioral approach, emerged within political science. It emerged as a protest against the normative and legal-institutional approaches. The behaviorists regard theory construction as their primary goal and believe that political scientists should focus their study on political behavior, not on laws and institutions. They think that the legal-institutional approach is inadequate because it focuses on the description of particular institutions and not on the development of scientific statements and theory. The behaviorists reject the normative tradition because they believe it is antithetical to the development of an empirical science. The behaviorist movement has initiated intense soul-searching within political science and has to some extent polarized the discipline's various factions. While the movement has profoundly affected political science, it has not been a victor. Political science was seriously challenged by the behaviorist movement during the late 1960s and the early 1970s. Although political science is becoming more theoretical and empirical, the older traditions are very much alive within the field today.

Each of the traditions within political science has concepts and generalizations that can be profitably incorporated into elementary and middle school social studies. However, the normative tradition, with its emphasis on values, can best be used when students are studying valuing and decision-making problems. The legal-institutional approach has dominated the discipline as well as those components of political science that are studied in the schools. Although students should be familiar with the legal codes and constitutions that affect political actors, the emphasis in school political studies should be on political behavior. Without a focus on behavior, students will get an unrealistic view of the ways our political system actually works, because laws are interpreted variously by different public officials and citizens.

Students should be introduced to political science concepts in the earliest grades, and they should gradually develop a better understanding of them in successive grades. To assure that students acquire political literacy in a sequential and developmental fashion, you should identify the political science concepts and generalizations you regard as essential for students to learn and choose appropriate content samples, teaching strategies, and materials to develop those understandings at the beginning of the year or when a curriculum guide is structured. Without such deliberate and early planning, the teaching of political understandings will be incidental and ineffective.

REFLECTION AND ACTION ACTIVITIES

1. What is the unique nature of political science? How does the political science "perspective" differ from the ways in which other social scientists view human behavior? What implications does your response have for planning political studies in the elementary and middle school grades?
2. How has political science been defined by different political scientists? Why do you think political scientists define their discipline differently? Which of the definitions of political science reviewed in this chapter do you think is the most useful? Why? Which do you feel is the least useful? Why? How might the definition of political science that teachers endorse affect their planning of political studies for elementary and middle school students?

3. Analyze several middle school civics textbooks. Tell whether the books represent the normative, legal-institutional, behavioral, systems, or postbehavioral approach. Document your response with excerpts from the books. Assume that you are teaching in a school in which one of these texts was adopted. Illustrate, with a lesson plan, how you would teach with the text and yet help students learn concepts and generalizations that the text does not illustrate or discuss.

4. Select one of the following generalizations and devise a series of activities (similar to the ones in this chapter) that can be used to teach it to students in the (a) primary grades, (b) middle grades, and (c) upper grades.

   a. In every society and institution, regulations and laws emerge to govern the behavior of individuals; individuals usually experience some form of punishment when authorities catch them breaking laws.

   b. Within every society, an individual or some group is authorized to make binding decisions and to allocate values.

   c. Many different types of political systems are used in various societies to determine public policy and to regulate behavior.

   d. Individuals are more likely to influence public policy when working in groups than when working alone.

 *internet links*

TEACHING POLITICAL SCIENCE

The Internet contains a rich array of resources on political science. The websites listed below can be used to teach legal, civic, and other dimensions of political science.

1. Division for Public Education of the American Bar Association (http://www. abanet.org/publiced/home.html). This site provides resources for students and educators and reflects the American Bar Association's mission to increase public understanding of the law and its role in society. Information on the Division for Public Education's programs such as Law Day and Mock Trials and its publications such as LRE Report and FOCUS on Law Studies are available online. This site is also linked to the homepage of the American Bar Association.

2. The Carl Albert Center (http://www.ou.edu/special/albertctr/). Educators can use this site for information on the U.S. Congress.

3. National Center for Policy Analysis: Idea House (http://www.public-policy. org/~ncpa/). This website serves as a gateway to an extensive array of information on public policy. Students can listen to a live briefing on global warming, read about both sides of congressional issues, and gain access to an extensive cybrary of information on public policy.

4. American Political Science Association On-Line (http://www.apsanet.org/). This site will primarily be of interest to teachers who are interested in political science as a profession. Information on political science journals, conferences, and opportunities for professional development can be accessed from this web page.

REFERENCES

Bottomore, T. (1996). *Political Sociology*, 2nd ed. Boulder, CO: Westview.

Deutsch, K. W. (1980). *Politics and government: How people decide their fate* (3rd ed.). Boston: Houghton Mifflin.

Easton, D. (1969). The New Revolution in Political Science. *The American Political Science Review, 63(4),* 1051–1061.

Easton, D. (1981). *The political system: An inquiry into the state of political science* (3rd ed.). Chicago: University of Chicago Press.

Easton, D. (1985). An approach to the analysis of political systems. In M. Feldman & E. Seifman, Eds., *The social studies: Structure, models, and strategies* (pp. 138–147). New York: Garland Publishing.

Galston, W. (1993). Political theory in the 1980s: Perplexity amidst diversity. In A. W. Finifter (ed.), *Political science: The state of the discipline II* (pp. 27–53). Washington, D.C.: American Political Science Association.

Isaak, A. C. (1988). *Scope and method of political science* (4th ed.). New York: Harcourt.

Milbrath L. W., & Goel, M. L. (1982). *Political participation: How and why do people get involved in politics* (Rpt. ed.). Washington, D.C.: University Press of America.

Saxonhouse, A. W. (1993). Texts and canons: The status of the "great books" in political theory. In A. W. Finifter (ed.), *Political science: The state of the discipline II* (pp. 3–26), Washington, D.C.: American Political Science Association.

Straayer, J. A., & Muessig, R. H. (1980). *The study and teaching of political science.* Columbus, OH: Merrill.

FOR FURTHER READING

Afro-Americans and the evolution of a living Constitution: Update on Law-Related Education, Vol. 12 (Fall 1988). This special issue includes articles by Mary Frances Berry, John Hope Franklin, and Derrick Bell.

Berry, M. F. (1995). *Black resistance/White law: A history of constitutional racism in America.* New York: Viking.

Brown, R. D. (1997). *The strength of a people: The idea of an informed citizenry in America, 1650–1870.* Chapel Hill: University of North Carolina Press.

Flexner, E., & Fitzpatrick, E. (1996). *A century of struggle: The woman's rights movement in the United States.* New York: Belknap.

Gardner, J. W. (1972). *In common cause: Citizen action and how it works.* New York: Norton.

Kegley, C. W., Jr., & Wittkopf, E. R. (1995). *American foreign policy: Pattern and process* (5th ed.). New York: St. Martin's Press.

Keller, C. W., & Schillings, D. (Eds.). (1987). *Teaching about the Constitution.* Washington, D.C.: National Council for the Social Studies.

Lamy, S. L., Meyers, R. B., Von Vihl, D., & Weeks, K. (1992). *Teaching global awareness with simulations and games.* Denver: University of Denver, Center for Teaching, International Relations Publications.

Parson, C. (1995). *Serving to learn, learning to serve: Civics and service from A–Z.* Thousand Oaks, CA: Corwin Press.

Shafritz, J. M. (1988). *The Dorsey dictionary of American government and politics.* Chicago: Dorsey Press.

Shiman, D. A. (1993). *Teaching human rights.* Denver: University of Denver, Center for Teaching, International Relations Publications.

Sinopoli, R. C. (1996). *From many, one: Readings in American political and social thought.* Washington, D.C.: Georgetown University Press.

CHAPTER 13

Economics: Structure, Concepts, and Strategies

*f*EATURE

AN ECONOMIC ANOMALY: THE WORKING POOR

Many Americans believe that any person who is willing to work hard can earn enough money to meet essential needs. They believe that all people may not be able to live in the best neighborhood or live the life style that they desire, but if they work they will not be hungry or homeless. The reality is that even though many people work every day, they live in poverty. The working poor have been defined as people who look for work at least 27 weeks out of the year even if they do not find work, heads of households who would remain below the poverty line even though they work 52 weeks a year, and hourly workers whose wages are at or below the minimum wage. The working poor include about 7 million Americans who hold more than one job, involuntary part-time workers who make up about 25 to 30 percent of the U.S. civilian labor force, and many people who work in service sector jobs like child care, food service, and home health (U.S. Census Bureau, 1995).

Increasing economic stratification in the United States complicates the problem of the working poor because, as distance grows between the social classes, poor people are viewed as less willing to work to improve their economic status and therefore deserve to be poor. In 1993 the bottom fifth of U.S. households received 4.1 percent of U.S. income while the top fifth of U.S. households received 47 percent (U.S. Census Bureau, 1995). This translates into a mean income for the bottom fifth of U.S. households of $9,739 and $111,017 for the top fifth. The top 5 percent of U.S. households had a mean income of $191,612 in 1993.

The disparity between the rich and the poor has increased over the years and is becoming more solidified. In 1993, 15.1 percent of the U.S. population lived in poverty. This means that 39.3 million people lived at the government official poverty level, which was $14,763 for a family of four (U.S. Census Bureau, 1995). The disparity between the rich and the poor also reflects age, race, and gender. These factors may also influence the ways in which the general public responds to the working poor. During the 1950s and 1960s most of the people who were classified as poor were elderly. However, in the 1990s poverty primarily entrapped the nation's children. In 1992, 21 percent of all of the children in the U.S. were poor, with 46 percent of African American and 39 percent of Hispanic children living in poverty (Swartz & Weigert, 1995). Gender is also an important variable in identifying the working poor. In 1990, African American (27.3%) and Hispanic (35.3%) females had the highest rates of poverty for wage-earners. White females constituted only 30 percent of all full-time workers, but they made up 41.5 percent of all poverty-wage workers. Females across all racial and ethnic groups constituted 38.7 percent of all full-time workers, and 56.5 percent of poverty-wage workers in 1990 (U.S. Census Bureau, 1995).

Images of the poor frequently do not reflect the reality of the lives of the working poor. Poor people are commonly depicted as people who are unwilling to work, not as people who are unable to find work or who work at one or more low-paying jobs. The social reality of the working poor is complex and cannot be fully understood and addressed from an economic perspective. Understanding, analyzing, and framing policy alternatives for addressing the problems of the working poor require an interdisciplinary perspective. Fashioning innovative public policy to respond to the needs of the working poor not only requires an understanding of the U.S. economy, but it also requires an understanding of how factors such as education, language barriers, and health issues influence the opportunity to work. Those factors have traditionally been viewed as variables addressed in disciplines such as sociology, medicine, and education. The working poor is an example of an economic problem that is blurring the boundaries between the disciplines.

THE ECONOMIC PERSPECTIVE

Each of the social sciences provides us key concepts and perspectives that can enhance our insights and understandings. Economics, too, enables us to see human behavior from a unique perspective. The major concept in this discipline is *scarcity*, and the science focuses primarily on how people try to satisfy their unlimited wants with limited resources. The major principle of the discipline is that there are not enough natural and human resources to satisfy all of people's wants. (See Figure 13.1). Economists study how people use limited resources to *produce, exchange,* and *consume goods and services.*

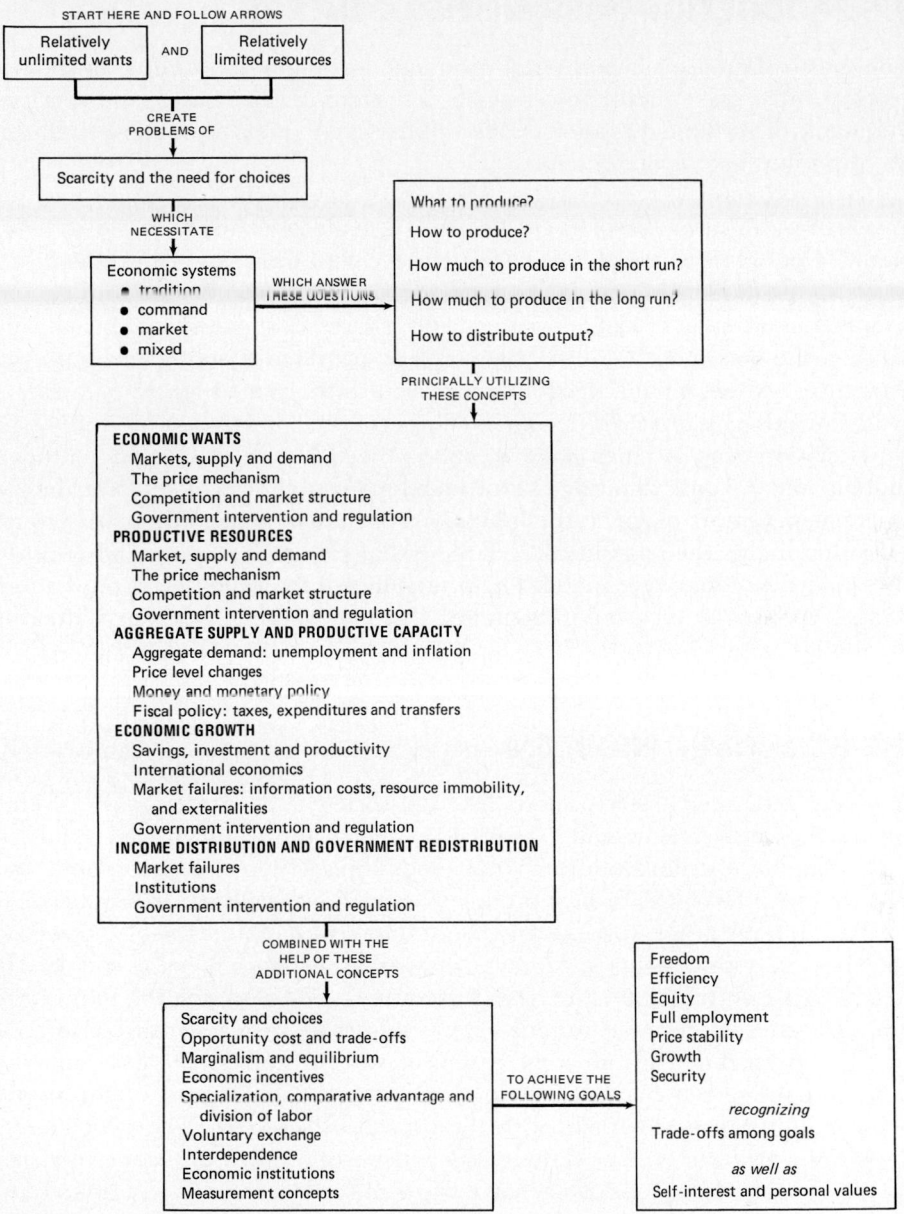

Figure 13.1
A schematic framework of economics: An approach to linking concepts.
Source: Reprinted from W. Lee Hansen, et al., *A Framework for Teaching Economics: Basic Concepts,* New York:
Joint Council on Economic Education, 1977, pp. 28–29. Used with permission of the Joint Council on Economic
Education.

THE PRODUCTION-POSSIBILITIES CONCEPT

Economists often use a hypothetical production-possibilities example to show how a society must make hard choices when determining what goods and services to produce with its limited resources. We will use such an example here to illustrate this important economic principle.

Society X has the resources and technological expertise necessary to provide universal health care to all of its citizens or to provide its armed forces with the most advanced equipment available. The society does not have the resources and technology to do both. If it decides to provide universal health care and the most advanced equipment available for the armed forces, the quantities of each will be less than the maximum amounts that could be provided if only one was provided. Therefore, as the amount of equipment given to the armed forces increases, the level of health care provided decreases. This economic principal is not only reflected in decisions that societies make; it is also reflected in decisions that families and students make. Understanding the production-possibilities concept can help students become more aware of the limitations of human and nonhuman resources. It also highlights the relationship between what can be gained and what must be given up when choices are made. The principle that underlies the production-possibilities concept is discussed in Standard 1 in The National Content Standards in Economics in Table 13.2.

THE ECONOMIC PROBLEM

The basic economic problem faced by every society is how to best use its limited resources to satisfy its wants and to assure its existence. Every human society must solve three related economic problems: What goods and services shall we produce and in what amounts? How shall they be produced? For whom shall they be produced?

Throughout history, people have used different methods to solve these problems. In determining what to produce and how to produce it, some societies have relied heavily on tradition (Banaszak & Brennan, 1983). Among the Hopi Indians of North America, corn was the most important crop, largely because traditionally corn had been raised and to some extent even venerated. In the past, cotton was the dominant crop in many of our southern states because of the cotton tradition in the South. Since the 1960s, with the growth of southern technology and the recognition by southerners of the disadvantages of a one-crop economy, farmers have diversified their crops. Every society to some extent relies on tradition to solve the three basic economic problems. Heilbroner (1989) notes that tradition can negatively influence an economy by limiting the flexibility and ability of the society to respond to large-scale rapid social and economic change.

In some societies, public authorities determine what goods and services are produced (Heilbroner, 1989). Dictators such as Castro, Hitler, and Franco not only exercised political control within their nations, but to a great extent they determined which goods and services would be produced and for whom they would be produced. Government control over the economy is more prevalent in communist countries than in the United States. However, as Heilbroner (1989) correctly points out, in every society the government influences what goods and services are produced as well as how they are distributed. Taxes are an example of how individual income is preempted by public authorities for public purposes. The degree of government influence varies among different nations.

THE MARKET ECONOMY

In the same year the Declaration of Independence was signed (1776), a book was published in Europe that signaled a revolution in the economic world. Adam Smith, the "father of economics," published *The Wealth of Nations*. Prior to the publication of this classic, the status of economic systems in the Western world had been largely shaped by a group of European writers known as the mercantilists. They thought that a sound economic system had to be tightly controlled by centralized authorities. Without such control within an economy, they believed, the results would be confusion, depression, and chaos. Adam Smith's seminal book challenged the ideas of these influential writers.

Smith believed that the best type of economic system resulted when the government maintained a "laissez-faire" or "hands-off" policy. Manufacturers would be forced to produce the goods consumers wanted; otherwise they would fold because of lack of sales. Only those goods that satisfied customers would remain on the market. Competition between producers and manufacturers would assure that prices would not become too high. Merchants who charged too much for their goods would go out of business because consumers would buy goods at stores with reasonable prices. The government could best help the economy, Smith argued, by leaving it alone.

Smith's ideas are embodied in the market economy, which is the economic system (in modified form) used in the United States and in most Western nations. In a market economy, consumers largely determine what goods and services are produced, and the quantities in which they are produced. During the 1970s and 1980s, the sales of Japanese cars in the United States and in other Western nations soared. Consumer demand for American-made cars dropped sharply. Consumers were increasingly buying Japanese cars because they believed they were more competitively priced, more fuel-efficient, and a better buy in general than many American cars. However, the U.S. economy is not a pure market economy. It is a mixed one.

THE MIXED ECONOMY

The federal government plays a large role in determining what goods and services are produced and sold in the United States. As American car manufacturers faced increasingly stiff competition from makers of Japanese cars in the 1980s, the U.S. government put pressure on Japan to reduce the number of cars it was exporting to the United States. The U.S. Senate gave the Chrysler Corporation, a major U.S. car manufacturer, loan guarantees of $1.5 billion to enable the company to stay in

profile

MILTON FRIEDMAN AND ROSE DIRECTOR FRIEDMAN

Free-Market Economists

Milton Friedman and Rose Director Friedman are influential proponents of market economies, free enterprise, limited government, and economic freedom. In 1976 Milton Friedman was awarded the Nobel Prize for his work in economics. He is currently a senior research fellow at the Hoover Institute and Paul Snowden Russell Distinguished Service Professor Emeritus of Economics at the University of Chicago. Rose Director Friedman is an economist and writer.

Both Friedmans have immigrant backgrounds. Milton Friedman is the son of Jewish immigrants, and Rose Friedman was born in Charterisk, Poland. The Friedmans met while they were in graduate school at the University of Chicago and were married on June 25, 1938. Over the years, they have collaborated on a number of writing projects, including *Price Theory: A Provisional Text, Capitalism and Freedom, Poverty: Definition and Perspective,* and *Tyranny of the Status Quo.* Their best-known book, *Free to Choose: A Personal Statement,* is also the title of their 10-week PBS series. *Free to Choose: A Personal Statement* explores the relationship between economic and political freedom and advocates for a free-market economy that would limit taxes to support minimal government, prohibit requirements for licensing professionals by accrediting agencies, encourage a vouchering plan for subsidizing education in private schools, and abolish the corporate income tax.

The free-market perspectives that are advocated by the Freidmans have had a significant influence on the field of economics and public policy. Milton Friedman has been honored by numerous economic organizations and is considered one of the foremost leaders of the Chicago School of Economics.

business. The federal government intervenes in the economy to protect consumers from items it considers harmful, such as diet drinks containing harmful chemicals, and unsafe toys.

You know how heavily subtle and often deceptive television, radio, and other advertising influences the wants of U.S. consumers. Many consumers in the 1950s used only a small number of basic detergents and soaps for household chores. However, the average middle-class household today uses a number of specialized cleaners and spot removers. The soaps used to clean the bathroom, the oven, woodwork, and to wash dishes are often different. These specialized desires and needs have been largely shaped by television commercials that many of today's shoppers spend hundreds of hours watching each year. The strong impact that the anti-smoking commercials had on smokers during the 1960s and 1970s is another example of how consumer wants are shaped by the mass media. Thus, consumers, the government, and the producers themselves all play a role in determining what goods and services are produced in the U.S. mixed economy.

Business firms largely determine how goods and services are produced in the U.S. economy. Their main goal is to produce the largest amount of goods and services for the smallest outlay of resources. Most large industries specialize in the products they make and have a division of labor within their plants. By producing only a few kinds of items and using a production-line technique to manufacture them, firms make maximum use of their resources. The U.S. federal government, as well as labor unions, to some extent influence how goods and services are produced. The government sets minimum safety standards and regulates the use of dangerous machines. Strongly organized unions, which are becoming less influential in U.S. society, demand specific kinds of working conditions, hours, and salaries.

How do we determine who within a market economy will get the goods and services produced? To a great extent, the persons who contribute most to the production of goods and services also consume or use most of them. Two persons with similar training and experience who do identical work at an automobile plant usually earn a comparable salary. They can buy about the same amount of goods and services each month. In principle, this is what happens in a pure market economy;

the goods and services that individuals receive are roughly comparable to the contribution they make to the total production of goods and services for the society.

Often this does not happen in a mixed economy, but to some extent it does. The salaries of workers in an automobile plant might be determined as much by the strength of their union as by the contribution they make to the production of society's goods and services. Consumers may be willing to pay very high salaries to some workers, such as sports and movie stars, whose contributions to the production of society's goods and services are not very important in a tangible or measurable sense. Experience, level of education, and how much consumers are willing to pay for a particular good or service might heavily influence a worker's salary. Because of certain societal values, the U.S. federal government often intervenes to upset the "natural" working of the market economy. Individuals with disabilities, retired workers, public officials, unwed mothers, and unemployed workers often receive a share of society's production pie even though they may contribute very little or nothing to the production of the goods and services they consume. Federal legislation also prevents children from working in industry. Children are perhaps the largest single segment of nonproductive consumers in the United States.

THE DEATH OF ADAM SMITH'S DREAM

Smith urged the government to keep its hands off the economy. He felt that, if left alone, the market system would result in a balanced, efficient, and just economy. When free-market economies developed within Western societies, it was not long before it was fairly clear that Smith's ideas were overly optimistic. Because merchants tried to make the highest profits with the least amount of resources, their interests were often contrary to those of consumers. Merchants therefore often used devious methods to get and keep sales; consumers often didn't have the choices Smith thought they would have. Monopolies emerged and merchants conspired to raise prices and to "beat the consumer." In the United States, railroads were among the first large monopolies. Federal antitrust laws unsuccessfully attempted to shatter such seats of power.

The government gradually assumed greater and greater responsibilities in the economic realm. The stock market crash of 1929 and the publication of John Maynard Keynes's *The General Theory of Employment, Interest, and Money* in 1936 were two significant events that helped to legitimize government intervention. The Depression of the 1930s painfully revealed the ills that could plague a market economy. Keynes's book suggested that because of the tremendous freedom that customers and business people have in a market system, "the total demand for new goods and services will sometimes be too large and sometimes too small to keep us at full employment." Thus, from time to time the government needed to intervene in order to spike up the economy. Even though Malthus and a few other writers had challenged Smith's laissez-faire theory prior to the 1930s, it had survived all criticisms with the help of such influential writers as David Ricardo and John Stuart Mill. But the tragic fate of Smith's powerful legacy was inevitable. The free-market economy was gradually replaced by a highly mixed one.

The roles that the federal and state governments play in the U.S. economy have increased greatly in recent years. In 1920, less than 10 percent of goods and services in the United States was bought by the government. In 1997, that figure was over 17.9 percent (Bureau of Economic Analysis, 1998). Big increases in spending for defense, education, and roads account for most of the large jump. The number of federal agencies regulating different parts of the economy has also increased by leaps and bounds. They range from the Food and Drug Administration, which regulates drugs and foods, to the Environmental Protection Agency, which administers antipollution legislation.

"I like the sound of it. Tell me more about deficit spending."
Source: Joseph Farris. Used with permission.

RESEARCH METHODS IN ECONOMICS

The Intellectual Experiment: A Public Method

Unlike most other social scientists, who make extensive use of the laboratory experiment and the structured interview, economists cannot conduct laboratory experiments, and the interview technique is not a major research strategy within the discipline. The most frequently used method in economics is the intellectual experiment (Reynolds, 1988).

Economists test hypotheses by assuming that all the variables are constant (or equal) except the variable whose effect they are trying to determine (the independent variable). Let's study an example. Professor Jones, an economist at State University, studies this problem: "What is the most important factor influencing consumer demand for compact cars?" She concludes that the price of compact cars is the most important factor. She bases her conclusion on the analysis of statistics that show the cost of compact cars and the number purchased within each of the last 10 years. What factors did Professor Jones assume to be equal or constant? She assumed that the income of consumers, the quality of compact cars, and the price of larger cars were constant variables. In other words, she assumed that of all the other factors that might influence consumer demand for compact cars, only the price varied.

In the real world (which the economist simplifies for research purposes) other factors often do not remain constant. In applying her generalization, Professor Jones may find that even though the price of compact cars increased significantly the following year, the number bought also increased. Several new American compact cars hit the market, and the hourly wages of consumers reached a new peak. These factors brought about an unexpected increase in the number of compact cars purchased.

NATURE OF ECONOMIC CONCEPTS

Economic concepts are probably more precise than those in any of the other social sciences. The meanings of such concepts as scarcity, production, and exchange are rather standard in the discipline (Samuelson & Nordhaus, 1997). This can easily be seen by examining one of the several dictionaries of economics. There is also a great deal of consensus about what the key economic concepts and generalizations are. The tables of contents in most introductory economics textbooks look very similar.

OBJECTIVITY IN ECONOMICS

Because most economic data are quantitative (such as the prices of goods, the number of hours that employees work, and hourly wage rates), data collection within the discipline tends to be more objective than in the other social sciences. Much of the data used by economists is compiled by such agencies as various departments of the federal government. Because of the use of models and the quantitative nature of economic research, statistics are often used to analyze data as well as to control variables that economists would otherwise be unable to control or hold constant. The quantitative nature of the data, the preciseness of the concepts, and the intellectual experiment method make it possible for one economist to replicate studies done by others.

ECONOMIC ANALYSIS AND POLICY ECONOMICS

Economists usually distinguish between two major approaches within the discipline. One approach is called economic analysis or positive economics. Its main goal is the development of scientific theory. High-level generalizations about the law of supply and demand, the law of diminishing returns, and the law of scarcity are examples of the products of this method of inquiry. The other approach is known as policy economics or normative economics. The goal of policy economics is to use the generalizations and theories developed in economic analysis to solve social problems that are largely economic in nature. This approach deals with such problems as "Should we reduce income taxes in order to stimulate the economy?" and "How can we best manage the economy so that we have sound welfare programs?" Bach (1987) suggests the following steps in policy economics: (1) Define the problem, (2) Map out the main alternative ways of achieving the desired goals, (3) Analyze carefully the alternative policies outlined in step two, and (4) Check your solution—both against flaws in your own analysis resulting from fallacies or blind spots, and against past experience.

Economics is both a science and an applied discipline. Economic analysis is scientific because the goal is to develop scientific theory. Policy economics is an applied field because it deals with value questions as well as with scientific knowledge. In order to determine the goals of an economy (such as in Bach's step 2), we must make one value choice instead of another. Thus value inquiry is an essential part of policy economics. There are difficulties when a discipline has both scientific and policy aspects. When economists make statements or recommendations, it is often not clear whether they are speaking as scientists, that is, basing their statements on scientific knowledge alone, or whether the statements are derived from a combination scientific-valuing process, that is, whether they reflect economists' personal biases.

The dual nature of the field is largely responsible for the reputation economists have for disagreeing among themselves. Someone once said, "If you laid all the economists in the world end to end, they would still not reach a conclusion." Although there is actually a great deal of agreement among economists about the nature of the discipline and its key concepts and principles, they have different values and ideas about what the proper goals of an economy should be, and they often, as is to be expected, disagree about policy issues. The public does not often make this distinction, largely because economists rarely make it themselves when they make public statements. When teaching economic studies in the elementary and middle school grades, you should help students discover how economic analysis can help policy makers determine the possible consequences of different courses of action, but emphasize that citizens, not economists, should determine the goals of the U.S. economy.

LEVELS OF ECONOMIC ANALYSIS

Economists derive generalizations about economic behavior at two levels. Macroeconomics focuses on large units, such as the economy as a whole or major divisions within it, such as government, households, and businesses. Microeconomics is concerned with specific economic units and a detailed consideration of the behavior of these individual units, such as the output of a specific product, the number of workers, or the revenue or income of a particular firm or household (McConnell, 1995).

Generalizations that are valid in macroeconomics are not necessarily valid on a small scale of analysis. For example, the fallacy of composition, a common fallacy made when citizens talk about economic problems, is assuming that what is true for the part is also true for the whole. A small manufacturer who lowered his prices might increase his sales and therefore his profit because consumers tend to buy more goods when prices decrease. However, if all the manufacturers within an economic system lowered their prices, their sales would not necessarily increase. Total input into the circular flow of income would be lowered and wages would be lowered as a consequence. People tend to buy less when they make less money. Our example illustrates the importance of distinguishing between these two levels of analysis.

ECONOMIC CONCEPTS

There is a lot of agreement about what the key concepts in economics are. Their definitions are also highly standardized. Almost any economist would regard the law of supply and demand and the law of diminishing returns as key economic ideas and would define them in much the same way as other economists. We define some of the key economic concepts below and describe activities that can be used to teach them to elementary and middle school students. A list of basic economic concepts, developed by the Joint Council on Economic Education, appears in Table 13.1.

Scarcity

Just as culture is the main concept in anthropology, and group is the key concept in sociology, scarcity is the most important concept in economics. All other economic principles and theories are related to it. The essence of this concept is that, while people have unlimited wants, the amount of resources within any society are limited (Kourilsky, 1983). Thus there are never enough goods and services to satisfy all wants. Consequently, people must make some hard choices when they decide what goods and services they will produce with their limited resources, how they will be produced, and how they will be distributed. When a society becomes wealthier and develops a higher level of technology, it is able to create more and better goods and services. However, scarcity continues because citizens' wants also increase.

Activities
1. Ask the students to make a list of all the things they would like for their birthdays or for another special occasion, such as Christmas or Chanukah. Ask them to narrow the list to the things they can realistically expect to get. Discuss why the two lists are different.

TABLE 13.1. *Basic Concepts in Economics*

Fundamental Economic Concepts

1. Scarcity
2. Opportunity Cost and Tradeoffs
3. Productivity
4. Economic Systems
5. Economic Institutions and Incentives
6. Exchange, Money, and Interdependence

Microeconomic Concepts

7. Markets and Prices
8. Supply and Demand
9. Competition and Market Structure
10. Income Distribution
11. Market Failures
12. The Role of Government

Macroeconomic Concepts

13. Gross National Product
14. Aggregate Supply
15. Aggregate Demand
16. Unemployment
17. Inflation and Deflation
18. Monetary Policy
19. Fiscal Policy

International Economic Concepts

20. Absolute and Comparative Advantage and Barriers to Trade
21. Balance of Payments and Exchange Rates
22. International Aspects of Growth and Stability

Measurement Concepts and Methods

Tables
Charts and Graphs
Ratios and Percentages
Percentage Changes
Index Numbers
Real vs. Nominal Values
Averages and Distributions Around the Average

Source: Reprinted with permission from Phillip Saunders (Chair), G. L. Bach, James D. Calderwood, and W. Lee Hansen, *A Framework for Teaching the Basic Concepts* (Master Curriculum Guide in Economics), 2nd ed. (New York: Joint Council on Economic Education, 1984), p. 11.

2. Interview parents about how family budgets are planned and managed.
3. Role-play a session of the state legislature in which budget allocations are made for such services as education, health, transportation, welfare, and crime prevention. Discuss ways the state legislature solves the problems that result from demands by citizens for increased services and fewer taxes.

There are never enough goods and services to satisfy all wants. The students in this photograph will have to confront the concept of scarcity as they plan a Student Council activity.
Source: Library of Congress, Washington, D.C.

Production

Production is the process of creating goods and services to satisfy human wants. The farmer who grows cotton and corn, the worker who works on an automobile assembly line, and the spouse who cooks and sews for a family are all producers. Workers who produce services, such as doctors, teachers, and service station attendants, are also producers.

When teaching about production, you can introduce these concepts: goods, services, and consumers. Goods are products that satisfy consumer wants. A service is work done that satisfies consumer wants. Books, food, toys, and automobiles are examples of goods. Teaching, washing windows, and nursing are examples of services. Consumers use goods and services to satisfy their wants and needs. Students should realize that every human being, in order to survive, must consume goods and services, and that these goods and services must either be produced by themselves or by someone else.

Activities
1. Make a list of the goods and services all human beings need to survive, such as food, shelter, and water. Discuss how these goods and services are obtained in your community.

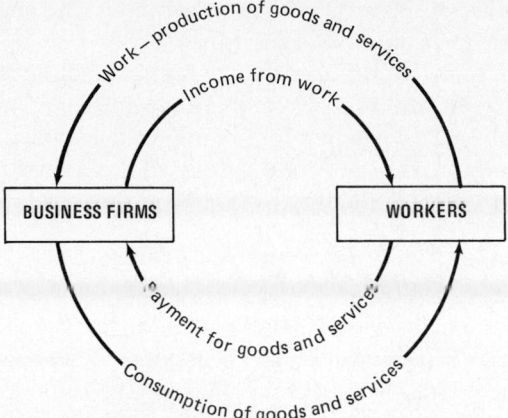

Figure 13.2
The circular flow of income.

2. List and discuss services the students produce, such as washing the dishes, mowing the lawn, cleaning the car, and selling newspapers.
3. Make a list of the goods and services the students consume. Compare the goods and services they consume with the ones they produce.

Interdependence

When an economic system is characterized by specialization and exchange, it is highly interdependent (Saunders et. al., 1984). Interdependence is relying on other producers for the goods and services needed to satisfy one's wants, and helping others to satisfy their wants by participating in the production of goods and services consumed. In colonial America, and in many preliterate societies, families were highly independent because they produced their own food and most of the other goods and services they needed. Early American farm mothers made many home remedies to treat their children's diseases and canned most of the family's foods. Sometimes members of families delivered the babies. Because workers in highly technological societies are so specialized, most families, communities, cities, regions, and nations cannot exist without relying on the goods and services produced by other workers and economic units.

The circular flow of income diagram (see Figure 13.2) illustrates both interdependence and the structure of a market economy. Money flows from business firms to workers. When workers produce goods and services for business firms, they are paid for their work. When they buy goods and services, the money they earn as salary is paid to the firms or to markets selling goods. Thus income continuously flows, and the people who produce goods and services also consume them.

Activities
1. Do a survey to find out what major goods and services are produced in the community and where the major markets are for these goods and services.

Discuss how the goods and services produced in the community help other communities, the nation, and the world.

2. Survey the foods served one day at home to discover where they were grown, packaged, and marketed. Share this information at school during a discussion of how interdependent communities, cities, and nations are.

3. Ask the students to describe how a group of them might survive if they were in a plane crash that landed in the middle of the woods in an unknown land.

Specialization and Division of Labor

Specialization occurs when an economic unit, such as an individual, a business, a region, or a country, produces a narrower range of goods and services than it consumes. Comparative advantage results from specialization when economic units produce those goods and services that they can produce most efficiently (Saunders et. al., 1984).

Division of labor is based on the principle of comparative advantage. It consists of dividing the production of goods and services into smaller parts so that each worker does a specific and specialized job. This process often involves an assembly-line technique. Usually each person who helps to manufacture an automobile makes or attaches only one part. Division of labor, or specialization, has both advantages and disadvantages. With specialization, goods are usually produced more quickly and efficiently. Workers also develop greater skills at performing their particular tasks because they practice the skills frequently. However, workers often have low morale and little pride in their work. If a large number of workers help to make a product, it is difficult for any one of them to gain a great deal of satisfaction from its production. With increased specialization, pride in workmanship tends to fade.

Activities
1. Divide the class into four equal groups. In two of the groups, make a sugar cookie using division of labor. In the other two groups, make the cookie without using division of labor. The class should keep time to determine which group makes the cookie in the least time.
2. Visit a fast food restaurant or another kind of business where division of labor is used. Discuss the observations in class.
3. View a videotape which shows the large number of workers involved in producing one type of goods, such as an airplane, car, or computer.

Voluntary Exchange

In a specialized market economy, individuals and other economic units produce more of a particular good or service than they can use or consume. To meet their needs for other goods and services, they must exchange the goods and services they produce with other workers. A worker who makes computers needs other goods and services—medical care, food, and shelter. A farmer who grows food might need a computer to help him on the farm. The computer worker and the farmer need each other's products. They could directly exchange a computer for food. This kind of exchange, called barter, was often used in traditional societies before forms

"I've called the family together to announce that, because of inflation, I'm going to have to let two of you go."
Source: Joseph Farris. Used with permission.

of money were developed. Because bartering is both awkward and inefficient, money was developed to make the exchange between workers easier and more efficient. Buyers and sellers make their exchanges in a market.

Activities
1. Have a county fair. Ask the students to make items in their art and shop classes and trade them for items made by others during the fair. The students should try to make the best possible items with as few resources as possible and market them at the highest possible prices.
2. Ask the students to bring some stickers or other items to class to trade with other students. Discuss some of the major observations they made about trading during this activity.
3. Ask the class to investigate whether there is a good or service needed or wanted by the students in the school that is not available and that they could provide by starting a business. If there is, work with the students to start a small business that sells goods such as paper, pencils, stickers, and notebooks.

inquiry strategy

LINKING CAREER AWARENESS TO SOCIAL AND ECONOMIC ISSUES

This lesson is designed to provide an opportunity for students to become more aware of how social and economic issues can influence career decisions. As a result of the lesson, students should increase their career awareness, refine their decision-making skills, and become more aware of the relationship between education and economic returns. Although this lesson has several predetermined objectives, its open-ended nature provides an opportunity for student-generated questions to surface. Efforts should be made to incorporate those questions into the lesson.

In order to efficiently execute this lesson, teachers will need to identify sources for the following information and have it available to share with students at the beginning of the lesson.

Population of the city in which the school is located
Data on the educational attainment of adults in the city
Median household income
Breakdown of occupations held by adults in the city

All of this information can be accessed through the U.S. Census Bureau's website, http://www.census.gov/cgi-bin/gazetteer. This website allows visitors to search by zip code, access data in numerous categories including those listed above, and view a map of the census tracts included in the zip code. Much of the information is also available in *Statistical Abstracts of the United States*.

The Census Bureau breaks down jobs into six major categories:

Managerial and professional specialty occupations
Technical, sales, administrative support occupations
Services occupations
Farming, forestry, and fishing
Precision production, craft, and repair occupations
Operators, fabricators, and laborers

Identify the type of occupations held by people in the community and the percentage of people in each occupation category. Once you have that information, you can assign each of the occupation categories to a team of students. Ask the students to research the specific jobs in each of the categories and the educational and other requirements for holding the jobs. Students can research jobs in their assigned category by reading library books, asking people in the community who have those jobs to be guest speakers in their classroom, and using the *Dictionary of Occupational Titles*. Ask students to review old magazines and newspapers for pictures of people working in the occupations they are researching. Once identified, the photographs can be cut out and mounted on cardboard and displayed around the room. Once they have completed their research, each of the teams should give an oral report to the class on their job category.

When the reports have been completed, explain to your students that for the next month they will experience what it is like to secure a job and support themselves.* Based on the information presented by the teams in their oral reports, identify the types of jobs held by people in the community. Each student should be given an identity that matches a worker in the community. The identity should include information on the person's educational level and the number of people in his or her household.

Each student will need to find a job. Then, based on the students' incomes, develop a budget indicating how much money they will pay for housing, day care if needed, food, and other necessities. Local newspapers and other local publications should be used as a source of information on potential jobs and the cost of housing, food, and day care.

To find a job, students should complete job applications and submit them to their teacher. Based on predetermined criteria such as neatness, experience, and education, the teacher determines whether the student gets the job.

As students encounter problems finding jobs, housing, or managing to live within their budgets, they will raise questions. The teacher should be prepared to discuss issues, such as homelessness and welfare reform, which may surface during this phase of the lesson. Those questions should be explored as part of the lesson. For example, when students find that they can't meet their housing costs and are unable to raise the money for rent, they may become homeless. This would present an opportunity to discuss that issue as well as ways in which the community could help people not only after but before they become homeless.

At the end of one month, each student should submit a report that answers two questions: (1) What was the most surprising thing that they learned during the month? and (2) What advice would they give a person with an identity similar to the one they assumed? Student responses to those two questions should be summarized in a chart and used for class discussion.

*Depending on the amount of time that can be devoted to this lesson, the class can continue this phase of the lesson longer than one month.

ECONOMIC GENERALIZATIONS

Because the key concepts in economics can be readily identified, it is not difficult to find generalizations showing the relationship between economic concepts. Generalizations that can be used to guide economic studies in the elementary and middle school grades are found in economics textbooks, in professional books on the teaching of the social studies, and in many curriculum guides in school systems throughout the nation. The following generalizations are representative of the types you can use to guide the planning of economic studies.

Scarcity

A conflict between unlimited wants and limited resources creates the need for decision-making.

Choices are based on the individual's value system, but the value systems are to a large extent culturally derived. Needs and wants are therefore culturally derived.

Interdependence

All families and family members in a community are dependent on one another. Division of labor refers to the separation of production into various jobs.

The growth of interdependence increases the problems of adjustment for the individual in the society, and it also increases the need for coordination through organization-managerial direction, and market mechanisms.

Voluntary Exchange

Individual producers of goods and services exchange with others to get the goods and services they need to satisfy their basic wants. • Individuals who contribute to the production process receive a share of the goods and services produced. • Price is a measure of the relative scarcity and need for goods, services, or resources. • Money is an institution to facilitate the operation of an exchange economy.

Market Economy

Consumers determine what is produced in a free economy, considering all the available alternatives. Advertising and the mass media often influence choices. • Government has increasingly become a participant in the market economy. It is a competitor and also a creator of economic opportunities.

ECONOMIC EDUCATION IN THE SCHOOLS

The Need for Economic Understanding

Economic problems and issues within a society divide large segments of the population. Part of our inability to find viable solutions to complex economic problems results from economic illiteracy on the part of both citizens and public officials. Because of their confusion about economic issues and problems, citizens often vote for candidates who make grand and unrealistic promises about economic reform. Candidates often make such promises out of ignorance, but just as often they make them merely to get votes and do not consider how they might deliver the promised reforms. Promising no new taxes is a campaign strategy often used by politicians to get votes.

To be able to judge the soundness of proposals for economic reforms, citizens must have a clear understanding of the nature of a mixed economy and an awareness of the complexity of modern economic systems. Because many students end their formal education when they leave the public schools, the schools must implement sound programs in economics education if future citizens are to intelligently influence economic policy and participate effectively in our political system. Almost all the social issues that societies face have economic aspects, and the economic perspective will help us to resolve them.

Although the economic point of view can help us to solve problems, economics cannot tell us whether we should have a guaranteed annual income for all families, or whether income taxes should be reduced or increased. However, economic concepts and principles can help us to predict the possible consequences of a guaranteed annual income or of an increase in income taxes. The discipline cannot tell us what the consequences of these actions will be; as we have suggested, economic principles, in common with other social science principles, depend on many variables. Nevertheless, even tentative knowledge can help us to make decisions on complex economic problems by revealing the probable consequences of different courses of action.

Economics education is complicated by the fact that students, like adults, have many misconceptions about the economic system. Often journalists, equally ignorant about economic matters, reinforce the common myths about the economy. Almost everyone is a self-styled economic expert. Economics and education probably have more experts than any other disciplines. For example, a common fallacy is the assumption that what is good for an individual situation is also good for the economy as a whole. When our economy is depressed, citizens often argue that the economy would recover if the government would simply stop spending money. Individuals can often improve their economic situation by saving a significant portion of their incomes, but much unemployment results when the government limits spending, because many people have government-related jobs. In some cases, it is necessary for the federal government to increase spending in order to stimulate a troubled economy.

Because money is such an important part of our lives (it is often said that money, not love, makes the world go 'round), reasoning on economic issues tends to become clouded by emotion. Citizens are often opposed to increasing taxes, yet keep demanding more efficient and extensive services from the city or federal government. Students should be helped to understand that more extensive public services mean higher taxes. The scarcity concept will help them to discover that you can't have your cake and eat it too. Citizens should demand honesty on the part of public officials and the most efficient services possible from the funds spent. However, expecting something for nothing and demanding efficient use of scarce resources are separate matters; the study of economics will help students to make this distinction.

A Sequential Program in Economics Education

The need for economic understanding is too important to be left to chance. While many gifted teachers help students view social studies content from an economic perspective, we can be assured that all students gain economic understanding only if we plan a specific program of instruction. This does not mean that a separate economics program should be implemented. We do not recommend this approach to economics instruction in the elementary and middle school. Rather, the social studies staff or teacher should identify a number of key economic concepts and related generalizations that can be taught with the content that constitutes the core of the social studies program. Economics is not specialized content but a unique way of viewing the content that presently constitutes the social studies curriculum. The key concepts and generalizations identified should be introduced in the earliest grades and further developed in other grades. Students will gain an increasing depth of understanding as they study economic concepts in successive grades in a spiraling fashion.

There are many opportunities for you to introduce and extend economic concepts with content that constitutes the traditional social studies curriculum. Let's consider how the concept of scarcity and a related generalization, "Every individual and society faces a conflict between unlimited wants and limited resources," might be introduced in kindergarten and further developed in successive grades. You could introduce this concept in kindergarten with a role-playing situation. In the situation, Mother and Father are trying to decide whether they should take a trip next summer or add a needed room to the house. They do not have enough money to do both. You could ask the students such questions as: "What is the problem in this situation?" "Why is there a problem?" "Why do you think Mother and Father can't do both things?" "Have you ever had to make a choice between two things?" "What did you decide to do?" "Why?" "What helped you to decide?" "If you were Mother and Father, what would you do?" "Why?"

The study of community helpers in the next grade could extend this concept. You could ask the students to name the services that the community provides (you might start by showing them pictures of the helpers in the community), to hypothesize about why more services are not provided, and to think of ways in which the present services could be extended and improved. You could then ask them why current services are not better or more extensive. You should help the students discover that a community has limited funds (derived from taxes), and that it cannot provide unlimited services, such as more street sweeping, more fire stations, or more police.

Topics such as food, clothing, transportation, and our state, traditionally parts of elementary social studies, also contain content that can further develop this concept. Investigating how people must make choices when buying clothing and why public transportation systems are inefficient in many of our cities, and becoming aware of the continuous search by state officials for additional funds to provide needed public services, will extend the concept of scarcity in later grades.

Production, goods, services, consumption, exchange, and interdependence are economic concepts that should also be built into the social studies program. To facilitate the teaching of these concepts and to extend students' understanding of an economic system, you can pose the three basic economic problems: What goods and services shall we produce and in what amounts? How shall they be produced? For whom shall they be produced? You can also help the students determine, through their inquiries, how the problems are solved by different kinds of societies. You should select societies that have different kinds of economies so that the students can derive the generalization that all human groups have solved these basic economic problems and have invented a wide variety of ways to solve them.

NATIONAL CONTENT STANDARDS IN ECONOMICS

The National Content Standards in Economics is an important tool for helping educators develop curricula that can enable students in grades K–12 to view issues from an economic perspective and better understand major economic principles, concepts, and generalizations. There are 20 economic content standards. Each standard includes a rationale, benchmarks, and instructional resources. The standards were developed by representatives from a coalition of organizations including the National Council on Economic Education (NEE), the National Association of Economic Educators, the Foundation for Teaching Economics, and the American Economic Association's Committee on Economic Education. Table 13.2 contains the economics standards.

TEACHING STRATEGIES

Generalization

> All members of a society are economically interdependent; individual producers of goods and services exchange with others to get the goods and services to satisfy their basic wants and needs.

Primary Grades

Have students compare the self-sufficiency of pioneers living on farms with the interdependence of people in today's society. Research the following questions: What was the source and process of obtaining butter in pioneer days? What is it today?

Lead the students into a discussion about how pioneer farmers obtained butter. Bring out the points that they would milk the cow, set the milk in a cool place to allow the cream to separate from the milk, and then place the cream in a churn and mix it until butter appeared. After churning, the butter was removed, washed, salted, and shaped. It was then used for eating and cooking. If it is possible to obtain whole, unprocessed milk in your area, bring some to school so that the students can see how the cream and milk separate. Then have students skim the cream from the top of the milk, place it in an old-fashioned churn if one is available, and churn the butter. If whole, unprocessed milk and a churn are not available, purchase thick cream from the grocery store and place it in a jar. Students can take turns shaking it until butter is obtained.

Next, show a videotape or a series of pictures that illustrate how butter gets from cows to the pupils' morning toast. If there is a dairy or creamery accessible, plan visits to these places. After the students have seen a visual presentation illustrating how milk is produced and have taken a field trip, have them develop a pictograph for the bulletin board showing the people and processes involved in the journey of butter to their tables.

The students can also make a pictograph illustrating the processing and consumption of butter during pioneer days and compare the production of butter during these two periods.

Discuss the following questions:

1. Are more people involved in processing butter now, or were there more during the pioneer period?
2. How do they help one another?
3. How would people in a pioneer town obtain butter?
4. How would we obtain butter if the plant workers who process it went on strike?
5. Is butter today better? Why or why not?

TABLE 13.2. *National Standards in Economics*

Students will understand that:

Productive resources are limited. Therefore, people cannot have all the goods and services they want; as a result, they must choose some things and give up others.

Effective decision-making requires comparing the additional costs of alternatives with the additional benefits. Most choices involve doing a little more or a little less of something; few choices are all-or-nothing decisions.

Different methods can be used to allocate goods and services. People, acting indvidually or collectively through government, must choose which methods to use to allocate different kinds of goods and services.

People respond predictably to positive and negative incentives.

Voluntary exchange occurs only when all participating parties expect to gain. This is true for trade among individuals or organizations within a nation, and among individuals or organizations in different nations.

When individuals, regions, and nations specialize in what they can produce at the lowest cost and then trade with others, both production and consumption increase.

Markets exist when buyers and sellers interact. This interaction determines market prices and thereby allocates scarce goods and services.

Prices send signals and provide incentives to buyers and sellers. When supply or demand changes, market prices adjust, affecting incentives.

Competition among sellers lowers costs and prices, and encourages producers to produce more of what consumers are willing and able to buy. Competition among buyers increases prices and allocates goods and services to those people who are willing and able to pay the most for them.

Institutions evolve in market economies to help individuals and groups accomplish their goals. Banks, labor unions, corporations, legal systems, and not-for-profit organizations are examples of important institutions. A different kind of institution, clearly defined and well-enforced property rights, is essential to a market economy.

Money makes it easier to trade, borrow, save, invest, and compare the value of goods and services.

Interest rates, adjusted for inflation, rise and fall to balance the amount saved with the amount borrowed, thus affecting the allocation of scarce resources between present and future uses.

Have your students engage in a block-building contest. Obtain two sets of blocks. One student will work with one set of blocks and two students with the other set. The rest of the class will observe the two teams to see which team can build a structure more quickly using all the blocks. Before they begin building, have the observers make predictions regarding which team will be finished first and why. Repeat the contest several times to see whether their predictions are verified each time. If the student who is working alone wins, ask the students why this happened. A possible response might be that the two people were not working well together. Ask the students what they observed as advantages and disadvantages of working alone and with a partner.

Show a videotape or a series of pictures depicting the construction of a modern-day house. Next, put a large picture of a new house in the center of a bulletin board. Have the students list and discuss the kinds of workers who would be

TABLE 13.2. *(Continued)*

Income for most people is determined by the market value of the productive resources they sell. What workers earn depends, primarily, on the market value of what they produce and how productive they are.

Entrepreneurs are people who take the risks of organizing productive resources to make goods and services. Profit is an important incentive that leads entrepreneurs to accept the risks of business failure.

Investment in factories, machinery, new technology, and the health, education, and training of people can raise future standards of living.

There is an economic role for government to play in a market economy whenever the benefits of a government policy outweigh its costs. Governments often provide for national defense, address environmental concerns, define and protect property rights, and attempt to make markets more competitive. Most government policies also redistribute income.

Costs of government policies sometimes exceed benefits. This may occur because of incentives facing voters, government officials, and government employees, because of actions by special interest groups that can impose costs on the general public, or because social goals other than economic efficiency are being pursued.

A nation's overall levels of income, employment, and prices are determined by the interaction of spending and production decisions made by all households, firms, government agencies, and others in the economy.

Unemployment imposes costs on individuals and nations. Unexpected inflation imposes costs on many people and benefits some others because it arbitrarily redistributes purchasing power. Inflation can reduce the rate of growth of national living standards because individuals and organizations use resources to protect themselves against the uncertainty of future prices.

Federal government budgetary policy and the Federal Reserve System's monetary policy influence the overall levels of employment, output, and prices.

Source: Reprinted from *Voluntary National Content Standards in Ecomonics,* copyright © 1997, National Council on Economic Education, New York, New York. Used with permission. Excerpts are reprinted from these pages: 1, 3, 4, 7, 9, 11, 13, 15, 17, 19, 20, 22, 24, 26, 28. 30, 33, 35, 36, 39.

needed to build the new house. After these have been listed, have students draw pictures of these workers, label them, and place them on the bulletin board around the house.

Use the homemaking corner of your classroom to illustrate the interdependence of family members. If you don't have a homemaking corner, assemble some appropriate props for the following role-playing situation. Have students role-play a working father, a working mother, a new baby, and a school-age child. While the rest of the class observes, have the students act out their parts in the homemaking corner according to their own interpretations. Ask the following questions and list responses on the board:

1. What jobs does each member of the family carry out?
2. How does each family member help the others?

3. Which family members do the most work? Why?
4. Are there other family members who could do more work? Who are they and what kind of work could they do?

Next, change the composition of the family by eliminating the father role. Discuss how the jobs of the mother and children might expand as a result of the elimination of the father role.

1. What additional work will the mother have to do?
2. What other jobs might the child do at home to help the family?

Have students role-play this family situation. Observers will list their observations, as in the first role-playing situation. Change the composition of the family a third time by eliminating the mother role and reinstating the father role. Discuss the same questions, and have the students act out their new family roles. The pupils will list their observations of jobs done by family members and how each member helps the others.

Discuss the similarities and differences among the different lists of family services. Ask, "What could we say was true of each family situation?" Rephrase the question as necessary to solicit responses indicating that the students recognize the interdependence of family members for services.

Intermediate Grades

A number of the goods and services needed by modern-day families are more easily obtained when families get together to pay for them. These goods and services are usually paid for with tax monies or when the people use them. Such services might include providing water, roads, electricity, schools, fire protection, street cleaning, police protection, health facilities, parks, street repair, stoplights, and bus services.

Have your students interview their parents to find out how many and what kinds of goods and services mentioned above are used by their families. Have students also find out what percentage of their family's taxes go for what items and which services are paid for directly when used.

After students have collected this information, pool the information, chart it as indicated here, and answer the questions that follow.

Goods and Services	Source of Revenue	Amount of Revenue
Electricity	Direct payment according to amount of kilowatts used	
Schools	Taxes	20%
.	.	.
.	.	.
.	.	.

1. Why is it to the mutual benefit of the people in the community to pay for these goods and services together?
2. Are there some goods or services listed that are no longer useful to the community as a whole, and that should be dropped or replaced? Support your answer with facts.
3. Are there some goods or services not listed that should be added and paid for by the entire community? Support your answer with facts.
4. In some communities a service that has been paid for directly upon use has had difficulty maintaining itself financially. Tax support has been proposed and added in some cases. Thus the service is both tax-supported and paid for directly. One such example is the transit system in Seattle, Washington. A city transit tax of 50 cents was added to the city electric light bill. The city made riding the bus more attractive by adding several Blue Streak Lines, which provided rapid service for those who work in the city. Have students examine their chart to determine whether there have been similar problems in their community. Then determine how the community solved the problem to the mutual benefit of most of its members. Research on this problem may require some exploration of the newspapers to determine what kinds of problems have existed and what action was taken. There may be a problem for which the solution is currently being sought. If this is the case, have your students research it and make proposals for its solution.

Present your students with the following situation:

Here are three people, each of whom has a problem. Ms. Cline owns a grocery store on the corner. It is just a small store, so she does all the work required to run it. The person who regularly delivers fresh vegetables to the store is ill, and the big delivery companies won't take Ms. Cline's order because it is too small. She will lose customers if she doesn't do something, because fresh vegetables of good quality are one of the main reasons people shop at her store. Ms. Cline calls her friend Mr. Hoboken, who owns his own truck, and asks for his help. Mr. Hoboken says that he can't help because his truck is broken down, and he probably won't be able to get it fixed for several weeks. The next day Mr. Hoboken's neighbor, Mr. Glass, comes to visit and says he lost his job as a mechanic two weeks ago. He hasn't yet been able to find new work. He has run out of funds and wonders whether Mr. Hoboken would be willing to let him have food on credit.

Ask the students to think about how these three people could solve their problems without using money. Then have three students dramatize the roles of the people in the story and show how they solved their problems.

Discuss the following questions:

1. Why were the three people unable to solve their problems alone?
2. Was the solution acted out by the three players a logical one?
3. How does the solution illustrate the interdependence of workers?
4. What are some other examples of interdependence you can think of?

Read the following situation to your students:

> At the beginning of summer vacation, Charles Abernathy built a new doghouse for his dog, Rags. His neighbor, Mr. Herman, liked it and asked Charles to build a similar one for his spaniel, Freckles. He told Charles he would pay him $60. Charles was very excited about this because he wanted to earn money for summer camp and maybe even enough to buy a Stingray bike. Before Charles completed the house for Freckles, another friend came by and asked Charles to build a doghouse for his spaniel, too. Then Ms. Hildreth dropped by and asked Charles to build a house for her Great Dane that would be twice the size of the others he had built. Ms. Hildreth offered to pay him $120 for the job. Before long Charles had orders for 25 doghouses: 20 regular-sized ones and 5 double-sized ones. He began to worry then, because it had taken him about a week to make the first one, including the sanding and painting. How would he ever be able to build 25 doghouses by himself?

After presenting the situation to the students, divide the class into four groups. Direct the groups to devise a very detailed solution to Charles's problem. The solution must be one that allows him to keep his commitment for building the doghouses and possibly to handle some more orders. After the groups have decided on their solutions, have a spokesperson from each group present the group's plan to the class. Discuss the merits of each plan and have the students vote for the one that would work best. Be sure the students support their arguments for and against the various proposals with good reasons.

Upper Grades

Have the students plan a car wash in order to earn money for a cause that is important to them or in order to sponsor some event at your school. Planning should include the following points:

1. What would be the best location for the car wash? Why? (Students may need to investigate the parts of town in which people would be most likely to need their cars washed.)
2. What points will need to be considered regarding the selection of the place to hold the car wash?
3. Would it be better to have several locations? Why or why not? If so, what should those locations be?
4. What would be the most efficient way for the responsibilities to be shared? Why? Why not just have each individual have a car wash in the area around his or her home?
5. What are the best sources of the supplies necessary for carrying out the car wash?
6. What would be the best price to charge for the service?
7. What would be the most effective kind of advertising?
8. Where should the advertising be distributed?
9. How long in advance of the sale should advertising be out?
10. Develop a chart representing the interdependence of the operation and the services provided.

Tell your students that they will be playing a game in which half of them will be working in buying teams of two for the Vroom Airplane Company. They will be buying the following items: aluminum, engines, tires, and electrical wiring. They will be negotiating with representatives, teams of two, of other companies in the United States and in other countries. Each company team selling a product will have a standard price per unit of measure for their goods. Each company team will have a recommended bargaining procedure. The major bargaining device is the promise to buy a certain number of planes. The company teams may negotiate within a range of $18 to $160 for the cost per unit of measure and may promise to buy from 0 to 25 planes. The following are the standard prices and recommended bargaining procedures suggested by company presidents to their sales representatives.

Aluminum
1. Adanac: $21 per unit measure
   If you buy from this foreign country, you receive an extra point because you will be furthering the international balance of payments.
   The president of the company recommends you order 15 new Vroom planes.
2. Lubeck Aluminum, U.S.: $15 per unit of measure
   If you buy their aluminum, they will give you a bonus of aluminum serving trays for food service use on your planes.

Engines
1. Jolyes Joyce: $300,000 per unit measure
   The president of the country in which this company is located will purchase 13 Vroom planes if you buy their engines.
2. Standard Electric: $296,355 per unit of measure
   Will guarantee a sale of 15 planes if you also purchase their wiring.

Tires and related rubber components
1. Goodday: $6 per unit of measure
2. F. B. Richgood: $9 per unit of measure

Electrical wiring
1. Standard Electric: $30 per unit of measure
2. Housevesting: $33 per unit of measure

   Their subsidiary, Ajax Airlines, will buy 5 planes.

Give the students an opportunity to get the constraints of their roles well in mind. Direct each buying team and selling team to keep very careful and accurate records, subject to audit, in order to substantiate their business negotiations. Designate four areas of the room with signs of the four negotiating companies. The Vroom teams will travel to the "offices" of the selling teams for conferences. After all the teams have made their purchases and sales, have each Vroom buying team present their business deal to the class, which will vote for the winning team. The team that obtains the lowest total cost per unit, therefore the lowest cost of production, and sells the most planes is the winner.

If there is a major industry or business in the area you live in, have your students write or visit it. Interview some of its representatives to determine some of the major supplies they use in production. Have the students ask:

1. Which supplies do employees of the company produce themselves?
2. Which supplies does the company order? From whom?
3. Where does the company get the materials for those items it makes itself?
4. Where do the suppliers get their raw materials?

When the students have collected this information, have them develop a large bulletin board illustrating the chain of goods and services that goes into the making of that product.

SUMMARY

Economics is primarily concerned with how people attempt to satisfy their unlimited wants with limited resources. The key concept in the discipline is scarcity; one of its major principles is that there are not enough resources for us to satisfy all of our wants. The production, exchange, and consumption of goods and services are also dominant concerns of the discipline. In their study of scarcity, economists try to determine how each society solves the three basic economic problems: What goods and services shall be produced and in what amounts? How shall they be produced? For whom shall they be produced?

The major research method used in economics is the intellectual experiment. In using this strategy, economists assume that all the variables are constant except those whose effect they are trying to ascertain. Economic concepts are probably more precise than those in any of the other social sciences. Not only is there a great deal of agreement about what the key concepts in economics are, but the definitions of economic concepts are highly standardized. The nature of economic concepts considerably facilitates the job of curriculum builders when they try to identify economic concepts for inclusion in the social studies curriculum. Furthermore, economic research tends to be more objective than research in any of the other social sciences; most economic data are quantitative. Highly statistical techniques are often used to analyze data in the discipline. We can identify two major approaches within the discipline: economic analysis and policy economics. The goal of economic analysis is to develop scientific generalizations and theory. The objective of policy economics is to use generalizations and theory to solve the economic problems that society faces. While economists usually agree on their scientific generalizations, they often make highly conflicting recommendations in the policy area, because they have different values and ideas about what the proper economic goals of society should be.

Because of the complex nature of society, there is a tremendous need for schools to help students develop economic literacy and understanding. Almost all the social problems pervasive in our society have economic aspects. Students will be able to make much more reflective decisions about political candidates, referenda, and economic proposals if they understand the general principles of our economic system.

Students should have experiences in the earliest grades that will help them to gain some understanding of economics. All the topics traditionally covered in social studies can be viewed from an economic perspective because economics does not consist of specific content but consists of a unique way of looking at human behavior. When students consider the family, the community, the state, and the world, they can be helped to view the problems from an economic perspective. Economic concepts and generalizations can also help students to understand more clearly many of the experiences that they have each day.

REFLECTION AND ACTION ACTIVITIES

1. What is the economic perspective? What key concepts do economists use in studying human behavior? How does the economic perspective differ from the conceptual tools used by other social scientists to study human behavior?
2. What are the three basic economic problems that must be solved by all societies? Illustrate, with a teaching plan, how students in the elementary grades can use a data retrieval chart to derive generalizations related to these three basic problems.
3. How did the ideas of Adam Smith differ from those of the mercantilists? In what ways were Smith's ideas overly optimistic?
4. What was the central argument set forth in Keynes's *The General Theory of Employment, Interest and Money*? Compare and contrast the ideas of the mercantilists, Smith, and Keynes. To what extent does the U.S. economy reflect the ideas of the mercantilists, Smith, and Keynes?
5. What is the intellectual experiment? Give examples of how an economist uses this method to study a problem. What are the advantages of this method? Disadvantages? Illustrate, with a teaching plan, how you would help students to understand this method of research.
6. Compare and contrast economic analysis and policy economics in terms of goals and research methods. Why is it important to distinguish these two components of the discipline? What contributions can each make to the social studies curriculum?
7. Analyze a teaching unit in your curriculum library. What economic concepts and generalizations does the unit contain? What economic concepts and generalizations would you add to or delete from the unit in order to make it more effective? How else would you change the unit to increase its quality?
8. Select one of the following generalizations and design a series of activities (similar to the ones in this chapter) that can be used to teach it to students in the (a) primary grades, (b) middle grades, and (c) upper grades.
   a. All members of a society are economically interdependent; individual producers exchange goods and services with others to get what they require to satisfy their basic wants and needs.
   b. The conflict between unlimited wants and limited resources means that individuals and societies must make difficult decisions about the utilization of scarce resources.

 *internet links*

TEACHING ECONOMICS

The Internet can bring up-to-date information on economic issues into classrooms. Teachers and students can use the Internet to increase their knowledge and understanding of economics as well as to gain access to information used by economists to analyze economic issues and develop economic forecasts. Examples of websites that can be used by teachers and students are listed below.

1. WebEc-WWW Resources in Economics (http://www.helsinki.fi/WebEc/WebEc.html). An extensive array of free information on economic and technological growth and change can be found at this website. In addition, WebEc contains a list of journals in economics, a calendar of events of interest to economists, and links to the web pages such as those listing information on Nobel Laureates in Economics.

2. Bureau of Labor Statistics (http://stats.bis.gov/). Labor statistics are maintained by the Bureau of Labor Statistics, an agency located within the Department of Labor. Teachers and students can access current and historical data on Average Price Data, Producer Price Index, Employment Cost Index, and 23 other surveys. This web page also links to other governmental information servers, including the treasury and justice departments.

3. Financial News can be found at the following sites:

   Business Week Online (http://www.businessweek.com). The cover story, table of contents, and other information reported in the weekly print edition of *Business Week* can be accessed from this web page. In addition, a wide selection of articles originally published in *Business Week* are available in a searchable archive.

   Black Online Enterprise. (http://www.blackenterprise.com). This web page was developed by *Black Enterprise* Magazine and contains business news and information on conferences, investments, jobs, and other resources for African American entrepreneurs, corporate executives, managers, and professionals.

   CNNfn: The Financial Network (http://cnnfn.com). This web page is a good source for data and analysis of current financial issues. Stock quotes, opening and closing figures for the djia, nasdaq, and bond markets can be found here.

REFERENCES

Bach, G. L. (1987). *Economics: An introduction to analysis and policy* (11th ed.). Englewood Cliffs, NJ: Prentice-Hall.

Banaszak, R. A., & Brennan, D. C. (1983). *Teaching economics: Content and strategies.* Menlo Park, CA: Addison-Wesley.

Bureau of Economic Analysis. (1998). [Online]. Available http://www.bea.doc.gov/bea/dn/niptbl-d.htm [1998, June 11].

Heilbroner, R. L. (1989). *The economic problem* (9th ed.). Englewood Cliffs, NJ: Prentice-Hall.

Kourilsky, M. L. (1989). *Understanding economics: Overview for teachers, experiences for students.* Menlo Park, CA: Addison-Wesley.

McConnell, C. R. (1995). *Economics: Principles, problems, policies* (13th ed.). New York: McGraw-Hill.

Reynolds, L. G. (1988). *Economics: A general introduction* (5th ed.). Homewood, IL: Irwin.

Samuelson, P. A., & Nordhaus, W. D.(1997). *Economics* (16th ed.). New York: McGraw-Hill.

Saunders, P., Bach, G. G., Calderwood, J. D., & Hansen, W. L. (1984). *A framework for teaching the basic concepts (master curriculum guide in economics)* (2nd ed.). New York: Joint Council on Economic Education.

Swartz, T. R., & Weigert, K. M. (1995). *America's working poor.* Notre Dame, IN: University of Notre Dame Press.

U.S. Census Bureau. (1995). [Online]. Available http://www.census.gov [1998, June 11].

FOR FURTHER READING

Amos, O. (1995). *Economic literacy: A comprehensive guide to economic issues from foreign trade to health.* Franklin Lakes, NJ: Career Press.

Children in the marketplace: Lesson plans in economics for grades 3 and 4 (2nd ed.). (1986). New York: Joint Council on Economic Education.

Davis, J. E. (1987). *Teaching economics to young adolescents: A research-based rationale.* San Francisco: Foundation for Teaching Economics.

Edwards, J. (1994). *Money: A thematic unit.* Westminster, CA: Teacher Created Materials.

Galbraith, J. K. (1977). *The age of uncertainty: A history of economic ideas and their consequences.* Boston: Houghton Mifflin.

Frey, B. S. (1992). *Economics as a science of human behavior: Towards a new social science paradigm.* Boston: Kluwer.

Heilbroner, R. L. (1987) *The worldly philosophers: The lives, times and ideas of the great economic thinkers* (6th ed.). New York: Touchstone.

Levy, F. (1996). *Teaching the new basic skills: Principles for educating children to thrive in a changing economy.* New York: Free Press.

Miller, S. L. (1988). *Economic education for citizenship.* Bloomington, IN: Social Studies Development Center.

Pleeter, S., & Way, P. K. (1993). *Economics in the news* (2nd ed.). New York: Longman.

Pool, J. C. (1997). *Macroeconomics: The big picture.* Winchester, VA: Durell Institute of Monetary Science at Shenandoah University.

Walstad, W. R., & Sanders, P. (1990). *The principles of economics course: A handbook for instructors* (11th ed.). New York: McGraw-Hill.

CHAPTER 14

Geography: Structure, Concepts, and Strategies

*f*EATURE

THE HISTORICAL GEOGRAPHY OF HISPANICS IN THE UNITED STATES

Geography can add an important dimension to students' understanding of history. The geography that underlies current and past settlement patterns of Hispanics in the United States provides contextual information that can help students better understand contemporary issues associated with English-only laws, bilingual education, and undocumented immigration.

Hispanics are becoming one of the largest ethnic groups in the United States. The Hispanic population in the United States increased from 14.6 million in 1960 to 22.35 million in 1990 (Wright, 1997). After Mexico, Spain, Argentina, and Columbia, the United States is the fifth largest Spanish-speaking country in the world. This feature examines how political, social, and economic factors influenced the population distribution of Hispanics from 1850 to 1990.

The first Europeans to permanently settle in the Southwest were from Spain. Santa Fe was founded by the Spanish in 1607. It became the capitol of New Mexico in 1610. By 1700 the Spanish had established missions in southern Arizona, and by 1716 they had settled in east Texas. By 1769 Spanish settlers had established a string of missions along the California coast.

In 1848 the Southwest became part of the United States under the terms of the Treaty of Guadalupe Hidalgo. In that treaty, the United States gained all the land north of the Rio Grande and north of a horizontal line drawn one marine league south of the Port of San Diego extending to the Rio Grande at El Paso. Five years later, as a result of the Gadsden Purchase, the U.S.–Mexico border in southern Arizona was established. In 1850, two years after the signing of the Treaty of Guadalupe Hidalgo, the Hispanic population in the Southwest was 101,050 with 69,500 Mexicans in New Mexico, 18,550 in Texas, 11,700 in California, and 1,300 in Arizona. Political power and the future of the region had been transferred from Mexico City to Washington, D.C. However, the hearts and minds of many of the people who lived in the Southwest remained connected to Mexican culture, language, and history. The familial links to Mexico that were a part of the Southwest in 1848 are still evident today.

In 1930 the Census Bureau created a new ethnic category for Mexicans. All people who were born in Mexico and who were not White, Negro, Native American, Chinese, or Japanese were categorized as Mexican. At that time, 1,422,533 Mexicans lived in the United States. Ninety percent of the Mexican population in the United States lived in the West, primarily in Texas.

Migration from Mexico continued with Mexicans serving as a primary source of labor to clear and till the land and to build irrigation canals. Between 1900 and 1935, approximately 700,000 people migrated to the United States from Mexico. Mexicans primarily migrated to three major areas: the sugar beet regions of the North and South Platte Rivers in Wyoming, Nebraska, and Colorado; the fruit and vegetable regions of the Arkansas River in Colorado and Kansas; and the cotton, fruit, and vegetable areas of the Sacramento, San Joaquin, and Kern Rivers In Central California.

By the 1930s, Mexicans were also being recruited to work in factories. More than 30,000 Mexicans were working in factories in the Chicago-Gary area in 1930. Most Hispanics, however, were primarily located in the West and were a small percentage of the population in the Midwest.

The Bracero program had a major influence on Mexican migration. It was a guest worker program that was in effect from 1942 to 1964. The program guaranteed transportation, food, housing, and a minimum wage for Mexican workers, who were called Braceros. As a result of the Bracero program, Mexicans workers moved to the Texas plains, the Yakima River Valley in Washington, and the Snake River Valley in Idaho. Even though the Bracero program provided a reliable source of labor, some farmers believed it was too expensive and had too many controls. They opted not to use the program and hired undocumented Mexicans who were less expensive and easier to control than Braceros.

During periods of recession, Mexicans in the Bracero program were repatriated or forcibly returned to Mexico. At the end of the Korean War, when few Mexican workers were needed, the United States established Operation Wetback to find and return undocumented workers to Mexico. The program repatriated over 3.8 million undocumented Mexicans. At the end of the recession, however, the demand for labor in several economic sectors, particularly agriculture, resulted in a termination of Operation Wetback and a return to previous levels of undocumented Mexican workers.

It is relatively easy for people in Puerto Rico to migrate to the United States because they are U.S. citizens. During the 1950s, Puerto Rican migration to the United States increased. The Puerto Rican presence on the East Coast changed the geographic distribution of U.S. Hispanics. In 1990, there were 2.7 million Puerto Ricans in the United States. Most Puerto Ricans lived in New York City, but large numbers also lived in New Jersey, Massachusetts, Connecticut, and Pennsylvania.

In 1930, 92 percent of U.S. Hispanics lived in the West. By 1960, 78 percent lived in the West, 17 percent lived in the Northeast, 4 percent lived in the Midwest, and one percent lived in the South. By 1990, 12.2 million Hispanics lived in the Northeast, Midwest, and South compared to 10.1 million in the West. Interestingly, in recent years, the direction of Puerto Rican emigration has been reversed.

In 1990, Cubans (4.8 percent) along with Mexicans (61.2 percent) and Puerto Ricans (12.1 percent) made up the largest percentage of the Hispanic population. Cubans began arriving in the United States in large numbers after the Cuban Revolution in 1959. The Cubans who arrived at that time were immediately granted refugee status and allowed to remain in the United States. After failed attempts to relocate the Cubans to other parts of the United States, south Florida became a center for Cuban Americans. Between 1959 and 1994, approximately 715,000 Cubans relocated to the United States, most to south Florida.

Until 1982, Central Americans, South Americans, and Dominicans were lumped together in the U.S. Census under the category of "Other" Hispanics. In 1990, 2 million Hispanic Americans in this category lived in the West, 1.5 million lived in the Northeast, 1.28 million in the South, and 279,000 in the Midwest. Beginning in 1982, the Census Bureau created a new category: Central and South American. In 1990, 2.8 percent of Americans were of Central or South American origin. This represents 13.8 percent of the Hispanic population. About three-fourths of all Dominicans lived in New York City (357,868) in 1990.

Until the 1960s, the U.S. Hispanic population was overwhelmingly Mexican and western. After 1965, changes in immigration laws led to increased migration from Central and South America. Many of these immigrants moved to eastern and southern states. By 1990, only 45 percent of Hispanics lived in the West. However, California (34.4 percent) and Texas (19.4 percent), two states that were part of Northern Mexico, continue to be regions where large numbers of Hispanics live. As more Hispanics immigrate to the United States, a more geographically and socially heterogeneous Latino population will be created. However, Mexican Americans will continue to be the dominant group among Hispanics for some time into the future. In 1990 Mexican Americans represented 60 percent of the Hispanic population, followed by Puerto Ricans in the mainland at 12 percent and Cuban Americans at almost 5 percent. These figures suggest that the legacy of Mexican culture, language, history, and familial ties will continue to be reflected in Hispanic issues and concerns.

Source: Adapted with permission from *Journal of Geography,* Vol. 96, No. 3, pp. 134–145. Used with permission of the National Council for Geographic Education.

THE GEOGRAPHIC PERSPECTIVE

Geography is one of the oldest social sciences. It dates back to the time of the ancient Greeks. The term geography comes from the Greek words *geo* (earth) and *graphein* (to write). Geography is an integrative discipline that brings together the physical and human dimensions of the world in the study of people, places, and environments. The earth's surface and the processes that shape it are its subject matter. Geographers are interested in the features that give a place its special character and differentiate it from other places. They strive to develop descriptions and explanations that carefully integrate people and the place and space in which they live by seeking answers to questions about where things and people are located, why they are located in particular places, and what difference their location makes (Gersmehl, 1995).

FIVE TRADITIONS

As we have noted in previous chapters, most of the social sciences are comparatively new; they emerged as distinct disciplines or fields of knowledge only within the past century. Geography, however, has a very long history. The ancient Greeks and Egyptians carefully observed the course of the sun and the stars, accurately charted the dimensions of their world around the Mediterranean, and recorded descriptions brought back by traders and travelers of the lands and people beyond their borders. Out of this long tradition of careful observation and study of the earth have come five different perspectives, or research interests, shared by many geographers. While each is somewhat different in its approach to the study of *place* and *space,* they are recognized and accepted by most geographers as being well within the mainstream of the discipline. Taken together, these five traditions reflect the broad scope of the field and the varied approaches used by geographers. Elements of each of these traditions may be found in the geography components of the social studies curriculum in the schools (Broek et al., 1980).

Physical Geography or the Earth Science Tradition

The study of the surface of the earth, particularly the arrangement and function of natural features, is physical geography. This study includes physical features, such as plains, valleys, mountains, and rivers; the weather and climate of the atmosphere (meteorology); the action of waves, tides, and currents (oceanography); and the vegetation and animal life of the earth. This approach has always been a strong one among geographers, particularly as they sought to collect and systematize the rapidly expanding knowledge of the world brought back by travelers and explorers. In large measure, these early studies and reports were descriptive.

Regional Geography or the Area Studies Tradition

Regional geographers study an area or region of the earth's surface that is homogeneous in terms of some specific criteria such as location, manufacturing, land forms, climate, economic activity, cultural trait, or ethnic origin of the people. The regional geographer asks: "What are the key features that give the region its character?" "How are these key features or criteria related to other features in the same or adjacent areas?" Thus, the regional geographer attempts to present as comprehensive a description and analysis of an area as possible. The regional approach is widely used in the elementary and middle schools. Three types of regions are most commonly studied: *physical regions*, in which the land features are basically alike; *cultural regions,* in which some aspect of culture or level of technology predominates; and *political regions,* which are grouped along the lines of territorial boundaries.

Cultural Geography or the Human-Land Tradition

Cultural geographers study the relationships between people and the environment. With this approach, sometimes called human geography or ecological geography, the geographer is specifically interested in the interrelations of cultural development and environmental conditions. The importance or use that we make of the physical and biotic features of the earth is a function of the attitudes, objectives, and technical skills of our culture. Thus, coal could be considered a "valuable natural resource" only when we had discovered it, learned what to do with it, and had the technology to produce it in usable quantities.

Spatial Geography or the Location Theory Tradition

Spatial geography centers on the location of places and the patterns of distribution. This tradition seeks to explain why features such as cities, mountains, or human populations are arranged as they are on the earth's surface, and why there are differences in the densities, dispersions, and patterns. Another major part of this tradition is the geometry of the earth's surface, which includes the study of maps and the design of map projections (cartography), and the precise location and mapping of places and surfaces of the earth (geodesy and geodetic survey).

Spatial geography often concentrates on developing theories of location. Spatial geographers have studied the central location of towns, the spatial interaction or movements of trade, people, and ideas, and the spatial structure of urban areas and their relation to surrounding areas. In marked contrast to the regional or cultural geographer, the spatial geographer is more likely to use quantified data and statistical methods to determine the interaction of a cluster of variables relating to economic activities. Perhaps more than any of the other geographic traditions described above, spatial geographers have attempted to develop high-order generalizations and to weave these into comprehensive theories about the location of place and space.

The Historical Geography Tradition

This is the study of the geographic change of a region as it has occurred over time. In contrast to the four approaches already described, historical geographers use time as the main dimension for studying spatial distributions and patterns on the earth's surface. They are chiefly concerned with how various features of the landscape appeared in the past and with the physical and human patterns that have

profile

DOREEN MASSEY

Geography Matters: The Intersection of the Social and Spatial

Doreen Massey is an internationally known human geographer whose research focuses on space and place. Massey's work includes but is not limited to theory building, examining analytical ideas, and data-gathering. It also includes what has been termed emancipatory geography or social action. Massey and her colleagues at the Open University in London, England, use the term "Geography Matters" to call attention to the human dimension of geography, to challenge power structures, and to question the authority of geographical accounts and explanations.

In her book *Space, Place, and Gender,* Massey bridges the divisions between social and natural categories in geography and links components of human and physical geography. Massey's understanding that social relations and economic relations are interconnected in complex ways is also reflected in her research on high-tech scientists who work in private industry in England. In that work she raises questions about the construction of masculinities at work and describes how the masculine poles of classic Western dualism, such as reason/nonreason, are enacted in the everyday work lives of men.

Doreen Massey's work is raising new questions and drawing connections between geographers and theorists in fields such as economics, political science, and sociology. Her work ensures that geography will continue to matter to people on the margins of society as well as those at its center.

combined to bring about a change in that landscape. Thus, the geographer shares with the historian the dimension of time—but in quite a different way. For example, a historian might consider the return of Lenin from exile as a key event in the Bolshevik Revolution of 1917, whereas a geographer might consider the elimination of private land holdings and the establishment of collective farms during the 1920s as marking a significant change in the geography of Russia.

In summary, these five traditions or approaches to geography—physical, regional, cultural, spatial, and historical—represent a broad range of research interests and methods of investigation within geography. Elements of each are used in the social studies curriculum at various grade levels; each helps to provide a balanced approach to the study of geography. Given these rich and varied traditions, there is little reason for teachers to rely so heavily on the memorization of place names, capital cities, and lists of products as the exclusive approach to geography.

THE DEVELOPMENT OF GEOGRAPHIC THEORY

Geographers tend to be more concerned with developing maximum understanding of individual areas rather than with the formulation of broad universal laws and principles. Consequently, there has been comparatively little growth in the formation of theory that systematizes sets of high-order generalizations or principles into a comprehensive explanation of complex phenomena. In this section we will briefly describe three prominent theories in geography: (1) location theory, (2) central place theory, and (3) spatial structure theory.

Location Theory

How can we explain why things are located where they are? Is there some relationship, for example, between the location of cattle grazing lands and the distance to a meat packing center? Or if we wanted to locate a new branch of a business or a manufacturing plant, could we determine an optimal location? These questions are the concern of geographers (and economists, too), who are now able to turn to a rather well-developed body of knowledge, called *location theory*, for appropriate answers or ways of finding answers.

Location theory has at various times been a rather broad umbrella for studies derived from the related fields of economics, urban studies, and transportation studies. Essentially, it is the study of the geography of economic activities. Put more broadly, it is the study of the effects of place and space on the organization of economic activities.

Central Place Theory

Central place theory has played a key role in studying the location of towns and cities in urban geography. Based on a study of the agricultural towns in south Germany, Christaller (1966) discovered that small villages tended to cluster about larger towns or cities in a rather hexagonal pattern. These larger towns served as the center for many important marketing, social, and cultural activities. The development of the railroad and, more recently, the interstate network of freeways and airways has greatly changed the growth and importance of many towns and cities, thus making Christaller's earlier concept of hexagonal trade patterns obsolete. Although many modifications have been made in central place theory, it remains an important component in the study of urban geography (Harper & Schmuddle, 1978).

Spatial Structure Theory

A third theory in geography that has considerable importance, especially in urban geography, is the spatial structure theory. In many ways this is an outgrowth of the central place theory. It conceives of space on the earth's surface as being ordered in a hierarchy of use and function. An expansion of the central place theory is that cities and towns are arranged in a functional hierarchy of ascending order, from the smallest hamlet through the town, the city, and finally to the large metropolitan center. Such theoretical patterns provide useful methods of examining and determining the ordered use of land and the patterns of various land usage.

Each of the three major theories—location, central place, and spatial structure—plays a useful role in describing, explaining, and predicting the complex events of the organization and interaction of place and space, especially as they relate to the field of urban geography. We will now discuss a number of the concepts that are central to the work of the geographer, ones that can serve as organizers for planning units in the elementary and middle schools.

GEOGRAPHIC CONCEPTS

The broad areas of location theory and spatial interaction, urban spatial patterns, cultural diffusion, and environmental perception represent some of the more prominent geographic emphases in the social studies curriculum. Central to them are a number of key social science concepts and related subconcepts such as location, spatial interaction, urban spatial patterns, internal structure of a city, cultural diffusion, and environmental perception. Each of these is discussed below. Examples of how each concept might be taught at various grades are given.

Location

One of the most essential tasks of the geographer is the location or identification of place and space. From earliest times, geographers have been concerned with the precise location of towns and rivers, great bodies of land or water, and other features. Systems of latitude and longitude, the distance between places expressed in miles, and measures of area all help to define or identify the location of particular places or spaces on the earth's surface. But the concept of location also includes several other closely related subconcepts that greatly extend the rather narrow meaning of precise location described above. These are site, situation, and environment.

Site refers to the location of a place in terms of its local internal features and resources. This may be the presence of a number of steep hills in a town, a winding river, sheltering hillsides, or the juncture of two main railroad lines. Such internal features are often key factors in studying the growth of a city, or related phenomena such as settlement patterns and the development of industry.

Situation refers to the larger context of a site. Thus, *situation* might refer to the location of a town within a valley and its surrounding hilly or mountainous country, or to the location of a larger city and its relation to the network of rail, air, and waterways that connect it to many other surrounding places. Thus, whereas *site* deals with the internal features of a place, *situation* deals with the external relations of the place and its interaction with other places.

The term *environment* is used to refer to the totality of both site and situation. In its broadest context, this includes the physical, biotic, and cultural features of the landscape and their interactions. Current usage of the term *environment* in the context of pollution and conservation of natural resources is too restricted and limited a use of the term. Students should use the term in its broadest meaning. *Cultural development* and *technological growth* are part of the total picture of the earth's surface.

Activities

1. In primary grades students can locate their school in terms of its site: for example, at the corner of Northfield Road and Clarkwood Street; near a lot of trees; close to the Granada apartments where I live.

2. Older students can use a map to identify the situation of their town: for example, surrounded on all sides by other small towns; a large freeway goes close by; the land is flat as far as you can see; part of Cuyahoga County that includes the city of Cleveland.

3. Use town maps with simple grid systems (letters along the top and bottom and numbers along the sides) to locate familiar landmarks: streets, schools, shopping centers, and so forth. Be sure students can use the system in both ways. They should be able to locate a street listed on the map index as Northfield Road, D-4, as well as to define the coordinates of a shopping center by tracing with their fingers (and later eyes alone) to the coordinates J-6.

4. In upper grades, ask students to describe the location of a city in terms of its environment. Cleveland, for example, might be described as being a major port city on Lake Erie with shipping links to the upper Midwest, Canada, and the Atlantic Ocean; rail, air, and highway connections to Chicago, St. Louis, and New York; steel mills and auto assembly plants; large and diverse ethnic populations; and an outstanding symphony orchestra and art museum.

5. With older students, use the latitude and longitude system of coordinates on the globe to teach the precise location of places (see Chapter 5). Locate New York, San Francisco, London, Canberra, Tokyo. (Note the many related concepts needed for a full understanding: hemisphere, Prime or Greenwich Meridian, east and west longitude, equator, north and south latitude, and degrees of a circle {actually a half-circle} around the earth.)

Spatial Interaction

Very few places on earth exist entirely alone, isolated, or wholly independent from one another. Instead, people form relationships with other places as they move from one place to another, engage in economic trade, provide services, or transmit ideas, learning, and culture. Geographers use the term *spatial interaction* to refer to the relationship of one place to another within the surrounding space and to the varying degrees of mutual dependence that may exist between places. Chicago, for example, is the hub of a great metropolis with links to a ring of surrounding cities in other states including Milwaukee, Rockford, Indianapolis, and Toledo. Thus, the relationship between these cities and the hub city, Chicago, is called *spatial interaction*. Geographers look for the links that aid or hamper the movement of people, trade, or ideas between these cities and for the pattern these movements create. They use the subconcepts *circulation* and *access* to help describe the relationships in spatial interaction.

Circulation refers to the patterns of movement between places. Valleys, mountain passes, interstate highways, rivers, canals, and airways are types of geographic features serving as paths for the circulation of people or trade. In contrast, deserts, lakes, mountains, large swamps, and jungle areas are surface features that may at one time have been barriers to the easy movement of people and goods. Modern technology now provides the means for overcoming them. Yet curiously, it is the same technology which now creates new barriers to circulation. Major freeways bypass whole areas of the countryside or the crowded cities. Many smaller towns and cities now find themselves almost cut off entirely from the movement of goods, people, and ideas by freeways that skirt around them to provide high-speed movement, uninterrupted by the flow of local traffic.

Access deals with the easy entry into and exit from the circulation patterns. Cities that are intermediate stops along a main railroad or airline route, that have port facilities on a river or seacoast, or that have entry and exit cloverleaves along a superhighway are all examples of places with good access to the circulation pattern. In contrast, many island areas have only limited ferry service to the mainland and people in vast, remote areas such as Alaska and parts of Australia are connected to the "outside" only by the irregular flights of local bush pilots. In addition, it is not uncommon for people whose towns have been bypassed by freeways to have to drive 20 or 30 miles to enter or leave a modern highway. Lastly, as these same modern, "limited access" freeways cut across large cities, they create great concrete walls that divide traditional neighborhoods, force a major rearrangement of social patterns, and often lead to urban decay. Thus, the modern technology that has helped us overcome some of the circulation limits of mountains and deserts presents new problems of access for small towns and inner-city urban areas.

Activities
1. Ask younger students to name cities or large towns near their homes where they go with their parents to shop, to go to movies or a museum, or to visit relatives. Ask them to describe how they get there and how long it takes.

The teacher can draw a simple outline map on a wall chart to show direction flow and pattern of movement (circulation).

2. Is there a large interstate highway nearby? Ask older students where it goes and what cities are along its route. How close (or far away) is the nearest entry (access)?

3. Using markers and plastic overlays, trace on a map the various connecting links to major cities in your area (highways, railroads, airlines). Are there some links that are seldom used or no longer exist? Why?

4. Using the same maps as in activity 3, trace the linkage for ideas and communications. Where is the nearest regional postal center which sorts, distributes, and forwards all mail? Plot the network of towns and local post offices that are served by the regional postal center. Where are the major and local television stations that serve your area located? Where are local and metropolitan newspapers published? How close or far away are these places?

5. Examine a map of your state or region that shows large interstate freeways. Are there bypassed towns or cities? Explain why and what is likely to happen to them in the future.

6. Have students interview parents or local merchants about how they were affected when a large freeway was built near or through their city or town.

7. Using a topographical or relief map, ask students to locate deserts, swamps, mountains, or large lakes. Investigate how these have been overcome or whether they still remain barriers today. Explain why.

Urban Spatial Patterns

The urban areas of the world provide geographers with an excellent opportunity to study the basic concept of *space* and how it is used. The concept *city,* for example, means a place providing many centralized and specialized services for itself and the surrounding area. The space or distance that people travel to work or shop in the city or to spend their leisure time there is called the city's *sphere of influence.* Put more specifically, what is the average distance a person drives or commutes to work in the city; the maximum distance? Conversely, this same concept applies to the space or distance that newspapers are delivered regularly from the city to outlying areas, that goods (both wholesale and retail) are normally delivered by trucks from city businesses, and by the distance of phone calls made regularly to and from the city. In short, how far beyond the corporate limits of the city does its influence extend? The space within the sphere of influence is variously known as the hinterland, the trade area, the supporting area, or the tributary area.

Another concept of key importance to the urban geographer is that of the town or city as a *central place.* Viewed as a kind of common marketplace, the town is organized to provide a variety of goods and services centralized within a single area. People will come a considerable distance to buy in this market what they cannot buy at a local cluster of convenience stores. Cities are much the same as towns, only on

inquiry strategy

GENDER AND MIGRATION

Gender blindness exists when concepts like migrant and immigrant are primarily presented as male constructs and when issues related to the lives of immigrants are presented from a male perspective and do not illuminate the experiences of women. Students can explore the idea of gender blindness by examining the extent to which social studies books present immigration as a male experience.

Most students study U.S. history, culture, and geography in the fifth and eighth grades. Issues of migration and immigration are typically covered in fifth and eighth grade social studies textbooks. In this lesson, students conduct a content analysis of a fifth and/or eighth grade social studies book.

Introduce the lesson by explaining that the students will be taking on the role of population geographers. Population geographers are concerned with the structure and change of human populations. Human geographers study births, deaths, migration, and immigration as well as political, social, and economic components of population structure and change. Note that while gender is recognized as an important factor in migration research, it wasn't until the 1970s that women emerged as objects of study in research on migration (Morokvasic, 1983). Prior to the 1970s, women immigrants tended to be cast in the roles of wives, daughters, and mothers rather than as independent actors.

To help students understand how gender blindness can result in inaccurate perceptions, share the following example. In the late 1800s, Irish women immigrated in larger numbers than Irish men. From 1871 to 1986 the net female Irish immigration was 1,511,500 compared to a net male migration of 1,502,535 (Diner, 1983). The two main destinations of Irish immigrants were Britain and the United States. In the United States among immigrant groups, the Irish had a female majority by 1900. Census records indicate that by 1900, women represented 54 percent of the Irish immigrants compared to 21 percent for Italian immigrants and 41 percent for German immigrants (Diner, 1983).

Divide your students into four work teams. Select a social studies book and assign each team a different section of the book to review. Ask students to read their sections and identify themes similar to the ones listed below. They should pay attention to the number of times and the ways in which immigrants are identified as men or women.

Themes related to immigrant group members:

in their country of origin
during migration and arrival in the United States
work activities outside the home
work activities within the home including child care
social life
other

TABLE 14.1. *Frequency Distribution of Theme Units by Category*

Theme Category: In their country of origin Theme Unit (write down all examples of this theme and indicate whether males or females were the focus of the discussion or illustration)		
1. 2. 3.	Males	Females
Theme Category: During migration and arrival in United States Theme Unit (write down all examples of this theme and indicate whether males or females were the focus of the discussion or illustration)		
1. 2. 3.	Males	Females
Theme Category: Work activities outside the home Theme Unit (write down all examples of this theme and indicate whether males or females were the focus of the discussion or illustration)		
1. 2. 3.	Males	Females
Theme Category: Work activities within the home including child care Theme Unit (write down all examples of this theme and indicate whether males or females were the focus of the discussion or illustration)		
1. 2. 3.	Males	Females
Theme Category: Social life Theme Unit (write down all examples of this theme and indicate whether males or females were the focus of the discussion or illustration)		
1. 2. 3.	Males	Females
Theme Category: Other Theme Unit (write down all examples of this theme and indicate whether males or females were the focus of the discussion or illustration)		
1. 2. 3.	Males	Females

After students collect their data, ask them to summarize their findings in a chart similar to the one in Table 14.1. Each team should present its findings. This could be done by asking a member of each team to serve on a panel in which findings from each section of the book are discussed. Once students have heard all the findings, ask them to write a statement in which they describe how immigration with respect to gender is represented in the text. If students believe that gender imbalance exists, they should generate a list of ways gender imbalance can be redressed in school texts. Conclude the lesson by having students write to the textbook publisher to share their findings and recommendations.

a much larger scale. But the distance people are willing to travel is proportionate to both the time and cost of the journey and the cost and availability of goods or specialized services. At some point, however, people decide to purchase locally or to travel to some other town where goods are available at a lower cost in terms of time and money.

The growth of large shopping malls over the past several decades, however, has brought about a major change in the geography of cities and has challenged the concept of the city as a central place. Built in outlying suburban areas with easy access to interstate freeways, the shopping malls are virtually small towns under one large roof with a year-round comfortable "climate." When a number of malls surround a city, they form a network of competing economic centers. Many people now do all their major shopping at a mall and seldom, if ever, go downtown to the older central business district. As a result, many downtown stores and businesses moved out of the cities, often to new, more convenient locations in the shopping malls. This has been a major factor in the decay of older cities. For urban renewal planners, the pressing question is how to revitalize the inner core of the cities to attract people to come downtown once again for shopping, professional services, commercial transactions, and recreation.

A development known as *gentrification* is contributing to the revitalization of the central cities. This process consists of the purchase and renovation of houses and stores in deteriorating inner-city communities by middle- and upper-class people. Gentrification, however, has some unfortunate social consequences. The lower-class individuals and small businesses who occupied the older, replaced housing and stores are displaced because they cannot afford to buy or rent the new and expensive properties. Despite its social costs, gentrification does attract young, affluent families, sometimes called *Yuppies*, to the central cities.

Not every city fits the model of a central place. Some cities do not have a central location, nor do they provide centralized services. However, they may have a special feature around which an urban area has developed. They are referred to as *special place* locations. Examples of special place locations are recreational centers such as Vail, Las Vegas, and Monte Carlo; mining centers such as Butte and Anaconda; and capital cities such as Olympia, Washington; Washington, D.C.; and Brazilia.

Finally, there is the concept of *urban sprawl*. This refers to the gradual growth of a city from urban to suburban to rural areas, and the buildup of the areas in between. It is the outward extension of the city through a series of concentric rings. Current efforts at urban renewal suggest some reversal of the outward movement pattern and a trend of return to the central area of a city, closer to the central business district. Town houses are seen by some as a desirable alternative to the long, congested commuting trip from the suburbs.

What happens when urban growth becomes so great that the urban sprawl from one city gradually merges with that of another large city, and there is almost a continuous belt of urban development stretching many miles? Such a combination of large metropolitan areas is called a *megalopolis*. A gigantic urban sprawl stretches for more than 600 miles from southern New Hampshire to northern Virginia, and includes the cities of Boston, New York, Philadelphia, Baltimore, and Washington, D.C. This is the largest megalopolis in the world.

Activities
1. Have students look at local newspaper stands. What newspapers are carried regularly? What paper comes from the city farthest away? Why do you think the store carries that newspaper? Compare the difference in amount and variety of advertising in the local paper and one from a large city. Explain the difference in the two papers.
2. Look in the front pages of a city telephone directory and study the map of local telephone exchanges. From how far out can you make a local call? At what point do the calls become long distance?
3. Look at the advertisements of several major department stores in newspapers of a large city. How far will they normally deliver purchases such as a sofa or a refrigerator?
4. Examine the map of a nearby city's metropolitan transit authority. How far out from the city do the commuter bus lines extend? Rail or subway lines? At what point do major expressways begin to get crowded with inbound commuter traffic heading toward a city?
5. Take a walking tour of a nearby town (or a driving tour of a large city). Jot down in a notebook evidence of centralized facilities or services—for example, large warehouses, grain elevators, railroad yards, large department stores, oil storage tanks, airports (including air cargo terminals). What smaller communities do these facilities serve?
6. Drive along a major highway leading out of a city. How can you tell when you have left the major urban area and entered the suburban residential area? Is there a clear boundary or a gradual transition? How far do you go until you reach a clearly rural area? Or do you begin to reach another urban area? Mark off these different areas on a local road map.
7. Study the classified advertisements in the Sunday paper from a nearby city. Are there any housing ads designed to encourage suburbanites to move back into the city? What special attractions do they offer? Would you move? Explain why?

Internal Structure of a City

So far we have discussed the location of cities and their external relations with other cities. Let us consider briefly several concepts related to the city itself. The internal structure of a city comprises the arrangement of the parts of the city and the function of those parts. The basic pattern of the streets of the city, its layout, refers to the grid pattern of the streets, as in Denver; or the radiating spokes, as in Washington, D.C., or Paris; or to the riverine pattern of Nashville, Tennessee. One of the most useful concepts is the *central business district* (CBD), which is the area marked by the convergence of transportation and commerce linkages. It is the major market center, the trade or business district. It is often referred to as *downtown* in contrast to the less commercial and more residential area often called *uptown*. Huge suburban shopping centers now compete with the CBD. These malls mark the outward expansion of the city and serve as nuclei for the urbanization of residential areas.

The circulation network consists of major streets or rapid transit lines (buses, streetcars, subways, elevated trains, and so forth) into, out of, and around the city. New freeways provide fast and easy access to the suburbs and beyond but also block off and isolate parts of the city by huge moats of concrete. Helicopters and air-taxis sometimes provide entirely new routes in the circulation network of the largest cities.

Another important concept for analyzing the internal structure of a city is its *land use patterns*. Most cities have clearly identifiable zones or sectors of differentiated use, such as the industrial area, the wholesale districts, the theater district, residential areas, the port or terminal transfer area, and the retail sales-banking-office area. The location of these sectors often depends on the location of transportation facilities for the movement of people, goods, and services to and from the area. The change from fixed means of transportation, such as railroads or streetcars, to the more mobile cars, buses, and trucks has produced a series of newer sectors. The older ones have been left to decay; the result is the growth of slums.

Finally, there is the *social variation* in the internal structure of a city. In cities all over the world, minority groups of differing national origins, color, or religion can be found set apart from the rest of the populace in distinctive ethnic communities. Whether they congregate willingly, for reasons of social and cultural identity, or because of discrimination, different ethnic cultures and traditions or use of a language other than English may characterize a neighborhood for several generations. These districts are often among the poorest in the city. Color, however, has been a far more insidious barrier to movement within or out of the city than religion, language, or national origin has ever been. The restriction of African Americans to certain areas of the cities by a variety of legal, economic, and social pressures has created one of our most urgent social problems.

Another aspect of social variation is the level of wealth or income that clearly divides residential areas into upper-, middle-, and lower-income home districts, each with different levels of density, availability of living space, and provision of public services. Similarly, the retail trade area falls into districts based on the wealth or purchasing ability of its clientele. High-fashion shops tend to be uptown, whereas stores carrying low-cost goods, pawn shops, and secondhand stores tend to be in the older, decaying parts of the city. Gentrification has affected the kinds of houses, stores, restaurants, and other types of businesses located in the central cities. The central areas of many cities are being renovated and revitalized. The huge and unfortunate growth in the rate of homelessness in the United States may result in part from the large number of poor people who have been displaced from their central city apartments and homes by gentrification.

Activities

1. Put a plastic overlay on a large map of a nearby city. Trace the main streets with colored pens. Is there a well-defined pattern to the arrangement of streets? How would you describe it?

2. Using a different overlay on the same map, mark off the main streets that contain most of the business offices and retail stores in a city or large town. This is the central business district (CBD).

3. Observe the flow of traffic in a large city or town, particularly during a commuter rush hour. What are the streets that carry most of the traffic into, out of, or across the city at various points? A map showing the routes of buses and the rail lines of a metropolitan transit system will also demonstrate the circulation network of a city.

4. Using the map you made of the CBD in activity 2 above, outline areas or zones of different land use patterns in different colors. For example, outline manufacturing areas, grain or oil storage areas, theater districts, or residential areas.

5. Can you locate various ethnic or cultural neighborhoods on a map? A good clue to look for as you drive around a city is the location of churches, community centers such as a Polish-American club, or ethnic food stores or restaurants. The yellow pages in a phone directory may also give some clues.

6. Make a walking (or driving) tour of the residential area of a nearby city. What characteristics of the houses or of the neighborhood distinguish higher-income areas from lower-income ones?

Cultural Diffusion

An important anthropological concept used by geographers and often neglected in school geography is *cultural diffusion*. It refers to the distribution of some cultural trait such as language, religion, or technological development within a particular area. The geographer interested in cultural diffusion asks: Where are such traits found? What is their dispersion? What is their density? Is the pattern of movement relatively fixed or highly mobile over time and space? What features of the earth's surface appear to be related to the diffusion (or restriction) of a particular cultural trait?

Many studies have traced the immigration and settlement patterns of French-Canadian and Scotch-Irish mill workers in New England, or of German and Scandinavian farmers in the Midwest. Others have traced the concentration or the spread of religious groups, the clustering of elderly citizens in certain areas, and the diffusion of rock music. While avoiding invidious comparisons, the alert and sensitive teacher can easily help students in the middle and upper grades to identify neighborhoods in which a different language is spoken, to plot the circulation range of a Spanish edition of a newspaper, to study the changing patterns of participation in such recreational areas as skiing, soccer, or camping, or to analyze the incidence of serious crime.

Activities

1. Locate areas of a city in which languages other than English are spoken, such as Spanish, Greek, or Arabic. (A phone call to the Board of Education offices might quickly tell you which schools hold bilingual classes for students or which hold classes in English for adults.)

2. Check in the phone directory or on the newsstands for a foreign language newspaper. Where is it sold locally? Is it written and published in that local community, or is it printed somewhere else and distributed nationally by mail to a network of ethnic communities? How long has the paper been in existence? (Your local library may also have copies of old foreign language newspapers that were once very popular in your city but are no longer published or sold there.)

3. Some sports, such as skiing, soccer, and gymnastics, have become increasingly more popular. Social geographers can trace the movement of such cultural changes. Check with the owner of a local sports store or a high school physical education department to find out where centers for such sports are located, who are the old hands and the newcomers at these sports, and how new interest was aroused and sustained. What part do various ethnic groups in the community play in supporting these sports?

4. Are senior citizens clustered in one or more distinct areas of your city? Visit a community planning agency for local census data that will show age, income levels, and type of housing for various census districts in your city.

5. Have students visit a home for elderly citizens where there are residents who come from different ethnic or cultural backgrounds. Interview residents to discover when and how they came to the city, where they lived, went to school, the jobs they held, and how things have changed (or remained the same) in their old neighborhoods.

Environmental Perception

The renewed concern of geographers for a better understanding of people and the environment has brought them into close contact with similar interests among psychologists and sociologists. Each has been concerned with the broad question "How do people view the world around them?" The feelings, attitudes, images, or ideas that result from cognitive structuring of physical and social environment are referred to as *environmental perception*. Geographers are especially interested in the differences in perception that different groups have of the same environmental area and in the distribution of such perceptions over space (Saarinen, 1970). For example, the perceptions of resource managers (city planners, zoning commissioners, conservationists, forest wardens, etc.) are often quite different from those of the resource users, the people most immediately concerned. Note that the common restrictions on the uses of watershed areas and water systems are often viewed quite differently by campers, naturalists, boaters, hunters, industrialists, loggers,

"Every time I pass through here, I get heartburn."
Source: Joseph Farris. Used with permission.

and those officials responsible for the reservoir and waterworks. Similar problems exist when parts of the land, especially urban areas, are perceived differently by various groups of people: the rich, the poor, African Americans, Whites, and various ethnic groups. Terms such as "across the tracks," "silk stocking neighborhood," and "snob hill" are common in our language and usually have negative connotations. Many towns and cities have sections in which particular ethnic groups have located. These areas are often referred to in a derogatory way as "coontown," "Jewtown," and the like. Mayors who are eager to drum up tourist trade may describe their city as an "exciting, fun city," but residents concerned with an alarming increase in crime may describe the same city as a "frightening jungle." A group of geographers, called *social geographers,* has given considerable attention to how different groups of people, such as ethnic minorities, new residents, children, elderly people, and hospital patients, view their environmental surroundings and how these views may change as people move from place to place over time.

Activities

1. In many areas local school buildings are being closed because of declining enrollment. What new uses are being suggested for the buildings or the land? How do various community groups perceive these new uses?

2. Boating is becoming an increasingly popular recreation on our lakes, rivers, and oceans. However, many state and federal agencies raise concerns about human safety, increased pollution, danger to fish and wildlife, disruption of the natural ecology, and the uncontrolled growth of resort areas. Role-play a public meeting where the conflicting claims of increased recreational use of public waterways are debated against the public interest concerns of governmental officials.

3. Have students interview various members of a community (e.g., residents, merchants, city officials, and so forth) for their perceptions about various parts of the city. Is there an upper-crust section, a tough area, a fashionable, stylish, or chic section, or a neighborhood that is referred to as "down and out" or "across the tracks"? How do they describe the downtown area (CBD) during the daytime? At night? Are there some areas where people are afraid to walk alone at night? Where they feel perfectly free and safe at any time? Are derogatory words used to describe some neighborhoods? Do city officials describe an area in one way, but residents or shop owners describe it quite differently? How would you account for such differences?

GENERALIZATIONS IN GEOGRAPHY

Geography has traditionally been more concerned with the development of descriptive and explanatory studies than with the formulation of empirical generalizations of wide universality. While there has been no lack of concepts within the discipline, they have served principally as organizing elements for analytical studies.

The generalizations that follow are directly related to the concepts discussed above. While some are predictive, most are descriptive or explanatory. Nevertheless, they represent appropriate end points for student learning in concept-oriented studies in geography. That is, classroom teaching should focus on a variety of student activities and content examples so that students may formulate the generalizations (or some approximations in their own words). They can then test their applicability to a number of other similar situations.

For teachers, generalizations such as these represent convenient starting points for planning and organizing instruction, gathering appropriate materials, and devising activities to engage students in direct learning experiences. Many textbooks and school district curricula developed in recent years use generalizations as organizing principles or themes to provide for a coherent and integrated sequence of geographic learning from grade to grade.

Location

Cities are located at places where there is easy access to one or more major routes of transportation.

As knowledge of science and technology increased, people were able to locate and map places on the globe with greatly increased accuracy.

Spatial Interaction

A variety of relationships exist between a city and the smaller towns surrounding it. These relationships are based on the exchange of trade, services, or ideas.

Technological change tends to alter the established relationships between cities and towns and to affect the movement of people, trade, and services.

Urban Spatial Patterns

A city's economic influence extends outward, to a wide area of the surrounding hinterland, and greatly affects the livelihood of many people.

Cities provide a centrally located trading place and a ready supply of goods and services not available in the surrounding area.

Internal Structure of a City

The transportation, commercial, and financial linkages of a city converge at one place to form a central trade or business district (CBD).

The change from fixed means of transportation, such as railroads or streetcars, to more mobile cars, buses, and trucks results in the growth of new sectors of the city and the eventual deterioration of older sectors, resulting in slums.

When immigrant or minority groups move into a city, they tend to congregate in clearly defined sections of the city in order to retain social or cultural identity and because of economic or social pressures.

Cultural Diffusion

The movement of people with culturally different traits is facilitated by improved transportation and changes in technology.

The interactions between an ethnically or culturally different group and the members of other groups in a community result in the gradual movement and exchange of cultural traits from place to place.

Geographical features of the earth such as oceans, mountains, and swamps tend to isolate certain people and cultural groups until they develop technological changes that permit them to conquer these barriers.

Environmental Perception

Groups of people view the environment differently, depending on the value or worth they place on its use.

The social conditions of a community will affect how its members or visitors perceive it.

Racial or ethnic biases affect how a person feels about or perceives a neighborhood where culturally different people live.

Students in this photograph are painting masks. Art can be a powerful tool for teaching geography concepts such as cultural diffusion and environmental perception.
Northshore Public Schools, Seattle.

GEOGRAPHY IN THE SCHOOL

Geography has long been a part of the elementary school curriculum. Together with history, it was the mainstay of the social studies program. Geography has been taught in a variety of ways: as a separate discipline with its own textbook and separate content matter, as part of a multidisciplinary approach with special emphasis on geography at one or more grade levels, and as related knowledge in a broad, interdisciplinary study.

Trends in teaching geography in recent years have reflected an integrated social science approach, focused around broad themes or major social issues. Certain geographic topics have typically received major emphasis at a particular grade level. For example, students usually study their town or city in grade 2, their state or region in grade 4, a regional or cultural approach to Europe, Asia, or Africa in grade 6, and urban geography and physical geography in grades 7–8. At other times, geographic content is integrated when the curriculum focuses more directly on history, as in the growth of the American nation in grade 5. Modern textbooks reflect these trends and organize content around relevant concepts and generalizations of geography. In a few places, geography is taught as a separate discipline.

A separate geography textbook is used, and the curriculum content is not integrated into a broader social science curriculum.

NATIONAL STANDARDS IN GEOGRAPHY

National standards in geography were established in 1995 through the collaborative efforts of the Association of American Geographers, National Council for Geographic Education, the National Geographic Society, and the American Geographic Society. The goal of the standards is a geographically informed person. Such a person would be able to see meaning in the arrangement of things in space; see relations between people, places, and environments; be able to use geographic skills; and apply spatial and ecological perspectives to life situations. The standards are divided into six essential elements and eighteen standards. The essential elements and standards are listed in Table 14.2.

SOME PERSISTENT ERRORS

While the teaching of geography has improved greatly in the last two decades—largely because of the interest and involvement of professional geographers in textbook writing and teacher training—old errors and misconceptions still persist. Outdated textbooks often convey a notion of geography as "exotic lands and strange people." We still find statements such as "geographic features determine how people make a living," a long-outmoded geographic determinism that fails to take into account people's ability to adapt or modify the environment through new technological developments. Nineteenth-century concepts of British colonialism still lock us into inaccurate and misleading terms, such as Middle East and Far East, which presume London is the center of the imperial world. Lastly, most classroom maps still use outdated Mercator projections that badly distort many parts of the earth, rather than some of the newer map projections, which are based on far more accurate photographs made from satellites orbiting in space.

TEACHING STRATEGIES

Generalization
Regions can be distinguished according to physical features.

Concepts
Region; physical features.

Primary Grades

The teacher begins by arousing interest with large colorful pictures of various geographic regions: tropical rain forests, deserts, tundra, marine climates, plains, Alpine mountains.

The teacher asks: "What are we looking at? Are these all the same? What is the same? What is different? What are the differences?" (Children might reply: hot, cold, dry, wet, plants, no plants, big mountains, and so on.)

After considerable discussion of similarities and differences, the teacher asks: "Could we put some of these pictures together in groups? Which ones seem to belong together?" Students get up and begin to move pictures to tables in different parts of the room. They sort and resort the piles of pictures, discussing similarities and differences, until they seem satisfied with each of the different piles of pictures.

The teacher asks: "What name could we call these different piles of pictures?" Children might reply: different kinds of places. Places that are different but that have the same kinds of things in them.

Teacher seeks to clarify: "What do you mean, different kinds of things?" Children reply: "Some places have lots of rocks; some have no rocks; some are all flat; some have lots of trees; that picture looks like a big jungle."

The teacher is satisfied that children have actually identified different geographic features to distinguish among the various groups of pictures they put together. The teacher instructs the class to call these different piles of pictures "different places that have the same kinds of things in them."

At various times during the next few days the children play with the pictures, challenging one another to sort and resort them into appropriate piles. Some children bring pictures from magazines into class and set up their own piles of "different places that have the same kinds of things in them." The teacher allows them to continue to use the awkward but correct title for groupings.

After several days or more, when the teacher is sure that all the children understand the process of sorting, grouping, and labeling the piles, the teacher asks: "Would you like to learn a special word that we use to name these different places that have the same kinds of things in them? We call these different places *regions*, and we call the same kinds of things *physical features*." The teacher repeats and practices the new words with the class. They seem proud to show off their new vocabulary (though a few still continue to stick with the phrase they learned first.)

Intermediate Grades

Regional studies are typically found in the intermediate grades, frequently grade 4. The students learned to form the basic concept of region in the primary grades and to distinguish common physical features as a criterion for the concept. Here we shall use the case study approach, so that students will see the region as a totality and will establish relationships between its many other features.

The teacher selects one example of a wet tropical forest area for which materials are available, for example, the Amazon rain forest, portions of the Hawaiian Islands, or other tropical islands.

The teacher shows a picture of one specific wet tropical region, such as the Amazon area, and asks, "What can we tell about this place from its picture?" (It probably rains a lot, it has a lot of plants and trees; there are probably only a few people there; there might be a big river there.) The teacher asks each student his or her reason for thinking that the idea is true and records the idea on the board.

TABLE 14.2. *National Geography Standards*

I. The World in Spatial Terms
Geography studies the relationships between people, places, and environments
by mapping information about them into a spatial context.
The geographically informed person knows and understands:
    1. How to use maps and other geographic representations, tools, and
       technology to acquire, process, and report information from a spatial
       perspective
    2. How to use mental maps to organize information about people, places, and
       environments in a spatial context
    3. How to analyze the spatial organization of people, places, and environ-
       ments on the Earth's surface

II. Places and Regions
The identities and lives of individuals and peoples are rooted in particular places
and the human constructs called regions.
The geographically informed person knows and understands:
    4. The physical and human characteristics of places
    5. That people create regions to interpret earth's complexity
    6. How culture and experience influence people's perceptions of places and
       regions

III. Physical Systems
Physical processes shape earth's surface and interact with plant and animal life to
create, sustain, and modify ecosystems.
The geographically informed person knows and understands:
    7. The physical processes that shape the patterns of earth's surface
    8. The characteristics and spatial distribution of ecosystems on earth's surface

IV. Human Systems
People are central to geography in that human activities help shape earth's
surface, human settlements and structures are part of earth's surface, and
humans compete for control of earth's surface.
The geographically informed person knows and understands:
    9. The characteristics, distribution, and migration of human populations on
       earth's surface
   10. The characteristics, distribution, and complexity of earth's cultural mosaics
   11. The patterns and networks of economic interdependence on earth's
       surface
   12. The processes, patterns, and functions of human settlement
   13. How the forces of cooperation and conflict among people influence the
       division and control of earth's surface

After they have done as much research and inferring as they can from the picture and from other sources such as reference books, letters from people in the
area, and stories about the area, the teacher asks, "What are the specific and special
things that work together to make the Amazon region what it is?"

The study of an entire region is designed to help students perceive the totality
of one particular place, people, or time, as opposed to the analytic approach, in
which students focus on one aspect—land forms or cultural adoptions. It is a

TABLE 14.2. *(Continued)*

V. Environment and Society
The physical environment is modified by human activities, largely as a consequence of the ways in which human societies value and use earth's natural resources, and human activities are also influenced by earth's physical features and processes.
The geographically informed person knows and understands:

    14. How human activities modify the physical environment
    15. How physical systems affect human systems
    16. The changes that occur in the meaning, use, distribution, and importance of resources

VI. The Uses of Geography
Knowledge of geography enables people to develop an understanding of the relationship between people, places, and environments over time—that is, of earth as it was, is, and might be.
The geographically informed person knows and understands:

    17. How to apply geography to interpret the past
    18. How to apply geography to interpret the present and plan for the future

Source: Reprinted with permission from *Geography for Life, National Geography Standards*. 1994. Washington, D.C.: National Geographic Society (1994), on behalf of the American Geographical Society, Association of American Geographers, National Council for Geographic Education, and the National Geographic Society, pp. 34–35.

geographic case study of a region. This case study could be focused on one point in time or it could focus on one region throughout time.

Upper Grades

This strategy is designed for use with students in upper grades, who may be studying urban geography and who may already have some historical knowledge of the westward movement in the United States. The purpose of this activity is to focus on one specific region and observe the role of its river in influencing where people settle. The teacher can use Memphis, Minneapolis, St. Louis, Detroit, Pittsburgh, or a similar city.

    In focusing on a river town, the students will observe how people can get goods and services more easily because of the river. They will observe the complete integration of the lives of the people and their needs with the role of the river.

1. *Concept Diagnosis.* The first objective for the students is to determine topics on which they want information about the city in question. The teacher might ask, "What kinds of information do you think you should have about the city, based on what you know about cities in general and about this city in particular?" These categories of knowledge can function as areas for committee research and for labels on a data retrieval chart to be constructed (see Table 14.3).

2. *Data Collection.* The teacher can then help the students record their data on a chart so that they can use it in generating hypotheses about the way in which the parts of the city are integrated.

TABLE 14.3. *The Influence of a River on a City*

Concepts	Memphis	St. Louis	Pittsburgh
Location			
Place			
Spatial Interactions			
Internal Structure			
Cultural Diffusion			
Impact of Technology			

3. *Generalizing.* The third stage of this investigation is the discussion of patterns that seem to appear in the data retrieval chart. The teacher asks whether the students see any patterns in the way things work together, and the whole class evaluates the possibility of patterns and the implications each pattern might have for the whole city or for individual parts of it. In free-flowing ways they can explore the values involved in the pattern.

4. *Definition of Problem.* This strategy follows quite naturally from gathering data regarding one particular city and from observing the relationships among people, goods, services, and regions. The purpose here, as it is in geography in general, is to understand the interactions of people, space, and time. In this instance the teacher may present the class with a specific problem. The problem may be related to the way people value the existing relationships of people and space and time. For example, the problem could be "Given that people have overcome their dependence on river transportation and considering the level of technology that exists today, what are the best ways in which we can plan locations of future cities?"

5. *Proposing Solutions—Value Clarification.* Once the problem has been defined, the teacher can form groups, or can allow the class to form its own structure for tackling the problem. By the upper grades, if the valuing process has been used before by the teacher, the students can go through the steps on their own and only later resume in a larger group to discuss their chosen solutions. For classes going through this process for the first time, the teacher could ask, "What are the possible alternatives available?" These could be listed vertically under the label: "Alternatives." The teacher could then ask, "What would the consequences be for each alternative suggested?" and some beginning ideas could be sketched out.

This kind of problem is open enough so that each student can approach it on an appropriate level of sophistication. Some pupils might want to research carefully the alternatives and probable consequences; others might wish to use whatever information they have available at the time. The only requirement is that the individual think through alternatives and consequences, and be able to provide a rationale for his or her choice or lack of choice.

SUMMARY

In this chapter we considered the role of the geographer and the five traditions of the discipline: physical, spatial, cultural, regional, and historical. We examined the place of geography among the social sciences and saw that it ranged widely in the continuum, close to the physical sciences at one end, and close to the humanities at the other. The regional method was seen as the principal research method of the geographer. It was approached in two quite different ways: the broad area study and the topical or systematic approach. In practice, however, the geographer actually uses both approaches. Quantitative methods and the use of maps, globes, and special cartographic projections constitute the special techniques and tools of research.

In discussing geography as a generalizing discipline, we pointed out that the geographer, perhaps because of the nature of the discipline, has tended to concentrate more on individual studies than on the development of general laws or theory. Out of these extensive studies on individual regions of the earth have come a large body of concepts, a group of generalizations of somewhat restricted application (mostly at the regional level), and a comparatively small body of theory. Three of these theories were discussed briefly: location theory, central place theory, and spatial structure and organization. A large number of concepts selected from the general area of urban geography were discussed in detail. Activities and strategies for teaching selected geographic concepts and generalizations were described.

REFLECTION AND ACTION ACTIVITIES

1. Summarize briefly each of the five traditions in the discipline of geography, and show how each contributes to the study of place and space. How can each tradition be reflected in elementary and middle school geography?
2. Compared with the other social science disciplines, geography has many concepts, comparatively few high-order generalizations, and only a very limited body of theory. How can you explain this situation?
3. Examine a social studies curriculum in a local school district. Does it reflect evidence of some of the newer trends in the development of geography education described in this chapter? In what areas is it deficient?
4. Look over a sampling of social studies textbooks from a local school district. What place is given to geography? What emphasis within geography does it reflect? To what extent does it provide materials for social inquiry, valuing, and decision-making as described in Chapter 1 of this book?

internet links

TEACHING GEOGRAPHY

Teachers can use the Internet to reveal exciting and interdisciplinary aspects of geography. The websites listed below can be used to teach social, cultural, and other dimensions of human geography. They weave anthropology, archaeology, history, and sociology into geography and provide data to examine spatial aspects of urban inequality, social welfare, and housing. The websites listed below also highlight the international nature of geography. They link students and teachers to geographers and databases in Great Britain, Australia, the Netherlands, and other places all over the world where cutting-edge work is being done in the field of geography.

1. The Center for World Indigenous Studies: Fourth World Documentation Project Archives (FWDP) (http://www.halcyon.com/FWDP/fwdp.html). The FWDP is an online library of texts and resources that document the struggle of indigenous peoples all over the world to regain and retain their rights. Full text of treaties, United Nations resolutions, tribal and inter-tribal agreements, and other documents can be downloaded from this site. It is an invaluable data source for exploring components of human geography, particularly historical geography.

2. HungerWeb (http://www.brown.edu/Departments/World_Hunger_Program/index.html). Educators can use this site to access primary data on hunger, food, poverty, and population. Information on specific countries is provided through links to virtual libraries and information centers all over the world. Data available from this site can be used to examine questions that are central to the work of economic geographers, social geographers, and cultural geographers.

3. Geographic Information Sciences/Remote Sensing/Statistics/Cartography (http://www.geo.gubc.ca/vgd/). This website provides a gateway to an extensive array of geographic information systems (GIS) resources. It is linked to the Virtual Geography Department, the U.S. Census Bureau, the University of Edinburgh's GIS home page, and other key (GIS) resources. Educators who are not familiar with GIS can access answers to frequently asked GIS questions from this site.

4. Athena: Curriculum: Earth (http://athena.wednet.edu/curric/land/todayqk.html). Students can use the data provided at this site to examine earthquake activity around the world. Updated earthquake data and map generators are provided for three sites. The data, provided in table format, include the date, time, location, and magnitude of the most recent global earthquake activity. Suggestions for student activities and links to other current earthquake information are also provided at this site.

REFERENCES

Broek, J. O. M., et al. (1980). *The study and teaching of geography*. Columbus, OH: Merrill.

Christaller, W. (1966). *Central places in southern Germany*. Englewood Cliffs, NJ: Prentice-Hall.

Diner, D. R. (1983). *Erin's daughters in America: Irish immigrant women in the nineteenth century*. Baltimore: Johns Hopkins University Press.

Geography Education Standards Project. (1994). *Geography for life: National geography standards 1994*. Washington, DC: National Geographic Society.

Gersmehl, P. J. (1995). *Why not here? Teaching geography to a new standard*. Indiana, PA: National Council for Geographic Education.

Harper, R. A., & Schmuddle, T. H. (1978). *Between two worlds: An introduction to geography* (2nd ed.). Boston: Houghton Mifflin.

Morokvasic, M. (1984). *Migration in Europe: Trends in research and sociological approaches*. London: Sage.

Saarinen, T. F. (1970). Environmental perception. In P. Bacon (Ed.), *Focus on geography: Key concepts and teaching strategies* (40th Yearbook) (pp. 63–69). Washington, D.C.: National Council for the Social Studies.

United States Census Bureau (Updated 2/27/1998). Resident population of the United States: Estimates, by Sex, Race, and Hispanic Origin, with Median Age. Internet.

Wright, J. S. (1997). *The New York Times 1998 almanac*. New York: Penguin.

FOR FURTHER READING

Joint Committee on Geographic Education of the National Council for Geographic Education and the Association of American Geographers (1984). *Guidelines for geographic education: Elementary and secondary schools*. Washington, D.C.: Author.

Nabhan, G. P. (1998). *Culture of habitat: On nature, culture, and story*. Washington, D.C.: Counterpoint.

Salvatore N. J. (Ed.). (1988). *Strengthening geography in the social studies* (Bulletin No. 81). Washington, D.C.: National Council for the Social Studies.

Zelinsky, W. (1992). *The cultural geography of the United States,* (revised ed.). Paramus, NJ: Prentice-Hall.

PART IV

Value Inquiry, Decision-Making, Citizen Action, and Assessment Strategies

Source: Northshore School District, Seattle

In previous chapters, we pointed out why higher-level scientific knowledge is essential for sound decision-making. However, knowledge in itself is not sufficient. Citizen actors must also be able to identify and clarify their values before they can take effective action to solve personal problems or influence public policy. Values deeply influence human behavior. The first part of Chapter 15 sets forth a rationale for value education and presents a value-inquiry model that you can use to help students to identify and clarify their values. Valuing activities are also described.

Once decision-makers have gained higher-level knowledge and clarified their values, they must synthesize their knowledge and values in order to determine their courses of action. The second part of Chapter 15 focuses on how decision-makers relate their derived knowledge to their values in order to make decisions and to determine courses of action on social issues. This part of Chapter 15 illustrates how skills and knowledge components discussed in earlier chapters can be applied to help citizen actors make reflective decisions and intelligently influence public policy. Activities and strategies that can help students gain proficiency in valuing and decision-making skills constitute an important part of Chapter 15.

To assure that the skills constituting decision-making and citizen action are mastered by your students, you must have effective ways to assess student achievement. Chapter 16 presents a number of techniques you can use to assess student behavior. Although assessment should be a continuous process in teaching, we focus on the topic here to emphasize its importance.

Valuing, Decision-Making, and Citizen Action

VALUE INQUIRY: NATURE AND APPROACHES

The Value Component of Decision-Making

While knowledge is an essential component of decision-making, it is not sufficient. To make reflective decisions, citizen actors must identify and clarify their values, and relate them to the knowledge they have derived. The valuing component is a very important part of the decision-making process; values often determine what knowledge an individual will accept or reject. Values also underlie the knowledge that is constructed by social scientists (Banks, 1998; Code, 1991). Value confusion often results in contradictory and confused citizen action.

The Nature of Values

A universally agreed on definition of value does not exist in either the social sciences or philosophy. Jary and Jary (1991) define values as "the central beliefs and purposes of an individual or society" (p. 688). Values, unlike attitudes and other beliefs, are not related to any specific things, persons, or groups, but are very general and influence a person's behavior toward a large class of objects or persons.

A value is also a standard for determining whether something is good or bad, and for judging one's own behavior. People learn their values, as they do most other beliefs and attitudes, from the persons in their social environment. Most values are not reflectively and independently derived. The social origin of values explains why most people socialized within the same culture, subculture, or social system are likely to have similar values.

Value Conflicts in Individuals and in Society

Most individuals socialized within modernized societies do not attain a set of clarified values but inculcate values that are contradictory and at odds with each other. This creates value confusion and value problems. Conflicting values are found within individuals as well as within the larger society. Both *freedom* and *equality* are part of the American creed, yet in practice these values often conflict. Landlords who want the freedom to rent to whomever they please may not rent to nontraditional families or to couples with young children, thus denying these individuals equality. Many of the nation's overarching values, such as *equality, justice,* and *freedom,* are also inherently contradictory in practice.

The value problems faced by youths in modernized democratic societies are especially acute. Much more than youths in traditional societies, they are faced with an infinite number of value alternatives from which they must choose, many of

Art activities can be used to stimulate discussions of value issues and problems.
Library of Congress, Washington, D.C.

which are contradictory. The mass media and the tremendous mobility within contemporary U.S. society expose today's youths to a wide variety of life styles and belief systems. Their problems are complicated by the fact that they are expected to move from childhood to adulthood within a short span of time, and therefore to live by two different sets of standards. Young people often become cynical when adults fail to live up to the ideals they expound. They interpret the failure of adults to live up to certain ideals as the absence of the ideals themselves. People can hold ideals, such as equality and honesty, without always living up to them. However, this is often difficult for young people to understand and appreciate.

Value Education in the Schools

Because many of the social and personal problems within U.S. society are rooted in value confusion, the school should play an important role in helping students to identify and clarify their values, and to make value choices intelligently. However, many teachers fail to help students deal with moral issues intelligently (Simon, Howe, & Kirschenbaum, 1995).

Some teachers treat value problems like invisible people. They deny their existence. They assume that if students get all of the facts correct, they can solve important social problems. These teachers practice the cult of false objectivity. Other teachers use an evasion strategy. When value problems arise in the classroom, they try to change to a safer topic. When issues such as genetic engineering, gay rights, and political scandals come up in the classroom, they are quickly and forcefully dismissed by teachers who use the evasion strategy.

Probably the most frequently used approach to value education in the elementary and middle school is the indoctrination of values considered correct by adults. Such values as justice, truth, freedom, honesty, and equality are taught along with legendary heroes, stories, rituals, and patriotic songs. A major goal of value inquiry in U.S. schools should be to help students develop a commitment to American creed values such as equality and human dignity. However, we cannot use an indoctrination approach when trying to help students develop a reflective commitment to democratic values. An indoctrination approach violates democratic values and does not help students develop a method for deriving and clarifying their own values.

The didactic inculcation of values is also unsound because it assumes that most value conflicts and problems result because students are unable to distinguish "good" from "bad" values. However, this is not the case. Students can rather easily distinguish good from bad. Most value problems result because students must often choose between two goods. For example, if a student's friend asked his opinion of a very poor drawing, he must decide whether to be honest or courteous. To be honest would hurt his friend's feelings, and he would therefore not be courteous. When teachers use didactic methods to teach students contradictory but equally "good" values, such conflicts are intensified.

Didactic methods are also unsound because they deny students freedom of choice and do not teach students how to derive, clarify, and justify their moral choices. While we should require students to defend their moral choices within the context of societal values such as human dignity and equality, each generation must have the opportunity to define the meanings of these idealized values. We cannot expect standards to guide a person's life unless those standards have been freely chosen from alternatives, and after thoughtful consideration of the consequences of the alternatives. Individuals must also be proud of the standards that guide their behavior (Simon, Howe, & Kirschenbaum, 1995). If teachers and other adults force values on students, students will not prize the values. The forced standards will have little influence on their behavior when they are out of the presence of authorities.

The Goals of Value Education

The major goal of value education should be to help students to develop a set of consistent, clarified values that can guide purposeful and reflective citizen action. This goal can best be attained by teaching students a method or process for deriving their values within a democratic classroom atmosphere. In this kind of democratic classroom, students must be free to express their values choices, determine how those choices conflict, examine alternative values, consider the consequences of different value choices, make value choices, and defend their moral choices within the context of human dignity and other American creed values. Students must be given an opportunity to reflectively derive their own values in order to develop a commitment to human dignity, equality, and to other democratic values. They must be given an opportunity to reflect on value choices within a democratic atmosphere in order to internalize values. Values must be freely chosen from alternatives, and after thoughtful consideration of the consequences of each alternative, before they can be internalized (Simon, Howe, & Kirschenbaum, 1995).

A VALUE INQUIRY MODEL

We have discussed the nature of values and presented and defended a position regarding value education that emphasizes reflective inquiry and uncoerced choice. We will now describe a valuing model consistent with the theory of social studies education presented in this book. You can use this model when teaching value lessons or giving students opportunities to increase their proficiency in decision-making skills.

Our valuing model is consistent with the position of value education defended above. It is a model that enables students to identify the sources of their values and those of others, to determine how values conflict, to identify value alternatives, to predict the consequences of alternative values, to freely choose from the values that they can identify, and to justify their moral choices in terms of American creed values such as equality and human dignity. To successfully implement this valuing strategy in the classroom, you must have a firm commitment to the belief that students must freely choose their own values. At the same time, students should be helped to discover the consequences of different values, be consistent in their value choices, be required to defend and justify their moral choices in terms of human dignity, and be willing to accept the consequences of and to act on their beliefs.

When you develop value inquiry lessons, you should consider seriously the age and developmental levels of your students. Students should not be required to reason morally beyond their stage of moral development. Most primary grade students will be unable to reason about complicated moral issues that involve high-level ethical principles. However, they can understand simple stories and dilemmas that involve values such as honesty, truth, and loyalty. Reflective and experienced teachers will carefully tune value lessons to their students' levels of moral and cognitive development.

1. Defining and Recognizing Value Problems: Observation-Discrimination

To intelligently reflect on values and to resolve issues, students must be able to recognize the value components of decision-problems and to distinguish definitional, value, and scientific problems. You can use case studies, incidents from novels and short stories, factual information, and open-ended stories to teach students to recognize the value components of decision-problems.

To help students develop skills in defining and recognizing value problems, you can read an open-ended story such as "Finders Weepers" (Shaftel & Shaftel, 1982) and ask such questions as "What is the problem in this situation?" "What things are important to the individuals in this story?"

Finders Weepers
In "Finders Weepers," an open-ended story by the Shaftels, Eddie, Pete, and Tom are visiting Eddie's uncle for a week. Uncle Ross told the boys to have fun and to enjoy the big lake but not to use the boat. While Eddie and Tom were swimming, Pete ignored his promise to Uncle Ross and rowed the boat onto the lake. While Eddie scolded Pete, all of the boys enjoyed using the boat. On the last day of their visit, the boat was missing. When they found it a mile away, it was badly damaged. It will take $30 to repair the boat. The boys have only $11 more than their bus fare home. In the bus station they find a wallet that contains $22 in cash and a check for $292. Pete argues strongly that they should keep the money and turn in the check and the wallet at the Lost and Found office at the bus station. Eddie argues just as strongly that they should not keep the money and should turn in the wallet with the money and the check at the Lost and Found office. They decide to vote on the matter. Tom must cast the deciding vote.

2. Describing Value-Relevant Behavior: Description-Discrimination

In this phase of value inquiry, the student names the behavior of the individuals in the problem story, event, or situation. Not every action or gesture needs to be described—only the behavior central to the problem under discussion. If the class is discussing an open-ended story such as "Finders Weepers," the students should briefly describe the behavior of the characters: Uncle Ross, Pete, Eddie, and Tom. They should not describe every word said by each character but should try to

profile

MAXINE GREENE

*A Light in
Dark Times*

Maxine Greene is described in a book by William Ayers and Janet Miller (1998) as a light in dark times. She is professor of philosophy and education and William F. Russell Professor in Foundations of Education (emerita) at Teachers College, Columbia University. Greene is an influential voice in philosophy of education and social thought. She has deepened our understanding of aesthetics, the arts, and literature as art. In her latest book, *Releasing the Imagination,* she explains how the arts can play a key role in building understanding across differences by encouraging new connections and perspectives. Greene (1995) writes, "I am drawn, by the lure of incompleteness to be explored, the promise inherent in any quest....There are always vacancies: there are always roads not taken, vistas not acknowledged. The search must be ongoing; the end can never be quite known" (p. 15).

summarize their behavior in one or two sentences. They might describe Pete's behavior in this way: "Pete was the first to use the boat. He wanted to take the money out of the wallet before turning it in at the Lost and Found office at the bus station." You can ask questions to help students accurately describe the relevant behavior in a problem situation: "What did Pete do?" "What did Eddie and Tom do?" When the students are describing behavior, they should make as few inferences as possible. Students should be taught to clearly distinguish *observation, inferences,* and *value judgments* during this phase of value inquiry.

3. Naming Values Exemplified by Behavior Described: Identification-Description, Hypothesizing

In this phase of value inquiry, the students try to name the values evidenced by the behavior described in step 2. To facilitate this phase of inquiry, you can list the behavior on the board in one column, and related values next to the behavior in another column. During this process, the students will make inferences and will not necessarily always agree on the values they see in the behavior described. While you should encourage independent thinking at this point, you should require the students to give reasons for the values they identify. This phase of inquiry requires the relating of behavior and values to be as accurate as possible even though the students may have limited information about the individuals in the problem situation.

In discussing the open-ended story "Finders Weepers," you can ask these questions during this phase of value inquiry:

> What does the behavior of Pete tell us about what is important to him?
> What was more important to Pete, honesty or getting out of trouble?
> What was most important to Eddie?
> What was most important to Uncle Ross?
> In our role-play of the story, what was most important to Tom?

4. Determining Conflicting Values in Behavior Described: Identification-Analysis

To help students discover that there are many value conflicts within our society as well as within individuals, you can ask the students to name conflicting values exemplified by particular individuals and evident in the behavior of different persons. When the class is studying "Finders Weepers," you can ask questions that help the students to describe Eddie's conflicting values. He did not want his Uncle Ross to get angry at him for using the boat. Yet he wanted to have fun. When Pete started using the boat, both he and Tom participated and enjoyed using the boat with Eddie. Eddie wanted both to have fun with the boat and to please his uncle. These desires were conflicting.

You can help middle-grade students to develop skills in identifying conflicting values by studying major historical decisions and the value conflicts experienced by past leaders. President McKinley anguished about whether to give the Philippines independence after the Spanish-American War in 1898 or to annex that nation to the United States. In an interesting and revealing document, he tells a church group how he walked the floor of the White House night after night and prayed before he decided to annex the Philippines to the United States. When studying this important decision, students can analyze the political, cultural, and ethical factors that influenced McKinley's decision. Some Americans were very unhappy with McKinley's decision. Samuel Clemens (Mark Twain) was one of them. The students could discuss ways in which the values of McKinley and Twain, in this situation, conflicted.

5. Hypothesizing about the Sources of Values Analyzed: Hypothesizing

During this phase of value inquiry, the students state hypotheses about the sources of the values they identified in step 3. As with all hypothesizing, you should require the students to give reasons for their statements. Hypotheses should be based on reason and evidence, and should not be ignorant guesses. This part of the inquiry process is designed to help students discover that most of our values are "caught" from persons within our environment and are not independently or reflectively derived. Once students are aware of the sources of their own values as well as those of other persons, they can more easily evaluate the soundness and appropriateness of these values in various situations.

When discussing "Finders Weepers," the students can hypothesize why Uncle Ross, Pete, and Eddie had different values. They can also hypothesize about why President McKinley and Mark Twain had different values related to the annexation of the Philippines, and why they consequently made different decisions. When students state hypotheses about the sources of values, they should give examples and evidence to support their ideas.

6. Naming Alternative Values to Those Exemplified by Behavior Observed: Recalling

Students should know that within our society are many value alternatives from which to choose. If they are to derive their own values and be proud of the choices they make, they must be aware of a wide range of alternatives. Without alternatives an individual cannot make choices. This phase of value inquiry is designed to help students discover value alternatives. When the students role-play "Finders Weepers," you can ask questions to help them identify value alternatives: "Eddie valued having fun and staying out of trouble more than some other things. What are some other things Eddie could have valued?" When the class is studying McKinley's decision regarding the Philippines, you could say: "We have said that McKinley highly valued giving the Filipino people the American way of life and maintaining American military strength in the Pacific region. What are some other things he could have valued?"

7. Hypothesizing about the Possible Consequences of Values Analyzed: Predicting, Comparing, and Contrasting

The following are important goals of value inquiry: (1) help students see that different values result in different consequences, (2) help students learn to accept the consequences of the values they hold, and (3) help students consider the consequences of different beliefs. During a discussion of "Finders Weepers," the students can discuss the possible consequences of Pete, Eddie, and Tom's keeping the money but turning the check and wallet in at the Lost and Found. One possibility is that they may face criminal charges when the wallet is returned to the owner. If they return the wallet with the money and the check, they may have to get loans from their parents to pay for the boat. They could possibly get part-time jobs to earn the money to pay off their loan. When discussing McKinley's decision about annexing the Philippines, the students could discuss the actual consequences of his decision (one consequence was a revolt against the United States) and hypothesize about what might have happened if McKinley had decided to support independence for the Philippines.

8. Declaring Value Preferences: Choosing

After the students have described the behavior of the individuals in the stories, cases, and situations studied, identified the values involved, determined how they conflict, and predicted the possible consequences, they should be asked to declare their personal value preferences. This phase of value inquiry is extremely important and should be handled sensitively.

During this phase of value inquiry, you should be careful not to condemn values inconsistent with your beliefs. This is not to suggest that you should remain neutral on value issues, but rather that you should not declare value preferences until the students have expressed their own choices. Unless you create a classroom atmosphere that allows and encourages students to express their true beliefs, value inquiry will become a game in which students will try to guess what responses you want them to make. However, once they are out of the classroom and among friends, they will act out and freely express their true beliefs. If your students know that you think that Pete, Eddie, and Tom should return the wallet, the money, and the check, you will be unable to teach a useful value inquiry lesson with "Finders Weepers." Value preferences must be freely made within a democratic classroom atmosphere, and after the student has thought reflectively about the consequences of different value positions.

9. Stating Reasons, Sources, and Possible Consequences of Value Choices: Justifying, Hypothesizing, and Predicting

While you are obligated to help students derive their values within a democratic classroom atmosphere, you also have a responsibility to help them determine the sources of their values, the reasons they embrace them, their possible consequences, and to defend their moral choices in terms of American creed values such as equality, justice, and human dignity. Reflective citizen actors have clarified values, know why they embrace their beliefs, and are aware of the sources and consequences of their values. Once students are keenly aware of both the sources and consequences of their values, they are more likely to consider embracing other beliefs and to act on those they hold. We also hypothesize that they are more likely to endorse such American creed values as justice and human dignity.

You can use questioning strategies to help students declare value preferences and defend their moral choices. During a study of "Finders Weepers," you can ask different students: "What do you think Pete, Eddie, and Tom should do with the wallet? Why? What did you consider in making your decision? What does your decision indicate you think is most important in this situation? Would you be willing to act on your decision? Is your decision a fair decision? Why or why not?" You have to be very careful when asking questions like these so they will not, in any way, abuse the students or punish them for freely expressing their beliefs and values. Students must be able to express their attitudes, beliefs, and values freely in order for value inquiry to take place.

Value Analysis and Clarification

The operations that comprise the valuing model we have discussed are summarized in Table 15.1 and Figure 15.1. You can use this model to teach students a process for valuing, to help them identify and clarify their values, and to justify their moral choices. Although the steps within this model are discussed separately, in practice they will not be clearly divided; they will be highly interrelated. For example, you may ask a student to describe value-relevant behavior and to name the values it exemplifies at the same time. However, we have separated these operations in our model to emphasize the contribution that each can make to the clarification and derivation of values. While students should be given practice in all the operations of the model, within a particular valuing lesson you may decide to deal with one or several of the processes. The operations can be taught separately or as a unit. We believe that students need both types of practice in order to develop proficiency in value inquiry skills.

VALUING STRATEGIES

You can use a variety of materials to give students practice in using the operations contained in our value inquiry model. Descriptive content in the social sciences, historical events, classroom and playground incidents, literature, art, photographs, open-ended stories, role-playing, videotape segments, and news stories are among the variety of materials that can be used. Below is a list of valuing strategies, grouped by grade levels, that you can use to help students increase their value

TABLE 15.1. *Banks Value-Inquiry Model*

1. Defining and recognizing value problems: Observation-discrimination
2. Describing value-relevant behavior: Description-discrimination
3. Naming values exemplified by behavior described: Identification-description, hypothesizing
4. Determining conflicting values in behavior described: Identification-analysis
5. Hypothesizing about sources of values analyzed: Hypothesizing (citing data to support hypotheses)
6. Naming alternative values to those exemplified by behavior observed: Recalling
7. Hypothesizing about the possible consequences of the values analyzed: Predicting, comparing, contrasting
8. Declaring value preference: Choosing
9. Stating reasons, sources, and possible consequences of value choice: Justifying, hypothesizing, predicting

inquiry skills. These strategies are examples only. You will think of many others that are equally appropriate for teaching value analysis and clarification skills.

Primary Grades

1. Students sometimes experience a dilemma about what to do when they find a stray animal, such as a cat or a dog. Discuss this incident with the class: Jerry was taking his dog for a walk when a little puppy came running up to him whimpering for affection. Jerry's own dog was very concerned about the puppy; his interest was shown by sniffing and licking the puppy. Jerry didn't want to leave the dog outside alone. However, he knew that his mother did not want the family to own more pets. It was obvious that the stray puppy did not have a home. What should Jerry do?

2. Susie has been trying to save enough money to buy a camera for almost a year. Although she saves a part of her small allowance each week, it doesn't seem as if she is ever going to save the $45 more needed to buy the camera. She would especially like the camera for her birthday party in two weeks. The bell that ends the school day had just rung when Susie saw the crisp new $50 bill on the playground. She picked it up quickly and hid it in her hand. What should Susie do?

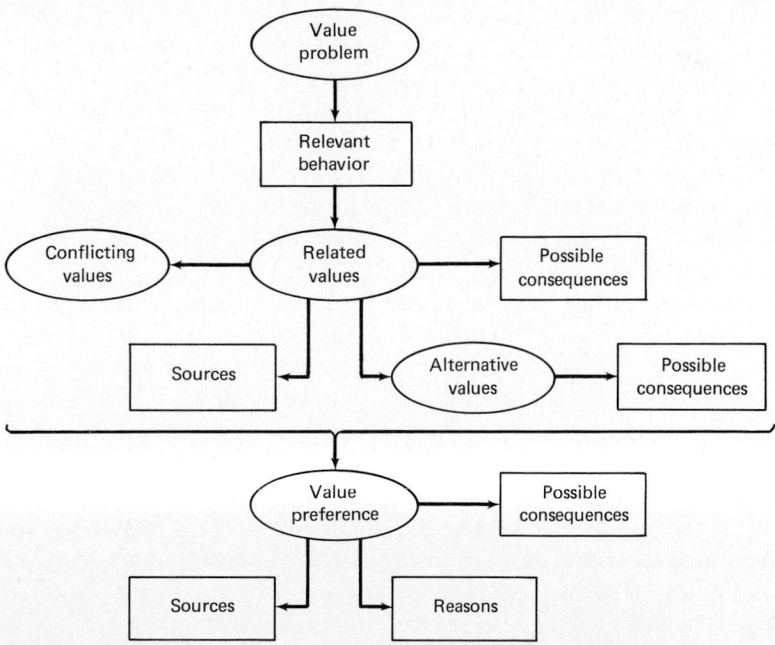

Figure 15.1
Operations of value-inquiry model, graphically illustrated.

3. Joe was looking at Kay when she copied from Carol's paper during the science test last Friday. On Monday Mr. Hinkle, the teacher, announced that, because Kay had gotten the highest score on the science test, he had chosen her to represent their class in the schoolwide science fair. Should Joe tell Mr. Hinkle about Kay's cheating last Friday?

4. Read to the class "Three Little Pigs." Ask them to name the values of the first little pig, the second little pig, the third little pig, and the wolf. Write these values on the board or butcher paper. Ask them to list the results of each set of values, as described in the story. Are these results realistic? Why or why not? Ask the students to act out or describe different endings for the story. Ask them to name the values of the characters in the story as they changed it in their descriptions or role-play.

Intermediate Grades

1. To help students identify values, pictures without captions can be used. Choose pictures that portray a value position. For example, a picture of a group carrying signs and picketing indicates that the group values public demonstration as a form of protest. Some of the protests against the war in Vietnam were violent. Show photographs of both peaceful and violent protests. Have the students identify the value positions of (1) the people protesting and (2) those they are protesting against. Either current or historical photographs can be used.

2. Ask the students to read arguments by leaders who say we need to increase our defense spending and by those who say we are spending too much money on defense and too little on domestic problems. Ask the students to identify the values of the various leaders and the possible consequences of their values. Ask the students to take a position on the defense spending controversy and defend it.

3. Lumber is an example of a quickly depleted natural resource. Ask the students to identify on a continuum the positions an individual might take regarding the appropriate use of trees and forest products. For example, one end of the continuum would indicate the total use of present lumber supplies for house-building, furniture, paper manufacture, and the use of logs in fireplaces. The other end of the continuum would indicate the conservationist position—favoring leaving all trees on the land, reforesting all places where forest fires and logging have depleted tree growth, and finding synthetic materials for all products now made of wood.

4. During their study of United States history, ask the students to read about Lincoln's decision to issue the Emancipation Proclamation in 1863. The Proclamation freed all the enslaved persons in the states that were in rebellion against the Union. What were the major factors that influenced Lincoln's decision? To what extent was his decision political? To what extent was it ethical? Also ask the students to examine the moral and political factors that influenced President Andrew Jackson's decision to support the Indian Resettlement Act of 1830, President Truman's decision to authorize the dropping of the atomic bomb on Japan in 1945, and

President Kennedy's decision to support an attempt to overthrow the Castro government in Cuba in 1961.

Upper Grades

1. Read the following situation to the class. A group of three students are in a field or out-of-the-way place smoking cigarettes. They are obviously experimenting to find the proper way to hold a cigarette. Inhaling the cigarette is difficult for them; they cough a great deal. They attempt to effect the casual air of experienced smokers. Later, one of the three students arrives home and is greeted by his father. The student casually walks into the house but doesn't get past his father's scrutiny. His father immediately notices the smell of smoke on the boy's clothes. The father asks the boy whether he has been smoking. Ask the students to role-play an ending to this situation and to discuss the value issues it raises.

2. During the early 1980s, capital punishment reemerged as a major national issue. It surfaced in large part as a response to the high crime rate in the United States. Several states reenacted the death penalty. At least one state began to execute the prisoners who had been sentenced to death in previous years. Ask the students to examine the arguments for and against the death penalty and to identify the moral, political, and social issues involved in the debate. Ask the students to take and defend a position on the issue.

3. Most of the cases that come to the United States Supreme Court involve competing value claims. Ask the students to identify some major historical and current cases that have come before the Court, the values that were in conflict, and the values the Court upheld. They should also examine the dissenting opinions in each case and identify the values exemplified in the dissents. Three examples of race relations cases that the students might study are (1) the *Plessy* v. *Ferguson* case (1896), in which the Court ruled that "separate but equal" facilities were constitutional; (2) the *Brown v. Board of Education* case (1954), in which the Court ruled that school segregation was "inherently unequal," thus reversing its own *Plessy* decision; and (3) the *Regents of the University of California v. Bakke* case (1978), in which the Court upheld the idea of affirmative action but ruled against strict racial quotas.

DECISION-MAKING AND CITIZEN ACTION STRATEGIES

Sequencing the Development of Decision-Making Skills

Students must be able to derive interdisciplinary knowledge using an inquiry process, and form and clarify their values, in order to make reflective decisions and to shape public policy. We will consider how a teacher or curriculum designer may plan the development of these skills, and the related decision-making skills: synthesis, prediction, and the affirmation of a course of action.

Teachers' development of these skills depends greatly on the social studies curriculum within their districts, their own interests, the resources available, and their students' backgrounds. Many teachers will find themselves in school districts where only social science inquiry units are part of the approved curriculum. Other teachers will believe that, while valuing and decision-making skills are important, social science inquiry should constitute the bulk of their social studies program. This book is designed to help teachers and curriculum designers with different points of view about the social studies curriculum.

Readers who are primarily interested in social science inquiry will find Chapters 9 through 14 of most interest. However, value inquiry and decision-making skills can be taught within the context of social science inquiry units and with social science and historical content. For example, while students are studying the American Revolution, you can ask the following kinds of questions:

Valuing Questions
1. What does the behavior of the British and the colonists tell us about what was important to them?
2. How were the things important to the British different from the things important to the colonists?
3. What were other things that the British and the colonists could have regarded as important?

Decision-Making
1. What were the alternatives open to the colonists?
2. What were the possible consequences of each alternative in question 1?
3. What evidence can you give to support your belief that the alternatives you state were possible?

Thus, one approach you can take to developing inquiry, valuing, and decision-making skills is to teach these skills within the context of social science inquiry units. Another approach is to identify a number of vital social problems or issues, list social science concepts related to the issues, and plan separate units to teach the concepts and the analysis of the issues related to the concepts.

The students could apply the knowledge they learned during the inquiry units when they decide on social issues. During the social issues units, they would develop proficiency in valuing and decision-making skills. Citizen action and participation projects could also be planned and implemented during the analysis of social issues, so that the students could take action on some of the decisions they make. For example, you may decide to teach conceptual units that will help students to decide on social issues related to animal cloning, a current war or international conflict, or race relations in the community. Concepts will be taught in the social science inquiry units that will enable students to make reflective decisions and to take citizen action related to these problems.

Once you have identified the social issues you plan to teach during the year, you should use the criteria for the selection of concepts found in Chapter 2. These criteria suggest that concepts should be accurate, have the power to organize a great deal of information and data, and be suitable for the students. While these criteria should be exercised, the relationship of the concepts to the social issues to be studied should be the most important criterion. This relationship will give students the knowledge they need to make decisions and take action on social issues. Such concepts as *power, international law, authority,* and *scarcity* might be developed to help the students analyze a current war or international conflict. By studying the concepts of power and authority, the students will be able to determine who has the authority to declare and lead us into war, and how citizens can exercise power to influence public policy regarding war. The concept of international law will help students discover how international laws are made and their usual consequences. Materials and activities related to the concept of scarcity will illuminate the way wars often affect the economy of a nation. For example, the students may discover that wars often increase prosperity and that the termination of wars often results in widespread unemployment.

We have discussed two major ways you might plan units to teach inquiry, valuing, and decision-making skills. These skills may be developed with deliberate questioning strategies within the framework of social science inquiry units. An alternative plan is to identify a number of social issues, structure conceptual units to give students the knowledge needed to make reflective decisions regarding them, and teach decision-making units related to the social issues at different points in the year.

Although both these plans have certain advantages or may be the only plans feasible for many teachers, we will propose another alternative. We believe this third alternative is the most effective way to structure learning experiences that enable students to develop proficiency in social science inquiry, value inquiry, decision-making, and citizen action skills. Although we will discuss this organizational plan separately, you should realize that it is highly related to the other plans discussed, and that its strategies can be used within the previously discussed plans. You will be able to adapt these procedures and our decision-making model to your own unique teaching situation, or you can use the procedures exactly as we describe them. We believe that the most effective organizational plan is the approach outlined below.

IDENTIFYING IMPORTANT SOCIAL ISSUES AND PROBLEMS

The first step in planning decision-making units, using the method we consider most effective, is to identify social issues that are of concern to the students and that are unresolved in the local community and the larger society. The issues should be pervasive and of enduring interest. Decision-making units should not be built around problems that are narrow or of only temporary concern. You can determine the pervasive social issues within a society by carefully studying the news media over a period of time, by being generally aware of the events within the community and society, and by listening to the students' conversations and class comments about their social and political worlds.

You can also use questionnaires and essays to determine what social issues are most important to your students and the community. Although social issues frequently vary within different time periods, some have been of enduring concern in modern society. These include political alienation, poverty, racial and gender inequality, pollution, and in recent years, concern about animal cloning and genetic engineering.

Teaching Decision-Problem Units

IDENTIFYING THE DECISION-PROBLEM

We will illustrate how a class may study a social issue, and through a decision-making process, decide what action to take regarding it. In a medium-sized industrial community called Riverdale, racial conflict has developed between African Americans and Whites. During the previous summer, an African American family moved into the predominantly White Riverdale neighborhood, and a racial confrontation occurred in which several persons were injured, including two White police officers. A number of citizens formed a group to campaign for an open-housing bill, but to date support for the movement has been meager. Race relations within the city are tense.

In response to federal legislation, a movement to desegregate the public schools by cross-busing began, but an anti–school desegregation movement emerged to defeat the attempts for desegregation and to recall the school board. The students in the sixth-grade class at Abraham Lincoln, an all-White school on the fringes of Riverdale, pose this problem: *"What action should we take regarding race relations in our community?"*

SOCIAL SCIENCE INQUIRY (RELATED KNOWLEDGE)

Because scientific knowledge is one essential component of the decision-making process, the teacher identifies social science concepts and related generalizations to help the students make reflective decisions about the issue. The teacher selects these concepts: *discrimination* from sociology, *conflict* from history, *culture* from anthropology, *specialization* from economics, and *power* from political science. Organizing generalizations related to the concepts are identified, and subideas related to the organizing generalizations and to race relations in the United States are stated. The key generalization and subideas for one of the key concepts follows.

Concept
Discrimination

Organizing Generalization
Groups are often the victims of discrimination because of age, gender, race, religion, and cultural differences.

Subideas
1. U.S. slavery was a form of discrimination.
2. African Americans have experienced discrimination in legal matters. The slave codes and laws such as the grandfather clause are examples.
3. African Americans have experienced discrimination in the administration of justice. The widespread lynching in the early 1900s is an example.
4. African Americans experience discrimination in the areas of voting and government.
5. African Americans experience discrimination in employment.

ORGANIZING FOR INSTRUCTION

You should identify the key concepts related to the social issue you wish the class to decide on, and state the organizing generalizations and related subideas. Then you are ready to formulate the teaching strategies and specify the instructional materials for the social science phase of the decision-problem unit. The concepts and materials should also be organized in a logical fashion.

In our example, you may wish to start the unit with the first key concept *(discrimination),* because the subideas related to this concept deal with the earliest period of race relations in the United States. Although decision-problem units need not be chronological, they should have some kind of logical organization. Another teacher using the concepts in our example may wish to start with the key concept *power,* and discuss the civil rights movement of the 1950s and 1960s (Halberstam, 1998). When organizing social issues units, you should consider the interests of the students, the availability of materials, your own interests, the relationships of the concepts, the content to be studied, and the social issue to be analyzed.

We illustrated in Chapter 2 how you can organize social science inquiry units. The same form of organization is appropriate for the social science phase of social issues units. You can divide a sheet of paper in half and write the key concepts and generalizations on one side of the paper, and the activities designed to develop the ideas on the other half, as illustrated in Table 15.2.

TABLE 15.2. *Organizing Social Issues Units*

Key Ideas	Activities
Concept: Discrimination *Organizing generalization:* Groups are often the victims of discrimination because of age, sex, race, religion, and cultural differences. *Subidea:* African Americans have experienced much discrimination in all phases of American life, including education, the administration of justice, and employment.	1. Read selections from *South Town, North Town,* and *Whose Town?* by Lorenz Graham. 2. View a videotape on Black slavery and list ways in which it was a form of discrimination. 3. Find copies of such documents as the slave codes and the grandfather clause, and role-play how they affected the lives of African Americans. 4. Compile statistics on the number of African Americans who were lynched during the early years of the 1900s. 5. Read and discuss accounts of the discrimination that African Americans experience in employment, school, and in the administration of justice today.

VALUE INQUIRY

After the students have had an opportunity to derive social science generalizations related to their decision-problem, they should undertake lessons that will enable them to identify, analyze, and clarify their values. For value inquiry exercises, you may use case studies clipped from newspapers and magazines, open-ended stories, photographs, role-playing activities, or moral dilemmas that the students and you write. Much of the factual material, which is covered during the social science phase of the unit, may also be used to help the students to form and clarify values related to the problem or issue being studied.

When teaching a decision-problem or social issue, you should use valuing strategies directly related to the issue under consideration. In our example unit, it would be inappropriate for you to ask the students value questions about such issues as water pollution and a current international conflict unless these issues were directly related to race relations in the United States or to African American–White relations in the students' local community.

Appropriate valuing activities for our sample unit would include:

1. Reading and discussing selections from the novels *Roll of Thunder Hear My Cry, Let the Circle Be Unbroken,* and *The Road to Memphis* by Mildred D. Taylor. This trilogy describes the problems, hopes, and dreams of an African American family in Mississippi from the 1930s to 1940s. These novels include many selections that are rich in value conflicts and dilemmas.
2. Reading about and discussing the moral crisis that surfaced during the Civil War. Speeches by the abolitionists and their opponents will highlight the moral crisis that the Civil War brought to national consciousness.
3. Reading and discussing the moral issues raised in Martin Luther King Jr.'s "Letter from a Birmingham Jail" (April 16, 1963), in which he responds to charges that he was an outside agitator in that city and defends his non-violent resistance tactics.
4. Reading and discussing the moral issues raised in Martin Luther King Jr.'s "I Have a Dream" speech, delivered on August 28, 1963, during the March for Jobs and Freedom in Washington, D.C.
5. Militant Black leaders, such as Malcolm X and Stokley Carmichael, became increasingly impatient with King's nonviolent tactics. Read speeches and documents by King, Malcolm X, and Carmichael and discuss the ways their values were alike and different.
6. Role-playing and discussing the desegregation of an all-White school.
7. Viewing and discussing pictures of nonviolent civil rights demonstrations during the 1960s (Halberstam, 1998).
8. Reading and discussing a news story about a race problem in the local community.
9. Reading about and discussing the value conflicts which surfaced when federal and state institutions implemented "affirmative action" plans to help eliminate job discrimination in the 1970s and 1980s (Ezorsky, 1991).
10. Discussing the anti–affirmative-action proposition approved by the voters in California in 1996.

DECISION-MAKING AND CITIZEN ACTION

After the students have derived social science generalizations and clarified their values regarding the social issue, you should ask them to list all the possible actions they could take regarding race relations in their community, and to predict the consequences of each alternative.

It is imperative that the alternatives and consequences be realistic and based on the knowledge students have mastered during the scientific phase of the unit. Alternatives and consequences should be intelligent predictive statements and not ignorant guesses or wishful thinking. You should require students to give data and reasons to support the alternatives and consequences they formulate. For example, a student who states that his or her class can solve racial problems in the community by going from door to door telling residents about the problems would obviously be dreaming. This statement is not meant to suggest that information would not contribute to the problem's resolution. In our example, it would be impossible for the students to think of actions that would solve the racial problems in their community. However, they might be able to take action that will help to improve their own racial attitudes.

The students can identify alternatives and possible consequences in chart form, as illustrated in Table 15.3.

DETERMINING A COURSE OF ACTION

After naming alternatives, predicting their consequences, and identifying the knowledge supporting the alternatives and consequences, the students should then order the alternatives according to their hierarchy of values. The decision-making process is illustrated in Figure 15.2.

The students should pose and answer this question: *Which course of action is most consistent with my most important values?* The students should identify their values and order them into a hierarchy during the valuing phase of the social issues unit. A group of students may decide that they value the worth and dignity of the individual above all else, and that their next most important value is equality. They should try to define their values operationally and relate them to the alternative courses of action they have stated. They must resolve such problems as: Is taking no action at all when African Americans are experiencing discrimination in our community consistent with our values about the worth and dignity of the individual? Are we not denying the worth and dignity of the individual when we deny people equal opportunities under the law, in employment, and in education? How can we act in ways consistent with the values we hold?

Another group of students may conclude that they value majority rule above all else. Because the majority of Whites in the community do not think that African Americans should have certain jobs or live in certain neighborhoods, taking no action about the situation would be consistent with their values. These students studied the results of a recent community racial attitude survey.

If a group of students reaches this conclusion after thoughtful reflection, your role is to help the students reanalyze the sources of their values, determine how

TABLE 15.3. *Alternative Actions and Possible Consequences*

Alternative Actions Regarding Race Relations in Our Community	Possible Consequences
1. Take no group action.	1. More hostilities may occur. 2. More persons may be injured in racial violence. 3. African Americans and Whites may further separate and form separate societies. 4. Our own school may become involved in a racial conflict over school integration. 5. We will not be criticized by conservative factions in the school and wider community. 6. African Americans may be denied more rights in our community.
2. Take group action to improve racial feelings in our classroom and school.	1. We may encounter hostility from administrators, other students, and teachers. 2. If we proceed carefully, we may improve race relations in our school, but they will not necessarily improve in the wider community. 3. We may interest other students and teachers in working to help improve race relations in the school or wider community.
3. Take group action to improve race relations in the wider community.	1. We might encounter hostility from community groups. 2. We might inflame racial feelings from such groups. 3. Unless we win the cooperation of our parents, they may work against or not support our efforts. 4. By working carefully and wisely with civic and religious groups, we might be able to positively influence racial feelings in the community.
4. Take no group action, but individually act to improve race relations.	1. Such action may have little effect on the racial problems in our community, but it may make us feel better because we may be acting in ways more consistent with our values than before. 2. Our individual actions may influence the action of other individuals, and thus our efforts would have more influence.

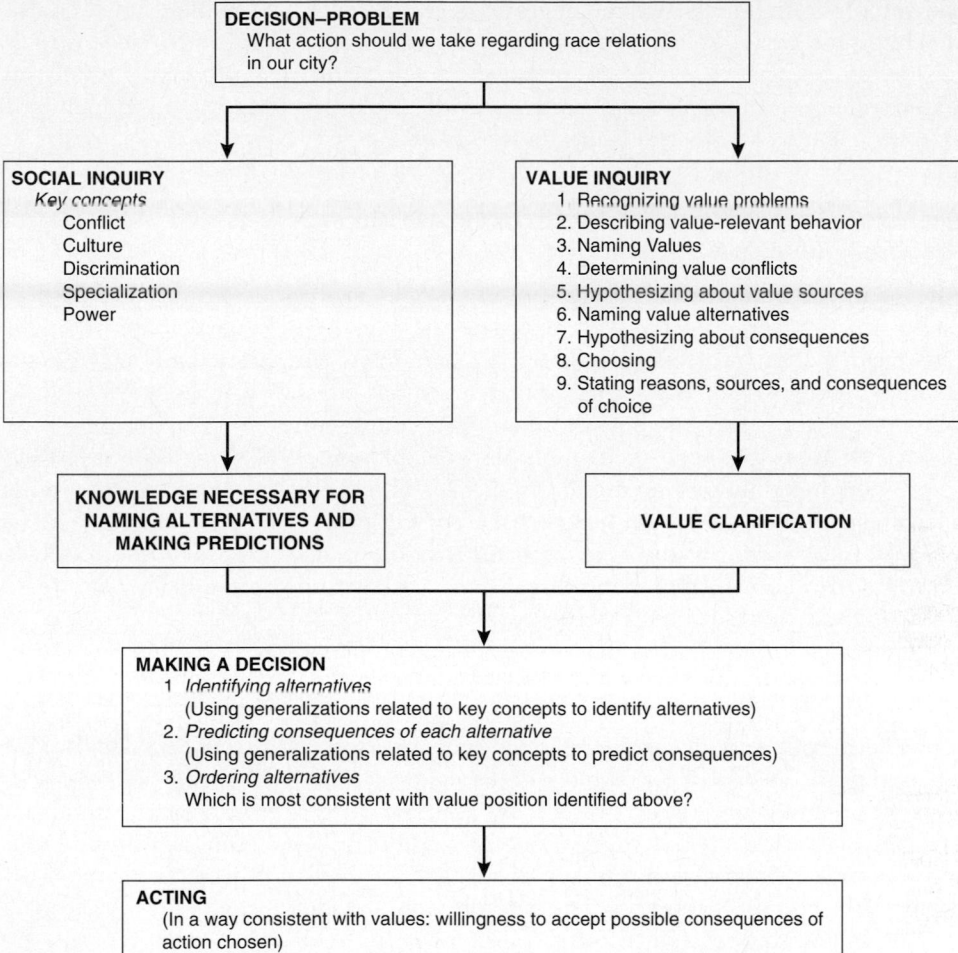

Figure 15.2
The decision-making process.

they may conflict with other values they hold or with American creed values such as equality and human dignity, and help them to identify the possible consequences of their beliefs. You should also help the students determine whether they can live with and be proud of the possible consequences of their value choices. To implement our theory of moral education, students must be allowed to make uncoerced decisions within a democratic classroom atmosphere. It is not an easy theory to implement. However, it is consistent with a democratic ideology and a commitment to human dignity, values which we endorse and on which our theory is based.

Students should be encouraged to make their own decisions, to accept responsibility for them, and not to rely on others, including teachers, to make decisions for them. While students should be encouraged to think independently about social issues, there will be situations in which students should and will make group decisions. Practice in group decision-making is desirable. In real-life situations, the individual must often participate in group decision-making. Skillful group decision-making is essential for civic competency in a democratic, pluralistic society. Also, if citizen action projects are to be planned and implemented, they will usually be undertaken in groups, although some individuals may decide to take independent action on some of the social issues the class studies.

PROVIDING OPPORTUNITIES FOR CITIZEN ACTION AND PARTICIPATION

After students have made decisions on important social issues, we should, whenever possible and practical, provide opportunities for them to participate in action and participation projects to implement their decisions. Participation gives students a greater sense of personal, social, and civic efficacy. Knowledge is of little value if it is not used to help solve human problems—especially in a period of our history when personal and societal problems loom large. While you will not be able to provide opportunities for students to act on all or perhaps most of the decisions they make (this would be neither possible nor desirable), the school, by cooperating with public and private agencies, can provide opportunities for students to act on some of their decisions. Traditionally, the social studies has educated students for civic apathy rather than for efficacy and action.

Citizen action and participation projects may take different forms. They may consist of volunteer services in the community, community studies having an action component, community research projects, internships, and citizen action designed to influence public policy at the regional, state, national, or international level. The age and grade level of the students will be major factors to be considered when citizen action and participation projects are planned. Internships in private and public agencies are usually not appropriate for students in the elementary and middle school grades. There are a number of successful internship projects, however, in many high schools. Elementary and middle school students can and do often participate in community service and research projects.

Students in the elementary and middle school cannot solve the major societal problems that very competent adults have been unable to solve. However, they can take some actions related to major social problems (Lewis, 1991). These actions will contribute in small ways to the improvement of their classrooms, schools, and communities. More importantly, however, such actions can help them to develop greater personal, social, and civic efficacy. Helping students to develop a greater sense of personal, social, and civic efficacy, and to develop greater skills in influencing their social and civic environments, should be the major goals of citizen action and participation projects and activities. Services to their communities should be an important but secondary consideration.

Citizen Action in the Community and School

When a social issue has divided a community, such as race relations in our example, it is probably best for students to confine their actions to their classroom, school, or to local situations (such as a club or church) where they do not run the risk of being publicly abused or ostracized. If a group of students becomes involved in a heated racial controversy in a sharply divided community, the school and the students may become vulnerable to severe attacks from extremist groups. Some students may independently decide to become involved in such a social issue in the community. However, they should act as individuals and not as agents of the school. Because the public school is very vulnerable in our society, it will be severely criticized if teachers and administrators do not exercise sound judgment in planning action and participation projects for students.

The most reasonable course of action for the students to take in our exemplary decision-problem unit may be to formulate a race relations program or ethnic studies lessons in their own school. They could start by working jointly with the principal, teachers, parents, and other persons in the school and neighborhood. The PTA may give the students needed help and support. Although the class, as a group, may decide on a course of action, no students should be forced to participate in a citizen action project or activity that they feel is contrary to their values and beliefs.

Because the school is a social institution with problems mirroring those of the larger society, students can practice shaping public policy by working to help eliminate problems in their classroom, school, or school district. They might start by studying and analyzing the problems within their classroom. To help students develop a sense of personal, social, and civic competency, you and your principal must be committed to the belief that students should participate in the making of school and other public policies.

Unless teachers and principals are willing to give students a role in the making of classroom and school policies, student action projects cannot be successfully implemented. Students who lack personal, social, and civic efficacy in their own school will be ineffective in shaping public policy and contributing to the solution of social problems in the wider community. Obviously, there are school policies that students cannot and should not be allowed to make or influence. School administrators and teachers must also conform to rules and laws made by higher authorities. However, when issues and problems such as discipline, dress codes, school assemblies, cafeteria food selection, fights on the playground, sexism, and racism arise in the school, student participation in the development of policy can help solve these problems, as well as help students develop a greater sense of personal, social, and civic efficacy. The nature and extent of student participation in school policy should be determined by the issue or problem, and by the maturity, knowledge, and interest that students have in the issue or problem.

Teachers who want to help students develop proficiency in citizen action skills should provide them with ample opportunities to clarify their policy goals and to learn how to exercise civic skills successfully. In a useful model (see Figure 15.3), Newmann (1975) identifies several essential components of an effective citizen action curriculum. It should help students to develop skills in (a) formulating policy goals, (b) working to rally support for those goals, and (c) resolving psycho-philosophic concerns. When students formulate policy goals using this model, they articulate and justify the moral choices involved in their policy and carry out policy research related to it. They explore and experiment with ways of exercising civic power when they work to rally support for their goal. Citizen action may cause philosophical and psychological dilemmas for individuals. Hence the need for the citizen action curriculum to help students to resolve psychological and philosophical concerns.

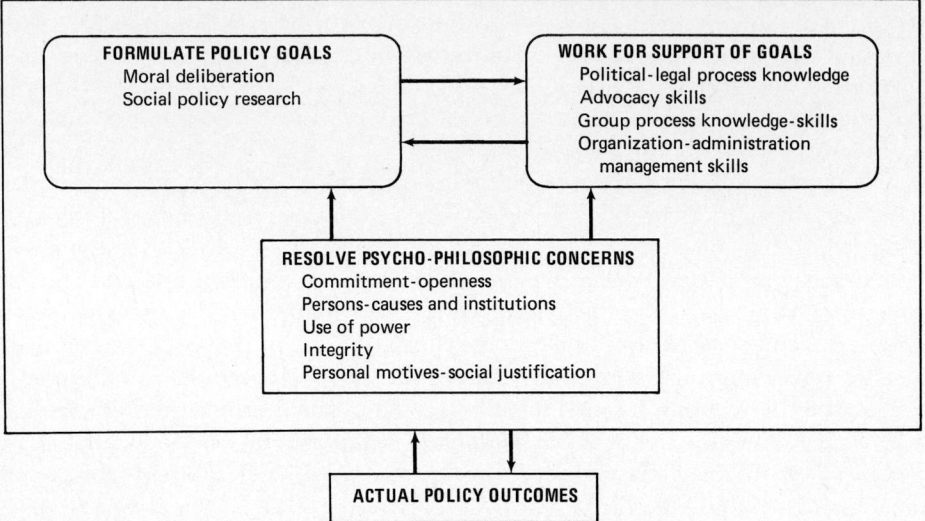

Figure 15.3
Areas of competence required to exert influence in public affairs.
Source: Fred N. Newmann, *Education for Citizen Action: Challenge for Secondary Curriculum,* copyright 1975, published by McCutchan Publishing. Reprinted by permission of the publisher.

Guidelines for citizen action and participation are presented in Table 15.4. Examples of citizen action and participation projects, grouped by grade levels, are presented below.

CITIZEN ACTION PROJECTS

Primary Grades

1. During a unit on the family, the students interviewed their parents and grandparents about what life was like when they grew up. Working with their teacher, the students developed a set of questions that each of them used in interviewing their parents and grandparents. The students who had grandparents who lived in another city conducted phone interviews.

2. When the students were studying about their community, they learned that pollution was a major problem. They decided they wanted to take some action about the problem. They saved all of the aluminum cans used in their homes and asked some of their neighbors to save those they did not want. They sold the aluminum cans to the Department of Ecology in their state for 34¢ per pound and used the money to buy plants and shrubs for their school yard.

3. A unit on the community in a second-grade class dealt in part with senior citizens in the community. The students became interested in the problems of senior citizens and raised the question: What can we do to help the

TABLE 15.4. *Guidelines for Citizen Action Projects*

1. The activities should be *meaningful* experiences, not merely projects in which students become involved just to say that they are participating in citizen action projects.
2. The *primary* goal of citizen action projects should be to provide experiences for the students whereby they can attain a sense of political effectiveness, and not just serve the community. However, the most effective projects contribute to the attainment of both goals.
3. Charity and other kinds of community help experiences are legitimate and potentially meaningful activities, although the projects should, as often as possible, help students to gain a sense of political effectiveness.
4. Students should participate in citizen action activities only after they have studied the related issue from the perspectives of the social sciences, analyzed and clarified their values regarding it, identified the possible consequences of their actions, and expressed a willingness to accept those consequences.
5. When problems within the school can be resolved through student action, participation in school activities should have priority over participation in projects in the wider community.
6. While group decision-making is legitimate and often desirable, no individual student should be required to participate in an action project that he or she feels is contrary to his or her values and beliefs.
7. The experience and age of the students should be considered when action projects are planned and implemented. Young children should confine their actions to their classroom, school, and family, or to other primary groups or secondary institutions in which they feel secure and that are supportive of their actions.
8. When citizen action projects are planned, the support of other teachers, students, school administrators, related community agencies, and members of the community should be solicited.
9. Students who wish to participate in citizen action projects should be allowed to have schedules conducive to such participation. The concept of the school should be broadened; activities needn't necessarily take place within the four walls of the school room.
10. When a community is seriously divided over a social issue and feelings within the community are intense, action projects should be confined to the classroom, school, family, or to other supportive institutions in which students feel secure.
11. Citizen action projects planned by student should not violate the laws and mores of a community.
12. Citizen action projects planned within the school should be consistent with American creed values and human dignity.
13. When citizen action projects are planned, the teacher should make every effort to help the students identify all the possible consequences of their actions, especially those actions that may have adverse consequences, either for the individual or the group.
14. Students who wish to engage in individual projects should not be discouraged, but should be helped to realize the fact that group action is usually more politically effective than individual action.
15. When citizen action projects are planned, the teacher should make every effort to minimize any physical, emotional, or psychological damage to the students. This can be accomplished largely by soliciting the cooperation of other persons in the school and wider community, and by carefully considering the possible consequences of different courses of action.
16. Citizen action projects in the social studies program should be nonpartisan. Although groups of students may decide to campaign for a particular candidate or issue, students with other beliefs and goals should have the option to plan parallel projects to support their beliefs and political choices.

senior citizens in our community? They decided to visit a senior-citizen home during the holiday season. They took gifts and sang holiday carols.

4. A third-grade class studied their city and learned that some people, in some parts of the city, often did not have enough food. There was a food bank that solicited donations of food for them. Each student saved a part of his or her allowance for several months to contribute money for a class food-bank donation. The class also chose the items it donated to the food bank.

5. A class studying family life in Colombia, South America, became concerned about poverty in other nations. The class decided that it wanted to make a donation to an agency that helped families in Latin America. They investigated different organizations and decided which would be the most appropriate to receive their donation. They raised the money for their donation by sponsoring a Walk-A-Thon at school. They asked neighbors to pledge 20¢ for each mile they walked.

Intermediate Grades

1. While they were studying an economics unit, the students pointed out that they always had trouble finding the specific brands of school supplies their teachers requested each September. They worked with their teacher and established and ran a school supply store in a vacant room in their school. They learned about wholesale prices, retail prices, and customer satisfaction. They also provided a needed service for their school.

2. A class that wanted to take a trip to their state capitol raised money with a series of car washes in their community. They observed their state legislature in action, talked to some of its members, and prepared a written report to share with the whole school.

3. A class wanted some new social studies software for use with the computers in their school. They raised money to buy it by selling spices to the people in their community.

4. A class conducted a comprehensive historical study of their community by interviewing senior residents and visiting museums, cemeteries, and other institutions. They wrote their findings in the form of a narrative history and shared it with the other classes in the school.

Upper Grades

1. When the school district faced a major budget problem, the students developed a campaign leaflet asking neighbors to vote for a special levy. They went to homes in their neighborhoods to distribute the leaflets and to ask citizens to support the special levy.

2. After studying a unit on the role of women in American life, the students in one class met and talked with the principal and the teachers about ways that the entire curriculum could include more content about women.

3. A group of students formed a Tutorial Club. The members of the club stayed one hour after school on designated days to tutor students who came to their Tutorial Center.

4. After studying the Bill of Rights and the Constitution, the students in one class sponsored a number of activities to promote the rights of students, including an assembly, a debate, and a guest lecture.

5. When the city was considering a proposal to name a street after Martin Luther King Jr., a class visited the City Council to present their support for the proposed legislation.

SUMMARY

Both scientific knowledge and clarified, reflectively examined values are necessary for citizen actors to make thoughtful decisions that will help to solve personal, social, and civic problems. Because of the conflicting and confused values in modern societies, schools need to help students develop clarified values consistent with American creed values, such as equality and human dignity. Students need to be taught a process for deriving and clarifying their values. We cannot expect people to affirm and to act on values that they have not chosen from alternatives within a democratic classroom atmosphere. The first part of this chapter describes a theory of value education, a related value inquiry model, and strategies for implementation in the classroom.

While valuing is essential in the decision-making process, citizen actors must also synthesize knowledge and values, and decide on a course of action consistent with their value choices. The second part of this chapter presents a rationale for decision-making and citizen action, an example of a decision-making unit, and examples of citizen action and participation activities. The major goal of citizen action and participation should be to help students to develop greater personal, social, and civic efficacy. Students will not be able to take action on many of the decisions they make in social studies classes. However, by working cooperatively with public and private agencies, you can provide students with some rich opportunities to implement a few of their decisions (Lewis, 1991). While citizen action and participation activities undertaken by students may make only small contributions to improving life in the community and solving social problems, they can contribute greatly to helping students acquire the attitudes and skills needed to influence their personal, social, and civic worlds.

REFLECTION AND ACTION ACTIVITIES

1. Locate a case study in a recent publication about an individual or group facing a decision-problem that has value components. The case may involve a White couple who are trying to decide whether to allow their children to be bused to a desegregated school, a young person who is trying to decide whether he or she should experiment with illegal drugs, or an organization that is trying to decide whether it should support an urban renewal project that will displace inner-city residents but result in a badly needed freeway. Using the author's valuing model, develop a valuing lesson plan around the case to teach to a group of students.

2. Pictures without captions are excellent tools for teaching value inquiry. Locate, in current magazines or on the Internet, a number of pictures that can evoke value questions. Mount the pictures and develop a series of questions (based on the value inquiry model

presented in this chapter) that you can ask students in order to develop their value inquiry skills.

3. Descriptive social science data can evoke value questions. Articles and accounts of the American Revolution, slavery, the Civil War, the Vietnam War, and contemporary social problems have much potential for value inquiry. Identify a selection in a social studies textbook and illustrate, with a teaching plan, how the selection can be used to help students to increase their value inquiry skills.

4. In your curriculum library, examine several social studies curriculum guides and textbooks and evaluate their value components. Do the materials include value inquiry objectives? Are the strategies for developing the objectives sound? In what ways would you modify the value components of these materials in order to make them more effective?

5. What role do values play in decision-making? What are the implications of your response for teaching decision-making skills?

6. What alternate unit plans can you use to help students gain proficiency in decision-making skills? Which plan do you think is the most effective? Why? Most practical? Why?

7. Identify a current social issue and construct a decision-making unit for students in the elementary or middle school grades. Include key concepts and generalizations related to the issue from the following disciplines: history, sociology, anthropology, geography, political science, economics, and psychology. Plan strategies for teaching value inquiry. Also include strategies for teaching pupils how to relate the key ideas to their values in order to make decisions. List possible courses of action that students might take on the issue, and their possible consequences.

8. Demonstrate your understanding of the following terms by writing or stating brief definitions for each. Also tell why each is important.

   a. values
   b. value inquiry
   c. value conflict
   d. value clarification
   e. didactic strategies
   f. Banks value inquiry model
   g. decision-making
   h. decision-problem
   i. enduring social issue
   j. personal efficacy
   k. social efficacy
   l. civic efficacy

REFERENCES

Ayers, W., & Miller, J. L. (Eds.). (1998). *A light in dark times: Maxine Greene and the unfinished conversation.* New York: Teachers College Press.

Banks, J. A. (1998). The lives and values of researchers: Implications for educating citizens in a multicultural society. *Educational Researcher,* 27(7), 4–17.

Code, L. (1991). *What can she know? Feminist theory and the construction of knowledge.* Ithaca, NY: Cornell University Press.

Ezorsky, G. (1991). *Racism and justice: The case for affirmative action.* Ithaca, NY: Cornell University Press.

Greene, M. (1995). *Releasing the imagination: Essays on education, the arts, and social change.* San Francisco: Jossey-Bass.

Halberstam, D. (1998). *The children.* New York: Random House.

Jary, D., & Jary, J. (1991). *Collins dictionary of sociology.* San Francisco: HarperCollins.

Lewis, B. A. (1991). *The kid's guide to social action.* Minneapolis, MN: Free Spirit.

Newmann, F. N. (1975). *Education for citizen action: Challenge for secondary curriculum.* Berkeley: McCutchan.

Simon, S. B., Howe, L., & Kirschenbaum, H. (1995). *Values clarification.* New York: Warner Books.

Shaftel, F. R., & Shaftel, G. (1982). *Role playing in the curriculum* (2nd ed.). Englewood Cliffs, NJ: Prentice-Hall.

FOR FURTHER READING

Cole, R. (1993). *The call to service: A witness to idealism.* Boston: Houghton Mifflin.

Jackson, P. W., Boostrom, R. E., & Hansen, D. T. (1993*). The moral life of schools.* San Francisco: Jossey-Bass.

Kirschenbaum, H. (1994). *One hundred ways to enhance values and morality in schools and youth settings.* Boston: Allyn and Bacon.

Lewis, B. A. (1991). *The kids' guide to social action.* Minneapolis, MN: Free Spirit.

Noddings, N. (1992). *The challenge to care in schools: An alternative approach to education.* New York: Teachers College Press.

Simon, S. B., Howe, L., & Kirschenbaum, H. (1991). *Values clarification: A handbook of practical strategies for teachers and students.* Chesterfield, MA: Values Press.

CHAPTER 16

Assessment Strategies

ASSESSMENT IN THE SOCIAL STUDIES

In what ways have Jane and Alexandra improved in their ability to form concepts and propose hypotheses? Under what circumstances have Chris, Rob, and Sonya demonstrated that they are progressing or experiencing problems? How well have the students accomplished the important goals of social studies? Questions such as these are the concern of assessing student learning in the social studies.

Subtle differences exist between *assessment* and *evaluation*. However, these concepts are frequently used interchangeably. Assessment is basically a formative process in which information on students' knowledge, skills, and understandings is fed back into the instructional process and used to improve instruction and student learning. Evaluation is basically a summative process in which teachers use information on students' knowledge, skills, and understandings to make value judgments about student performance. *Test* and *measurement* are two other terms that are commonly used when discussing assessment. A test is a formal, systematic procedure for gathering information. Most tests are paper and pencil procedures. Measurement is the process of assigning numbers or quantifying performance.

In this chapter we will use assessment in a broad sense to refer to information-gathering processes that can help teachers (1) formulate clear and precise goals, (2) set appropriate and attainable criteria that reflect what students have had an opportunity to learn, (3) gather data about the instructional process that can provide a basis for diagnosing what students know and can do, (4) provide feedback to students, (5) modify the curriculum and instruction, and (6) report the data to students, parents, and administrators in clear, meaningful, and accurate ways. When used in this way, assessment fulfills an important role in the teaching-learning process.

Many techniques and devices can be used in assessment. Some are informal teacher-made measures; others are formal methods or standardized tests. Some examples include observation reports, anecdotal records, reports of group discussions, collections of students' work, class diaries, logbooks, teacher-made tests, committee reports, class projects, checklists, attitudinal measures, and standardized national tests or assessment inventories. All of these provide evidence or data on which assessment can be based.

"There's no doubt I'll be failing you, Seymoure. Meanwhile, I hope to see some improvement in your work!"
Source: Joe E. Buresch. Used with permission.

PERFORMANCE-BASED ASSESSMENT

Performance-based assessment is an important outcome of the standards movement. Many advocates of national standards believe that performance-based assessment is a logical consequence of content standards and that content standards would be meaningless without a means to measure their achievement. They argue that as new curriculum frameworks are developed, performance standards should also be developed. Performance standards provide concrete examples and explicit definitions of what students need to know and be able to do in order to demonstrate proficiency in the skills and knowledge specified by content standards. Content standards and performance expectations are discussed in chapters 9, 12, 13, and 14.

Performance-based assessment, which is frequently called authentic assessment, is based on examples of student behavior in "real-world" situations instead of indirect estimates of learning goals such as paper and pencil assessments. Debates, exhibitions, teacher observations, videotapes of performances, inventories of student work, portfolios, and essays are examples of authentic assessments. Short answer, matching, true-false, and multiple-choice tests are examples of paper and pencil assessments. Paper and pencil assessments are frequently used at the end of a unit to gather information on student mastery of curriculum goals and objectives and to assign grades. They are popular for these purposes because they are objective and can cover a large number of content items. However, it is important to remember that paper and pencil assessments are only one component of a full assessment program.

Assessment should be used to improve student learning and instruction as well as to evaluate students. When used exclusively to evaluate students, its potential to improve curriculum and instruction and student learning is limited. The performance tasks that flow out of authentic assessment are designed to gather data about student progress and lead to improvements in curriculum and instruction. By integrating assessment into the natural flow of classroom activity and not limiting it to the end of an instructional period, authentic assessment becomes an integral part of teacher planning and student learning.

Evaluating students without an emphasis on improving student learning and helping teachers plan effective instruction raises historic concerns related to fairness and equity. Unequal resources in school facilities and materials, unequal access to knowledge, and other inequalities in learning opportunities can contribute to unequal results on high-stakes tests. This lack of opportunity to learn can lead to low-income students and students of color bearing the consequences of low scores in the form of delayed kindergarten entry, grade retention, placement in lower tracks, and denial of diplomas. Thus, initial inequalities can be compounded when assessment focuses on what students should know and be able to do rather than on what students know and can do as a result of their educational experiences. Students should not be held accountable for skills and knowledge they have not had an opportunity to learn.

Scoring rubrics can provide a means for teachers to consider whether they are holding students accountable for learning subject matter for which students have not had adequate instruction. Checklists, which are the simplest type of scoring rubric, are discussed in this chapter. Scoring rubrics can be used by teachers to assess student products, record observations of student behavior, and assess the effectiveness of the curriculum and teaching approaches. When scoring rubrics indicate students are meeting or not meeting performance standards, teachers will not only have data on student behavior, but they will be able to tie that behavior to specific activities and components of the curriculum. Scoring rubrics can also provide students and parents with information on student performance. When used by students in the form of self-evaluations, scoring rubrics can reduce confusion about performance criteria and can help students to focus their behaviors on learning objectives and to take responsibility for completing assignments. Scoring rubrics that provide information gathered from teacher observations, student samples, and student self-evaluations provide a rich source of data for parent conferences. They allow teachers to share specific information about students' progress and problems. They can also provide a departure point for teachers to explain the purpose of school assignments and what parents can do to support the achievement of their children.

When integrated into instructional planning and viewed as a continuous process, performance-based assessment has the potential for improving student learning. The major goals of student assessment should be to help teachers, parents, and students better understand what students know and can do, encourage students to continue to strive for further growth, and provide information that can help improve the curriculum and instruction.

INSTRUCTIONAL OBJECTIVES: A TECHNIQUE FOR ASSESSMENT

It is virtually impossible to evaluate learning in social studies if the instructional goals or objectives are not clearly stated at the outset. Indeed, you might think of objectives and assessment as opposite sides of the same coin. The more clearly and precisely you state the objectives, the more likely you will be able to obtain precise data on student learning and the effectiveness of the curriculum and instructional process. Using this approach, you can specify objectives in terms of students' performance or behaviors that are readily observable and that can be easily assessed by a criterion measure of acceptable performance. Behavioral (or performance) objectives specify the behaviors you expect students to exemplify. These are examples of objectives stated in behavioral terms.

> The student is able to:
> *recall* the cardinal directions.
> *estimate* population growth.
> *form* the concept of population density.

Note that the italicized words above are quite specific and indicate well-defined intellectual processes. The processes have been discussed earlier in this text. They indicate clearly what the student is expected to do. You can use a checklist or an observation form to verify that students have had an opportunity to learn the tasks and to identify the level at which the task is performed.

In contrast, vague or ambiguous words do not provide help for assessment because they do not identify readily observable learning behaviors. Here are examples of vague or ambiguous objectives.

To *know* the major rivers and capital cities.
To *understand* the growth of large cities.
To *appreciate* the importance of transportation routes.

Despite the fact that such words as know, understand, and appreciate are commonly used as objectives, they give no evidence of a specific outcome that can be easily recognized and used as a basis for assessment.

Developing Instructional Objectives in Social Studies

Stating an objective in behavioral or performance terms means that the objective must tell what the students are doing when they demonstrate their achievement of the objective. Table 16.1 consists of action verbs classified as cognitive or affective processes or as social studies skills. Each of these is a recognizable action that you can observe and record on a checklist or an observation record. These action words are combined with appropriate social studies content to complete the objective as shown in Table 16.2.

CRITERIA OF ACCEPTABLE PERFORMANCE

Performance objectives are usually stated in ways such that the demonstrated performance is either evident or it is not. In the checklist shown in Figure 16.1, an individual student's progress is reported in terms of objectives accomplished. Note that Jerri Ann has not yet developed the concept *population density*. Rather than grade it with a traditional F, it is simply left blank, indicating that it still must be accomplished.

Here is where the teacher must make several important instructional decisions. Must every student accomplish every objective? If not, then how many and which ones shall constitute a basic or minimal mastery of the goal? Has enough of the important content been learned to provide a basis for future learning? Are some content goals essential prerequisites that cannot be omitted? Generally, teachers set a mastery goal of 80 percent of a lesson's major objectives. This includes all those that are considered minimum essentials. Figure 16.2 shows a class record of goals accomplished. Note that item 1 is marked with an asterisk to indicate that it is an essential. All students have accomplished it.

Given the need to individualize instruction and to provide higher levels of accomplishment for various students, several other approaches to setting criteria measures are possible. The simplest approach is to increase the quantities in the examples given above, for example, nine out of 10 responses correct, 100 percent accuracy, or the same task completed in a shorter time. Such criteria test for greater retention, accuracy, or speed of learning, but the learning task remains essentially

TABLE 16.1. *A Sample of Strong Action Verbs*

Cognitive Processes	Affective Processes	Social Studies Skills
to recall	to prefer	to construct (a model)
to recite	to choose	to draw (a map)
to describe	to believe in	to interpret (symbols)
to identify	to react positively or	to locate (countries)
to compare	negatively toward	to identify (time
to contrast	to response to	zones)
to evaluate	to judge as good or	to measure (distance)
to solve	bad	to determine (slope
to apply	to approve	from a contour map)
to observe	to comply with	to translate (color
to analyze	to acclaim	codes)
	to react with pleasure	to show distortion of
		various map
		projections

TABLE 16.2. *Combining an Action Verb with Social Studies Content*

The student will be able to . . .

recall ...the names of the continents

compare ...population distributions

develop the concept of ...population density

apply ...the principles of a grid coordinate system to a hypothetical country

estimate ...population growth

point out ...areas of greatest distortion on a Mercator projection

explain why ...windward slopes receive greater precipitation than leeward slopes

judge as good (or bad) ...a system of land tenure

react with sympathy ...to evidence of hunger or poverty

be moved to action ...to improve environmental quality

prefer (or choose) ...a flood control project over preserving a district as a wilderness area

develop the generalization that ...people's use of the land in a given region is a function of the attitudes, objectives, and technical skills of the population

the same. There is no qualitative increase in the intellectual level of learning or in social studies content goals.

Qualitative increase in the learning level may be accomplished by specifying more complex, sophisticated, and higher-order processes of cognitive or affective learning. We refer you back to the discussion of Bloom's Taxonomy of Educational Objectives in Chapter 4. The list of key words given at each of the levels of the taxonomy can be used as verbs for specifying instructional objectives at different cognitive levels. Examples of affective processes are listed in Table 16.1.

As a result of this unit of work on _____ *population* _____
                                              (TOPIC)

_____ *Jerri Ann* _____ is able to.
         (STUDENT'S NAME)

		Comments
1. Recall the names of the seven continents.	X	
2. Compare the population distribution patterns of New York, Chicago, and Seattle.	X	
3. Develop the concept "population density."		
4. Apply the principles of a grid coordinate system to a hypothetical country.	X	*See attached map completed in class*

Figure 16.1
Individual progress report.

As result of this unit of work on _____ *population* _____
                                             (TOPIC)

the students are able to

	Chris	John	Mark	Robert	Connie	Matt	Stuart	Carolyn	Allison	Joey	Jay Dee
* 1. Compare population distribution.	✓	✓	✓	✓	✓	✓	✓	✓	✓	✓	✓
2. Explain the concept of "population density."	✓		✓	✓			✓		✓		
3. Apply principles of the grid coordinate system.	✓			✓		✓		✓			✓

Figure 16.2
Class progress report.

Here are examples of instructional goals which specify more complex tasks:

Given data from the 1970, 1980, 1990, and 2000 censuses, the student will be able to construct a bar graph showing the change in population for the following cities: New York, Cleveland, Chicago, and Pittsburgh. The student will propose several hypotheses that could explain the changes in population.

Students can project an estimate of the population of the same cities in 2010 using the same data from the 1970, 1980, 1990, and 2000 censuses. Assume that there are no changes in basic demographic trends.

Another approach to setting different levels of performance is to require a more creative approach to the task. For example, the criterion may be to present two or more different approaches or solutions to the same problem, rather than to seek a single, convergent solution. To use some of the higher-level thinking processes we discussed in Chapters 3 and 15, students may be asked to provide two or more alternate solutions in a decision-making situation. Each might be equally feasible or might solve the problem, although one might be preferable to the other.

IS THE MINIMUM ALSO THE MAXIMUM?

As an outgrowth of public demands that schools be more accountable for student performance (or the lack of it), many states have established statewide minimum competency tests in basic skill areas. Passing these tests is often a prerequisite for high school graduation. Many educators have expressed concern that the basic or minimum levels of performance specified will become, by default, the maximum as well. You need to be alert to this danger and to be sure to specify goals that, while tailored to individual differences, stress imagination, creativity, and higher thought processes. You must challenge students so that (to paraphrase Tennyson) their reach exceeds their grasp, else what are schools for? The National Council for the Social Studies' (NCSS) Social Studies Standards, summarized in Table 1.3, can help you avoid this problem. The NCSS standards include performance expectations for the early, middle, and high school grades. The performance expectations tie assessment to the 10 overarching curriculum themes identified in the standards.

METHODS OF ASSESSMENT

There are many methods of assessment you may use to assess student performance. They range from informal observation and simple checklists to formally administered standardized tests and national evaluation programs. Some of the most commonly used techniques include:

Autobiographies	Committee reports	Performance charts
Activity records	Collections of student work	Portfolios
Attitudinal measures		Questionnaires
Anecdotal records	Class projects	Semantic differential tests
Behavior journals	Group discussions	
Cumulative records	Interviews	Sociometric measures
Class diaries	Log books	Standardized tests
Charts	National assessment tests	Teacher-made tests
Checklists	Observation records	

In order to provide a more systematic framework for discussing the techniques listed above, we have chosen to focus our discussion of assessment strategies on several major dimensions of the social studies. This approach will put the assessment techniques into an appropriate context and will show how more than one method can be used to gather data on the same goal.

EVALUATING THE RESULTS OF SOCIAL INQUIRY: FACTS, CONCEPTS, GENERALIZATIONS, AND THEORIES

We have placed a heavy emphasis on the importance of social inquiry and its products (Chapter 3), questioning strategies (Chapter 4), and a variety of specialized social studies skills (Chapter 5). In the following sections we will describe a variety of assessment measures that are both simple and effective for gathering data on student performance in these areas. Notice that we place emphasis on simplicity and ease of use. Our experience is that when assessment measures are complex, time-consuming, or difficult to administer, teachers simply will not use them, no matter

"You're not living up to your potential!"
Source: Joseph Farris. Used with permission.

how much potential data they promise. It is far better to use a variety of information measures on a regular and systematic basis than to rely on one or two assessment tasks during the term.

In Chapter 3 we discussed the products of social inquiry: facts, concepts, generalizations, and theories. You can use a variety of techniques to assess whether students have acquired these important learning products and whether or not they can use them in making reflective decisions. Some of these include:

Anecdotal records	Group discussions	Checklists
Teacher-made tests	Samples of student work	Class projects

Anecdotal Records

An anecdotal record is a brief, factual record of a student's performance, noting what a student has done but avoiding judgmental inferences. Table 16.3 illustrates a few entries from Manuel's record. The entries are related to learning the concept of historical time. He is in the fifth grade.

This extract from an anecdotal record relates Manuel's progress in developing the notions of order and sequence as parts of the concept of chronological (or historical) time. It has the advantage of providing a detailed record of learning diagnosis and what was done to develop the prerequisite notion of sequence. The obvious disadvantage is that careful reporting, even though brief, does take time to do. Yet the analytic detail in Manuel's case is of far more value than a simple checklist that only shows he has not mastered the concept.

Group Discussions

Group discussions are often an important vehicle for having a class formulate generalizations about several samples of data that have been logged into a data retrieval

TABLE 16.3. *Anecdotal Record*

Sept. 25 Manuel seems to have trouble with the concept of *historical time* and a sense of chronology.

Sept. 26 Today I worked separately with Manuel. He read a story about Columbus. He could retell most of the important facts in correct sequence.

Oct. 1 Class began to develop a time line of European explorers who came to America. Manuel helped draw in the lines and markers for 100-year intervals.

Oct. 2 Rosalie worked with Manuel to make up a list of explorers. Needed much practice to put them in order. He is still confused and uncertain about how to arrange years in order.

Oct. 4 M. put explorers and dates on 3 × 5" cards and moved them back and forth on his desk. Success! This worked. He could now arrange them from earliest to latest and vice versa. He now has the idea of sequence. But the notion that 1492 is over 500 years ago still has no meaning for M.

chart for easy study and analysis. See, for example, Table 5.3, "The Political System in Three Nations." Assuming that research groups have filled in the chart with data from the three countries, discussion will no doubt be lively as students compare and contrast political experiences under the three political systems. Using an informal checklist like that shown in Table 16.4, you can evaluate both the process of arriving at the generalization and the validity of the generalization itself. The students arrived at the following generalizations:

1. In each of the three societies, some individuals and groups are authorized to make decisions that all citizens must obey.
2. The ways in which the three nations determine which groups will make binding political decisions differ.

As is evident from Table 16.4, the criteria for assessment relate to both the process of forming the generalization and its validity. The teacher listens carefully to the discussion and checks off the items as the discussion goes along or at its end. When students have had some experience with the process of generalizing, they can use the same checklist as a means of self-assessment. Notice that the criteria refer almost entirely to the data base and the students' use of it, thus helping to make the assessment as objective as possible, yet keeping the instrument informal.

The same process can be used with simpler content and with younger students. In Chapter 10, for example, we discussed the concept of *role* and how it was developed within the family. In many primary grades, a class studies families in its own community and then studies families in other parts of the world for a cross-cultural comparison. The chart shown in Table 16.4 could easily be modified with simpler language to assess generalizations formed about roles of mothers and fathers in various parts of the world (e.g., our town, Japan, and Nigeria). Table 16.5 shows a modified version for use in primary grades.

Here again, the emphasis is on the students' development and use of the data about mothers' roles in different cultural settings, but the checklist's language is simplified. The chart could be filled out entirely by the teacher, or the students could determine whether the criteria had been met through group discussion. Students could enter the check marks with the teacher's help.

Paper and Pencil Assessments

Paper and pencil assessments are one of the most widely used forms of assessment of social science facts, concepts, generalizations, and theories. There are many formats, including true/false (or yes/no) responses, multiple choice, sentence completion (fill in the blanks), and open-ended essays. They are relatively easy to give and to score and most teachers believe them to be impartial or objective.

There are limitations, however, that must be considered. Good test items require students to think carefully before answering, and they are not easy to construct. Too often, test items deal only with low-level thought processes or with trivial content knowledge. Moreover, the skills needed for taking objective tests are often not the same skills developed in learning the content. Students must learn to "psych out" what the teacher expects in the test items and to work under the pressure of time limits.

Because many of the technical aspects of constructing teacher-made tests are beyond the scope of this book, we shall provide here only a few illustrations of sample test items. Each of the items shown in Table 16.6 is keyed to a social science concept that forms the organizing focus of a unit on water resources. The items were also written at various levels of Bloom's Taxonomy to test a wide range of higher-level thinking abilities.

TABLE 16.4. *Checklist for Student Discussion of a Generalization*

Criteria	Yes	No	Comments
1. Are all data accurate?			
2. Are there data from all three samples, U.S., U.K., and Russia.			
3. Are comparisons and contrast based on the data?			
4. Do the data support the generalization?			
5. Is it accurate (true) for all three samples?			
6. Are there obvious exceptions that might disprove it.			
7. Is it stated as a testable statement?			

TABLE 16.5. *Generalization Checklist for Primary Grades*

Criteria	Yes	No	Comments
1. Do we have information about mothers' roles in all three places?			
2. Are there things that are the same in all places?			
3. Are there things that are different?			
4. Do we have facts to back up our statements?			
5. Are the statements true in all three places?			

TABLE 16.6. Sample Test Items Written at Various Levels of Bloom's Taxonomy

Taxonomy Level and Concept	Test Item
1. Knowledge (watershed)	A watershed is a a) wet region of land b) building for storing water c) marshy area d) land area that drains into a stream or river or lake
2. Application (landform)	The best name for this group—*mountain, plateau, hill*—is a) region b) landform c) area d) town
3. Application (river system)	People can control the flow of water by a) planting trees and building dams b) building dams and filtering water c) using water meters and planting trees d) filtering water and planting trees
4. Comprehension (landforms)	Which of the following have caused natural changes in landforms? a) roads and highways b) glaciers and fast streams c) dynamite and rainfall d) running water and irrigation
5. Comprehension (supply and demand)	As more people draw on the same water supply, the amount of available water tends to a) increase b) decrease c) remain the same d) evaporate
6. Application (watershed)	Which of the following would you consider when searching for a water supply for a large city? a) the closest stream and pure water b) a natural lake c) pure water d) an abundant supply and pure water
7. Analysis (population)	Population decreases in a community most likely result from a) decline in the number of businesses b) betters schools in the community c) better jobs elsewhere d) decline in businesses and better jobs elsewhere
8. Analysis (supply and demand)	Examine the conclusions given below. Using the charts in Figure 16.3, decide which statement is the best conclusion. a) City A is a rapidly growing community and does not have enough water for the people. b) City B is entitled to help from the state as it has the greatest need for a new water supply. c) City C is experiencing many problems with water shortage.
9. Analysis (supply and demand)	Choose the statement that explains your conclusion. a) City A is near to us and we have relatives there. If they want more water they should have it. b) The governor lives in City B, and therefore they need help from the state to provide them with a new water supply. c) Many people have moved into City C, and the rainfall has been constantly decreasing. d) All three cities need more water due to growth in population. e) All three cities are experiencing water problems due to decreasing rainfall.

TABLE 16.6. *(Continued)*

Taxonomy Level and Concept	Test Item

Factory and Fish

A committee has been working on a problem of what to do about a large factory in their town. This factory is polluting the river, and as a result many of the fish in the river have died. Some of the townspeople think the factory should be made to move out of town. Other townspeople think the factory is more important than the fish. Many people in town work there.

10. Evaluation (technology)

What do you think the committee should do? Choose the best solution.
a) The factory should be made to move out of the town.
b) The factory should be allowed to stay and operate as it is.
c) The factory should be allowed to stay if it installs a purifying plant.

11. Evaluation (technology)

Choose the statement below that best explains the solution you chose for question 10.
a) The plaint should be made to move. If it moves, there are other jobs in other factories for the workers. They will only have to travel a short distance.
b) The factory should be allowed to stay. The job is more important than the fish. People who fish can fish in other streams.
c) They should install a purifying plant. No matter where the plant moves, it will have to do this, as no one will allow the plant to pollute the river.
d) The town should help to pay for the purification plant because many townspeople fish in the river.
e) Make the plant move because we don't want factories dirtying our town. Besides, the more factories, the more people and we might have to build a new school.

12. Synthesis (supply and demand, river systems, watershed, landforms, technology, population)

Suppose that a large city is in need of a new water supply. Briefly describe the factors you would consider in searching for this supply.

13. Synthesis (supply and demand, river systems, watershed, landforms, technology, population)

Suppose you are told by the town council that it thinks your town will not have an adequate water supply in 10 years. Outline a plan to test whether its belief is true or false.

Source: Adapted from Alberta P. Sebolt, "The Consequences of a Test for Concept Learning and Identification of the Cognitive Processes Required," *Curriculum Model No. 1: Water Resources* (ERIC Document No. ED 040 892).

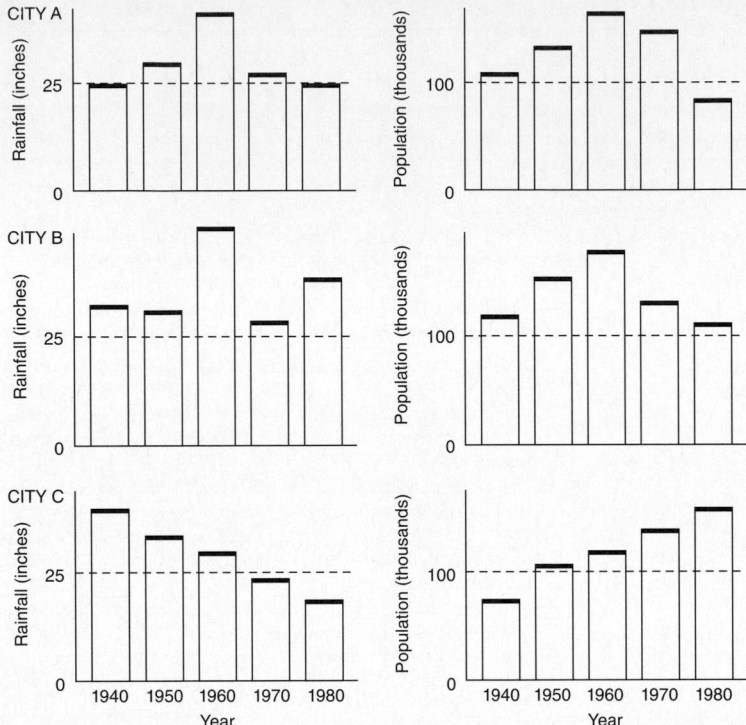

Figure 16.3
Rainfall and population graph for three different cities. Each of these cities has asked the state to help them find a new supply of water. The state says they can help only some of the cities this year.

Hints for Writing Test Items
To help you write test items for teacher-made tests, here are a few hints to keep in mind.

True/False Items
1. T/F items are best used to test knowledge recall or comprehension level knowledge.
2. Use this type only for information that is genuinely true or false. Avoid material that may be open to interpretation.
3. Avoid words like *always, sometimes,* or *never.* They tend to confuse or raise suspicions in the students' minds.
4. Keep the sentences short, clear, and positively stated.
5. Avoid negatives such as not, none, or neither-nor.
6. Use yes/no for younger students. This prevents confusion in writing the letters T and F.

Samples:
1. __T__ Albany is the capital of New York.
2. __F__ The earth is the center of the universe.
3. __F__ Chicago is a city on the Gulf of Mexico.

Sentence Completion
1. Fill in the blanks are best used for very specific knowledge recall items.
2. The main statement should contain enough information to give the students an idea of the response sought.
3. Decide what alternative responses you will accept as correct. (Be prepared for surprises from some students!)
4. Decide whether you will penalize for incorrect spelling.

Samples
1. The city in Japan with the largest population is _____ .
2. _____wrote the Declaration of Independence.
3. Congress makes our national laws. It is made up of two parts, the House of Representatives and the _____.

Multiple Choice Items
1. These can be used to test a wide variety of higher-level thought processes. See examples in Table 16.6.
2. Be sure that alternatives represent reasonable choices that will require students to choose carefully among them. Avoid obviously wrong or absurd choices.
3. Don't intentionally try to trick or mislead students with cunningly worded items. Questions should be forthright even if difficult.
4. Avoid items that test obscure trivia.
5. Vary the place of the correct response. Don't establish a pattern that the third response is always the correct one.

Essay Tests
1. Essays provide the best test of learning at the analysis, synthesis, and evaluation levels.
2. Give clear directions about what is expected, how the theme or topic should be handled, and the maximum length.
3. Prepare a short list of criteria for judging the essay and use it as a basis for grading and for giving feedback to the students on their performance. If necessary, list factual data that must be presented for correct response.
4. If possible, grade the essay blind (i.e., without knowing the student's name) to help increase objectivity.
5. Place a premium on unusually creative responses; encourage independence of thought and judgment; reward provocative and highly original thinking.

See Table 16.6, items 12 and 13, for samples.

In summary, paper and pencil tests are good measures for assessing students' learning of facts, concepts, generalizations, and theories. If carefully designed, they can be used to evaluate a wide range of thinking levels. Remember, however, that such tests have as many weaknesses as they do strengths; they are not necessarily superior to the many other informal measures mentioned above. A good checklist, like those shown in Tables 16.4 and 16.5, can produce more useful assessment data than a number of hastily prepared tests dealing only with factual recall or low-level thinking processes.

ASSESSING THINKING SKILLS

Throughout this book, and particularly in Chapter 5, we have stated that thinking skills are an important component of the social studies curriculum. It is equally important to evaluate whether or not students have developed such skills and how well they are able to use them.

In Chapter 5, we discussed a number of thinking processes, including describing, inferring, analyzing, conceptualizing, generalizing, applying generalizations to new situations, and making decisions. More authentic assessments, in which students use or apply what they have learned, will allow teachers to incorporate higher-order thinking into assessment. Formal tests are better used to assess the product or outcome of the thinking process. More authentic assessment can include:

Charts	Checklists	Group discussions	Anecdotal records
Interviews	Observations	Samples of student work	Student log books

Describing

The activities suggested on pp. 129–130 all require students to observe some activity and record what they saw. Thus, a list dictated to a teacher by young children or a log describing what pupils ate in the cafeteria, the major activities that the class participated in during a field trip, or who did the shopping on Saturday morning become the primary sources of evidence. What is important is the criteria applied to the lists. A checklist might include questions or criteria such as:

1. Were all events recorded?
2. Did anything unusual happen?
3. Did you notice any kind of pattern of events?
4. Do others agree the record is accurate?
5. Is sufficient detail given to create a mental image?
6. Is vocabulary expressive yet still accurate?

Note that the activities suggested range from observing and counting food choices at lunch to describing characteristics of French impressionist painting, or the ways women are depicted on TV commercials. Thus, students must learn not only how to describe in objective detail (what and how many), but also how to describe in qualitative terms, using rich and varied vocabulary, yet still retaining accuracy. A checklist developed with the above criteria provides a good measure for assessing describing skills.

Making Inferences

To make an inference means to draw a conclusion or make a deduction from facts or observations. Here again, authentic tasks provide good assessment devices. Building on the activities mentioned above for describing, you can examine charts or logs with students. You can ask questions to nudge the students into giving an explanation or interpretation of who brought more groceries on Saturday morning, men or women:

How do you explain this situation?
What can you conclude from these facts?
Why might there be more women (or men) shopping at this time?
What might men (or women) be doing at that time?
Could you conclude that women like to shop more than men?
Could you conclude that it is a woman's role to do the grocery shopping on Saturday morning?

The above questions are designed to tease out inferences from the students, and to derive meaning from their observations. For more advanced students the criteria are stated in logical terms:

Are the inferences logically deduced from the data?
Are other conclusions equally plausible? (Many men work on Saturdays; therefore, women do the shopping.)
Has the inference gone beyond the data to support it?

In summary, the teacher observes group (or individual) discussions carefully, using a checklist based on the above criteria to record evidence of students' ability to make inferences.

Analyzing Information

When students analyze information, they identify its parts and establish logical relationships between the parts and the whole. In teaching the skills of analyzing social science material, we most often want students to separate facts from opinions, assumptions, or conclusions. Another skill is the ability to determine whether facts are presented to support a conclusion or generalization. Lastly, it is important that students be able to analyze materials such as films, posters, slogans, or TV commercials to recognize such forms as stereotypes, propaganda, racism, chauvinism, or saber-rattling.

Checklists offer one of the simplest ways of assessing students' progress in analyzing information, as shown in Table 16.7. Teacher-made tests can also be used to evaluate a student's ability to analyze information. For example:

Directions

Read the article "Teddy Roosevelt Urges War with Spain." It appeared in the *New York World* in 1898.

1. The statement that the USS Maine exploded in Havana harbor is a (an):

_____fact   _____conclusion

_____inference   _____assumption

2. The statement that all the Cuban people support immediate independence from Spain is a (an):

_____fact   _____assumption

_____conclusion   _____inference

3. Teddy Roosevelt's statements about American power and might, his claim of sole right to control the Caribbean, and his call for an immediate attack on Spanish forces are called:

_____prejudice   _____sarcasm

_____jingoism   _____propaganda

Conceptualizing

The role of concepts in social science inquiry has been discussed at length in Chapter 3, and two strategies for concept formation and concept attainment were presented in Chapter 5. Teacher-made test items for concept learning have already been presented in Table 16.6. Here we are concerned with the skill of conceptualizing.

TABLE 16.7. *Checklist for Analyzing Information*

Jane is able to:	Yes	No	Comments
1. Identify facts and relate to generalizations.			
2. Distinguish inferences from facts.			
3. Point out unstated assumptions.			
4. Determine whether facts support a conclusion.			
5. Recognize propaganda, bias, and chauvinism.			
6. Identify sarcasm, satire, and irony.			
7. Identify main theme and subtopics.			

Once again, one of the easiest and most direct sources of evidence regarding students' ability to form or attain concepts is close observation of individuals or small groups while they are directly involved in the process. The checklist shown in Table 16.8 takes its format directly from the elements of the strategy.

If the deductive concept attainment strategy had been used, the teacher would follow the basic strategy shown in Table 5.2. The teacher evaluates the students' mastery by asking them to identify examples of the concept from a list of examples and nonexamples of it. The student then defines the concept. For example:

> Which of the following are transportation vehicles?
> _____ automobile   _____ airplane
> _____ bicycle   _____ ship
> _____ bed   _____ helicopter
> _____ rickshaw   _____ seesaw

The students might define *transportation vehicle* as "a thing you can get on or into that will take you somewhere faster than you could walk there." They might also add, "You can get on a bed or a seesaw, but it doesn't take you anywhere." Obviously, the phrasing is that of young children, but the essence of the definition is there.

ASSESSING DECISION-MAKING AND CITIZEN ACTION

In Chapter 15, we developed a rationale and presented a variety of strategies for decision-making and citizen action. We also discussed the skills related to these two

TABLE 16.8. *Checklist for Concept Formation*

Julie is able to:	Yes	No	Comments
1. Observe and list data.			
2. Put similar things together in groups.			
3. Identify what characteristics are common in each group.			
4. Rearrange things into other groups if other characteristics seem obvious or more logical.			
5. Give a name or label to the group.			
6. State a definition of the group that correctly applies to things in the group.			

TABLE 16.9. *Chart for Evaluating Decision-Making Ability*

A. Decision-problem: _____

B. Related knowledge (identify concepts and generalizations):_____
_____
_____

C. Value position (clarification and identification):
_____

D. Identifying alternatives: Predicting consequences of each:

_____   _____

_____   _____

_____   _____

_____   _____

E. Ordering alternatives (which is most consistent with value position identified above?):

1. _____

2. _____

3. _____

4. _____

F. Acting (in a way consistent with values, willingness to accept possible consequences of action chosen):

_____
_____
_____

areas in Chapter 5. Here we shall present briefly a number of assessment tasks that can be used with these important processes. They include:

Charts	Checklists	Student diaries
Anecdotal records	Student logs	Attitudinal measures
Case study reports	Interviews with students	

Our model for the decision-making process is presented in Figure 15.2. Table 15.3 shows how a variety of alternative courses of action and their possible consequences might look when put in chart or poster form. Table 16.9 is a chart for assessing decision-making ability. It provides a means to log in all the essential components of the process and identify what is missing. A checklist such as shown in Table 16.10 records student performance on the process.

TABLE 16.10. *Checklist for Evaluating Decision-Making Skills*

Sonya is able to:	Yes	No	Comments
1. Identify related knowledge appropriate to the problem.			
2. Identify and clarify values involved and own position.			
3. List alternative course of action.			
4. Predict possible consequences.			
5. Rank other alternatives consistent with value position.			
6. Choose a course of action consistent with values.			
7. Act on decision; willing to accept possible consequences.			

ASSESSING CITIZEN ACTION AND PARTICIPATION

As we discussed in Chapter 15, students should have opportunities to follow up decision-making processes with direct involvement in some form of citizen action or participation. The key goal of the social studies program is to help students develop a greater sense of personal, social, and civic efficacy. In short, students should develop strong and positive attitudes that (1) they can make important and worthwhile contributions to dealing with social problems; (2) they can work effectively with others to solve such problems; and (3) when working with others, they can find effective means to influence public policy. Put even more simply, students who have had good experiences with citizen action programs in schools should develop strong beliefs that (1) "I have something worthwhile to say, so I will speak out"; (2) "Together we can get something done about this"; and (3) "My vote counts and we can fight City Hall."

None of the above statements should suggest a naively simplistic approach to the problem of citizen participation in government. We are fully aware of the power and importance of money, lobbies, and special interest groups, entrenched bureaucracies, election politics, and political alignments. What we are more concerned about are the pervasive citizen attitudes of apathy, helplessness, and alienation from the entire political process. Such attitudes are expressed in statements like "What good will it do? Who will listen to me? I can't get any answers at City Hall. My vote won't count. You can't fight City Hall. Politicians control things."

In evaluating the role of citizen participation and action, you must pay close attention to the students' expression of feelings, beliefs, and attitudes about participation in the political process. In assessing the wide array of activities suggested in Chapter 15, you may use authentic tasks such as:

Student diaries	Role-playing	Student interviews
Attitudinal measures	Class logs	Anecdotal records
Student reports		

The important point in using the above measures is that you must look for expression of student beliefs or attitudes or create situations, such as role-playing or class dramas, in which such attitudes can be expressed.

An attitudinal scale like the one shown in Table 16.11 is a useful device. The scale is designed to measure the strength of attitudes and runs from "strongly agree" through "uncertain" to "strongly disagree." The open-ended questions at the end of the inventory provide further opportunity for students and feedback on the class project and their role in it.

ASSESSING MAP AND GLOBE SKILLS

As we pointed out in Chapter 5, map and globe skills are very important elements in the social studies program. Students must not only know what types of maps are available, but also how to use them, and what limitations they have. But first, a word

TABLE 16.11. *Attitudinal Measure for Citizen Action*

Name: Alexandra	Project: Visits to Elderly at Peterson House				
Attitude	**SA**	**A**	**U**	**D**	**SD**
1. This project was important to me.					
2. I felt free to discuss it in class.					
3. I made some good suggestions in planning the class visits.					
4. The director of the Peterson House was interested and helpful in getting this project started.					
5. Planning with others in the group helped make the plan workable.					
6. I believe we did something useful.					
7. I am willing to get involved in another project like this.					

What I liked best: _____

What I liked least: _____

Things we could do better: _____

of caution. Many teachers and those citizens involved with back-to-basics groups seem to have placed an inordinate and excessive emphasis on map and globe skills, particularly the rote memorization of place location—countries, rivers, and capital cities—cardinal directions, and latitude and longitude using antiquated Mercator style maps. Perhaps it is a desire to return to the "good old days" of what they learned in school, or perhaps a belief that this knowledge is fixed, true, and certain and can be tested objectively. Important though map and globe skills are, they are not the entire curriculum, and emphasis on them should be kept within the perspective of the total social studies curriculum.

A number of the assessment tasks we have already described can be used to assess map and globe skills. These include:

Teacher-made tests	Student-made maps or scale models
Checklist	Standardized tests

Paper and Pencil Assessments

These are the most common assessment measures. The several types discussed above and illustrated in Table 16.6 lend themselves well to evaluating map and global skills. Avoid the tendency, however, of having too many knowledge-recall questions simply because they are so easy to construct.

Student-Made Maps

Here is another good source of data for assessment. You can devise checklists to evaluate a neighborhood map, such as shown in Figure 5.2, using criteria such as these:

1. Are the major streets shown?
2. Are they correctly related to one another?
3. Are major buildings correctly placed and marked with proper symbols?
4. Can students show where they live on the map?
5. Can students mark cardinal directions?

Building Scale Models

All too frequently teachers shy away from class projects such as constructing models of physical features of the land using sand tables, clay, papier-mâché, or other construction materials, or building scale models of a landscape, a mountain range, or a model of a local town. Perhaps these teachers fear the projects will be too messy, take too long to complete, or create too much confusion in an otherwise well-ordered classroom. Too bad! For students (and adults too!) love to "goof around" in gooey papier-mâché or in soft, wet clay. It appeals to the tactile sense of the fingers and helps to develop a keen sense of height and depth, smooth and rugged, that no set of colors on a topographical map can convey. What a tremendous way to teach scale in three dimensions: build coastlines, indent harbors, create great mountain ranges, and smooth out wide flat plains.

Models can be assessed with a student-developed checklist much like the one below:

1. Is the general contour accurate?
2. Are physical features generally correct in shape, location, and relative size?
3. If a scale of miles or altitude were used, would the model be generally accurate?

Note that the criteria do not emphasize precise accuracy, only a general sense of accuracy and a reasonable attention to scale (in the case of older students). Remember that the goal is to have fun learning about geography, not to become expert cartographers. We certainly wish to encourage this form of learning when evaluating map and globe skills.

ASSESSING TIME AND CHRONOLOGY CONCEPTS AND SKILLS

Time and chronology concepts and skills are among the most difficult in the social studies, largely because they are abstract, difficult to comprehend, and have few concrete referents in the life experience of students. We provided a number of activities in Chapter 5. Because these skills tend to be abstract, teachers should place more emphasis on informal measures than formal ones. Too often test items tend to be at the knowledge-recall level only. Some of the assessment measures that can be used include:

Anecdotal records   Teacher-made tests   Checklists
Class projects (e.g., time lines or family genealogy charts)

In Table 16.3 we gave an extract of an anecdotal record and used the concept of chronology to illustrate how it could be used as an assessment measure. The student's progress in learning the concepts of order and sequence are carefully noted by the teacher. This could be supplemented by a checklist of other specific concepts and skills.

The Family Genealogy Chart

This is another device for teaching the concept of time as it relates to family and social history. Here, chronological time can be extended in meaning from "long, long ago" (or "once upon a time" when reading stories) to so many generations ago. This can also be stated as "how many grandparents ago?" The teacher can ask relevant questions that provide criteria for assessment using a checklist:

1. Does the chart show several generations?
2. When looking at a family photo of mother, daughter, grandmother, and great-grandmother, can students define the concept *generation*?

3. Using the photo mentioned above, can students take the date when each person was born and place it on a timeline?
4. Using the timeline developed above, can students calculate the average number of years in a generation?
5. Can students correctly place significant national or world events on the family timeline?

Criteria such as these provide abundant data to assess the growth of the concepts *generation* and *chronology.* They also provide data to evaluate the skills of placing significant social and national events in chronological order and establishing meaningful personal relationships among them.

ASSESSING GROUP SKILLS

Group skills are an essential goal of the social studies program, yet it is surprising how often they are ignored as specific areas for teaching and assessment. We discussed in Chapter 5 many ways of developing skills for working in groups, including both leadership and group membership (participant) rules. Some useful forms of assessment are:

Teacher observation	Student interviews	Anecdotal records
Role-playing	Checklists	Autobiographical records
Attitudinal measures		

Checklists are frequently used for evaluating group skills. Students must learn not only how to lead, but also how to participate effectively when someone else is leading the group. Table 5.5 presents a form for evaluating group skills.

Attitudinal measures are another means for evaluating growth in group skills. A self-assessment measure such as that shown in Table 16.12 can be a useful device to use in conjunction with a student conference to help the student relate his or her own perceptions of group performance to those of the teacher or other members of the group.

The self-assessment chart in Table 16.11 presents a number of very important leadership criteria that can indicate areas of accomplishment or needed growth. More importantly, it provides a good yardstick for testing a student's own perceptions against those held by members of the group (which may not always be as positive as one's own). Conversely, a student who is trying out a leadership role for the first time may also receive positive feedback and encouragement to help develop a stronger self-concept and a willingness to take a leadership role again.

Because people cannot be leaders in every situation, a similar self-assessment chart could be developed for group membership or participation skills using some of the characteristics for effective groups shown in Table 5.4. Such a chart is shown in Table 16.13.

TABLE 16.12. *Self-Evaluation Form for Group Leadership*

Name: Neil M.		Role: Leader of Map-Making Group			
Attitude	SA	A	U	D	SD
1. I enjoy being a leader.					
2. I work easily with others in the group.					
3. I believe the group respects me when I am the leader.					
4. I am willing to let others be in charge of part of the work.					
5. I am willing to listen to suggestions from others.					
6. I am good at keeping the group at a task to complete its work.					
7. I can accept criticism from others without getting upset by it.					
8. I can praise or compliment others for good work.					
9. I can give help or encouragement to those who may need it.					
10. I am able to develop a good group spirit; that *we* met *our* goal.					

ASSESSING WRITING SKILLS

Writing skills are a very important part of the social studies program. While they are principally taught in the language arts, they need to be reinforced in the social studies. In Chapter 5 we discussed four types of writing: (1) summary, (2) synthesis, (3) analytic and critical, and (4) creative. Many activities were described for each type of writing. Some assessment tasks that can be used to assess writing skills include:

Essay tests	Samples of student work	Scripts for class plays
Committee reports	Checklists	Imaginary diaries of famous people

Summary Writing

While being able to write accurate summaries is an important skill, it is too often overemphasized. The other three forms mentioned above are often neglected.

TABLE 16.13. *Attitudinal Measure for Citizen Action*

Name: David E.			Role: Member of Map-Making Group		
Attitude	**SA**	**A**	**U**	**D**	**SD**
1. I can offer suggestions easily.					
2. I help keep the group focused on the task.					
3. I support the leader when he or she is right.					
4. I can work cooperatively with others in the group.					
5. I make positive and constructive criticisms.					
6. I feel good about our group and what it is doing.					
7. I enjoy working with other people in a group, even if I am not the leader.					

Criteria for summary writing might include:

1. Major points included.
2. Limited in detail.
3. Brief, to the point.
4. Conclusions or recommendations clearly listed.

Synthesis Writing

Synthesizing is an important skill that builds on summary writing. But a synthesis is not achieved by adding two summaries together with a few linking words or sentences. Students must give evidence of being able to:

1. Summarize in their own words two or more sources.
2. Show relationships between ideas or views expressed.
3. Identify points of agreement or disagreement, strengths or weaknesses, pros or cons.
4. Quote directly, or paraphrase longer quotes.
5. List references in a simple manner.

Analytical and Critical Writing

This is a goal most teachers like to aim for, but students get too little actual experience and even less assessment of it. These skills have been discussed at length in

Chapter 5, and assessment tasks for analytic thinking have been suggested in an earlier section of this chapter on thinking skills. Checklists for assessing student written work should include such criteria as:

1. Determining perspective or point of view
2. Separating fact from inference or opinion
3. Identifying bias, propaganda, or stereotypes
4. Relating minor parts to main idea or theme
5. Making judgments about the quality of facts presented, or ideas expressed
6. Making judgments about the overall worth or merit (or lack of it) of a speech, book, play, or report, using some criteria as the basis for critical judgment

Creative Writing

Unlike the other forms of writing discussed above, creative writing gives free rein to a student's creative and expressive talents. While it may involve some summary and some synthesis, these are only vehicles for expressing thoughts and feelings in new and novel ways. The activities suggested on p. 155 provide excellent opportunities for writing expressively and creatively about actual or likely historical events. Checklists for assessing creative writing might include such criteria as:

1. Novelty of approach
2. Imaginative portrayal of events or characters
3. Expressive and varied dialogue
4. New, imaginative solutions to old problems
5. Several solutions, each solving the problem, but in a different and perhaps novel way

SUMMARY

This chapter has described a variety of techniques for assessing instruction in social studies. These involve formal as well as informal approaches, with emphasis on such measures as checklists, performance charts, teacher-made tests, anecdotal records, and attitude measures. In each case we stressed the importance of developing relevant criteria and using these as means of assessing student progress toward instructional goals.

We discussed a number of forms of teacher-made tests, such as true/false, sentence completion, multiple choice, and essay questions. We identified strengths, weaknesses, most appropriate uses, and gave many examples of each type. In the last section we discussed ways of evaluating each of the social studies skills discussed in Chapter 5. These included thinking skills, map and globe skills, time and chronology skills, group skills, and writing skills. Throughout the chapter we made frequent cross-reference to ideas and activities developed in other parts of the book and related assessment tasks to them.

REFLECTION AND ACTION ACTIVITIES

1. Examine a curriculum guide from a local school district. How are instructional objectives expressed? If they are not written in behavioral or performance terms, try to rewrite some of them using the techniques presented in the first part of this chapter.

2. Teachers frequently use paper and pencil assessments such as multiple choice, true/false, completion, or essay tests. What are some of the strengths and weaknesses of each type?

3. We have listed a variety of performance-based assessment techniques in this chapter, such as checklists, anecdotal records, and attitudinal scales. What strengths and limitations do such measures have compared to the paper and pencil assessments mentioned in question 2 above?

4. A group of students is preparing a play about a family in Massachusetts in 1820 that is considering moving westward to Ohio. What criteria and what techniques might you propose to assess this play? (Hint: Consider it from the point of view of social studies content, thinking skills, group skills, and creative writing.)

5. Students in the second grade have been studying their local community. The class has decided to make a model of the town on a large table. What criteria and techniques would you use to assess this project? Be sure to include group leader/member skills.

6. Demonstrate your understanding of the following key concepts and terms by writing or stating a brief definition for each of them. Give an example of each.

    a. assessment
    b. evaluation
    c. behavioral/performance objective
    d. criteria for assessment
    e. anecdotal record
    f. attitudinal measure
    g. analytical skills
    h. creative writing

FOR FURTHER READING

Airasian, P. W. (1996). *Assessment in the classroom.* New York: McGraw-Hill.

Beyer, B. K. (1987). *Practical strategies for the teaching of thinking.* Boston: Allyn & Bacon.

Beyer, B. K. (1988). *Developing a thinking skills program.* Boston: Allyn & Bacon.

Gardner, H. (1993). *Multiple Intelligences: The theory in practice.* New York: Basic Books.

Hunkins, F. P. (1989). *Teaching thinking through effective questioning.* Needham Heights, MA: Christopher-Gordon Publishers.

McCollum, S. L. (1994). *Performance assessment in the social studies classroom. A how-to book for teachers.* Joplin, MO: Chalk Dust Press.

Valencia, S. (Ed.). (1998). *Literacy portfolios in action.* New York: Harcourt Brace.

Wiggins, G. (1993). *Assessing student performance: Exploring the purpose and limits of testing.* San Francisco: Jossey-Bass.

Index